CHET & DIANE TOOLE
616 VIA DEL SUR
MESQUITE, TX 75150

THE LETTERS OF JOHN THE APOSTLE

THE LETTERS OF JOHN THE APOSTLE

AN IN-DEPTH COMMENTARY

by

DONALD W. BURDICK

MOODY PRESS
CHICAGO

© 1985 by
THE MOODY BIBLE INSTITUTE
OF CHICAGO

All rights reserved. No part of this book may be reproduced in any form without permission in writing from the publisher, except in the case of brief quotations embodied in critical articles or reviews.

Except where indicated otherwise, all Scripture quotations in this book are from the *New American Standard Bible,* © 1960, 1962, 1963, 1968, 1971, 1972, 1973, 1975, and 1977 by the Lockman Foundation, and are used by permission.

Greek quotations cited in this book are from the United Bible Societies Greek Testament, 3d edition text. This work is published by arrangement with the German Bible Society, Stuttgart, and is used by permission.

The use of selected references from various versions of the Bible in this publication does not necessarily imply publisher endorsement of the versions in their entirety.

Library of Congress Cataloging in Publication Data

Burdick, Donald W.
   The letters of John the Apostle.

  Bibliography: p.
  Includes index.
  1. Bible. N.T. Epistles of John—Commentaries.
I. Bible. N.T. Epistles of John. 1984. II. Title.
BS2805.3.B88   1985   227'.94077   83-23808
ISBN 0-8024-2356-6

1 2 3 4 5 6 7 Printing/GB/Year 90 89 88 87 86 85

Printed in the United States of America

To Violet, gentle companion in ministry for more than forty years, and to Sharon and Douglas, the children with whom God blessed our home

Acknowledgments

The author and publisher wish to express gratitude to the following sources of quotations and special material.

The Johannine Epistles, by C. H. Dodd. The Moffatt New Testament Commentary. London: Hodder and Stoughton, 1946. Excerpts reprinted by permission of Hodder and Stoughton Limited.

The Johannine Epistles, by A. E. Brooke. The International Critical Commentary. Edinburgh: T. & T. Clark, 1863. Excerpts reprinted by permission.

The Epistles of John, by B. F. Westcott. Grand Rapids: Eerdmans, 1950. Excerpts reprinted by permission.

The Ante-Nicene Fathers, edited by Alexander Roberts and James Donaldson. Grand Rapids: Eerdmans, 1950-51. Used by permission.

The Nicene and Post-Nicene Fathers, edited by Philip Schaff and Henry Wace. Grand Rapids: Eerdmans, 1952-53. Used by permission.

Selected quotations from *The Tests of Life,* by Robert Law. Reprinted 1968 by Baker Book House and used by permission.

Contents

Chapter	Page
Preface	ix
Abbreviations	xi

Part 1: The First Epistle of John/Introduction

1. The Background of 1 John — 3
2. The Authorship of 1 John — 7
3. Date, Place, and Recipients of the Epistle — 38
4. The Occasion and Purpose of the Epistle — 49
5. The Character and Content of the Epistle — 68

Part 2: The First Epistle of John/Commentary

6. Introduction: The Reality of the Incarnation, 1:1-4 — 95
   First Cycle: The Christian Life Viewed as Fellowship with the Father and Son, 1:5—2:28 — 115
7. Fellowship Tested on Ethical Grounds, 1:5—2:11 — 117
8. Two Digressions, 2:12-17 — 171
9. Fellowship Tested on Christological Grounds, 2:18-28 — 192
   Second Cycle: The Christian Life Viewed as Divine Sonship, 2:29—4:6 — 224
10. Sonship Tested on Ethical Grounds: The Practice of Righteousness, 2:29—3:10a — 226

11. Sonship Tested on Ethical Grounds: Love for Fellow Believers, 3:10*b*-24	259
12. Sonship Tested on Christological Grounds, 4:1-6	291
Third Cycle: The Christian Life Viewed as a Closely Woven Integration of the Ethical and the Christological, 4:7—5:12	314
13. The Ethical Test, 4:7—5:5	316
14. The Christological Test, 5:6-12	364
15. Conclusion: Great Certainties of the Christian Life, 5:13-21	384

Part 3: **The Second Epistle of John**

16. Introduction to 2 John	413
17. Commentary on 2 John	419

Part 4: **The Third Epistle of John**

18. Introduction to 3 John	441
19. Commentary on 3 John	446
Bibliography	467
Index of Subjects and Persons	476
Index of Scripture	481
Index of Authors	486

Preface

This volume is intended to serve both those who know New Testament Greek and those who do not. Consequently, every Greek expression that appears is accompanied by an English translation, either the NASB or my own rendering (which appears in italics). My particular focus in writing was on the biblically literate layman, the student in the college and seminary classroom, and the pastor in his study.

The format of the commentary grew out of more than thirty years of teaching Greek exegesis. Those who work in that area are all aware that there are several procedures basic to all exegetical practice, namely, the study of syntax, the examination of word meanings, and the analysis of thought content. Exegesis may and should involve the structure of the author's thought pattern, especially if the exegete is preparing to preach from the passage under study.

In addition, I have long been impressed by the effective use of paraphrase in bringing out additional color in Greek grammar and words. Dr. Vincent Brushwyler, former General Director of the Conservative Baptist Foreign Mission Society, very aptly employed the paraphrase of the Greek text, even in the pulpit. Anyone who has used the commentaries of J. B. Lightfoot will remember that he used paraphrase as an integral part of his studies in the prison epistles of Paul. (Cf. *St. Paul's Epistle to the Philippians*, p. 110.)

It was out of such considerations that the arrangement of the present commentary arose. Syntactical and lexical studies are treated together under the heading Exegetical Commentary; the analysis of the thought content of a passage is designated Theological Commentary; the paraphrase naturally becomes the Paraphrastic Commentary; and the analytical outline is the Structural Commentary.

The Theological Commentary is intended to be two-pronged in nature, first dealing with the meaning of the passage for John's day, and then discussing its meaning for our day.

It is hoped that the Structural Commentary will prove helpful, not only as an aid in following John's thought through a given passage, but also as a basis for developing sermonic outlines for that passage.

Those who are familiar with Greek grammar will note that the commentary employs the eight-case system throughout. Preference for this system rather than the five-case system is based on arguments advanced by A. T. Robertson, *(A Grammar of the Greek New Testament in the Light of Historical Research,* pp. 446-49) and H. E. Dana and Julius R. Mantey, *(A Manual Grammar of the Greek New Testament,* pp. 32-34, 65-66). In addition, although merely a utilitarian reason, the eight-case system is easier to use because of its simplicity of classification. Each case grouping is more unified and more clearly related to the basic idea of that case.

Finally, I must express sincere appreciation to my wife for her long patience with the hours upon hours of my time that the writing of this commentary consumed; to Sarah Lyons, Shelley Shobe, Verla Webb, and Freda Rasko for typing, not only the English text, but the Greek as well; and to Moody Press for bearing with me through many necessary delays.

Abbreviations

Literary Abbreviations

ASV	*American Standard Version* (1901)
Beck	*New Testament in Language of Today* (Beck)
Gr.	Author's translation of the Greek (short, literal translations of a word or phrase are indicated by italics)
H.E.	*Ecclesiastical History of the Second and Third Centuries*, Eusebius of Caesarea (c. A.D. 260-340)
Heb.	Translation of Hebrew
KJV	King James Version
LXX	Septuagint
Mag.	*Letter to the Magnesians* (A.D. 117), Ignatius
Moffatt	*A New Translation* (Moffatt)
Montgomery	*Centenary Translation of the New Testament in Modern English* (Montgomery)
Mss.	Manuscripts
NASB	*New American Standard Bible*
NEB	*New English Bible*
NIV	*New International Version*
Phillips	*New Testament in Modern English* (Phillips)
RSV	*Revised Standard Version*
RV	*Revised Version*
Smyr.	*Letter to the Smyrnaeans* (A.D. 117), Ignatius
TEV	*Good News for Modern Man* (Today's English Version)
Trall.	*Letter to the Trallians* (A.D. 117), Ignatius

Williams	Charles B. Williams, *New Testament, A Translation in the Language of the People*
κτλ.	et cetera

MANUSCRIPT SYMBOLS

ℵ	Sinaiticus, fourth-century codex. Good quality of text, of the Alexandrian group.
A	Alexandrinus, fifth-century codex. Except for the gospels, it contains the Alexandrian text similar to ℵ and B.
B	Vaticanus, fourth century. Very good quality of text, of the Alexandrian group.
C	Ephraemi, fifth-century codex. Representative of all major texts, often agrees with the Byzantine group (poorer text-type).
D	Bezae, fifth- or sixth-century codex, which does not contain the Johannine epistles. Chief representative of the Western text-group, known for its many variations.
K	Mosquensis, ninth- or tenth-century codex. Characterized by numerous text corruptions, generally of the Byzantine group.
L	Angelicus, a ninth-century codex. Mainly Byzantine in text-type.
P	Porphyrianus, a ninth-century codex. In the catholic epistles, Alexandrian in text-type.
ψ	Athous Laurae, an eighth- or ninth-century codex. Largely of the Alexandrian text-type, generally agreeing with either ℵ or B or both.
33	A minuscule codex from the ninth or tenth century. A good representative of the Alexandrian group of manuscripts.
81	A minuscule codex from A.D. 1044. A superior manuscript, generally of the Alexandrian text-type.
614	A minuscule codex from the thirteenth century. Contains many early Western-type readings.

PART 1
The First Epistle of John
Introduction

1
The Background of 1 John

W. M. Ramsay aptly styled the Anatolian peninsula as a bridge stretching between Asia and Europe,[1] across which moved invasions and migrations traveling from East to West and from West to East. Of at least equal importance was the cultural flow that likewise streamed into and across this natural link between the two worlds. In a sense, Anatolia, or Asia Minor, could be likened to a no man's land between the Hellenic and the Oriental. It was "neither fish nor fowl," yet it was both. Ramsay said, "One feels inclined . . . to describe the west coast as Greek, the plateau within Taurus as the Debatable Land, and the country beyond Taurus as Eastern and Asiatic."[2] Although this may be an oversimplification, as Ramsay himself recognized, it does allow for a better understanding of the nature of Anatolian culture.

Asia Minor was a meeting place of ideas, philosophies, and religions. This was especially true in the period often designated as the Hellenistic age, which lasted roughly from 300 B.C. to A.D. 300. Hans Jonas divided these six centuries into two periods of equal length. He spoke of "the Hellenization of the East" from 300 B.C. to 1 B.C. and "the orientalization of the West" from A.D. 1 to A.D. 300.[3] Of course, this too is oversimplification, for orientali-

1. W. M. Ramsay, *Luke the Physician*, p. 105.
2. Ibid., p. 114.
3. Hans Jonas, *The Gnostic Religion*, pp. 3-27 (esp. p. 18).

zation of the West was occurring to some extent prior to 1 B.C., just as Hellenization of the East continued after A.D. 1. In general, however, the classifications suggested by Jonas are acceptable.

Asia Minor, then, was of necessity in constant cultural turmoil, continually being agitated by influences from both East and West. Consequently, the order of the day in the Anatolian peninsula—perhaps more so there than any other place in the ancient world—was syncretism.

As a result of continuing research and an increasing number of newly discovered materials, there is more awareness today than ever before of just how syncretistic the centuries immediately before and after the birth of Christ were. W. C. van Unnik, in discussing the Nag Hammadi manuscripts, wrote: "One must continually reckon with the fact that under the Roman Empire a host of religions and systems of thought were intermingled, and often in the strangest amalgam. It was the age of syncretism."[4] Apart from the Judaeo-Christian sphere, the world was religiously inclusivistic. There was always room for a new religion, provided of course that it was not of an exclusive nature. Syncretism, however, did not merely express itself in a mood of tolerance toward other faiths. Its characteristic expression was in the combination of various ideas and beliefs from different sources to form new or aberrant religions. This was the age of the developing mystery religions, the age of the occult, the age of the proliferation of Gnostic sects.

The same was true of philosophical systems. A Philo could mingle Judaism with Platonic and Stoic concepts. The astrological fatalism of the East "could be clothed in the garments of Stoic cosmology with its doctrines of sympathy and cosmic law."[5]

What was true of Asia Minor as a whole was equally true of Asia, its most illustrious province, where one found a wide variety of religions and systems of thought. Along with the native gods of the area, Asians worshiped deities imported from such places as Greece, Rome, Egypt, and Syria. A survey of some of the major cities of the province reveals the variegated nature of the Asian religious picture. In Ephesus the place of prominence was given to Artemis, the fertility goddess whose temple was regarded as one of the world's seven wonders. Smyrna had a very zealous Jewish

---

4. W. C. van Unnik, *Newly Discovered Gnostic Writings*, Studies in Biblical Theology, no. 30, p. 29.
5. Jonas, p. 22.

The Background of 1 John 5

element that caused the Christians of the city much trouble (Rev. 2:9). The Imperial Cult also flourished here.

The city of Pergamum was known for its temple of Asklepius, the god of healing sometimes called "the Pergamene god."[6] The patron goddess of the city was Athena, and with her were worshiped Zeus and Dionysus. It was here in 29 B.C. that the Imperial Cult had its first appearance in the province of Asia when permission was granted to build a temple in honor of Augustus. And it was from this city that the Cult spread throughout the province.

Sardis was known for its temple of Cybele, a goddess of fecundity whose worship stemmed from the highlands of Phrygia. In Hierapolis people revered the Phrygian Leto, a nature goddess corresponding to Cybele and often identified with her. The patron deity of the city was Apollo. In addition Judaism had a strong foothold here. The tutelary deity of Laodicea was Zeus. In Colossae numerous pagan deities were honored, including the Egyptian Isis and Serapis, the Ephesian Artemis, the Greek Demeter, and the Phrygian Men.

The intellectual and religious atmosphere of Asia, like that of the Mediterranean world in general, was constantly being stirred by currents and cross-currents. Dualism was in the air. From Persia came its religious expression, with contrasts between light and darkness, and good and evil. From Greece came its philosophical expression, with the antithesis of spirit and matter. From Babylonia came astrology and its stress on the fatalistic power of the heavenly bodies over the lives of men. From Palestine came Judaism, both normative and occult. Also from the Jews came Christianity with its doctrine of the divine-human Savior, who united in the mystery of the incarnation both matter and spirit, flesh and deity.

It was to be expected that the church, encircled as it was by this variety of faiths and ideas, would sooner or later begin to feel their influence. It is not surprising, therefore, to find that the syncretistic spirit of the age attempted to involve Christianity, in spite of its exclusiveness, in the process of amalgamation that was going on everywhere. As a result the church faced not only the problem of opposition from without, from such competitors as the mystery religions and the Imperial Cult, but it also was confronted with the more subtle danger of infiltration by persons and concepts foreign to its fundamental nature.

6. Merrill F. Unger, *Archaeology and the New Testament*, p. 277.

The beginnings of that infiltration were not long in coming. Those are reflected in Paul's letter to the Colossians, which seems to have been aimed at a very early stage of the syncretizing process that later crystallized into the Gnosticism of the second and third centuries. The same kind of error is also referred to in the pastoral epistles (1 Tim. 1:3-4; 4:1-3; 6:20-21) and probably in Jude and 2 Peter. By A.D. 90 that kind of heresy was beginning to take on a more definite form that deviated from the traditional doctrine of the Person of Christ as well as from the biblical emphasis on a holy life.

Aware of the growing threat of those syncretizing pressures, John became increasingly concerned. It was becoming apparent that the churches needed a written refutation of the heresy in order to confirm the believers in their knowledge and belief of the truth. Christians had to be assured at those very points where the incipient heresy was laying its emphasis. Consequently, moving under the leadership and inspiration of the Holy Spirit, John wrote a document for circulation among the churches of Asia.

Thus, out of a background of syncretism, confusion, and heresy came one of the most delightful yet hard-hitting writings of the New Testament. Although it was originally penned to meet the need of the churches of first-century provincial Asia, in the wisdom and providence of God 1 John has proved its worth throughout the succeeding centuries to believers everywhere. Its importance for present-day Christians can hardly be overestimated.

2

The Authorship of 1 John

The foregoing chapter has proceeded on the assumption that 1 John was written about A.D. 90 by John the apostle to the churches of Asia for the purpose of counteracting incipient Gnosticism. It is obvious that this assumption contains debatable elements. For example, many today would not be willing to grant that this letter actually came from the pen of an apostle. It is therefore necessary to investigate the validity of this and other assumptions.

Modern Views Concerning Authorship

In the Johannine debate of the nineteenth and twentieth centuries, the question of the authorship of the Johannine literature has developed a number of complexities. Various theories have been advanced concerning the part, if any, that the apostle John played in the production of the writings. Questions have arisen about the relationship of the gospel to the epistles and the Apocalypse. Did they all come from the same author? If not, who were the different authors? What was the relationship of the apostle to the beloved disciple and to the evangelist? Were they the same person, two different persons, or three different persons? In fact, when one considers the number and complexity of the numerous possible interpretations, he is liable to be overwhelmed by the situation. This state of affairs comes partly because the gospel and the epistles do not specifically name any author.

Various classifications of the modern authorship theories have been employed. One of the simplest is that used by A. M. Hunter[1] and followed by Harold S. Songer.[2] Those writers arrange the various theories into the following categories: (1) non-apostolic, (2) mediate, and (3) apostolic.

NON-APOSTOLIC VIEW

As early as 1901, P. W. Schmiedel was asserting that the writer of the fourth gospel was an anonymous person of the province of Asia, writing sometime after A.D. 132. First John was thought to be from a different author and 2 and 3 John from still another writer (or writers), although probably from "the same school of thought."[3]

In 1910, B. W. Bacon concluded that the gospel was not written by John the apostle or John the elder, but by an unknown Ephesian.[4]

In the 1930s, James Moffatt argued that the names of the authors of the Johannine literature can no longer be known. He suggested that John 1-20 was written by "one of the anonymous early Christian authors . . . who were willing to sink their names into their great cause and subject."[5] A second unknown individual was said to have edited chapters 1-20 and added chapter 21. It was this unknown editor who supposedly wrote 1 John.[6] Second and 3 John were penned by an unknown presbyter, who also could conceivably have composed the Apocalypse.[7] It is clear that in Moffatt's thinking nothing that has traditionally been ascribed to John the apostle was actually written by him.

In more recent years, Rudolf Bultmann advanced a theory of fourth gospel origins that involved the employment of three liter-

---

1. A. M. Hunter, *Interpreting the New Testament 1900-1950*, p. 85.
2. Harold S. Songer, "The Gospel of John in Recent Research," *Review and Expositor* 62 (Fall 1965): 418-20.
3. *The Encyclopedia Biblica*, 1901 ed., s.v. "John, Son of Zebedee," by P. W. Schmiedel.
4. B. W. Bacon, *The Fourth Gospel in Research and Debate*, p. 532.
5. James Moffatt, *An Introduction to the Literature of the New Testament*, p. 570.
6. Ibid., p. 594.
7. Ibid., pp. 479-80.

ary sources.[8] The author of the gospel was not John the apostle but an unnamed former follower of John the Baptist. In composing the gospel the anonymous writer is said to have used (1) a sayings source containing "revelation discourses" stated in Semitic language, (2) a signs source made up of miracle stories, which can be found in John 1-12, and (3) a passion and resurrection source. These sources were skillfully edited, woven together, and supplemented by the unknown evangelist to produce our fourth gospel.

According to Bultmann, 1 John was not composed by the same person. Whoever the writer of the epistle was, he is said to have used a prior written source that was Gnostic in nature, edited and annotated to bring it into harmony with "ecclesiastical tradition." Bultmann suggests that 1:5—2:27 was originally an independent writing done in "rough draft,"[9] but 2:28—5:12 was made up of fragments, perhaps all written by the same author and added to 1:5—2:27 by the author or by his disciples.

MEDIATE VIEW

A number of scholars, especially in more recent years, have attempted to retain the values of the traditional view of apostolic authorship while at the same time considering arguments advanced against authorship by the apostle John. They steer a course between the horns of what appears to them to be a dilemma by suggesting that the Johannine literature was written by followers of the apostle. John's influence, his witness to events and statements, and his interpretation of those events and statements were thus embodied to a greater or lesser degree in the Johannine writings. However, because John himself did not actually pen the documents, additions and variations also arose. As a result, the main thrust of the writings was Johannine, but non-Johannine elements also are to be found. Four significant volumes were published in English during the fifties and sixties advocating this mediate view. How this general view of authorship varies from scholar to scholar can be readily seen in the following overviews.

In 1955 C. K. Barrett's first edition of *The Gospel According to John* appeared, arguing for the mediate theory of authorship. Barrett saw the beloved disciple (John 13:23; 21:7, 20) as John the

---

8. Rudolf Bultmann, *The Gospel of John: A Commentary.* See especially the Introduction by Walter Schmithals, pp. 6-9.
9. Rudolf Bultmann, *The Johannine Epistles*, Hermeneia, pp. 1-3.

apostle who migrated to Ephesus and there composed some apocalyptic writings. Disciples of the apostle produced the Johannine literature after John's death. One pupil used John's apocalyptic works to compose the Apocalypse. Another (or two others) wrote the epistles. And still another—the boldest thinker of all— wrote the gospel. Barrett declares him to be "perhaps the greatest theologian in the history of the church." Later, others in the Johannine circle edited the gospel and added chapter 21. Because of the disciple's references to the beloved disciple John, the gospel came to be known as the work of the apostle.[10]

In 1966 Raymond E. Brown, a Catholic scholar, published the first volume of his *Anchor Bible* commentary on the gospel of John. In it he set forth a rather detailed form of the mediate view of authorship, involving five stages in the development of the gospel. Like Barrett, he identified the beloved disciple as John the apostle, whose authority stood behind the gospel. He was responsible for stage one in the growth of the tradition. Stages two through four in the development involved the preaching of John's disciples. Finally, an outstanding disciple actually composed the book. Stage five was a final redaction of the Gospel by a member of the Johannine school. Brown ascribed the epistles of John to the same circle.[11]

Another volume advocating a mediate theory was published in English in 1968. Written by the Catholic scholar Rudolf Schnackenburg, this commentary attempts to "do justice both to the tradition of the ancient church about the authorship and what we know from the work as we have it before us."[12] Schnackenburg insists that the apostle John was the authority who stood behind the fourth gospel, though he himself did not write it. He was the inspiration for a school of writers who composed the Johannine literature, and from him came data concerning Christ's life as well as the interpretation of events and discourses. The actual writer is

10. C. K. Barrett, *The Gospel According to St. John* (New York: Macmillan, 1955), pp. 113-14.
11. Raymond E. Brown, *The Gospel According to St. John* (i-xii), The Anchor Bible, vol. 29 (Garden City, N.Y.: Doubleday, 1966), pp. XXXIV-XXXVI, XCVIII-CI. In a more recent volume, however, Brown has changed his mind. The beloved disciple was not John the Son of Zebedee. See *The Community of the Beloved Disciple* (New York: Paulist Press, 1979), p. 33.
12. Rudolf Schnackenburg, *The Gospel According to St. John*, Herder's Theological Commentary on the New Testament (New York: Herder and Herder, 1968), 1:103. In the same place Brown (see note 11 above) indicates that Schnackenburg has also changed his mind.

said to have been a Hellenistic disciple of the apostle, a disciple of Christ but not one of the Twelve. It was he who mediated and interpreted the tradition concerning Jesus. The Johannine school injected this writer into the gospel account as the beloved disciple in the place of the apostle John. Traditional materials and personal interpretations were compiled partly by the disciple and partly by his followers to produce the earliest copy of the fourth gospel. This in turn went through various stages of redaction.[13] According to Schnackenburg, the Johannine epistles are to be ascribed to the same school of writers.[14]

Finally, the mediate view of Oscar Cullmann, as set forth in his 1976 study *The Johannine Circle*, denies apostolic authorship of the gospel, but sees John the apostle as the authority on which the author of the gospel relied. The actual writer was the beloved disciple, a former follower of John the Baptist who became a disciple of Jesus, but not one of the Twelve. In his composition of the gospel the author drew on his own memory and on oral tradition. His disciples (the so-called Johannine school) completely revised what he had written. To them also (but not to the evangelist) may be credited the epistles and possibly the book of Revelation.[15]

APOSTOLIC VIEW

The view that holds John the apostle to have been the author of the Johannine literature goes back to the early church and was held almost unanimously until the rise of modern critical scholarship. In favor of the traditional view, such names as Martin Luther, John Calvin, B. F. Westcott, F. L. Godet, A. Plummer, and Robert Law (on 1 John) may be cited.

13. Ibid., pp. 101-4. See also Rudolph Schnackenburg, "On the Origin of the Fourth Gospel," in *Jesus and Man's Hope*, 1:239-43.
14. Schnackenburg, *The Gospel According to St. John*, 1:103.
15. Oscar Cullmann, *The Johannine Circle* (Philadelphia: Westminster, 1976), pp. 53-87. Also see R. Alan Culpepper, *The Johannine School: An Evaluation of the Johannine School Hypothesis Based on an Investigation of the Nature of Ancient Schools* (Missoula, Mont.: Scholar's Press, 1975). Culpepper studied a number of ancient schools such as the Pythagorean, The Academy, The Lyceum, and The Stoa and concluded that there is reason to believe that a Johannine school also existed. For a brief survey of the Johannine school theory, see D. A. Carson, "Historical Tradition in the Fourth Gospel: After Dodd, What?" *Gospel Perspectives*, vol. II, edited by R. T. France and David Wenham (Sheffield, England: JSOT Press, 1981), pp. 132-34.

More recent scholars who have defended apostolic authorship include William Hendriksen, Donald Guthrie, John R. W. Stott, Leon Morris, and J. A. T. Robinson.[16] The views of the last two of these men will be commented on in brief.

Morris, in his *Studies in the Fourth Gospel*, devotes a lengthy chapter to "The Authorship of the Fourth Gospel," in which thirty-five pages are given to a discussion of Westcott's concentric argument for apostolic authorship.[17] He says, "What I propose to do is to take Westcott's powerful statement of the conservative case, and see, if we can, what modern advance has done to it."[18] After a thorough discussion of each of Westcott's five points in the light of modern scholarship, Morris concludes "the fact is that the massive argument of Westcott has not been decisively refuted. Modifications in detail are demanded, but few of the main points have been really overthrown. Westcott these days is not so much controverted as by-passed."[19] (The main points of Morris's study will be considered in the latter part of this chapter.)

Especially noteworthy is the declaration of Robinson for apostolic authorship. He concluded his essay, "The New Look on the Fourth Gospel," with the following:

> Is there a real continuity, not merely in the memory of one old man, but in the life of an on-going community, with the earliest days of Christianity? What, I think, fundamentally distinguishes the "new look" on the fourth Gospel is that it answers that question in the affirmative. But if we do assert this continuity, it is obviously going at one and the same time to reduce the necessity for making everything depend upon apostolic authorship *and* to make us much more open to its possibility.[20]

16. William Hendriksen, *The Gospel of John*, New Testament Commentary (Grand Rapids: Baker, 1954), pp. 3-31; Donald Guthrie, *New Testament Introduction* (Downers Grove, Ill.: InterVarsity, 1970), pp. 241-71, 864-69; J. R. W. Stott, *The Epistles of John*, Tyndale New Testament Commentaries (Grand Rapids: Eerdmans, 1964), pp. 13-41; Leon Morris, *Studies in the Fourth Gospel* (Grand Rapids: Eerdmans, 1969), pp. 215-92; Morris, *Commentary on the Gospel of John*, The New International Commentary on the New Testament (Grand Rapids: Eerdmans, 1971), pp. 8-30; J. A. T. Robinson, *Redating the New Testament* (Philadelphia: Westminster, 1976), pp. 254-311.
17. B. F. Westcott, *The Gospel According to St. John* (Grand Rapids: Eerdmans, 1954), pp. ix-lii.
18. Morris, *Studies in the Fourth Gospel*, p. 218.
19. Ibid., pp. 264-65.
20. J. A. T. Robinson, *Twelve New Testament Studies*, Studies in Biblical Theology, no. 34, p. 106.

The "new look" that Robinson described views the tradition behind the fourth gospel as of potentially equal historicity to that on which the Synoptic gospels rest. The gospel of John is as trustworthy a witness for the Jesus of history as for the Jesus of faith. This "new look," Robinson declared, will make people more open to the possibility that John the apostle wrote the gospel that bears his name.

In his later volume, *Redating the New Testament,* Robinson clearly comes out for apostolic authorship. Referring to the writings of Brown and Cullmann, he reminds us that Brown argued that the beloved disciple was John the apostle but denies that John was the writer of the gospel. On the other hand, Cullmann argues that the beloved disciple was the author of the gospel but denies that he was John the apostle. Robinson's comment concerning the positions held by the two men is, "I believe that both men are right in what they assert and wrong in what they deny."[21]

John the Elder as Author

It has often been suggested in modern times that the author of all or part of the Johannine literature was John the Elder. This theory is based on the fact that the author of 2 and 3 John designates himself as "the elder," and on the assumption that Papias spoke of two Johns, one a disciple and the other an elder. In a quotation preserved by Eusebius, Papias is recorded to have said:

> If then, anyone came who had been a follower of the elders, I questioned him in regard to the words of the elders,—what Andrew or what Peter said, or what was said by Philip, or by Thomas, or by James, or by John, or by Matthew, or by any other of the disciples of the Lord, and what things Aristion and the Presbyter John, the Disciples of the Lord, say. For I do not think that what was gotten from books would profit me as much as what came from the living and abiding voice.[22]

On the basis of such items as the differences between the fourth gospel and the Synoptics, numerous scholars have thought it necessary to reject the apostolic authorship of the gospel and Johannine epistles. In the subsequent search for the identity of the writer, students were struck with the fact that the author of 2 and

21. Robinson, *Redating the New Testament,* p. 310.
22. Eusebius *H.E.* 3. 39.

3 John, whoever he may have been, called himself "the elder" (2 John 1; 3 John 1). It was also felt necessary to attempt to explain how the so-called Johannine literature had come to be ascribed to John the apostle in the first place. Papias's statement about John the Elder provided the clue that led to a new authorship theory. Eusebius long ago (c. A.D. 260-340) found reason to see two Johns in Papias's statement.[23] The various items—the rejection of apostolic authorship, the author's self-designation as elder, the statement of Papias, and the explanation of Eusebius—seemed to fit together like pieces of a jigsaw puzzle. The result was inevitable; many cast their vote for John the Elder as author of the Johannine gospel and epistles.

A better understanding of the case for and against apostolic authorship can be obtained by examining the use of the term *elder* in 2 and 3 John and in the statement of Papias. The designation *elder* may be used in at least three different ways: (1) of an older person, (2) of a respected older Christian leader whatever his official position, or (3) of a church official. That the author of the two epistles was merely referring to himself as "the old man" is unthinkable. But he could have been using the title that Christians had given to him as the oldest and most respected Christian leader known to them. It would in this case be a title of loving respect.

Some, however, have thought it strange that one of the twelve apostles should also have been an elder in the official sense. The office of apostle was not limited to a local church; the office of elder, on the other hand, was a local church office. Consequently, it may be viewed as unthinkable that such a significant person as an apostle should also be classed as an elder, a lower and more limited official in comparison.

It should be remembered, however, that tradition places John in Ephesus during his later years. It is entirely possible that he may have functioned as one of the elders in the local assembly. It would have been an honor for the church in Ephesus to have such an illustrious elder, and it certainly would not have been beneath the dignity of the aged apostle to serve in that capacity. Note that Peter referred to himself as an elder (1 Pet. 5:1). True, C. H. Dodd says the use of the term by the apostle Peter "belongs to a different context, and cannot usefully be cited as a parallel."[24]

23. Ibid.
24. C. H. Dodd, *The Johannine Epistles*, The Moffatt New Testament Commentary, p. lxix.

The Authorship of 1 John   15

This, however, is not as certain as Dodd makes it sound. There is no reason both Peter and John may not be using the term *elder* in an official sense. It certainly is plain that Peter designated himself both as apostle (1 Pet. 1:1) and as elder (1 Pet. 5:1). If such a double office was valid in Peter's case, it is possible that John, too, may have functioned in both capacities. In humility he may have preferred to understate his position when communicating with his beloved Asian Christians.

The essential element in the theory of John the Elder as author is the statement of Papias. Neither Papias nor Eusebius said anything explicitly or implicitly that would suggest John the Elder as the author of any of the Johannine literature. In the first place, Papias does not explicitly state that there were two individuals named John; also Eusebius goes no further than to suggest that Papias had two persons of that name in mind. Any identification, therefore, of a person called John the Elder with the author of the Johannine writings is purely arbitrary.

Did Papias refer to one person, John the apostle who was also an elder, or was he distinguishing between the apostle and another John who was an elder? The term *elder* occurs three times in the quotation. The first two instances have been interpreted in two different ways. Papias said, "If, then, anyone came, who had been a follower of the elders, I questioned him in regard to the words of the elders—what Andrew or what Peter said. . . ." The Greek text of the last clause reads τοὺς τῶν πρεσβυτέρων ἀνέκρινον λόγους Τί Ἀνδρέας ἢ Τί Πέτρος εἶπεν. . . . ("I inquired as to the words of the elders, what Andrew or what Peter said.") Some translations insert the word *about*—"I used to inquire as to the words of the Elders [about] what Andrew or Peter said. . . ."[25] Such a translation suggests that there were three levels of individuals—Papias, the elders, and the apostles—and that Papias asked the elders what the apostles said.

There is no justification for the insertion of the word *about*, for no corresponding term occurs in the Greek text. Such an insertion alters the natural meaning of Papias's statement. In reality, the interrogative expression, "What Andrew or what Peter said," is in apposition to λόγους, "words." To view it as similar to a prepositional phrase—"the words of the elders *about* what Andrew or what Peter said"—is to go beyond the plain meaning of the Greek text.

25. A. H. McNeile, *An Introduction to the Study of the New Testament*, p. 284.

Papias was actually referring to all of the apostles as elders. Thus, the term is being used to refer to older respected leaders regardless of office. This could be the usage that was intended in 2 and 3 John—a designation for the aged and respected apostle John.

The third occurrence of the term appears with the second use of the name John: "and what things Aristion and the presbyter John, the disciples of the Lord, say." The word here translated "Presbyter" is the same word previously translated "elder" (πρεσβύτερος). It may have been used in the same way—to refer to an older, respected leader (namely John the apostle), or it could conceivably have been used differently—to indicate a local church official such as Peter was (1 Pet. 5:1).

If Papias had in mind but one person named John, he must have purposely used two different tenses for the word *say*. In the first instance it was the aorist εἶπεν, "said," but in the second occurrence it was the present λέγουσιν, "say, are saying." While it must be granted that he could have been speaking of two persons with the same name, this interpretation is by no means demanded by the construction of the passage. It is equally possible that his reference was to one and the same John, spoken of under two differing circumstances. In the first case, his past words are in view—what he said in days gone by. However, since John evidently outlived all the other apostles, he alone of the Twelve still may have been living and speaking during Papias's early years. The second reference to the apostle would then be speaking of John's latter years when he was either an elder or an older respected leader in the Ephesian church and a contemporary of Papias.

It can be concluded that: (1) nothing demands the belief that there were two Asian leaders named John, (2) the term *elder* in John's case may simply have been an expression of loving respect, (3) it was not at all inconsistent for an apostle to hold the local church office of elder, and (4) there is no evidence proving that a John other than the apostle produced the Johannine literature.

THE QUESTION OF UNITY OF AUTHORSHIP

Up to this point the authorship of the Johannine writings has been discussed in general. There are, however, differing opinions as to whether or not these books had identical authors. I. Howard Marshall thinks there is an overwhelming probability that the three Johannine epistles came from the same hand, but he indicates it is improbable that many scholars today hold to the common authorship of the gospel and epistles.[26]

As has been noted, a common view today is that the Johannine writings came from "the Johannine circle," to use Cullmann's designation. That is, although the writings were written by different individuals, they all originated in a homogeneous community where theology and religious expression were fairly well stereotyped.

Until 1937, when Dodd published his article "The First Epistle of John and the Fourth Gospel," scholars were generally agreed that the author of the gospel was also the author of the epistles. Dodd, however, presented extensive and detailed arguments against such an authorship.[27] Because of the high respect held for Dodd's scholarship and the widespread influence of his article, careful consideration must be given to his arguments.

THE POSITION OF C. H. DODD

In 1946 Dodd's commentary *The Johannine Epistles* appeared, in which he augmented his already weighty arguments against identity of authorship.[28] His case is threefold. His study of the two Johannine writings convinces him that there are noticeable differences in (1) style and vocabulary, (2) religious background, and (3) theological outlook.

Although Dodd recognizes a similarity of style, he finds a definite difference. There is, he believes, a subtly varied rhythm in the gospel, but in the first epistle the sameness often becomes monotonous. First John lacks the glow, the intensity, and the subdued sense of excitement that is found in the gospel. Dodd recognizes that those are subjective judgments, and thus he supports them by certain grammatical, syntactical, and lexical comparisons. On the one hand, it is said the epistle uses certain favorite grammatical constructions excessively; on the other, it has a much smaller number of compound verbs, particles, prepositions, adverbial particles, conjunctions, and Aramaic idioms. All of this would tend to reduce the style of the writer to a monotonous sameness. A vocabulary count shows the epistle to employ some forty words that

26. I. Howard Marshall, *The Epistles of John, The New International Commentary on the New Testament,* pp. 31-32.
27. C. H. Dodd, "The First Epistle of John and the Fourth Gospel," *Bulletin of the John Rylands Library* 21 (April 1937): 129-56.
28. Dodd, *The Johannine Epistles,* pp. xlvii-lvi.

do not appear in the gospel, and the gospel to employ over thirty terms not found in the epistle.

In two respects Dodd thinks the gospel and first epistle differ in the religious background or atmosphere each seems to reveal. The gospel makes rather extensive use of the Old Testament, both in direct quotations and in allusions, but the epistle has no quotations and only one explicit reference to the Old Testament. It is further asserted that the clear evidence of Semitisms in the gospel is almost totally absent from the epistle. Instead, 1 John gives free play to the Hellenistic element. Expressions such as "God is light" (1 John 1:5) and "God is love" (1 John 4:8) are said to be neither Christian nor Jewish, but Hellenistic.

The theological outlooks of these two writings are also claimed to be at variance. In each of three areas the theology of the epistle is thought to be more primitive. In eschatology Dodd thinks 1 John reveals a primitive expectation of an early return of Christ; the gospel, he is sure, represents a more developed theology in which an imminent return is replaced by a realized eschatology. The redemptive aspects of theology are also stated more primitively in the epistle than in the gospel. The epistle views Christ's death as an expiation ("propitiation," 1 John 2:2; 4:10) for sin, but the gospel sees it as the glorification of Christ and the defeat of Satanic powers. Finally, the two productions seem to differ in their conceptions of the Holy Spirit. First John manifests the primitive or popular view of the Spirit as being "the spirit of prophecy—that is to say, an afflatus, or 'inspiration,' granted to certain individuals, 'prophets' by whom the truth of the gospel is confirmed to those who hear (Acts 5:32; cf. 1 John 5:6)."[29] In contrast, the fourth gospel exhibits a much higher doctrine of the Spirit. He is the author of regeneration (John 3:5-8), the comforter ("helper," John 14:16-17), the witness to Jesus (John 15:26), and the one who convicts men's hearts (John 16:8-11).

On the basis of these differences Dodd asserts: "The simplest hypothesis . . . seems to be that the author of the Epistle was a disciple of the Evangelist and a student of his work. He is not a mere imitator, but he has become possessed by certain of his master's ideas, though not going the whole way with him; and he has caught something of his style and manner, though with a difference."[30]

29. Ibid., p. 96.
30. Ibid., p. lvi.

AN ANALYSIS OF DODD'S POSITION

In response to Dodd's denial of a unity of authorship, several significant analyses have been published. Three studies in particular are worthy of note. In 1947 W. F. Howard's "The Common Authorship of the Johannine Gospel and Epistles" appeared.[31] This was followed the next year by W. G. Wilson's "Examination of the Linguistic Evidence Adduced Against the Unity of Authorship of the First Epistle of John and the Fourth Gospel."[32] Another similar analysis was presented in 1955, written by A. P. Salom and entitled, "Some aspects of the Grammatical Style of 1 John."[33] All these writers have pointed out some of the inherent weaknesses of Dodd's arguments.

Concerning the subjective judgment that the first epistle lacks the subtly varied rhythm, the glow, and the subdued excitement of the gospel, it should be noted that such differences may be the result of a difference in the nature and purpose of the two writings. The gospel is a record of the activities and teachings of Jesus, accompanied by the evangelist's interspersed interpretations. All of that makes for variety. The epistle, however, contains no recitation of events or discourses. It is solidly didactic in nature with no variation from narration to public address to interpretation. Its purpose is not inherently conducive to the subtle variety of rhythm that Dodd finds in the gospel. In general such differences as the subtle variety of rhythm perhaps are indicative, not necessarily of a difference in authorship, but only of purpose, subject matter, and occasion.

The specific linguistic variations have been thoroughly analyzed by Wilson in the article cited above. He compared the two Johannine writings with those of Luke, and demonstrated statistically that the difference in the number of prepositions employed in 1 John and the gospel is not as great, proportionately, as that to be found in Acts and the third gospel. The variation in the number of particles in the two Johannine productions is even less than the variation in Paul's recognized epistles. The difference between

---

31. W. F. Howard, "The Common Authorship of the Johannine Gospel and Epistles," *Journal of Theological Studies* 48 (Jan. 1947): 12-25.
32. W. G. Wilson, "An Examination of the Linguistic Evidence Adduced Against the Unity of Authorship of the First Epistle of John and the Fourth Gospel," *Journal of Theological Studies* 49 (July 1948): 147-56.
33. A. P. Salom, "Some Aspects of the Grammatical Style of I John," *Journal of Biblical Literature* 74 (June 1955): 96-102.

1 John and the gospel in the number of compound verbs employed is considerably less than that same difference between 1 John and the Synoptic gospels. He further demonstrates that compound verbs occur in considerably greater number in narrative sections of the New Testament than in epistolary sections. Against Dodd's argument based on the forty words appearing in the epistle but not in the gospel and the thirty words appearing in the gospel but not in the epistle, Wilson found there is actually more variation in vocabulary between 1 Corinthians and Philippians than between John and 1 John.[34]

More recently Nigel Turner has analyzed the style of the Johannine Epistles as compared with the style of the gospel and has concluded that "the stylistic considerations in favour of unity are indeed overwhelming."[35] He then proceeds to list numerous phrases, words, and stylistic features common to both the gospel and the epistles. Turner singles out such features as the repetition of grammatical constructions, scarcity of particles, prevalence of asyndeton, and synonymous and antithetical parallelism. He concludes the section by asserting: "I John is not likely to have been a linguistic imitation of John, for the last thing its author aims at is literary effect."[36]

Dodd's argument based on the very limited use of the Old Testament in the epistle as compared to such use in the gospel does not take note of two significant considerations. First, an author who is sensitive to his readers will attempt to adjust his writing to meet them where they are. If they are largely Gentiles, he will probably not make extensive use of Jewish materials. That is evident in Paul's epistle to the Philippians, who were quite certainly Gentiles. The letter contains no quotations from the Old Testament and but one possible allusion (2:10-11). The same situation seems to be the case in 1 John. The very last verse of the epistle, "little children, guard yourselves from idols," points to Gentile recipients. Second, it is noteworthy that the Old Testament quotations in the gospel occur largely in the discourses of persons whom the author quotes rather than in the narration itself.[37] It would therefore seem that the author of the Johannine writings was not as much given to Old Testament usage as were the persons he wrote about.

34. Wilson, pp. 149-50.
35. James Hope Moulton, et al., *A Grammar of New Testament Greek*, 4 vols. (Edinburgh: T & T Clark, 1908-76), vol. 4: *Style* by Nigel Turner, p. 133.
36. Ibid.
37. Guthrie, pp. 879-80.

The presence of what Dodd calls "Semitic colouring" in the gospel and its absence in the epistle must likewise be viewed in the light of the purposes of the two writings. The gospel relates history that occurred in a Semitic environment. Its discourses were originally uttered in Aramaic. In fact, the total atmosphere of the story of Jesus Christ is Semitic in nature. The first epistle, however, was written for a Gentile readership. It was not written to relate a Semitic narrative, but rather to meet the threat of a heresy that was largely non-Jewish in its origin. What Hellenistic thought there is in the epistle (and Dodd seems to have made a stronger case for it than the facts justify)—is necessary because of the strong Hellenistic character of the heresy involved.

It is, moreover, doubtful that a very telling case can be made for the assertion that John's statements "God is light" (1 John 1:5) and "God is love" (1 John 4:8) are Hellenistic in form. It must not be forgotten that in the fourth gospel Christ is recorded as saying "I am the light of the world" (8:12). The author may be merely echoing the assertion of the Lord. And since the discovery of the Dead Sea Scrolls, John's use of the terms *light* and *darkness* is seen as reflecting the religious background of Palestine during the first century. Such terms can no longer be characterized as Hellenistic in source. Furthermore, if those two statements (1 John 1:5; 4:8) are Hellenistic, it would seem necessary also to class Jesus' declaration "God is spirit" (John 4:24) as Hellenistic.

Dodd's claim that the first epistle's theology is more primitive than the gospel's is open to serious question. In the first place it seems rather strange that the theology of one whom Dodd identifies as a disciple of the evangelist should be more primitive than the theology of the evangelist himself. It is obvious that the idea of the gospel's eschatology being more advanced than the epistle's is a result of Dodd's preoccupation with the theory of realized eschatology. Although there are elements of truth to be found in this theory, it is a mistake to allow it to obscure clear evidences of a sudden future return of Christ to raise the dead and to execute judgment. To interpret John 5:28-29 strictly in terms of realized eschatology is to ignore the natural meaning of Christ's claim. This eschatology is as primitive as that of 1 John 3:2, "We know that, when He appears, we shall be like Him, because we shall see Him just as He is."

Although it is true that Christ's death is presented in the gospel as His own exaltation and His defeat of satanic powers (12:23, 31; 13:31), this is not at all contradictory to the propitiatory aspect of the cross. We must not overlook the obvious sacrificial significance of John 1:29, "Behold, the Lamb of God who takes away the sin of the world!" Propitiation is also implied in the context of John 3:16, in which Jesus is described as "lifted up," referring to His crucifixion (v. 14). The purpose of this event was to rescue men from destruction and give them everlasting life (vv. 15-16). Again this act of Christ is connected with deliverance from condemnation (vv. 17-19). Thus, the death of Christ enables the believer to escape the just wrath of God (v. 36). In reality this is propitiation, although the term itself is not used here. (See also John 6:51; 10:11, 15; 11:49-52).

Dodd's understanding of the epistle's doctrine of the Holy Spirit also appears to be inadequate. He says that in 1 John the Spirit is not presented "in fully personal terms" as He is in the fourth gospel and the Pauline epistles. However, although the Spirit is referred to by the seemingly impersonal term "anointing," it is clear that this "anointing" performs the personal act of teaching (1 John 2:20, 27). Again, in 1 John 5:8, the Spirit fulfills the personal work of bearing witness. In the context of 4:4 it is entirely proper to understand "He who is in you" as referring to the Holy Spirit and His indwelling ministry of power and wisdom, ideas that are very similar to Paul's concept of the Spirit (1 Cor. 2:10-16; Eph. 3:16).

By way of positive evidence, Howard points out that 1 John was written to enable Christians to face the threats of heresy, and therefore it was necessary to assure them of the guarantee that the inner witness of the Spirit provides. For this reason the epistle's teaching concerning the Spirit differs from that in the gospel. Yet, even in this area there is distinct similarity. Howard insists "it would be hard to find any words more truly in keeping with the teaching of the farewell discourse than the two verses, 'And hereby we know that he abideth in us, by the Spirit which he hath given us,' and 'Hereby know we that we dwell in him, and he in us, because he hath given us of his Spirit' (1 John 3:24; 4:13)."[38]

It is impossible to escape the theological unity that flows through the depths of both books. When one carefully examines the alleged differences between the books, one finds they are the kind of variations that result from different occasions, different purposes, and different content, not from a difference in authorship. When the style, vocabularly, and theology of the two books are compared, the evidences of identity of source are impressive.

---

38. Howard, p. 23.

These two books clearly reveal common authorship when properly examined. This brief survey is sufficient to show that the weightiest attempt to prove a difference of authorship has not achieved its goal.[39] In addition it may be argued that 2 and 3 John show markedly close relationship with 1 John and with the gospel. Second John continues to deal with the same problem of false teachers that is discussed extensively in 1 John (cf. 1 John 2:18-23; 4:1-6; 2 John 7-10). Second John uses terminology that is identical to that used in 1 John, as evidenced by the following:

REPEATED WORDS AND PHRASES

1 John	2 John
τῶν πλανώντων—*the ones deceiving* (2:26)	πλάνοι—"deceivers" (v. 7)
ἐξεληλύθασιν εἰς τὸν κόσμον—"have gone out into the world" (4:1)	ἐξῆλθον εἰς τὸν κόσμον—"have gone out into the world" (v. 7)
ὃ μὴ ὁμολογεῖ—"which does not confess" (4:3)	οἱ μὴ ὁμολογοῦντες—"who confess not" (v. 7, KJV)
Ἰησοῦν Χριστὸν ἐν σαρκὶ ἐληλυθότα—"Jesus Christ having come in flesh" (4:2)	Ἰησοῦν Χριστὸν ἐρχόμενον ἐν σαρκί—"Jesus Christ coming in flesh" (v. 7)
τοῦτό ἐστιν τὸ τοῦ ἀντιχρίστου—"this is the spirit of the antichrist" (4:3)	οὗτός ἐστιν ὁ πλάνος καὶ ὁ ἀντίχριστος—"This is the deceiver and the antichrist" (v. 7)
οὗτός ἐστιν ὁ ἀντίχριστος—"This is the antichrist" (2:22)	

---

39. For further discussion of unity of authorship see A. E. Brooke, *The Johannine Epistles*, The International Critical Commentary, pp. i-xxvii; Stott, pp. 16-24; Marshall, pp. 31-42.

It should also be noted that 2 John and 3 John are tied together by the common designation of the author as "the elder" (2 John 1; 3 John 1), as well as by very similar concluding passages (2 John 12-13; 3 John 13-15). And the gospel and all three epistles are linked by a common use of typically Johannine terminology:

Love—John 13:34-35; 1 John 2:7-11; 3:10-24; 4:7—5:3; 2 John 5; 3 John 1, 6
Truth—John 1:17; 3:21; 14:6, 17; 1 John 1:6-7; 2:4, 21, 27; 4:6; 2 John 1-4; 3 John 8, 12
Walking in truth—1 John 1:6; 2 John 4; 3 John 3-4
Joy—John 16:24; 17:13; 1 John 1:4; 2 John 12; 3 John 4

Having surveyed the reasons for holding that the epistles and the gospel of John were written by the same author, the external evidence concerning the identity of the author must be examined.

EVIDENCE FROM EARLY NON-CANONICAL WRITERS

Probably the earliest specific statement that ascribes authorship to the apostle John was made by Irenaeus of Lyons (c. A.D. 130-200), who wrote his *Refutation and Subversion of Knowledge Falsely So Called* about A.D. 185.[40] In 3.16. 5, this church Father says, "but Him who was born it knew as Jesus Christ the Son of God, and that this same suffered and rose again as John, the disciple of the Lord, verifies. . . . For this reason also he has thus testified to us in his Epistle: 'Little children, it is the last time.' " A loose quotation of 1 John 2:18-22 follows. The authorship of the epistle is ascribed to "John, the disciple of the Lord," *disciple* being a term often used in a broader sense than the word *apostle,* to refer to any follower of Christ. However, the preceding context makes it plain that Irenaeus was speaking of that John who was one of the Twelve. The remainder of the chapter is a discussion of statements from the apostles that contradict the adoptionist ideas of the Valentinians and other Gnostics. It is therefore certain that Irenaeus held that 1 John was written by John the apostle, and not by some other Christian of the same name.

At about the time when Irenaeus was writing, the Muratorian Canon was composed. This fragment is usually dated somewhere between A.D. 170 and A.D. 215; both Edgar J. Goodspeed and

---

40. Edgar J. Goodspeed, *An Introduction to the New Testament,* p. 279.

Moffatt put it about A.D. 200.[41] Concerning the author of our epistle, the Canon says, "What marvel, therefore, if John so constantly brings forward particular [matters] also in his Epistles, saying of himself: 'What we have seen with our eyes and heard with [our] ears and our hands have handled, these things we have written to you.'"[42]

This comment concerning John's epistles is preceded by a description of the occasion that gave rise to the fourth gospel. The Muratorian fragment explains, "The fourth [book] of the Gospels is that of John [one] of the disciples." It seems clear from the context that the term *disciples* is here equated with *apostles* and thus refers to the Twelve.

Clement of Alexandria (c. A.D. 155-215), whose writings are also dated about A.D. 200,[43] leaves no room for doubt concerning the identity of the John who wrote the first epistle. He describes 1 John 2:18-19 as "the word of the Apostle John."[44]

Tertullian also (c. A.D. 155-222), writing about A.D. 200,[45] was equally pointed in ascribing 1 John 4:1-3 to "the Apostle John."[46] It is clear that at the end of the second century the identity of John the apostle as author of 1 John was solidly established in Italy, Gaul, North Africa, and Alexandria.

A few years later Origen of Alexandria (c. A.D. 185-253) added his testimony to the growing list that held John the apostle to be the author. He was quoted by Eusebius as saying, "Why need we speak of him who reclined upon the bosom of Jesus, John, who has left us one Gospel, though he confessed that he might write so many that the world could not contain them? . . . He has left also an epistle of very few lines; perhaps also a second and a third; but not all consider them genuine."[47] Although it is true that Origen did not use the term *apostle*, his description of John as the one who reclined on the bosom of Jesus would seem to suggest that he had one of the Twelve in mind.

About the same time Cyprian of Carthage (c. A.D. 200-258) spoke specifically for apostolic authorship: "And the Apostle John, remembering this charge, subsequently lays it down in his epistle:

41. Ibid., p. 324; Moffatt, p. xxiv.
42. Daniel J. Theron, *Evidence of Tradition*, p. 109.
43. Goodspeed, p. 324; Moffatt, p. xxiv.
44. Clement of Alexandria *Stromata* 3. 6. 45.
45. Merrill C. Tenney, *The New Testament, An Historical and Analytic Survey*, p. 434.
46. Tertullian *Against Marcion* 5. 16.
47. Eusebius *H.E.* 6. 25. 9, 10.

'Hereby,' says he 'we do know that we know him, if we keep his commandments.' "[48]

From Alexandria again came further confirmation in the interesting words of Dionysius, bishop and head of the Alexandrian catechetical school (c. A.D. 200-265). Concerning the John who wrote the Apocalypse, he said, "But I cannot readily admit that he was the apostle, the son of Zebedee, the brother of James, by whom the Gospel of John and the Catholic Epistle were written."[49]

In the first half of the fourth century Eusebius of Caesarea (c. A.D. 260-340) completed his well-known *Ecclesiastical History of the Second and Third Centuries* about A.D. 324-26.[50] His statement concerning 1 John provides a significant summary with which to end this survey of external evidence. He wrote, "But of the writings of John, not only his Gospel, but also the former of his epistles, has been accepted without dispute both now and in ancient times."[51] This statement is a direct declaration that no one anywhere up to that time had rejected the gospel or the first epistle. It further implies that these two writings were received as productions of John. In addition the context reveals that Eusebius was speaking of John the apostle.

It was, therefore, the universal opinion of the church throughout the second and third centuries that John the apostle was the author of the first epistle. No voice was raised in opposition to that view; no other person was suggested as author. It was furthermore commonly assumed that the same John wrote both the fourth gospel and the first epistle.

EVIDENCE FROM THE JOHANNINE LITERATURE

The internal evidence must now be examined in order to ascertain whether it confirms the unanimous testimony of the early church that the first Johannine epistle was written by the apostle John. It is almost unnecessary to point out that neither the epistle nor the gospel make such a claim explicitly. Any evidence that is elicited from these books will of necessity be indirect.

The evidence yielded by an inductive study of the epistle itself

---

48. Cyprian, *Epistles* 24. 2.
49. Eusebius *H.E.* 7. 25.7.
50. Goodspeed, p. 128; Moffatt, p. xxix.
51. Eusebius *H.E.* 3. 24. 17.

will be considered first. Then, on the basis of the convincing arguments for the common authorship of the two books, the evidence for the apostolic authorship of the gospel will be surveyed.

JOHANNINE GREEK STYLE

The Greek of the Johannine gospel and epistles is of a unique character. With a simplicity of syntactical structure, an absence of literary polish, and a limited vocabulary, it combines a certain crispness, a forceful directness, and lucidity of expression, resulting in a most effective end product. Such characteristics are entirely in keeping with what is known of the apostle John. Apparently he had not enjoyed the advantages of extended schooling of any kind. This is indicated both by his family occupation, fishing, and by the comment of Luke that Peter and John were recognized to be "uneducated and untrained men" (Acts 4:13), a description that referred to their lack of formal education. It would therefore be expected that, if in the process of time John learned to write in Greek, his style would be simple and nonliterary.

According to Nigel Turner, this is the type of Greek found in the Johannine writings. He says:

> The style of the Epistles, together with that of the Gospel, is one of extreme simplicity all through, with some monotony of construction. . . . Like the fourth evangelist, he is a cultured man but his Greek is elementary . . . and repetitive . . . , as if it were the style of an old man.[52]

Guthrie sees such characteristics as possible reflections of advanced age. He says, "There is, moreover, a style of language with its somewhat limited powers of expression, its limited vocabulary, and its lack of literary polish, which is not surprising in an aging man to whom maturity of thought was much more important than elegance of expression.[53]

Scholars have also recognized the Semitic character of Johannine Greek. Turner, for example, says, "Although I John has no O.T. quotations, there is evidence that the Greek is Jewish, without however being exclusively Aramaic or Hebrew."[54]

---

52. Nigel Turner, *Style*, p. 135.
53. Guthrie, p. 189.
54. Ibid.

Barrett, writing on the gospel, says, "Perhaps it is safest to say that in language as in thought, John treads, perhaps not unconciously, the boundary between the Hellenic and the Semitic."[55] Marvin Vincent characterized John's style in both gospel and epistle as being "animated with a Hebrew genius."[56] Law refers to "the generally Hebraic type of composition . . . [saying] I am not sure that the closeness with which the style has been moulded upon the Hebraic model, especially upon the parallelistic forms of the Wisdom Literature, has been sufficiently recognized."[57]

One of the features of the epistle is its use of antithetical parallelism (1:6-7, 8-9; 2:4-5, 9-10 etc.). This, as Law points out, is an indication of the epistle's relationship to the Old Testament. While not necessarily certain, it is most natural that such Hebrew color should be an indication of the nationality of the writer. The simplicity of style in combination with the Hebraic spirit that animates Johannine Greek would fit John the apostle, a native of Palestine, a born Jew, brought up in a bilingual world, and living and writing in Greek-speaking Asia.

EYEWITNESS TESTIMONY

An unbiased, first-time reading of the opening verses of the epistle (1:1-4) produces the conclusion that the author was explicitly claiming to have been an eyewitness of at least a portion of the life and ministry of Christ. This impression is confirmed by the further statement of 4:14.

However, Dodd, in the interest of his theory of authorship, argues that these passages do not indicate the writer himself was a literal eyewitness of the life of Christ.[58] There are several possible interpretations of John's use of the pronoun *we* in 1:1-4. He may be using an editorial *we*, in which case he really meant *I*. He may have been referring to a group of eyewitnesses of which he was a part, namely, the apostles. Or he may have been employing the homiletical *we*, in which the speaker identifies himself with Christians in general. The latter view is supported at length by Dodd.

It is clear, unless one is bent on supporting a previously adopted position, that 1:1-4 makes a distinction throughout between the *we*

---

55. Barrett, p. 11.
56. Marvin R. Vincent, *Word Studies in the New Testament*, 2:20.
57. Robert Law, *The Tests of Life*, p. 2. Cf. Otto A. Piper, "I John and the Didache of the Primitive Church," *Journal of Biblical Literature* 66 (Dec. 1947): 442.
58. Dodd, *The Johannine Epistles*, pp. 9-16.

of authorship and the *you* of readership. These four verses are a very distinct unity: Dodd designates them as the "Exordium."[59] The general theme of the section is that the author had received certain information and was now declaring it to his readers. This was being done so that the readers could enter into fellowship with the author and with God the Father and the Son. Starting with the evident fact that verse 4 refers to the author ("we write"), the author's train of thought may then be followed in reverse to verse 1. If the "we" of verse 4 is the *we* of authorship, then it is necessary to understand that the "we" of verse 3a is the *we* of authorship and the "you" is the *you* of readership—"we proclaim to you." But if this be granted, then the "we have seen" of verse 3a likewise refers to the author in distinction from the readers. The "we" who write in verse 4 is the same as the "we" who declare in verse 3a, and the "we" who declare in verse 3a is the same as the "we" who have seen in verse 3a. To carry this analysis back one step further, it is noted that there is a parallel between verses 2 and 3. What the author has said in verse 2 he has picked up again in verse 3 with an added statement of purpose. Notice that in the second verse he has said, "we have seen and bear witness and proclaim to you," and in verse 3 he repeats, "what we have seen and heard we proclaim to you." It is plain that the same distinction evident in verses 3 and 4 between the author and the readers is present in verse 2.

In the same manner, the "we" of verse 1 is tied to the "we" of verses 2, 3, and 4. In verse 2 the author says, "the life was manifested, and we have seen," a statement that is obviously parallel with, and explanatory of, verse 1. If the "we" of verse 2 is the "we" of authorship, there can be little doubt that the "we" of verse 1 has the same meaning. The "we" who have heard, seen, looked upon, and handled is the "we" of verse 4 who wrote the epistle. Thus, the author has made a distinction between the "we" of verse 1 and the "you" of verse 4. Verse 1, then, does not speak of "the whole Church to which the apostolic witness belongs."[60] If such were the case, the passage would be involved in the ridiculous situation in which the whole church ("we") was writing to itself ("you"). It is much easier to accept the more natural interpretation, which sees the author as an eyewitness, than to adopt Dodd's unnatural interpretation in order to avoid the eyewitness claim.

59. Ibid., p. 1.
60. Ibid., p. 16.

Therefore, careful interpretation finds that the epistle came from the pen of an eyewitness, and although such interpretation does not explicitly identify the author, it is in harmony with the testimony of the early church Fathers that John the apostle wrote the book.[61]

AUTHORITATIVE MANNER

The tone of a book is able to provide valuable information about the author. Although it does not explicitly indicate his name, it is capable of supplying corroborative evidence. First John bears an unmistakable air of authority. Its author wrote as one who knew whereof he spoke and who at least assumed that he had the proper authority to speak thus. This authoritative manner is evident throughout the book from the first verse to the last. In 1:1-2 it is the authority of the eyewitness; in 1:3 it is the authority of one who had previously entered the fellowship that he offers his readers. The author assumes the right to outline spiritual standards and categories (1:6-8, 10; 2:4-5), to set forth truth and to distinguish it from error (2:22-23), and to issue commands that he obviously expected to be obeyed (2:15, 24, 28; 4:1; 5:21). Whereas others might, and did, possess such authority and exercise it in their writings, there was no one to whom it was more becoming than to an apostle. Hence, in the authoritative tone of the epistle we find another corroboration of the church Fathers' witness to John as the author.

EVIDENCE OF ADVANCED AGE

The tone of 1 John also seems to suggest that its author was an elderly man. The repeated use of the diminutive τεκνια, "little children," is best understood as the endearing term of a spiritual father for his beloved children (2:1, 12, 28; 3:7, 18; 4:4; 5:21). As Theodor Zahn has pointed out, the author admonished all, young and old, as children, in language that "befits only an old man."[62] This, too, is in harmony with the information from the early church writers concerning John's latter years, when as an aged apostle he ministered to the Christians of Asia.

---

61. For a thorough discussion of the eyewitness evidence see Stott, pp. 26-34.
62. Theodor Zahn, *Introduction to the New Testament*, 3:356.

MARKS OF A "SON OF THUNDER"

By the Lord's own designation John and his brother James came to be known as the "Sons of Thunder" (Mark 3:17), a title that cannot be dismissed as a meaningless nickname. There is good reason to understand it as descriptive of the personalities of those two fishermen. It was John who forbad the exorcist to cast out demons in Jesus' name because he did not follow Christ and His disciples (Mark 9:38). And it was the sons of thunder who wanted to call down bolts of lightning to destroy the inhospitable Samaritans (Luke 9:54). John was not the overly kind, softhearted apostle of love some people assume him to have been. His eyes could flash with the lightning of righteous anger and his voice could echo with the thunder of threatened judgment.

Although many have mistakenly assumed 1 John to be an epistle of tender love, of sweetness and gentleness with no rebuke, such is not the case. In a number of specific points is is obviously the epistle of the son of thunder. Everett F. Harrison lists bluntness and severity of language as one of the letter's characteristics.[63] If a man professes to be what in reality he is not, John does not cover his hypocrisy with nice terms. He declares such a person to be a liar who neither possesses nor practices the truth (1:6; 2:4). False teachers are called antichrists (2:18) and liars (2:22). Again the author designates them as false prophets (4:1). The same kind of blunt forcefulness is evident in the sharp either-or categories the writer sets up. He who knows Christ keeps His commandments; he who does not keep His commandments does not know Him (2:3-4). He who loves his brother dwells in the light; he who hates his brother has lived all his life in darkness (2:9-11). To love the world excludes any possibility of loving the Father (2:15).

A forceful personality cannot readily be concealed. It is inevitably reflected in a person's style of speaking and writing. To this rule 1 John is no exception. Whoever wrote the epistle was obviously a blunt and vigorous individual—a son of thunder. Again the internal evidence is in harmony with the external. Both point to John the apostle as author.

MARKS OF INTIMACY

In the gospels the apostle John is seen as a member of an inner circle of three disciples who sustained a more intimate relationship

---

63. Everett F. Harrison, *Introduction to the New Testament*, p. 415.

with Jesus than the other nine. When the Master entered the house of the synagogue ruler whose daughter had died, He took Peter, James, and John with Him (Mark 5:37 ff.); again it was those three who were allowed to witness the transfiguration (Matt. 17:1 ff.); and when Christ came to the experience of Gethsemane the same trio of disciples entered with Him into the garden where in agony He struggled with the awful reality that lay immediately before Him (Matt. 26:36 ff.).

Exactly why the Lord chose those three for greater intimacy, we cannot be sure. Perhaps it was because they were among the earliest to have become associated with Him, but that cannot be the whole reason, because on that basis Andrew also should have been included. Certain personality traits may well have been involved as bases for our Lord's choice. In the case of John there was, no doubt, what William Alexander called a transparent honesty, "a deep, almost terribly severe view of truth."[64] Evidence of this characteristic is seen, not so much in the gospels, as in the first epistle.

There is indication in the fourth gospel, however, of a certain warmth of personality for John, of a loving intimacy, and of a mystical turn that may be termed deep spirituality. Notice the following facts concerning him:

- He is singled out as the disciple whom Jesus loved (John 13:23; 21:20)
- He reclined at the last supper in the position nearest to Christ (John 13:23; 21:20)
- He was the disciple to whom Jesus committed the care of His mother (John 19:25-27)

All three items are clear indications of the loving warmth of personality that has previously been ascribed to him. The first two items, and perhaps the third as well, are also evidences of the depth of John's spirituality.

In the first epistle signs of the same traits of character are seen. The author speaks of physical contact with the Savior in 1:1: "our hands handled." His references to seeing (1:1-3), hearing (1:1, 3), and fully experiencing the life of Christ (1:2) are also in agreement with what we know of John in the gospels. The mystical aspect of John's spirituality is paralleled by the stress on abiding in

---

64. William Alexander, *The Epistles of St. John*, The Expositor's Bible, p. 55.

Christ or being in Him (2:5-6, 24, 27-28; 3:24; 4:13). Also in harmony with the gospel picture of John is the emphasis on love. In three sections, each longer and more specific than the preceding one, 1 John insists on the absolute necessity of love as a mark of the genuine believer (2:9-11; 3:10*b*-24; 4:7—5:3). In short, it may confidently be affirmed that the epistle is exactly the kind of writing one would expect to come from the John of the gospels.

APOSTOLIC AUTHORSHIP OF THE GOSPEL

Inasmuch as we have concluded that the epistle and the gospel were written by the same person, arguments for the authorship of the gospel have bearing on the authorship of the epistle as well. The external evidence for the gospel is similar to that for the epistle, including such testimonies as those of Irenaeus, Tertullian, Clement of Alexandria, the Muratorian Canon, Dionysius of Alexandria, and Eusebius. In addition, we may cite statements of Theophilus of Antioch (c. A.D. 170) and the Anti-Marcionite Prologue to John (c. A.D. 175).

The internal evidence for the apostolic authorship of the gospel is most thoroughly stated in Westcott's classic commentary, compiled between 1883 and 1887 but first published in 1908.[65] His line of reasoning has been followed, with variations, by numerous writers. It proceeds in concentric circles from the outer layer of evidence to the center point—the conclusion that the author of the gospel was John the apostle.

In 1969 Leon Morris examined the Westcott arguments in the light of the findings of modern Johannine scholarship. His conclusion was that "the massive argument of Westcott has not been decisively refuted."[66] It has been altered in minor points, but the main points still stand. The following paragraphs will survey the Westcott argument and briefly take note of the findings of Morris.

Westcott's case consisted of five main points. First, the author of the gospel was a Jew, as is shown by his intimate knowledge of Jewish life, customs, and language. For example, he explains the meaning of Semitic terms (1:38, 41); he knows of Samaritan-Jewish antipathy (4:9); he understands the popular Jewish attitude

---

65. B. F. Westcott, *The Gospel According to St. John*, pp. ix-lix. Cf. George Salmon, *An Historical Introduction to the Study of the Books of the New Testament*, pp. 257-68.
66. Morris, *Studies in the Fourth Gospel*, pp. 264-65.

toward women (4:27); he knows that the last day of the Feast of Tabernacles is the great day (7:37). Here Morris finds that modern scholarship does nothing but reinforce the Westcott argument. Aramaic studies since Westcott's time have served to strengthen the case for the Semitic background of the gospel.[67]

Westcott's second point was that the author was a Jew of Palestine, a fact revealed by his knowledge of minute details of Palestinian geography and landmarks. For example, the author knows Capernaum is down (about 690 feet below sea level) from Cana (about 1,000 feet above sea level) (2:12); he knows there is much water in Aenon (3:23); he is familiar with the pool near the sheep gate (5:2); he knows the Sea of Galilee also is called the Sea of Tiberias (6:1); he is acquainted with the Temple environs (8:20; 10:23); Bethany is accurately located "about fifteen furlongs" from Jerusalem (11:18, KJV).

Morris's survey of modern writers shows that, apart from Barrett in *The Gospel According to John*, more recent studies have served to confirm the idea that John was a Palestinian Jew. R. D. Potter is cited as concluding that "we have in this Gospel . . . the narrative of a reliable witness, a Palestinian Jew."[68] Morris also quotes Brown's conclusion to his study of the thought lying behind the gospel. He says, "In sum, then, we suggest that into Johannine theological thought patterns has gone the influence of a peculiar combination of various ways of thinking that were current in Palestine during Jesus' own lifetime and after his death.[69]

The third point in the Westcott argument is that the author was an eyewitness, a fact deduced from the minute details that mark his writing. Incidental actions of persons are related, with the names of those involved (6:5-7; 12:21-22; 13:23-26; 14:5, 8-9); details of time are given (1:29, 35, 43; 2:1; 3:2; 4:40, 52); numerical facts are supplied (2:6, 20; 4:18; 5:2, 5; 6:19).

Morris admits, "This part of Westcott's case is vigorously disputed in recent times,"[70] and he refers in particular to objections from Barrett, who makes it a point to attempt to refute eyewitness evidence, arguing that the author may have added incidental de-

---

67. Ibid., p. 221-24.
68. R. D. Potter in *Studia Evangelica*, vol. 1 (Berlin, 1959), p. 331, as cited by Morris, *Studies in the Fourth Gospel*, p. 230.
69. Raymond E. Brown, *The Gospel According to John* (i-xii), p. LXIV, as cited by Morris, *Studies in the Fourth Gospel*, p. 233.
70. Morris, *Studies in the Fourth Gospel*, p. 237.

tails to his work "in order to give it verisimilitude."[71] However, Morris shows that Barrett's standard for eyewitness evidence, by its very nature, would rule out any and all eyewitnesses.[72] In response, Morris refers to A. J. B. Higgins[73] and R. A. Edwards[74] as modern scholars who see the incidental details (pointed to as evidence of an eyewitness) as being so deeply rooted in the tradition as to be an integral part of it.[75]

Westcott's fourth point argues that the author was an apostle. He says this is a necessary conclusion from the restricted nature of some of the events decribed, for example, the author's detailed account of Christ's first contact with some of His future disciples (1:35-51), the journey through Samaria (4:1-45), and the discourses spoken to the disciples alone (chaps. 13-17). More important is that the author knows the very emotions of Christ (11:33; 13:21), as well as His reasons for speaking and acting (2:24-25; 4:1; 5:6, etc.). He also knows some of the innermost thoughts of the Lord (6:6, 61, 64; 13:1, 3, 11, etc.).

Morris recognizes that that kind of evidence is not treated by modern scholars. While admitting that those passages cited above do not actually prove the author to have been an apostle, he points out that such evidence fits well with apostolic authorship and thus serves to corroborate other evidence.[76]

The final point in the argument of Westcott declares the author to have been John the apostle. This specific identification is based on statements assigning the gospel to the disciple whom Jesus loved (21:20, 24). It is to be assumed that the disciple so described would be one of the inner circle—Peter, James, or John. Peter is excluded because he is distinguished from the author (21:20-24), and James is excluded because he was martyred long before the gospel could have been written. At the center of these concentric circles of argument is the one person who best fits the internal evidence, John the apostle.

71. C. K. Barrett, *The Gospel According to St. John*, p. 104, as cited by Morris, *Studies in the Fourth Gospel*, p. 237.
72. Morris, *Studies in the Fourth Gospel*, p. 238.
73. A. J. B. Higgins, *The Historicity of the Fourth Gospel* (London, 1960), pp. 17f., as cited by Morris, *Studies in the Fourth Gospel*, pp. 239-41.
74. R. A. Edwards, *The Gospel According to St. John* (London, 1954), p. 7, as cited by Morris, *Studies in the Fourth Gospel*, p. 242.
75. See also D. A. Carson, "Historical Tradition in the Fourth Gospel: After Dodd What?" pp. 131-32.
76. Morris, *Studies in the Fourth Gospel*, p. 245.

After analyzing Westcott's arguments, Morris again looks at the objections raised by Barrett,[77] the most weighty of which is that it is not probable that a man would refer to himself as "the disciple whom Jesus loved." Although Morris recognizes the strength of this objection, he responds by declaring it to be "a subjective estimate," one that "is countered by the reflection that it is not a designation that a man would naturally use of someone else!"[78] In a footnote Morris points out that Brown admits that if one accepts the claim that the gospel is based on eyewitness testimony, the identification of the beloved disciple with John the son of Zebedee is the most likely hypothesis.[79] To this opinion may be added that of F.-M. Braun who, although holding to a mediate theory of authorship, identifies the beloved disciple as John the apostle.[80] Robinson, as noted before, declares that the beloved disciple and John the son of Zebedee were one and the same.[81]

A concluding note on the historicity of the fourth gospel is in order. In recent years there has developed, as Robinson terms it, a "new look on the fourth Gospel."[82] There is a greater readiness today to accept the independence of the Johannine tradition. Robinson says, "if the Johannine stream is independent of the Synoptists, then potentially it is as near the source as any of the other independent streams of tradition."[83] Along the same line Hunter quotes T. W. Manson as saying, "It is no longer possible to say, 'If the Fourth Gospel contradicts the Synoptists, so much the worse for the Fourth Gospel.' "[84] Referring to the studies of P.-H. Menoud, E. Ruckstuhl, and B. Noack, Robinson concludes, "In John we are dealing with a man who is not piecing together written sources but placing his stamp upon the oral tradition with a sover-

---

77. Barrett, p. 98-99.
78. Morris, *Studies in the Fourth Gospel*, p. 251.
79. Raymond E. Brown, *The Gospel According to John*, p. XCVIII, as cited by Morris, *Studies in the Fourth Gospel*, p. 252, n. 97.
80. F.-M. Braun, *Jean le Théologien*, p. 396f. as cited by Rudolf Schnackenburg, *The Gospel According to St. John*, 1:101.
81. Robinson, *Redating the New Testament*, p. 310.
82. Robinson, *Twelve New Testament Studies*, pp. 94-106.
83. Ibid., p. 96. Robinson first made this statement in 1957 (cf. A. M. Hunter, *According to John*, p. 14); nineteen years later he has gone so far as to declare his acceptance of apostolic authorship of the fourth gospel (*Redating the New Testament*, p. 310).
84. T. W. Manson, *Rylands Bulletin*, May 1947, as quoted in A. M. Hunter, *Interpreting the New Testament 1900-1950*, p. 90.

eign freedom. Indeed, he *is* his own tradition. As Menoud puts it, it is as if he is saying to us from beginning to end: 'La tradition, c'est moi!' "[85]

In the light of the current flux and the new view of the fourth gospel that has emerged, it is not unreasonable for a theological conservative to conclude that the arguments decidedly favor John the apostle as the author of both the fourth gospel and the first epistle.

---

85. Robinson, *Twelve New Testament Studies*, pp. 97-98.

3

Date, Place, and Recipients of the Epistle

In chapter 1 it was assumed that 1 John was written about A.D. 90 in the Roman province of Asia to the major churches of that province. It is the purpose of this chapter to provide the supporting facts upon which these assumptions rest.

DATE AND PLACE OF WRITING

Any determination of the date of 1 John must take into consideration a number of items, such as the question of the priority of the fourth gospel or the first epistle, the testimony of tradition, the content of the epistle, and the development of heresy in the early church. Although the nature of the evidence prevents pinpointing a specific year, such considerations can and do suggest a general period of time during which John penned his first epistle.

THE QUESTION OF PRIORITY

Various suggestions have been offered explaining the relationship of 1 John to the fourth gospel. Some have thought that the epistle was written at the same time as the gospel and served as a sort of covering letter introducing the larger work, or that 1 John was a preface to the gospel and thus immediately preceded it. Others, arguing for the priority of the gospel, have contended that

1 John was intended to popularize the contents of the gospel or to refute its Gnostic use, or to soften elements in the gospel that had proved offensive to the church.

That the two books were not written simultaneously to the same audience seems evident from a comparison of their declared purposes. The gospel states, "But these have been written that you may believe that Jesus is the Christ, the Son of God; and that believing you may have life in His name" (John 20:31). The epistle, however, declares "These things I have written to you who believe in the name of the Son of God, in order that you may know that you have eternal life" (1 John 5:13). The gospel assumes a readership in need of evangelization; the epistle assumes a readership of believers who need bases for the assurance of their salvation. Consequently, Lightfoot's idea that 1 John was a cover letter for the gospel seems out of the question. The only way in which the two books could be explained as originating simultaneously would be to assume that they had different readers in view.

The arguments for the priority of 1 John have been most completely set forth and explained by A. E. Brooke,[1] and listed succinctly by Guthrie.[2] The weightiest argument for gospel priority is the fact that many passages in the epistle are made more understandable when viewed against the background of statements in the gospel (cf. 1 John 2:23 and John 15:23ff.; 1 John 2:27 and John 14:26; 1 John 3:8 and John 8:44).[3] It is chiefly on the strength of this argument that the majority of scholars have concluded that the gospel is the earlier of the two works. However, in so doing, many show caution. Westcott was willing to state confidently only that "the Epistle presupposes in those for whom it was composed a familiar acquaintance with the characteristic truths which are preserved for us in the Gospel."[4] And Brooke says, "Even if we need the Gospel to explain the Epistle, the readers of it may have had their necessary commentary in the author's oral teaching."[5] That a previous acquaintance with John's teachings is

---

1. A. E. Brooke, *A Critical and Exegetical Commentary on the Johannine Epistles,* The International Critical Commentary, pp. xix-xxii.
2. Donald Guthrie, *New Testament Introduction,* pp. 881f.
3. For additional arguments for the priority of the gospel, see Henry Alford, *The Greek Testament,* 4:169; Karl Braune, "The Epistles General of John," in *A Commentary on the Holy Scriptures,* 9:16; Brooke, pp. xxiiiff.
4. B. F. Westcott, *The Epistles of St. John,* p. xxxi.
5. Brooke, p. xxiv.

needed is certain, for in a number of places the epistle assumes knowledge of distinctively Johannine ideas.

John's stress upon love as Christ's new commandment (John 13:34-35; 15:12, 17) is assumed to be already familiar to the recipients of the epistle (1 John 2:7-8; 3:11; 4:21). The equally Johannine emphasis on eternal life (John 3:15-16, 36; 10:28; 17:2-3) is also referred to as a concept well-known to the readers (1 John 2:25; 5:13, 20). It is asserted (1 John 2:13-14) that they have known Christ as the One who has existed from "the beginning" (cf. John 1:1-2). And it is taken for granted (1 John 2:20-21, 27) that they are aware of the teaching ministry of the Holy Spirit (John 15:26; 16:13-14). These facts at least show that the recipients of 1 John were thoroughly acquainted with his distinctive emphases. It is quite possible that even more is indicated.

A careful verse-by-verse comparison of 1 John with the gospel reveals that at least eighty percent of the verses in the epistle reflect concepts to be found in the gospel. This finding confirms the assertion that the readers were previously familiar, at the least, with Johannine teaching, but it also strengthens the probability that they possessed that teaching in the written form of the fourth gospel. Therefore, although the priority of the gospel cannot be demonstrated as proven fact, it can be shown to be probable. Brooke views the possibility of a later date for the composition of the gospel as "extremely unlikely,"[6] thus opting for a later date for the epistle rather than an earlier one.

THE TESTIMONY OF TRADITION

Although the writers of the early church do not comment specifically concerning the date of 1 John or its place of origin, they do make a number of statements that have a general bearing on that question.

Irenaeus discusses the writing of the first three gospels and then says, "Afterwards, John, the disciple of the Lord, who also had leaned upon His breast, did himself publish a Gospel during his residence at Ephesus in Asia."[7] Eusebius likewise, after commenting on Matthew, Mark, and Luke, adds, "And when Mark and Luke had already published their Gospels, they say that John, who had employed all his time in proclaiming the Gospel orally, finally

6. Ibid., p. xxvii.
7. Irenaeus *Against Heresies* 3. 1. 1.

proceeded to write."⁸ Irenaeus, in his refutation of the Gnostics by use of apostolic tradition, wrote, "Then, again, the Church in Ephesus, founded by Paul, and having John remaining among them permanently until the times of Trajan, is a true witness of the tradition of the apostles."⁹ Referring to John as the one "who beheld the apocalyptic vision" (the book of Revelation), Irenaeus explained, "For that was seen no very long time since, but almost in our day, towards the end of Domitian's reign."¹⁰ Eusebius follows his discussion of the persecution under Domitian with the statement, "It is said that in this persecution the apostle and evangelist John, who was still alive, was condemned to dwell on the island of Patmos in consequence of his testimony to the divine word."¹¹ In the same chapter Eusebius explains that that persecution was in process during "the fifteenth year of Domitian," which was A.D. 96, the last year of his reign. In a later section, this early church historian further testifies: "At that time the apostle and evangelist John, the one whom Jesus loved, was still living in Asia, and governing the churches of that region, having returned after the death of Domitian from his exile on the island."¹² Clement of Alexandria is quoted as saying: "For when, after the tyrant's death, he returned from the isle of Patmos to Ephesus, he went away upon their invitation to the neighboring territories of the Gentiles, to appoint bishops in some places, in other places to set in order whole churches, elsewhere to choose to the ministry some one of those that were pointed out by the Spirit."¹³

There is no definite information in the church Fathers concerning the date when John first came to Ephesus. The latest reference to him in the New Testament, apart from the statement of his exile in the Apocalypse (1:9), is Paul's word in Galatians 2:9 placing him in Jerusalem at the time of Paul's visit to Jerusalem with Barnabas and Titus. If this was the occasion of the missionary conference of Acts 15, the date would be about A.D. 50.

Prior to the destruction of Jerusalem the Christians are said to have fled from the doomed city to find refuge in Pella.¹⁴ However, John next appears in Ephesus, as the above-quoted statements

---

8. Eusebius *H. E.* 3. 24. 7.
9. Irenaeus *Against Heresies* 3. 3. 4. Cf. 2. 22. 5.
10. Ibid., 5. 30. 3.
11. Eusebius *H. E.* 3. 18. 1.
12. Ibid., 3. 23. 1.
13. Ibid., 3. 23. 6.
14. Ibid., 3. 5. 3.

from the church Fathers indicate. In the absence of any more accurate information it may assumed that the apostle took up his residence there about the time of Jerusalem's destruction (A.D. 70). It appears that instead of going to Pella, he, along with Andrew and Philip, settled in Asia. The failure of Paul's Timothy letters to mention John's presence at Ephesus, as well as the need for Timothy to be stationed there (1 Tim. 1:3ff.), are evidences that John had not yet come to Asia when Paul wrote (A.D. 63-67).

While in residence there John wrote the fourth gospel. It may be inferred from Eusebius's above quoted remark that the book was composed after a number of years of Asian ministry. This might place the origin of the gospel as late as the eighties, perhaps between A.D. 85 and A.D. 90. Therefore, based on the previous conclusion that 1 John came after the gospel, it would appear necessary to date the epistle later than A.D. 85.

The latest possible date is determined by Polycarp's quotation of 1 John 4:23 in his *Letter to the Philippians* (chap. 8). Although there have been attempts to prove otherwise, it is quite certain that that Philippian letter was written about the time of Ignatius's death, that is, about A.D. 116. It is probable, however, that John did not live until A.D. 116. An earlier death seems likely because he would have been well over 100 years of age by the time of Ignatius's martyrdom. Also, the statements of Irenaeus, Clement of Alexandria, and Eusebius that John lived until the times of Trajan (A.D. 98-117) may best be taken to imply that he died early in Trajan's reign. Both his age and these statements of the church Fathers would indicate that the latest date for the epistle would be about A.D. 100.

On the basis of tradition it may be concluded that 1 John was written sometime between A.D. 85 and A.D. 100. Since tradition indicates that the gospel was written at Ephesus, that John dwelt at Ephesus prior to his exile to Patmos, and that he returned there after his banishment, it seems most likely that 1 John also originated in that city.

INTERNAL EVIDENCE

As in the case of tradition, internal evidence may provide clues to help place the book chronologically.

One cannot escape the constantly recurring evidence that the author possessed an intimate knowledge of his readers and their problems. His affectionate "little children" (τεκνία) is one of the most evident signs of familiarity (2:1, 12, 28; 5:21; see also the

Date, Place and Recipients of the Epistle 43

term "beloved" [ἀγαπητοί] in 3:2, 21; 4:1, 7, 11). The writer knows their spiritual condition (2:12-14, 21); he is aware of the dangers confronting them (2:26; 4:1). He speaks to them as one who has been among them in the capacity of a revered spiritual father for a number of years, which would confirm the conclusion that the epistle probably originated after A.D. 85.

Alexander Ross sees in the tone of the book a suggestion that the author wrote in his later years: "The whole tone of the Epistle would seem to indicate that it is the work of a man of mature years and of mellow Christian character, who, out of the depths of a profound experience through many years of the riches of the grace of Christ, addresses his frequent loving exhortations as to his "little children."[15] Intangible as this tone may be, it is a further confirmation of the conclusion that the epistle originated in the last quarter of the first century.

That John wrote some time before the period of the Ignatian letters is apparent from a comparison of the church life reflected in the epistles of Ignatius with that reflected in the Johannine letters. Dodd says, "The ecclesiastical situation in the province of Asia, as represented in these epistles (the Johannine epp.), seems earlier than the situation represented in the Epistles of Ignatius, A.D. 115.... The Epistle of Clement to the Corinthians (about A.D. 96) seems to reflect a situation at Corinth comparable with that presupposed in our epistles."[16] In Ignatius's day the power and prestige of the bishop was much more pronounced than in the day of the Johannine epistles. First John gives no stress to the episcopal idea at all, and in 2 and 3 John the only term employed of any church leader is the title of elder, which John applies to himself. In Ignatius there is constant stress on submission to the bishop who is compared to God the Father, whereas the elders are made to be like the apostles.[17] In Clement the Corinthians are rebuked for having dismissed bishops without cause, but there is no noticeable exaltation of the episcopal office. In fact, it appears that the offices of elder and of bishop are still viewed as one and the same.[18]

A comparison of the heresy confronted by the church in A.D.

---

15. Alexander Ross, *The Epistles of James and John*, The New International Commentary on the New Testament, p. 118.
16. C. H. Dodd, *The Johannine Epistles*, The Moffatt New Testament Commentary, p. lxvii.
17. Ignatius *Mag.* 6.
18. *I Clem.* 44.

115-116 with that of the times of John's letters also shows the latter writings to come from a somewhat earlier day. As Guthrie says, "The letter (I Jn.) belongs to a period when Gnosticism is certainly on the horizon, although not as yet fully developed."[19] In Ignatius a full-blown Gnosticism is not yet seen either; nevertheless there is evidence that the teachings of the Docetists had arrived at a more solid state than in John's day (cf. 1 John 1:1ff.; 2:18-19, 22; 4:2-3 and *Trall.*, 10. 1; *Smyr.*, 2. 1; 5. 2).

Finally, it has been pointed out by Karl Braune and others that there is no hint of any persecution in 1 John.[20] This might suggest a time after the death of Domitian (A.D. 96) or, as is more probable, before the beginning of the Domitianic persecutions, which according to Eusebius occurred in the latter part of the Emperor's reign.[21]

CONCLUSION

A date for the epistle then is determined on the one hand by the probable priority of the gospel, which may be placed between A.D. 85 and 90, by the evidence of the author's long-standing, intimate knowledge of the readers, and by the indications of the advanced age of the writer. These factors all argue against an earlier date. On the other hand, the date is determined by tradition that seems to suggest John lived until the time of Trajan (A.D. 98), by the extreme old age of John made necessary if it is assumed the letter was written in the second century, by the evidence of an earlier ecclesiastical situation than that of Ignatius's day, by the indications of an earlier stage of Gnostic development, and by the lack of evidence of persecution. These factors all argue further against a later date. It would seem therefore that an intermediate date between A.D. 90 and 95 would best fit all the data surveyed.

Chiefly on the basis of evidence from the church Fathers it is further concluded that John wrote his first epistle while living at Ephesus.

RECIPIENTS OF THE EPISTLE

It is especially important to ascertain as clearly as possible the identity of the intended recipients of 1 John. No New Testament book originated in a vacuum. In every case the writings arose to

19. Guthrie, p. 205.
20. Braune, p. 15.
21. Eusebius *H. E.* 3. 18.

meet specific needs of people surrounded by specific circumstances. Consequently, to know who the recipients of 1 John were and what their spiritual conditions and needs were is to be better qualified to understand the epistle addressed to them.

EVIDENCE FROM THE EPISTLE

1. *Their religious background.* A survey of 1 John reveals several facts concerning the persons addressed, one of the most obvious of which is that they were Christians. The clearest statement of their faith appears in 2:12-14, where John in a repetitive sequence of declarations asserts that the readers had experienced forgiveness, that they knew both Father and Son, that God's word dwelt in them, and that they were victorious over the devil. This one passage alone is sufficient to establish beyond a doubt the fact of their Christian faith. Further examination of this and other statements reveals something of the quality and duration of their experience.

It seems clear that at least some of them had been followers of Christ for a number of years. That they had possessed knowledge of the old/new commandment "from the beginning" (2:7-8) suggests that considerable time had elapsed since they first responded to the gospel message (cf. 3:11). The same impression is gained from 2:24, where John urges his readers to let the truth they had "heard from the beginning" continue to dwell in them. It is evident from a number of passages that those believers had received spiritual instruction, even extending to eschatological details. They knew the truth (2:20-21); they knew something of the doctrine of the atonement (3:5); they knew something of the moral fruits of the gospel (3:15); and they were familiar with the doctrine of antichrist (2:18; 4:3). It is furthermore quite clear that the readers were not immature in faith or in life. They were victorious over the devil (2:13-14); they were strong (2:14); they possessed an experiential understanding of God's truth (2:14); and they were taught by the indwelling Holy Spirit (2:20, 27). As a result of such spiritual maturity, John did not find it necessary to rebuke his readers, but only to exhort and warn gently. The strong language of the epistle is not directed against the intended readers, but against the false teachers who threatened them.

2. *Their ethnic background.* There has been some question as to whether John's readers were Jews or Gentiles. In the main, discussion of this point centers on the closing exhortation, "Little children, guard yourselves from idols" (5:21). Although the reference

to idols seems to point to Gentile readers, some have suggested that the term may be used figuratively to refer to "the chimeras of false teaching, which are as empty and misleading as the objects before which the pagans bow."[22] That interpretation would remove any suggestion that the readers were Gentile and would leave the door open for a Jewish readership. Robinson supports the latter view by reminding us that the epistle refers to Cain as though the readers were familiar with the Old Testament story. It is further pointed out that, whereas Paul lays stress on confessing Jesus as Lord, John emphasizes confession of Jesus as Christ; the epistle insists that one must have the Son in order to have the Father (2:22); the terms used in condemnation of the heresy are all Jewish terms (idolatry, 5:21; false prophecy, 4:1, antichrist, 2:18; 4:3); and the moral strictures of the epistle are Jewish (3:4; 5:16). Robinson, therefore, believes that the Johannine epistles as well as the gospel were written to Greek-speaking Diaspora Judaism.[23]

There are, however, other arguments that favor a Gentile destination for the epistle. First, it is more natural to understand the reference to idols in its literal sense, since nothing in the context indicates it is to be given any other connotation. Second, the absence of any Old Testament quotations must not be passed over lightly. If the heresy combated in 1 John had as many Jewish connections as Robinson claims, it is quite strange that the Old Testament was not used in refuting the heresy. Third, the Jewish terms and usages that do occur are quite natural when it is remembered the author was himself a Jew, steeped in Jewish religious influence, and that the Christian faith, as the flower of Old Testament religion, adopted many Jewish terms and usages as customary expressions of truth.

What evidence there is concerning the question of Jewish or Gentile recipients seems to favor the latter. However, it is quite possible that the readers included both Diaspora Jews and native Gentiles. That would be a most natural situation anywhere outside Palestine, as an analysis of the converts on Paul's missionary journeys shows.

3. *Their geographical location.* Inasmuch as the locale of the readers is not stated in the epistle, any attempt to identify them on the

---

22. Everett Harrison, *Introduction to the New Testament*, p. 420.
23. J. A. T. Robinson, *Twelve New Testament Studies*, Studies in Biblical Theology, no. 34, pp. 130-37.

Date, Place and Recipients of the Epistle 47

basis of internal geographical evidence must be based on inference. It is possible that the absence of any specific identification is, in itself, an indication that no single locality is in view. This is confirmed by the fact that no personal greetings were sent.

It would seem reasonable to deduce from the general nature of the epistle that it was intended for a number of churches. There is evidence, however, that the recipients possessed a certain homogeneity. They were believers who each possessed a number of the same spiritual characteristics. They also were confronted with a common spiritual peril—the threat of heresy. These facts suggest the intended recipients were located in several towns within a certain well-defined geographical area with the churches bound together by similar sociological factors.

Further it must be added that, although he does not address them by name, John knows his readers somewhat intimately. His affectionate "little children" (2:1, 28; 3:7, 18; 4:4; 5:21) and "beloved" (3:2; 4:1, 7, 11) reveal a close personal relationship, as does his detailed knowledge of their spiritual condition (see above). Therefore, John wrote to a group of churches in a fairly well-defined area where he was personally and affectionately known. Beyond this point the internal evidence does not go.

EVIDENCE FROM NONCANONICAL WRITINGS

The earliest confirmed uses of 1 John are found in the writings of Polycarp of Smyrna (c. A.D. 116) and Papias of Hierapolis (c. A.D. 120-160). Although the epistle may have been equally well known in a number of other areas in those early years, it is likewise possible that its appearance in Asia first of all means that it was sent to the churches of that province. If such was the case, it would agree with the deduction that the letter was sent to a group of churches in an area bound together by common sociological and geographical factors. Such a description would be true of the congregations of provincial Asia.

As was previously shown in the discussion of date and place of writing, John spent his latter years in Ephesus and apparently wrote his first epistle from that city. His activity while residing there seems to have been made up largely of ministry among the churches of Asia. This included oral proclamation of the gospel, according to Eusebius,[24] as well as church administration.[25] Clem-

---
24. Eusebius *H. E.* 3 24. 7.
25. Ibid., 3. 23. 1.

ent of Alexandria indicates that John traveled among the churches in areas surrounding Ephesus for the purpose of choosing men for the ministry, appointing bishops, and dealing with church problems.[26] The apostle's relationship to Asia is further confirmed by the address and contents of the Apocalypse. The book of Revelation was specifically sent to "the seven churches which are in Asia" (1:11, KJV). In addition, the contents of the second and third chapters of Revelation seem to imply a close tie between the author of the book and the churches addressed.

John's preaching, his administrative work, and his literary activity all had to do with the Asian churches. Because 1 John gives evidence of having been written for a number of churches, the most reasonable suggestion concerning the intended recipients is that the letter was addressed to the churches of provincial Asia, among which John exerted apostolic influence during his later life.

Surveying the evidence, both from the epistle and from other sources, leads to the conclusion that John's first letter was written from Ephesus, sometime between A.D. 90 and 95, to the churches of the Roman province of Asia. No other conclusion harmonizes the available facts about date, place, and recipients as well as this traditional view does.

---

26. Ibid., 3. 23. 6.

4

The Occasion and Purpose of the Epistle

In the study of the background of a New Testament epistle, few other factors are quite as significant as the occasion that called the letter into existence. Seeing the epistle in the light of the needs and problems of the first century will reveal how it should be applied to the needs and problems of today.

It was assumed in the first chapter that 1 John was written to counter an early form of Gnosticism. The basis for such an assumption will now be discussed.

Occasion

The epistle itself will first be examined to discover elements of the occasion mirrored there. These elements will then be compared with data from the early noncanonical writings to ascertain more exactly the situation at which the letter was aimed.

EVIDENCE FROM THE EPISTLE

Although the author may have had several needs in view when he wrote, it is apparent there was one overriding problem that called for treatment. Throughout the epistle there is evidence that John's readers were confronted with teachers of doctrinal error. John pointedly declares, "These things I have written to you concerning those who are trying to deceive you" (2:26). The present tense participle πλανώντων is undoubtedly a conative present used to describe an attempted action.[1] The threat of those deceivers may also be seen in 1:3 where John says, "What we have seen and heard we proclaim to you also, that you also may have fellowship with us." Behind this simple declaration of purpose may be discerned the efforts of the false teachers to win the believers over to heretical doctrines and thus to sever their fellowship with the apostle. John, therefore, seeks to fortify the doctrinal foundation of that fellowship in order to counteract the teachers' activities.

The apostle is not referring to an isolated instance, nor to a limited number of false teachers. On the contrary, he asserts that there are many such occasions and he characterizes the teachers as antichrists, saying, "Children, it is the last hour; and just as you have heard that antichrist is coming, even now many antichrists have arisen" (2:18). Again, describing them as false prophets, he says, "Beloved, do not believe every spirit, but test the spirits to see whether they are from God; because many false prophets have gone out into the world" (4:1). Because of the many propagators of error, it was more than a remote possibility that the readers would be accosted by them.

At one time those teachers had been within the churches, apparently as professing believers. They were not opponents who came from without with the intent of attacking and destroying the churches. They were one-time members who began their propagation of error within the sphere of Christian fellowship. However, it appears that because they did not find there a ready acceptance of their ideas, they withdrew from the fellowship of the churches. John refers to their departure, saying, "They went out from us, but they were not really of us; for if they had been of us, they would have remained with us; but they went out, in order that it might be shown that they all are not of us" (2:19). It was because of the fundamental difference between those "antichrists," as John calls them, and the orthodox believers that the heretics withdrew. However, the apostle further explains that their withdrawal produced an additional result. It showed clearly that the errorists were really not to be considered as representative of the Christian community. The divine intention in the break was to make a clear demarcation between the genuine and the spurious.

Although the false teachers no longer were active members of

---

1. F. Blass and A. Debrunner, *A Greek Grammar of the New Testament*, trans. and ed. Robert W. Funk, 3d rev. ed., sec. 319.

the churches, they did not completely sever relationships. It was their persistent influence from without that made it necessary for John to write. Apparently they continued to press the claims of their teaching upon individuals within the churches. Second John seems to indicate that they traveled about in the guise of Christian teachers and attempted to gain entrance to those who had not yet been instructed concerning their error (2 John 7-11).

John uses strong terminology in his description of those opponents of the truth. The term "antichrist" (2:18, 22) shows that in the apostle's mind they were in reality against Christ. He also calls them false prophets (4:1). In both the Old and New Testaments a prophet is a person who speaks under the influence of inspiration. He is inspired by a spirit, either from God or from the devil. That John regarded those prophets as moved by an evil spirit seems evident from his use of the term *spirit* in 4:1-6. They were inspired by the spirit of error, which is also characterized as the spirit of antichrist. Thus, their teachings and motivation are treated as satanic in source.

As John viewed it, the very core of the heresy was an erroneous concept of the Person of Christ. Because Christology is at the heart of orthodox Christianity, it is possible to use it as the criterion by which to distinguish the false from the true. John has done that in several passages of his epistle, the clearest of which are 2:22-23 and 4:2-3. In the former he says, "Who is the liar but the one who denies that Jesus is the Christ? This is the antichrist, the one who denies the Father and the Son. Whoever denies the Son does not have the Father; the one who confesses the Son has the Father also." Here the test question is, Do you believe that Jesus is the Christ? That John is not using the term *Christ* in the Old Testament messianic sense is apparent from verse 23, where he employs "Son" interchangeably with "Christ." The same interchange is found in a comparison of 4:15 and 5:1. The first of those two verses speaks of God dwelling in the believer, and the second has to do with being born of God. The second experience, regeneration, is in reality the initiation of the first experience, divine indwelling. And both experiences are the product of believing in Jesus—in 4:15 as the Son of God, and in 5:1 as the Christ. It is therefore reasonable to conclude that John uses the term *Christ* synonymously with the designation *Son of God*. Thus, at the very heart of the error being combated in this epistle is the denial that Jesus is the Son of God, the pre-existent second Person of the Trinity.

This denial is stated in a slightly different way in 4:2-3, "By this you know the Spirit of God: every spirit that confesses that Jesus Christ has come in the flesh is from God; and every spirit that does not confess Jesus is not from God; and this is the spirit of the antichrist, of which you have heard that it is coming, and now it is already in the world." Here the test question concerns the confession of the incarnation. The Asian churches were being confronted with a denial of the full humanity of Christ, a denial that the Christ had actually possessed a body of flesh.[2] John does not go beyond this point in the description of the heresy. He does not delineate any of the "positive" elements of the heretical Christology. Consequently we have only his refutations of the false teachers to use in identifying the error.

First John 1:1 and 5:6 also seem to refer to a common error. However, in these verses the author is not as explicit as in the two previous passages. The emphatic declaration of first-hand information with which the epistle begins may have been intended as a positive refutation of the Christology of the false teachers. John's insistence that he had heard, seen, looked at, and handled "what was from the beginning" (1:1) seems to indicate that his readers were being confronted with a denial by the false teachers of the validity of John's experience and doctrine. The heretics may have refused to accept the teaching that the flesh-and-blood Jesus and the pre-existent Son were one and the same person. Again nothing is said about what they did believe about Jesus; only their denial is hinted at.

Doctrinal error, however, was but one side of the heresy mirrored in 1 John. Theological deviation was accompanied by moral deviation. That is apparent from the repeated insistence that those who walk in darkness, who do not keep His commandments, and who continually practice sin, are not of God. After declaring

---

2. Raymond Brown, *The Community of the Beloved Disciple*, pp. 112-13, sees the denial that Jesus Christ has come in the flesh (4:2-3) as an indication that John's opponents placed such an emphasis on the divine in Jesus that the human side of His person was minimized. In that case, that Jesus had a real human body was not what the opponents were denying. Instead they denied that Jesus' human existence was significant for salvation. What was important, they said, was that the Son had brought eternal life to people when He became incarnate. The reason that Brown finds this interpretation to be preferable to the commonly held view that the opponents denied Christ's incarnation is that several recently found Gnostic manuscripts seem to indicate that some Gnostics, at least, accepted an actual incarnation. The *Tripartate Tractate* (I 113:37), for example, speaks of an "unbegotten, *impassible* Word *[Logos]* who came into being in the flesh," (cited by Brown, p. 112).

that God is light in 1:5, John says, "If we say that we have fellowship with Him, and yet walk in the darkness, we lie and do not practice the truth" (1:6). In 2:4 the term "fellowship" is replaced by the term "know," and "walk in darkness" is replaced by "does not keep his commandments," and in 3:8 the one who practices sin is said to be of the devil. On the positive side, the one who sustains a vital relationship with God walks in the light (1:7), obeys His commandments (2:3, 5), and practices righteousness (2:29; 3:7, 9).

Behind this moral weakness lies a very inadequate view of sin, in fact, a denial of sin. In 1:8 John speaks of those who may profess that they do not have sin, and in 1:10 of those who may profess that they have not committed any acts of sin. When read in context, these verses obviously cannot be understood as referring to persons claiming sinless perfection, as that term is understood today. John has in mind people who walk in darkness, disobey God's commands, and practice sin, and yet who claim that they neither are sinful nor guilty of committing sin. How they explain their claim the epistle does not make clear. Whether or not their view of sin grows out of their theology is not stated. All that is known is that John is combatting an antinomianism that, in some way, insists that sin is not sin and that the sinner is not sinful.

One more characteristic of the heretics seen in the epistle needs to be examined. John lays repeated stress on love for fellow believers, an area in which the heretics apparently were drastically lacking. This is clearly seen in the strong language employed in 2:9-11: "The one who says he is in the light and yet hates his brother is in darkness until now. The one who loves his brother abides in the light and there is no cause for stumbling in him. But the one who hates his brother is in the darkness and walks in the darkness, and does not know where he is going because the darkness has blinded his eyes." Even more bluntly emphatic is John's declaration in 3:14-15: "We know that we have passed out of death into life, because we love the brethren. He who does not love abides in death. Everyone who hates his brother is a murderer; and you know that no murderer has eternal life abiding in him." It is plain that these two verses are not accusing believers of lovelessness. Believers know they have passed from death to life because they love the brothers. There is, however, another group in view that hates the brothers, and in the light of the main thrust of the whole epistle it seems most logical to identify that group as those who deny the incarnation and who have explained away the

Judaeo-Christian view of sin. The false teachers departed from the Christian circle of fellowship (2:18-19), and it is reasonable to assume that that occurred as a result of a deep and abiding antipathy toward those who would not receive their heretical ideas. A decision concerning the probable identity of this and other above-mentioned errors must await an examination of the heresies circulating in the early church at the end of the first century.

THE HERESIES OF THE EARLY CHURCH

1. *The Judaizers.* The earliest heresy to invade the infant church was the attempt made by the Judaizers to syncretize Judaism and Christianity. The first response the church made to that endeavor took the form of a council held in Jerusalem (Acts 15), as a result of which a letter was sent to the Gentile churches of Syria, Cilicia, and Antioch informing them of the decision of that official gathering (Acts 15:23-29). A major document, Paul's epistle to the Galatians, was also written in refutation of the Judaistic heresy.

A comparison of the false teaching reflected in 1 John with that combated in Galatians does not reveal any basic similarities. Although some have suggested that John's statement concerning the confession of Jesus as the Christ is indicative of a Judaistic heresy, it is evident that John does not use the term *Christ* in the Jewish messianic sense. He employs it as interchangeable with the expression *Son of God*. In addition, it is impossible to accuse the Judaizers of being in any sense antinomian as the heretics of 1 John were. On the contrary, they stressed the keeping of the law, both moral and ceremonial. Furthermore, there is every reason to believe that the influence of the Judaizers in the church did not persist beyond the destruction of Jerusalem. The period in which the Johannine literature arose was much later than the time when the Judaizers flourished.

2. *The Gnostic sects.* The second great heresy of the early church was really not a single, unified school of thought. It was a complex phenomenon. From the latter half of the first century on into the second and third centuries there appeared a number of heretical systems that have been generally categorized as Gnostic. Some of those systems were ascetic, others were antinomian; some were docetic in their Christology, others were adoptionist. Greater still is the variety when the smaller details of the various Gnostic schools are compared.

Gnosticism reached its full flower in the second century and persisted into the third. In order to understand its central principles that flower will first be examined and then consideration will be given to the root from which the flower developed.

As the term *gnosis* (knowledge) suggests, Gnosticism was a religion centered in knowledge, and that knowledge was viewed as redemptive in nature, the result, not of study or research, but of revelation from a higher plane. The highest form of knowledge for the Gnostic was the knowledge of self. Robert Grant explains, "This is the first and most important point in defining Gnosticism. It is a religion of saving knowledge, and the knowledge is essentially self-knowledge, recognition of the divine element which constitutes the true self."[3]

Basic to the Gnostic philosphy was a dualistic belief that matter is evil and spirit is good. If matter is evil, it follows that this world is bad. The body and its world of materiality constitute a prison in which the soul is incarcerated and from which it needs to be redeemed. The Gnostics believed that originally they had been spiritual beings dwelling in a higher world, but because of circumstances not of their making and beyond their control they fell into this world of sinful ignorance and materialism. Redemption from such a miserable state is the result of *gnosis*. This *gnosis* is not gained by research, but by revelation imparted by a divine redeemer who descends into this world to reveal and to redeem. Often this redeemer is identified as Jesus, who then re-ascends to the transcendent deity, thus defeating the evil spirit beings and making it possible for those who would be redeemed also to ascend to God.[4] When a person becomes aware of what he once was and what his present condition is in this world, and of the possibility of returning to that original spiritual state and how that return can be made, that knowledge in itself becomes his redemption.[5]

From these basic and general elements the confusing variety of Gnostic systems grew. They sought to explain how this evil world came into existence without involving the Absolute in evil. Usually that was accomplished by postulating a series of spiritual beings called aeons who emanated from the Absolute. It was one of those

---

3. Robert M. Grant, *Gnosticism and Early Christianity*, p. 10.
4. John W. Drane, "Gnosticism and the New Testament 1" *TSF Bulletin* 68 (Spring 1974): 8; Edwin M. Yamauchi, *Pre-Christian Gnosticism*, pp. 29-30.
5. For fuller discussions of the basic tenets of Gnosticism see Robert M. Grant, *Gnosticism and Early Christianity*, pp. 6-13, and by the same author, *Gnosticism*, pp. 13-19. Also John W. Drane, "Gnosticism and the New Testament" 1, pp. 6-9.

aeons that was responsible for the emergence of the God of the Old Testament, who in turn created matter. Some reacted to the evil nature of their world-prison by an extreme asceticism, attempting thereby to free themselves from defilement. Others went to the opposite extreme of unbridled libertinism, reasoning that the God who created the world also instituted the Mosaic law, and therefore if man would be free from the evil of the world, he must break all of the Creator's commandments. In so doing the Gnostic adherent thought he was acting in harmony with the Absolute God.

Such an attitude toward the Old Testament God expressed itself in numerous criticisms designed to depict Him as a malicious God rather than the God of holiness and love. One Gnostic source says:

> What kind of God is he? First, he envied Adam that he ate from the tree of knowledge. Second, he said to Adam "Where are you?" God has no foreknowledge, since he did not know that. Afterward he said, "Let us cast him out of this place so that he will not eat from the tree of life and live forever." Thus, he has shown that he is a malicious envier . . . He said, "I am a jealous God. I will bring the sins of the fathers on the children to the third and fourth generation." And he said, "I will harden their hearts and blind their minds so they will neither know nor understand the things that are said." But he said these things to those who believe in and serve him![6]

The Gnostic view of the Person of Christ also took a variety of forms. It was generally held by all Gnostics that the Christ was one of the aeons, but the manner of His emanation varied from system to system. Some said the Christ came upon the human Jesus at His baptism and left Him just before His death. By that view they avoided any vital link between the heavenly Christ and evil flesh. The Christ merely rested upon Jesus; He was not integrally related to the man of flesh and blood, and thus was not defiled by evil. Other Gnostics have become known as Docetists from the word δοκέω *("I seem, I appear")*. Those persons declared that the Christ did not really become incarnate, but only appeared to have a body. The Christ whom the disciples viewed in bodily form was really only a phantom.

There has been considerable disagreement concerning the origins of Gnosticism. Some, such as Rudolf Bultmann, have spoken

---

6. *Testimony of Truth.* Claremont Coptic Gnostic Project, IX 3 47, 14-48, 15, cited by Pheme Perkins, *The Gnostic Dialogue*, pp. 16-17.

of a pre-Christian Gnosticism that supposedly influenced Christian doctrine to a significant degree.[7] Others have insisted on limiting the term to a description of the fully developed systems of such second-century teachers as Basilides and Valentinus. Both views contain truth, but at the same time both views were extremely over-simplified. It is certainly true that Gnosticism did not spring up overnight at the beginning of the second century. It had its antecedents. It was syncretistic in nature and drew upon various sources, some pagan, some Jewish, and some Christian. Some of these elements can obviously be traced back to pre-Christian days. Gnosticism, then, had both pre-Christian and Christian origins. The doctrine of the Gnostic redeemer is an example of the latter. Grant declares: "The most obvious explanation of the origin of the Gnostic redeemer is that he is modelled after the Christian conception of Jesus. It seems significant that we know no redeemer before Jesus, while we encounter other redeemers (Simon Magus, Menander) immediately after his time."[8]

Although it is true that Gnosticism in its mature form is not found prior to the second century, all will grant that the roots of the plant are to be found prior to that time. During the latter half of the first century a development was taking place that eventuated in the full-grown Gnosticism of the second century. Some may want to go no further than to designate this phenomenon as a "syncretism."[9] Others may prefer to call it "proto-Gnostic" or "incipiently Gnostic" or "Gnosticizing" as does Grant.[10] Still others, such as Quispel and W. F. Albright, will argue that "Gnosticism had already developed some of its most pronounced sects before the Fall of Jerusalem, and there is no reason to date the emergence of the Sethians and Barbelo-Gnostics after the end of the first century A.D."[11]

Brown thinks that the "secessionists" against whom 1 John

---

7. However, see Edwin M. Yamauchi, *Pre-Christian Gnosticism: A Survey of the Proposed Evidences* and Richard N. Longenecker, and Merrill C. Tenney, eds., *New Dimensions in New Testament Study*, "Some Alleged Evidences for Pre-Christian Gnosticism," by Edwin M. Yamauchi, pp. 46-70.
8. Grant, *Gnosticism*, p. 18; cf. Grant, *Gnosticism and Early Christianity*, pp. 61-69.
9. Johannes Munck, "The New Testament and Gnosticism," in *Current Issues in New Testament Interpretation*, ed. William Klassen and Graydon F. Snyder (New York: Harper, 1962), pp. 234-37.
10. Grant, *Gnosticism*, p. 14.
11. W. F. Albright, "Recent Discoveries in Palestine and the Gospel of John," in *The Background of the New Testament and Its Eschatology*, ed. W. D. Davies and D. Daube (Cambridge: Cambridge University Press, 1956), p. 163.

warns, having left the "more conservative side of the Johannine community," rapidly moved in the direction of docetism, Montanism, Cerinthianism, and Gnosticism.[12] In fact, he believes that the Johannine adversaries may have served as catalysts in the development of second-century Gnostic systems.[13]

By whatever name and in whatever stage of development, the phenomenon later known as Gnosticism most certainly was present and exerting its influence during the last two decades of the first century.

At that time the system of Simon Magus would have been a live option. Grant writes:

> Is it not likely, then, that Simonian Gnosticism arose chiefly after the destruction of the temple, even though Simon the Samaritan magician was at work a generation earlier? Admittedly we cannot trace the precise development of Simonian doctrines and say which are early and which are late. But it seems likely to me that as a system Simonianism is a late first-century creation.[14]

If Irenaeus's identification is correct, that Simon, who later instituted the first Gnostic system,[15] was the magician encountered by Peter in Samaria (Acts 8:9-24). Simon reportedly taught that he was the Supreme Father of all, who had appeared among the Jews as the Son, among the Samaritans as the Father, and among other nations as the Holy Spirit. He bought a prostitute named Helena out of slavery in Tyre and claimed she had been the first conception of his mind, from whom were generated the angels and archangels. Those in turn detained her in the lower regions of space, where she was forced to be confined in one female body after another, at last becoming a common prostitute. Simon is said to have represented himself as having come to deliver her and confer salvation upon men.

If the "Clementine Homilies" are historically accurate, they provide a more detailed description (ii. 22-25) of Simon's rise to leadership.[16] Here he appears along with the woman Helena as an associate of John the Baptist. When John was killed, Simon was finally recognized as John's successor, in fact, as the Christ. Proof

---

12. Raymond E. Brown, *The Community of the Beloved Disciple*, p. 24; Brown, *The Epistles of John*, The Anchor Bible, vol. 30, p. 105. See also John W. Drane, "Gnosticism and the New Testament" 2 *TSF Bulletin* 69 (Summer 1974): 6.
13. Brown, *The Epistles of John*, pp. 59, 65, 104.
14. Grant, *Gnosticism and Early Christianity*, p. 89.
15. Irenaeus *Against Heresies* 1. 23.
16. Grant, *Gnosticism*, pp. 25-27.

that he was the Standing One (the Christ) came when a rival tried to strike him with a staff and found that it passed through his body as if he were smoke. This account would seem to suggest a docetic view of Simon.

There are two reasons for assuming that Simon and his followers tended toward antinomianism. The first is his association with the prostitute Helena. The second is the statement of Irenaeus that "the mystic priests belonging to this sect both lead profligate lives and practice magical arts."[17] In summary, then, it appears that Simonianism was in some sense docetic in its view of the Redeemer and antinomian in its concept of morality.

Mention should also be made of the Nicolaitans, who are referred to both by Irenaeus and in the Apocalypse. What they taught is not revealed in available sources. All that is known is that they lived "lives of unrestrained indulgence."[18] Whether they actually were Gnostics cannot be judged; however, the fact that Irenaeus includes them may indicate that they were. Reference to them in the Apocalypse shows they were present in Asia during the closing decade of the first century.

Of major importance are the person and teaching of the Egyptian Jew, Cerinthus. That he and John were contemporaries seems evident from the account of their near encounter at a public bath in Ephesus. Irenaeus refers to Polycarp as the source of his information, saying: "There are also those who heard from him that John, the disciple of the Lord, going to bathe at Ephesus, and perceiving Cerinthus within, rushed out of the bath-house without bathing, exclaiming, 'Let us fly, lest even the bath-house fall down, because Cerinthus, the enemy of the truth, is within.' "[19]

This Cerinthus apparently came to Ephesus from Egypt where he had been educated. He taught that the primary God did not make the world, but that a lesser Power, who was ignorant of the absolute God, was the creator. Jesus was not virgin born but was the proper son of Joseph and Mary, Cerinthus said. After His baptism the Christ descended upon Him from the supreme God in the form of a dove, after which Jesus declared this unknown God to men and worked miracles among them. Prior to Jesus' death the Christ departed from Jesus, and the latter died and rose again.[20]

According to the accounts of Epiphanius and Philaster, Cer-

---
17. Irenaeus *Against Heresies* 1. 23. 4.
18. Ibid., 1. 26. 3. (Cf. Rev. 1:6, 15.)
19. Ibid., 3. 3. 4.
20. Ibid., 1. 26. 1.

inthus was at least partially favorable to Judaism.[21] He would therefore not seem to be antinomian in his view of morality. However, Dionysius of Alexandria set forth an opposite view, saying: "And as he was himself devoted to the pleasures of the body and altogether sensual in his nature, he dreamed that the kingdom would consist in those things which he desired, namely, in the delights of the belly and of sexual passion."[22] This much is certain: Cerinthus is a clear example of early Gnostic-style teaching that was both contemporary with John and present in provincial Asia.[23]

It is not out of place to move slightly beyond the lifetime of the apostle John in attempting to ascertain the religious currents flowing at the end of his life. The letters of Ignatius, which were written as the Antiochean bishop was being escorted across Asia Minor on his way to a Roman martyrdom, may with reasonable certainty be dated between A.D. 115 and 117. In these early epistles Ignatius reveals the kind of heresy with which he had been confronted in Antioch prior to his arrest. There is no doubt that it was docetic in its Christology.

The terms used to describe the teachings of those Antiochean heretics make it clear that they did not merely deny that Christ became incarnate. In addition they asserted that although He did not actually take on a body of flesh, He seemed to have a human form and He seemed to suffer and die. That is suggested in the strong assertions of the reality of Christ's humanity. To the Trallians Ignatius wrote, "Stop your ears, therefore, when anyone speaks to you at variance with Jesus Christ, who was descended from David, and was also of Mary; who was truly born, and did eat and drink. He was truly persecuted under Pontius Pilate; He was truly crucified, and [truly] died."[24] In the following chapter Ignatius reveals the reason for his affirmation of the incarnation. There are those, whom he calls "unbelieving," who say "that He only seemed to suffer."[25] A bit further on, Ignatius asserts, "But if these things were done by our Lord only in appearance, then am I

---

21. A. E. Brooke, *A Critical and Exegetical Commentary on the Johannine Epistles*, pp. xlviff.
22. Eusebius *H. E.* 3. 28. 5.
23. For a thorough analysis of what may be known about Cerinthus, see Brown, *The Epistles of John*, pp. 65-68, 766-71.
24. Ignatius *Trall.* 9. Cf. Ignatius *Smyr.* 1.
25. Ignatius *Trall.* 10. Cf. Ignatius *Smyr.* 2.

also only in appearance bound."[26] And again he asks, "For what does any one profit me, if he commends me, but blasphemes my Lord, not confessing that He was [truly] possessed of a body?"[27]

There is good reason for believing that at the time the good bishop of Antioch wrote, the docetic heresy was not a new phenomenon in Antioch.[28] It appears that the presence of Docetism in Antioch may be dated considerably earlier than A.D. 115-117. How early it began to exert an influence in the city on the Orontes is not known, but a figure of at least five or ten years previous to Ignatius's death is certainly not unreasonable.

THE HERESY REFLECTED IN 1 JOHN

1. *Review of its main points.* The heresy combated in John's first epistle was, as previously seen, perverted in its Christology and woefully deficient in its morality. It denied that Jesus was the Christ, the pre-existent Son of God. It was not necessarily a denial of the historicity of Jesus, nor of the existence of the Christ, but it was a denial that the two were to be identified as one and the same Person. Such a disavowal was a repudiation of the incarnate Jesus of whom the apostles had intimate knowledge. In the area of morality the heresy was decidedly antinomian, not a careless kind of antinomianism, but a reasoned, purposeful kind. Even though those heretics walked in darkness, they insisted that they neither committed sin nor possessed a sinful nature.

2. *Comparison with early Gnosticism.* An early kind of Gnostic teaching contemporary with John was that of Cerinthus.[29] The church Fathers, it will be remembered, indicate that at one time John and Cerinthus were both living in Ephesus. It is, therefore, not surprising to find agreement between the heresy dealt with in 1 John and the one taught by Cerinthus. The insistence that Jesus Christ came both by water and by blood rather than by water only (1 John 5:6) could very well be a reference to Cerinthus's teaching that the Christ came upon the human Jesus at His baptism (water) and left Him just before His death (blood). The denial that Jesus is the Christ (1 John 2:22) is also in agreement with Cerinthus's distinction between Jesus and Christ.

26. Ignatius *Smyr.* 4.
27. Ignatius *Smyr.* 5.
28. Virginia Corwin, *St. Ignatius and Christianity at Antioch,* p. 29.
29. Brown, *The Community of the Beloved Disciple,* p. 150 (note 291), says Cerinthus "is consistently listed among the first gnostics."

In view of the afore-mentioned facts it is reasonable to assume that at least one form of the false teaching confronting the Asian churches was that of Cerinthus. This identification has the support of numerous writers, from the time of the early church to the present day. Irenaeus was the first to state that John combated the error of Cerinthus. He wrote concerning the fourth gospel: "John, the disciple of the Lord, preaches this faith, and seeks by the proclamation of the Gospel, to remove that error which by Cerinthus had been disseminated among men, and a long time previously by those termed Nicolaitans, who are an offset of that 'knowledge' falsely so called."[30]

Nicolaitanism (Rev. 2:6, 15) was another heresy of John's day that showed some similarity to Cerinthianism. That both the Apocalypse and Irenaeus describe the Nicolaitans as decidedly antinomian agrees with John's reference to persons who deny sin. It thus may be that in addition to perverted Cerinthian Christology, John had in mind perverted Nicolaitan morality.

As already shown, Simonianism also was quite probably in circulation by the end of the first century. The teachings of Simon, however, find no definite parallels in 1 John. The one point at which there is agreement is in morality. Both Simonianism and the heresy combated in 1 John were antinomian. Hence there is the possibility that some of the heretics reflected in 1 John were Simonians.

One question remains in attempts to identify the heretics of 1 John, What part, if any, did Docetism play in the circumstances that occasioned the epistle? A comparison of John's statements with those of Ignatius is helpful. The bishop of Antioch spoke explicitly of those who not only denied the reality of Christ's coming in the flesh, but who also asserted, "that He only seemed to suffer"[31] and that the things He did were done "only in appearance."[32] In addition Ignatius says that they did not confess that "He was [truly] possessed of a body."[33] This is clearly Docetism.

In 1 John there is no such clear evidence of docetic Christology. John merely indicates that the false teachers denied that Jesus Christ, the pre-existent Son of God, came in human flesh. He says nothing of mere apparent suffering or of only appearing to do

---

30. Irenaeus *Against Heresies* 3. 2. 1.
31. Ignatius *Trall.* 10.
32. Ignatius *Smyr.* 4.
33. Ignatius *Smyr.* 5.

certain things. The apostle's silence at this point does not prove that a docetic Christology was not in view; it leaves the door open for either possibility. However, it should be noted that 1 John 1:1 may be refuting Docetism. John's exmphasis on hearing, seeing, and handling the Word of life may be insisting that the Word was incarnate. However, Pheme Perkins says that "Gnostics never deny that Jesus has a body which can be seen, handled and touched." She adds:

> I Jn seems to be using the language of "seeing, hearing, and touching" to evoke personal presence and to establish the claim that only their tradition derives from that presence. In the Johannine tradition, there is no break between the earthly and the risen Jesus or between Jesus and what the community came to understand about him through the spirit (e.g. Jn. 14:26; 16:13).[34]

There is, however, another possible interpretation of the evidence. Since it seems apparent that Gnosticism assumed a variety of forms, it may be that here is evidence of two different Gnostic views: one that denied an actual incarnation (reflected in the Ignatian letters) and one that accepted the incarnation (reflected in the *Gospel of Truth* [CG I *3* 30, 27-31, 20; *NHLE:* 43f.], referred to by Perkins). Brown points out that "docetism came in many shades," and he cites several docetic statements from the Nag Hammadi writings to illustrate this variety.[35]

That there is a similarity between the opponents in 1 John and those of Ignatius is suggested by Brown. He finds the closest parallels to the Johannine secessionists in the Ignatian docetists, a fact that he finds not surprising if Ignatius was referring to situations that existed "only some ten years after the Johannine Epistles were written."[36]

3. *Conclusion.* The churches of Asia were being troubled with one or more forms of early Gnosticism. Quite certainly the teaching of Cerinthus was one of those forms. In addition, some kind of antinomianism was being propagated, perhaps Nicolaitan or Simonian in origin. It is also possible that some of the false prophets circulating among the churches were teaching Docetism. As a

---

34. Pheme Perkins, *The Johannine Epistles,* p. 10.
35. Brown, *The Community of the Beloved Disciple,* pp. 105-6.
36. Brown, *The Epistles of John,* p. 58 (note 137).

result the believers were in danger that they might break fellowship with the apostolic circle and cast their lot with the false teachers.

Purpose

Inasmuch as the specific occasion for writing was the presence of one or more forms of earlier Gnosticism, the primary purpose of John was to counteract the pressures that the false teachers were bringing to bear upon the Asian Christians.

A WARNING

The apostle seeks to impress upon the minds of his readers a warning concerning the danger that threatens them. Consequently, in hard-hitting terms he describes the false teachers, calling them antichrists and liars (2:18-23). Following this he explains, "These things I have written to you concerning those who are trying to deceive you" (2:26).

A SERIES OF TESTS

John wants his "little children" to be able to identify their enemies, and so he provides a series of tests by which they may be able to distinguish the false from the true. The first of these is the Christological test, which appears in several forms. The false teachers may be identified by their denial "that Jesus is the Christ" (2:22), or by their failure to confess "that Jesus Christ has come in the flesh" (4:2). Such persons are not of God; they are motivated by the spirit of antichrist (4:3).

In view of the antinomian forms of Gnosticism that were threatening the Asian churches, the apostle provides his readers with an additional means of distinguishing the spurious from the genuine. This is the test of morality, which is introduced in 1:5-10 and most specifically stated in 3:4-10. Here the person who engages in the habitual practice of sin is identified as a member of the devil's family rather than the family of God (3:10).

And finally, John points to the test of attitude. The false teachers are not open toward the proclamation of truth by members of the apostolic circle. The apostle writes: "They are from the world; therefore they speak as from the world, and the world listens to them. We are from God; he who knows God listens to us; he who is not from God does not listen to us. By this we know the spirit of truth and the spirit of error" (4:5-6). Furthermore, this attitude toward the teachers who speak the truth is also extended to believers in general. The heretics are to be identified by their lack of love toward the brothers (2:9, 11; 3:10-15).

AN ANTIDOTE

The third aspect of John's primary purpose is his obvious intention to provide an antidote for his readers to the heretical pressures they were experiencing. It was his stated aim to assure them of their genuine Christian experience. The Gnostic insistence that only those who possessed *gnosis* were redeemed no doubt unsettled some Christians so that they began to wonder if simple faith was enough to save. Believers could be made to feel inadequate by the haughty Gnostic attitude of superiority, with the result that they might be tempted to give serious consideration to Gnostic claims. Consequently John wrote to assure them that they were God's children and that they had eternal life by faith in the Son of God.

In summarizing his overall purpose John says, "These things I have written to you who believe in the name of the Son of God, in order that you may know that you have eternal life" (5:13). Because of the position of this verse, standing as it does at the head of the concluding section of the epistle, it is clear that John intended the statement to refer to the whole book. More specifically, he used the very same criteria that served as tests by which to identify the false teachers as tests for the assurance of the genuine believer. That is, a person may know he is born of God if he believes the truth about Jesus Christ, God's Son (2:23; 4:2; 5:1); if he is practicing righteousness—otherwise characterized as keeping His commandments—and is walking in the light (2:29; 3:9-10; 2:3, 5; 1:7); and if he is loving the other members of God's family (2:10; 3:10, 14; 4:7; 5:1). A person who passes these tests and thus has solid ground for assurance is not very liable to succumb to the pressures of any false teachers.

AN INDIRECT POLEMIC

Some have characterized 1 John as a polemic against Gnosticism, but such a characterization requires examination. Two facts should be remembered. First, the letter was not addressed to the Gnostics, but to the Asian Christians. There are, in reality, three parties involved in the situation: the author, the recipients, and the false teachers. The author wrote to equip the recipients to withstand the false teachers. Thus, in this sense the letter is only indirectly polemical.

In the second place, the epistle does not devote the bulk of its treatment to the negative refutation of Gnosticism. There are several pointed declarations concerning the false teachers (2:18-19, 22-23, 26; 4:1, 3, 5-6), but by far the greater portion of the book is positive in nature. John's method was to combat error by declaring truth and seeking to inculcate it in the lives of people. Westcott well said: "St. John's method is to confute the error by the exposition of the truth realised in life. His object is polemical only so far as the clear unfolding of the essence of right teaching necessarily shews all error in its real character."[37]

In the final analysis, there is very little in the letter that is not directly related to John's primary purpose of counteracting the pressures brought to bear by Gnostic teachers. Brooke recognizes this fact when he says, "It is probably true that the writer never loses sight altogether of the views of his opponents in any part of the Epistle."[38]

A number of biblical scholars have taken a different view of John's intent. They have insisted that, although the polemical clearly played a part in the origin of the epistle, it is not to be viewed as primary. A distinction is made between the edificatory and the polemical. Brooke, for example, insists that the main purpose of the apostle was to stir up in his readers the enthusiasm and love that had grown cold through the years. It is his assumption that the major problem confronting John was not the possibility that the false teachers might seduce and deceive the Christians of Asia. The real danger was the cold, traditional, half-hearted spiritual condition of those believers. Therefore, Brooke declares that John speaks not primarily as a theologian, but as a pastor.[39]

One wonders, however, whether the idea of the "loss of their first love" really comes from 1 John or whether it was not, in fact, suggested by the letter of Christ to the Ephesian church found in Revelation 2:1-7. There is little in the first epistle that explicitly supports the view that John's Christian audience had lost its early

---

37. B. F. Westcott, *The Epistles of John*, p. xxxix.
38. Brooke, p. xxvii.
39. Ibid., pp. xxvii-xxx. Cf. Everett F. Harrison, *Introduction to the New Testament*, pp. 413f.

enthusiasm and had become merely nominal. On the contrary John commends his readers for their spiritual condition. He is urging them not to lose the warm vital experience they now enjoy (2:24, 27). Their danger is that the deceivers may penetrate their spiritual defenses, destroy their confidence in the gospel preached by the apostles, and draw them away from the faith. John writes, not as a theologian or as a pastor only, but as both. There is no good reason for making any distinction. The apostle has a pastor's interest in his people, and as a capable pastor should do he employs theology in the pastoral ministry of warning and strengthening the believers.

5

The Character and Content of the Epistle

Before engaging in a verse-by-verse analysis of an epistle like 1 John, the interpreter will do well to attempt to secure a bird's-eye view of the book as a whole. Both approaches—the analytic and the synthetic—are necessary for a full understanding of any book of the Bible. The one complements the other, and neither one is complete without the other.

THE FORM OF THE WRITING

Considerable difference of opinion has existed concerning the classification of 1 John. Serious question has been raised as to its epistolary nature, chiefly because it does not have the customary introduction and conclusion found in most epistles (cf. Col. 1:1ff.; 4:7-18). Wilhelm Michaelis called it a treatise; Edward Reuss, a homiletical essay; Ebrard, a sort of dedicatory epistle for John's gospel;[1] Moffatt, a tract or pastoral manifesto in vague epistolary form;[2] Dodd, an informal tract or homily;[3] Westcott, a pastoral

---

1. Karl Braune, "The Epistles General of John," in *A Commentary on the Holy Scriptures*, 9:12.
2. James Moffatt, *An Introduction to the Literature of the New Testament*, pp. 538-39.
3. C. H. Dodd, *The Johannine Epistles*, The Moffatt New Testament Commentary, p. xxi.

rather than a letter;[4] George C. Findlay, a homiletical epistle;[5] R. E. O. White, an open letter;[6] H. E. Dana, not a letter but an encyclical in epistolary form;[7] and Law, a true letter.[8] In spite of the absence of the usual epistolary introduction and conclusion, there are several valid reasons 1 John should be regarded as an epistle rather than a tract or a homily. It has been argued that the book was intended for the Asian churches in general and an encyclical would be of a general nature, without the personal greetings and information of an epistle addressed to a specific church.

The epistle to the Hebrews is a good example of a writing that lacks the typical epistolary introduction. It begins in a manner quite similar to the way 1 John opens. However, because Hebrews concludes in standard epistolary form, there is no doubt concerning its classification. James, on the other hand, closes as abruptly, if not more so, as 1 John, without any greetings, personal information, or benediction. But the introduction clearly identifies it as an epistle. Now, if it is possible for an epistle to lack either an epistolary introduction or conclusion, it is also conceivable that an encyclical epistle may lack both introduction and conclusion.

As an encyclical 1 John would tend to have some similarity to a treatise or an essay. Also because it was, no doubt, intended to be read to the churches, and because it contains pastoral counsel and exhortations (as do also such epistles as James and 1 Peter), 1 John has some of the marks of a homily. However, given an epistolary introduction and conclusion, the form of the book would never be questioned.

The deciding factor must of necessity be the manner in which the writing refers to its author, its recipients, and itself. First John has an author who refers to himself as "I" or "we" addressing persons whom he designates as "you." In the first five verses the writer refers to himself (and perhaps his associates) seventeen times, using the first person pronouns ἡμῶν, "our," and ἡμετέρα, "our," and verbs in the first person plural (ἀκηκόαμεν, "we have heard," μαρτυροῦμεν, "we proclaim," etc.). He refers to his readers four times by the second person pronouns

---

4. B. F. Westcott, *The Epistles of St. John*, p. xxx.
5. George C. Findlay, *Fellowship in the Life Eternal*, p. 59.
6. R. E. O. White, *Open Letter to Evangelicals*, p. 15.
7. H. E. Dana, *The Epistles and Apocalypse of John*, p. 14.
8. *International Standard Bible Encyclopedia*, 1939 ed., s.v. "The Epistles of John," by Robert Law.

ὑμεῖς, "you," and ὑμῖν, "to you," and by a verb in the second person plural, ἔχητε, "you may have." He also declares that he is writing (γράφομεν, "we write") to them (1:4). Although he does not begin with the standard epistolary introduction, the opening statements nevertheless demand that the writing be viewed as a letter. These same characteristics carry throughout the book.

On the basis of such data 1 John should be classified as a bona fide New Testament epistle. More specifically, it should be described as encyclical or circular in nature and pastoral in function.

THE THEOLOGY OF THE EPISTLE

At the close of the nineteenth century, George B. Stevens wrote, "No type of New Testament teaching has more individuality than the Johannine; none has characteristics at once more marked and more difficult to define."[9] It is not an exaggeration to say that the difference between Johannine and Pauline theology is as clear as the difference between summer and winter. This is not to suggest any disharmony between the two, for there is none. It is only to assert that each has its own distinctive characteristics that make it stand out in sharp relief against the other.

THE DOCTRINE OF GOD

John's distinctive teaching concerning God the Father is set forth in two unique statements. In 1 John 1:5 the author declares, "God is light." It is obvious that the term *light* is a metaphorical representation of one of God's essential characteristics. In the succeeding context (1:6-10) there is evidence that the author has used the metaphor ethically rather than metaphysically. He speaks of certain qualities of life, which he describes as walking in the light and walking in the darkness (1:6-7). His conception of light is clearly practical. Light is moral goodness; darkness is moral evil. This is further borne out by the discussion of the confession of sin in 1:8-10. God, in His essence, is absolute moral goodness, a concept that involves the ideas of holiness, righteousness, and truth.

This declaration, "God is light," serves as a standard of comparison by which John would show what the conduct of the Christian should be. That the believer is related to God, both in fellow-

---

9. George B. Stevens, *The Johannine Theology*, p. 2.

ship (1:5-7) and by birth (2:29-3:10), demands that he must be like God in holiness and righteousness.

The second unique statement concerning God is the declaration, "God is love" (4:8). More than an assertion that God is loving or that He loves, this is an affirmation concerning the essential nature of God, what He is in His essence. All that He is, and thus all that He does, is conditioned by ἀγάπη, "love," that intelligent, self-determined, self-communicating disposition toward others that actively seeks their highest good.[10] And because God is ἀγάπη essentially, He is the source of ἀγάπη on the human plane as well. Consequently, all who are related to Him by spiritual birth likewise possess and manifest ἀγάπη.

These two statements, "God is light" and "God is love," are actually not distinct and separate. In the essence of God they coalesce, so that He may be characterized as holy love. In his excursus on "The Correlation of Righteousness and Love," Law says, "The conclusion, then, at which I arrive is that Righteousness and Love are coterminous in area; that as little can Righteousness exist without Love as Love, truly so called, without Righteousness."[11]

Upon this understanding of the Divine Being, one of the epistle's major theses is founded. What God is in Himself is determinative of what His child will be, for He imparts to His child His own characteristics. Joseph Bonsirven explains: "Mystic that he was, saint John could only conceive of the moral and religious life of the Christian as a participation in the life of God, his virtues only as a sharing of the divine characteristics: the love, the truth, the righteousness which are in the Christian spring from the love, from the truth, from the righteousness which are in God." (Our translation.)[12]

Thus the person who exhibits the qualities of love, truth, and righteousness demonstrates that he has been born of God; the one who lacks these virtues shows that he is not a child of God.

THE DOCTRINE OF CHRIST

The Christology of 1 John revolves around two poles of equal importance: the Savior's humanity and His deity. Referring to "the

---

10. Gerhard Kittel, ed., *Theological Dictionary of the New Testament*, 1964-76, s.v. "ἀγαπάω, ἀγάπη, ἀγαπητός," by Gottfried Quell and Ethelbert Stauffer.
11. Robert Law, *The Tests of Life*, p. 84.
12. Joseph Bonsirven, *Épitres de Saint Jean*, vol. 9, *Verbum Salutis*, p. 30.

great Christological thesis" of the epistle, Law wrote, "That thesis is the complete, permanent, and personal identification of the historical Jesus with the Divine Being who is the Word of Life (1:1), the 'Christ' (4:2) and the Son of God (5:5)."[13]

His deity is set forth by several expressions, of which the most direct is the designation *son*. This term is applied to Christ twenty-one times in 1 John. In the introduction to the epistle, He is called "the Word of life" (1:1), an expression that is clearly related to John's use of the term λόγος, "word," in the prologue to his gospel. It is plain that λόγος is a designation of deity, for John says, "In the beginning was the Word, and the Word was with God, and the Word was God" (John 1:1). That the epistle uses the term λόγος in the same sense is indicated by the similar employment of the words "with God" (John 1:1-2) and "with the Father" (1 John 1:2). Also, in both passages "the Word" is associated with "the life" (John 1:4; 1 John 1:1-2).

It is apparent that John intended his readers to view the Son as on an equal plane with God the Father. In his grand finale of great Christian certainties he declares, "We know that the Son of God has come, and has given us understanding, in order that we might know Him who is true, and we are in Him who is true, in His Son Jesus Christ. This is the true God and eternal life" (1 John 5:20). As Bonsirven points out, John's statement seems to designate both the Father and the Son as "the true God and eternal life."[14]

The epistle asserts the fact of the pre-existence of the Son. He is said to have existed from the beginning (1:1; 2:13-14); He is referred to as "the eternal life, which was with the Father" (1:2); and He is declared to have been sent into the world, a statement that also assumes pre-existence (4:9-10, 14).

In keeping with His deity, although not a direct declaration of it, are the indications of Christ's sinlessness. First John 3:5 plainly declares "In Him there is no sin," and this denial is backed up by positive assertions that He is righteous (2:1) and pure (3:3).

One of the foremost assertions of the epistle is that "Jesus is the Christ" (2:22; 5:1). Although it is true that Χριστός, "Christ" is the translation of מָשִׁיחַ (*māshiaḥ*) and was employed to designate the Messiah of Old Testament prophecy (Acts 17:3), there is good reason to believe that John has here used the term in a different

---

13. Law, p. 91.
14. Bonsirven, pp. 34-35.

sense. As shown previously, the declaration, "Jesus is the Christ," is equivalent to the statement, "Jesus is the Son of God" (4:15).[15] The Gnostic Christ was not the Jewish Messiah; he was instead an emanation from the unseen God, an aeon of the Pleroma.[16] It is therefore reasonable to expect that John, in refutation of the heretics, used the term *Christ* in a related sense to refer to the preexistent, only-begotten Son of God, the λόγος who was with the Father and who is Deity (John 1:1).

The second pole around which the Christology of 1 John revolves is that of Christ's humanity. Although not explicitly mentioned as often as his deity, the human nature of Jesus is nevertheless one of the major emphases of the epistle. John places significant stress upon the bodily reality of the man Jesus by the striking periodic sentence with which he opens his letter: "What . . . we have heard, what we have seen with our eyes, what we beheld and our hands have handled, concerning the Word of Life . . . we proclaim to you" (1:1-3). By the use of repetition and the Greek perfect tense, the apostle emphatically insists that he has witnessed the reality of Christ's humanity and that the memory of that reality is still clearly with him when he writes some sixty years later.

So important is the doctrine of the Savior's humanity that it is employed as a criterion for discerning the false prophet from the true (4:1-3). The prophet who comes from God confesses that Jesus Christ has come in flesh, but the prophet who denies Christ's coming in flesh is inspired by the spirit of antichrist.

In contrast to the false teachers, John insists on the incarnation of the Son of God, the mystery of the divine Christ coming in human flesh—not coming *upon* human flesh, but coming in such an integral union with humanity that the result was one indivisible person, Jesus Christ (4:2)—not coming in the phantasmal semblance of human flesh, but in flesh that was real to sight, hearing, and touch (1:1).

THE DOCTRINE OF THE HOLY SPIRIT

The teaching of the epistle concerning the Holy Spirit is somewhat limited. The author seems to assume that his readers are

---

15. Bonsirven, p. 34.
16. George Ladd, *A Theology of the New Testament*, p. 611.

already familiar with the Person and work of the Spirit, as would be natural if they were in possession of the fourth gospel, especialy chapters 14-16.

The Holy Spirit is seen in 1 John as a distinct person performing activities that assume the attributes of personality. He teaches (2:27), and He bears witness (5:7).[17] That the Spirit is distinct from the Father and the Son is evident from 2:20, 27; 3:24; 4:13. He is said to be an anointing from the Holy One (2:20) and thus not identical with the latter (cf. 2:27). In 3:24 God the Father (cf. v. 23) has given us His Spirit (cf. 4:13).

Although the Spirit is distinguished from the Father and Son, He is nevertheless viewed as being on a par with them. He is called the Spirit of God (4:2), and like the Son (John 14:6) He is described as truth (1 John 2:27; 5:7). The intimate relationship between Father and Spirit is seen in that the possession of the Spirit is evidence that God indwells the believer (3:24; 4:13).

As noted above, the activities of the Spirit are twofold, teaching and bearing witness. However, it is possible that John also refers to the indwelling work of the Spirit when he says, "Greater is He who is in you than he who is in the world" (4:4). The first pronoun "He" may be taken as referring to Christ, but in the context it would seem better to understand it as referring to the Holy Spirit. Another important aspect of the Spirit's work is the combating of error (4:1-7). This He does by teaching the believer all truth (cf. 2:20, 27), by bearing witness to Christ (5:7-8), and by motivating the believer's confession of the incarnation (4:2).

One may well ask what John means by statements in 2:20 and 27 indicating that the anointing of the Holy Spirit results in an enlightenment of some kind. George Ladd points out that this illumination is not reserved for the elite few. It is for all believers. Nor is it a "direct, unmediated illumination by the Spirit." Instead, "it is an inner work of the Spirit that enables a man to perceive the truthfulness of the Christian tradition."[18]

In 1 John, then, in spite of the scarcity of reference to the

---

17. There is a difference in verse divisions at 5:6-7. The NASB, ASV, Moffatt, and the RSV maintain a shortened verse 6. On the other hand, the United Bible Societies Greek Text and Montgomery, Williams, Beck, TEV, and NIV also include in v. 6 the words, καὶ τὸ πνεῦμα . . . ἡ ἀλήθεια, *and it is the Spirit . . . the truth*. This commentary is following the NASB in this and other instances where there are slight differences in versification.

18. Ladd, pp. 610-11.

Spirit, He played a very important part in the Asian churches' battle against the incipient Gnostic heresy.

THE DOCTRINE OF SIN

Although the epistle does not present a complete treatment of the doctrine of sin, nevertheless in proportion to the length of the letter its references to sin are numerous. John deals with sin's source, nature, and universality.

It is assumed that the devil is responsible for the origin of sin. Those who practice sin are said to come *from the devil*, (ἐκ τοῦ διαβόλου), who in turn is described as sinning "from the beginning" (3:8). That the term *beginning* is not used in any absolute sense seems obvious; otherwise God would of necessity be the creator of a sinful being and thus the author of sin, which is inconceivable.[19] The phrase ἀπ' ἀρχῆς, "from the beginning," would appear to refer more naturally to the beginning of the human race. This would agree with the statement of Christ that the devil "was a murderer from the beginning" (John 8:44), which probably has reference to the incitement of the murder of Abel. In the epistle, too, the context of 3:8 speaks of Cain's relationship to the "wicked one" and his slaughter of Abel (3:12).

John indicates that the devil brings his evil influence to bear both on the individual and on the world. That sin in the individual is traceable to Satan may be deduced from such statements as, "We know that no one who is born of God sins; but He who was born of God keeps him and the evil one does not touch him" (5:18), and, "I am writing to you, young men, because you have overcome the evil one" (2:13). It is apparent that sin in the individual is the result of the devil's hold upon a person, and victory over sin is in reality victory over the devil himself. The declaration that "the whole world is lying in the evil one" (5:19, author's translation) makes it clear that the same evil influence extends to the whole world.

John employs several terms that are indicative of the nature of sin. In the first chapter it is metaphorically described as *darkness* (1:5-7), by which he refers to the absence of moral goodness, holiness, righteousness, and truth. The second term used to characterize sin is *lawlessness* (ἀνομία, 3:4). Sin is the transgression of

19. Stevens, pp. 140-45.

law, not merely of the Mosaic law, but of the eternal divine law, the moral standard that flows from the divine nature and to which all beings are responsible. The third term descriptive of sin is *unrighteousness* (ἀδικία). In 5:17 all unrighteousness is declared to be sin, a concept not far removed from that set forth in 3:4. In both terms, lawlessness and unrighteousness, the violation of a moral standard is involved: in the first instance, the standard is conceived of as law; in the second instance, it is justice or that which is right. Whichever term is used, the ultimate reference is to God's standard of right and wrong, a standard that is expressive of His own character. In the final analysis John views sin as the failure, or refusal, to be conformed to the divine nature.

Because of Paul's emphasis on the forensic element of the gospel one would correctly expect to find the judicial aspect of sin stressed in his writings (Rom. 1:18, 32; 2:1-9; Gal. 3:10). John's characteristic affirmation of the experiential aspect of the gospel (regeneration and eternal life) might lead one to assume that his treatment of sin would be solely experiential. Such, however, is not the case. Law has pointed out that sin may be viewed ethically or judicially and "in the Epistle each of these aspects of sin is strongly presented."[20] The judicial view is most clearly seen in 2:1-2 where the terms *advocate* and *propitiation* occur. The need for an intercessor and for propitiation is based on a penal understanding of sin (cf. 4:10). The concept of sin as transgression of law (3:4) is likewise judicial, as is the idea of sin that results in death (5:16-17).

John also sees sin as a principle or power at work in the nature of man. In reference to Christ he says, "In Him there is no sin" (3:5). Our Lord was not infected with any inherent depravity, so that not only did He not commit sin, but neither did He possess the nature of sin. The same aspect of sin may be in view in 1:8, "If we say that we have no sin, we are deceiving ourselves."

The epistle in a number of places speaks of sin as specific overt acts. It may safely be assumed that whenever the plural noun occurs such is the meaning. "If we confess our sins, He is faithful and righteous to forgive us our sins" (1:9). "And He Himself is the propitiation for our sins" (2:2; cf. also 2:12; 3:5). The verb ἁμαρτάνω, "I sin," may also be used to indicate specific acts, as it is in 1:10, "If we say that we have not sinned, we make Him a liar," and in 2:1, "My little children, I am writing these things to you that you may not sin" (aorist, ἁμάρτητε).

---

20. Law, p. 129.

The Character and Content of the Epistle   77

Most important for the understanding of John's teaching concerning sin is the concept of sin as habitual practice. This usage occurs in 3:6, 8-9: "No one who abides in Him sins; no one who sins has seen Him or knows Him. . . . the one who practices sin is of the devil; for the devil has sinned from the beginning. . . . No one who is born of God practices sin, because His seed abides in him; and he cannot sin, because he is born of God." In these verses the practice of sin is expressed in two ways. In verse 6 John employs the present tense verb forms ἁμαρτάνει and ἁμαρτάνων to depict the continued action of sinning. The second expression to denote continual sinning is ποιῶν τὴν ἁμαρτίαν, *to commit sin.* This is said to be true of the devil (v. 8), but not of the Christian (v. 9).

A seeming contradiction in 1 John is resolved by this recognition of the force of the present tense as compared with the aorist tense. The believer does not sin habitually (3:9), but he may and does commit acts of sin (2:1) that need to be confessed and forgiven (1:9). For John this distinction is important in distinguishing the genuine believers from the libertine false teachers who are seeking to lead Christians astray. A person who is truly regenerate, although not sinlessly perfect, will not habitually live in sin.

Some object to such an explanation, based, as it is, on the distinction between the present and aorist tenses.[21] However Ladd is surely right when he says:

> This is a very plausible and consistent interpretation and cannot be rejected because it is based on grammatical subtleties. Tense in Greek did mean something. The tense of 2:1 is aorist; the goal of the Christian life is that one shall commit no sin. In experience the dominance and practice of sin is broken; but this does not mean sinless perfection.[22]

The universality of sin, meaning not merely that it is found everywhere, but that all are sinners and all commit sin, is clearly taught in 1:8, 10. The whole world is declared to be guilty of sins and in need of propitiation (2:2).

The puzzling question of the nature of the sin unto death will be treated in the commentary on 5:16-17.

---

21. I. Howard Marshall, *The Epistles of John. The New International Commentary,* p. 180.
22. Ladd, p. 615.

THE DOCTRINE OF SALVATION

From the divine point of view redemption involves propitiation, a doctrine John treats twice in his epistle. He declares, "He Himself is the propitiation for our sins; and not for ours only, but also for those of the whole world" (2:2), and "He loved us and sent His Son to be the propitiation for our sins" (4:10). What is involved in John's doctrine of propitiation may be discerned by examining kindred passages in the epistle. For instance, John explains that Christ "appeared in order to take away sins" (3:5). Although it may be possible to find the sacrificial idea of bearing sin (αἴρειν, "to take away") in this verse, such a meaning is not required.[23] All the passage clearly states is that Christ came to remove sins. Other passages of the letter must be consulted in order to determine the method of accomplishment. Somewhat similar is the assertion that "the Son of God appeared . . . that He might destroy the works of the devil" (3:8). From the first part of the verse it would seem unquestionable that those works are both the sins the devil himself commits and the ones he incites others to commit.

The method by which sin is removed is seen in 3:16, "We know love by this, that He laid down His life for us." The laying down of Christ's life involved the shedding of His blood, and John explains what that shedding of blood accomplished. He says, "The blood of Jesus His Son cleanses us from all sin" (1:7). Thus these passages taken in combination teach us that sins are removed (3:5), or cleansed (1:7), by Christ's act of laying down his life for us (3:16).

This background allows for a closer look at John's doctrine of propitiation. The word ἱλασμός has been rendered both as "propitiation" and as "expiation." In the first case it is God who is propitiated; in the second it is sin that is expiated. Some have rejected the first translation in favor of the second for fear that God may be depicted as an arbitrarily angry being whose petty irritability must be pacified by sacrifice. Although it is certain that the Judaeo-Christian God cannot be so described, yet the idea of propitiation must not be discarded simply on this account. The background of the Septuagint usage of the ἱλασμός family of terms must be taken into consideration. Morris has shown that the Septuagint regularly uses these terms to express the idea of propi-

---

23. Stevens, pp. 167f.

tiation.[24] This was also its normal usage in secular Greek. Furthermore, propitiation does not necessarily demand the understanding that the deity is arbitrarily angry over petty and selfish grievances. The anger that calls for propitiation may be perfectly justified. It is therefore unreasonable to interpret ἱλασμός in the light of pagan usage when such usage is clearly contrary to the biblical doctrine of God. The meaning of propitiation must be viewed against the background of what the Bible teaches concerning divine justice and wrath. As moral governor of the universe, God directs His wrath against those who violate His law (3:4), not in an arbitrary fashion but on the basis of justice. Stevens explains: "The Biblical idea is that the obstacle to forgiveness lies in his essential righteousness which so conditions his grace that without its satisfaction God cannot, in self-consistency, forgive."[25]

Biblical propitiation, then, is the satisfaction of divine justice resulting in the diversion of divine wrath from the sinner. Furthermore, in the New Testament propitiation is not only demanded by divine justice if sin is to be forgiven, but it is provided by divine love. Law put the matter in capsule form: "Propitiation is no device for inducing a reluctant deity to forgive; it is the way by which the Father in heaven restores His sinning children to Himself."[26]

It should also be noted that in both occurrences of ἱλασμός in 1 John it is followed by the preposition περί, "concerning," rather than the objective genitive ἁμαρτιῶν, "of sins," which would be the case if sins were the object of propitiation.

In John's doctrine of propitiation, then, God is propitiated concerning sin by the death of Christ. His justice, outraged by the violation of His law (3:4), is satisfied by the shedding of Christ's blood (1:7) and thus He can forgive sins. It is in this sense that sins are taken away (3:5).

As indispensable as the teaching of propitiation is in 1 John, it is

24. Leon Morris, *The Apostolic Preaching of the Cross*, pp. 125-85; cf. Hans-Georg Link and Colin Brown, "Reconciliation, Restoration, Propitiation, Atonement," in *New International Dictionary of New Testament Theology*, ed. Colin Brown, 3:148-63. Stevens, pp. 181-84; J. R. W. Stott, *The Epistles of John. The Tyndale New Testament Commentaries*, pp. 82-83; David Hill, *Greek Words and Hebrew Meanings*, pp. 23-48; Roger R. Nicole, "C. H. Dodd and the Doctrine of Propitiation," *Westminster Theological Journal* 17 (1954-55): 117-57.
25. Stevens, p. 183.
26. Law, p. 162.

not the most weighty soteriological theme of the epistle. At the very heart of John's doctrine of salvation lie the kindred concepts of regeneration and eternal life. No truth is more basic for an understanding of 1 John than that of regeneration. It is the foundation of John's teaching concerning the family of God, moral likeness between the believer and God, and thus the grounds for assurance of eternal life. Law wrote concerning John's doctrine of life:

> Its predominance is complete; it is the centre to which every idea in the Epistle is more or less directly related. And, indeed, its unique development of the Christian conception of Life and Regeneration may be set beside its doctrine of the moral nature of God and its doctrine of the Incarnation, as one of the three great contributions of Johannine thought to the teaching of the New Testament.[27]

John's doctrine of new birth and subsequent eternal life begins with the assertion: "Whoever believes that Jesus is the Christ is born of God" (5:1). The believer, therefore, is a child of God (3:1-2, 10). The word used to designate this relationship is τέκνον, "child," which is related to the verb τίκτω, "I bear." Also of interest in this connection is the author's favorite term of endearment, τεκνία (2:1, 12, 28; 3:7, 18; 4:4; 5:21). This is a diminutive form of τέκνον, literally meaning "little born ones," comparable to the Scottish *bairns*, as Scofield has pointed out.[28] God's children are conceived of as a spiritual family. They are bound together by ἀγάπη, that love that finds its only source in God (4:7-8) and thus is a characteristic mark of the family. "Whoever loves the Father loves the child born of Him" (5:1). Of equal significance is the family characteristic of the practice of righteousness (3:9-10) and victory over the world (5:4-5). The reason God's children are of necessity marked by righteousness is that God's seed—the life principle that also carries the hereditary characteristics—dwells in them (3:9).

Related to the concept of the divine family are the ideas of fellowship, knowing God, dwelling in God, and God indwelling the believer. The person who is in harmony with the message of the epistle has fellowship with the Father, with the Son, and with the apostolic circle (1:3). He is the one who is walking in the light

---

27. Ibid., p. 184.
28. C. I. Scofield, et al, eds. *The New Scofield Reference Bible*, p. 1342.

as God is in the light (1:5-7). John is not here distinguishing between two levels of Christian experience; he is instead distinguishing between those who are of God and those who are not of God, between the saved and the unsaved. The believer is in the divine fellowship; the unbeliever is outside that sphere. In the same way, the Christian is characterized as one who knows the Lord in personal experience (2:3-4), who is dwelling in Him (2:5-6, 24, 27-28; 3:6), and who is indwelt by Him (3:24; 4:13, 15-16; 5:20).

Integrally related to the doctrine of regeneration is the concept of eternal life in 1 John. In the absolute sense this life is not merely a vital force, it is a Person who was manifested to the apostles, who in turn saw the life and bore witness concerning it (1:1-2). From a comparison of the prologue of the gospel of John (1:1-2, 4, 14) and the introduction to the epistle, it is clear that John refers to Christ as "the eternal life" (cf. John 14:6). The Father also is so designated (5:20).

The believer is promised eternal life (2:25), and it is said that God sent His Son "that we might live through Him" (4:9). Believers can truthfully say, "God has given us eternal life" (5:11). Because "life is in His Son" (5:11) and because Christ is "the eternal life" (1:2) John declares: "He who has the Son has the life; he who does not have the Son of God does not have life" (5:12). These statements tell us that eternal life is embodied in the Person Jesus Christ and that it may be received in the present. It would therefore appear that the term refers to more than unending life. Although the word αἰώνιος, "eternal," demands the inclusion of the temporal aspect in any explanation of the concept of eternal life, the qualitative aspect is at least equally important. Eternal life is unending life marked by those qualities inherent in Christ Himself. John's final statement of purpose, which undoubtedly refers to the entire epistle, is found in 5:13, "These things I have written to you who believe in the name of the Son of God, in order that you may know that you have eternal life."

In the final analysis one of the chief purposes of John's treatment of the doctrine of salvation is to provide the believer with grounds for the assurance of eternal life. When placed in a logical sequence, the first of these grounds is belief in Jesus as the divine Christ come in human flesh to be Savior (2:22-23; 4:2-3; 5:1, 10-12, 20). Although some twentieth-century evangelicals have attempted to make this the only ground for assurance, John declares that there is an additional test. It involves the practice of righteousness and of love for other Christians. The person who is born of God lives a life of righteousness (2:29); he does not habitually commit sin (3:9). Although he may commit individual acts of sin (2:1), he does not live in sin as the natural sphere of his life. Furthermore, the person who has eternal life demonstrates love for his fellow believers (2:9-11; 3:14-17). After discussing the nature of true ἀγάπη (3:16-18), the apostle declares, "We shall know by this that we are of the truth, and shall assure our heart before Him" (3:19). Here again, the basis for assurance is not perfection in love, but a general pattern of loving the brothers, whereas the general pattern of hating the brothers shows that a person has never received eternal life (3:14-15). According to 1 John, then, the one who passes these two tests—the doctrinal test of belief, and the ethical test of righteousness and love—has solid grounds for assurance.

THE DOCTRINE OF LAST THINGS

Because of John's emphasis on present experience neither the gospel nor the epistle contains extensive eschatological data. There is, however, no basis for assuming that eschatology is absent from those books. John certainly expected a future consummation of the age, which would include the coming of antichrist, the second advent of Christ, resurrection, judgment, and eternal life. The advocates of realized eschatology have not succeeded in reducing such literal future events to mere present spiritual experiences.

Even the term *eternal life* contains an eschatological aspect, as already suggested. Although one cannot but recognize the significant qualitative force of this expression, the quantitative element must not be overlooked. The word αἰώνιος, "eternal," certainly has temporal significance. The contrast in John 3:16 between perishing and having eternal life demands an understanding of life as a continuing experience not to be terminated by destruction. The epistle provides confirmation of this interpretation in the words of 2:17, "The one who does the will of God abides forever."

In contrast, John sees the world as already "passing away" (παράγεται, 2:17), a suggestion that the day will come when the evil system of godlessness will come to its destined end, whereas God's people will continue for eternity.

Eschatology may be defined as the doctrine of last things, and as such it sustains an important relation to John's expression "the last hour" (ἐσχάτη ὥρα, 2:18). John saw time moving toward a climax, with his own day as the final period before that climax. It was not that the apostle was mistaken in assuming the end was near. Such an assertion overlooks the New Testament concept of the present age. The entire period between the two advents of Christ is the last time when seen in the overall picture of God's redemptive program. For Jews and early Christians time was divided into two ages, this age and the age to come (Matt. 12:32), and the coming age was to be the age of the Messiah and His reign upon the earth. The time between the two advents, therefore, is the last segment of the present age.

John bases his statement that it is the final hour upon the presence of false teachers in the world (2:18), which is in agreement with Christ's description of the present age. In the opening section of the Olivet discourse Jesus instructed His disciples regarding what to expect during this age so they would not mistake those events as signs of the end of the age (Matt. 24:4-14). The age was to be marked by false Christs (vv. 4-5), wars (vv. 6-7), calamities in nature (v. 7), persecution (vv. 9-10), false prophets (v. 11), and wickedness (v. 12). Jesus warned, however, "That is not yet the end" (v. 6), "all these things are merely the beginning of birth pangs" (v. 8), "and this gospel of the kingdom shall be preached in the whole world for a witness to all nations, and then the end shall come" (v. 14). Thus the entire period between the two advents of Christ is a time of upheaval in religion, international affairs, nature, and morality. Therefore, in 1 John 2:18 the apostle, remembering the words of Jesus, singles out one element, false teachers, as proof that this is in the last period of the present age.

The only New Testament writer to use the term *antichrist* is the apostle John, and his employment of the word is limited to his first two epistles (1 John 2:18, 22; 4:3; 2 John 7). Although this specific designation is not found elsewhere in the New Testament, the concept is present under the designation "man of lawlessness" in 2 Thessalonians, and "the beast" in Revelation. Thus, when John writes, "you heard that antichrist is coming," he may well have been referring to Paul's previous teaching concerning the man of lawlessness.[29]

There is a sense in which the term *antichrist* is spiritualized in 1 John. It is clear the apostle recognized that sometime in the future a man would arise who would be the personal culmination of all opposition to Christ. In this ultimate sense, the antichrist is

---

29. Ladd, p. 613.

neither an influence nor a movement among men; he is to be a person. However, something of what he will be is already present in the world today. It is present in the heretics who spread erroneous concepts of Christ's Person and work. "This is the antichrist, the one who denies the Father and the Son," writes John in 2:22. Specifically, he could say of the early Gnostics in Asia, "Even now many antichrists have arisen" (2:18). In a similar manner the spirit that shall be fostered by the end-time antichrist has been present throughout the age. John sensed it in the false teachers of his day and wrote, "Every spirit that does not confess Jesus is not from God; and this is the spirit of the antichrist, of which you have heard that it is coming, and now it is already in the world" (4:3). To the apostle the spirit of antichrist was a kind of afflatus that motivated false prophets similar to the manner in which God's Spirit motivates his prophets (4:1). If this is to be taken literally, and there is no reason it should not be, it is reasonable to infer that the spirit of antichrist is in reality the spirit of the devil and his servants inspiring men in their opposition to Christ.

The subject of the second advent itself is mentioned specifically in but two passages, and in those it is not introduced as a major topic of discussion. In 2:28 it is advanced as a reason for abiding in Christ, and in 3:2-3 it is mentioned in order to show the future glory of divine sonship. Christ's coming will be a manifestation or appearance of One who has not been visibly present (note the verb φανερωθῇ, v. 2). It is also described as a παρουσία, "coming," the technical term for the glorious coming of a king (2:28). This, incidentally, is the only occurrence of the latter term in the Johannine writings. Although there is no uncertainty as to the fact of His coming, the time is indeterminable. Such is the force of ἐάν, "if," which should be translated "whenever" both in 2:28 and 3:2.

The first epistle touches on two other events closely associated with Christ's return. The process of salvation, begun at conversion and continued in the life-long experience of progressive sanctification, will come to its completion at the second advent. Although one cannot now know all that this involves, "we know that . . . we shall be like Him" (3:2). The fact that "we shall see Him just as he is" suggests bodily likeness as the result of resurrection; the mention of the present purifying effect of this hope (3:3) suggests moral likeness as the result of completed sanctification. When Christ returns the believer will be delivered from the last tinge of depravity and his body will be transformed to be like the resurrection body of the Lord.

Also associated with the second coming of Christ is the subject of judgment. John does not explicitly indicate what aspect of judgment he has in mind, nor does he reveal any details of the eschatological sequence of events. He merely alludes to judgment in the process of discussing the fruit of love (4:17). The presence of love in the believer's life demonstrates our likeness to Christ—"as He is, so also are we in this world" (4:17), and this in turn will produce bold confidence in the day of judgment. Likeness to Christ is proof of membership in God's family, and thus, there is no need to fear either the Judge or the issues of the judgment.

THE STRUCTURE OF THE EPISTLE

It is commonly agreed that the organization of 1 John is most difficult to discover. This is true because of the intricate interrelation of its major concepts resulting in a closely knit fabric that is not easily unraveled. For example, notice the theme of love as it reappears repeatedly in ever new and varying associations. It is intimately related to walking in the light (2:9-11), to assurance (3:14, 19), to obedience (3:23; 5:2-3), to regeneration (4:7), to the knowledge of God (4:7-8), and to belief in Christ (4:14-16; 5:1).

A second reason for the difficulty involved in discovering the structure of the book lies in the kind of transitions John employs. Rather than being clearly marked, they are subtle and unobtrusive, often occurring in the middle of a statement. Plummer likens them to "the changes in dissolving views." He adds, "We know that we have passed on to something new, but we hardly know how the change has come about."[30]

The difficulty incurred in discovering the epistle's organization is also due in part to the aphoristic nature of many of its statements. Dodd says: "The striking aphorisms which are the most memorable things in the epistle do not usually emerge as the conclusion of a line of argument. They come in flashes and their connection with the general line of thought is sometimes only hinted at."[31] John's writing may be characterized as intuitive rather than analytic and deductive. And whereas the structure of analytic composition is most easily discernible, the organization of intuitive writing is by no means as obvious.

Having recognized the problems inherent in any attempt at

---

30. A. Plummer, *The Epistles of St. John*. The Cambridge Greek Testament for Schools and Colleges, p. liii.
31. Dodd, p. xxii.

tracing the thought development of 1 John, it should be stated that such an attempt is not impossible. In fact a thorough study of the epistle shows it to be most carefully and intricately organized. When the pattern of the book is discerned, it is recognized as a veritable piece of art. In many ways it is similar to a musical composition made up of several recurring themes around which interesting variations are developed, with each new treatment rising to greater heights than the previous one. The conclusion is a grand finale in which the main theme of the piece is repeatedly sounded with spine-tingling force. Numerous writers have described the structure as a spiral. Law explains, "It is like a winding staircase—always revolving around the same centre, always recurring to the same topics, but at a higher level."[32] The same writer also uses the term *contrapuntal* to characterize John's method.

A survey of the developing understanding of the epistle's structure reveals that until about 1750 the consensus of opinion was that the book is without any discoverable structure. One of the first to set forth a scheme of organization was J. A. Bengel (1687-1752) who divided the book into three sections: Exordium, 1:1-4; Discussion, 1:5-5:12; Conclusion 5:13-21.[33] Although the artificiality of Bengel's trinitarian arrangement must be recognized, his main divisions are fundamental to any valid system of organization for the epistle. Wilhelm De Wette (1846)[34] proposed the following outline:

I. Introduction, 1:1-4
II. Three exhortations, 1:5—5:21
   A. The first exhortation, 1:5—2:28
   B. The second exhortation, 2:29—4:6
   C. The third exhortation, 4:7—5:21

Theodor Häring's analysis (1892), which was for the most part adopted by Brooke,[35] is a most commendable piece of work. He found two theses, the ethical and the Christological, presented in the epistle as evidence that a person is regenerated and in fellowship with God. These two theses are set forth in a "triple presentation." The main points in the outline are given by Brooke somewhat as follows:

I. Introduction, 1:1-4

---

32. Law, p. 5.
33. J. A. Bengel, *Gnomon of the New Testament*, 5:141.
34. Henry Alford, *The Greek Testament*, 4:172.
35. A. E. Brooke, *A Critical and Exegetical Commentary on the Johannine Epistles*, The International Critical Commentary, pp. xxxiv ff.

II. First presentation of the two tests of fellowship with God, 1:5—2:27
   A. Ethical thesis, 1:5—2:17
   B. Christological thesis, 2:18-27
III. Second presentation of the two theses, 2:28—4:6
   A. Ethical thesis, 2:28—3:24
   B. Christological thesis, 4:1-6
III. Third presentation of the theses, 4:7—5:12
   ("Intentional intermingling of the two leading thoughts in two sections.")
   A. First explanation of the two ideas as now combined. Love based on fatih . . . proof of knowing God and being born of God, 4:7-21
   B. Second explanation of the connected thoughts. Faith as the base of love, 5:1-12
   C. Conclusion, 5:13-21

In 1909, without having seen Häring's breakdown of the epistle, Law suggested that John establishes three tests set forth in a threefold cyclical form.[36] His outline is given briefly.

I. Prologue, 1:1-4
II. First cycle: The Christian life as fellowship with God conditioned and tested by walking in the light, 1:5—2:28
   A. Walking in the light tested by righteousness, 1:5—2:6
   B. Walking in the light tested by love, 2:7-17
   C. Walking in the light tested by belief, 2:18-28
III. Second cycle: The Christian life as that of divine sonship, 2:29—4:6
   A. Sonship tested by righteousness, 2:29—3:10*a*
   B. Sonship tested by love, 3:10*b*-24*a*
   C. Sonship tested by belief, 3:24*b*—4:6
IV. Third cycle: Closer correlation of righteousness, love, and belief, 4:7—5:21
   A. Love, 4:7—5:3*a*
   B. Belief, 5:3*b*-21

The outline suggested by Stott is obviously similar to that of Law.[37] Its Major portion consists, like Law's outline, of three applications of the same three tests—the moral, the social, and the doctrinal.

36. Law, pp. 7-24.
37. J. R. W. Stott, p. 55.

Still more recent analyses of the structure of the epistle are those of Marshall and Brown, neither of which reveals any relationship to the kind of structure suggested by Law. Marshall's outline is as follows:

Prologue—the Word of life. 1:1-4
Walking in the light. 1:5-2:2.
Keeping his commands. 2:3-11.
The new status of believers and their relation to the world. 2:12-17.
A warning against antichrists. 2:18-27.
The hope of God's children. 2:28—3:3.
The sinlessness of God's children. 3:4-10.
Brotherly love as the mark of God's children. 3:11-18.
Assurance and obedience. 3:19-24.
The spirits of truth and falsehood. 4:1-6.
God's love and our love. 4:7-12.
Assurance and Christian love. 4:13-5:4.
The true faith confirmed. 5:5-12.
Christian certainties. 5:13-21.[38]

Brown thinks the structure of 1 John is built on the pattern of the gospel of John, and therefore he detects the following structural plan in the epistle:

I. The Prologue (1:1-4).
II. Part One (1:5—3:10): The gospel that God is light, and we must walk in the light as Jesus walked.
III. Part Two (3:11—5:12): The gospel that we must love one another as God has loved us in Jesus Christ.
Conclusion (5:13-21): A statement of the author's purpose.[39]

The analysis that will be employed in this commentary is obviously built upon previous ones, especially those of Häring and Law. Comparison will show that the following outline is both a simplification and a refinement of those two.

ANALYSIS

I. Introduction: The reality of the incarnation, 1:1-4.
   A. The substance of the apostolic declaration, 1:1-2.

---

38. I. Howard Marshall, p. 26.
39. Raymond E. Brown, *The Epistles of John*. The Anchor Bible, 30:124.

B. The purpose of the apostolic declaration, 1:3-4.
 II. First cycle: The Christian life viewed as fellowship with the Father and the Son, 1:5—2:28.
   A. Fellowship tested on ethical grounds, 1:5—2:11.
      1. Fellowship demands moral likeness, 1:5-7.
      2. Fellowship demands confession of sin, 1:8—2:2.
      3. Fellowship demands obedience, 2:3-6.
      4. Fellowship demands love of fellow believers, 2:7-11.
   B. Two digressions, 2:12-17.
      1. An assumption concerning the readers, 2:12-14.
      2. A warning concerning loving the world, 2:15-17.
   C. Fellowship tested on Christological grounds, 2:18-28.
      1. A contrast of heretics and believers, 2:18-21.
      2. The Christological test, 2:22-23.
      3. The key to continuing fellowship, 2:24-28.
III. Second cycle: The Christian life viewed as divine sonship, 2:29—4:6.
   A. Sonship tested on ethical grounds, 2:29—3:24.
      1. Sonship demands practice of righteousness, 2:29—3:10*a*.
      2. Sonship demands love of fellow believers, 3:10*b*-24.
   B. Sonship tested on Christological grounds, 4:1-6.
      1. A warning against false prophets, 4:1.
      2. The Christological test, 4:2-3.
      3. The test of listening, 4:4-6.
 IV. Third cycle: The Christian life viewed as a closely woven integration of the ethical and the Christological, 4:7—5:12.
   A. The ethical test, 4:7—5:5.
      1. The source of love, 4:7-16.
      2. The fruit of love, 4:17-19.
      3. The necessary association of love for God and love for one's brother, 4:20—5:1.
      4. The evidence that one loves God's children, 5:2-3*a*.
      5. The possibility of obeying God, 5:3*b*-5.
   B. The Christological test, 5:6-12.
      1. The coincident witness of historical facts and the Holy Spirit, 5:6-9.
      2. The experiential witness of eternal life, 5:10-12.
  V. Conclusion: The great certainties of the Christian life, 5:13-21.
   A. Certainty of eternal life, 5:13.
   B. Certainty of answered prayer, 5:14-17.

C. Certainty of victory over sin and the devil, 5:18.
D. Certainty of the believer's relation to God, 5:19.
E. Certainty of the incarnation, 5:20.
F. A concluding exhortation, 5:21.

This outline is marked by two major characteristics. First, it finds three cycles of thought in the epistle, and second, it sees two tests, the ethical and the Christological, in each cycle. Some have described such an arrangement as too artificial, but this criticism can be accurate only if examination of the book shows that it is not so organized. However, there is evidence that the book does indeed contain cycles of thought. They are indicated, for example, by the three well-defined treatments of love (2:7-11; 3:10*b*-24; 4:7—5:3), as well as by the three distinct sections that are Christological in nature, dealing with belief of the truth concerning the Person of Christ (2:18-28; 4:1-6; 5:6-12). These two series, it will be noted, occur in cyclical fashion as follows: love (2:7-11), belief (2:18-28), love (3:10*b*-24), belief (4:1-6), love (4:7—5:3), and belief (5:6-12).

Our outline lists two tests in each cycle, the ethical and the Christological, but Law claims there are three, the tests of righteousness, love, and belief (Christological). It is agreed that one test obviously is the test of belief. The question is, however, whether there are two additional tests, righteousness and love, or only one, the ethical. Although Law's outline may at first commend itself to the student of 1 John, further examination favors the dual rather than the triple arrangement.

In support of two tests are the following factors:

- John's summary of the divine command (3:23)—it is twofold, including belief and love, but not righteousness.
- John's use of the concept of obedience to the divine command—evidence that one knows Christ is found in the keeping of His commandments (2:3-4); and in the context immediately following, the commandment is to love one another (2:7-8). This would seem to tie together Law's tests of righteousness and love as one and the same.
- The relation of loving the brothers to walking in the light (2:9-11)—the test of fellowship is walking in the light (1:5-7), which in its context appears to be the practice of righteousness or the opposite of sin (cf. 1:8—2:2). However, in 2:9-11, the test of walking in the light is love of the brothers. This also

would suggest that there is but one criterion in mind, namely the ethical, including both the practice of righteousness and the practice of love.
- The sudden transition from the practice of righteousness to the love of the brothers (3:10).
- The fruits of hatred (3:12, 15) and of love (3:16-17)—hatred produces evil deeds; love produces good.
- The beginning of the third cycle with the subject of love (4:7 ff.)—John opens the two previous cycles with the discussion of righteousness (1:5—2:6; 2:29—3:10a). However, the third cycle almost completely omits the practice of righteousness if this is not included in the test of love.
- Gnosticism's dual deviation—It is a well-known fact that this early heresy was characterized basically by deviations in Christology and in morality.

It has been suggested that the structure of 1 John is best described as a spiral.[40] R. C. H. Lenski represents it as an inverted pyramid or cone that rests upon its apex and ascends in ever-widening circles depicting the advance in height and breadth made by each new cycle of thought. The following is an adaptation of Lenski's diagram.

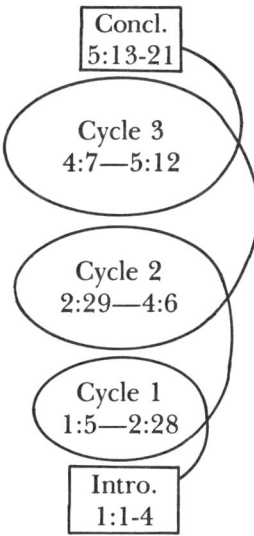

---

40. Dodd, pp. xxi-xxii. R. C. H. Lenski, *The Interpretation of the Epistles of St. Peter, St. John and St. Jude,* pp. 366-67. Albert Curry Winn, *Test of Real Christianity,* p. 15.

A comparison of this diagram with the analytical outline will reveal the significance of the various parts of the spiral. The introduction, which sounds the keynote of a valid Christology, provides the foundation upon which the whole structure rests. The various themes of the epistle are all dependent upon the truth of the incarnation. In each of the three cycles of thought the discussion revolves around two points of reference: (1) the correct view of Christ, and (2) the resultant ethic. Belief in the incarnate Son of God produces regeneration (5:1), which in turn issues in a life characterized by righteousness and love. It must not be assumed, however, that the second and third cycles are mere repetitions of the first. As the diagram reveals, the second cycle advances in the height and breadth of its thought beyond the first, and the third cycle beyond the second. New facets of Christological and ethical truth are added in each succeeding cycle until the concluding section is reached, where repeated stress is laid on the assurance that is produced by belief in the incarnate Christ and by the resulting life of righteousness and love.

PART 2
The First Epistle of John Commentary

6

I. Introduction: The Reality of the Incarnation, 1:1-4

First John begins in a manner calculated to capture the reader's attention. Instead of employing the standard epistolary introduction, the author plunges directly into the heart of his subject—affirmation of the Person of Christ. The Gnostic heresy, which the epistle combats, was characterized by attacks on this very foundation of the Christian faith. It is to this fundamental error that John devotes his opening statement—not by refuting, but by asserting the truth concerning Christ's Person in striking, unequivocal terms that would be impressed indelibly upon the mind of the reader. Thus he sets the tone for the entire book, which revolves around a Christological center point. Faith in Jesus Christ, the divine-human Savior, results in regeneration (5:1), and regeneration in turn results in Christian love (4:7) and the practice of righteousness (3:9).

The structure of these introductory verses is somewhat involved, as numerous commentators have noted. However, the unusual nature of the arrangement serves to make the declaration the more striking. The first sentence is periodic in form, being so laid out that its complete idea is not apparent until the reader reaches the third verse. The entire first verse is in reality the direct object of the main verb ἀπαγγέλλομεν, "we proclaim" (v. 3). The second verse is parenthetical and is intended to lay stress on the manifestation of the living Word, on the revelatory nature of the incarnation. After the break introduced in verse 2, it is necessary to employ repetition (ὃ ἑωράκαμεν καὶ ἀκηκόαμεν, "what we have seen and heard") to pick up the main thought once more. The author then proceeds to state two aspects of his purpose in writing the epistle. The course of thought may be represented as follows: (1) the substance of the apostolic declaration, 1:1-2, and (2) the purpose of the apostolic declaration, 1:3-4.

EXEGETICAL COMMENTARY (1:1-4)

(The exegetical sections of the commentary are aimed specifically at the explanation of the Greek text. They are most characteristically concerned with the syntax of the text and with the study of the Greek words the author has employed. Although discussion of the theology of the passage cannot be completely excluded, the attempt is made in these sections to keep it at a minimum.)

A. THE SUBSTANCE OF THE APOSTOLIC DECLARATION, 1:1-2

1:1. Ὃ ἦν ἀπ' ἀρχῆς, "what was from the beginning."[1] Attention is immediately drawn to the use of the neuter relative pronoun ὅ, "what," with which the epistle begins. Inasmuch as a preliminary reading leads to the assumption that the phrase refers to the Person of Christ, one might have expected to find a masculine pronoun. Such, however, is not the case. The neuter was no doubt chosen for a specific reason and therefore ought not to be referred, directly at least, to the Person of Christ. The same form of the pronoun occurs in three succeeding parallel constructions, which in turn are followed by the prepositional phrase, περὶ τοῦ λόγου τῆς ζωῆς, "concerning the Word of life." Consequently, the neuter relative pronoun refers to what concerns the *Word of life,* the attributes, speech, and actions of the God-man. It is to the manifestation of the divine Word in flesh that John refers, and not directly to the Person of the Word. This use of the neuter pronoun is much more expressive than the masculine form would have been. The Person of Christ cannot be excluded, for it is necessarily assumed, but in addition there is the reminder of all

---

1. The Exegetical Commentary is treated phrase by phrase, with each phrase stated in Greek and in English. The Greek text is taken from the third edition of *The Greek New Testament* edited by Kurt Aland, et. al. and published by the United Bible Societies.

Introduction: The Reality of the Incarnation   97

that He was as the manifestation of God in human flesh. And, more specifically, John has in mind *what* he is proclaiming (ἀπαγγέλλομεν, v. 3). It is his announcement concerning the God-man that is the substance of the neuter relative, ὅ. Marshall explains that the neuter refers to "the Christian message which was incarnate in Jesus."[2] Thus it is both impersonal and personal.

The term ἀρχῆς, "beginning," may have reference to any one of three time periods. (1) Eternity past. It may be taken as a term for that distant past, prior to creation, which to the limited human point of view may be conceived of as the beginning. This is not to say that God or eternity can be described as having a beginning, but it is to view eternity past as prior to all things, and thus as the period of beginning. (2) The period of creation. This, clearly, was a time of beginning when the world as it is now known came into being. (3) The time of the incarnation. John could have had in mind the beginning of the Christian era marked by the coming of the eternal Word into human flesh to be our Savior.

ἀπ' ἀρχῆς is used a second time in 2:7, where the author states that his readers had possessed the command to love since the beginning of the gospel or, at least, since the beginning of their experience of the gospel. However, the declaration of 1:1 seems to be much more vast in its scope than the mere sixty years, more or less, involved in the statement of 2:7. Furthermore, the similarity of the opening line of the epistle to that of the fourth gospel suggests that the term is used in the same sense in both passages. And it is clear that John 1:1 cannot be referring to the incarnation or to the beginning of the gospel. That it does not refer to creation seems also to be indicated by the absence of the article with ἀρχῆς, which suggests that a particular point of time is not in view. It seems best, therefore, to understand ἀρχῆς as descriptive of eternity past, and this view is supported by the statement that the Word was πρὸς τὸν πατέρα, "with the Father" (1 John 1:2) and πρὸς τὸν θεόν, "with God" (John 1:1).

In the gospel (1:1) John describes the divine interpersonal relationships prior to creation (ἐν ἀρχῇ, "in the beginning"), but in the epistle (1:1) he speaks of the existence and relationships of the Word from eternity past until the time when John wrote (ἀπ' ἀρχῆς, "from the beginning"). The verb ἦν, "was,"

---

2. I. Howard Marshall, *The Epistles of John, The New International Commentary on the New Testament*, p. 101.

gives evidence of having been carefully chosen to make it clear that the Word of life was in existence from all eternity past. John does not use ἐγένετο, "became," because there never was a point when He was not, nor a time when He came into existence.

ὃ ἀκηκόαμεν, "what we have heard." Various suggestions concerning the reference of the first person plural have been offered by commentators: (1) it is an editorial "we," (2) it refers to John and Christian leaders in Ephesus who would vouch for the facts John was setting forth, (3) it includes the readers as well as the author, that is, the whole church,[3] and (4) it speaks of John and the other apostles. The fourth view has the bulk of the evidence in its favor. The very nature of the experiences described—hearing, seeing, touching—demands persons who were eyewitnesses, which automatically eliminates the readers and the church as a whole. John could have been using the epistolary "we," but because the New Testament emphasizes that the apostles as a group were witnesses of the historicity of the Christ event, the fourth view seems preferable (cf. Luke 24:48; Acts 1:22; 2:32; 3:15; 5:32; 10:39, 41). John declares not merely the isolated opinion of one man, but the united testimony of the whole apostolic group.

The perfect tense of the verb ἀκηκόαμεν, "we have heard," is most significant, referring as it does to action completed in the past, the results of which continue to the present. In this instance, that which continued must have been the memory of what was heard, the echo of which continued to ring in John's ears. The tense, therefore, is John's way of insisting on the reality of what was heard as well as the accuracy of the report.

ὃ ἑωράκαμεν τοῖς ὀφθαλμοῖς ἡμῶν, "what we have seen with our eyes." The perfect tense is here applied to the act of seeing, with the suggestion that what was seen some sixty years previously still lingered before the mind's eye. John had not forgotten what his eyes had seen when he walked and talked with Christ. Bonsirven caught the spirit of John's perfect tense when he said, "That image is always engraved in their hearts."[4] The addition of "with our eyes" makes it clear that the author is referring to literal sight with the physical eyes. It is no spiritual vision of which he speaks.

---

3. C. H. Dodd, *The Johannine Epistles*, The Moffatt New Testament Commentary, pp. 9-16.
4. Joseph Bonsirven, *Épitres de Saint Jean*, vol. 9, Verbum Salutis, p. 72 (my translation).

ὃ ἐθεασάμεθα, "what was beheld." There are two significant facts to be noted in connection with this verb. First, it is an apparent repetition of the idea expressed in ἑωράκαμεν, "we have seen." Although the two verbs are sometimes employed interchangeably,[5] θεάομαι may be used in a more specialized sense to describe that "careful and deliberate vision which interprets . . . its object."[6] Again it sometimes refers to physical sight that produces a supernatural impression.[7] Inasmuch as John has used both words in this same series of clauses, it is clear that he did not intend them to be understood synonymously. θεάομαι was added to emphasize the careful, inspective kind of seeing with which the disciples examined the revelation of God in Jesus Christ. They scrutinized Him so thoroughly that they had no doubt concerning His physical reality. (Cf. θεάομαι in John 1:14 where John declares, "We beheld his glory.") The second fact to be noticed is that the author abruptly changes from the perfect tense (ἀκηκόαμεν, ἑωράκαμεν) to the aorist (ἐθεασάμεθα). Such a shift could not have been without purpose. Instead of stressing the continuing results as he did in the perfect tenses, John here points up the historicity of the act of looking upon Jesus.

καὶ αἱ χεῖρες ἡμῶν ἐψηλάφησαν, "and our hands handled." ψηλαφάω is the culmination of a progressive series that includes hearing, seeing, examining, and handling. Each act adds more weight to the evidence for the reality of the incarnation. Here again an aorist verb is used, which looks back to the specific act of touching the body of Christ. It has often been suggested that both aorists refer to the postresurrection experience of the disciples' examining Jesus visually and handling Him with their hands. On two occasions He invited them to touch His resurrection body that they might know the reality of it. In Luke 24:39 Christ said, "Touch (ψηλαφήσατε) me," and in John 20:27 Thomas was directed to touch the wounds in the Lord's hands and side. However, in the context of 1 John 1:1, the apostle is not trying to prove the reality of the resurrection. His point here is that Jesus was most surely incarnate in a "flesh-and-bones" body, not that He was raised again. The specific statement that the handling was done *with our hands* makes it clear that John is not speaking of merely brushing against Jesus; he has in view rather the purpose-

---

5. William F. Arndt and F. Wilbur Gingrich, trans. and eds., *A Greek-English Lexicon of the New Testament*, by Walter Bauer, p. 353.
6. G. Abbott-Smith, *A Manual Greek Lexicon of the New Testament*, p. 203.
7. Arndt and Gingrich, pp. 353-54.

ful taking hold of Christ as in a careful examination of His body. περὶ τοῦ Λόγου τῆς ζωῆς, "concerning the Word of life." The KJV translation, "of (περί) the word of life," is too weak and general. John is proclaiming (ἀπαγγέλλομεν, v. 3) what was from the beginning, what they had heard, seen, and so forth, *concerning* the Word of life (v. 1). The term λόγος has been understood in two senses: (1) as referring to a message such as the message of the gospel, and (2) as referring to the second Person of the Trinity, the divine Logos. Reasons for holding the former view have been advanced by Westcott[8] and Dodd[9] among others. However, the weight of the evidence favors the personal meaning of the term. In the first place, John uses λόγος in John 1:1, 14 in a manner that can only be understood personally; and he uses it in a passage that in many ways is parallel to the preface to his first epistle. The two passages are tied together by the terms ἀρχή ("beginning"), πρὸς τὸν θεόν/πατέρα ("with God/the Father"), ζωή ("life"), and λόγος ("word"). Second, the neuter relative pronouns of 1 John 1:1 do not demand that λόγος be interpreted impersonally because the pronouns refer to *that which* John declares *concerning* the Word of life. The relative pronoun ὅ, "what," refers to the manifestation, but the expression τοῦ λόγου τῆς ζωῆς, "the Word of life," refers to the person who was manifested. Third, the parenthetical explanation in verse 2 demands the personal interpretation. Here John further defines what was manifested to them and what they are declaring, namely, the eternal *life that was with the Father.*

Controversy concerning the source from which John drew the term λόγος goes back to the second century when the Alogoi rejected the fourth gospel and the Apocalypse because of the use of λόγος in those books. In modern times the term has been variously traced to the Old Testament, to Philo, and to Stoic philosophy. Numerous Old Testament passages contain the expression *word of the Lord,* and in some it is personified. In Psalm 33:6 the word of the Lord becomes the agent of creation. This passage is paralleled in Hebrews 11:3, "By faith we understand that the worlds were prepared by the word of God." The wisdom of God also is personified in Proverbs 8:22-31 and described as participating in creation. John's use of λόγος as an intermediate agent in creation (John 1:3) would therefore be an apt one for the

---

8. B. F. Westcott, *The Epistles of John,* pp. 6-7.
9. C. H. Dodd, pp. 3-6.

Introduction: The Reality of the Incarnation

Jewish understanding. It would also find a response in the mind of the thinking Gentile world as well. Philo had used the term to refer to the impersonal intermediate agency by which God made the world. Stoic philosophers also employed the word to describe the immanent principle of reason which, according to their system, pervades the universe. John, therefore, adopted a term familiar both to the Hebrew and Greek ear. Stripping it of its false associations, he filled the word with theological meaning to describe the true agent of creation and communication between God and men.

λόγος is a most fitting term to express what John has in mind. By its very nature it speaks of revelation. The spoken word is the revelation of the mind of the speaker and thus of the speaker himself. In the same way the λόγος reveals God to man. This is especially seen in John 1, where it is declared that the Word who was in essence deity became incarnate (1:1, 14). This is declared to be necessary because no man has ever seen God (1:18). Christ, the Word, is the revelation of the unseen God.

A clear distinction between the λόγος of John's theology and the uses of Philo and Stoicism is indicated by the qualifying words τῆς ζωῆς, "of life." The Word is the living Word, the source of life, in fact life itself, as verse 2 reveals. Thus, the genitive τῆς ζωῆς is a genitive of apposition, *the Word* who is *the Life*. (Cf. John 1:4; 11:25; 14:6.)

1:2. καὶ ἡ ζωὴ ἐφανερώθη, "and the life was manifested." Verse 2 is a parenthesis separating the direct object clauses of verse 1 from the main verb ἀπαγγέλλομεν in verse 3. John's intent is to explain more fully what had been witnessed personally (v. 1) and how it had been witnessed. The use of καί, "and," introducing a coordinate clause, rather than γάρ, "for," followed by a subordinate clause, is characteristically Johannine. (Cf. the ten similar occurrences of καί in John 1:19-28.) Instead of τοῦ λόγου τῆς ζωῆς, "the word of life," (v. 1), John changes to the more direct ἡ ζωή, "the life." Whereas λόγος refers to the revelation, ζωή designates that which was revealed. To call Him *the Life* is far more than to say that He is living or that He gives life. It is rather to declare that Christ *is* essentially the Life. The verb ἐφανερώθη is a constative aorist viewing the action as a whole,[10] comprehending not only the birth of the God-man but spanning all of

---

10. H. E. Dana and Julius R. Mantey, *A Manual Grammar of the Greek New Testament*, p. 196.

Christ's life on earth. It is the historical event of the incarnation that is described by the word φανερόω. It was due to the divine initiative alone in manifesting the Life that the apostles were able to hear, see, examine, and touch the Word made flesh.

καὶ ἑωράκαμεν, "and we have seen." (See discussion on v. 1.)
καὶ μαρτυροῦμεν, "and bear witness." The meaning of this verb rests on the four verbs of verse 1: ἀκηκόαμεν, ἑωράκαμεν, ἐθεασάμεθα, and ἐψηλάφησαν. In order for a person to bear witness he must have had personal experience such as those verbs describe. Bultmann indicates that the verb μαρτυρέω referred to legal testimony, especially that of an eyewitness.[11] That it was no momentary testimony the apostles bore is evident from the present tense μαρτυροῦμεν, which is employed to depict continued action. For John the activity of witnessing had spanned some sixty years, and it was still going on at the time of writing this epistle. The same can be said for the tense of the following verb.

καὶ ἀπαγγέλλομεν ὑμῖν, "and proclaim to you." It is not repetitious for John to add this verb, for whereas the preceding one speaks of personal testimony, this word describes a more or less official announcement. The apostles had been selected to be witnesses concerning the life of Christ (Acts 1:21-22), but they were also appointed to go forth with an authoritative proclamation of the message of Christ. That proclamation is not to be limited to the declaration of this epistle. John had in view the ministry of the apostles across the years. Some have drawn a distinction between ἀπαγγέλλομεν (v. 2) and ἀναγγέλλομεν (v. 5), but this is unwarranted in the light of the biblical and extrabiblical usage of the two words.[12]

τὴν ζωὴν τὴν αἰώνιον, "the eternal life." Here John further describes the Life that was manifested and now is being proclaimed by him and his associates. The repetition of the article serves to stress both the noun ζωήν, "life," and the adjective αἰώνιον, "eternal," making the latter to function substantivally—"the life, the eternal life." Brooke, commenting on Weiss's statement that αἰώνιος is always used in the New Testament to mean endless duration, says: "It would be truer to say that it *never* has the sense of endless duration. . . . It can only mean 'belonging to the age' of which the writer is speaking or thinking, and so

---

11. Rudolf Bultmann, *The Johannine Epistles*, Hermeneia, p. 7.
12. Gerhard Kittel, ed., *Theological Dictionary of the New Testament*, 1964-76, s.v. "ἀγγελία, ἀγγέλλω, ἀναγγέλλω, ἀπαγγέλλω, κτλ.," by Julius Schniewind.

Introduction: The Reality of the Incarnation

comes to mean possessed of the characteristics of that age. If the 'age to come' is supra-temporal, then αἰώχιos denotes that the subject which it qualifies has this characteristic."[13] This statement, although it has an element of truth, is much too radical. The word αἰών was used in biblical Greek in two senses: (1) to designate eternity or unending time, and (2) to refer to a long but limited period of time. It was used with the first meaning especially in statements concerning God. The adjective αἰώνιos is likewise capable of being employed in both senses. However, in the New Testament it almost always speaks of that which is eternal (Rom. 16:26; 2 Cor. 4:18; Heb. 9:14).[14] John, therefore, does not use αἰώνιον here merely in the sense of "spiritual" life, as Brooke suggests.[15] τὴν ζωὴν τὴν αἰώνιον carries the dual concepts of quantity and quality. It is unending life, but it is also life marked by such qualities as spirituality, glory, and abundance, and which may be possessed in the present as well as in the future. In 1 John 1:2 this life is personified in Him who is its source and its substance. In Himself, He *is* eternal life, both quantitatively and qualitatively conceived.

ἥτις ἦν πρὸς τὸν πατέρα, "which was with the Father." The pronoun that introduces this clause is not merely a simple relative pronoun. It is compounded of the relative and the indefinite pronouns and here carries the idea of quality as well as identity. It may be rendered, "who by his very nature, who is such as."[16] That eternal Life, the second Person of the Trinity, was by His very nature in personal fellowship with the Father. Rather than σύν or μετά John chose to use πρός because it speaks not merely of personal presence but of active communion. The root idea of πρός is that of *facing*,[17] and it speaks of motion toward something or someone. This passage may therefore be paraphrased by saying that Christ "was in active, face-to-face fellowship with the Father." One can readily hear the echo of John 1:1, ὁ λόγοs ἦν πρὸς τὸν θεόν, "the Word was with God," where the use of the article with θεόν identifies the person of deity, God the Father, rather than the quality of deity.[18]

καὶ ἐφανερώθη ἡμῖν, "and was manifested to us." From

---

13. A. E. Brooke, *The Johannine Epistles,* The International Critical Commentary, p. 6.
14. Kittel, s.v., "αἰών, αἰώνιos," by Hermann Sasse.
15. Brooke, p. 6.
16. Arndt and Gingrich, p. 591.
17. Dana and Mantey, p. 110.
18. Ibid., p. 140.

eternity past the Life was in face-to-face fellowship with the Father, but this condition was altered by the incarnation when Christ was manifested to men. The repetition of ἐφανερώθη in this verse shows that John was intent on stressing the manifestation he saw. (See previous comments on the first occurrence of the verb.)

B. THE PURPOSE OF THE APOSTOLIC DECLARATION, 1:3-4

1:3. ὃ ἑωράκαμεν καὶ ἀκηκόαμεν, "what we have seen and heard." (See comments on verse 1.) After the parenthetical explanation of verse 2, John repeats in reverse order two verbs from verse 1 for the purpose of clearly tying the direct object clauses of that verse to the main verb ἀπαγγέλλομεν, "we proclaim," of verse 3.

ἀπαγγέλλομεν καὶ ὑμῖν, "we proclaim to you also." Concerning the verb, see comments on verse 2. There are several possible explanations of καί: (1) it may mean *even*, but this is unlikely, (2) it may mean *also* referring to the fact that John had declared the message to others and now he is declaring it *also* to the readers of this epistle, (3) it may mean that "we" as well as others are making this declaration to "you," or (4) it may have the apostles in view. They had arrived at the truth by witnessing the incarnation; now John is declaring it to his readers that they *also* may possess the truth. The probability of the fourth view is confirmed by the following clause.

ἵνα καὶ ὑμεῖς κοινωνίαν ἔχητε μεθ' ἡμῶν, "that you also may have fellowship with us." Ἵνα with the subjunctive ἔχητε, "may have," refers to the purpose of John and his associates in declaring what they had seen and heard. It is with the intent that the readers *also* may continue to experience the sacred fellowship that the apostles enjoyed. The present tense verb (ἔχητε) is significant. An aorist tense would mean "to come to have, to get, to obtain," but the present tense means "to continue to have." John's desire is that the fellowship they enjoy may continue to be their experience—that it will not be hindered by the influence of false teachers. Κοινωνία, "fellowship," is related to κοινός, "common," used in secular Greek to refer to things held in common, such as common ownership, the common property of a married couple. It is also employed in the New Testament in this sense (Acts 2:44; 4:32). Κοινωνός describes a fellow participant, one who has something in common with someone else. Luke 5:10 states that James and John were partners (κοινωνοί) with Peter. Κοινωνία therefore means "fellowship, participation, partnership."[19] In contrast to μετοχή it pictures an active participation, not mere passive sharing.[20] In 1 John κοινωνία describes a fellowship based on a common faith in the incarnate Son of God. Because of that faith held in common the believers are participants in a common interpersonal relationship with God and with one another. Law explains:

> The common basis of both "fellowships," the human and the divine, is found in the knowledge of God in Christ (John 17:3) which is given to men in the facts of the Incarnate Life. By their participation with the Apostle in the possession of that knowledge, his readers also will enter, or enter more fully, into the "fellowship" which he possesses with the Father and the Son.[21]

The preposition μετά (μεθ') speaks of the relationship of distinct individuals who maintain their separate identities even while in close association. The first person plural pronoun ἡμῶν, "us," refers to the apostles. John desires to prevent the heretical teachers from attempting to sever the bond of fellowship between the readers and the apostles.

καὶ ἡ κοινωνία δὲ ἡ ἡμετέρα, "and indeed our fellowship." Although there is disagreement concerning the functions of καί and δέ, it seems best to regard the former as emphatic and the latter as connective. Further emphasis is present in the repetition of the article ἡ and in the use of ἡμετέρα, "our," rather than the genitive of the personal pronoun (ἡμῶν, "of us"). John has chosen the strongest terms to lay stress on the nature of the apostolic fellowship. The full force of his words could be represented in English as follows: "and certainly the fellowship of which I have spoken, that which is ours." The fellowship John desires as a continuing experience for his readers is no commonplace association. It is a most remarkable relationship.

μετὰ τοῦ πατρὸς καὶ μετὰ τοῦ υἱοῦ αὐτοῦ Ἰησοῦ χριστοῦ, "with the Father, and with His Son Jesus Christ." Here again μετά is used rather than σύν to express the association of the distinct persons involved. The occurrence of μετά with the article before both πατρός, "father," and υἱοῦ, "son," serves first to

---

19. Kittel, s.v., "κοινός, κοινωνός, κτλ.," by Fredrich Hauck.
20. Brooke, p. 8.
21. Robert Law, *The Tests of Life*, p. 371.

distinguish between the Father and the Son, and then to place them on the same plane with each other. Furthermore, John makes it clear that the Son of God is none other than the man Jesus Christ. This identification leaves no room for any kind of Gnostic distinction between the divine Son and the human Jesus.

1:4. καὶ ταῦτα γράφομεν ἡμεῖς, "and these things we write." Previously (vv. 2-3) John had spoken of the broader witness and declaration that had been and still was being carried to people everywhere. In this verse, however, he narrows down the declaration to the recipients of this epistle. The ταῦτα, "these things," of verse 4 seems most naturally to refer to the items John has been discussing in verses 1-3. The content of the declaration spoken of in verses 2-3 would thus be the same as the content of ταῦτα (v. 4). The only difference is that the latter was addressed to a much more circumscribed group of people. Instead of the plural γράφομεν, "we are writing," one might have expected that John would have used the first person singular γράφω as he does later on in the epistle (2:1, 12 ff.). However, the plural looks back to the plural verbs of verses 1-3, where the apostles are included as eyewitnesses, although it is obvious γράφομεν refers more specifically to John, depicting him as the representative of the apostolic group.

ἵνα ἡ χαρὰ ἡμῶν ᾖ πεπληρωμένη, "so that our joy may be made complete." Employing a clause previously used by our Lord (John 16:24), John states one aspect of his purpose in writing this epistle. (Cf. John 15:11; 17:13; 2 John 12.) His comprehensive statement of purpose is found in 5:13. There are also additional, subsidiary purposes stated in 1:3-4 and 2:1. However, they are all intimately related. If, as a result of this epistle, the readers come to enjoy an experience of more intimate fellowship with the Father and the Son (1:3) and do not allow the fellowship with other believers to be marred or broken by the inroads of false teachers, the author will be overjoyed.

The manuscripts are at variance concerning the personal pronoun (ἡμῶν, "our"/ὑμῶν, "your") following χαρά, "joy." The better witnesses favor ἡμῶν. Furthermore, because ὑμῶν appears to be more natural, early scribes might have been led to change the text from ἡμῶν to ὑμῶν. More careful consideration of John's statement reveals that the second person form makes very good sense. He writes for the benefit of his readers who are to him both τεκνία, "little children," (2:1) and ἀγαπη-

Introduction: The Reality of the Incarnation 107

τοί, "beloved" (3:2). If those dear ones profit from what John writes, he will rejoice abundantly. In fact, that would be his greatest joy (3 John 4).

The periphrastic ᾖ πεπληρωμένη is filled with more meaning than can be conveyed by an English translation. A perfect periphrastic is usually intensive in force, laying stress on the continuing results of a completed action.[22] Literally the construction means "to be in the state of having been filled." The author wrote in order that he might be in the state of fullness of joy as he saw his beloved children responding to the truth.

THEOLOGICAL COMMENTARY (1:1-4)

(The theological sections of the commentary deal specifically with the meaning of the passage, first for John's original readers, and second for the church of our day. Under this heading the content of the passage is treated more comprehensively than in the exegetical section.)

A. THE HISTORICAL BACKGROUND

John does not explicitly declare that these introductory verses are directed against any group or teaching, yet in the light of the whole epistle it appears that even in these opening lines he is refuting error. Although 1 John was not written as a polemic directed to the heretical teachers (see Chapter 4), it was penned to warn believers of that erroneous system of thought (2:26).

It seems apparent that John and his readers were confronted with the Christology of Cerinthus, who taught that Jesus was a mere human being and that the Christ was a divine aeon or emanation from the absolute Deity, which associated itself with the human Jesus during his earthly ministry. That association was said to have lasted from Jesus' baptism until His crucifixion, being marked at its beginning by the descent of the dove (Matt. 3:16) and at its termination by the words, "My God, my God, why hast thou forsaken me?" (Matt. 27:46).

It is also probable that Docetism in its more characteristic form was abroad during the latter period of John's life. Not many years following the writing of this epistle, Ignatius was busy combating the docetic assertion that Christ did not possess a real physical body, that He only appeared to be incarnate, that He was in

---

22. Dana and Mantey, p. 232.

reality a kind of phantom who successfully played the part of a flesh-and-blood human being.[23]

In neither of those views did the divine Christ actually become human; there was no real identification of God with man. Thus, there was no actual substitutionary atonement. In the Cerinthian view the Christ left the human Jesus before the latter died; in the docetic view Christ, being a kind of phantom, only seemed to die.

B. THE JOHANNINE REFUTATION

John's refutation in these introductory verses is entirely positive. There is no attack, no denial, no criticism of any adversary; yet no more forceful refutation of the heresy could be imagined. Simply by the forthright, positive declaration of the Christological truth, the author directs a hard-hitting blow at the error. Instead of denying what the Gnostics taught, John affirms the truth and advances eyewitness testimony to support it.

1. *The substance of the apostolic declaration,* 1:1-2. In verses 1-2 the author lays stress on the tradition that was being handed on by the apostles. They were the eyewitnesses who had seen, heard, and even handled the incarnate Son of God. Their testimony was superior to all the vagaries of the Gnostics. In fact the latter could cite no witnesses whatsoever to prove their theories of Christology. The church Fathers, following the Johannine pattern, repeatedly cite the testimony of apostolic tradition. That the church possessed that tradition, whereas the heretics did not, proved the former to be genuine and the latter spurious.

In opposition to the Docetists who denied the reality of Christ's body, John emphasizes the care with which the apostles examined the incarnate Christ. Their examination included the senses of hearing, sight, and touch. As surely as they knew that their senses did not lie, they knew that He was not a phantom. Furthermore,

---

23. Raymond Brown, *The Community of the Beloved Disciple,* p. 112, refers to several of the Nag Hammadi manuscripts which reflect such Docetic views of Christ. The *Trimorphic Protenoia,* 13. 50. 12-15, quotes a heavenly Word as saying, "I put on Jesus. I bore him from the cursed wood and established him in the dwelling places of his Father, and those who watch over their dwelling places did not recognize me." *The Apocalypse of Peter,* 7. 81. 15-25, describes a living Jesus as laughing at those who persecuted the external Jesus. Again, Brown in *The Epistles of John,* The Anchor Bible, 30:58, n. 137, cites the *Letter of Peter to Philip* 8. 136. 20-22; 139. 15-23; NHL 396-97) as saying that Jesus came and was crucified but was not recognized by some. "They thought he was a mortal man, whereas he is a stranger to suffering."

Introduction: The Reality of the Incarnation

John insists that the memory of what they heard, saw, and felt had not faded with the passing of the years. It was indelibly fixed in the consciousness, giving lasting validity to their witness.

In opposition to the teaching of Cerinthus, John insists that what the apostles carefully examined was identical with "what was from the beginning" (v. 1). It is not possible to separate the one from the other. The Person who was manifest in human flesh was the One who existed in eternity past in face-to-face fellowship with God the Father.

The apostolic declaration concerned the One whom John designates as the Word, the One who is the revelation of God, who is Himself life and the source of life, Creator as well as Revealer. He is no mere emanation from Deity; He is Deity.

2. *The purpose of the apostolic declaration*, 1:3-4. In its wider scope the purpose of the declaration was to cultivate fellowship. It was to attempt to make sure that the hearers would continue in apostolic communion and so to preserve them from being drawn into the heretical circle. The Gnostics were by nature divisive. They not only separated themselves from the apostolic fellowship (2:19), but they also sought to influence others to break away. The two circles of fellowship are evident in succeeding passages of the epistle. John speaks of the family of God and the family of the devil (3:10); he writes about two groups of hearers, one tuned to listen to the world and the other tuned to hear the truth (4:5-6); and he distinguishes between those who love the people of God and those who hate them (2:9-11; 3:10-15; 5:1).

By his declaration of the truth concerning the incarnation, John would provide the basis for a fellowship that includes God the Father, God the Son, the apostles, and believers in general. Such a fellowship is only possible to those who accept the apostolic testimony that Jesus Christ is the God-man, the eternal Son of God become incarnate.

More specifically, John writes this epistle with the hope that its acceptance and application will bring fullness of joy to his own heart. This will come as he sees his dear children (τεκνία) founded upon the truth of the incarnation, bound together with all believers everywhere in a unique divine fellowship, and thus securely fortified against the heresy.

C. THE PRESENT-DAY APPLICATION

Although the church today is not confronted with first-century incipient Gnosticism, these verses have application in varying degrees to the combating of twentieth-century errors. E. C. Hoskyns was surely right when he said concerning the gospel of John: "The modern reader will therefore not apprehend the Fourth Gospel as its author meant it to be apprehended if he concludes that it was against, say, Gnosticism, or Docetism, or Ebionitism, or even against the Jews, and rests satisfied with that explanation, without at the same time recognizing that those ancient movements of religion are still deep-seated and destructive factors in our common life."[24]

Recognizing this principle of interpretation, Stott says the emphasis of these verses is applicable to the empirical scientist, the demythologizing radical, and the subjective mystic. All such persons need to realize that the invisible and intangible things of God are revealed through visible and tangible historical events.[25]

With Lenski we may also find an application of these verses to those who today deny the deity of Jesus.[26] During the first century Cerinthus viewed Jesus as being a mere man upon whom the divine Christ came for a time. Although the person who currently denies the deity of our Lord may not believe in the descent of a divine Christ, nevertheless his denial of deity does parallel that of Cerinthus.

Charles Ryrie, commenting on Johannine theology, says: "Philosophic arrogance (as in liberalism), may attempt to disentangle eternal truth from its historical shell (as in Barthianism), and neglect of the Jesus of History and His example (as sometimes in fundamentalism) are all echoes of contemporary gnosticism. They make the study of Johannine theology particularly relevant in our day."[27] In view of such twentieth-century denials, we must emphasize the apostolic testimony that the human Jesus whom the disciples personally knew is the same Person who existed from the beginning, the Eternal Life who was manifested among men. If, as Cerinthus asserted, it was only the human Jesus who died, then His death was no more efficacious than that of any other man. The denial of our Lord's deity is also the denial of the atonement. By this single denial Christian theology is radically altered so that it is no longer truly Christian.

24. Edwin Clement, Hoskyns, *The Fourth Gospel*, p. 49.
25. John R. W. Stott, *The Epistles of John, The Tyndale New Testament Commentaries*, p. 61.
26. R. C. H. Lenski, *The Interpretation of the Epistles of St. Peter, St. John and St. Jude*, p. 374.
27. Charles Ryrie, *Biblical Theology of the New Testament*, p. 312.

Introduction: The Reality of the Incarnation 111

John has made it clear that genuine Christian fellowship is based upon a common acceptance of the apostolic testimony concerning the incarnation (1 John 1:3). Therefore, without the common possession of faith in the God-man, Jesus Christ, there can be no spiritual fellowship, for the very foundation of such fellowship is lacking. So today, genuine Christian fellowship can only exist among individuals who hold to both the deity and humanity of Jesus Christ. To deny the reality of the incarnation is to reject the very foundation of the Christian faith. Without this truth there can be no such thing as Christian faith, and consequently without it there can be no Christian fellowship. It is not possible, then, for individuals or organized groups to have biblical fellowship with those who do not agree on the fundamentals of the Christian faith.

In addition, application of this passage may be made even more directly to that group of present-day cults that are gnostic in character, namely Christian Science, New Thought, the Unity School of Christianity, and the Theosophical Society. The basic factor that binds these four religious systems together is their view of Christology. All of them separate Christ from the human Jesus, making the former to be some kind of divine consciousness that, although latent in all men, was fully developed in the man Jesus.

Mary Baker Eddy, the founder of Christian Science, said, "The word Christ is not properly a synonym for Jesus."[28] She further declared: "Jesus is the name of the man who, more than all other men, has presented Christ, the true idea of God, healing the sick and the sinning and destroying the power of death. Jesus is the human man; and Christ is the divine idea; hence the duality of Jesus the Christ."[29]

New Thought, a close parallel to Christian Science, takes a similar view of the relationship of Christ and Jesus. Henry Wood writes: "Christ is the name of sonship—God in us. Jesus personally expressed that relation, supremely, ideally. . . . The Christ represents the universal and eternal divine sonship—the highest possible inner consciousness. . . . It was locally and historically expressed in full degree through the personality of Jesus, but by no means limited to him."[30]

The Unity School of Christianity, which seems to have somewhat common roots with Christian Science and New Thought,

---

28. Mary Baker Eddy, *Science and Health with Key to the Scriptures*, p. 333.
29. Ibid., p. 473.
30. Henry Wood, *New Thought Simplified*, p. 182.

also separates Christ from Jesus. It declares, "By Christ is not meant the man Jesus."[31] This group further explains its view of Christology in an older (c. 1920s) issue of *Unity* magazine:

> The Bible says that God so loved the world that he gave his only begotten Son, but the Bible does not here refer to Jesus of Nazareth, the outer man; it refers to the Christ, the spiritual identity of Jesus, whom he acknowledged in all his ways, and brought forth into his outer, until even the flesh of his body was lifted up, purified, spiritualized and redeemed. Thus he became Jesus Christ, the Word made flesh.[32]

The Theosophical Society is not hesitant to recognize Gnosticism as one of the sources of its system of thought. It refers to the early Gnostics as "the intellect and heart of the Church," whose insights became buried under the misunderstandings of the ignorant majority.[33] Theosophists say that the Christ has come many times in the persons of great world teachers who "have been appearing at propitious times since humanity began existence."[34] Hence the Christ was merely a divine awareness resident within the man Jesus just as it is within all men.

There is another way in which Christian Science is at variance with 1 John. Eddy and her followers also deny the reality of matter, declaring it to be "nothing beyond an image in mortal mind."[35] If this be true, it is obvious that Christ's physical body was only an illusion. Such denial rules out any possibility of an atoning death because death also, according to Mrs. Eddy, is nothing but an illusion. The eternal Christ did not suffer in the flesh, and even the human Jesus only appeared to suffer in order to give men a better understanding of love.

PARAPHRASTIC COMMENTARY (1:1-4)

(The purpose of the Paraphrastic Commentary is to present an expanded paraphrase, drawing upon the fruits of study of both the exegetical

---

31. *Unity*, no. 2, p. 146, as cited by Walter R. Martin, *The Kingdom of the Cults*, p. 280.
32. *Unity*, vol. 57, no. 5, p. 464, as cited by Martin, p. 280. (Quotation used by permission of *Unity* magazine, Unity School of Christianity, Unity Village, Missouri.)
33. W. Rogers, *Elementary Theosophy* (Wheaton, Ill.: Theosophical Press, 1956) p. 22, as cited by Martin, p. 223.
34. Ibid., pp. 260-63, as cited by Martin, p. 227.
35. Mary Baker Eddy, p. 116.

Introduction: The Reality of the Incarnation 113

and the theological sections of the commentary. Hence, the following rephrasing of 1 John 1:1-4 is in reality a commentary in brief.)

(1) The things which have to do with that One who is the Life, the very expression of the Father's nature—what existed from eternity past, what we apostles heard and still rings in our ears, what we saw with our own eyes and continues to linger in our mental vision, what we carefully examined, what our very hands handled. (2) [for He who in His essence is Life was revealed to us, and we saw and still remember Him, and we are bearing eyewitness testimony. Yes, we are officially proclaiming to you the Life which, both quantitatively and qualitatively, is eternal, who by His very nature was in active, face-to-face fellowship with God the Father and now has been revealed to us]—(3) the things we saw and heard and still vividly recall we are officially declaring to you as well, in order that you may actively participate with us in that close association that is based upon a common faith in the incarnate Son of God. And, to be more specific, the fellowship that we apostles are enjoying is a fellowship with both God the Father and God the Son. (4) One purpose for writing this letter to you is so that, because of your response to its warnings and assurances, we may continue in a state of abundant joy.

STRUCTURAL COMMENTARY (1:1-4)

(If a commentary is to fulfill its mission, it is important that it carefully trace the biblical writer's train of thought through each section under consideration. A most effective method of accomplishing this goal is that of the analytical or content outline, which enables the student to see at a glance the structure of the passage. The following outline is a more detailed development of that which has been employed in the text of the exegetical commentary.)

I. Introduction: The reality of the incarnation, 1:1-4
   A. The substance of the apostolic declaration: That which has to do with the Word, the Life, 1:1-2
      1. What has existed since eternity past, 1:1*a*
      2. What the apostles heard, 1:1*b*
      3. What they saw, 1:1*c*
      4. What they carefully examined, 1:1*d*
      5. What they handled, 1:1*e*
   [Parenthesis, 1:2
      1. The manifestation of the Life, 1:2*a*
      2. The eyewitnesses of Life, 1:2*b*
      3. The apostles' proclamation of the Life, 1:2*c*]

B. The purpose of the apostolic declaration, 1:3-4
   1. The purpose of the universal witness of the apostles, 1:3
      a. Stated: that you may have fellowship with us, 1:3*a-b*
      b. Explained: our fellowship is with the Father and the Son, 1:3*c*
   2. The purpose of this specific declaration (the letter)—abundant joy for the writer, 1:4

II. First Cycle: The Christian Life Viewed as Fellowship with the Father and Son, 1:5—2:28

From the introduction (1:1-4) John moves without a break in thought into the first major section of the epistle. The groundwork has been laid, the keynote sounded, and now he proceeds to unfold the argument of the book. The first cycle (1:5—2:28) conceives of the Christian life as a divine-human fellowship, an idea first introduced in the previous section (1:3), but now to be developed more fully. As the apostle indicates in the introduction, such a fellowship is based upon a valid Christology. He affirms the reality of the incarnation (1:1-2) as a foundation for this divine-human relationship (1:3). The same idea is taken up again in the first cycle of the argument (2:18-28), where John bluntly asserts the absolute necessity of believing in the incarnation. Only the person who confesses that Jesus is the incarnate Christ has any relationship to God the Father (2:22-23).

Although the term κοινωνία, "fellowship," occurs only at the beginning of the cycle (1:6-7), several parallel expressions are used throughout the section, making it evident that the idea of fellowship pervades the whole. These synonymous clauses are:

ἐγνώκαμεν αὐτόν, "we know him," 2:3 (cf. 2:4, 13-14)
ἐν αὐτῷ ἐσμεν, "we are in him," 2:5
ἐν αὐτῷ μένειν, "to abide in him," 2:6 (cf. 2:24, 27-28)

The epistle as a whole is characterized by a series of tests advanced to distinguish the genuine believer from the spurious. Sensing this motif, Law entitled his commentary on the theology and text of 1 John *The Tests of Life* (pp. 5-24). Whereas Law suggested three tests—righteousness, love, and belief—this commentary prefers to regard them as two in number: the ethical (1:5—2:11) and the Christological (2:18-28).

The first major section of the epistle revolves around two main points of reference, the ethical (1:5-2:11) and the Christological (2:18-28), both of which constitute conditions requisite to any fellowship with God. It is necessary both to believe in the incarnate Son of God and to walk in the light if one is to particpate in the divine κοινωνία. On the one hand, belief in the incarnation is prerequisite to entering the sphere of fellowship; on the other, walking in righteousness and love is the necessary evidence of such belief.

7
Fellowship Tested on Ethical Grounds, 1:5—2:11

Fellowship can only be experienced by those who possess something in common. Hence, inasmuch as God is light, those who are in fellowship with Him will manifest a similarity of character and practice. The absence of this quality of life belies any claim, no matter how insistent, to communion with God. If fellowship is a reality it will be evidenced by moral likeness (1:5-7), by readiness to confess one's sin (1:8—2:2), by obedience to God's commands (2:3-6), and by love for God's people (2:7-11).

Exegetical Commentary (1:5—2:11)

FELLOWSHIP DEMANDS MORAL LIKENESS, 1:5-7

1:5. καὶ ἔστιν αὕτη ἡ ἀγγελία, "and this is the message." Καί, "and," links the new section closely with the preceding one, with the result that the basic ideas of the introduction flow almost imperceptibly into the first major division of the argument. In verse 3 John has said, "what we have seen and heard [ὃ ἑωράκαμεν λαὶ ἀκηκόμεν] we proclaim [ἀπαγγέλλομεν] to you." Here in verse 5 he carries on the same idea using similar terms (ἀγγελία, ἀκηκόαμεν, and ἀναγγέλλομεν). Ἀγγελία, "message," is the foundation word upon which ἀπαγγέλλομεν (v. 3) and ἀναγγέλλομεν (v. 5), "we . . . announce," are based.

ἦν ἀκηκόαμεν ἀπ' αὐτοῦ, "which we have heard from Him." This clause reveals the source of the message. It was *from Him*, that is, from Christ as the preceding context indicates. John has been writing about that which concerned the incarnate Word (v. 1), and it was that that the apostles had been declaring (v. 3). In verse 5 he identifies one element of their message. Furthermore, the repetition of ἀκηκόαμεν, "we have heard," from verse 1 confirms the relationship of the declarations in verses 1-3 and verse 5. There is no record that Jesus ever explicitly declared that "God is light." It is entirely possible, however, that this is a statement of Jesus not recorded in the gospels. In that case John was recalling it from memory and recording it here for the first time (cf. Acts 20:35). Or perhaps Bonsirven is right in suggesting that the message (ἀγγελία) "sums up the teaching of the Master and the general impression left by his doctrine."[1] Christ described Himself as light (John 8:12; 9:5; 12:35-36, 46). He addressed God as "Holy Father" (John 17:11), as "righteous Father" (John 17:25), and as "true" (John 7:28; 8:26), all of which are qualities included in the metaphorical use of the term *light*. That God is light and the possessor of light is also an Old Testament concept (Pss. 27:1; 36:9; 43:3; 104:2; Isa. 58:8). As in verses 1-3, the perfect tense of ἀκηκόαμεν speaks of a past completed action with results continuing to the present. What the apostle had heard was still resounding unforgettably in his ears.

καὶ ἀναγγέλλομεν ὑμῖν, "and (we) announce to you." No valid distinction is to be found between ἀπαγγέλλομεν (vv. 2-3) and ἀναγγέλλομεν (v. 5). Although such a difference could be supported by the etymology of the two verbs, in actual usage they had come to be employed interchangeably.[2]

ὅτι ὁ θεὸς φῶς ἐστιν, "that God is light." This pregnant clause sets forth the content of the message John is passing on to his readers. The absence of the article with φῶς, "light," serves a double purpose. It makes it clear that ὁ θεός, "God," is the subject and φῶς is the predicate nominative, thus ruling out the interpretation that light is God. In addition the anarthrous usage makes the statement qualitative. God's nature is described as possessing the qualities of light. It is obvious that φῶς is not employed

---

1. Joseph Bonsirven, *Épitres de Saint Jean*, vol. 9, Verbum Salutis, p. 85 (my translation).
2. Gerhard Kittel, ed., *Theological Dictionary of the New Testament*, 1964-76, s.v. "ἀγγελία, κτλ.," by Julius Schniewind; Rudolph Bultmann, *The Johannine Epistles*, Hermeneia, p. 15, n. 2.

in a literal sense. It is superficial to attempt, as some do, to explain away the metaphorical usage by saying that God Himself is the reality of which earthly light is the reflection.[3] As true as this may be, it overlooks the common biblical practice of representing God in anthropomorphic or physical terms. The Old Testament speaks of the arm of God (Isa. 52:10) and the eye of the Lord (2 Chron. 16:9). God is described as a rock and a tower (Ps. 18:2). In each of these expressions the biblical author is attempting to represent deity in terms understandable to man. There is no necessity to see in the term *light* anything more than a simple figurative use intended to enable finite man better to understand the infinite God.

Because John does not explicitly state what aspects of light he has in mind, it is necessary to study his usage of the term. The word is employed in the gospel of John as one of the metaphorical designations of Christ. There the light is seen pitted against the darkness (1:4-9), but the darkness was not able to overcome it (κατέλαβεν, v. 5). The light has come into the world and evil men prefer the darkness and hate the light, whereas he who practices the truth comes to the light (3:19-21). Jesus declares Himself to be the light of the world who enables men to cease walking in darkness and to possess the light of life (8:12; 9:5; 12:46). In these passages two characteristics of light seem to be predominant. The term is used (1) concerning truth and (2) in connection with practice (3:20-21). The one who practices evil (ὁ φαῦλα πράσσων) hates the light, but the one who practices the truth (ὁ δὲ ποιῶν τὴν ἀλήθειαν) comes to the light. The light is antagonistic to evil, but it is in harmony with truth and good deeds. Light would seem, therefore, to be the standard of truth, righteousness, and holiness, especially as seen in Christ Himself.

Bonsirven suggests three senses in which God may be described as being "light." Light represents divine glory and majesty; it speaks of divine illumination or revelation; and, above all, it depicts moral rectitude.[4]

The Dead Sea Scrolls also use the term light in an ethical sense. *The Manual of Discipline* says: "The origin of truth lies in the Fountain of Light, and that of perversity in the Wellspring of Darkness. All who practice righteousness are under the domination of the Prince of Lights, and walk in ways of light; whereas all who practice perversity are under the domination of the Angel of

---

3. B. F. Westcott, *The Epistles of St. John*, p. 17.
4. Bonsirven, pp. 86-88.

Darkness and walk in ways of darkness."[5] Here also light is related to truth and to the practice of righteousness. The same is suggested by inference in John 3:20-21, where the opposite of practicing the truth is the practice of evil.

Dodd and Marshall point out the widespread use of the concept of light in Greek philosophy, Zoroastrianism, Philo, the Dead Sea Scrolls, and the Gnostic systems.[6] It is clear that the theological and philosophical use of the term was widespread and commonplace in the first-century world. Its prominent place in the Qumran literature (so similar to its employment by John) not only aids in the understanding of the apostle's meaning, but also counters any insistence that the Johannine writings are products of the later Hellenistic church.

It would seem, then, that John's term *light* includes the elements of truth and moral rectitude. It may be concluded that God in His essence is holiness. In 1 John 4:8 John also declares God in His essence to be love. Thus God essentially is holy love. (See comments on 4:8 for fuller discussion.)

καὶ σκοτία ἐν αὐτῷ οὐκ ἔστιν οὐδεμία, "and in Him there is no darkness at all." John here reveals his penchant for contrast of the positive and the negative. In reality the statement is an antithetical parallelism of the kind often found in Hebrew poetry. The term σκοτία, "darkness," is to be understood as the opposite of φῶς, "light," and thus as referring to falsehood and moral evil. It includes any moral imperfection, whether in nature, attitude, or practice. In this instance, because John denies that there is any darkness *in Him*, the stress is on imperfections of nature and attitude. That both light and darkness are used in a moral sense is clear from the following context (1:6-10) as well as from the association of light with love in 2:9-11.[7]

The denial is made more than doubly strong by the words οὐκ, "not," and οὐδεμία, "no." First, the two words make up a kind of double negative, which in Greek serves to strengthen the denial. In addition, the term οὐδεμία is in itself a forceful denial

---

5. Theodor H. Gaster, trans., *The Dead Sea Scriptures*, "The Manual of Discipline," IQS 3:19-21.
6. C. H. Dodd, *The Johannine Epistles*, The Moffatt New Testament Commentary, pp. 18-19; I. Howard Marshall, *The Epistles of John*, The New International Commentary, p. 109.
7. See also Additional Note on "The symbolism of light in Scripture" in John R. W. Stott, *The Epistles of John*, Tyndale New Testament Commentaries, pp. 70-72.

made up of the negative οὐ and the cardinal numeral μία. Literally it means *not one*. Thus there is not one bit of darkness in God, not the slightest trace of moral evil. He is absolutely holy and true.

1:6. ἐὰν εἴπωμεν, "if we say." John is setting forth a hypothetical case, as the use of the subjunctive mood indicates. It is also noteworthy that he includes himself by using the first person plural, thus revealing the humility with which he approaches the problem. Here the "we" is the "we" of identification with the readers, whereas in 1:1-4 it was the "we" of identification with other eyewitnesses. This is the first of five occurrences extending through the end of the chapter in which ἐάν, "if," with the subjunctive mood is used. In each instance John proposes a hypothetical but possible case and then draws a deduction from the case. No doubt some of these hypothetical statements (vv. 6, 8, 10) represent claims made by the false teachers. These conditional sentences are arranged antithetically, stating the negative, the contrasting positive, and—in the second series—the negative again.

Negative (v. 6)—"*walk in the darkness*"
Positive (v. 7)—"*walk in the light*"

Negative (v. 8)—"*say we have no sin*"
Positive (v. 9)—"*confess our sins*"
Negative (v. 10)—"*say that we have not sinned*"

ὅτι κοινωνίαν ἔχομεν μετ᾿ αὐτοῦ, "that we have fellowship with Him." The claim is one of having fellowship as a continuing experience, as John indicates by the present tense ἔχομεν, "are having." The experience of fellowship is that of sharing something held in common (κοινός, "common"; cf. on 1:3). The preceding verse shows that the antecedent of αὐτοῦ, "Him," is God. This is one of the claims of the early Gnostics. Other claims are found in 1:8 ("we have no sin"), 1:10 ("we have not sinned"), 2:4 ("I have come to know Him"), 2:9 (I am "in the light"), 2:22 ("Jesus is not the Christ," Gr.).

καὶ ἐν τῷ σκότει περιπατῶμεν, "and *yet* walk in the darkness." The second part of the hypothetical activity is the walk, paralleling the claim ἐὰν εἴπωμεν, "if we say." Here again the action, as indicated by the present tense περιπατῶμεν, "walk," is linear referring to the continuing walk of the speaker. περιπατέω is a common figurative term to describe the process of living. Hence, John is describing the speaker's living continually in darkness. σκότει, "darkness," in this context refers to that which is antithetical to the very being of God. As in verse 5, it has moral connotations signifying the absence of truth and holiness and thus the presence of error and moral evil. To walk in darkness is to live habitually in the very sphere (locative case ἐν τῷ σκότει) of error and sin. The article τῷ is used to particularize darkness in sharpest contrast to the light (τῷ φωτί, v. 7). John here uses language that is quite parallel to that of the Dead Sea Scrolls. *The Manual of Discipline* discusses those who "walk in ways of light" and those who "walk in ways of darkness." It is said that the aim of "the spirit of perversity" is to see to it "that a man walks entirely in ways of darkness."[8]

ψευδόμεθα καὶ οὐ ποιοῦμεν τὴν ἀλήθειαν, "we lie and do not practice the truth." Just as the conditional clause contained two elements, speech and action, so does the independent clause. ψευδόμεθα, "we lie," corresponds with εἴπωμεν, "we say," and οὐ ποιοῦμεν τὴν ἀλήθειαν, "we do not practice the truth" answers to περιπατῶμεν, "we walk." Both verbs, ψευδόμεθα and ποιοῦμεν, are in the present tense depicting continuing action. ποιοῦμεν (from ποιέω, *to do*) thus comes to refer to a continual practice. The article τὴν before ἀλήθειαν particularizes the noun and connects it to a specific body of truth, in this case Christian doctrine.

The idea of practicing the truth is also found in John 3:20-21 where it is set in opposition to the practice of evil deeds. Truth there is not so much intellectual as it is practical and moral. It is truth that springs from the character of God and is intended to be expressed in the lives of His people.

1:7. ἐὰν δὲ ἐν τῷ φωτὶ περιπατῶμεν, "but if we walk in the light." The second hypothetical case is positive in nature. It concerns walking in the light in contrast to the practice of walking in darkness. Here again the verb περιπατῶμεν is a present tense, which indicates a habitual pattern of life. Life is living in the sphere (ἐν τῷ φωτί, locative case) of the light. The article points out a particular light, and in this case looks back to the nature of God who is light (v. 5). To walk in the light is to live in the sphere characterized by truth and holiness that come from God and are therefore God-like.

ὡς αὐτός ἐστιν ἐν τῷ φωτί, "as He Himself is in the light." Not only does John describe God as being light (v. 5), but

---

8. Gaster, "The Manual of Discipline," 3:20-21; 4:11.

he adds that God is *in* the light (cf. 1 Tim. 6:16). He exists in the sphere of truth and holiness, and therefore our lives are to be lived in that same sphere. That the reference is to God the Father is evident from the description of Jesus as υἱοῦ αὐτοῦ, "His Son." The presence of the pronoun αὐτός, "He Himself," is emphatic.

κοινωνίαν ἔχομεν μετ' ἀλλήλων, "we have fellowship with one another." We are reminded once again by the etymology of the word κοινωνίαν (κοινός, *common*) that fellowship is based upon something held in common. It requires that there be a community of experience, possession, or nature; without such community there can be no genuine fellowship. In this context that which is held in common is expressed by the symbolical term *light*. The verb ἔχομεν, present tense, speaks of the continuing experience of fellowship—*we are having*.

To keep on walking in the light is to keep on having fellowship. But who are the parties referred to by the reciprocal pronoun ἀλλήλων, "one another"? In verse 6 it is fellowship with God that is in view, but the antithetical statement of verse 7 is not completely parallel, for μετ' ἀλλήλων does not most naturally refer to fellowship between the believer and God, but rather of fellowship between believers. In the final analysis, however, fellowship with one another involves fellowship with God. As Bonsirven points out, the fellowship of the saints is "a gauge and a sign of the divine fellowship."[9] That fellowship with other believers implies fellowship with God is confirmed by two facts: (1) the obviously intended parallelism between verses 6 and 7, and (2) the description of fellowship in verse 3 as being both with men and with God.

καὶ τὸ αἷμα Ἰησοῦ τοῦ υἱοῦ αὐτοῦ καθαρίζει ἡμᾶς ἀπὸ πάσης ἁμαρτίας, "and the blood of Jesus His Son cleanses us from all sin." The better Greek manuscripts (א B C) omit χριστοῦ. The remaining expression τοῦ Ἰησοῦ τοῦ υἱοῦ αὐτοῦ, "of Jesus His Son," is thus an assertion directed against Cerinthus who distinguished between the man Jesus and the divine Son. The verb καθαρίζει, "cleanses," being in the present tense, speaks of a linear action just as does περιπατῶμεν, "we are walking." The habit of continually walking in the light is accompanied by a continual cleansing from sin as opposed to a once-for-all cleansing sometimes called positional sanctification.

After describing what some of the Corinthians once were (forni-

---

9. Bonsirven, p. 90 (my translation).

cators, idolators, adulterers, etc.), Paul says, "But you were washed, but you were sanctified, but you were justified" (1 Cor. 6:11). Each of those verbs is in the aorist tense, indicative mood, depicting an action that had occurred at a point in the past. At the time when the Corinthian believers had first trusted Christ they were washed clean. However, in addition to positional sanctification the believer experiences progressive sanctification, which involves a continuing growth in holiness as sin is purged from the life. That καθαρίζει refers to progressive sanctification rather than positional sanctification (or justification) is indicated by its present tense form. This interpretation is confirmed by verse 9 where καθαρίζω occurs in conjunction with ἀφίημι, "forgive." The cleansing is thus distinguished from forgiveness.

Henry Alford, drawing upon Düsterdieck, says that John views the blood of Christ as providing victory over sin, "being a purifying medium, whereby we gradually, being already justified, become pure and clean from all sin. And this application of Christ's blood is made by the Spirit which dwelleth in us." He further describes the experience as being that of "the inherent righteousness of Christ, wrought in us gradually in sanctification."[10] The word καθαρίζω and its related forms have a long history in the religions of the past in which they were used to describe ritual and cultic cleansing. In the New Testament, however, the emphasis is on personal and moral cleanness. Christ's death is the propitiation that atones for sin and makes a new purity available.[11]

πάσης ἁμαρτίας, "all sin," because of the absence of the article, means *every* in the sense of *any*. It is not every last sin, but any sin that may occur.[12] This is the same as saying that the construction stresses kind rather than particular identity. There is no sin, whatever its nature or degree, that is beyond the cleansing power of the blood of God's Son.

FELLOWSHIP DEMANDS CONFESSION OF SIN, 1:8—2:2

1:8. ἐὰν εἴπωμεν, "if we say." (See comments on v. 6.)
ὅτι ἁμαρτίαν οὐκ ἔχομεν, "that we have no sin." The

---

10. Henry Alford, *The Greek Testament*, 4:428.
11. Kittel, s.v. "καθαρός, καθαρίζω, κτλ.," by Friedrich Hauck and Rudolph Meyer.
12. James Hope Moulton, *A Grammar of New Testament Greek*, 4 vols.: vol. 3: *Syntax*, by Nigel Turner, p. 199.

important question here concerns the precise meaning of ἁμαρτίαν, "sin." Law insists that John refers to the guilt of sin.¹³ However, when this verse is compared with verse 10 (οὐχ ἡμαρτήκαμεν, "we have not sinned") it appears more reasonable to view verse 8 as having to do with the principle of sin and verse 10 the acts of sin. This denial of the depravity of sin is tantamount to denying that one *is* a sinner. The present tense speaks, not of the past unregenerate state when unbelievers might have refused to recognize sin's reality, but of the present state of professing believers who make such a denial. This claim is probably the response of the Gnostic to the accusation that he is walking in the darkness (v. 6).

ἑαυτοὺς πλανῶμεν, "we are deceiving ourselves." The verb πλανάω in its primary sense means "to lead astray," and in the passive, "to go astray." It is used of the sheep that wandered from the other ninety-nine (Matt. 18:12). The basic idea is that of leading one away from the right way. Examination of its New Testament occurrences reveals that it pictures major error rather than incidental mistakes. (Cf. Matt. 24:4—"take heed that no man leads you astray" [RSV]; Jas. 5:19—"wander from the truth" [NIV]; 1 Pet. 2:25—"ye were as sheep going astray" [KJV]; 1 John 2:26—"those who are trying to lead you astray" [NIV]; Rev. 2:20—"she . . . leads my bond-servants astray"; Rev. 12:9—"Satan, who leads the whole world astray" [NIV].) The part played by the agent is doubly stressed. First, the position of ἑαυτούς in the sentence is emphatic and second, the reflexive pronoun is stronger than the direct middle. It is not that a person has been deceived without his knowing it, but that he has led himself astray. Bultmann says that it is not "a simple mistake," but instead is "misdirected self-understanding."¹⁴ And Bonsirven describes the deception as "more or less voluntary and culpable."¹⁵

καὶ ἡ ἀλήθεια οὐκ ἔστιν ἐν ἡμῖν, "and the truth is not in us." As in verse 6 John uses the articular noun ἀλήθεια to point out that specific body of truth, both moral and soteriological, that God has revealed to His people. This truth includes "the message" (ἡ ἀγγελία) of verse 5, that "God is light," and it is identical with "His word" in verse 10. John declares that those

---

13. Robert Law, *The Tests of Life*, p. 130. However, see the response to Law's view in Brooke, *A Critical and Exegetical Commentary on the Johannine Epistles*, The International Critical Commentary, pp. 17-18.
14. Bultmann, p. 21.
15. Bonsirven, p. 94 (my translation).

who deny that they possess the sin principle have never received God's revealed truth into their souls. One cannot be saved unless he recognizes that he is sinful and needs to be saved.

1:9. ἐὰν ὁμολογῶμεν τὰς ἁμαρτίας ἡμῶν, "if we confess our sins." For the fourth time John sets up a hypothetical case introduced by ἐάν with the subjunctive mood. The verb ὁμολογῶμεν is an iterative present depicting the practice of confessing after each act of sin. Etymologically the word means "to speak (λέγω) together" (ὁμοῦ), and thus "to agree with" and then "to admit." This is the only place in the New Testament where ὁμολογέω refers to the confession of sin. It is used most frequently in connection with the confession of Christ or of truth about Him (eleven times). Three times it means *to admit*. In John 1:20 it appears in contradistinction to ἀρνέομαι, "I deny" (John admitted that he was not the Messiah). Its usage with reference to sin is somewhat similar because it refers to the admission of sin rather than the denial of it, as in 1 John 1:8, 10. The compound verb ἐξομολογέω is used similarly of confession of sins in Matthew 3:6. In both instances (1 John 1:9; Matt. 3:6) the open verbal acknowledgement of sin is in view. Nothing is said about the persons to whom confession is to be made. However, since God is the One who is being appealed to for forgiveness, it is certain that the confession is made to Him. Note that the admission does not concern sin as depraved nature, but rather acts of sin (τὰς ἁμαρτίας, "sins"), as the article τάς and the plural form of the noun clearly indicate.

πιστός ἐστιν καὶ δίκαιος, "He is faithful and righteous." The foundation upon which the assurance of forgiveness rests is indicated in these two attributes of God. His faithfulness and righteousness are not dependent on confession. Instead, upon confession He is found to be faithful and righteous. God's faithfulness is commonly viewed in Scripture as His loyalty to His promise (cf. Heb. 10:23; 11:11). He has established His covenant in which He pledges Himself to forgive sins (Jer. 31:34, "I will forgive their iniquity, and their sin I will remember no more").

In addition God is righteous, a characteristic not to be viewed merely as an extension of faithfulness. God's righteousness is His moral self-consistency. He always acts in uprightness in keeping with His own character. Consequently, since He is light (v. 5), sin must always be viewed as it really is—a violation of the divine standard, and it must be recompensed according to its true nature. Sin can only be forgiven when its penalty has been paid; then

Fellowship Tested on Ethical Grounds 127

God is free in perfect righteousness to forgive all who seek remission (cf. Rom 3:25-26). By the same token, since Christ has fully atoned for sin, God is bound by His righteousness to forgive all who repent and confess their sins. Marshall rightly declares, "If the conditions are fulfilled God would be wrong to withhold forgiveness."[16]

ἵνα ἀφῇ ἡμῖν τὰς ἁμαρτίας, "to forgive us our sins." The conjunction ἵνα may be used either in a final or nonfinal sense.[17] However, since it is clear that God is not faithful and righteous only for the purpose of forgiving sins, the final sense may be dismissed as irrelevant to John's meaning. Brooke argues that the usage here is not telic, insisting rather that it is definitive, in which case it should be translated as an infinitive, "to forgive." This contention is supported by a long list of examples, none of which is actually parallel to 1 John 1:9.[18] It is better, however, to interpret ἵνα in this passage as introducing a result clause, because forgiveness is in reality the result of God's faithfulness and righteousness rather than the definition of those attributes. "God is faithful and righteous *so that* he forgives."[19]

Ἀφῇ, from ἀφίημι, "I forgive," speaks very naturally of a legal obligation against someone. It was often used in the papyri of releasing a person from a legal obligation such as a debt.[20] This carries over into the New Testament where Jesus tells the story of a man who forgave his servant a debt (δάνειον ἀφῆκεν αὐτῷ, "forgave him the debt," Matt. 18:27). In like manner God promises to forgive the debt of sin to those who confess. In passages such as the one under consideration where ἀφίημι speaks of forgiveness, it takes the accusative of the object (τὰς ἁμαρτίας, "sins") and the dative of the person (ἡμῖν, "us").[21] (Cf. Luke 11:4.) In this case the article τάς with ἁμαρτίας is rightly translated as a possessive, "our sins."[22]

καὶ καθαρίσῃ ἡμᾶς ἀπὸ πάσης ἀδικίας, "and to cleanse us

---

16. Marshall, p. 114.
17. William F. Arndt and F. Wilbur Gingrich, trans. and eds. *A Greek-English Lexicon of the New Testament*, by Walter Bauer, pp. 376-78; H. E. Dana and Julius R. Mantey, *A Manual Grammar of the Greek New Testament*, pp. 248-49.
18. Brooke, pp. 19-20.
19. A. T. Robertson, *A Grammar of the Greek New Testament in the Light of Historical Research*, p. 998. Maximilian Zerwick lists this verse as an instance in which ἵνα should be translated as ὥστε, "so that." See *Biblical Greek*, sec. 352.
20. Kittel, s.v., "ἀφίημι, κτλ.," by Rudolph Bultmann.
21. Ibid.
22. Dana and Mantey, p. 148.

from all unrighteousness." The verb καθαρίσῃ, "cleanse," views sin as defilement that is to be removed, and it is we ourselves who are defiled and in need of cleansing as the accusative pronoun ἡμᾶς makes clear. As was indicated in the discussion of verse 7, the cleansing, both in verse 7 and verse 10, is tantamount to progressive sanctification. Westcott calls it the "progressive hallowing of the Christian which follows after to the end of life."[23] Πάσης ἀδικίας, "all unrighteousness," is similar to πάσης ἁμαρτίας, "all sin," in verse 7. It means any unrighteousness of any kind or degree. Ἀδικίας is failure to measure up to δικαιοσύνη, "righteousness," the standard of rightness.

1:10. ἐὰν εἴπωμεν, "if we say." See comments on verse 6.

ὅτι οὐχ ἡμαρτήκαμεν, "that we have not sinned." In contrast to the statement of verse 8 (ἁμαρτίαν οὐκ ἔχομεν, "we have no sin"), which denies the possession of a sinful nature, this denial is a claim never to have committed any sins. The perfect tense verb refers to the past and with the negative it includes all of past time up to the lastest minute. It claims that one is now in the state of never having committed sin. It is therefore a denial that one has ever sinned, not merely a claim to have reached the state where one no longer commits sin.

ψεύστην ποιοῦμεν αὐτόν, "we make Him a liar." The position of ψεύστην, "liar," in the clause is emphatic and holds up to view the terrible accusation being leveled against God. It is none other than the designation that Christ gave to the devil (John 8:44). This is more than a declaration that God *lies;* it is the erroneous charge that He *is* a liar in character. Basic to the whole redemptive revelation of God is that all men without exception are sinners who commit sin. This fact God declares in the Old Testament as well as the New. Paul's sad description of the human race in Romans 3:10-18 is made up of a series of quotations from various parts of the Old Testament, starting with:

> There is none righteous, not even one;
> There is none who understands,
> There is none who seeks for God;
> All have turned aside, together they have become useless;
> There is none who does good,
> There is not even one.
> (Rom. 3:10-12 [cf. Psalm 14:1-3])

---

23. Westcott, p. 25.

From verse 5*b* to here in verse 10 the third person pronouns "He," "Him," and "His" all refer to God the Father, as is made clear by the identification in verse 5*b* of God as light and the designation of Jesus as "His Son" (v. 7).

καὶ ὁ λόγος αὐτοῦ οὐκ ἔστιν ἐν ἡμῖν, "and His word is not in us." This statement is parallel to that of verse 8, ἡ ἀλήθεια οὐκ ἔστιν ἐν ἡμῖν, "the truth is not in us," the difference being that the *word* is the *truth* that has been spoken or revealed. Thus it is God's communicated truth that is not in us. This means His redemptive message has not been appropriated and thus does not dwell in us. Ἐν ἡμῖν, "in us," speaks of a most intimate relationship. (Cf. 2:5-6, 24, 28; Eph. 1:1, 6; 2:13.)

2:1. τεκνία μου, "My little children." It is apparent that John has purposely used the term τεκνίον predominantly. (It occurs seven times in 1 John in comparison to παιδίον, "little child," which appears only twice.) The word is a diminutive form related to the verb τίκτω, "I bear." Thus τεκνία are "little born ones," an expression that reminds us of the Scottish term *bairns*.[24] It is in harmony with John's emphasis on being born of God (2:29; 3:9; 4:7; 5:1, 4, 18). First John views the people of God as a family in which God is Father and believers are His children living in a relationship of love toward each other. By reason both in the basic meaning of τεκνία and its diminutive form it is a term of endearment most fitting for the elderly John to use in addressing his beloved people, whether they are actually his children in the faith or not.

ταῦτα γράφω ὑμῖν, "I am writing these things to you." Although ταῦτα, "these things," may refer to the whole epistle, it is certain that its most specific reference is to the immediately preceding context in which John has been discussing that God is light (truth and holiness) and that the believer must walk in the light (1:5-7). The insistence that no one truthfully can deny his sin (1:8, 10) must not be interpreted as in any way condoning sin.

ἵνα μὴ ἁμάρτητε, "that you may not sin." Rather than to permit or encourage sin, John's purpose was to combat it. Ἁμάρτητε (from ἁμαρτάνω, *I sin*) is an ingressive aorist indicating that the apostle does not want his readers ever to commit even one act of sin. It is significant that the present tense is not used here. John is not merely aiming at the cessation of the practice of sin

---

24. C. I. Scofield et al, eds. *The New Scofield Reference Bible*, p. 1342.

(present tense), but at the eradication of every act of sin. His goal is nothing less than perfection.

καὶ ἐάν τις ἁμάρτῃ, "and if anyone sins." The conjunction καί may in some contexts bear an adversative meaning;[25] therefore, inasmuch as the word joins two antithetical clauses here, it is better to translate it "but" (NIV) rather than "and." John is not unrealistic in expecting absolute perfection on the part of his readers. Although the goal is perfection, he recognizes the weakness of the flesh. However, he does not allow for the continual practice of sin. He makes provision for individual acts of sin as the aorist ἁμάρτῃ indicates. He says, "If anyone commits an act of sin"; it is noteworthy that he changes from the first and second persons to the third person, which seems to make the possibility a little more removed from the persons to whom he is writing.

παράκλητον ἔχομεν, "we have an Advocate." Παράκλητον, "advocate," originally and literally carried the passive meaning of "one who is called to come to one's side as a helper." As the usage of the word expanded, it came to be used of a variety of helping activities. Thus the word, as applied to the Holy Spirit in John 14:16, 26; 15:26; 16:7, is best translated "helper," a term sufficiently comprehensive to include the varied ways in which the Spirit assists the believer. Here in 2:1, however, a specific kind of aid is in view, as follows. One of the most common uses of the term in extrabiblical Greek was to refer to a helper in a legal trial, not an attorney but one who appeared in court in behalf of another, a friend of the defendant called in to testify to the character of the latter.[26] Christ is the Friend of the defendant and comes before God the Judge to intercede for the believer who has committed an act of sin.

A parallel term to *advocate* is *high priest,* which is applied to Jesus in the epistle to the Hebrews. Both the advocate and the high priest were intercessors on behalf of others. In Hebrews 2:17 Christ is designated as "a merciful and faithful high priest [who makes] propitiation for the sins of the people." Similarly in 1 John 2:1-2 Christ is called our Advocate and "the propitiation for our sins." This ministry is graphically portrayed in Hebrews 9:24. There is an additional aspect of high priestly ministry found in Hebrews that John does not stress. That is Christ's sympathetic

---

25. Dana and Mantey, p. 250.
26. Arndt and Gingrich, pp. 623-24; William Barclay, *New Testament Words,* pp. 215-22.

understanding and his ability to help those who are tempted because He was tempted in similar manner (Heb. 2:18; 4:15-16). Christ's intercessory work is also referred to in Romans 8:34. For a thorough treatment of παράκλητος see the lengthy discussion by A. E. Brooke.[27]

πρὸς τὸν πατέρα, "with the Father." This speaks of an intimate relationship. See comments on 1:2. The root meaning of πρός is "facing,"[28] suggesting a close face-to-face kind of relationship between the Advocate and the Father. Because Christ is one with the Father, His intercession is certain to be effective.

Ἰησοῦν Χριστὸν δίκαιον, "Jesus Christ the righteous." Three characteristics of the Lord are suggested by these terms. The name Ἰησοῦν speaks of His humanity by which He is identified with us and thus can function as our representative. Χριστόν in 1 John refers not so much to His Messiahship in the Hebrew sense as to His deity, (see earlier discussion on the term) by virtue of which He is in face-to-face fellowship with the Father. Δίκαιον appears in the predicate position and literally means "Jesus Christ being righteous." John does not merely declare that there is an advocate whose advocacy is righteous; he describes Christ Himself as being righteous, which is an essential quality of His being.

2:2. καὶ αὐτὸς ἱλασμός ἐστιν περὶ τῶν ἁμαρτιῶν ἡμῶν, "and He Himself is the propitiation for our sins." The pronoun αὐτός is used for emphasis to point out that the One who is our advocate is Himself the propitiation for our sins. Normally the priest and the sacrifice are distinct and separate. Here they are one and the same.

Ἰλασμός has fared badly at the hands of many modern interpreters who insist it be translated "expiation" rather than "propitiation." However, this insistence is based on a misconception of the attributes of God, which in turn has led to a misinterpretation of the ἱλασμός family of words both in the LXX and the New Testament. We have shown previously that ἱλασμός can and should be translated "propitiation." (See discussion in chapter 5, pages 78-79.) Christ is not only the propitiator, but He is the propitiation that satisfies the offended justice of God so that the believer may be forgiven. It is noteworthy that ἱλασμός is here followed by περί τῶν ἁμαρτιῶν, *concerning sins,* rather than by the objective genitive case as would be expected if the passage

---

27. Brooke, pp. 23-27.
28. Dana and Mantey, p. 110.

were speaking of the expiation *of* sins. It is God who is propitiated with regard to sins; it is not sins that are expiated.[29] The context also is significant here, as Houlden points out when he notes that both παράκλητος (v. 1) and ἱλασμός (v. 2) carry the idea of "winning over the party to whom appeal is made or sacrifice offered."[30] In the latter case, Christ died to propitiate God's wrath against sin; in the former case He intercedes when one of His own sins.

οὐ περὶ ἡμετέρων δὲ μόνον, "and not for ours only." The salvation offered by Christ is not restricted to any one class of people as was that of the Gnostics.

ἀλλὰ καὶ περὶ ὅλου τοῦ κόσμου, "but also for those of the whole world." The strong adversative conjunction ἀλλά, "but," throws this clause into marked contrast with the preceding one. John is firmly denying any limited nature of the atonement and is affirming that it is applicable to the sins of all people. It is necessary to supply the words *those of* in order to maintain the parallelism that ties this clause to the previous one. In each case the propitiation concerns sin—individually and the sins of the whole world. Κόσμου, "world," in this context speaks of the world of people, just as in John 3:16. Elsewhere (1 John 2:15-17) John employs the term in an ethical sense to depict the evil world order that is organized against God.

FELLOWSHIP DEMANDS OBEDIENCE, 2:3-6

2:3. καὶ ἐν τούτῳ γινώοκομεν ὅτι ἐγνώκαμεν αὐτόν, "and by this we know that we have come to know Him." The preposition ἐν is used with the locative case to mean "in" and with the instrumental case to mean "by, by means of." The context here demands the latter meaning. Τούτῳ, "this," may refer either to the preceding context or to that which follows. (In 3:16 it points to the succeeding context, but in 3:19 it looks to the preceding context.) In 2:3 the explanation of τούτῳ is found in the clause ἐὰν τὰς ἐντωλὰς αὐτοῦ τηρῶμεν, "if we keep his commandments." The ἐάν does not speak of the condition for knowing Christ; rather it describes the condition for *ascertaining* that one knows Him.

29. On the meaning of ἱλασμός in this passage see Leon Morris, *The Apostolic Preaching of the Cross*, pp. 205-7.
30. J. L. Houlden, *A Commentary on the Johannine Epistles*, Black's New Testament Commentaries, p. 62.

The two verbs meaning "to know," γινώσκω and οἶδα, occur repeatedly in this epistle (γινώσκω—twenty-five times; οἶδα—fifteen times) revealing the stress John has placed on knowledge in combating the false gnosis that threatened believers. In Classical Greek these two words were consistently distinguished from each other. οἶδα spoke of knowledge grasped directly or intuitively by the mind, whereas γινώσκω referred to knowledge gained mediately by experience or instruction.[31] Many have assumed that this kind of distinction consistently governs all New Testament occurrences of the two verbs. Among those who have held to this view are Lightfoot, Godet, H. Cremer, Westcott, Law, Plummer, Brooke, Robertson, Vincent, Lenski, and Hendriksen. Others such as Dodd, J. H. Bernard, H. Seesemann, Barrett, Nigel Turner, and Morris, have concluded that the distinction between the two verbs no longer existed in Hellenistic Greek. As with many things, the truth seems to lie between the two extremes. A study of the Pauline usage of these verbs leads to the conclusion that Paul usually followed the Classical pattern, but that in 18 out of 153 uses the verbs were used interchangeably. Consequently, "each occurrence must be examined independently and interpreted in the light of its own context."[32]

Several examples in 1 John indicate that John also interchanged the two words at times. In 2:3 γινώσκω is used in its classical sense of knowledge gained mediately through observation of objective acts—the keeping of God's commandments. By this one discerns that he has come to know Christ. In 2:29 John says, "If you know (εἰδῆτε) that He is righteous, you know (γινώσκετε) that everyone also who practices righteousness is born of Him." However, in a parallel passage (5:15) John writes, "And if we know (οἴδαμεν) that He hears us . . . we know (οἴδαμεν) that we have the requests which we have asked from Him." In both instances the second occurrence of the word *know* speaks of knowledge based on reflection. Again, in 3:14 John says, "We know (οἴδαμεν) that we have passed out of death into life, because we love the brethren." But in 3:19 he states, "We shall know (γνωσόμεθα) by this [the fact that we love in deed and truth, v. 18] that we are of the truth, and shall assure our heart before Him." Both

---

31. Abbott-Smith, *A Manual Greek Lexicon of the New Testament*, pp. 92-93.
32. Richard N. Longnecker and Merrill C. Tenney, eds., *New Dimensions in New Testament Study*, "Οἶδα and Γινώσκω in the Pauline Epistles," by Donald W. Burdick, p. 354.

statements of assurance are based on the fact of love for fellow believers, but again in one instance οἶδα is used and in the other γινώσκω appears. Such comparisons demand that we recognize that these terms may be employed interchangeably, or they may be used with the Classical distinctions in mind. Each occurrence must be examined individually.

John reflects the Hebrew concept of knowledge, not as theoretical and speculative, but as experiential. The Hebrew יָדַע means "to know" or "to come to know" by experience. Bultmann says, "Knowledge is not thought of in terms of possession of information. It is possessed only in its exercise or actualization."[33] So John says that God is known through obedience to His will rather than in theory. Law says, "The proof of this 'knowing' God is active sympathy with His will,—keeping His commandments."[34]

Ἐγνώκαμεν is a perfect tense form that literally means *we have come to know and as a result we are continuing in that knowledge*. It seems best to view it as an intensive perfect placing stress on the continuing results. Thus, it may properly be translated like the present tense "we know."[35] To whom does the pronoun αὐτόν refer? To the Father or the Son? In 1:6-7, John speaks of fellowship with God, and therefore it may be assumed that 2:3 is talking about knowing God the Father. However, the last person to be identified specifically in the preceding context is Christ (v. 1), and it is clear that the pronoun αὐτός (v. 2) must refer to the Son. The same pronoun in verse 6 (αὐτῷ) is paralleled with ἐκεῖνος, a peculiarly Johannine designation for Christ (cf. 3:3, 5, 7, 16; 4:17), and He is said to have *walked*, referring to His incarnate activity. In addition, it may be noted that Christ Himself often spoke of His commandments (John 13:34; 14:15, 21; 15:10, 12). It would seem then that, even though *God's* commandments would appear to be the more natural usage here, John must be referring to knowing *Christ* and obeying His commands. It should be noted, however, that Bultmann and others argue that αὐτόν must be God.[36] Dodd insists that it makes little difference,[37] and F. F. Bruce points out that to know Christ is to know God.[38]

33. Kittel, s.v. "γινώσκω, κτλ.," by Rudolph Bultmann.
34. Law, p. 211.
35. Bonsirven, p. 100, n. 1.
36. Bultmann, pp. 24-25; Marshall, p. 122; F. F. Bruce, *The Epistles of John*, pp. 38-39.
37. Dodd, p. 31.
38. Bruce, p. 51.

That John does not speak merely of a correct Christology but of a personal relationship is evident from the accusative of direct object with ἐγνώκαμεν. The text reads, "We have come to know *Him*," not "We have come to know *about* Him." ἐὰν τὰς ἐντολὰς αὐοῦ τηρῶμεν, "if we keep His commandments." This conditional clause sets forth the test by which one can ascertain whether or not he is personally acquainted with Christ. The evidence of such acquaintanceship is the continuing, habitual activity (present tense τηρῶμεν) of keeping His commandments. Τηρέω, "I keep," depicts watchful care. Thus τηρῶμεν represents a careful concern lest one should break the commandments.

John employs the word ἐντολή, "commandment," similarly in 2:7-8 and 3:22-24. In the former passage the commandment is to love (cf. John 13:34-35), and in the latter it is to believe in Christ and to love one another. However, the context immediately preceding 2:3 would seem to suggest that the commands here referred to are not to be limited to belief and love, but are to be viewed as including divine moral imperatives in general. However, the command to love is probably uppermost in John's mind, as verses 7-8 seem to indicate. Keeping these commandments, therefore, is equal to walking in the light (1:6-7) and practicing righteousness (2:29; 3:7, 9).

2:4. ὁ λέγων ὅτι Ἔγνωκα αὐτόν, καὶ τὰς ἐντολὰς αὐτοῦ μὴ τηρῶν, "The one who says, 'I have come to know Him,' and does not keep His commandments." In chapter 1 John introduces his statement with ἐὰν εἴπωμεν, "if we say," but in 2:4, 6, 9 he uses the article and participle ὁ λέγων, "the one who says." The latter expression is more individual and specific than the former and serves to point out both the Gnostic deceivers and their actual claims. It is as though John had actually heard the heretics make their empty boasts. Law says, " 'He that saith, I know Him' is not an arrow shot at a venture, but has a definite mark in the Antinomian intellectualist for whom his self-assured knowledge of Divine things superseded all requirements of commonplace morality."[39] The use of the present tense pictures a continued claim to know Christ. As is common in Greek language, ὅτι is recitative, being the equivalent of the quotation marks that introduce a direct quotation. On ἔγνωκα αὐτόν, "I have come to know him," see on ἐγνώκαμεν, "we have come to know Him"

---

39. Law, p. 210.

(v. 3). Although it is possible that the καί may be continuative ("and"), inasmuch as the claim (λέγων) is contrary to the practice (τηρῶν) it seems better to translate the conjunction as adversative *(but)*. By his choice of the present tense τηρῶν John shows that he has in mind the habit of not keeping the commandments. On τὰs ἐντολάs and τηρῶν, see on verse 3.

ψεύστης ἐστίν, καὶ ἐν τούτῳ ἡ ἀλήθεια οὐκ ἔστιν, "is a liar, and the truth is not in him." John does not say merely that the one whose practice and profession are contradictory is deceived, but he insists that such a one's character is that of a deceiver (ψεύστης ἐστίν, "he is a liar"). He also does not possess the truth. As in 1:8, ἡ ἀλήθεια, "the truth," refers to the specific body of truth, both soteriological and moral, that God has revealed. It is that understanding of spiritual things that realizes genuine knowledge of Christ must be accompanied by a life of obedience. More than that, the truth is viewed as a dynamic within a person that itself produces a life of obedience to the divine commands. Ἐν τούτῳ, "in this one," is stronger than ἐν αὐτῷ, "in him," in that τούτῳ is a demonstrative pronoun that particularly refers to a certain person. Brooke is correct in saying that when οὗτοs (τούτῳ) refers to something in the preceding context it denotes it *"as previously described."*[40] Literally the phrase means *in this one*, the one who dares to make such a claim while his life is marked by disobedience.

2:5. ὃs δ' ἂν τηρῇ αὐτοῦ τὸν λόγον, "but whoever keeps His word." John moves from the specific ὁ λέγων (v. 4) to the indefinite ὃs δ' ἂν, "whoever," showing that whereas he points out the actual claim of a specific heretic in verse 4, in verse 5 he includes all genuine believers. No particular individual is in mind here. Knowledge of God is not limited to the elite few whom the Gnostics designated as "the spiritual"; instead it is available to all who have real faith. The main indicator that a person knows God is that he habitually keeps (present tense, τηρῇ) the word of Christ (αὐτοῦ τὸν λόγον). The position of the pronoun αὐτοῦ before the article and noun is intended to stress that the word is *His*. It is clear from the parallelism that the commandments of verses 3-4 are related to the word of verse 5. In fact, the terms *commandment* (2:3-4), *truth* (1:8; 2:4), and *word* (1:10; 2:5) all are somewhat equivalent to each other. Truth denotes reality as it is known by God; the word is that portion of truth God has chosen to make

40. Brooke, p. 31.

known; the commandments are the moral imperatives included in God's revealed word. Thus, because both the truth and the word dwell in the believer (1:8, 10; 2:4), it is also true that the commandments of Christ indwell him. As a result the indwelling commandments (truth, word) express themselves in outward obedience (practicing the truth, 1:6; keeping commandments, 2:3-4; keeping His word, 2:5).

ἀληθῶς ἐν τούτῳ ἡ ἀγάπη τοῦ θεοῦ τετελείωται, "in him the love of God has truly been perfected." One would have expected that the parallelism of this verse with verse 4 would call for the conclusion, "truly this man knows Christ." Instead John advances beyond mere knowledge to love—love in its perfected state. To emphasize the reality of this completed love, the apostle has placed ἀληθῶς, "truly," first in the clause, and thus in no uncertain terms throws the reality of the genuine believer's love in sharp contrast to the Gnostic's empty boast that he knows Christ. On ἐν τούτῳ, see on 2:4.

For the first time in this epistle John introduces the concept of ἀγάπη, "love," which hereafter functions as one of the major themes of the book. Opinions have varied concerning the meaning of the phrase ἡ ἀγάπη τοῦ θεοῦ, "the love of God," as to whether the genitive τοῦ θεοῦ is subjective, objective, or merely descriptive. Westcott argues that it is subjective, referring to God's love for the believer.[41] Brooke understands the construction to be an objective genitive, speaking of the believer's love of God.[42] And Law, who combines all three views, explains that it is neither the subjective nor the objective genitive considered separately, but it is a descriptive view that "unites both in a common conception—the love which is the nature of God (4:8), and which is the nature also of those who are 'begotten of Him' (4:7)."[43] However, although the truth found in each of these views and in Law's composite explanation must be recognized, the context of 2:5 seems to indicate that the objective view best explains John's meaning. In 2:3-6 he is discussing obedience to the commandments as evidence that a person knows Christ. Here in verse 5 obedience is evidence of perfected love. A similar statement occurs in 5:3, "For this is the love of God, that we keep His commandments." Now, all of this

---

41. Westcott, pp. 48-49. Cf. R. C. H. Lenski, *The Interpretation of the Epistles of St. Peter, St. John and St. Jude,* p. 408.
42. Brooke, p. 32. Cf. A. Plummer, *The Epistles of St. John,* The Cambridge Greek Testament for Schools and Colleges, p. 38.
43. Law, p. 212. See also Marshall, pp. 124-25 and Westcott, pp. 48-49.

reminds one of the statements of Christ in John 14: "He who has My commandments and keeps them, he it is who loves Me" (v. 21). "If anyone loves Me, he will keep My word" (v. 23). "He who does not love Me does not keep My words" (v. 24). Consequently, 1 John 2:5 means that love for God has been perfected in the one who is living a life of obedience.

But in what sense is the believer's love brought to a state of perfection, as the perfect tense τετελείωται, "has been perfected," suggests? Surely, no believer reaches perfection in any area during this life. Instead of perfection in love, John is expressing a principle that he develops more fully in a later passage (3:16-18), namely, that love is incomplete if it produces no deeds of love. The completion of love is obedience. Law explains: " 'Perfected' love, in the phraseology of the Epistle, signifies, not love in a superlative degree, but love that is consummated in action. Bearing fruit in actual obedience, Love has been perfected: it has fulfilled its mission, has reached its goal."[44]

ἐν τούτῳ γινώσκομεν ὅτι ἐν αὐτῷ ἐσμεν, "By this we know that we are in Him." Ἐν τούτῳ, "by this," is to be construed as being instrumental, as in 2:3, rather than locative. However, whereas the phrase in 2:3 points to the statement that follows, here it looks back to the preceding context. The ὁ λέγων, "the one who says," that opens 2:6 introduces a new claim, which makes it necessary to relate ἐν τούτῳ to that which goes before.[45] Τούτῳ points to the entire concept of keeping Christ's word as the consummation of one's love for God. Love expressing itself in obedience is the means of knowing that one is in Him (ἐν αὐτῷ ἐσμεν). In the light of the discussion in 2:3-4, it would have been natural to expect John to say, "By this we know that we know Him," as in verse 3. Instead, he uses a parallel expression that explains more fully what he means by knowing Christ. To know Him is to be in Him, that is, to be in an intimate, mystical relationship with Him. This is no casual, superficial acquaintance; it is a relationship of intimate fellowship. To be in Him (ἐν αὐτῷ εἶναι) and to abide in Him (ἐν αὐτῷ μένειν) are parallel to the phrase ἐν Χριστῷ that is characteristic of Paul's concept of our union with Christ. To be saved is to experience this intimate relationship. (Cf. John 15:4-7; 17:21, 23, 26; 1 John 2:24, 27-28; 5:20.)

44. Law, pp. 212-13.
45. Bultmann, p. 26.

2:6. ὁ λέγων ἐν αὐτῷ μένειν, "The one who says he abides in Him." Verse 6 constitutes a summary statement of the test of obedience. An intimate relationship with Christ will manifest itself in Christlikeness. As in 2:4, the specific ὁ λέγων is applied to the believer rather than to the false teacher. John desires to be just as specific in regard to the truth as he is concerning error. Ἐν αὐτῷ μένειν, "to dwell in Him," is a fuller development of ἐν αὐτῷ ἐσμεν, "we are in Him." Μένω, "I dwell," speaks of a permanent and intimate relationship rather than a temporary, superficial association. Bultmann explains, "In oldest Greek usage, it is usually a matter of remaining at an objectively established place, for an objectively determined time, even if this period extends into infinity."[46] The word does not describe a closer, more intimate relationship with Christ (sometimes referred to us as "the abiding life") enjoyed only by the more devoted Christian. All believers are in Christ and abide in Him. John undoubtedly drew the concept from Christ's words as recorded in John 15, where the picture is one of the fruitbearing branch that stands in a continuing, vital relationship to the vine. The present tense μένειν serves to strengthen the linear idea inherent in the verb itself. No short-lived union is in view here. This is the claim to be experiencing an ongoing relationship of intimacy with the Lord. It is clear from the remainder of the verse that αὐτῷ, "him," must refer to Christ.

ὀφείλει καθὼς ἐκεῖνος περιεπάτησεν καὶ αὐτὸς [οὕτως] περιπατεῖν, "ought himself to walk in the same manner as He walked." The person who claims to be remaining in Christ is under a continual obligation, as the present tense ὀφείλει, "he ought," shows. In addition both the meaning of the verb περιπατεῖν, "to walk," and the tense (present) depict linear action. Thus, the one who claims to be remaining in Christ is under continual obligation to keep walking as Christ walked. This is parallel to walking in the light (1:7) and keeping commands (2:3-5). On the figurative significance of περιπατέω, see on 1:6. The similarity called for is not merely a broad, general likeness, but is rather an exact duplication. Καθώς means "just as," in comparison with ὡς, which means "as." In the light of Johannine usage it is clear that ἐκεῖνος, "that one," points to Christ (cf. 1 John 3:3, 5, 7, 16; 4:17 where the NASB translates ἐκεῖνος as "He"). So paramount was the Lord in John's thought that He could be designat-

---
46. Bultmann, p. 26.

ed by the remote demonstrative pronoun and it would be perfectly clear whom the apostle had in mind. Αὐτός, "himself," stands in contrast to ἐκεῖνος, serving to distinguish the believer from his Lord; the copy from the original. The aorist περιεπάτμσεν, "he walked," is constative and thus views the exemplary conduct of Christ as a whole. It is like a snapshot of that righteous life.

FELLOWSHIP DEMANDS LOVE OF FELLOW BELIEVERS, 2:7-11

2:7. ἀγαπητοί, οὐκ ἐντολὴν καινὴν γράφω ὑμῖν, "Beloved, I am not writing a new commandment to you." The KJV reading "brethren" (ἀδελφοί) is based on the inferior Byzantine type of text (K L and many others). The superior reading ἀγαπητοί is supported by the Alexandrian text (ℵ A B C P). John uses four terms of endearment in this epistle, all of which are closely related to the basic theology of the book (τεκνία, ἀγαπητοί, παιδία, ἀδελφοί). ἀγαπητοί, "beloved," first occurs in 2:7 where the apostle introduces the subject of love for fellow Christians. Those who are called upon to love one another are given a living example in John's love for them. ἀγαπητοί is related to ἀγάπη, "love," and ἀγαπάω, "I love." This family of words was not widely used in secular Greek prior to the time of the New Testament. Other words for affection had developed associations that made them undesirable as expressions of the love of God and of His people. Ἀγάπη, however, was ideally suited to serve such a purpose. In secular Greek it represented a love in which the mind analyzes and the will chooses the object to be loved. Thus it is not a term wholly given to emotion, but it involves the whole man, emotions, intellect, and will. Ἀγάπη is a deliberate, free act that is the decision of the subject rather than the result of unbidden, overpowering emotion. It was often used in contexts demanding the translation, "to show love," which indicates that it is not a possessive but a giving love.[47] How well such a term describes the love of God! He in sovereign freedom set His love upon man, not because man's loveliness commanded His love, but because He in grace chose to show His love by giving His Son. And in like manner Christians should love one another. Christian love is "not simply a wave of emotion; it is a deliberate conviction of the mind issuing in a deliberate policy of the life."[48]

---

47. Kittel, s.v. "ἀγαπάω, κτλ.," by Ethelbert Stauffer.
48. Barclay, p. 22.

Because the intellect and the will are primarily involved in ἀγάπη, God can command love for one another. In obedience to God's command and enabled by His Spirit, the mind and will are then set to love the brother in Christ, not because his attractiveness calls forth love, but simply because one chooses to love him. He may be ever so lacking in loveliness; nevertheless, one wills to love him because God has commanded it and because this is the nature of regenerated members of God's family. This is the idea underlying the vocative epithet, ἀγαπητοί, with which John addresses his readers.

The word order, placing οὐκ ἐντολὴν καινήν first, is noteworthy. In the first place, the negative negates the direct object more than the verb. In the second place, the position of the object before the verb indicates emphasis, inasmuch as the usual practice in biblical Greek was to place the verb as near the beginning of the clause as possible.[49] John has thrown the new commandment in as strong a contrast as possible with the "old commandment" (ἐντολὴν παλαιάν). Not a *new commandment,* but an *old commandment.*

Commentators have debated the identity of this commandment unnecessarily. The words ἐντολὴν καινήν are an exact parallel to the words of Jesus in John 13:34, ἐντολὴν καινὴν δίδωμι ὑμῖν, ἵνα ἀγαπᾶτε ἀλλήλους, "A new commandment I give to you, that you love one another." Furthermore, the following context in 1 John 2 proceeds to discuss love for one's brother (vv. 9-11). It is obvious that John is building upon Christ's command to His disciples to love one another.

Since Christ explicitly called this commadment new, how then can John deny its newness? The answer to this question must take the meaning of καινήν, "new," into consideration. In contrast to νέος, which means new in *time,* καινός means new in *kind.* Richard C. Trench explains that that which is καινός is "the qualitatively other," while that which is νέος is the numerically other. Καινός may describe that which is novel or strange in contrast to that which is known or familiar.[50] Thus when John says that the commandment is not καινήν he means that it is not a novel or strange kind of commandment. The reason this is true is given in the remainder of 2:7.

ἀλλ ἐντολὴν παλαιὰν ἣν εἴχετε ἀπ' ἀρχῆς, "but an old commandment which you have had from the beginning."

---

49. Moulton, pp. 347-48.
50. Richard C. Trench, *Synonyms of the New Testament,* pp. 213-14.

That the commandment was not new and strange is confirmed by the fact that they had possessed it for a long time. When Christ first gave the commandment it was new in kind, not because they had never before been commanded to love (cf. Lev. 19:18), but because they had never before been commanded to love as Christ loved (John 13:34 15:12, 17). The newness was in the new and lofty example of Christ's love.

Ἀλλά, "but," is a strong adversative conjunction that places the ideas of new and old in emphatic contrast. John wants his readers to know that, rather than introducing a new duty, he is reminding them of an old familiar obligation. Παλαιάν, "old," is that which is ancient, which has been present for a long time. How long the commandment had been in their possession is determined by ἀπ' ἀρχῆς, "from the beginning." The same phrase occurs in 1:1 referring to Christ's pre-existence, but here in 2:7 the meaning must be more limited. Some have suggested that it speaks of the beginning of mankind; others, the beginning of the law.[51] However, the verb εἴχετε, "you have had," seems to demand that the ἀρχῆς must have been during the lifetime of John's readers. It could conceivably refer to the beginning of the gospel sixty years earlier when Christ first gave the command (John 13:34). Still more natural is the view that interprets the beginning as being the initiation of the readers' Christian experience, that is, from the time when they themselves first heard the message. Since that day they had been in continuous possession of the command. The imperfect tense εἴχετε is durative in sense, indicating possession of the commandment from a starting point right up to the present moment. The imperfect is here used where a perfect tense might have been expected, but the intention of the author apparently was not to depict the continuing results of receiving the commandment, but to indicate the constant possession of the command through the years.

ἡ ἐντολὴ ἡ παλαιά ἐστιν ὁ λόγος ὃν ἠκούσατε, "The old commandment is the word which you have heard." This explanation makes it yet clearer that the beginning spoken of must have been within the lifetime of the readers (ἠκούσατε, *you heard*).[52] "The word" (ὁ λόγος) was the apostolic message that contained this command of Christ. The KJV addition of a second "from the beginning" (ἀπ' ἀρχῆς) at the end of this verse is not supported by the better manuscripts (ℵ A B C P).

51. Plummer, p. 40.
52. Bultmann, p. 27.

Only the inferior Byzantine text (K L and other mss.) has the repetition.

2:8. πάλιν ἐντολὴν καινὴν γράφω ὑμῖν, "On the other hand, I am writing a new commandment to you." John is dealing in paradox. When the commandment is looked at from one point of view, it is not new, novel, or strange—his readers had possessed it from the beginning of their Christian experience. But, when it is looked at from another point of view, it *is* new. It is in that sense that πάλιν, "again," is used, not to introduce a new subject but to call for a second look at the same subject. The remainder of the verse explains in what sense this not-new commandment is new.

ὅ ἐστιν ἀληθὲς ἐν αὐτῷ καὶ ἐν ὑμῖν, "which is true in Him and in you." Since the relative pronoun ὅ, "which," is neuter it cannot modify ἐντολήν, which is feminine. It must, therefore, refer to the newness of the command. It is that newness "which is true in him and in you."

Αὐτῷ must refer to Christ as it obviously does in 2:2-6. This is also confirmed because He was the one who first gave the new commandment. The newness was true in Christ in that His death was a new and unique demonstration of the selfless, self-giving love of God. In Him for the first time the world saw what ἀγάπη really is. Christians are to love others as *Christ* loved, not merely as they love themselves or as they would like to be loved.

Plummer points out that the repetition of the preposition ἐν, "in," implies that in the case of the readers the newness is true in a different sense from that in which it was true in Christ.[53] Explanation is given in the remainder of the verse.

ὅτι ἡ σκοτία παράγεται καὶ τὸ φῶς τὸ ἀληθινὸν ἤδη φαίνει, "because the darkness is passing away, and the true light is already shining." The conjunction ὅτι indicates that what follows is an explanation of the previous assertion. The explanation seems to refer, not to ἐν αὐτῷ, "in Him," but to ἐν ὑμῖν, "in you," because there is no sense in which the darkness is passing away in Christ. Such a departure of darkness can only be true in redeemed men. On the use of ἡ σκοτία, "the darkness," as a figurative term for falsehood and moral evil, see on 1:5. Notice that the presence of the article identifies the darkness as the particular darkness previously referred to and thus known to the readers. It is wickedness and error as contrasted with truth and holiness. The KJV translates παράγεται, "is past," a rendering that

---

53. Plummer, p. 41.

fails to recognize the significance of the present tense linear action. A more accurate representation would be, "the darkness is passing away." It has not already passed away as the KJV suggests, nor is its passing something wholly confined to the future. It is even now in process of passing away. It is best to view παράγεται not as a passive voice but as a middle that stresses the part the subject of the verb plays in the action of passing away. The darkness contains within itself the seeds of its own dissolution, and thus it is of itself passing away. (See on 2:17.)

In its place the true light is shining. On the meaning of φῶς, "light," see on 1:5. Note that as with σκοτία the article is used with φῶς. The article does not require that the light be viewed as personal, referring to Christ. Inasmuch as the darkness is not personal, the light is no doubt also impersonal, referring to the gospel in its broadest sense as the truth of God that results in true holiness.

The qualifying adjective ἀληθινόν, "true," refers to that which is genuine in contrast to the counterfeit or spurious. However, in Hellenism that genuineness is what is real because it is heavenly and eternal rather than earthly and temporal.[54] Thus the light is not of this world, nor is it the spurious light of Gnosticism. It is instead the genuine light of the gospel. The repetition of the article before ἀληθινόν equally distributes the emphasis between the noun and its adjective and may be translated "the light, the true one."[55] Greater emphasis is thus placed on the genuineness of the light.

The present tense verb παράγεται, "is passing away," is paralleled by the present tense φαίνει, "is shining." Just as the darkness is in the process of passing away, so the true light is in the process of shining. This is true in the world at large. As more and more people submit to the gospel, darkness recedes and light advances. That this process is John's meaning here is evident from the preceding prepositional phrase, ἐν ὑμῖν, "in you." After saying that the newness of the commandment is true in you, the apostle explains in the causal clause (ὅτι ἡ σκοτία . . .) how this is true. As the believer daily grows in love, he experiences the newness of the commandment because love penetrates more of his being and his relationships. And this is not something that must be waited for until the coming of Christ—it is "already" (ἤδη) in process.

---

54. Kittel, s.v. "ἀληθινός," by Rudolph Bultmann.
55. Dana and Mantey, p. 152.

2:9. ἡ λέγων ἐν τῷ φωτὶ εἶναι καὶ τὸν ἀδελφὸν αὐτοῦ μισῶν, "The one who says he is in the light and yet hates his brother." John here picks up the theme of character tests again. This time the test has to do with whether or not a person loves his brother. In 1:6-7 the test concerns walking in the light; in 1:8-10 it is a question of admitting one's sin; and in 2:3-6 the test is obedience. In each instance the test is stated in both negative and positive fashion. All of these tests, including the test of love (2:7-11), are ethical in nature. For ὁ λέγων see on 2:4. No doubt the Gnostic claim is in view here. The idea of light is suggested by the statement concerning the true light in verse 8, but it is more closely related to the concept of walking in the light in 1:7. There περιπατέω suggests the activity of life carried on in the sphere of light, an activity characterized by truth and holiness (cf. on 1:5). Here εἶναι, "to be," suggests existence in the sphere of light. On the lips of the Gnostic, however, such a statement may have been merely a claim to possess the truth (γνῶσις, *knowledge*).

The participle μισῶν is in parallel construction with λέγων and is modified by the same article. John describes one who is claiming to be in the light and at the same time is hating his brother. The present tense of μισῶν pictures a continuing attitude of hatred rather than a momentary fit of anger. Questions may be raised concerning the force of the term μισέω in this passage. Is it strong antipathy or mild dislike? In the Sermon on the Mount Jesus uses the contrasting terms *hate* and *love* in the milder sense of dislike and preference (Matt. 6:24). In 1 John, however, there is good reason to believe that the term *hatred* carries the full weight of strong antipathy. This is obvious in John's assertion that the one who hates his brother "is a murderer" (3:15), by which the apostle means that such a person harbors a murderous attitude in his heart. Thus the attitude that belies the claim to be in the light is one of full-blown, murderous hatred.

Τὸν ἀδελφὸν αὐτοῦ, "his brother," may be understood in one of several ways: (1) as referring to a blood brother, (2) as referring to any fellow human being, or (3) as referring to a spiritual brother. It is true the Bible teaches love for brothers in all three categories. However, in 1 John there is evidence the author limits the term to the third meaning. This letter is the family epistle that stresses regeneration and views believers as the children of God. The statement of 5:1 is significant in this regard. John writes, "Whoever believes that Jesus is the Christ is born of God; and whoever loves the Father [the one who begot, Gr.] loves the child born of Him." Here the circle of love is the circle of regeneration. But such restriction does not minimize the necessity to love all men, which is certainly God's desire for believers, as clearly taught elsewhere in Scripture (Matt. 5:43-48; 22:39; Rom. 13:8-10). However, John's reason for limiting love in this epistle to the family of God is determined by his purpose, which is to use the presence or absence of such love as a test of family membership. The one spoken of here clearly fails this family test. The singular τὸν ἀδελφόν is to be taken, not as referring to a specific individual, but as a general term meaning a fellow Christian. Note the use of the plural τοὺς ἀδελφούς in 3:14, 16.

ἐν τῇ σκοτίᾳ ἐστὶν ἕως ἄρτι, "is in the darkness until now." Whereas the claimant insists that he is living in the sphere of the light, in reality he is in the darkness. His vaunted claim to the light of truth and knowledge (γνῶσις) is completely nullified by his continuing attitude of hatred for God's people, for hatred is a characteristic of darkness, not of light; and it is a sign of being unregenerate. This state of unregeneracy is confirmed by the phrase ἕως ἄρτι, "until now." Ἕως is used here as an improper preposition pointing to the end of a period of time. John does not indicate any point of beginning, but he does identify the terminus *ad quem* by use of the adverb ἄρτι, "now, this moment." Therefore, the person who is hating the people of God is in the darkness right up to the latest moment, and he has never been in any condition other than spiritual darkness.

2:10. ὁ ἀγαπῶν τὸν ἀδελφὸν αὐτοῦ ἐν τῷ φωτὶ μένει, "The one who loves his brother abides in the light." It is noteworthy that John does not introduce this statement with ὁ λέγων, as he does the preceding verse. Here it is not the profession but the reality that is in view, since the one who dwells in the light actually does love his brother. John employs the present tense (ἀγαπῶν) to show that love for one's brother is to be a continuiing reality rather than a momentary or sporadic experience. On τῷ φωτί, "the light," see on 1:5. To dwell in the light is more than merely to be in the light. Μένω speaks of remaining, of staying in a place, of living permanently in a certain location rather than being a transient. The present tense of the verb (μένει), with its linear action, confirms the idea of permanency. So the one who entertains a continual attitude of love toward fellow believers is a permanent resident within the sphere of the light.

καὶ σκάνδαλον ἐν αὐτῷ οὐκ ἔστιν, "and there is no cause for stumbling in him." The term σκάνδαλον is a later form of the Classical Greek σκανδάληθρον, the stick in a trap on which the bait was placed. Both words also were used of the trap itself. However, in the Greek of the LXX σκάνδαλον also came to refer to a stumbling block.[56] For examples of usage as a snare or trap see Joshua 23:13; Psalms 140:5; 141:9, and for usage as a stumbling block, Leviticus 19:14; Psalm 119:165. When these two concepts are brought to 1 John 2:10, the context seems to favor the idea of a stumbling block rather than a snare. An additional question remains to be answered concerning those in whose pathway the stumbling block is placed. There are three possible interpretations: (1) it may refer to a stumbling block placed in the way of another person; (2) it may mean that there is no stumbling block in the light (ἐν αὐτῷ, "in it"); or (3) it may be speaking of a stumbling block in one's own pathway. View one is favored because that is said to be the most natural use of σκάνδαλον. It may also be argued that inasmuch as the context deals with love for fellow Christians, the first interpretation would be most acceptable. All that can be said in favor of view two is that it is a possibility. From the viewpoint of the context, explanation three seems to be the most appropriate. In 2:11 John says that the one who hates his brother does not know where he is going because the darkness has blinded his eyes. This suggests that he, and not another, may stumble over some unseen object in the way. So, in contrast, verse 10 says there is nothing within the person who loves his brother that will result in his own downfall.

2:11. ὁ δὲ μισῶν τὸν ἀδελφὸν αὐτοῦ, "But the one who hates his brother." The conjunction δέ, "but," serves here as an adversative, throwing verse 11 into contrast with verse 10. On μισῶν and ἀδελφόν, see on 2:9. Three statements are made concerning the one who hates his brother, each of which further emphasizes that hatred is sure evidence of a life lived in spiritual darkness.

ἐν τῇ σκοτίᾳ ἐστίν, "is in the darkness." This phrase reiterates the idea of 2:9.

καὶ ἐν τῇ σκοτίᾳ περιπατεῖ, "and walks in the darkness." See on 1:6.

καὶ οὐκ οἶδεν ποῦ ὑπάγει, "and does not know where he is going." This third statement advances beyond the epistle's previous declarations concerning those in darkness. It is a verbatim repetition of Jesus' words in John 12:35. Whereas the two preceding statements in verse 11 identify the state and the activity of the

---

56. Barclay, p. 251.

one who hates his brother, this statement speaks of his destination. ὑπάγει literally means "he is departing." Thus the one who continually hates his fellow Christians is not aware of what his destiny is or of the way by which he is traveling. Blindly he moves on through the darkness toward the "blackness of darkness" (KJV), which will be forever (Jude 13).

ὅτι ἡ σκοτία ἐτύφλωσεν τοὺς ὀφθαλμοὺς αὐτοῦ, "because the darkness has blinded his eyes." Ὅτι introduces an explanatory clause. Where a perfect tense would normally be expected, John purposely chose to use an aorist (ἐτύφλωσεν, "blinded") to indicate a definite, past action. The blindness is no recently initiated state, but one that is of long standing. This agrees with the implication of ἕως ἄρτι, "until this moment" (v. 9). Because of the overlapping of the Greek aorist and the English perfect tenses it is best to translate the verb "has blinded" (cf. John 12:40; 2 Cor. 4:4).

Theological Commentary (1:5—2:11)

A. THE HISTORICAL BACKGROUND

1. GNOSTIC ANTINOMIANISM

There is both internal and external evidence that John wrote his first epistle in refutation of an antinomian heresy that divorced religion from morality, or at least, viewed morality as unnecessary to religion.

Internal evidence of such a viewpoint is found in 1:5-7 and 2:3-6. The hypothetical situation described in 1:6 is a clear suggestion that John's readers were confronted with persons who were making an obviously inconsistent claim. They were saying, "We are having fellowship with God," while at the same time living in error and sin. The same evidence, clothed in somewhat different terminology, appears in 2:4. There, by his specific identification of the speaker (ὁ λέγων), John seems to suggest that he had actually heard the claim he is about to cite. In this instance the errorist forthrightly declares, "I know Christ," but an examination of his life reveals that he is not living in obedience to the divine commands. There again the claim to an intimate relationship with the Lord is not accompanied by conformity to His will. Although the error being combated is not named, it is certain that it was antinomian in nature, a refusal to submit to the divine standard of righteousness.

According to the writings of the church Fathers some forms of the Gnostic heresy were antinomian. Irenaeus described the practices of some of the early second-century heretics in the following way: "Others, on the other hand, starting from Basilides and Carpocrates, introduced promiscuous intercourse and many marriages and indifference about eating meats sacrificed to idols; they said that God does not really care about these matters."[57] Both of those Gnostic teachers lived shortly after John's time. Clement of Alexandria and Jerome place Basilides during the reign of Hadrian (A.D. 117-138).[58] The Nicolaitans were actually contemporary with John in Asia Minor, as we learn from Revelation 2:6, 15. Concerning them Irenaeus says that they lived "lives of unrestrained indulgence."[59] Perhaps the main person against whom 1 John was directed was Cerinthus, a man who, if Dionysius of Alexandria was correctly informed, was "devoted to the pleasures of the body and altogether sensual," expecting that the future kingdom would consist of "the delights of the belly and of sexual passion."[60] According to Polycarp, Cerinthus was present in Ephesus at the same time as John.[61] Furthermore, Irenaeus specifically states that John wrote his gospel "to remove that error which by Cerinthus had been disseminated among men, and a long time previously by those termed Nicolaitans, who are an offset of that 'knowledge falsely so called.' "[62] In addition, it is possible that John had in mind another antinomian error called Simonianism.[63]

2. GNOSTIC DENIAL OF SIN

Closely related to Gnostic antinomianism was the denial of sin both in nature and practice (1 John 1:8—2:2). John's readers were apparently faced with persons who claimed that they did not possess sinful natures (1:8) and consequently that they had never committed acts of sin (1:10).

An attempt to understand such assertions requires an explanation of the rationale of Gnostic antinomianism. Their libertine practices were not merely the product of unrestrained lust; the antinomians at least sought to justify themselves by their philos-

---

57. Irenaeus *Against Heresies* 1. 28. 2.
58. A. H. McNeile, *An Introduction to the Study of the New Testament*, p. 340.
59. Irenaeus *Against Heresies* 1. 26. 3.
60. Eusebius *H.E.* 3. 28. 5.
61. Irenaeus *Against Heresies* 3. 3. 4.
62. Ibid., 3. 11. 1.
63. Ibid., 1. 23. 4.

ophy. Within fifty years after the writing of 1 John such a philosophy was held by Carpocrates. It was said that matter, which is evil, was created by the Demiurge, a remote emanation from the Absolute. That Demiurge was said to be the God of the Old Testament, who not only created matter but also gave the Mosaic commandments. Consequently, if one would oppose the creator of evil matter, one must purposely break his commandments.[64] Clement of Alexandria quotes the Antitactae, a branch of Gnostic libertines who held similar views, as saying: "Therefore, even we ourselves are set in opposition to him to avenge the Father, and act contrary to the will of the second. Since then, the latter has said, 'Thou shalt not commit adultery,' let us, say they, commit adultery to abolish his commandment."[65]

Irenaeus gives a further development of the Carpocratian view, saying:

> They have reached such a pitch of madness that they say that it is in their power to do whatever is irreligious and impious, for they say that actions are good and bad only in accordance with human opinion. In the transmigrations into bodies, souls ought to experience every kind of life and action. . . . The souls which in a single life on earth manage to participate in all sins will no longer become reincarnate but, having paid all their "debts" will be freed so that they no longer come to be in a body.[66]

To the Gnostic there was no sin; there was only ignorance of where men came from, of who they were, and of what they could become. What is commonly called sin is in reality the exact opposite in that by doing it one may thwart the Demiurge and achieve that perfect "knowledge" that brings salvation.

Inasmuch as such a view existed among the Gnostics a short time after John's day, there is some justification in assuming that the beginning of such a philosophy may have been behind 1 John 1:8, 10. This assumption is supported by the fact that Cerinthus, John's contemporary, also held that the world was not created by the primary God, but by a lesser Power who was ignorant of the primary God.[67] It is but a short step to the additional assertion

---

64. Robert M. Grant, *Gnosticism and Early Christianity*, p. 95.
65. Clement of Alexandria *Stromata* 3. 4. 34.
66. Irenaeus *Against Heresies*, 1. 25. 3.
67. Ibid., 3. 11. 1.

that the commandments of that lesser Power are as evil as the material creation.

About A.D. 140 the Gnostic Valentinus set forth a somewhat different philosophy of antinomianism. He divided mankind into three groups: the material, the animal, and the spiritual. The material will of necessity perish; the spiritual, who have attained perfect gnosis, will be saved; and the animal can be saved if it makes the right choices and exerts the proper effort.[68] Irenaeus said of the Valentinians:

> On this account, they tell us that it is necessary for us whom they call *animal* men, and describe as being *of* the world, to practice continence and good works, that by this means, we may attain at length to the intermediate habitation, but that to them who are called "the spiritual and perfect" such a course of conduct is not at all necessary. For it is not conduct of any kind which leads into the Pleroma, but the seed sent forth thence in a feeble, immature state, and here brought to perfection.[69]

With such a view of their nature, it would have been easy for those Gnostics to have denied committing any sin. Being essentially spiritual they were not *themselves* defiled by any deeds of the material body.

3. GNOSTIC LOVELESSNESS

John's statements in 2:7-11 suggest that his readers were also troubled by persons claiming to be in the light, but who were actually filled with antipathy for the people of God (2:9, 11). They apparently were moving, or had moved, in the circle of Christian fellowship, for John speaks of hating one's "brother." (See Exegetical Commentary on 2:9.) In addition, John's statement in 2:19 that "they went out from us" confirms that at least for a time these false teachers had been included in the Christian circle. In spite of this relationship, their lives were marked by hatred rather than love.

In the writings of the postapostolic period there is evidence that the Gnostic heretics fit the description drawn from 1 John. They moved among God's people posing as bona fide Christian teachers, yet they really despised those who were faithful to the apostol-

68. Ibid., 1. 6. 1, 2.
69. Ibid., 1. 6. 4.

ic tradition. What Irenaeus said concerning the Gnostics of his day was probably also true to some extent of their forerunners in John's time: "And committing many other abominations and impieties, they run us down (who from the fear of God guard against sinning even in thought or word) as utterly contemptible and ignorant persons, while they highly exalt themselves, and claim to be perfect, and the elect seed."[70]

Ignatius also comments on the lovelessness of the Gnostics of his day (died A.D. 117), saying: "But mark ye those who hold strange doctrine touching the grace of Jesus Christ which came to us, how that they are contrary to the mind of God. They have no care for love, none for the widow, none for the orphan, none for the afflicted, none for the prisoner, none for the hungry or thirsty."[71]

B. THE JOHANNINE TESTS

Confronted with this kind of false teacher, the Christians of the province of Asia were in danger of becoming, at the least, thoroughly confused, and perhaps of being led astray. Who could one trust? Who was speaking the truth? In a day when the religious air was full of all kinds of ideas and beliefs, how could the true way be recognized? To meet this crying need John set up a series of tests, all of which may be grouped under two general headings, the ethical and the Christological. In this section (1:5—2:11), the tests are ethical.

1. FELLOWSHIP DEMANDS MORAL LIKENESS, 1:5-7

The meaning of fellowship. The key word binding 1:5—2:28 together is κοινωνία, *fellowship.* Although the term is used to describe the relationship between believers (1:3, 7), its ultimate and primary reference is to the relationship between God and His people. Some have viewed John's purpose in this section to be the cultivation of this divine-human fellowship among his readers. Consequently, both the person who is not enjoying such fellowship and the person who is in fellowship are understood to be Christians. The contrast in verses 6-7, according to this view, is between a believer out of fellowship with God and a believer in fellowship with Him.

70. Ibid., 1. 6. 4.
71. Ignatius *Smyr.*, 6. 2.

However, as much as fellowship with God needs to be cultivated, this is not the apostle's aim in 1:5—2:28. In John's theology the Christian life in its very essence *is* fellowship with God. The contrast, then, is between one who is a genuine Christian and one who professes to be but is not. This interpretation is corroborated by the usage of the synonymous term γινώσκειν, "to know," in 2:3-4. To have fellowship with God is to know Him; not to be in a relationship of fellowship is not to know Him. Christ declared, "This is eternal life, that they may know Thee, the only true God, and Jesus Christ whom Thou hast sent" (John 17:3).

The early Gnostics whom John was refuting claimed to be in fellowship with God; in response the apostle established a test by which that claim could be verified—"the test of likeness." The test grows out of the basic concept in κοινωνία, the concept of a common possession or experience. In order for two persons to have fellowship, they must hold something in common. Since in the divine-human relationship God is the sovereign party, He alone determines the necessary basis of fellowship between God and man. This basis is determined, not arbitrarily, but by what God Himself is, as John asserts in his declaration "God is light."

The standard of comparison. The apostle explains that his statement concerning the nature of God came *from Him,* that is, from the incarnate Word described in 1:1-4. The declaration "God is light," was either an explicit statement of Christ, or it was a summation of His teaching about God.

The terms *light* and *darkness* used in a moral sense would not be strange to Christ or to John, as shown by their frequent occurrence in the documents from Qumran.

In some Gnostic systems, such as the Mandaean, light and darkness played a significant part. It was held that there were two eternal principles, one Light and the other Darkness. The existing world was characterized by Darkness into which Light entered as an altogether foreign element. The world of light was said to be "a world of mildness without rebellion, a world of righteousness without turbulence, a world of eternal life without decay and death, a world of goodness without evil. . . ."[72] It may, therefore, be that John chose to employ the terms *light* and *darkness* in order to make his refutation of incipient Gnosticism more effective.

The declaration that "God is light" is set forth as a standard in John's test of likeness. As was previously indicated in the Exegeti-

---

72. Hans Jonas, *The Gnostic Religion,* p. 57.

cal Commentary on 1:5, light is a metaphor used to represent truth and holiness. Therefore God is essentially true and holy. In John's test of likeness, the standard of comparison is the nature of God Himself. Anyone who professes to be in His fellowship must to some degree be like Him in this regard and manifest holiness.

The structure of 1:5-7. The sequence of thought in this section is typically Johannine, revealing the apostle's love of contrast. The standard of comparison established in verse 5 serves as the foundation for the two following verses. In verse 6 John sets up a negative hypothetical example, and in verse 7 a positive one. In verse 6 he suggests the case of professing Christians who fail to pass the test of likeness. Whereas God is light and absolute moral perfection, the persons professing fellowship are walking in darkness and are living lives of habitual sin. Thus the claim to fellowship is proved to be false.

In contrast John sets up the hypothetical example of persons who are walking in the light. This practice of truth and righteousness becomes the proof of genuine fellowship. God is light, and they walk in the light; God in His essence is holiness, and they, as a habit, practice holiness.

The definition of walking in darkness and walking in light. It has already been suggested that the term *walking* is a metaphor expressive of those activities composing one's life. Both the tense of the verb (present) and the meaning of the word itself convey the idea of continual activity. It is the habit of life that is in view. Thus, to be walking in darkness is to be living habitually in error and sin. Likewise, to walk in the light is to carry on one's life in the sphere of truth and holiness, to engage in the habitual practice of righteousness.

This does not mean that every action of those who walk in darkness is evil, although the constant direction of life is toward sin, and the general practice is the performance of wickedness. By reason of general Christian influence in the world and because of the knowledge of right and wrong, the person walking in darkness will undoubtedly do some good things.

It may be asked whether the expression "walking in the light" is simply another way of speaking of sinless perfection. Taken by itself the expression could be so interpreted. However, there are indications in the context that this is not John's meaning. He speaks in 1:7 of continual cleansing (present tense καθαρίζει) by the blood of Christ. If the person walking in the light were sinlessly perfect, such continual cleansing would be unnecessary. Perfection is not expected, for allowance is made for individual acts of sin into which the believer may fall. (See additional treatment in the following discussion of 1:8—2:2.)

The refutation of incipient Gnosticism. Whereas the Gnostic insisted that the question of morality has no bearing upon one's relation to God, John declares forcibly that the two cannot be divorced. He insists that fellowship with God will invariably be accompanied by a life of righteousness. The Gnostics, however, were known for their high claims and their low living. They claimed themselves to be the *pneumatikoi*, the spiritual ones, whereas other men were the *sarkikoi*, the carnal ones. The Gnostics claimed special esoteric knowledge that resulted in salvation. At the same time, however, many Gnostics were antinomian and lived in all kinds of sin, especially the sin of sexual immorality. John's point is that low life disproves the validity of lofty claims.

In addition he declares that they "do not practice the truth" (v. 6). By this interesting statement the apostle binds together in closest unity doctrine and life. Truth cannot be merely a matter of profession. Truth held genuinely must work itself out into practice; if there is no practice of truth, then that truth is not genuinely accepted. If the esoteric gnosis were genuine truth genuinely held, it would most surely result in holy living.

Indirectly John includes a secondary refutation of Gnosticism. In verse 7 he speaks of the blood of Jesus, a statement which by itself constituted no problem for the Cerinthian Gnostic. Jesus was a flesh-and-blood man who shed His blood on a cross. However, when John adds the words τοῦ υἱοῦ αὐτοῦ, "His son," the Cerinthian system comes under attack, for the man Jesus was not held to be the Son of God. Jesus was a man of flesh, and flesh is always evil. God is spirit, and spirit is always good. The two are and must ever be, according to that system, poles apart. But John places them in closet union: the flesh-and-blood Jesus is God's Son.

2. FELLOWSHIP DEMANDS CONFESSION OF SIN, 1:8—2:2

The structure of 1:8—2:2. The Johannine technique of throwing the negative and the positive into contrast with each other is again apparent here. However, whereas in 1:6-7 the structure of contrast was negative-positive, in 1:8-10 the form is negative-positive-negative. In verse 8, the first negative hypothetical example is the case of persons who profess to be without indwelling sin. As in verse 6, such persons fail the test—they are self-deceived and do not possess the truth. In verse 9 the positive hypothetical example is the case of those who, as a habit, admit their sins. Such persons pass the test and are favorably viewed as the subjects of divine forgiveness and cleansing. In verse 10 the second negative example is that of people who claim that they have never committed acts of sin. Because of their refusal to admit their sins, they fail the test of confession, and in so doing they make God out to be a liar while revealing themselves to be destitute of truth.

Following the statement of the test of confession, John explains the theology upon which the confession of sin rests (2:1-2), namely the two facts of Christ's propitiation for sins and His intercession in heaven.

The Christian's attitude toward sin. Of necessity the practice of walking in the light involves one's attitude toward sin. As mentioned under the definition of walking in the light, John was not thinking in terms of sinless perfection as evidenced by his statement concerning the continued cleansing from sin for all who are walking in the light (1:7). However, it is in 1:8—2:2 that this allowance for acts of sin is more clearly revealed. Here the apostle indicates that those who walk in the light must not deny their sinful natures (1:8) or their sinful acts (1:10). Instead they must make it a practice to confess their sins in order that they may be forgiven and cleansed (1:9).

Thus, one can readily see why fellowship with God demands the practice of walking in the light. Fellowship is possible only if the two parties are in some measure alike. God is light and the believer walks in the light. However, when the Christian's walk in the light is disrupted by sin, confession is necessary to restore the marred fellowship to its intended condition.

John's use of forgiveness in 1 John 1:9 is to be distinguished from Paul's use in a passage such as Colossians 1:14. There Paul's use of forgiveness is *forensic*. It is initial forgiveness that follows faith in Christ and that comprises the negative aspect of justification. When God justifies the one who trusts in Christ He performs two legal acts: (1) He declares the believer's sins—past, present, and future—all to be forgiven on the basis of Christ's shed blood, and (2) He imputes to the believer the perfect righteousness of Christ. Why then does that forgiven believer need any further forgiveness? Why did John write about continued confession and consequent forgiveness to those who were already forgiven (1:9; cf. 2:12)? The answer is that John is not speaking of *forensic* forgiveness, as does Paul, but of *filial* forgiveness. He is writing to those who have been forgiven the guilt of sin once for all and who are now the children of God. It is not necessary that the guilt question be raised again, but it *is* needful that that which had disturbed the fellowship between Father and child be removed. And it is with this restoration of undisturbed communion that the *filial* forgiveness of 1 John 1:9 is concerned.

Since sin must be confessed in order to restore disturbed fellowship, it is obvious that the Holy Spirit through John commands us to avoid sin. The prohibition against sin becomes even plainer in 2:1*a*, where the author bluntly declares, "My little children, I am writing these things to you that you may not sin" (aorist tense ἁμάρτητε, *commit one act of sin*). Thus, the genuine believer's attitude toward sin is one of opposition. His aim is to avoid committing even one act of sin. His normal pattern of life is one of practicing righteousness, and when he fails in this he confesses his sin and secures restoration of fellowship with God.

The theology that underlies this confession is set forth in 2:1*b*-2. John speaks first of the advocacy of Christ before the Father on behalf of Christians (v. 1*b*), following which he refers to Christ's propitiatory work (v. 2). In the actual order of both logic and occurrence, propitiation precedes advocacy, so that, as Calvin put it, "Christ's intercession is the continual application of His death to our salvation."[73] But the apostle is approaching the subject from the vantage point of the occasion when the Christian commits an act of sin. It is at that point that advocacy occurs. The sinning Christian sees the advocacy first and then the prior act of propitiation on which the advocacy of Christ rests.

It is significant that the Advocate is described as "Jesus Christ the righteous." For Christ's advocacy of the believer's cause to be effective, it is imperative that He be perfectly righteous. An advocate must himself have a reputable character, and One who dies as the propitiation for the sins of others must Himself be without sin.

Forgiveness, both forensic and filial, rests upon the propitiatory sacrifice of Jesus Christ. By His death He satisfied the justice of God in that He fully paid the penalty for sins. Thus, for those who will have it, there is peace with God. And the preservation of a continuing relationship of peace and fellowship depends, at least in part, upon the present heavenly advocacy of Christ. He is carrying on a continual intercessory ministry in God's presence (cf. Heb. 7:25—"He always lives to make intercession for them").

---

73. Cited in Stott, p. 82.

John says that if the believer does commit an act of sin (aorist ἁμάρτῃ) the remedy is found in the Advocate.

Although the advocacy of Christ is limited to believers ("we have an Advocate," 1 John 2:1), the propitiation is worldwide in its scope (v. 2). As Bonsirven has said, "Jesus has poured out his blood for all men, he has virtually purchased the whole world; to benefit from that purchase it is sufficient to be united to the Redeemer."[74] John has no limited atonement here. Christ's death is adequate in its scope and intent to save all men, but it is efficacious only for those who by faith receive its benefit.

The refutation of incipient Gnosticism. The test of confession (1:8— 2:2) like the test of likeness (1:5-7), was set up in opposition to the false teachers who were attempting to seduce John's readers. It is apparent that they were persons who denied their own sinfulness, insisting that they neither possessed a sinful nature (1:8) nor committed sinful acts (1:10). As was previously shown (earlier in this Theological Commentary, section A.2.), this denial may well have been based on the belief that there is no such thing as sin since the Gnostic, who was spiritual, was not touched by the deeds of the material body.

In response, John declared that the denial of sin reveals the tragic condition of those who make such claims. Whereas they professed to be among the spiritual ones who were sure of salvation, John leveled a fourfold indictment at them:

    (1) They were self-deceived, 1:8
    (2) They did not possess the truth, 1:8
    (3) They were calling God a liar, 1:10
    (4) They were devoid of God's Word, 1:10

The heretic, then, failed the test of confession of sin and was shown to be, not merely a false teacher, but also one who has not known God's truth or His salvation.

3. FELLOWSHIP DEMANDS OBEDIENCE, 2:3-6

The structure of the passage. These verses repeat what has already been stated in 1:5-7. There are two differences, however, that justify the repetition. First, different terms and figures of speech are employed; second, 2:3-6 advances beyond 1:5-7 by adding the suggestion that obedience is related to love (2:5).

---

74. Bonsirven, p. 28 (my translation).

John opens this new section by stating the basic principle of the test of obedience, namely that obedience to Christ's commandments is proof that a person knows Him (v. 3). Then follow the two examples of the test in John's typical negative-positive form. The one who professes to know Christ but who does not obey fails the test and is shown to be a liar (v. 4), but the one who does obey passes the test and is assured that he knows Christ (v. 5). The section is concluded with a restatement in different terms of the basic truth of the test: Dwelling in Him must be accompanied by living as He lived (v. 6).

The basic teaching of the passage. Although the word *fellowship* does not occur in 2:3-6, the idea is by no means absent. Instead of κοινωνία, John employs several parallel terms, the first of which is γινώσκειν, "to know" (vv. 3-4). In biblical usage the word *know* speaks of knowledge gained by experience. Thus to know Christ is to be acquainted with Him through personal relationship, or to be in fellowship with Him. Again John speaks of being "in Him" (v. 5). This prepositional phrase is descriptive of an intimate mystical relationship to Christ, the closest kind of fellowship. The expression "abides in Him" (v. 6) is the same in meaning, with the exception that it carries the added idea of permanency.

Bultmann points out that, whereas the actual word *fellowship* occurs only in 1 John 1:3, 6, 7, the idea is found throughout the epistle.[75] Bonsirven explains that κοινωνία is a Pauline term, whereas John usually speaks in such concrete expressions as being in God, dwelling in God, possessing God, knowing God, and seeing God.[76] (See 1 John 2:23, 24.) It is clear that John consistently views the Christian life as one of fellowship with God. It is also clear, therefore, that 2:3-6 further develops the theme begun in 1:5-7. Here, as in the foregoing passage, John sets up a test by which the claim to have fellowship may be verified.

To put it concisely, that test is obedience to Christ's commands. To know Christ is to obey Him (v. 3). This is parallel to the teaching of 1:5-7 that to have fellowship with God is to be like Him. The concepts of walking in the light (1:7) and keeping His commandments (2:3) are closely related if not identical in sense. Both speak of the practice of truth and righteousness.

The key to understanding the rationale of this test is found in the word ἀγάπη, "love" (v. 5.). Obedience is said to be the fruit

---

75. Bultmann, p. 13.
76. Bonsirven, p. 78. See also Bruce, pp. 38-39.

of love. This is the meaning of ἡ ἀγάπη τοῦ θεοῦ τετελείωται, "the love of God has truly been perfected" (v. 5). Love, when it is allowed to bring forth its proper end product, produces obedience. It is assumed that he who knows the Lord, who is in fellowship with Him, also loves Him. There can be no divine-human fellowship without love, for to know God is to love Him. And by the same token to love Him is to obey Him. Thus, the test of obedience is a valid test. Knowing Him means loving Him; loving Him means obeying Him; therefore knowing Him is evidenced by obedience.

In 2:6 John returns to the idea of likeness, which he introduced in 1:5-7. The claim to be dwelling in Christ ought to be accompanied by a Christ-like walk. In chapter 1 this was called walking in the light. There can be no genuine intimate relationship such as dwelling in Him unless there is also a similarity of life. Paul asks, "What partnership have righteousness and lawlessness? Or what fellowship has light with darkness?" (2 Cor. 6:14). Those living in fellowship with the Lord will also be walking in the light as He did.

The refutation of Gnosticism. Because of its emphasis on salvation by knowledge (γνῶσις), the heresy being refuted by John came to be called Gnosticism. The profession, "I know Him," (v. 4) was no doubt the proud boast of the heretics.

John, therefore, has put their claim to the test in order to discover the true nature of the knowledge they professed. There is a kind of knowledge that does not affect life, which therefore may be described as speculative or theoretical. What is known of the antinomian Gnostics clearly shows that the knowledge they possessed did not result in obedience and holy living. It was only speculation *about* God, not experiential knowledge *of* God. Thus the test of obedience demonstrated that their claim to know God was false. John's readers were to place no confidence in the Gnostics' high-sounding boasts.

The ground for Christian assurance. These verses not only contain a refutation of the Gnostic error; they also provide a solid foundation for the assurance of those who are true believers. The idea of assurance is set forth by the use of γινώσκομεν (vv. 3, 5). Here it is not the *claim* to know the Lord that is in view. Instead it is the firm knowledge that one *does* know Him. In the thinking of some persons assurance is based solely upon a profession of faith in Christ, and surely such a profession is necessary to any genuine assurance. However, the NT also provides other bases for assurance. In this passage, for example, John declares that continuing obedience to the Lord is solid ground for assurance that we know Him.

4. FELLOWSHIP DEMANDS LOVE OF THE BROTHERS, 2:7-11

The structure of the passage. This new section is introduced in a unique manner (2:7-8), and employs paradox to point up the test of love that follows (2:9-11). As a foundation for the test the author refers us to Christ's commandment to love one another (John 13:34-35) and makes the paradoxical statement that the command is both old and new.

Following this introductory description, the duty of love is employed as a test of spiritual experience. As in 1:8-10, the apostle uses the pattern of negative-positive-negative, with the second negative expressing more advanced truth than the first. The claim stated in verse 9 and assumed in verses 10-11 is the claim to be "in the light," and it is this profession that is put to the test. Verse 9 declares that if the claim is accompanied by hatred rather than love, the claim is false. Such a person is in darkness rather than light. Verse 10, assuming the same claim, states that if it is accompanied by love for one's brother, the claim to be in the light is valid. Verse 11 restates the negative with further explanation of the condition of the person who fails the test of love.

The scope of the old-new commandment. A cursory reading of 1 John 2:7-11 and John 13:34-35 may leave one with a very superficial view of the scope of Christian love. Two considerations, however, reveal something of the fuller dimension that characterizes this mark of Christ's disciple. First, consider the prominent place given to love by both Christ and John. Our Lord commanded that His followers love each other as He loved them, and He singled out this one item as the characteristic mark for His disciples (John 13:34-35). Furthermore, John selected love as a major evidence of a life lived in the light (1 John 2:10). Second, both Christ and Paul indicate that love is in reality all-inclusive in its scope. Jesus, after identifying the two greatest commandments as being to love God completely and to love one's neighbor as one's self, declared, "On these two commandments hang all the law and the prophets" (Matt. 22:40, KJV). And Paul speaks in similar terms when he says:

> Owe nothing to anyone except to love one another; for he who loves his neighbor has fulfilled the law. For this, "YOU SHALL NOT

COMMIT ADULTERY, YOU SHALL NOT MURDER, YOU SHALL NOT STEAL, YOU SHALL NOT COVET," and if there is any other commandment, it is summed up in this saying, "YOU SHALL LOVE YOUR NEIGHBOR AS YOURSELF." Love does no wrong to a neighbor; love therefore is the fulfillment of the law.

(Rom. 13:8-10)

It is readily apparent from the words of Christ and Paul that the command to love is in reality an ethical command. It involves the sum total of man's duty to God and man. To love, therefore, is the same as to walk in the light (1:5-7) or to obey Christ's commands (2:3-6). He who loves his fellow Christian will in no way harm him; instead he will seize every opportunity to do good to him (3:16-18).

It is noteworthy that John singles out love for one's brother rather than love for God as a test of being in the light. As has been indicated in the Exegetical Commentary, the term *brother* refers to a fellow believer. No doubt love for the brother is selected as a test because it is more readily discernible than love for God. In specific acts of love toward one's brother can be seen concrete evidence that one is in the light (2:9-11) and thus in fellowship with God (1:5-7).

In John's thinking there are close relationships between love and light on the one hand and hatred and darkness on the other. Love is characteristic of light. In fact, love in its broadest sense is the equivalent of light. On the other hand, hatred is one of the characteristics of darkness. If love is the fulfillment of the law, hatred is the breaking of the law; if love is the attitude that does good to another whenever possible, hatred is the attitude that does harm whenever possible. These diametrically opposite relationships are evident in 2:8 where John says that the new commandment is true in the believers "because the darkness is passing away, and the true light is already shining." Here the true light is associated with the truth of the love-commandment, and by the same token the darkness may be associated with hatred as verses 9 and 11 indicate.

The passing of the darkness and the advance of the light are phenomena true in the lives of individual believers. These related phenomena are also true on a broader scale. The new age is advancing and the old age is declining. The phenomena of the coming age are already being increasingly experienced as a foretaste of the future. Therefore, the old age is already beginning to experience advance notice of its destruction and defeat. This is not to suggest any optimistic view that the world is getting better and better. It is to assert that in Christ the eschatological future is already making itself felt today. Bruce says: "As long as the new age is inaugurated but not yet consummated (as it will be by the *parousia* of Christ), the old age is still in being. Believers who belong spiritually to 'that age' live temporally in 'this age.' Although 'the true light' is already shining, the darkness has not passed completely away; it is in process of 'passing away.' "[77]

It will be noted that John puts his tests in statements that are "either-or" in nature. One either loves or he hates; there is no shading of attitudes between the two extremes. This may seem to be disregarding the degrees of feeling that must exist between outright love and outright hatred. However on the one hand John is talking about the unbeliever or heretic who, because of his opposition to truth, actually hates those who hold the truth. On the other hand, John refers to those who cherish the truth of God and thus have a deep affinity toward others who also hold the truth dear. Westcott says, "There is a simple choice between 'for' and 'against,' that is essentially between 'love' and 'hatred.' "[78]

The refutation of Gnosticism. The apostle's primary purpose in this section is not to cultivate Christian love among God's people, as needful as that may be. As in the foregoing sections, he is continuing to mount an offensive against the Gnostic heresy, this time by attacking their lovelessness. John shows his readers that the genuine may be distinguished from the spurious by the presence or absence of love. A person might claim to have fellowship with God and to be dwelling in the light, but the acid test is the test of love for the people of God. If a teacher came who professed to be in the light, but who showed antipathy for Christian people, John declared that his profession was not to be believed. He was a liar and was destitute of the truth. Thus the Gnostics who, according to Irenaeus, treated Christians "as utterly contemptible and ignorant"[79] and who, according to Ignatius, had "no care for love,"[80] were shown to be liars who had never known the truth of God.

---

77. Bruce, p. 55.
78. Westcott, p. 55.
79. Irenaeus *Against Heresies* 1. 6. 4.
80. Ignatius *Smyr.* 6. 2.

C. THE PRESENT-DAY APPLICATION.

1. SPECIFIC APPLICATIONS

Christian Science. Perhaps the most direct present-day use of 1 John 1:5—2:11 would be to apply it to a Gnostic-type cult such as Christian Science. In addition to denying the reality of matter, this cult also denies the existence of sin. In answer to the question "Is there no sin?", its founder Mary Baker Eddy wrote:

> All reality is in God and His creation, harmonious and eternal. That which He creates is good, and He makes all that is made. Therefore the only reality of sin, sickness, or death is the awful fact that unrealities seem real to human, erring belief, until God strips them of their disguise. They are not true, because they are not of God. We learn in Christian Science that all inharmony of mortal mind or body is illusion possessing neither reality nor identity though seeming to be real and identical.[81]

Such a denial of the existence of sin is parallel to the Gnostic denial of sin. The reasoning behind the two denials is different, but the end result is similar. Gnosticism viewed matter as real and as essentially evil, while antinomian Gnostics insisted that what traditional Christianity called sin was a commendable way of defeating the lesser Power who had created evil matter. By such action one could ultimately be delivered from the material body and be restored to the original state of pure spirit. Christian Science, however, denies the reality of both matter and sin.

The context in which 1:8-10 is set makes it clear that John's concept of sin is that which flows out of the OT. Sin is the breaking of God's commandments (2:3-6), not the error of assuming the reality of unrealities (matter, sin, and death), as Christian Science would claim.

Sinless perfection. Another specific application of 1:8-10 may be made in reference to persons who claim sinless perfection of one kind or another. Although such a profession today rests upon a different basis than the Gnostic denial of sin, there is sufficient similarity to make John's refutation applicable to both.

The present-day perfectionist bases his claim upon the concepts of suppression or eradication of sin. He does not deny the reality of sin as the Christian Scientist does, nor does he insist that he has

---

81. Mary Baker Eddy, *Science and Health with Key to the Scriptures,* pp. 472-73.

never sinned as the Gnostic did. The perfectionist does claim, however, that he has attained that point in his Christian experience at which sin has been completely removed. The Wesleyan doctrine makes a distinction between sin and infirmity. According to H. Orton Wiley, sin is the willful and knowing violation of God's law, but infirmity is involuntary transgression of law, done because of ignorance or human weakness.[82] Distinction is also made between inbred sin or inherited depravity and sin as willful transgression. Entire sanctification, it is said, eradicates the inbred sin or depravity. Wiley uses such terms as "thoroughly purged, extirpated, eradicated and crucified."[83] Thus the sanctified believer is no longer indwelt by sin. As a result he has ceased to commit willful acts of sin. Infirmities (involuntary, unknowing transgressions) are still present, but these are not viewed as sins.

It is clear that 1 John makes no such distinction between sin and infirmity. Speaking to Christians, John declares, "If we say that we have no sin, we are deceiving ourselves, and the truth is not in us" (1:8). Adam Clarke, the renowned Wesleyan commentator and theologian, says concerning this verse, "This is tantamount to ver. 10: *If we say that we have not sinned.*"[84] In Clarke's thinking, both verses refer to sin committed prior to regeneration and 1:9 is, therefore, an appeal to the unregenerate to confess their sins and be justified and cleansed. However, it was not without reason that John wrote, "we have no sin" in verse 8 and "we have not sinned" in verse 10. The verb ἔχομεν (v. 8), "have," speaks of possession, not of *sins* as in verse 10, but of *sin*. The claim that the *principle* of sin is not possessed is the point John makes. Then in verse 10 he speaks of committing acts of sin, and the perfect tense verb used with the negative means "we have not sinned" *ever*. Consequently the two verses refer to persons who deny the possession of indwelling sin and the commission of acts of sin in the past and right up to the last minute before the claim is made. Such persons are deceived and devoid of the truth of God, according to John.

It is plain that verse 8, when taken at face value, forcibly refutes any claim to the eradication of depravity or sin of any kind, and verse 10 disproves the assertion that one has reached the point at which he no longer commits acts of sin. (First John 3:4 defines sin

---

82. H. Orton Wiley, *Christian Theology*, 2:507.
83. Ibid., pp. 488-89.
84. Adam Clark, *The New Testament of Our Lord and Savior Jesus Christ . . . A Commentary and Critical Notes*, 2:904.

as the transgression of law, whether willful and knowing transgression or not.)

The new morality. A third specific application to the present day concerns what has become known as "the new morality." According to the proponents of this view, morality is no longer to be governed by an external standard, such as the Ten Commandments; instead, standards of right and wrong become subjective and relative. The rightness or wrongness of an act is dependent upon the attendant circumstances and upon the rational judgment of the persons concerned. Premarital or extramarital sex relations are held to be morally acceptable if the parties involved love each other and if no one is harmed by the action. And such an idea has been propagated by some members of the clergy as a valid Christian viewpoint. The source of this way of thinking is a philosophy of relativism and pragmatism that insists there are no fixed, timeless standards of right and wrong. Although the Judaeo-Christian ethic is viewed as able to provide some guidelines, it is not the unchanging absolute that is binding in every situation.[85]

But John sees moral standards as fixed and unchanging because they are light (1:5) and men are expected to walk in the light (1:7), to obey Christ's commands (2:3-5) and to live a life patterned after His life (2:6). According to John there can be no such thing as a genuine experience of fellowship with God that is not accompanied by a life of obedience and righteousness. The antinomianism of the new morality finds no more place in the Christian system than the antinomianism of Gnosticism found.

Psychological and related excuses. It has become rather common to try to explain away responsibility for acts once regarded as sinful. The explanation is usually psychological or physiological in nature. Alcoholism loses its moral connotation because it is viewed merely as an illness. Homosexuality is no longer viewed as sinful because the homosexual is "born that way." To such excuses Stott replies: "John's affirmation is equally applicable today to those who deny the fact or guilt of sin by seeking to interpret it solely in terms of physiological, psychological or social causes."[86]

2. GENERAL APPLICATIONS

Although John's original intent was much more specific, application of 1 John 1:5—2:11 may also be made to broader areas of life. Moral likeness (1:5-7), confession of sin (1:8-2:2), obedience

---

85. Joseph Fletcher, *Situation Ethics, the New Morality,* pp. 26-31.
86. Stott, p. 77.

(2:3-6), and love for fellow Christians (2:7-11) are set forth in the epistle as marks that distinguish the genuine Christian from the counterfeit. It is possible, however, to make secondary applications by using these passages as encouragement to Christians to manifest these characteristics and thus to demonstrate the reality of their profession. Since the failure to live lives of holiness at the least indicates broken fellowship with God, we must be careful to live habitually in the light (1:5-7). Since the practice of confession of sin is a necessary activity of one who walks in the light, Christians need to give diligent attention to habitual confession of sins into which they fall (1:8—2:2). Since knowledge of Christ is proved by obedience, God's people ought to make it their aim always to do His will (2:3-6). Since love for fellow Christians is a mark of genuine believers, we must cultivate a constant attitude of love toward all brothers in Christ (2:7-11). And, of course, in all of these areas there is always room for improvement.

As we allow the Holy Spirit increasingly to produce these characteristics in our lives, we will have solid ground for assurance that we are in saving relationship to God. Since such traits are only possible to those whom God has regenerated and who are indwelt by the Holy Spirit, their continuing presence in the life of a professing Christian is concrete proof that he is a child of God.

Paraphrastic Commentary (1:5—2:11)

(5) When Christ was here on earth he told us what we are now making known to you, namely, that God in His essence is moral perfection and He does not possess even the slightest trace of evil. (6) Since this is true, if we profess to be in a relationship of saving fellowship with Him while we are living habitually in sin, we are being deceitful and we are not living in accordance with God's life-changing truth. (7) If, however, our lives are marked by the habitual practice of holiness just as Christ's life was, this is proof that we are in a relationship of saving fellowship, being continually cleansed from every sin by the atoning sacrifice of Jesus the Son of God.

(8) Suppose we should claim that we do not have sinful natures. In that case we would only be deceiving ourselves and revealing that we are devoid of saving truth. (9) Or suppose on the other hand that we are in the habit of admitting our sins to God. We would then find that He is true to His promise and that He acts in accord with the standards of justice so that He restores the relationship disturbed by our sins and washes away the defilement of every kind of wickedness. (10) Again, let's suppose we boast that we have never committed one act of sin. Such a claim actually accuses God

of lying in declaring that "all have sinned." And what is more, it becomes evident that we do not possess God's revealed truth.

(2:1) My dear children, my aim in sending this letter is that you will not commit even one act of sin. However, if anyone does commit sin, we have a Friend in heaven's court who will speak on our behalf. His name is Jesus Christ; He is truly righteous. (2) Furthermore, He Himself is the atoning sacrifice that fully meets the just demands of God and thus turns away His wrath, not only with regard to our sins, but also potentially with regard to those of everyone everywhere.

(3) Since there are many who are boasting of spiritual knowledge, let me tell you how we may be sure that we know Christ. Such assurance is based upon continued obedience to His commands. (4) On the one hand, the person who claims to know Christ but who is not habitually obeying Him is a deceiver, devoid of saving truth. (5) But, on the other hand, if anyone makes it a practice to live in accordance with Christ's word, beyond a doubt his love for God is shown to have reached the stage of fruitful maturity. And this is clear proof that we are in vital union with Christ. (6) The one who claims to be continuing in such union is under an abiding obligation to live daily just as Christ Himself lived.

(7) Dear friends, the directive that I am sending you is not really new and different; instead it is an old and familiar command that you have had since you first heard the gospel message. (8) There is a sense, however, in which it is new, both in Christ's unique example of love and in your daily experience of it as the light steadily advances on the retreating darkness in your life. (9) Now, love also serves as a test of spiritual life, so that a person who is claiming to be living in the light but is harboring a murderous attitude toward his fellow Christian reveals that he has always been in sin's darkness and remains there right up to this present moment. (10) But the one who maintains a constant attitude of love for his fellow believer demonstrates that he is dwelling in God's light and he will not stumble over obstacles in his path. (11) Again, that one who has a murderous attitude toward his fellow Christian is in a state of darkness, he is carrying on life's activities in darkness, and he cannot see the way before him because without light he is like a blind man.

STRUCTURAL COMMENTARY (1:5—2:11)[87]

II. First cycle: The Christian life viewed as fellowship with the Father and the Son, 1:5—2:28

---

87. For previous section of the outline, see pp. 112-14.

Fellowship Tested on Ethical Grounds 169

A. Fellowship tested on ethical grounds, 1:5—2:11
  1. Fellowship demands moral likeness, 1:5-7
    a. The standard of comparison, 1:5
    b. The test of likeness applied, 1:6-7
      (1) Negative results 1:6
        (a) The claim: fellowship with God, 1:6*a*
        (b) The practice: walk in darkness, 1:6*b*
        (c) The conclusions, 1:6*c*
      (2) Positive results, 1:7
        (a) The practice: walk in light, 1:7*a*
        (b) The conclusions, 1:7*b*
  2. Fellowship demands confession of sin, 1:8—2:2
    a. The test of confession applied, 1:8-10
      (1) Negative results, 1:8
        (a) The claim: no depravity, 1:8*a*
        (b) The conclusions, 1:8*b*
      (2) Positive results, 1:9
        (a) The practice: confession of sins, 1:9*a*
        (b) The assured results: forgiveness and cleansing, 1:9*b*
      (3) Negative results, 1:10
        (a) The claim: never sinned, 1:10*a*
        (b) The conclusions, 1:10*b*
    b. The theological foundations of confession, 2:1-2
      (1) Christ's intercessory work, 2:1
        (a) John's desire for his readers: that they sin not, 2:1*a*
        (b) God's provision for those who do sin: an Advocate, 2:1*b*
      (2) Christ's propitiatory work, 2:2
        (a) For our sins, 2:2*a*
        (b) For the sins of everyone, 2:2*b*
  3. Fellowship demands obedience, 2:3-6
    a. General statement of the test, 2:3
      (1) The subject of the test: knowledge of Christ, 2:3*a*
      (2) The requirement of the test: obedience, 2:3*b*
    b. The test applied, 2:4-5
      (1) Negative results, 2:4
        (a) The claim: to know Christ, 2:4*a*
        (b) The practice: disobedience, 2:4*b*
        (c) The conclusions, 2:4*c*
      (2) Positive results, 2:5

(a) The practice: obedience, 2:5*a*
(b) The conclusions, 2:5*b*
c. Summary statement—Union with Christ demands likeness to Christ, 2:6
4. Fellowship demands love of fellow believers, 2:7-11
   a. The command to love described, 2:7-8
      (1) It is old, 2:7
         (a) A possession since conversion, 2:7*a*
         (b) An element of the gospel message, 2:7*b*
      (2) It is new, 2:8
         (a) Christ manifested a new kind of love, 2:8*a*
         (b) Love is ever new in the believer's daily experience, 2:8*b*
   b. The test applied, 2:9-11
      (1) Negative results, 2:9
         (a) The claim: to be in the light, 2:9*a*
         (b) The practice: hatred, 2:9*b*
         (c) The conclusion: the claimant has always been in darkness, 2:9*c*
      (2) Positive results, 2:10
         (a) The practice: love, 2:10*a*
         (b) The conclusions, 2:10*b*
      (3) Negative results, 2:11
         (a) The practice: hatred, 2:11*a*
         (b) The conclusions, 2:11*b*

8

B. Two Digressions, 2:12-17

From 1:1 through 2:11 John's train of thought has proceeded without interruption. At verse 12, however, the orderly course of his argument is broken by a distinct digression in which he states his assumption concerning the spiritual condition of his readers (2:12-14). This is followed by a second digression containing a warning against loving the world (2:15-17).

In the previous sections of his letter the apostle has spoken bluntly about persons who falsely claimed to be in fellowship with God (1:6; 2:4) and to be without sin (2:8-10). He has denounced such individuals as self-deceived liars who neither possess nor practice the truth. He has also spoken of those who hate their fellow believers (2:9-11), and he has declared that they are and always have been lost in spiritual darkness.

At this point John pauses to assure his readers that those hard-hitting statements are not directed against them. He has been writing *to* them, not *about* them. He is addressing them as genuine believers who possess a saving knowledge of Jesus Christ. His purpose is not to shake their assurance of salvation; instead it is to confirm their confidence.

The second digression (2:15-17) is more difficult to relate to its context. This is not to say, however, that there is no contextual connection. John here warns believers against loving the world, not the people of the world, but the world as a system of evil, set in opposition to God. In the section immediately preceding these digressions, love for fellow Christians is discussed (2:7-11). There, love for believers is commended; here (2:15-17), love for the world is condemned. It is clear from 4:5 that the false teachers against whom John writes have a vital affinity with the world. It is their sphere of origin and activity, as it is likewise the domain of Satan. Hence, any vestige of love for the world that still remains in our hearts must be smothered.

EXEGETICAL COMMENTARY (2:12-17)

1. AN ASSUMPTION CONCERNING THE READERS, 2:12-14

2:12. γράφω ὑμῖν, τεκνία, "I am writing to you, little children." The present tense verb makes it clear that John is referring to the letter he is currently writing. Concerning τεκνία, "little children," see comments on 2:1. This designation is followed in succeeding clauses by the terms πατέρες, "fathers," and νεανίσκοι, "young men" (vv. 13, 14). Some have interpreted these terms as referring to physical ages; others, to spiritual ages. Some have seen three age groups here; some, two groups; and still others, one group. Against the view that John had three age groups in mind, it may be argued first that elsewhere in 1 John τεκνία does not refer to the very young alone, but is a term of endearment addressed to all believers (2:1, 28; 5:21). The same is also true of παιδία, "children" (2:14; cf. 2:18). In the second place it should be noted that the order in which the three terms appear is not the natural order—children, youths, fathers. Instead John's order is children, fathers, youths. For these two reasons it would seem preferable to understand τεκνία, "little children," and παιδία, "children," as referring to all believers and πατέρες, "fathers," and νεανίσκοι, "young men," as speaking of the older and younger believers, whether physically or spiritually or both. J. L. Houlden suggests that the terms "fathers" and "young men" may have been equivalents of "elders" and "deacons."[1]

ὅτι ἀφέωνται ὑμῖν αἱ ἁμαρτίαι διὰ τὸ ὄνομα αὐτοῦ, "because your sins are forgiven you for His name's sake." Ὅτι, "because," obviously must not be taken as referring to the sole

---

1. J. L. Houlden, *A Commentary on the Johannine Epistles*, Black's New Testament Commentaries, pp. 70-71.

reason for writing, nor is it speaking of the immediate occasion for penning the epistle. The primary reason for writing 1 John was to warn against the heresy of an incipient Gnosticism, but this John does *because* (ὅτι) the recipients are God's children and need to be instructed concerning the doctrinal error that is confronting them. They have experienced the forgiveness of sins in the past and are now in the state of having been forgiven (ἀφέωνται, perfect tense). The term *name* (ὄνομα) is used in Scripture to express the nature and character of the person to whom the name belongs. In this case the reference is no doubt to Christ rather than to God the Father (cf. Theological Commentary on 2:12). Among the many passages where the term is used to refer to the character of the person named are Psalms 44:5; 52:9; 54:1; John 1:12; Acts 3:16; 3 John 7. The same understanding apparently lies behind the translation, "for his sake" (1 John 2:12), which appears in the RSV and in the versions of Williams and Beck.

2:13. γράφω ὑμῖν, πατέρες, "I am writing to you, fathers." See comments on verse 12. The fathers are those who are older in the faith as well as in physical age. It had been almost forty years since Paul had first proclaimed Christ in the Ephesian synagogue (Acts 18:19). Thus, some of John's readers may well have been believers of long standing. The term also speaks of authority.

ὅτι ἐγνώκατε τὸν ἀπ' ἀρχῆς, "because you know Him who has been from the beginning." Concerning ὅτι see comments on verse 12. The perfect tense ἐγνώκατε, *you have known*, indicates that these men had come to know in the past and, as a result, they still know the one who is from the beginning. Inasmuch as this usage seems to be intensive, placing stress on continuing results, the verb may be translated as a present, "you know." Concerning the experiential nature of knowledge in Hebrew usage see comments on 2:3. The fathers whom John addresses possess knowledge, not merely of facts, but of a Person. And it is not said that they merely know *about* Him, but that they know *Him*. John's assurance was particularly meaningful in the first century due to the presence of Gnostics who made loud claims to knowledge of God.

Τὸν ἀπ' ἀρχῆς, "Him who has been from the beginning," standing by itself, could refer to God the Father. However, its meaning in 1 John is clearly established by its use in 1:1, where it is obvious that the expression refers to Christ. These mature persons had not been taken in by the Christological error of the heretics. That these words refer to Christ is further confirmed by the reoccurrence of the phrase in verse 14. There it is preceded by the statement, ἐγνώκατε τὸν πατέρα, "you know the Father." It is doubtful that the apostle would engage in what Marshall calls "awkward repetition" by referring to the Father in two successive statements.[2]

γράφω ὑμῖν, νεανίσκοι, "I am writing to you, young men." See comments on verse 12. The young men are those who are younger in the faith as well as physically. Νεανίσκος commonly referred to a person between twenty-four and forty years of age. Women are not mentioned because of the subordinate place assigned them in biblical times.

ὅτι νενικήκατε τὸν πονηρόν, "because you have overcome the evil one." On ὅτι see comments on verse 12. The perfect tense verb describes these young men as victors. They have overcome in the past, and as a result they now are overcomers. This description aptly fits youth with its vigor and vision. The same verb appears in 5:4-5, where the believer is described as overcoming the world, and in Revelation 2-3, where seven promises to overcomers are given. Although some manuscripts (ℵ 209) have the neuter τό, the evidence strongly favors the masculine τὸν πονηρόν. These youths did not merely overcome the abstract principle of evil; they overcame Satan himself, the source and personification of all evil. In contrast to κακός, which speaks of the absence of goodness, πονηρός describes "the positive activity of evil,"[3] the desire to affect and to infect others with one's wickedness.

ἔγραψα ὑμῖν, παιδία, "I have written to you, children." The better manuscripts (ℵ A B C L P and many others) support the aorist ἔγραψα, *I wrote*, whereas the present γράφω, *I am writing*, is found in K and a few others. Several ingenious suggestions have been advanced as explanations of the change from the present tense γράφω in verses 12 and 13 to the aorist tense ἔγραψα in verse 14. Some have suggested that the present tense refers to the epistle and the aorist looks back to the gospel of John.[4] Others understand the present to refer to the epistle in process of composition and the aorist to that part of the letter already written.[5]

---

2. I. Howard Marshall, *The Epistles of John*, The New International Commentary on the New Testament, p. 139.
3. Richard C. Trench, *Synonyms of the New Testament*, pp. 303-4.
4. Alexander Ross, *The Epistles of James and John*, The New International Commentary on the New Testament, pp. 162-63.
5. A. E. Brooke, *The Johannine Epistles*, The International Critical Commentary, p. 41.

Even more imaginative is Law's theory that John was interrupted after writing the first triplet in which he used the present tense. When he resumed writing again he picked up the train of thought with the aorist tense ἔγραψα, *I wrote*.[6] It seems best, however, to interpret ἔγραψα as an epistolary aorist. This usage, which appears occasionally in Greek writers, looks at the writing from the viewpoint of the reader, whereas the present tense views it from the standpoint of the writer.[7] Inasmuch as the English language has no such idiom, it is best to translate it as a present tense ("I write") rather than a past. This avoids the kind of misunderstanding found in the unacceptable views mentioned above. The reason for repeating the triplet was to place particular emphasis on the author's confidence in the genuineness of his readers' salvation experience. And in order to avoid the monotony of mere repetition, John used the epistolary aorist in the second triplet instead of the present tense.

A further attempt at variety is seen in the employment of παιδία, which is synonymous with τεκνία (v. 12). Both words are to be interpreted as referring to the entire Christian community rather than to the younger believers only (cf. 2:18). Whereas τεκνία (from τίκτειν, "to bear") views the children as born into the family, παιδία depicts them as subordinate to the authority of their elders.[8] Like τεκνία, παιδία is a diminutive form used here in the sense of endearment.

ὅτι ἐγνώκατε τὸν πατέρα, "because you know the Father." On ὅτι see comments on verse 12. On ἐγνώκατε see on verse 13. In verse 12 John characterizes his little children as those who have been forgiven; in verse 13 he describes the same group as knowing the Father. That is, they know God, not merely as God, but as the Father who loves and cares for His own.

2:14. ἔγραψα ὑμῖν, πατέρες, ὅτι ἐγνώκατε τὸν ἀπ' ἀρχῆς, "I have written to you, fathers, because you know Him who has been from the beginning." See verse 13.

ἔγραψα ὑμῖν, νεανίσκοι, "I have written to you, young men." See verse 13.

ὅτι ἰσχυροί ἐστε, "because you are strong." On ὅτι see verse 12. Strength is a normal characteristic of the age (24-40

---

6. Robert Law, *The Tests of Life*, p. 309.
7. H. E. Dana and Julius R. Mantey, *A Manual Grammar of the Greek New Testament*, p. 198; C. F. D. Moule, *An Idiom Book of New Testament Greek*, p. 12.
8. B. F. Westcott, *The Epistles of John*, pp. 60-61; A. E. Brooke, p. 43.

years) represented by νεανίσκος. The word ἰσχυρός is built on a root that speaks of *ability* and *power*. It places stress on the actual power that one possesses rather than on the mere principle of power.[9] John addresses those who possess the strength and virility of youth. That it is spiritual vigor that he has in mind is indicated by the two further characteristics he sites.

καὶ ὁ λόγος τοῦ θεοῦ ἐν ὑμῖν μένει, "and the word of God abides in you." Λόγος here does not refer to a book, but to the message, the truth of God. See 1:8, 10 where ἀλήθεια, "truth," and λόγος, "word," seem to be used in a parallel sense, the difference being that the *word* is the communicated *truth*. Thus, these young men were strong because they possessed the truth that God had communicated to them. It was dwelling in them continually (μένει, present tense). John sees this indwelling as an abiding, intimate relationship rather than a temporary or spasmodic interest in the truth. Cf. on 2:6.

καὶ νενικήκατε τὸν πονηρόν, "and you have overcome the evil one." See comments on verse 13. The young men have overcome because they are strong, and in turn, they are strong because God's truth is indwelling them.

2. A WARNING CONCERNING LOVING THE WORLD, 2:15-17

2:15. μὴ ἀγαπᾶτε τὸν κόσμον μηδὲ τὰ ἐν τῷ κόσμῳ, "Do not love the world, nor the things in the world." Μή when used with the present imperative, as in μὴ ἀγαπᾶτε, forbids an action assumed to be already in progress.[10] John, therefore, is taking it for granted that his readers are loving the world to some extent, and he is urging them to put a stop to this evil practice. The word κόσμος, "world," has the basic idea of order or arrangement. It is the antithesis of chaos. It is used in several different senses in the New Testament: (1) the universe, the sum total of creation (John 17:24), (2) the earth, the inhabited world (Rom. 1:8), (3) the people, all who dwell on the earth (1 John 2:2), and (4) the evil world order controlled by Satan and set in opposition to God. It is this latter, ethical, sense that appears in the passage currently being considered. Westcott defines this usage of the term as refer-

---

9. Gerhard Kittel, ed., *Theological Dictionary of the New Testament*, 1964-76, s.v. "ἰσχύω, ἰσχυρός, κτλ.," by Walter Grundmann.
10. Dana and Mantey, pp. 301-2; F. Blass and A. Debrunner, *A Greek Grammar of the New Testament*, sec. 336 (3). Maximilian Zerwick, *Biblical Greek*, secs. 246-47.

ring to "the order of finite being regarded as apart from God."[11] Law calls it "the social organism of evil."[12] The term involves all that goes into making up the organized system of evil on this earth. It includes such elements as all unregenerate men, their thoughts, attitudes, purposes, and desires; all influences and forces that are opposed to God; and the patterns of evil practice that characterize life apart from God. Findlay has well said, " 'The world' is not made up of so many outward objects that can be specified; it is the sum of those influences emanating from man and things around us which draw us away from god."[13] It is, basically, the expression of unregenerate humanity. Westcott explains that "Man fallen impresses his character upon the order which is the sphere of his activity, and thus the 'world' comes to represent humanity in its present state, alienated from its Maker, and so far determining the character of the whole order to which man belongs."[14]

Dodd identifies the world as "simply the pagan society in which he (the writer) and his readers necessarily moved." He further speaks of the temptation "to conform as far as possible to the practices and customs of pagan neighbors."[15]

It is noteworthy that John chose to use ἀγαπάω rather than φιλέω to describe love for the world. That the latter would not be out of place is evident from the use of φιλία, "friendship," in James 4:4. Love may be viewed as warm-hearted affection (φιλία), or it may be thought of as an intelligent, purposeful attitude of esteem and devotion (ἀγάπη). Bultmann says that John used ἀγαπάω here in its usual Greek sense of "to take a fancy to, to place a higher value on, as in Jn. 3:19; 12:43; II Tim. 4:10." He is calling for an intelligent evaluation of the world and a purposeful determination *not* to esteem this evil system as a thing of value.[16]

"The things in the world" (τὰ ἐν τῷ κόσμῳ) are not primarily material items, although these may be involved. As the next verse explains, John has in mind men's attitudes—including attitudes toward material things—rather than the material objects themselves.

11. Westcott, p. 63.
12. Law, p. 148.
13. George G. Findlay, *Fellowship in the Life Eternal*, p. 199.
14. B. F. Westcott, *The Gospel According to St. John*, 1:64-65.
15. C. H. Dodd, *The Johannine Epistles*, The Moffatt New Testament Commentary, p. 41.
16. Rudolf Bultmann, *The Johannine Epistles*, Hermeneia, p. 33, n. 19.

ἐάν τις ἀγαπᾷ τὸν κόσμον, "If any one loves the world." The present tense, ἀγαπᾷ, supposes a continuing practice of esteeming the world to be of supreme value. This is a hypothetical case John sets up in support of the prohibition with which verse 15 opens.

οὐκ ἔστιν ἡ ἀγάπη τοῦ πατρὸς ἐν αὐτῷ, "the love of the Father is not in him." There are three possible interpretations of ἡ ἀγάπη τοῦ πατρός: it may refer to love that comes from the Father (ablative of source), it may refer to the Father's love for the person involved (subjective genitive), or it may speak of the person's love for the Father (objective genitive). The preceding context speaks of love for the world and is no doubt parallel to the expression ἡ ἀγάπη τοῦ πατρός. Consequently, it seems best to understand the construction as an objective genitive. Love for the Father "is not in him" (οὐκ ἔστιν . . . ἐν αὐτῷ). This is more than to say that he does not love the Father (οὐκ ἀγαπᾷ τὸν πατέρα). Instead John denies that love for God is in him as a continuing principle and emphasizes this further by placing οὐκ ἔστιν, "is not," first in the clause.

2:16. ὅτι πᾶν τὸ ἐν τῷ κόσμῳ, "For all that is in the world." The conjunction ὅτι indicates that the following clause explains the reason for the preceding statement. John now explains why love for the world excludes love for God. Πᾶν and οὐκ (v. 16*b*) combined produce a universal negative—"nothing that is in the world" is from God.[17] The following three phrases, ἡ ἐπιθυμία τῆς σαρκός, "the lust of the flesh," etc., being in apposition to πᾶν τὸ ἐν τῷ κόσμῳ, "all that is in the world," are elucidations of what is meant by the latter phrase—not material things, but rather attitudes.

ἡ ἐπιθυμία τῆς σαρκός, "the lust of the flesh." Ἐπιθυμία, "lust," is a common New Testament word, appearing almost always with an evil connotation, although on occasion it is used of proper desires (Luke 22:15; 1 Thess. 2:17). In secular Greek from the time of Plato the term came to have a distinctive sense, especially among the Stoics. The latter listed it along with ἡδονή, φόβος, and λύπη as one of the four chief passions that are the result of "a wrong attitude to possessions." In the New Testament ἐπιθυμία is *desire as impulse* carrying the sense of urgency; it is *anxious self-seeking*; and it is lust in that "the thought

---

17. A. T. Robertson, *A Grammar of the Greek New Testament in the Light of Historical Research*, pp. 752-53; Blass and Debrunner, sec. 302 (1); Moule, p. 182.

of satisfaction gives pleasure and that of non-satisfaction pain."[18] Thus, John has in mind the passionate desire of the flesh for immediate self-satisfaction.

The genitive τῆς σαρκός, "of the flesh," is clearly a subjective genitive. It is not desire *for* the flesh; instead it is the desire that springs *from* the flesh. Σάρξ appears in numerous passages of the New Testament and with numerous connotations. Some of its usages are to refer to the material that covers the bones of the body, to refer to a human being, and to refer to human nature. In addition, John and especially Paul use σάρξ to describe the corrupt, sinful tendency resident in man's nature. In opposition to this the Gnostic and others in John's day held that the literal flesh was itself evil. The flesh of the material body may be an instrument of sin, but it is not in itself sinful. Paul points up the dignity of the body in 1 Corinthians 6 when he declares that the believer's body is for the Lord (v. 13), it will be raised up in the resurrection (v. 14), it is a member of Christ (v. 15), and it is a temple of the Holy Spirit (v. 19). The body and its flesh are amoral, being susceptible to both sinful and holy use. In 1 John 2:16, the lust of the flesh speaks of the lower aspect of sinful human nature and in at least one passage of the Dead Sea Scrolls the term flesh is used in this ethical sense. The *Manual of Discipline* says "if I stumble because of the sin of the flesh, my justification is in the righteousness of God which exists for ever."[19]

καὶ ἡ ἐπιθυμία τῶν ὀφθαλμῶν, "and the lust of the eyes." As compared with the lust of the flesh, this expression refers to the higher aspect of sinful human nature. Ὀφθαλμῶν, "eyes," is to be taken literally as referring to the organs of sight, but also to the craving of the corrupt human nature for things that the eyes see, whether good or bad. There are two possibilities of interpretation here. He may refer to the desire to appropriate the things seen. In that case, the lust of the eyes may well overlap the lust of the flesh. Or he may be speaking of the desire that is satisfied by simply "feasting" the eyes upon the object in view. The latter interpretation seems to be preferable.

καὶ ἡ ἀλαζονεία τοῦ βίου, "and the boastful pride of life." Ἀλαζονεία, *proud pretension*, is a pregnant term containing the ideas both of pride and pretension. It is closely related to ἀλαζών, "braggart," a person who extols his own virtues or

---

18. Kittel, s.v. "ἐπιθυμία, ἐπιθυμέω, " by Friedrich Büchsel.
19. A. Dupont-Sommer, *The Essene Writings from Qumran*, I QS 11:12.

accomplishments beyond the limits of truth and propriety.[20] Thus, ἀλαζονεία is the proud and boastful pretension to be more than one really is. An additional aspect of the term is observed in James 4:16 where the context speaks of an arrogance that assumes one's independence of God. It is the proud assumption that our destinies are determined solely by ourselves rather than by divine sovereignty.

When the New Testament speaks of spiritual or eternal life, it employs ζωή, which refers to life in itself as a vital principle. Βίος is used to depict life in one of the following aspects: (1) the duration of life (1 Pet. 4:3), (2) the manner of life—life-style (2 Tim. 2:4), or (3) the means of life.[21] Examples of this last usage occur in the gospels. In Mark 12:44 the widow is described as putting "her whole *living*" (RSV) into the treasury. In Luke 15:12 the father "divided unto them his *living*" (KJV). Usage (1) above clearly does not fit this passage. Tracing John's argument, he first condemns the desire for immediate self-satisfaction ("lust of the flesh"), then the desire for a more passive, visual satisfaction ("lust of the eyes"), and finally either a boasting life-style or a boasting about wealth and possessions ("pride of life"). The logical progression would go from *desire for* through to actual *possession of* wealth—not merely to a boasting life-style. Therefore John probably had the third usage—means of life—in mind when he used βιος. Further support is lent to this since the apostle clearly uses the word this way in 1 John 3:17. So the proud pretension here spoken of has to do with material possessions. It is the spirit boastfully confident in material things rather than in God that assumes that life consists of worldly possessions (cf. Dan. 4:30; Luke 12:16-21). John bluntly points out the fallacy of such an attitude in verse 17*a*.

οὐκ ἔστιν ἐκ τοῦ πατρὸς ἀλλ᾽ ἐκ τοῦ κόσμου ἐστίν, "is not from the Father, but is from the world." The KJV translations, "of the Father" and "of the world," are too vague. John's preposition ἐκ with the ablative case obviously has reference to source. The attitudes described do not come from God; instead (ἀλλά, "but," the stronger Greek adversative conjunction) they come from the evil world system that Satan has set in opposition to God.

---

20. For a graphic description of the ἀλαζών, see Dodd's quotation of the Greek philosopher Theophrastus (c. 371-287 B.C.), Dodd, p. 42.
21. Colin Brown, ed., *The New International Dictionary of New Testament Theology*, s.v. "Life," by Hans-George Link; Trench, pp. 88-89; William F. Arndt and F. Wilbur Gingrich, trans. and eds., *A Greek-English Lexicon of the New Testament*, p. 141.

2:17. καὶ ὁ κόσμος παράγεται καὶ ἡ ἐπιθυμία αὐτοῦ, "and the world is passing away, and also its lusts." On κόσμος, "world," see comments on verse 15. On ἐπιθυμία, "lust," see on verse 16. It is noteworthy that the tense of παράγεται, "is passing away," is present, suggesting that the process of dissolution is even now going on. It is not a judgment limited to a future cataclysmic destruction. The voice of the verb, being middle, stresses the part the subject plays in the action of passing away (cf. on 2:8).[22] By its very nature evil is self-destructive, and bears within itself the seeds of its own deterioration; its attitudes and practices are the very devices by which it is being destroyed.

ὁ δὲ ποιῶν τὸ θέλημα τοῦ θεοῦ μένει εἰς τὸν αἰῶνα, "but the one who does the will of God abides forever." John sets God's will in contrast to the lust and proud pretension of the world. Ποιῶν, *doing*, is present tense describing the continuing practice of God's will. Obedience to God is the persistent characteristic of the one who possesses saving knowledge of Christ (cf. 2:3-6). Μένω speaks of permanency, whether of dwelling, or continuing in a given state, or of persistence in life itself. Inasmuch as John places μένει in contrast to παράγεται, "is passing away," it is clear that here he has in mind the permanancy of continuing existence. Whereas the evil world order is passing away, God's child will live forever (εἰς τὸν αἰῶνα, "forever"). On αἰώνιον, *eternal*, see on 1:2. By a threefold combination the author stresses the permanency of the one who obeys God. The futuristic use of the present tense denotes continuation into future time; the verb μένω in itself speaks of continued existence; and the phrase εἰς τὸν αἰῶνα indicates the unending character of that existence.

THEOLOGICAL COMMENTARY (2:12-17)

A. AN ASSUMPTION CONCERNING THE READERS, 2:12-14

1. THE STRUCTURE OF 2:12-14

This section is unique in the epistle because of its carefully structured repetitive nature. It contains six statements in which

---

22. G. Abbott-Smith, *A Manual Greek Lexicon of the New Testament*, p. 338, identifies the verb as a middle; Kittel, s.v. "ἀγωγή, παράγω, κτλ.", by Karl Ludwig Schmidt, calls it either middle or passive; A. Plummer, *The Epistles of St. John*, Cambridge Greek Testament for Schools and Colleges, p. 53 says that the verb is middle rather than passive in both 2:8 and 2:17; and Dodd, pp. 45-46, speaks of "the self-destructiveness of our present civilization."

the main verb of the main clause is one of two forms of γράφω, "I write." The present tense occurs in the first three statements, and the epistolary aorist occurs in the second three statements. It seems apparent that John, by repetition, was emphasizing the truth set forth in these six statements. It also appears that in the last three statements he switches to the aorist tense to avoid excessive monotony in his repetition.

Another aspect of structure in these verses is the three groups—children, fathers, and young men—who are addressed twice. Again the repetition must be for the sake of emphasis. This is most plainly to be seen in the repeated assertions that the fathers "know Him who has been from the beginning" and that the young men "have overcome the evil one." The three groups addressed may represent the three periods of life—infancy, youth, and adulthood. However, in the Exegetical Commentary reasons were given for understanding the terms as follows:

> Children—all of John's addressees
> Fathers—older believers
> Young men—younger believers

We may conclude that John adopts this unique structure to assure his readers forcibly that he does not doubt the reality of their Christian experience. This interpretation is confirmed by Dodd's explanation that John is here pointing out "the characteristic notes of the new age," namely, the forgiveness of sins, the knowledge of God, and victory over the powers of evil. These truths, he says, echo "the central tradition of the Gospel."[23]

2. FORGIVENESS FOR HIS NAME'S SAKE

Forensic forgiveness. In a previous section distinction was made between forensic and filial forgiveness. The latter is seen in 1:9 where forgiveness removes all obstacles to intimate communion between the child of God and his heavenly Father. This aspect of forgiveness does not have to do with the guilt of sin but merely with disturbed fellowship. Forensic forgiveness, on the other hand, is a once-for-all occurrence canceling the guilt of a person's sins—past, present, and future. It takes place when a person first exercises faith in Christ as Savior, always being coupled with the

---

23. Dodd, pp. 36-37.

imputation of the righteousness of Christ. Forensic forgiveness and imputation respectively comprise the negative and positive aspects of justification.

When John says, "I am writing to you, little children, because your sins are forgiven you . . ." (2:12), he is speaking of the once-for-all, forensic forgiveness of justification. It is another way of saying, "I am writing to you because you are saved." And it is to these people, for whom all the guilt of sin has been completely and finally forgiven in the past, that John writes 1 John 1:9. There he speaks of repeated acts of confession and the resultant experiences of filial forgiveness.

The basis for forgiveness. According to 2:12 the forgiveness of believers' sins is "for His name's sake." It may be taken for granted that the name referred to is the name of Christ. Somewhat similar is our Lord's instruction to pray in His name (John 14:13-14; 15:16; 16:23-24, 26). Both prepositional phrases speak of the reception of benefit on the basis of the merit of someone else. In the case of prayer in Christ's name, the petitioner makes his request, not in his own name and on his own merit, but in the name and on the merit of Christ. He asks for things for which only Christ has the right to ask; and he receives the things he asks for just as though Christ Himself had made the request.

In this manner also the forgiveness of believers rests on Christ's merit and His atoning work, not on anything they may do or be in themselves. Forgiveness of sins is received on the basis of what He is and what He did on Calvary; it is not an arbitrary act on God's part; it is an action performed in just response to the merit of Christ's person and atoning work—granted because of His name.

3. THE NATURE OF SAVING KNOWLEDGE

Three times in this section John declares that his readers possess knowledge of the Father or the Son (vv. 13-14). No doubt this stress on spiritual knowledge was evoked by the incipient Gnosticism confronting John's readers at the close of the first century. To counteract these false claims of knowledge, the apostle assures his readers that they possess knowledge of the true God and of His Son.

However, the knowledge of the children of God is far different from the professed knowledge of the Gnostic. The latter was theoretical. It was, as Grant has pointed out, "essentially self knowledge."[24] Only as a man came to know himself—his origin, his present condition of imprisonment in the flesh, and his destiny—could he be saved, according to the Gnostic. This is a far cry from the saving knowledge of which the New Testament speaks. Jesus declared, "And this is eternal life, that they may know Thee, the only true God, and Jesus Christ whom Thou hast sent" (John 17:3). Such knowledge is not merely factual; it is personal. The Christian knows God and Jesus Christ in an I-Thou relationship. This is the kind of knowledge of which John speaks in 1 John 2:13-14 where he declares that his readers know both the Father and the One who has been from the beginning.

Furthermore, the Judaeo-Christian concept of knowledge is experiential. The Hebrew word יָדַע characteristically spoke of knowledge that was empirical and experiential, and it affected one's life. The experiential nature of knowledge is seen in the use of the term יָדַע to refer to sexual relations or to describe a personal relationship such as knowing someone "face to face."[25] Christian knowledge is this type of knowledge that grows out of personal experience, and it in turn influences one's life. The Christian knows because the truth has been actualized in his life and is not mere theory. In addition, such knowledge becomes so genuinely the possession of its recipient that it acts as a life-changing force. This is why John can insist, as he does in 2:3-4, that to know the Lord is to obey Him. The speculative knowledge of the Gnostic did not possess such life-changing power. Thus, while he loudly claimed lofty spiritual knowledge, he continued to walk in the darkness of sin. God's people today need to beware of such self-deception. They must make sure that their knowledge is personal and experiential rather than merely factual, theoretical, or speculative.

4. THE CONCEPT OF VICTORY

It is common to conceive of the victorious life as the ideal toward which every Christian should strive. The result is the repeated exhortation to be an overcomer. And within limits this concept is biblical.

However, John holds to a fuller concept of victory. He speaks of it as an already accomplished fact rather than an ideal. He wrote

---

24. Robert M. Grant, *Gnosticism and Early Christianity*, p. 10.
25. Gerhard Kittel, s.v. "γινώσκω," by E. D. Schmitz. 2:395

to the young men among his readers because they *had* overcome the wicked one (2:13-14). The tense used in both verses is the perfect, viewing the action as an already accomplished fact with existing results at the time of writing.

This same concept of victory is found in 4:4, "You are from God, little children, and have overcome them; because greater is He who is in you than he who is in the world." In this context the ones whom John's readers have overcome are the false prophets mentioned in 4:1, along with the errors they propagated.

The definitive statement of John's doctrine of victory is found in 5:4-5, where he categorically declares: "For whatever is born of God overcomes the world; and this is the victory that has overcome the world—our faith. And who is the one who overcomes the world, but he who believes that Jesus is the Son of God?" The child of God is not *exhorted* to be victorious; he is *declared* to be victorious by virtue of his faith in Christ as God's Son. The initial victory over the world comes when a person first trusts Christ as Savior (v. 4), but this is only the beginning of conquest for there is continuing victory in continuing faith (v. 5).

Walter T. Conner explains:

> The initial victory constitutes the guarantee of continuous victory. The faith that linked the Christian initially to God in Christ has all the potentialities of victory over the world that will be needed during the course of warfare here on earth. There is not, however, anything in that initial act of faith that constitutes any kind of mechanical guarantee of further and continuous victory over the world. Such continuous victory must be won, day by day, by faith in God and striving against evil.[26]

Thus, the victory John speaks of as an already accomplished fact is the initial victory that accompanies regeneration. It is a victory over Satan (2:13-14), falsehood and error (4:4), and the system of evil the New Testament designates by the term *world* (5:4-5). When a person trusts Christ as Savior, this act constitutes defeat of all the forces that are set to keep him bound in blindness and sin.

The continuing aspect of victory to which Conner refers is sometimes described today as the victorious life. Exhortations to this kind of living are both biblical and necessary. Although it is certain that John is speaking of initial victory in 2:13-14, there is good reason to believe that he also has the continuing aspect of victory in mind. The statements, "You are strong," and "The word of God abides in you," appear to be explanations of the source of their victory. God's word and their own spiritual strength as regenerated men enabled them to overcome the devil. Such remarks would seem to depict the continuing battles and victories of the Christian life rather than the initial victory of faith.

B. A WARNING CONCERNING LOVING THE WORLD, 2:15-17

1. THE CONTENT OF THE SECOND DIGRESSION

This second parenthetical section is made up of a prohibition followed by two reasons for complying with it. Assuming that his readers are to some extent caught in the web of the world's appeal, John urges them to change their attitude toward it, to stop loving (μή with the present imperative) this evil system. The first reason for such a change is found in the antagonism that, by the very nature of the situation, exists between God and the world (vv. 15b-16). They are set in diametric opposition to each other. This is seen in John's insistence that (1) the love of the world and the love of God are mutually exclusive (v. 15b) and (2) no part of the evil world system comes from God (v. 16).

The second reason for responding to John's injunction is that the world is destined for dissolution (v. 17). Even now deterioration is in process, and the day is fast coming when the world will cease to be. For these reasons it is both inconsistent and foolish for the believer to give his love to it.

2. THE ORGANIZATION OF THE COSMOS

The basic idea of the term κόσμος, "world," is that of order, of separate parts that have been arranged in a neat, pleasing, appropriate, or logical fashion. The world, therefore, can describe the orderly arrangement of the universe. It also came to be used in the restricted sense of the earth, then of the inhabited earth, and then of humanity. Inasmuch as man and his activities are basically evil and stand under God's condemnation, κόσμος came to refer to "the sum of the divine creation which has been shattered by the fall."[27] It includes such intangible but real elements as evil mo-

---

26. Walter T. Conner, *The Epistles of John*, p. 117.
27. Kittel, s.v. *κοσμέω, κόσμος, κτλ.*, by Hermann Sasse. 3:868-80.

tives, plans, influences, patterns of thought and activity, and the very spirit of wickedness.

In this derived meaning, however, the basic idea of order is not lost. It is still cosmos rather than chaos. In surface appearance the evil world may seem to be nothing but massive confusion. Men's aims and desires appear constantly to be in conflict with one another. But upon more careful examination, one discovers that the seeming disorder is in reality *organized* confusion. There is a method in the world's madness. Behind it all, the New Testament informs us, stands the evil mastermind who has planned and organized the whole system of evil to serve his own purpose.

Jesus in John 12:31 (KJV) calls the devil "the prince of this world," and in Matthew 12:24-26 He speaks of Satan's kingdom. In Ephesians 2:2 Paul relates "the course [ways, spirit] of this world" to "the prince of the power of the air, of the spirit that is now working in the sons of disobedience." This relationship is again seen in Ephesians 6:11-12. In verse 11 Paul urges preparedness for standing against "the schemes of the devil." Further explanation is then given in verse 12 where our battle is said to be against the rulers (ἀρχάς), the authorities (ἐξουσίας), the world-rulers (κοσμοκράτορας) of this darkness, and the spirit-forces (πνευματικά) of evil in the heavenlies. The terms ἀρχάς, ἐξουσίας, and κοσμοκράτορας all speak of organized authority and rulership, and the word κοσμοκράτορας in particular suggests that the κόσμος is under the sway of this organized authority.

Close scrutiny reveals a unity of plan and a concentration of purpose in all of the evil that characterizes this world. As in guerrilla warfare, there are no orderly companies of combatants marching into the fight, no clearly drawn lines of battle, no orthodox methods of military procedure. Yet no one denies that even in guerrilla warfare there is organization, pattern, and unity of purpose. This evil world is a carefully masterminded structure of opposition to God and righteousness with an overall program and pattern. The apparent chaos is in reality cosmos.

3. THE ANTAGONISM BETWEEN GOD AND THE WORLD

In 2:15-17, antagonism between God and the world is suggested by two statements. First, love of the world and love of the Father are said to be mutually exclusive (v. 15*b*), and second, the sinful desires and attitudes present in the world do not find their source in God but in the world (v. 16). This antagonism is more clearly evident in such passages as John 15:18-19; 17:16; 1 John 4:5-6; James 4:4.

The world is set in diametric opposition to God because this is the fundamental trait of its organizer, the devil. In his age-long warfare the world is a major instrument that Satan constantly employs in his attempt to thwart and disrupt the purposes of God. By it he strengthens his hold on lost humanity, and its allurements become a snare even to the people of God. It is an ever-increasing arsenal of ammunition and weapons designed for attack against the forces of righteousness.

When seen in this light the truth of John's statements becomes obvious. To love the world is to love the enemy of God. Thus, it is totally unreasonable to love God and the world at the same time (2:15b). So clear-cut are the lines of difference, so bitter is the antagonism that John can assert that he who loves the enemy of God, the world, cannot love God. James makes a similar declaration: "Friendship with the world is hostility toward God" (4:4). And Jesus said, "No one can serve two masters; for either he will hate the one and love the other, or he will hold to one and despise the other. You cannot serve God and Mammon" (Matt. 6:24).

Such statements paint the picture in sharpest contrast. No allowance is made for any middle ground. There is no continuum stretching from one extreme to the other. This style of writing is characteristic of John, the son of thunder. However, although he uses sharp contrast to add force to his statements, he seems to be aware that there are degrees of love and hatred. The greater the love for the world, the less for God, and vice versa. That John recognized this fact is seen in that he commands *believers* to stop loving the world (2:15a, μή with the present imperative). He assumes these genuine children of God had been loving the world. Being children of God they, of necessity, must also have loved God. Nevertheless, in verse 15b, John speaks of love for God as supreme devotion that excludes all antagonistic loyalties. This is the ideal, and when one sees the world in its total antagonism to God, as John did, the issue stands out in sharpest definition. Either one loves God supremely and hates the world, or one does not love God at all.

4. THE FUTURISTIC DIMENSION IN VERSE 17

In the Exegetical Commentary on this verse, it has been shown that the disintegration of the world and its lust is now in progress

(Greek present tense). This, however, is only part of the picture, for John's statement not only speaks of a present process, it also implies a future consummation. Because things now are in the process of passing away, they will someday cease to be. Such an implication is suggested by the statement "the one who does the will of God abides forever" (v. 17).

John looks beyond the present to the day of Christ's coming, to the destruction of the evil world system, to the establishment of the eternal kingdom of righteousness, and to the banishment of Satan to the eternal lake of fire. The full and final accomplishment of this process will come with the last judgment (Rev. 20:11-15) and the appearance of the new heaven and earth (Rev. 21:1). Then, the world that seems to be so desirable today will no longer compete for the affection of God's people. Even today, however, the very fact of its transitory nature should cancel its appeal.

5. THE GNOSTICS AND THE WORLD

It is quite possible that, even in this parenthetical section of warning against the world, John had in mind the teaching and practice of the same false teachers combatted elsewhere in the epistle. Dodd points out that the kind of teaching John opposed "made for compromise."[28] By its very nature Gnosticism was syncretistic and inclusivist, seeking to make Christianity acceptable to the world of the day by adjusting it to fit current dualism (the matter-is-evil, spirit-is-good philosophy). With regard to morality, it tried to make a place within the Christian system for unbridled libertinism.

In our day Christians still need to beware of the temptation to accommodate their faith to current viewpoints and practices. We must not be taken in by the temptation to adjust biblical teaching to fit the value systems of the present world; to rationalize a materialistic lifestyle; to adjust moral standards subtly so they are not as radically out of step with the times; to revamp our statement of theology so it will be more widely accepted; to employ methods of biblical critics in order to make conservative scholarship more respected in scholarly circles. These are today's subtle temptations to worldliness that parallel the worldliness of their Gnostic forerunners in John's day.

Such viewpoints are not from God, but from that evil system

28. Dodd, p. 43.

that both John and Paul designate the *world*. For the Gnostic the evil world was the world of matter; for John it was the organized system of evil controled by Satan and set in opposition to God—a system that is just as operative today as it was in John's day.

PARAPHRASTIC COMMENTARY (2:12-17)

(12) In writing this letter to you, dear children, I am not suggesting that you are in spiritual darkness. On the contrary, I am sure that all of you have experienced the forgiveness of your sins on the basis of Christ's person and work. (13) As for those of you who are older, I am addressing you with the confidence that you are personally acquainted with the one who has existed since eternity past, namely Jesus Christ. Those of you who are younger I am addressing with the knowledge that you have conquered the devil and as a result are now overcomers. (14) In order to leave no doubt, let me repeat. My children, when you read this I want all of you to know that I have written to you with the assurance that you know God the Father experientially. As I have said, you who are older must realize that I have written to you as those who personally know Him, God's Son, who has existed from eternity past. And you younger Christians, be assured that I have sent this letter to you knowing that you possess spiritual power, that God's truth is resident in your hearts, and that you are victorious over Satan.

(15) Stop setting your esteem and devotion on the godless world order and all that it includes. It is not possible for a person to be supremely devoted both to the godless world and to God. (16) This is true because everything that is involved in this evil world system—such things as the inordinate longing to satisfy the lower nature, the overpowering desire to feast the eyes upon that which is not pleasing to God, and the boastful confidence in material possessions—does not find its source in God, but in the evil world itself. (17) This wicked world with all of its evil desires is already on the way to total disintegration, but the person who makes it his practice to obey God will live eternally.

STRUCTURAL COMMENTARY (2:12-17)[29]

B. Two digressions, 2:12-17
   1. An assumption concerning the readers, 2:12-14
      a. First series of assurances, 2:12-13*b*
         (1) Address to all readers: their sins are forgiven, 2:12

---

29. For previous section of the outline, see pp. 168-70.

(2) Address to older readers: they know Christ, 2:13*a*
(3) Address to younger readers: they have conquered Satan, 2:13*b*
   b. Second series of assurances, 2:14
      (1) Address to all readers: they know the Father, 2:14*a*
      (2) Address to older readers: they know Christ, 2:14*b*
      (3) Address to younger readers: 2:14*c*
         (a) They are strong
         (b) They are indwelt by God's word
         (c) They have conquered Satan
2. A warning concerning loving the world, 2:15-17
   a. Command to stop loving the world, 2:15*a*
   b. Reasons for obeying the command, 2:15*b*-17
      (1) Antagonism between the world and God, 2:15*b*-16
         (a) Love for the world excludes love for God, 2:15*b*
         (b) Worldly attitudes do not find their source in God, 2:16
      (2) Transitory character of the world, 2:17

9

C. Fellowship Tested on Christological Grounds, 2:18-28

In 1:5—2:11 John has set forth the ethical test of a person's salvation experience. Now in 2:18-28, continuing to view salvation as fellowship with God, he advances the doctrinal test. The one who enjoys this saving relationship of fellowship is the one who believes that Jesus is the Christ, the Son of God. In sharp contrast, the false teachers denied this truth and thereby revealed that they had no personal relationship with God.

Inasmuch as the term *fellowship* does not occur in this section, it is reasonable to ask if John is still dealing with that subject. Careful study of the passage shows that although the word does not appear, the concept of fellowship is most certainly present. The Christian life is viewed as the experience of continuing in the Son and in the Father (2:24, 27-28). In each instance the verb employed is μένω, "to abide, to remain, to dwell." To dwell in the Father and in the Son is the most intimate kind of fellowship, and this fellowship is to be equated with eternal life (2:25).

Saving fellowship with God is closely related to belief of the truth concerning the incarnation. In fact, it is the one who holds meaningfully to that truth who dwells in the Father and Son (v. 24). This is another way of saying that one must believe in Christ as the incarnate Son of God in order to be saved.

In setting forth the Christological test John discusses the contrast between the heretics and the believers (2:18-21), the Christo-

Fellowship Tested on Christological Grounds

logical test itself (2:22-23), and the key to continuing fellowship (2:24-28).

EXEGETICAL COMMENTARY (2:18-28)

1. A CONTRAST BETWEEN HERETICS AND BELIEVERS, 2:18-21

2:18. παιδία, ἐσχάτη ὥρα ἐστίν, "children, it is the last hour." John here refers to his readers as παιδία, addressing them endearingly as subordinate to and dependent upon himself. The term suggests that the readers are such that they need the counsel and warning the apostle is about to give. The author is justified in so addressing them in view of his advanced age and long experience as an apostle with the authority implicit in that office.

The absence of the article in the expression ἐσχάτη ὥρα has been taken by some to refer to the general character of the time.[1] John would be saying that it is an eschatological kind of period, a time of crisis, a last-hour kind of time, rather than pointing to a specific period as *the* last hour. The absence of the article, however, allows for definiteness rather than quality if the expression has become technical or stereotyped.[2] It is also possible that the context may indicate that an anarthrous noun is definite. Both of these latter two conditions are true of ἐσχάτη ὥρα. The common occurrence of the parallel expressions ἐσχάταις ἡμέραις, "last days" (Acts 2:17; 2 Tim. 3:1; cf. Heb. 1:2; 2 Pet. 3:3) and ἐσχάτου τῶν χρόνων, "last times" (1 Pet. 1:20; cf. Jude 18) is ample justification for the omission of the article even though the expression is definite. Furthermore, in the context immediately preceding this verse, John refers to the eschatological fact that the world is passing away but God's people will remain forever. In addition, his reference to the coming antichrist in 2:18 points to a specific eschatological time. In spite of the absence of the article, therefore, there is good reason to believe the apostle has used ἐσχάτη ὥρα to refer to a specific time period rather than to the general character of the period.

καὶ καθὼς ἠκούσατε ὅτι ἀντίχριστος ἔρχεται, "and just as you heard that antichrist is coming." καθώς means "just as" in contrast to ὡς, which simply means "as." The fact of the coming

---
1. B. F. Westcott, *The Epistles of John*, p. 69.
2. H. E. Dana and Julius R. Mantey, *A Manual Grammar of the Greek New Testament*, p. 149.

antichrist finds a distinct parallel in the existence of many current antichrists. The only occurrences of the term ἀντίχριστος in Scripture are found in the Johannine epistles (1 John 2:18, 22; 4:3; 2 John 7). These are apparently the first uses of the word in literature.[3] The preposition ἀντί may mean "against" or "instead of." In the majority of its usages in compound words the meaning is "against." In some instances it refers to substitution (ἀνθύπατος, "proconsul"—one who serves in place of the consul; ἀντιβασιλεύς, "viceroy"). Rarely, a compound of ἀντί may be capable of meaning either "against" or "instead of." For instance, ἀντιστράτηγος may refer to an opposing general or to a propraetor (one who acts in place of the praetor), but it cannot indicate both at the same time. It is possible in some cases that, due to the meaning of the compound word, the preposition may seem to carry both meanings. A substitute Christ is, in the very nature of the case, an opposition Christ. That ἀντίχριστος may refer to a counterfeit Messiah may be suggested by such passages as Matthew 24:5; 2 Thessalonians 2:4; and Revelation 13:15.

The present tense ἔρχεται is no doubt a futuristic present, which assumes the future coming of antichrist to be as certain as a present reality.

καὶ νῦν ἀντίχριστοι πολλοὶ γεγόνασιν ὅθεν γινώσκομεν ὅτι ἐσχάτη ὥρα ἐστίν, "even now many antichrists have arisen; from this we know that it is the last hour." The perfect tense verb γεγόνασιν means that many antichrists have come and continue to exert their influence in the world and even on the church. The reference here is not to the future antichrist but to the numerous Gnostic teachers who were threatening the Asian Christians with their error. It was the presence of these vendors of error that assured John (γινώσκομεν, "we know") that it was the last hour.

2:19. ἐξ ἡμῶν ἐξῆλθαν, ἀλλ' οὐκ ἦσαν ἐξ ἡμῶν, "They went out from us, but they were not really of us." John employs a striking play on words and phrases in the contrast between the first ἐξ ἡμῶν and the second ἐξ ἡμῶν. The preposition ἐκ (ἐξ) is used in two different senses in this statement. The first occurrence is locational. The false teachers were once present within the local fellowship of believers, but they

---

3. Gerhard Kittel, ed., *Theological Dictionary of the New Testament*, s.v. "χρίω χριστός, ἀντίχριστος," by Walter Grundmann; C. H. Dodd, "*The Johannine Epistles,*" The Moffatt New Testament Commentary, p. 48.

Fellowship Tested on Christological Grounds 195

"went out from" that fellowship (ἐξῆλθαν, aorist indicative). The active voice verb shows that they left of their own accord. The second occurrence of ἐκ is descriptive of character. It speaks of source. Bultmann points out that it is characteristic of John to describe the nature of a thing by indicating its origin.[4] For example, to say that "no lie is of the truth" (1 John 2:21) is to indicate that a lie, by its very nature, has nothing in common with truth. (See also 3:8-10; 4:1-3.) Thus, in 2:19 ἐξ ἡμῶν means that they did not come "from us," they did not share the same spiritual life, they were not essentially of the same kind. The heretics and the believers had nothing in common. The strong conjunction, ἀγγά (ἀλλ), "but," emphasizes the fact that, although these teachers were once outwardly in the fellowship of the church, they were not really believers.

εἰ γὰρ ἐξ ἡμῶν ἦσαν μεμενήκεισαν ἂν μεθ' ἡμῶν, "for if they had been of us, they would have remained with us." The words "no doubt" in the KJV have no parallel in the Greek text and probably arise from an attempt to translate the untranslatable particle ἄν. Here ἐκ is linked with the preposition μετά (μεθ'), "with." Whereas the ἐκ speaks of identity of origin, μετά speaks of the mutual relationship of persons in the outward fellowship of the church. Marshall points to the pluperfect μεμενήκεισαν, "they would have remained," as indicating that the persons involved would have remained until the time of John's writing.[5] This contrary-to-fact statement is built upon the principle that genuine believers persevere in the faith and in their association with other believers. Thus John establishes another test of spiritual genuineness. In the words of Bruce, "Continuance is the test of reality."[6] Those who willfully turn from the truth show that a work of grace has never been begun within them. Those who persevere do so because God has regenerated them and continues to work within them.

ἀλλ ἵνα φανερωθῶσιν ὅτι οὐκ εἰσὶν πάντες ἐξ ἡμῶν, "but *they went out,* in order that it might be shown that they all are not of us." The words, *they went out,* are italicized to indicate that they have been supplied by the NASB in order to complete the meaning. Such ellipsis is not uncommon in John's

---

4. Rudolf Bultmann, *The Johannine Epistles*, Hermeneia, p. 36, n. 6.
5. I. Howard Marshall, *The Epistles of John*, The New International Commentary on the New Testament, p. 152, n. 3. See also Robert Law, *The Tests of Life*, p. 378.
6. F. F. Bruce, *The Epistles of John,* p. 69.

writing (John 13:18; 15:25). In each omission it is reasonably clear what words were taken for granted by the apostle. The purpose clause, ἵνα φανερωθῶσιν, "in order that they might be made manifest," does not speak of the Gnostics' purpose in leaving the church, but of the divine intention to make a clear distinction between truth and error. The KJV rendering, "that they were not all of us," seems to indicate that some of the heretics were in spiritual association with the believers, but not all were. Such a translation does not do justice to the text. When οὐ, "not," and πᾶς, "all," occur in the same clause the sense is often that of a universal negative, "no one." Westcott and Brooke explain that when the verb stands between the οὐ and the πᾶς, as it does here, the negation is always universal rather than partial. Examples are John 3:16; 1 Corinthians 1:29; 1 John 2:21; Revelation 21:27.[7] Thus John says that it was the divine intent that the heretics by their departure might make it clear that "none of them belonged to us" (NIV).

2:20. καὶ ὑμεῖς χρῖσμα ἔχετε ἀπὸ τοῦ ἁγίου, "But you have an anointing from the Holy One." The position of ὑμεῖς, "you," coming as it does immediately after the introductory conjunction, makes the word strongly emphatic. John is setting the believers in sharp contrast with the antichrists of verses 18-19. The presence of such contrast suggests that the conjunction καί, which introduces the verse, should be translated adversatively as in the AV, RSV, NASB, and NIV. "Many antichrists have come," says John, "but as for you, you have an anointing."

The author no doubt used the word χρῖσμα, "anointing," in contrast to the usage of ἀντίχριστοι, "antichrists." The basic word here is χρίω, "I anoint." It is from this term that Χριστός, "Christ," the anointed one, comes. There is a sense in which believers are *christs,* (anointed ones), for they have been anointed with the Holy Spirit.[8] Whereas the Gnostics are antichrists, the believers are christs. In the Old Testament, anointing with oil was the symbol of power conferred for an office such as the priesthood (Ex. 29:7) or the monarchy (1 Sam. 10:1). What in the Old Testament was limited to the chosen few, in the New Testament is the privilege of every believer.

7. Westcott, p. 72; A. E. Brooke, *A Critical and Exegetical Commentary on the Johannine Epistles,* The International Critical Commentary, p. 54. See also on 1 John 2:16.
8. A. Plummer, *The Epistles of St. John,* Cambridge Greek Testament for Schools and Colleges, p. 60.

Although John does not explicitly identify the anointing, most commentators assume that the term refers to the Holy Spirit.[9] Dodd, however, suggests that the anointing is the Word of God. He argues that since the anointing gives knowledge of God and is a "prophylactic against false teaching," it is best to view it as being the Word of God. In his mind, to rest spiritual understanding on the indwelling Holy Spirit is much too subjective.[10] Marshall more recently has suggested that the anointing is both Spirit and Word.[11] The Holy Spirit in believers' hearts enables them to apprehend the Word. This combination view was first advanced by Ignace de la Potterie.[12]

However, the hermeneutic that sees a double meaning where none is clearly indicated is questionable. Furthermore, there is no Scripture that refers to the Word of God as an anointing. The application of the term to the Word is based on certain assumed similarities such as the fact that both the anointing and the Word of God are said to remain in the believer (2:14, 27). The argument that the work of the indwelling Holy Spirit is too subjective to be trustworthy loses its force in light of Paul's declaration, "The Spirit Himself bears witness with our spirit that we are children of God" (Rom. 8:16). Jesus also informed His disciples that the Spirit would teach them all things (John 14:26). The subjective teaching ministry of the Holy Spirit has its place and value, just as the objective work of the truth of God does. In 1 John 2 both are emphasized—the Word of God in verse 24 and the Spirit of God in verses 20 and 27. The Spirit is the anointing who enables the believer to appropriate and understand the truth of God. The Spirit is the agent in this process, and the truth is the object being appropriated.

Distinction must be made between the anointing—the Holy Spirit—and its source—"the Holy One." The latter term may refer either to God the Father or to Christ inasmuch as both are so designated in other passages. The Father is called the Holy One

---

9. John R. W. Stott, *The Epistles of John*, Tyndale New Testament Commentaries, p. 110; Brooke, p. 56; Westcott, p. 73; Bruce, p. 71; Plummer, pp. 59-60; R. C. H. Lenski, *The Interpretation of the Epistles of St. Peter, St. John and St. Jude*, p. 435.
10. Dodd, p. 63.
11. Marshall, p. 155.
12. Ignace de la Potterie, "Anointing of the Christian by Faith," in *The Christian Lives by the Spirit*, ed. I. de la Potterie and S. Lyonnet (Staten Island, 1971), pp. 79-143 (80, n. 4), as cited by Marshall, p. 155.

in such Old Testament passages as 2 Kings 19:22 and Job 6:10, and Christ is so designated in Mark 1:24 and Acts 2:27; 3:14. Although it is true that on one occasion Christ promised that He would send the Holy Spirit to His disciples (John 16:7), in reality it is the Father who sends the Spirit at the request of, and in the name of, the Son (John 14:16, 26). It seems more probable, therefore, that the expression, "the Holy One" in 1 John 2:20 refers to God the Father.

καὶ οἴδατε πάντες, "and you all know." The KJV translation, "ye know all things," appears to be an extreme statement. The better manuscripts have πάντες (ℵ B P Ψ) rather than πάντα (A C K 33 81 etc.), which changes the statement to read, "you all know." It has been argued that πάντα, "all things," is the more difficult reading since no one knows all things. On the other hand πάντες may be viewed as the more difficult since it leaves οἴδατε without an object—"you all know"—and thus may be a bit clumsy. This was the majority view of the editorial committee of the United Bible Societies' *Greek New Testament.*[13] Therefore, on the basis of both external and internal evidence πάντες is favored. In contrast to the Gnostics who boasted that they alone possessed true spiritual knowledge, John assured his readers that the believers—all of them, not merely the elite few—were the possessors of such knowledge by virtue of the possession of the Holy Spirit.

The use of οἴδατε, "you know," rather than γινώσκετε is to be expected. John is saying that all believers possess knowledge rather than that they all are acquiring knowledge.

2:21. οὐκ ἔγραψα ὑμῖν ὅτι οὐκ οἴδατε τὴν ἀλήθειαν, ἀλλ ὅτι οἴδατε αὐτήν, "I have not written to you because you do not know the truth, but because you do know it." The verb ἔγραψα is an epistolary aorist as in 2:14, referring to the epistle that John was currently writing. It was not penned because he assumed spiritual ignorance on the part of his readers. The article with ἀλήθειαν marks out the truth as that body of doctrine that is distinctively Christian. In 1 John the focus is on Christology and especially on the incarnation. The believers know these things and should be able to distinguish between the teachings of the errorists and those of the apostles. John does not write to impart new truth but to alert them to the danger and to urge them to apply the truth they already possess.

καὶ ὅτι πᾶν ψεῦδος ἐκ τῆς ἀληθείας οὐκ ἔστιν, "and

---

13. Bruce M. Metzger, *A Textual Commentary on the Greek New Testament*, p. 710.

because no lie is of the truth." The words πᾶν and οὐκ are to be combined as in the KJV to form a universal negative. The author is not saying, "Not every lie is of the truth," which would be a partial negative allowing for the possibility that some lies may be of the truth. Instead he is insisting that "no lie is of the truth" (see 2:19 on universal negatives). The preposition ἐκ, "out of," speaks of source or parentage. No lie comes from the truth because like begets like, and falsehood and truth are radically incompatible. The expression τῆς ἀληθείας is made definite by the use of the article, indicating that the author is not referring to truth in general but to that body of truth that is distinctively Christian. The Gnostic lie cannot rightly claim to be drawn from that corpus of doctrine proclaimed by Christ and His apostles. The denial of Christ's incarnation is diametrically opposed to apostolic truth.

The third occurrence of ὅτι in verse 21 may either be taken to mean "that," as in the KJV, or "because." If it means the former, John writes since his readers know two things: (1) the truth and (2) *that* no lie comes from the truth. If it means "because," he is writing for two reasons: (1) *because* his readers know the truth and (2) *because* no lie comes from the truth. Although Alford and Plummer argue extensively for translating the word as "because," their arguments are not convincing.[14] It is better to understand John as saying that he writes to the Asian Christians since they know the truth and they know *that* no lie can come from the truth.[15] They are aware that the true and the false are so radically different that they must not, and indeed cannot, be mingled. There is no room for compromise or tolerance in the realms of truth and falsehood. Since they possess this basic knowledge, John can write urging them to act in accordance with what they already know.

2. THE CHRISTOLOGICAL TEST, 2:22-23

2:22. τίς ἐστιν ὁ ψεύστης εἰ μὴ ὁ ἀρνούμενος ὅτι Ἰησοῦς οὐκ ἔστιν ὁ Χριστός; "Who is the liar but the one who denies that Jesus is the Christ?" The absence of a connecting particle, with which most Greek sentences begin, helps to create a certain abruptness here. John's purpose in this striking rhetorical question is to identify the antichrists concerning whom he has

---

14. Henry Alford, *The Greek Testament* 4:452; Plummer, pp. 61-62.
15. Marshall, pp. 156-57, n. 30.

been speaking. They are the ones who deny that Jesus is the Christ. These two designations—"Jesus" and "Christ"—are more significant than mere names. Χριστός had originally referred to the Messiah predicted in the Old Testament and long expected by the Jews. But the Cerinthian Gnostics held Jesus to be a mere human being, while the Christ was the divine aeon that came upon Jesus at His baptism and left Him just prior to His death. John uses the term *Christ* as a parallel to the designation *Son* (2:22; 5:1, 5). Thus, to deny "that Jesus is the Christ" is to deny that the human Jesus and the divine Christ are united in one person, the incarnate God-man.

The Greek text carries the article before the noun ψεύστης and should be translated "the liar," thus pointing up the unique character of this deceiver. His is the lie that exceeds all other lies in its awful significance, for his denial strikes at the very heart of the gospel. To deny the incarnation is to deny the validity of Christian truth altogether. If Jesus were not the God-man, at the same time fully God and fully man, He could not be the Savior. He must be fully man to die for man, and He must be fully God for His death to be of sufficient value to atone for sin.

The literal rendering of the Greek text reads, "Who is the liar if not the one who denies. . . ." In other words, if this denier is not the liar, no one is. This is a striking way of declaring that the Gnostic teachers are the greatest deceivers of all. The apparently contradictory double negative of the text—"Who is the liar except the one *denying* that Jesus is *not* the Christ," ὁ ἀρνούμενος ὅτι Ἰησοῦς οὐκ ἔστιν ὁ Χριστός—is resolved by viewing the denial as a direct quotation, ". . . denying, *saying*, 'Jesus is not the Christ.'" According to Law, this "imparts a tone of special aggressiveness to the negation" by quoting the very words of the denial.[16] The present tense participle ἀρνούμενος, "denying" (vv. 22-23), makes it clear that the denial is not an isolated event, but is a continuing practice. ἀρνέομαι, "to deny," is used in two slightly different senses in the verse. First, a fact—"that Jesus is the Christ"—is denied; second, persons—"the Father and the Son"—are denied. In the second instance to deny is to refuse or reject the Son and, thereby, the Father. However, as Heinrich Schlier points out, to deny the truth about the Son is to deny (reject) the Son.[17]

16. Law, p. 379.
17. Kittel, s.v. "ἀρνέομαι," by Heinrich Schlier. 1:470.

οὗτός ἐστιν ὁ ἀντίχριστος, ὁ ἀρνούμενος τὸν πατέρα καὶ τὸν υἱόν, "This is the antichrist, the one who denies the Father and the Son." The demonstrative pronoun οὗτος is more pointed than the English personal pronoun "he," which appears in the KJV. John declares, "This one is the antichrist," referring back to the liar who denies that Jesus is the Christ. It is not reasonable to understand the expression ὁ ἀντίχριστος as referring to the personal antichrist who is to come at the end of the age, even though the noun is preceded by the article. Instead the article must refer to a specific manifestation of the spirit of antichrist in some outstanding heretical teacher such as Cerinthus. The denial is thus seen not merely as erroneous thinking but as diabolically inspired.

John now reveals that the denial that Jesus is the Christ is also a denial of the Father, a fact clearly stated in the following verse. Later Gnostics referred to God as the Supreme Ruler, the Ineffable God, the Unapproachable God, the Abyss, and even as the First Father and the Unknown Father. However, God was so far removed from the world that He could only have contact with it through a series of emanations. Gnostics knew nothing of the intimate Father-child relationship of which John speaks.

Whereas, in the first part of verse 22 Jesus is assumed to be "the Christ," in the latter part of the verse He is referred to as "the Son." It is clear that the two designations are parallel and thus that the term Χριστός is used to refer to the deity of Jesus, rather than His Messiahship in the Old Testament sense of the term.

2:23. πᾶς ὁ ἀρνούμενος τὸν υἱὸν οὐδὲ τὸν πατέρα ἔχει, "Whoever denies the Son does not have the Father." John here employs another universal negative, πᾶς . . . οὐδέ, which should be translated, "No one who denies the Son has the Father either." See comments on 2:19. The force of οὐδέ is two-pronged. The οὐ combines with πᾶς to produce a universal negative; the δέ functions adverbially to mean "either." The one who has rejected the Son has rejected the Father as well. To have (ἔχει) the Father is to possess Him as father just as it is customary to speak of having a human father or having a friend. Ἔχει τὸν πατέρα, then, speaks of a parent-child relationship, which can only be entered through Christ (John 14:6) as the only revelation of the Father (John 1:18). Hence, if Jesus is not God's Son, man has no personal revelation of God.

ὁ ὁμολογῶν τὸν υἱὸν καὶ τὸν πατέρα ἔχει, "the one who confesses the Son has the Father also." In the KJV these words appear in italics, indicating that they do not appear in the Greek text. They do, however, occur in ℵ A B C P and in numerous versions. The omission in such later manuscripts as K and L was no doubt due to the repetition of the words τὸν πατέρα ἔχει, which resulted in the scribal error known as *homoioteleuton*. When two lines ended in the same word or words, the copyist's eye sometimes jumped to the end of the second line and omitted the previous material in that line.[18]

The word *confesses* is the translation of ὁμολογῶν, present tense participle of ὁμολογέω, "I confess." Like the denial, the confession is a continuing practice. The use of ὁμολογέω and ἀρνέομαι, "I deny," in antithetical position was a common Hellenistic practice that came to be employed in the New Testament as well. Ὁμολογέω combines the ideas of solemn affirmation and public proclamation of one's faith (Mt. 10:32).[19]

3. THE KEY TO CONTINUING FELLOWSHIP, 2:24-28

2:24. ὑμεῖς ὃ ἠκούσατε ἀπ' ἀρχῆς ἐν ὑμῖν μενέτω, "as for you, let that abide in you which you heard from the beginning." This new subdivision begins with the personal pronoun ὑμεῖς employed to show emphatic contrast—"as for you." Commentators have debated the case and usage of the word with little unanimity. Some identify it as an independent nominative, not grammatically connected to the remainder of the sentence, intended to show strong emphasis.[20] Others view it as a vocative case.[21] The former identification is preferable, but either way the construction is a striking indication of contrast between the heretics (vv. 22-23) and the believers (v. 24). Note the repetition of the construction in verse 27. The word οὖν, "therefore" (KJV), is not found in such major manuscripts as ℵ A B C.

The aorist tense ἠκούσατε, "you heard," is a constative aorist that views the entire period "from the beginning" until the present time as a single occurrence. The words ἀπ' ἀρχῆς, "from the beginning," indicate that the aorist cannot simply refer to the point at which they first heard. In this case, therefore, it is best to translate ἠκούσατε, "you have heard."

18. Bruce M. Metzger, *The Text of the New Testament*, pp. 189-90.
19. Kittel, s.v. "ομολογέω, κτλ.," by Otto Michel. 4:207-10.
20. H. E. Dana, *The Epistles and Apocalypse of John*, p. 44.
21. Lenski, p. 438.

John has previously used ἀπ' ἀρχῆς in two different senses. In 1:1 and 2:13-14, he describes Christ as the One who has been "from the beginning." In 2:7 believers are said to have possessed the new-old commandment "from the beginning." When describing the existence of Christ, the phrase extends back to eternity past; the second usage goes back to the beginning of the readers' Christian experience. So here in 2:24 John is speaking of the gospel that the Asian Christians had heard across the years since they first believed. This is the apostolic tradition with special emphasis placed on the incarnation, the fact that "Jesus is the Christ" (v. 22).

Ἐν ὑμῖν μενέτω, "Let that abide in you," is a graphic way of exhorting the readers to continue believing. The present tense verb μενέτω, "let that abide," is doubly durative. Both the tense and the meaning of the verb call for continuing action. By personifying the truth as living in the believer, the expression portrays a more intimate relationship to the truth than the word *believe* would convey. It describes truth as being at home within the believer.

ἐὰν ἐν ὑμῖν μείνῃ ὃ ἀπ' ἀρχῆς ἠκούσατε, καὶ ὑμεῖς ἐν τῷ υἱῷ καὶ ἐν τῷ πατρὶ μενεῖτε, "If what you heard from the beginning abides in you, you also will abide in the Son and in the Father." When the apostle speaks of letting the truth "abide in you," he is not talking about merely subscribing to a creedal statement. As the second half of verse 24 indicates, the presence of indwelling truth results in a continuing vital relationship with God. This assumes a meaningful acceptance of, and interaction with, the truth.

The KJV misses the force of the repetition of the verb μένω, "to abide" (dwell, continue, remain), which occurs three times in verse 24. Instead of using three different renderings, as the KJV does ("abide . . . remain . . . continue"), it would be much more representative of the force of the original to use one translation throughout the verse: "As for you, let that which you have heard from the beginning *dwell* in you. If that which you have heard from the beginning *dwells* in you, you also *will dwell* (progressive future) in the Son and in the Father." The repetition of μένω continues in verses 27-28, thus pointing up one of the dominant ideas of 1 John 2:18-28.

The word "also" (καί) does not mean "you in addition to others," but serves to add the experience of dwelling in God to that of allowing the truth to dwell in them.

The order, "in the Son and in the Father," is not unintended. Normally the order would be reversed, but "the Son" is placed first, indicating that He is the key to any relationship with God (John 14:6).

2:25. καὶ αὕτη ἐστὶν ἡ ἐπαγγελία ἣν αὐτὸς ἐπηγγείλατο ἡμῖν, τὴν ζωὴν τὴν αἰώνιον, "and this is the promise which He Himself made to us: eternal life." A superficial reading of the passage may leave one with the impression that this verse is parenthetical rather than intimately connected with the context. Further consideration leads to the conclusion that the experience of dwelling in the Son and the Father is here described as an eternal relationship—eternal life.

The demonstrative pronoun αὕτη is shown by its feminine gender to refer to τὴν ζωὴν τὴν αἰώνιον, "eternal life," rather than to the experience of dwelling in God (v. 24). If the latter were the case, the pronoun would have been neuter instead of feminine. Nevertheless, whereas the pronoun looks forward rather than backward, the conjunction καί, "and," ties verse 25 to verse 24, indicating that dwelling in the Son and in the Father is the same as possessing eternal life.[22] Eternal life has two aspects, the chronological and the qualitative. It is a quality of life that is experienced both now and eternally. In verse 26 the emphasis is on the present qualitative aspect. The personal pronoun αὐτός is used for emphasis and should be rendered "he himself." Christ Himself is the One who promised eternal life (John 3:15-16; 6:40, 47; 17:3).[23]

2:26. ταῦτα ἔγραψα ὑμῖν περὶ τῶν πλανώντων ὑμᾶς, "These things I have written to you concerning those who are trying to deceive you." It is certain that ταῦτα, "these things," does not refer merely to the two immediately preceding verses, for these do not mention the false teachers. Although there may be a sense in which the whole epistle up to this point is in view, it is most logical to refer ταῦτα to the specific section John has just written (2:18-25). These verses contain the most extended explicit reference to the heretics thus far in the epistle. The summary declaration of verse 26 serves to round off the section containing the Christological test of spiritual genuineness.

As in 2:14, 21 the aorist is not historical, pointing back to a past letter, but epistolary, referring to the present letter from the viewpoint of the time when the recipients will read it. The verb

---

22. Marshall, p. 161.
23. Dana, p. 161.

πλανώντων, which the KJV translates "seduce," literally means "to cause to go astray." In 1 Peter 2:25 the readers are described as sheep going astray. There is, however, no indication in 1 John that the Asian Christians were actually being led astray by the Gnostic teachers. It is best, therefore, to view πλανώντων as a tendential present and to translate it "are trying to lead you astray."²⁴ The present tense of the participle makes it clear that the Gnostic effort was a real and continuing threat.

2:27. καὶ ὑμεῖς τὸ χρῖσμα ὃ ἐλάβετε ἀπ' αὐτοῦ μένει ἐν ὑμῖν, "and as for you, the anointing which you received from Him abides in you." In this verse John expands on the truth that he introduced briefly in verse 20. Like verse 20, this verse begins with καὶ ὑμεῖς, "and as for you," which depicts emphatic contrast with the statement immediately preceding. As in verse 24 ὑμεῖς is an independent nominative, adding to the forcefulness of the contrast.²⁵ Again, as in verse 20, the adversative sense of the context demands that καί be translated "but." "These things I write to you concerning those who are trying to deceive you. But as for you. . . ." On τὸ χρῖσμα, see on verse 20. The aorist ἐλάβετε, "you received," points back to the specific occasion of conversion when they received the gift of the Holy Spirit (Acts 2:38). John assumes that every Christian is given the Holy Spirit when he believes. The prepositional phrase ἀπ' αὐτοῦ, "from him," could refer to God the Father or to the Son. The Father is the originating giver of the Holy Spirit (John 14:16-17), but Christ also promised to send the Spirit to the disciples (John 16:7). In 1 John 2:20, it is most natural to understand "the Holy One" who gives the anointing (Holy Spirit) as the Father. However, in 2:27 there is reason to believe that John has reference to the Son as the one who provides the anointing. This conclusion is based on the use of the third person singular pronouns in the context of verse 27. In verse 25, it is the Son (αὐτός, "He Himself") who promised eternal life (John 3:15-16; 6:40, 47; 17:3). In verse 27*b*, ἐδίδαξεν, "He taught," refers to the Son (see later comments, this verse). That the phrase "in Him" (ἐν αὐτῷ) also refers to Christ is made clear by verse 28. Here, the One in whom believers remain is described as coming again. Surely, this is Christ, not God the Father.

John does not exhort his readers to *let* the Holy Spirit remain in

---

24. Dana and Mantey, p. 186. The ASV, RSV, NASB, NEB, NIV, and TEV all translate the verb as tendential.
25. Dana and Mantey, p. 70.

them. Instead, he declares that the Spirit *is* remaining in them (μένει—present indicative). That this indwelling is no temporary matter is indicated both by use of the present tense and by the linear idea residing in the verb itself.

καὶ οὐ χρείαν ἔχετε ἵνα τις διδάσκῃ ὑμᾶς, "and you have no need for anyone to teach you." The conjunction ἵνα in this passage cannot be understood in the telic sense, for the idea of purpose does not fit the passage. Instead, it is used as the equivalent of ὅτι, simply meaning *that*. When examined by itself, this clause may appear to rule out all human teachers. However, that this cannot be the author's intent is evident from the following facts: (1) John himself was engaged in teaching in this very letter, (2) Paul speaks of pastor-teachers, the gift of Christ to the church (Eph. 4:11), and (3) Paul also speaks approvingly of the gift of teaching (Rom. 12:7). Consequently, John must mean that his readers need no additional teaching such as the supposedly advanced teaching offered by the Gnostics. What they had already been taught under the influence of the Spirit was complete, and nothing more could be added to it. The Gnostics went beyond the truth, but the believer was to remain in the truth (2 John 9).

ἀλλ' ὡς τὸ αὐτοῦ χρῖσμα διδάσκει ὑμᾶς περὶ πάντων, καὶ ἀληθές ἐστιν καὶ οὐκ ἔστιν ψεῦδος, καὶ καθὼς ἐδίδαζεν ὑμᾶς, μένετε ἐν αὐτῷ, "but as His anointing teaches you about all things, and is true and is not a lie, and just as it has taught you, you abide in Him." This statement begins with the strong adversative conjunction, ἀλλά (ἀλλ') "but on the contrary," revealing the force with which the apostle rejects the idea that his readers need any additional human instruction. The KJV reading, "the same anointing," is a translation of τὸ αὐτὸ χρῖσμα found in manuscripts A K L. The better manuscripts (ℵ B C P) have τὸ αὐτοῦ χρῖσμα, "his anointing," referring to Christ, as do the expressions, ἀπ' αὐτοῦ (v. 27a) and ἀπὸ τοῦ ἁγίου (v. 20). It is His anointing because it comes from Him. The present tense διδάσκει, "is teaching," speaks of the continuous instruction the believer receives from the Spirit. It is not merely on certain occasions that the Spirit teaches, but it is an ever-present experience.

Although various interpreters differ concerning the matter, it seems most reasonable to view καὶ ἀληθές ἐστιν καὶ οὐκ ἔστιν ψεῦδος, "and is true and is not a lie," as a parenthetical explanation.[26] The contrast of the positive ("true") and the nega-

---

26. Law, p. 382; Westcott, p. 80.

tive ("lie") is a typically Johannine means of emphatic declaration. It is evident that the apostle is pointing up truth as one of the primary attributes of the Holy Spirit, no doubt remembering that Jesus designated Him "the Spirit of truth" (John 14:17; 16:13). The use of διδάσκω, "I teach," first in the present tense and then in the aorist, is significant. In the first instance the continuing teaching ministry of the Holy Spirit is in view. Some interpret the aorist as a constative usage having reference to the whole past ministry of the Spirit from the time of the readers' conversion up to the present. Such a meaning, however, seems to border on being superfluous. A more acceptable explanation is that, whereas the first occurrence of διδάσκω refers to the Holy Spirit, the second refers to the teaching of Christ. (So translated in NEB, Beck, and Phillips). This interpretation provides a more adequate explanation of the repetition of the verb and of the change of tense. The aorist indicative points back to the historical fact of Christ's teaching. Furthermore, John elsewhere records Christ's command to abide in Him (John 15:4-10). The change from ὡς, "as," to καθώς, "just as," may also indicate a change of persons: "As the Holy Spirit is now teaching you . . . and just as Christ taught you. . . ."

The KJV "ye shall abide" is the translation of μενεῖτε, the reading in such manuscripts as K and L, but superior manuscript evidence (ℵ A B C P) favors the present tense μένετε. Whether this form is indicative or imperative is open to debate, and there are reputable exegetes on both sides of the question. On the one hand, it is argued that the mood is indicative because the previous occurrence of the verb in this same verse is indicative. On the other hand, the verb is said to be imperative because it is imperative in verse 28. It is more reasonable for the apostle to repeat the imperative in verse 28 than it would be for him to *declare* in verse 27 that the recipients are dwelling in Him and then in the very next sentence (v. 28) to *command* them to dwell in Him. Houlden points out that μένω in this context acquires a meaning similar to that of the related term ὑπομονή, *perseverance*.[27] So then, John is calling for perseverance in the faith.

The words "in Him" (ἐν αὐτῷ) may be taken to refer to dwelling in the Holy Spirit. However, it is clear that the same phrase in verse 28 refers to dwelling in Christ since His παρουσία

---

27. J. L. Houlden, *A Commentary on the Johannine Epistles,* Black's New Testament Commentaries, p. 81.

("coming") is mentioned. Furthermore, as has been previously shown, Christ Himself urged His disciples to abide in Him (John 15:4-10).

2:28. καὶ νῦν, τεκνία, μένετε ἐν αὐτῷ, ἵνα ἐὰν φανερωθῇ σχῶμεν παρρησίαν, "and now, little children, abide in Him, so that when He appears, we may have confidence." The words "and now" (καὶ νῦν) indicate that the author is completing a line of thought and preparing to move to a new subject. On τεκνία, see comments on 2:1. His command to his beloved children is that they should keep on dwelling in Christ. Both the present tense and the inherent meaning of the verb call for continuing action. By repeating the command to keep on dwelling in Christ (cf. v. 27), John rounds off the section dealing with the Christological test of one's salvation (2:18-28). The purpose (ἵνα, "in order that") for continuing to dwell in Christ is that they may be ready for His coming. The Greek ἐάν literally means "if." However, the general teaching of the New Testament leaves no room for doubt concerning the *fact* of Christ's coming; only the *time* is indefinite. It was possible that He might have come during the lifetime of the readers. In a number of passages such as this, ἐάν can only mean "whenever" (1 John 3:2; John 8:16; 12:32; 14:3). It is the last hour (2:18) and Christ's coming is drawing near, but the exact time of His appearance cannot be known. However, whenever He does come, the believer will want to be prepared to stand before Him without shame.

The aorist tense φανερωθῇ, "he appears," points to the suddenness of Christ's coming. It will not be a process; instead, it will occur in a moment. At that point (aorist σχῶμεν, "we may have") John wants his readers to have confidence. This is neither an ingressive aorist (Robertson) nor an effective or culminative aorist (Lenski). It simply points to the fact of the possession of confidence at that time when Christ appears. It is interesting that John switches from the second person μένετε, "abide," to the first person, σχῶμεν, "we may have." This could indicate that John will not be ashamed when Christ comes if the Asian Christians are abiding in Christ. More probably, he is simply identifying himself as a fellow Christian with his readers. He like them must abide in Christ if he is to avoid shame at Christ's return.

The word παρρησίαν, "confidence," has an honored history. It was used in the Greek political sphere to describe the freedom of speech (πᾶs—"all," ῥῆσιs—"speech") that was the prized privilege of the citizens of a democratic city-state. The only persons who were allowed to speak in the assembly (ἐκκλησία) of a democracy were the full citizens. Παρρησία was thus viewed as the highest of privileges. The term referred, not only to the right of speech, but also to the courage to speak with candor. It came thus to be used in the moral sense of an openness to God, a fearlessness and confidence that allowed one to speak freely to Him in prayer. In an eschatological sense it describes appearing before Christ at His coming without shame or fear. It presupposes saving faith, a close spiritual relationship, and faithful obedience to His commands.[28]

καὶ μὴ αἰσχυνθῶμεν ἀπ' αὐτοῦ ἐν τῇ παρουσίᾳ αὐτοῦ, "and not shrink away from Him in shame at His coming." In Greek literature παρρησία was sometimes described as the opposite of αἰσχύνη, "shame," and this is the contrast John makes here. Αἰσχυνθῶμεν is used in this passage as a middle voice rather than a passive, and should be translated, "may *be* ashamed," rather than "may be *put* to shame." It is not that shame comes "from Him" (ἀπ' αὐτοῦ), but that the one who lacks παρρησία will turn "from Him" in shame. Plummer says, "We see the averted face and shrinking form, which are the results of the shame clearly indicated in the Greek. 'Turn with shame *from* Him' and 'Shrink with shame *from* Him' have been suggested as renderings."[29]

There are three primary terms used in the New Testament to describe Christ's coming: (1) αποκάλυψις, which is an "unveiling," a "revelation," (2) ἐπιφάνεια, an "appearing," and (3) παρουσία, a "presence, coming." The latter term, which is used only here by John, had become a technical term to describe the visit of a ruler. Preparations were made to receive the dignitary with pomp and adulation. Streets and highways were put in the best of repair; luxurious gifts were presented; and addresses of praise and gratitude were delivered. The term was also used in pagan circles of visits of the gods to men.[30] It was, therefore, natural that the word should be adopted by Christians to describe the coming of their God and King. John does not want the coming of our Divine Ruler to be a matter of shame but one of confidence and assurance in His presence.

28. Kittel, s.v. "παρρησία, παρρησιάζομαι," by Heinrich Schlier. 5:858-71.
29. Plummer, p. 67.
30. Kittel, s.v. "παρονσία, πάρειμι," by Albrecht Oepke. 5:858-71.

THEOLOGICAL COMMENTARY (2:18-28)

A. THE HISTORICAL BACKGROUND

The one Gnostic teacher known to be located in Ephesus during John's residence there was the Egyptian Jew Cerinthus.[31] Although there is no detailed account of his teachings, the general outlines of Cerinthian doctrine are provided for us by Irenaeus. 1 John 2:18-28 may have been occasioned by such teaching as Cerinthus's. John's reference to the denial that Jesus *is* the Christ (v. 22) seems to reflect the Christology of Cerinthus, and the declaration that to deny the Son is also to deny the Father (v. 23) may well be directed against the doctrine of the Unknown Father.

B. THE JOHANNINE REFUTATION

As has been pointed out elsewhere, the epistle of 1 John is addressed *to* the Asian believers but is directed *against* the early Gnostic heresy. In 1:5—2:11 John is concerned with the ethical deviation of his opponents as an indication that they do not know God. At the same time the apostle gives ethical grounds for assurance to those who are in saving relationship with Him. In 2:18-28 the apostle's concern is with the doctrinal deviation of the heretics as proof that they do not know the Father. Christology is the particular doctrine at stake here (2:22). Again John points out the basis of assurance for those who have a saving relationship with God (2:23).

1. THE CONTRAST BETWEEN HERETICS AND BELIEVERS, 2:18-21

John begins this section by warning his readers concerning the false teachers, whom he calls antichrists. They are, he says, an indication of living in the last period of this age. These heretics once were present in the Christian community, no doubt appearing to be genuine believers. In due time, however, their counterfeit nature was revealed by their withdrawal from the fellowship.

In contrast to the errorists, the apostle characterizes the genu-

---

31. Irenaeus *Against Heresies*, 3. 3. 4.

ine members of the Christian community as having been anointed by the Holy Spirit and therefore knowing spiritual truth. Contrary to the claims of the false teachers, John's readers are by no means deficient in knowledge, for they are the recipients of divine instruction.

The last hour (2:18). In the treatment of this verse in the exegetical commentary, reasons were given for believing that the expression "the last hour" refers to a specific period of time rather than merely to a characteristic or quality evident in John's day. It may, therefore, speak of the very end of the age, those few years that immediately precede the Lord's return. However, if that was John's meaning, it is obvious that he was mistaken, for Christ did not come then.

Dodd plainly says that John was indeed mistaken in declaring that it was "the last hour." "We have no reason," says Dodd, "to suppose that the writer intended any but a literal sense." However, Dodd continues, although in one sense it was "an illusion," in another sense it was not.[32] Although it was not literally true that the end of the age was about to break on them, there was in that expectation an underlying spiritual truth. The figure of antichrist represents the power of evil present in the world, but Christ's resurrection reveals His power to defeat the evil. In this sense eschatology is realized now rather than in some future age.

Dodd's realized eschatology suffers from at least two deficiencies. First, it is incomplete. It is true that Christians live in an eschatological age and experience benefits that are eschatological in nature—a taste of tomorrow's blessings today. Spiritually eschatology is being "realized" today, but only in a preliminary form. Eschatology will be realized literally when the age finally comes to its end and the literal antichrist appears, followed by Christ Himself coming in bodily form to establish His kingdom. Dodd's interpretation is but half of the story.

In the second place, Dodd's declaration that John's literal understanding of the end of the age was an illusion does more damage to the trustworthiness of Scripture than even he himself is ready to accept. He wants to find spiritual value in what John has written, but at the same time he declares John to have been mistaken. If the apostle was in error about the literal antichrist and end of the age, how can one be sure that there is any spiritual value in his

32. Dodd, p. 51.

mistaken view? It is entirely possible that when one shoots down the literal meaning, one likewise shoots down the spiritual significance.

Christ and the apostles followed the Jewish custom of dividing time into two ages: the present age, characterized by evil, and the coming age, to be marked by righteousness. The event that was expected to bring down the curtain on the old age and to usher in the new was the coming of the Messiah.

The present age had begun with the fall of Adam and was still continuing in the time of John. However, recently—within John's lifetime—a significant event had taken place. The Messiah had come in lowly fashion and had died on a Roman cross after promising to return again. The present evil age was still a current reality, but a change had occurred. Christians now found themselves between the two advents of the Messiah. The time from Adam to Christ had been the preparatory period when God was making ready for the Savior to come. Now that Christ had come, the time between the two advents was looked upon as being eschatological—the last hour.

In His prophetic discourse on Mt. Olivet (Matt. 24) Christ had foretold the kind of things that would mark the period between His two comings: false Christs (v. 5); wars, famines, earthquakes (vv. 6-7); persecution (vv. 9-10); false prophets (v. 11); and abounding wickedness and spiritual declension (v. 12).

Paul also characterized the last days with a similar list (2 Tim. 3:1-9) and warned young Timothy to turn away from the kind of persons he described (v. 5). Thus Paul viewed his time as at least the beginning of the eschatological period.

John refers to these types of eschatological characteristics when he explains that it is the last hour because many antichrists are on the scene. In a later passage he calls them false prophets, the exact term used by Christ in Matthew 24:11.

Bonsirven follows Bede in understanding that the last hour is the time between the incarnation of Christ and (as he calls it) "the end of the world." Accordingly, for John the last hour was that period of time during which Christ will overcome Satan and establish His reign. Prior to the incarnation, Satan's rule as prince of this world was not seriously threatened, but now the time period has dawned during which he will be defeated once-for-all. Foreseeing this, the devil puts forth great effort to prevent his downfall. This furious activity is expressed in the many antichrists or false teachers who are attacking the truth of God and the people of God.[33]

The doctrine of antichrist (2:18-19). Although the only biblical writer who uses the term "antichrist" is the apostle John (1 John 2:18, 22; 4:3; 2 John 7), the concept is set forth by other inspired authors as well.

In Daniel 7 the apocalyptic figure of a little horn is used to depict a powerful future king who will rise up in opposition to God and His people (vv. 8, 24-25). The period of his dominance is said to be "a time, two times [Hebrew dual form], and half a time" (v. 25, RSV). In the book of Revelation (12:14) the same expression, along with the parallel figures 42 months (11:2; 13:5) and 1,260 days (11:3; 12:6), is used in reference to the dreadful time of world upheaval that will precede Christ's coming to set up His kingdom. It would appear, therefore, that the little horn is the great future opponent of Christ who is depicted as the beast in Revelation 11:7; 13ff.; 17:3-17; 19:19-20. Paul likewise speaks of a future figure called the man of lawlessness "who opposes and exalts himself above every so-called god or object of worship" (2 Thess. 2:3-4). The little horn of Daniel 7 is brought to his destruction when the one like the Son of man is given everlasting world dominion (vv. 13-14, 26-27). The man of lawlessness of 2 Thessalonians 2 is destroyed by the command of Christ at His coming (v. 8). And the beast of Revelation comes to his end when he and his armies attack Christ at His second advent (Rev. 19:19-20).

It is to this sinister person that John refers in 1 John 2:18 when he says, "you heard that antichrist is coming." It was common knowledge among believers that Christ's second advent would be preceded by a period of terrible trouble known as the Great Tribulation and by the appearance of a vicious archenemy of Christ whom the latter will destroy at His coming.

John, however, uses the term *antichrist* in the plural (1 John 2:18) to describe persons who were living at the end of the first century. The context (vv. 19, 22) makes it clear that he has in mind the heretical teachers who were preying upon the Asian believers. These are not to be identified with the great final antichrist of Daniel, Thessalonians, and Revelation. However, they are similar in that they are opponents of Christ, and the many anti-

---

33. Joseph Bonsirven, *Épitres de Saint Jean*, vol. 9, *Verbum Salutis*, p. 125.

christs are actually inspired by the spirit of the final antichrist. Thus they are advance copies or previews of that diabolical figure who is to come. John repeats this concept in 4:3, where he declares concerning anyone who denies the incarnation of Christ, "this is the spirit of the antichrist, of which you have heard that it is coming, and now it is already in the world." Paul voiced a similar view when he wrote, "For the mystery of lawlessness is already at work; only he who now restrains will do so until he is taken out of the way. And then that lawless one will be revealed . . ." (2 Thess. 2:7-8).

Genuine spiritual knowledge (2:20-21). John does not assume spiritual ignorance on the part of his readers. Therefore, his purpose in writing is not to impart information to them. Instead, he takes it for granted that they do know the truth, and he writes to stir up their minds and to help them to analyze the false teaching in the light of the spiritual understanding they possess. Spiritual knowledge, according to John, derives from two sources: the teaching ministry of the Holy Spirit (2:20, 27) and the teaching of the apostles (2:24).

John assumes two facts concerning his readers. They all possess the Holy Spirit and they all have knowledge (2:20). The second assumption seems, at least in part, to be based upon the first; their knowledge comes from the Spirit. In 2:27 the apostle explicitly declares that the anointing teaches them with regard to all things.

This teaching ministry of the Spirit is not to be understood as the impartation of information. It is true that Christ promised the apostles that the Holy Spirit would teach them all things, including the remembrance of His previous instruction (John 14:26) and the impartation of new truth (John 16:13). These promises, however, seem to have been given with reference to the writing of inspired Scripture, rather than being guarantees of this kind of instruction for all believers.

Instead, the Spirit's teaching has to do with the comprehension of spiritual truth when one is confronted with it. The Holy Spirit enables the believer to appreciate and receive the truth by spiritually orienting the believer's mind. For example, certain individuals have the ability to appreciate good music; others show a complete lack of such an endowment. In the spiritual realm, the ability to receive and comprehend truth, rather than being innate, is imparted by the Holy Spirit.

The second source from which spiritual knowledge derives is the teaching of the apostles. John urges his readers to retain that which they had heard from the beginning (2:24). This was the body of truth passed on from the apostles to become the basic teaching of the church. Acts 2:42 (KJV) refers to it as "the apostles' doctrine." It consisted of specific information such as the facts of Christ's death and resurrection, as well as the significance of these events.

In John's doctrine of spiritual knowledge the teaching of the Holy Spirit and the impartation of factual information by the church go hand in hand. Neither, by itself, is sufficient. For spiritual understanding, factual information is necessary. Christianity is based upon historical facts structured around a framework of objective truth. However, such information only becomes meaningful as the Holy Spirit enables a person to receive, comprehend, and appreciate the truth.

Thus, John assumed that his readers had become the recipients of the facts of the Christian faith and of the instruction of the Holy Spirit. Consequently, they needed no additional merely human instruction (2:27). They possessed a knowledge of the truth (2:20), and in the light of this knowledge they were to judge every teaching they encountered.

The apostle's statements concerning knowledge are especially meaningful when viewed against the background of the current heresy and its stress on higher, esoteric knowledge. Gnostics insisted that they possessed knowledge that the uninitiated Christian did not have. They claimed that it is through knowledge that the soul is saved from its state of ignorance. When the soul comes to know its own true nature—a spirit-being come from the ineffable God—and its destiny—deliverance from ignorance and material imprisonment—then it finds redemption.

To believers who were confronted with such teaching and who may have been fearful that they were deficient in spiritual understanding, John gave assurance that they knew the truth (2:20) and thus needed no additional instruction (2:27). Because they had received the anointing of the Holy Spirit, they possessed true spiritual understanding and were continually being taught by none other than the divine Instructor Himself.

2. THE CHRISTOLOGICAL TEST, 2:22-23

As Law has pointed out, 1 John is a book of tests by which one can determine who is of God and who is not.[34] Although Law

---

34. Law, pp. 208-9.

finds three tests in the epistle, reasons have been given for believing that there are but two, the ethical and the doctrinal, or Christological. One statement of the Christological test is given in 2:22—"Who is the liar but the one who is denying, saying, Jesus is not the Christ? This is the antichrist" (Gr.). This test seems aimed specifically at Cerinthus, who made a distinction between the human Jesus and the divine Christ. John's statement rests on the premise that they comprise one person, Jesus Christ the God-man. He who believes that Jesus Christ is God incarnate has God as His Father, but he who denies that Jesus is the incarnate Son of God is a forerunner of the archenemy of Christ who will appear at the end of the age.

One of the main features of Cerinthus's system was the concept of the Unknown Father; in spite of the gross error of Gnosticism, there is an element of truth in this concept. John declares that no man has ever seen God (John 1:18). To the unbelieving Pharisees Jesus said, "You know neither Me, nor My Father" (John 8:19). God indeed is unknown to unregenerate man, and the only way that He can be known is through His self-revelation. John says, "The only begotten God, who is in the bosom of the Father, He has explained Him" (John 1:18). And to the unbelieving Pharisees Jesus explained, "If you knew Me, you would know My Father also" (John 8:19). Bultmann points out that to honor the Son is to honor the Father (John 5:23); to know the Son is to know the Father (John 8:19; 14:7); to hate the Son is to hate the Father (John 15:23); to see the Son is to see the Father (John 14:9); and to believe in the Son is to believe in the Father (John 12:44).[35] Thus, Jesus is the revelation of the Father, which means that anyone who denies Christ refuses God's revelation of Himself. The Gnostic who denied that Jesus is the Christ (the Son) rejected the only possiblity of knowing the Father. Consequently, although he talked of redemptive knowledge, God remained unknown to him.

3. THE KEY TO CONTINUING FELLOWSHIP, 2:24-28

The verb μένειν ("to remain, continue, dwell, abide") appears six times in various forms in 1 John 2:24-28. It would therefore seem that the concept of remaining is crucial in this section. The heretical teachers were not marked by remaining: they defected

---

35. Bultmann, p. 38, n. 6.

from the fellowship (2:19). On the contrary, remaining is the mark of the believer. Stott says, "Endurance is the hallmark of the saved."[36]

The key: Continuing belief of the truth (2:24). By the expression, that "which you heard from the beginning," John refers to the original message of the apostles, first brought to the province of Asia by Paul and his associates. John urges his readers to retain this time-honored truth in contrast to the newly-concocted vagaries of the heretics. Traditional Christianity is valued because, rather than being new, it goes back to authoritative sources and also because it has stood the test of time. The tradition passed on from person to person in the early years was carefully guarded and preserved because it carried the authority of the apostles from whom it came.

To allow the truth to dwell in one's self is to continue to possess it in a meaningful and intimate way. It is to persist in sincere belief of the truth. The fact of the incarnation of God's Son with its redemptive significance is to be cherished and retained regardless of whatever new winds of teaching may come. This persistent belief that Jesus is the incarnate Christ is the key to continuing fellowship with God.

The result of continuing belief of the truth (2:24). The readers are explicitly assured that continuing to hold to the truth results in a continued intimate relationship (dwelling) with Father and Son. This is John's way of describing the experience of the saved. To be in Christ is to be saved. To dwell in Christ is to continue in the experience of salvation. That this is what the writer has in mind is confirmed by the reference in the following verse (2:25) to eternal life. To dwell continually in the Father and the Son is to possess eternal life. And the key to this eternal relationship is persistent belief of the truth that Jesus is God's incarnate Son. These verses make it clear that the abiding life is not an experience limited to those Christians who are living in a close, more intimate fellowship with the Lord. Instead it is a term that describes the experience of all believers. To believe the truth is to abide or dwell in the Son and the Father. Verse 24 provides a basis for understanding Christ's use of the term μένω, "abide, dwell," in John 15:4-7. In fact, John's use of the term in 1 John 2:24-27 no doubt stems back to Christ's use.

John uses the word μένειν again in 2:27 of the indwelling Holy

---

36. Stott, p. 105.

Spirit. Although the presence of the Spirit is not here said to be a result of permitting the truth to dwell within them, it is taken for granted that the readers are indwelt by the Spirit. As other Scriptures indicate, this experience of the indwelling Spirit is also the product of faith (Gal. 3:2; Eph. 1:13). Thus, the message dwells in the believer, and as a result the believer dwells in the Father and the Son, and the Spirit in turn indwells the believer. Perhaps no word other than μένειν could as adequately represent the intimacy of the relationship that exists between the believer and the triune God.

The exhortation to continue (2:27-28). As suggested in the exegetical commentary, verse 27 closes with an exhortation to keep on dwelling in Christ. This is repeated in verse 28 and emphasized as a necessary preparation for the second coming of the Lord. To those who hold to the doctrine of the security of the believer this may seem to be an unnecessary exhortation. If the believer is secure in his position in Christ, he need do nothing to maintain that position. Those who reject the doctrine of the eternal security of the believer, however, will seize upon this exhortation as an indication that the believer's security is dependent upon his effort.

Neither of these reactions is in accord with the teaching of the New Testament. On the one hand, the Lord Himself plainly taught that the believer is absolutely eternally secure in his salvation. In John 10:28 He declared, "I give eternal life to them; and they shall never perish." This categorical denial is the translation of the Greek double negative, οὐ μή, plus the idiom for the concept of eternal duration (εἰς τὸν αἰῶνα). It should be rendered, "They shall by no means ever perish." This is looking at the matter from the divine side of the picture with the believer preserved in absolute security.

On the other hand 1 John 2:27-28 looks at the matter from the human point of view. The believer *does* persevere. He keeps on following the good Shepherd (John 10:27). He is responsible for maintaining his relationship to Christ as the Holy Spirit teaches (1 John 2:27). God guarantees the believer's security, but the Christian's regenerated will persists in maintaining a saving relationship with the Lord. And this is accomplished by holding persistently and meaningfully to God's redemptive truth (1 John 2:24).

The outward evidence of continuing belief (2:19). John declares concerning the defectors, "If they had been of us, they would have remained with us." Although it was spoken of heretical teachers, this statement declares a principle that is true of believers. Those who are genuine members of the Christian circle will continue in the circle. Defection is the evidence that one's profession was not genuine. There is an inner cohesiveness among believers that binds them inseparably together in the same spiritual family with the same Father, and indwelt by the same spiritual life. When one leaves the circle of God's people altogether, it is an indication that he never did belong to the family of God.

An apostate is not one who was once regenerated and later ceased to be a child of God. Instead, he is a person who has made a profession of being saved but who has never had a genuine experience of salvation. In due time the superficial profession wears thin, and, because there has been no genuine inner experience of Christ, he falls away. Apostasy, then, is an indication that the defector was never "of us" (1 John 2:19). On the other hand, those who are "of us" will continue. John's word for *continue* is μένειν. Thus, there is an external continuing (2:19) just as there is an internal continuing (2:27-28), and the two are integrally related. The one who continually dwells in the Father and the Son will also continue in the fellowship of God's people.

The pervasive theme: fellowship. The first cycle of thought in the epistle revolves around the concept of fellowship with God. The idea is first mentioned in the introductory verses when John says: "What we have seen and heard we proclaim to you also, that you also may have fellowship with us; and indeed our fellowship is with the Father, and with His Son Jesus Christ" (1:3). This theme is then picked up as the characterization of the Christian life in 1:5—2:28. To be a Christian is to have fellowship with Him; not to experience such fellowship is not to be saved.

The claim to have such fellowship is put to the test in 1:6-7, where the apostle declares that the person who is experiencing genuine fellowship with God will manifest the same by a life of moral goodness (walking in the light).

The term *fellowship* (κοινωνία) does not occur in chapter 2, but a careful look will reveal that the idea is there. In 2:3-4 John sets up the test of obedience by which a Christian can discern whether or not he knows Christ. To know a person is closely related to being in fellowship with him. In 2:5 John speaks of being "in Him" and in 2:6 of dwelling "in Him." These two expressions describe an intimate relationship that may be equated with fellowship. Again in 2:24 the author explains that if a person believes the time-honored message of the gospel, he will dwell "in the Son, and in the Father." Also, in 2:27-28 the believer is twice exhorted to dwell in Christ. As in 2:5-6, such expressions speak of the most intimate kind of relationship.

Thus, whether it is explicitly called *fellowship* or is described by other terms such as *knowing Christ* or *dwelling in Christ*, the concept of fellowship as a designation of the Christian life pervades the first major section of the epistle (1:5—2:28).

C. THE PRESENT-DAY APPLICATION

1. THE GNOSTIC CULTS

First John 2:18-28 has a most direct bearing upon the Gnostic-type cults of the present day. As we explained in the theological commentary on 1:5—2:11, these cults include Christian Science, New Thought, the Unity School of Christianity, and the Theosophical Society.

The Gnostic denial, "Jesus is not the Christ" (2:22, Gr.), is echoed explicitly in the teachings of these four present-day cults. As previously pointed out, Eddy said, "Jesus is the human man; and Christ is the divine idea; hence the duality of Jesus the Christ."[37] Wood of New Thought writes, "Christ is the name of sonship. . . . It was locally and historically expressed in full degree through the personality of Jesus, but by no means limited to him."[38] The Unity School of Christianity likewise distinguishes between Jesus and Christ: "By Christ is not meant the man Jesus."[39] And the admittedly Gnostic Theosophical Society teaches that the Christ has come at many times in history in the persons of great teachers. Of such, Jesus was merely an outstanding example.[40]

Concerning all who advocate such doctrine, John writes, "Who is the liar but he who is denying, saying, Jesus is not the Christ? This one who denies the Father and the Son is the antichrist" (1 John 2:22, Gr.). As in the first century, those who today make such a denial are the opponents of Christ. Though they may profess to be His followers, they are characterized by the same spirit that will mark the coming antichrist.

---

37. Mary Baker Eddy, *Science and Health with Key to the Scriptures*, p. 473.
38. Henry Wood, *New Thought Simplified*, p. 182.
39. *Unity*, No. 2, p. 46, as cited by Walter R. Martin, *The Kingdom of the Cults*, p. 280.
40. Martin, p. 280.

Perhaps 1 John 2:19 may also be applied to those who defect from traditional Christianity to one of the Gnostic cults. When a person who has professed faith in Jesus Christ afterward becomes a committed member of a cult that denies that Jesus is the Christ, he gives evidence that he apparently was not really "of us." Neither his faith in Christ nor his experience of regeneration were authentic. Genuineness of spiritual life will manifest itself in perseverance in both inner experience and outward association.

It is, however, to be granted that there may be temporary situations in which a person may for a time enter into a superficial relationship with an antichristian cult and then return to his original allegiance to Christ. But where a wholehearted and continuing relationship to the cult is established, it is reasonably certain that the prior relationship to Christ was superficial. It is impossible for both commitments to have been wholeheartedly genuine.

2. LIBERAL CHRISTIANITY

From the days of the older Modernism until the present time, there have been many who wear the guise of Christianity but who deny the deity of Jesus Christ. The Christological test of 1 John 2:22-23 applies in principle to such persons, as well as to the Gnostics of the first and the twentieth centuries. In John's usage, to deny that Jesus is the Christ is to deny that Jesus is the Son, as the interchange of the two terms in 2:22 reveals.

Our day is marked by a widespread desire to throw off all that is traditional. In the minds of many, if it is old it is fallacious. The statements of John are the exact reverse of this current mood. He asserts that if it is old it is true; but if, on the contrary, it is a newly introduced teaching not in agreement with the tradition of the apostles, it is error and must be refused. Such an assertion rests upon the conviction that the traditional teaching had been adequately demonstrated to be true and authoritative, as Hebrews 2:3-4 clearly indicates. Consequently, it is as important today as at the end of the first century to hold firmly to the truth of traditional Christianity, centering as it does in the fact of the incarnate Savior. There is no other way to come to God but through the Son of God made flesh and crucified for all mankind.

PARAPHRASTIC COMMENTARY (2:18-28)

(18) My children, we are living in the final period of this present age, between the two advents of Christ. Just as you have been

taught that at the very end of the age the diabolical archenemy of Christ will appear, even now many of his forerunners are on the scene. This is why we are sure that we are in the final period of the age. (19) These forerunners of the antichrist once moved in Christian circles, but they withdrew because they were not really one with us. If they had been one with us, they would have continued in the fellowship of the believers; but they left in accordance with the divine purpose to make it clear that none of them really belonged to our circles.

(20) But you—in contrast to these antichrists who boast of their supposed knowledge—you have the Holy Spirit, whom God has poured out upon us, and all of you therefore possess genuine knowledge of spiritual things. (21) My reason for writing this letter is not that I think that you are lacking in the knowledge of Christian doctrine; on the contrary I am writing to you because you have a thorough grasp of Christian truth and you are well aware that it is impossible that any false teaching should be the product of that truth.

(22) Who is the deceiver par excellence, if it is not the one who is persistently voicing the denial, "Jesus is not the divine Christ"? This one, who is repudiating not only God the Son but God the Father as well, is the present-day manifestation of the coming antichrist. (23) No one who is disclaiming that Jesus is God's Son has God as his Father either. The person who is openly acknowledging that Jesus is the Son also has God as his Father.

(24) As for you, let the apostolic teaching continue to dwell in your hearts. If you do this, you also will continue in a saving relationship with both God the Son and God the Father. (25) And this is what Christ Himself has guaranteed to us, life that is not temporary but eternal. (26) All these things that I am writing to you have to do with the heretical teachers who are bent on lending you astray from the path of truth. (27) But as for you, the Holy Spirit whom Christ has poured out upon you is continually dwelling within you, and you have no need for anyone to give you new or advanced instruction beyond that which you have already received under the Spirit's influence. But on the contrary, as you are continually being taught concerning these things by the Spirit that Christ has poured out upon you—and He is altogether true—and even as Christ Himself taught during His earthly ministry, keep on living in intimate relationship with Him. (28) Before leaving the matter let me urge you again, my dear children, maintain your intimate relationship with Christ, so that whenever He makes His appearance we may be boldly confident and not turn in shame from Him at His royal coming.

Fellowship Tested on Christological Grounds

STRUCTURAL COMMENTARY (2:18-28)[41]

C. Fellowship tested on Christological grounds, 2:18-28
  1. A contrast between heretics and believers, 2:18-21
     a. The heretics, 2:18-19
        (1) Their presence is an eschatological sign, 2:18
        (2) Their defection is proof of their true nature, 2:19
     b. The believers, 2:20-21
        (1) God has anointed them, 2:20a
        (2) They possess genuine spiritual knowledge, 2:20b-21
  2. The Christological Test, 2:22-23
     a. A negative statement of the test, 2:22-23a
        (1) The one who denies that Jesus is the Christ is the liar, 2:22a
        (2) He is an antichrist, 2:22b
        (3) He does not have God as Father, 2:23a
     b. A positive statement of the test: to confess that Jesus is God's Son is to have God as Father, 2:23b
  3. The key to continuing fellowship, 2:24-28
     a. Continued belief of the truth, 2:24-25
        (1) Exhortation to persistent belief, 2:24a
        (2) Result of persistent belief: a continuing relationship to God, 2:24b
        (3) Christ's promise of a continuing relationship, 2:25
     b. Continued relationship to Christ, 2:26-28
        (1) Heretical teachers counteracted by the divine Teacher, 2:26-27a
        (2) Believers exhorted to continue their relationship to Christ, 2:27b-28
           (a) The bases of the exhortation, 2:27b
              (1a) The Spirit's teaching
              (2a) The Spirit's trustworthy character
              (3a) Christ's teaching
           (b) The purpose of the exhortation, 2:28

---

41. For previous section of the outline, see pp. 190-91.

Second Cycle: The Christian Life Viewed As Divine Sonship, 2:29—4:6

Moving in spiral fashion John begins in 2:29 to follow again the same path he has already traveled in the first cycle of the epistle (1:5—2:28). However, that he is not merely repeating himself is apparent from two characteristics of this second cycle. First, instead of viewing the Christian life as fellowship with God, as he did in the first cycle, the apostle now describes it as divine sonship. To be a Christian is to have been born into the family of God. This characterization of the Christian life is an advance beyond the concept of fellowship. The family relationship is a much closer relationship, grounded as it is in the process of procreation. Family members are not merely companions who are united by common interests and experience. They are bound together by birth.

Another characteristic of the second cycle that elevates it above the previous one is that, although the same tests of the Christian life—ethical and Christological—are discussed, they are given fuller development than in the previous section, and are viewed from different perspectives.

As in the first cycle where the term κοινωνία, "fellowship," occurred only at the beginning of the section, so here the various forms of the expressions, ἐκ τοῦ θεοῦ γεγέννηται, "he has been born of God," and τέκνα τοῦ θεοῦ, "children of God," occur only in the earlier portion of the cycle. The concept of divine sonship, however, runs throughout the cycle. Not only does John declare that the one who lives a life of righteousness has been born of God (2:29; 3:9), he also says that children of God are to be distinguished from the children of the devil by the fact that God's children love one another and Satan's children do not (3:10). Thus, righteousness and love are marks of those who have been born into the family of God. In the Christological section (4:1-6), the phrase, ἐκ τοῦ θεοῦ, "from God," occurs six times. The preposition ἐκ, "from, out of," speaks of source. To be *from God* is the same as to be *born of God* (γεγεννημένος ἐκ τοῦ θεοῦ).

The second cycle is divided into two main sections, the ethical (2:29—3:24) and the Christological (4:1-6).

A. SONSHIP TESTED ON ETHICAL GROUNDS, 2:29—3:24

In this section sonship is being submitted to the ethical test. Whether a person has been born into the family of God can be ascertained by the presence of family likeness in that individual's life. The underlying idea of the passage is that of spiritual birth. Just as in human procreation the life and characteristics of the parents are passed on to their offspring, so in spiritual birth the divine life and characteristics are inherited by everyone born of God.

It is furthermore assumed by the author that the divine characteristics are not only inherited but also manifested. Thus, it is possible to ascertain by the presence or absence of these traits whether a person is a child of God. Stated proverbially, the principle running through this section is "Like father, like son." He who is a child of the devil manifests the devil's likeness; he who is a child of God manifests the divine likeness.

The characteristics John singles out for use as ethical tests are righteousness and love. Anyone who is a member of God's family will live a life of righteousness (2:29—3:10*a*) and will love God's people (3:10*b*-24).

10

Sonship Tested on Ethical Grounds: The Practice of Righteousness, 2:29—3:10a

In this section John clearly demonstrates that righteousness is the identifying mark of the family of God. After establishing the basic standard for the test (2:29), he marvels at the wonderful privilege of divine sonship (3:1-3). In the remainder of the passage (3:4-10a), the apostle discusses the family trait of righteousness, showing why the practice of sin is incompatible with divine sonship (3:4-8) and even going so far as to declare it to be impossible (3:9). In 3:10a he concludes with a summary statement.

EXEGETICAL COMMENTARY (2:29—3:10a)

SONSHIP DEMANDS THE PRACTICE OF RIGHTEOUSNESS, 2:29—3:10A

2:29. ἐὰν εἰδῆτε ὅτι δίκαιός ἐστιν, "If you know that He is righteous." As in 1:5, the opening verse sounds the keynote for the section that follows. There it was the declaration, "God is light"; here it is the fact, "He is righteous." In each instance, the opening assertion serves as the standard for the test set forth in the following verses. The conjunction ἐάν, "if," may seem to have been an unhappy choice. Inasmuch as it is certain that "He is righteous," it may seem that the author should have used εἰ, which assumes the following condition to be true. However, ἐάν does not necessarily imply doubt. It may refer to a known fact

Sonship Tested on Ethical Grounds: Practice of Righteousness 227

which, for rhetorical purposes, is stated in a potential mood. Such a usage is not at all uncommon in English.

John here uses οἶδα and γινώσκω in their classical sense.[1] He says, "If you know as an assured fact (εἰδῆτε) that He is righteous, you will logically conclude (γινώσκετε) that anyone who practices righteousness has been born of Him." The knowledge expressed by γινώσκετε is arrived at by reflection on the knowledge expressed by εἰδῆτε. (See fuller discussion at 2:3.)

Opinions vary concerning the identity of the person designated as "righteous." Some insist that the obvious reference of the previous verse to Christ and His coming demands that the expressions, "He is righteous" and "born of Him," must also refer to Christ.[2] Others say that there is a sudden change within verse 29 from Christ ("He is righteous") to God the Father ("born of Him").[3] Still others assert that both expressions refer to God the Father.[4] The difficulty with the first view is that the New Testament nowhere explicitly speaks of believers being born of Christ. They are "born of God" (1 John 3:9; 4:7; 5:1, 4), and "born of the Spirit" (John 3:8), but never born of Christ. Instead they are represented as Christ's brothers and joint heirs with Him in the family of God (Rom. 8:17). Furthermore, 3:1-2 refers to believers as "children of God," not of Christ; and the Father is the One who bestows the great love-gift of sonship. Therefore, the expression, "born of Him," must speak of God the Father. Consequently, it is most reasonable to understand that "He is righteous" likewise has reference to the Father since it appears in the same sentence. The change from Christ to God then occurs between verse 28 and verse 29.

---

1. Bultmann lists 1 John 2:29 as a passage where γινώσκω and οἶζιδα are used as full equivalents. [Gerhard Kittel, ed., *Theological Dictionary of the New Testament*, 1964-76, s.v. "γινώσκω, γνῶσις κτλ.," by Rudolph Bultmann.] Seeseman says, "But it (οἶδα) can also be synon. with γινώσκω; in the abs. use in the *koine* it is hard to establish any distinction in meaning." [Kittel, s.v., "οἶδα, " by Heinrich Seeseman.] However, on the classical sense of these two verbs in 2:29, see John R. W. Stott, *The Epistles of John*, Tyndale New Testament Commentaries, p. 117; B. F. Westcott, *The Epistles of St. John*, p. 82; A. E. Brooke, *A Critical and Exegetical Commentary on the Johannine Epistles*, The International Critical Commentary, p. 67.
2. Westcott, p. 83.
3. Rudolf Bultmann, *The Johannine Epistles, Hermeneia*, p. 45; I. Howard Marshall, *The Epistles of John*, The New International Commentary on the New Testament, pp. 167-68, notes 11 and 13.
4. Stott, p. 117; Robert Law, *The Tests of Life*, p. 384.

The term δίκαιος, "righteous," refers basically to conformity to a standard. In Greek usage it spoke of one "who observes custom," one "who observes legal norms," one who "observes laws."[5] In the LXX God is described as δίκαιος, "The One who is infallibly consistent in the normative self-determination of His own nature."[6] His actions, His declared standard of right and wrong, and His own nature are ever in perfect harmony. John does not here use the term δίκαιος in the Pauline sense of the righteousness that God imputes to believers, nor is he speaking of the justice or fairness of God who keeps His promise and forgives (1 John 1:9). Instead he is thinking of rightness of character and of action on God's part. God is always self-consistent: "He cannot deny Himself" (2 Tim. 2:13). He does what is according to His character, because He does what is right.[7]

γινώσκετε ὅτι καὶ πᾶς ὁ ποιῶν τὴν δικαιοσύνην ἐξ αὐτοῦ γεγέννηται, "you know that every one also who practices righteousness is born of Him." The verb γινώσκετε, "you know," may either be indicative or imperative. In favor of the latter it has been argued that the presence of imperatives in 2:28 (μένετε, "abide") and 3:1 (ἴδετε, "behold," KJV) suggests that γινώσκετε is also imperative. Such an argument is purely arbitrary, for nothing in the context demands a series of imperatives. The knowledge that God's children will bear the family likeness of righteousness is not something that John's readers were unlikely to possess. In fact, the apostle has already declared that they all have spiritual knowledge (2:20-21). Consequently, it would not have been necessary to command or exhort something that was already a fact.

Manuscripts ℵ A C P insert καί, "also" between ὅτι and πᾶς, whereas B K L omit the word. If the insertion is original, then the text would indicate that just as God is righteous, so *also* the members of His family will manifest righteousness. John makes it clear by the use of the present tense participle ποιῶν that he is not thinking of an isolated act of righteousness but its habitual practice. This is the life pattern of the members of God's family.

The phrase ποιῶν τὴν δικαιοσύνην, "doing righteousness," is a Hebrew expression appearing in the Old Testament as היטיב (Lev. 5:4; Jer. 4:22; 13:23), or as עֲשֵׂה-טוֹב (Ps. 34:14; 37:27) "to do good." The noun δικαιοσύνην, "righteousness," is preceded by the article

---

5. Kittel, s.v. δίκαιος, by Gottlob Schrenk. 2:182.
6. Ibid., p. 185.
7. Law, p. 68.

τήν, thus particularizing the righteousness the author has in mind. An abstract noun by its very nature is indefinite and general, but when it is preceded by an article the sense of the noun is restricted to a particular application.[8] In this instance the specific righteousness referred to is that that characterizes God the Father and is passed on to His children as a family characteristic. The perfect tense γεγέννηται, "has been born," describes an action completed in the past with results continuing to the present. This is an intensive use of the perfect tense, placing emphasis on the continuing results,[9] and represented in the NASB by the rendering, "is born of Him." The one who is making righteousness the practice of his life has been regenerated in the past, and as a result he is now a child of God who reveals the family trait of righteousness. The source of his birth is depicted by the preposition ἐκ (ἐξ), "out of," and the ablative case αὐτοῦ, "Him."

Both Bultmann and Houlden, among others, refer to the idea of rebirth in the Gnostic Corpus Hermeticum, (ch. XIII).[10] Bultmann goes so far as to suggest that the idea comes from Gnostic circles. It is, of course, possible that John might have used a Gnostic term in his refutation of Gnosticism. However, it is more probable that Gnostics borrowed from John since Christ had employed the concept of birth in reference to the believer (John 3:3, 5) and in reference to unbelieving Jewish leaders (John 8:42-44). It is quite evident that John drew the designation "children of the devil" (1 John 3:8, 10) from John 8:44.

3:1. Ἴδετε ποταπὴν ἀγάπην δέδωκεν ἡμῖν ὁ πατήρ, "See how great a love the Father has bestowed upon us." The mention in the preceding verse of being born of God stirs within John a deep sense of amazement, which he expresses in ἴδετε ποταπὴν ἀγάπην, "See how great a love." Ἴδετε is an aorist imperative calling for immediate action: *"Look (at once) at the kind of love. . . ."* The word bristles with urgency and excitement, and all the more so when followed by ποταπήν—originally meaning "from what country," this word came to be a stronger synonymn of ποῖος, "of what kind." It commonly expresses amazement and wonder at the nature of the item being described. One of the disciples used it

---

8. H. E. Dana and Julius R. Mantey, *A Manual Grammar of the Greek New Testament*, pp. 141-42.
9. Ibid., p. 202; Joseph Bonsirven, *Épitres de Saint Jean*, vol. 9, *Verbum Salutis*, p. 140.
10. Bultmann, pp. 45-46; J. L. Houlden, *A Commentary on the Johannine Epistles*, Black's New Testament Commentaries, p. 89.

when calling Jesus' attention to the greatness and the magnificence of the temple buildings and the stones of which they were constructed (Mark 13:1). Similarly, John here exclaims, "Consider what wonderful love!"[11]

That which gives rise to John's amazement is well expressed by the word ἀγάπην, "love," a term that describes the attitude of God toward sinful man. It is not a strongly emotional word. Instead it describes an attitude in which the intellect and the will are predominant. God loves the sinner, not because He is drawn to him by his lovableness, but because, in spite of man's unloveliness, God sets His mind and will on seeking man's highest good. This is what is amazing about God's love. "God demonstrates His own love toward us, in that while we were yet sinners, Christ died for us" (Rom. 5:8). For further explanation of ἀγάπην see on 2:7.

The location of ὁ πατήρ, "the Father," at the end of the clause is a means of emphasis. The fact that God the Father would condescend to love man is stressed as a reason for amazement. Notice that John does not merely say that the Father loved man, but that He has given (δέδωκεν) love, which is a much stronger way of declaring the fact. God did not merely show love; He has actually imparted love to man.

ἵνα τέκνα θεοῦ κληθῶμεν· καὶ ἐσμέν, "That we should be called children of God; and such we are." Ἵνα, "that," cannot have a telic force here, for God did not love in order that believers might be called His children. Rather, the conjunction is nonfinal or definitive, and as such it explains what God's love does. It transforms those who believe into children of God. They are "called" (κληθῶμεν) God's children—this is their reputation. The KJV "sons" is not justified by the Greek text, which has τέκνα, "children." John does not stress the legal relationship of a son (υἱός) but the natural relationship of a child (τέκνον). In John's theology of regeneration and eternal life the term τέκνον is of singular importance. The term here appears without the article, thus calling attention to the character rather than the identity of the readers. They are "God-children—a divine progeny."[12]

The better Greek manuscripts (ℵ A B C P) contain the words καὶ ἐσμέν, "and . . . we are," after the clause ἵνα . . .

---

11. William F. Arndt and F. Wilbur Gingrich, trans. and eds., *A Greek-English Lexicon of the New Testament*, by Walter Bauer, pp. 694-95; F. Blass and A. Debrunner, *A Greek Grammar of the New Testament*, sec. 298 (3).
12. H. E. Dana, *The Epistles and Apocalypse of John*, p. 49.

Sonship Tested on Ethical Grounds: Practice of Righteousness 231

κληθῶμεν, "that we should be called children of God."[13] The designation, "children of God," is not an empty name; it is in accord with reality. John's "and . . . we are" is an exultant exclamation of assurance. Not only are believers *called* God's children, they actually *are* His children.

διὰ τοῦτο ὁ κόσμος οὐ γινώσκει ἡμᾶς ὅτι οὐκ ἔγνω αὐτόν, "For this reason the world does not know us, because it did not know Him." The phrase, "for this reason," is the translation of διὰ τοῦτο, "on account of this." No doubt the antecedent of the neuter pronoun, τοῦτο, "this," is the fact that believers are the children of God.[14] They are radically different from the world, because they are members of God's family and the world is related, not to God, but to the devil. The term κόσμος, "world," has several different uses in the New Testament (see on 2:15). Inasmuch as John speaks of the world as a knowing agent ("does not know"), it would appear that he is thinking of persons. On the other hand, since the world does not know God or His children, it seems that John has reference to the evil world system that is estranged from, and in opposition to, God. Thus, "world" here must depict the unregenerate people who belong to the evil world system. They are related to the world rather than to the family of God. Therefore, they do not know those who are in God's family. To know (γινώσκειν) a person is not only to recognize him, but to understand him, to appreciate him, and to be in a friendly relationship with him. Such knowledge is experiential, growing out of personal contact. Because of the deep gulf between the children of God and the world, no such relationship is possible.

A futher explanation of this estrangement is introduced by ὅτι, "because." The pronoun αὐτόν, "him," has been taken to mean God the Father (Alford, Brooke), Christ (Law, Stott), and God manifested in Christ (Westcott). John's habit of referring to Christ by use of the personal pronoun is well known (cf. 2:8, 12, 27; 3:3, 5-6). Furthermore, the aorist ἔγνω, "knew," points to a particular point in past time when the world did not know Him. It

---

13. For a thorough discussion of the reasons for including the words καὶ ἐσμέν, see J. Harold Greenlee, *Introduction to New Testament Textual Criticism*, pp. 126-28.
14. Scholars are divided as to whether διὰ τοῦτο refers back to the fact that we are God's children or forward to the following ὅτι clause. Those who see it as referring back are Westcott, p. 96-97; Bultmann, p. 48, n. 17; and Marshall, p. 171, n. 25. Those who say it refers forward are Brooke, p. 81; Houlden, (with reservation), p. 90; and the NIV.

would be most natural to see here a reference to Christ's reception at His first coming. If the world did not receive Christ when He was here in the flesh, believers should not expect any better reception than He received (John 15:18-16:4).

3:2. ἀγαπητοί, νῦν τέκνα θεοῦ ἐσμεν καὶ οὔπω ἐφανερώθη τί ἐσόμεθα, "Beloved, now we are children of God, and it has not appeared as yet what we shall be." On ἀγαπητοί, "beloved," see on 2:7.

The adverb νῦν, "now," is placed first in its clause, as is οὔπω, "not . . . yet," in the next clause, in order to emphasize the contrast between the present and future aspects of the believer's state. What Christians are now is a reality; what they shall be has not yet been revealed. The noun τέκνα should be translated "children," not "sons" (KJV). See on 3:1.

The καί, which introduces the second clause, is clearly adversative in sense: "Now we are the children of God, *but* what we shall be has not yet been manifested." The aorist ἐφανερώθη is here better translated as an English perfect, "has been manifested," rather than as a simple past.[15]

οἴδαμεν ὅτι ἐὰν φανερωθῇ ὅμοιοι αὐτῷ ἐσόμεθα, ὅτι ὀψόμεθα αὐτὸν καθώς ἐστιν, "We know that, when He appears, we shall be like Him, because we shall see Him just as He is."

The conjunction "but" (δέ, KJV) is the translation of an inferior text (K L). The better manuscripts (ℵ A B C P) omit δέ. Although details concerning what the believer shall be have not yet been revealed, there is some knowledge about the matter. The use of οἴδαμεν here is evidence that in Koine Greek οἶδα and γινώσκω were somtimes used interchangeably. John declares "We know that . . . we shall be like Him, *because* we shall see Him just as he is." The knowledge is deduced from the fact that we shall see Him. If the strict distinction between the two verbs were being observed, γινώσκω would have been the proper term to use to express a deduction from an established fact. Originally οἶδα referred to the fact of knowledge without any indication of the manner in which it was received, whereas γινώσκω reflected the means by which the knowledge came, whether by experience, perception, or deduction from facts already possessed.[16] For fur-

---

15. A. T. Robertson, *A Grammar of the Greek New Testament in the Light of Historical Research*, pp. 847-48; Law, pp. 386-87.
16. Law, pp. 364-67.

Sonship Tested on Ethical Grounds: Practice of Righteousness 233

ther discussion, see on 2:3 and 2:29.

For ἐάν, see on 2:28.

Of major import is the determination of the subject of φανερωθῇ, the aorist, passive, subjunctive of φανερόω, "I manifest." The translators of the KJV thought the subject should be personal and rendered it as "he," no doubt referring to Christ. The NEB has translated the verb "it is disclosed." The pronoun "it" refers back to τί ἐσόμεθα, "what we shall be." A number of commentators (Alford, Robertson, David Smith, Stott, Lenski, etc.) favor this translation. Two major reasons have been advanced: (1) The proximity of the same verb in the first part of the verse (ἐφανερώθη, "it has . . . appeared"), the subject of which is obviously the clause τί ἐσόμεθα, leads to the probable thought that the subjects of the two verbs (ἐφανερώθη, v. 2a; φανερωθῇ, v. 2b) would be the same: "What we shall be has not yet been manifested. We know that whenever it is manifested. . . ." and (2) The absence of both of the pronouns commonly used to refer to Christ (αὐτός, 2:2; ἐκεῖνος, 3:5, 16) leads to the assumption that if the subject had been Christ, it would have been necessary to use one of those pronouns to make it clear that the subject of the second verb, φανερωθῇ, was not the same as the subject of the first verb, ἐφανηρώθη.

Although these reasons are not insignificant, other considerations are more weighty: (1) The context shows that John is laying stress on the appearances of Christ. In 2:28, His second coming is referred to (φανερωθῇ), and in 3:5 and 8 His first coming is pointed out (ἐφανερώθη), (2) The following verse (v. 3) is referring to Christ as the two pronouns (αὐτῷ and ἐκεῖνος) make clear. Therefore the αὐτόν of verse 2b must refer to Christ, and, following the same line of reasoning, the subject of φανερωθῇ must be Christ, and (3) It is more to be expected that John would identify the time of the believer's complete Christlikeness as being the second coming rather than the time when "it is disclosed" (NEB).[18]

Commentators likewise disagree concerning the reference of the words "like Him," with some suggesting that the pronoun

---

17. Henry Alford, *The Greek Testament*, 4:461; A. T. Robertson, *Word Pictures in the New Testament*, 6:220-21; David Smith, "The Epistles of John," *The Expositor's Greek Testament*, 5:183; R. C. H. Lenski, *The Interpretation of the Epistles of St. Peter, St. John and St. Jude*, pp. 451-53.
18. Commentators favoring the view that the subject refers to Christ are: Brooke, p. 82; Bonsirven, p. 148, n. 1; Westcott, p. 98; Marshall, p. 172; Law, p. 387.

refers to God and others that it denotes Christ. However, although it is true that the Christian is to be like God (Eph. 5:1), the New Testament more commonly speaks of likeness to Christ (Rom. 8:29; 2 Cor. 3:18; Phil. 3:20-21). Furthermore, the demonstrative pronoun ἐκεῖνος, which the KJV translates "he" in verse 3, is one of John's favorite designations of Christ (cf. 3:5, 16; 4:17). Therefore, since ἐκεῖνος, "he," in verse 3 refers to Christ, it is more reasonable to view αὐτόν, "Him," in verse 2 as likewise speaking of Christ. Ὅμοιοι, "like," is a word of qualitative comparison. Whereas ἴσος speaks of equality in such maters as size, number, or value, ὅμοιος speaks of similarity in qualities and characteristics. Believers can never be *equal* to Christ, since He is infinite and they are finite; but they can and will be *similar* to Him in holiness and in resurrection bodies.

The second ὅτι, "because," in verse 2 introduces a dependent clause that modifies either the main clause, οἴδαμεν . . . ,"we know. . . ," or the object clause, ὅτι . . . ὅμοιοι αὐτῷ ἐσόμεθα, "that . . . we shall be like Him." If it is the former, the meaning is that knowledge concerning future likeness to Christ is based on the already established fact that "we shall see Him just as He is." But if the causal clause modifies the object clause, John says that "we shall be like Him," *because* "we shall see Him just as He is." In this case it is the vision of Christ that transforms one into Christ's likeness. However, it is more natural for the dependent clause to modify the main clause unless the sense of the statement demands that it modify another dependent clause, and in this context no such demand is apparent. Futhermore, the passage is concerned with the knowledge of *what* believers shall be like in the future rather than the question of *how* the transformation is to be brought about. Thus, because he knows that believers shall see Christ, John is sure that they shall be made like Him. Only those who are like Christ will see Him just as he really is. Καθώς, being composed of κατά and ὡς, means "according as, just as." It is a stronger word of comparison than the simple ὡς, "as."

3:3. Καὶ πᾶς ὁ ἔχων τὴν ἐλπίδα ταύτην ἐπ' αὐτῷ ἁγνίζει ἑαυτὸν καθὼς ἐκεῖνος ἁγνός ἐστιν, "And every one who has this hope fixed on him purifies himself, just as He is pure." John's use of πᾶς ὁ, "every one who," both in his gospel and in this epistle, seems always to set aside "the claims of some party or other who claimed special privileges or exemptions for

Sonship Tested on Ethical Grounds: Practice of Righteousness   235

themselves."[19] In this case the Gnostic regarded himself as above any such moral restraints. Although he might claim a future hope in some form, his life of continuing sin revealed the falseness of his profession. Without exception, the possession of the hope produces purity.

The antecedent of the pronoun ταύτην, "this," is the assurance that believers shall both be like Christ and see Him as he really is (v. 2). A clear distinction must be made between the use of hope (ἐλπίς) in the New Testament and the common present day use of the term. New Testament hope is a confident expectation; it is assurance concerning something that is yet future. This is far different from the current employment of the term to express a wish or desire that may or may not be realized. The KJV translation, "in him," may be misleading. The phrase is not intended to locate the hope within the believer. Instead it speaks of the foundation upon which (ἐπ' αὐτῷ, "upon Him") the hope rests. It is a confident expectation founded upon Christ. Similar expressions, with the verb ἐλπίζω instead of the noun ἐλπίς, are found in Romans 15:12; 1 Timothy 4:10; 5:5.

Ἁγνίζει, "purifies," and ἁγνός, "pure," are not to be restricted here to abstention from sexual immorality as in 2 Corinthians 11:2. In comparison to ἅγιος, the term ἁγνός came to refer to cleanness with regard to general morality. In the LXX ἁγνός often carries the connotation of integrity.[20] John's use of the present tense ἁγνίζει indicates that the hope of Christ's coming results in a continuing process of purification. That the cleansing is not automatic is apparent from the fact that the possessor of the hope purifies himself. On καθώς, see on verse 2. Ἐκεῖνος, here as in other similar Johannine passages, refers to Christ (1 John 2:6; 3:5, 7, 16; 4:17). Such usage in reference to well-known personalities was not uncommon. The Pythagoreans are said to have referred to Pythagoras after his death by the pronoun ἐκεῖνος.[21] Note that John does not say that Christ purifies Himself, for He is, and always has been, pure.

3:4. πᾶς ὁ ποιῶν τὴν ἁμαρτίαν καὶ τὴν ἀνομίαν ποιεῖ, καὶ

---

19. Brooke, p. 83.
20. Colin Brown, ed., *New International Dictionary of New Testament Theology*, 1975-78, s.v. "Pure, Clean," by H. Baltensweiler.
21. Arndt and Gingrich, p. 239.

ἡ ἁμαρτία ἐστὶν ἡ ἀνομία, Everyone who practices sin also practices lawlessness; and sin is lawlessness." Concerning πᾶς ὁ, "everyone who," see 3:3. John repeatedly employs this expression in this section (2:29; 3:3-4, 6, 9). The πᾶς ὁ of verse 4 is set in bold contrast to that of 2:29. In both instances, the present tense participle ποιῶν, "doing," is used, contrasting those who are doing acts of righteousness with those who are doing acts of sin. John has in mind the habitual practice of righteousness and of sin. In 2:29—3:3 he discusses the fact that being born of God results in the practice of righteousness. Then assuming a negative viewpoint in 3:4-10*a*, he argues that the practice of sin is incompatible with the experience of regeneration.

The KJV translation, "committeth," is misleading in that it suggests a point action rather than the continuing practice indicated by the Greek present tense. Furthermore, the expression "transgresseth . . . the law" does not adequately represent the force of the original. The NASB translation is superior ("Everyone who practices sin also practices lawlessness"), not merely referring to an instance of lawbreaking, but to the continued, habitual performance of lawless acts. Both ἁμαρτίαν, "sin," and ἀνομίαν, "lawlessness," are preceded by articles, indicating that John is not thinking qualitatively. Rather he uses the articles with the two nouns to point to the classes of sin and lawlessness as two inclusive concepts rather than as single occurrences.

Having identified the practice of sin as the practice of lawlessness, John then turns to a more formal statement of definition: "sin is lawlessness." There is no justification for introducing this clause with the word "for" (KJV). The Greek καί may mean "and" or "indeed" here. Since both nouns in this copulative sentence are accompanied by articles, it is clear that they are equal and interchangeable. However, it is more natural to take ἁμαρτία, "sin," as the subject and ἀνομία, "lawlessness," as the predicate nominative that defines ἁμαρτία. Thus, sin is by its very nature lawlessness. Etymologically, ἁμαρτία means a missing of the mark, a failure to hit that at which one has aimed. It is the general word for sin of any kind. ἀνομία, however, is a stronger term, referring not merely to the absence of law, but to the purposeful disregard of law. Sin, then, is not merely a failure to measure up or a weakness; it is an active and purposeful refusal to conform to law. The principle of sin is in reality the principle of lawlessness. No particular code of laws, such as the Mosaic system, is in view here. Instead the apostle speaks generally of lawlessness as the repudiation of the expressed will of God. Law says, "In other words, to sin is to assert one's own will as the rule of action against the absolutely good will of God."[22] W. Gutbrod finds the idea of rebellion or revolt in the term ἀνομία.[23] And Bonsirven says, "By the word *anomia* the ancients designated the disposition of revolt against moral standards."[24]

The crucial point at which John was aiming was the insistence of the false teachers that the Gnostic could be indifferent to acts of sin, that he could engage in any and all kinds of action and still be in communion with God. What was sinful according to Judaeo-Christian standards, the Gnostic viewed as amoral. It was this attitude that the apostle denied. He asserted that sin is not a matter concerning which one can be indifferent. Sin is actual revolt against the revealed will of God. Hence, no one by any so-called esoteric knowledge of God is relieved of the obligation to obey God's will. Bultmann suggests that John's use of ἀνομία indicates that even the false teachers understood lawlessness in a heinous sense as serving the devil.[25] In the context of 1 John 3:4-10a, sin is rebellion, it is to take one's stand against God, it is to side with God's enemy, the devil.[26]

3:5. καὶ οἴδατε ὅτι ἐκεῖνος ἐφανερώθη ἵνα τὰς ἁμαρτίας ἄρῃ, "And you know that He appeared in order to take away sins." John appeals to the knowledge that all Christians possess by virtue of the anointing they have received (cf. οἴδατε, "you know," 2:20). Concerning the use of ἐκεῖνος, "that one," with reference to Christ, see on 2:6 and 3:3. The aorist tense ἐφανερώθη, "He was manifested," refers to the historical fact of the incarnation. That John does not say, "He was born," but "He was manifested," suggests that he has in mind prior existence rather than the inititation of existence.

The purpose (ἵνα) of Christ's coming was "to take away sins." ἄρῃ is another aorist referring to the act of Christ by which sins were removed. Although it is possible to find the concept of bearing sin, or the guilt of it, in αἴρω (see John 1:29), that does not seem to be the meaning here. Instead John is referring to acts of sin that Christ came to remove. This is suggested by the context that speaks of practicing sin (vv. 4, 6, 8-9) and practicing right-

---

22. Law, p. 133.
23. Kittel, s.v. "ἀνομία," by W. Gutbrod. 4:1086.
24. Bonsirven, p. 154 (my translation).
25. Bultmann, p. 50.
26. Marshall, pp. 176-77.

eousness (vv. 7, 10). Most significant is the fact that Christ came "to take away sins" (plural, referring to acts of sin). Bultmann points out that this purpose is parallel to that of destroying the works of the devil (v. 8).[27] John thus makes it clear that acts of sin are not compatible with being born of God. And this is true because Christ's purpose in coming was to remove such acts. If any similarity to the Old Testament sacrificial system is to be found here, perhaps the closest resemblance is to the ritual of the scapegoat (Lev. 16:22).

The KJV translation, "our sins," was no doubt based on manuscripts available to its translators that contained the word ἡμῶν, "our." However, there is better evidence for omitting the pronoun (A B P). In that case the article τάs before ἁμαρτίας may well be used possessively as was common in both classical and koine Greek.[28] And if this was John's intention, how much more inconsistent is the practice of sin seen to be in light of the understanding that it was "our" sins Christ came to take away?

καὶ ἁμαρτία ἐν αὐτῷ οὐκ ἔστιν, "and in Him there is no sin." The Greek word order is impressive. Literally, it would be translated, "and sin in him there is not," placing the emphasis on the word ἁμαρτία, "sin." John does not merely assert that Christ did not commit sin. His denial is more basic than that. It is that Christ did not possess a sinful nature. If God's Son was altogether sinless, then God's children should have nothing to do with sin. It is not compatible with their family relationship. Inasmuch as the first part of the verse speaks of Christ's incarnation, it might be expected that the author would use the imperfect tense ἦν "was," rather than the present tense ἔστιν "is." John, however, is referring, not merely to the past sinlessness of Christ, but to the fact that He *is* sinless—past, present, and future. It is an essential characteristic of His person. The absence of the article before ἁμαρτία places the stress on the qualitative aspect—not the act of sins, but the sin principle is in view. Christ does not possess a sinful nature.

3:6. πᾶς ὁ ἐν αὐτῷ μένων οὐχ ἁμαρτάνει, "No one who abides in Him sins." The declaration of verse 6 is a logical deduction from the statements of verse 5. Since Christ came to remove sins and since there is no sin in Him, it is obviously true that the one who dwells in him will not engage in habitual sin.

---

27. Bultmann, p. 50.
28. Dana and Mantey, p. 148.

Sonship Tested on Ethical Grounds: Practice of Righteousness

Like verses 3 and 4, this verse begins with πᾶς ὁ, which is better translated "everyone who" than "whosoever" (KJV). See on 3:3. When used in connection with a negative, in this case οὐχ, the πᾶς and the negative combine to give a universal negative, "no one." The expression ἐν αὐτῷ μένων, "dwelling in Him," has previously appeared in similar forms in 2:6, 24, 27-28. The discussion of these passages has shown that the distinction between dwelling in Christ and not dwelling in Him is the distinction between being saved and not being saved. It is not a distinction between two levels of Christian experience (see Theological Commentary). Both the present tense and the meaning of the verb μένω speak of continued dwelling. Inasmuch as it is evident that ἐκεῖνος, "that one," and ἐν αὐτῷ, "in Him," in the preceding verse refer to Christ, there is no reason to doubt that ἐν αὐτῷ in this verse likewise has reference to Christ.

The KJV rendering, "Whosoever abideth in him sinneth not," seems to demand sinless perfection on the part of the Christian, which would be in contradiction to John's clear statement in 1:8—2:2 that the believer is not sinless. However, granting the tense of the verb ἁμαρτάνει its proper force removes the seeming contradiction. Since the present tense depicts linear action, John does not say that the Christian does not commit a single act of sin. That idea would be represented by the aorist tense. Instead he declares, "No one who is dwelling in Him is continually sinning." Westcott comments on this verb: "It describes a character, 'a prevailing habit' and not primarily an act."[29] In this connection, David Smith writes, "The believer may fall into sin but he will not walk in it."[30]

πᾶς ὁ ἁμαρτάνων οὐχ ἑώρακεν αὐτὸν οὐδὲ ἔγνωκεν αὐτόν, "no one who sins has seen him or knows him." John continues his custom of emphasis by contrasting negative and positive statements. As in Hebrew antithetical parallelism, the second member of the contrast provides added information concerning the first member. The expression ἐν αὐτῷ μένων, "dwelling in Him," in the first line of the parallelism is expanded by the two verbs, ἑώρακεν, "has seen," and ἔγνωκεν, "has known," in the second line. Thus it is clear that dwelling in Christ is tantamount to seeing him and knowing Him.

---

29. Westcott, p. 104.
30. Robertson Nicoll, gen. ed., *The Expositor's Greek Testament*, "The Epistles of John," by David Smith, 5:184.

Again, the universal negative construction (πᾶς . . . οὐχ, "no one") is used to exclude everyone who fails to pass the test. As in the first half of the verse the verb ἁμαρτάνω appears in the present tense describing the habit of sinning. A single act of sin does not indicate that a person has not seen Him or known him, but continual sinning does.

The two verbs ἑώρακεν, "has seen," and ἔγνωκεν, "has known," are not to be taken as identical in meaning. To see someone is more superficial than to know someone. To see a person is to view his external likeness, but to know a person is to become familiar with the characteristics of his personality. To the Hebrew, and to the Christian as well, knowledge was bathed in experience. Rather than being theoretical, it was experiential. Knowledge of Christ, then, comes by the experience of His presence. The verb γινώσκω is ingressive in its meaning. It speaks of the obtaining of knowledge rather than its possession.[31] It often means something like "to come to know." In verse 6 it could be translated "he has not come to know Him." By adding the word ἔγνωκεν, "he has known," John may be unobstrusively discrediting the Gnostic teachers who claimed special knowledge, but whose lives were marked by sinful practices. The perfect tense of these two verbs employed with the negative conjunction, οὐδέ, provides a strong and comprehensive denial. The viewpoint from which the Greek perfect tense looks at an act is that of present time, while the action is set forth as completed in past time. The apostle declares concerning the habitual sinner that, as of the present time, he has not seen or known Christ, which is the same as saying that he has *never* seen or known Him.

3:7. τεκνία μηδεὶς πλανάτω ὑμᾶς, "Little children, let no one deceive you." At this point John makes a direct application of the theme of this section to his readers. On τεκνία, see 2:1. Although some manuscripts have παιδία (A C P), superior evidence (ℵ B K L) favors τεκνία. This term is most appropriate in a context where the emphasis is on being born of God. πλανάτω, "deceive" (KJV), literally means, "lead astray." See on 2:26. Although μή, "not," with the present imperative usually calls for the cessation of an action already in progress, this does not seem to be the case here. There is no evidence that John's readers were actually being de-

---

31. Longenecker, Richard N. and Tenney, Merrill C., eds., *New Dimensions in New Testament Study*, "Οἶδα and Γινώσκω in the Pauline Epistles," by Donald W. Burdick, p. 344.

ceived. Instead the apostle may well be urging them to continue not allowing anyone to lead them astray.[32]

ὁ ποιῶν τὴν δικαιοσύνην δίκαιός ἐστιν, καθὼς ἐκεῖνος δίκαιός ἐστιν, "the one who practices righteousness is righteous, just as He is righteous." This statement is the basic fact concerning which John does not want his readers to be deceived. Here again, as in 2:29, it is the continued practice of righteousness (ποιῶν, present tense) that is indicated, rather than one righteous act. Here also, as in 2:29, δικαιωσύνην, "righteousness," is preceded by the article revealing that a particular righteousness is being pointed out. Obviously, it is the righteousness characteristic of Christ, which is the mark of God's family, and which is the product of the new birth.

The practice of righteousness is not said to make one righteous. If that were true, the Greek would read δίκαιος γίνεται, "becomes righteous," rather than δίκαιός ἐστιν, "is righteous." Righteous conduct is the sign of righteous character. On δίκαιος, see on 2:29. It is expected that the child of God will be righteous "just as" (καθώς) "that one" (ἐκεῖνος) is righteous. Although some, such as Alford, interpret ἐκεῖνος as referring to God the Father, the preceding context (v. 5) indicates that the pronoun refers to Christ. καθώς does not indicate that the Christian is righteous to the same *extent* as Christ; this would be impossible for finite man. Instead the believer is said to be righteous in the same manner Christ is. In the family of God, the children of God are like the Son of God.

It may well be that John wrote this warning because the Asian believers were threatened by heretical teachers who claimed to be righteous simply because of professed esoteric knowledge. Theirs was not a righteousness of life; instead their conduct was marked by continual sin. John's warning against being led astray seems to suggest that this was the case. In response to such teaching he points out what genuine righteousness is. It is more than position or standing; it is conduct. The one who is truly righteous is the one who is consistently performing righteous deeds. Righteousness is not merely a matter of position; it is of necessity also a matter of life.

3:8. ὁ ποιῶν τὴν ἁμαρτίαν ἐκ τοῦ διαβόλου ἐστίν, ὅτι ἀπ' ἀρχῆς ὁ διάβολος ἁμαρτάνει, "the one who practices sin is of the devil; for the devil has sinned from the

---

32. Robertson, pp. 853-54.

beginning." The KJV "committeth sin" may well be taken to mean that anyone who commits a single act of sin is of the devil. It should be noted, however, that, as in verse 7, the participle ποιῶν is in the present tense and thus speaks of the person who is continually committing sin. His whole pattern of life is one of sin. The word ἁμαρτίαν, "sin," is preceded by the article, as is δικαιοσύνην, "righteousness" (v. 7). Inasmuch as verses 7 and 8 are set in antithetic parallelism to each other—the one being positive and the other negative—it seems that the articles before the two nouns serve to heighten this contrast. It is *the* righteousness on the one hand and *the* sin on the other. These are the distinguishing marks of the two families. The righteousness that John has in mind is *the* righteousness characteristic of God and coming from God; the sin referred to is *the* sin characteristic of the devil and which finds its source in him.

The phrase ἐκ τοῦ διαβόλου, "of the devil," is parallel to γεγεννημένος ἐκ τοῦ θεοῦ, "born of God" (v. 9; cf. 2:29). Both ἐκ and the ablative case speak of source, and although the Scripture does not use the expression *born of the devil*, Jesus did say, "You are of your father the devil" (John 8:44). Satan is the spiritual source of the one who is habitually committing sin. The practice of sin was originated and introduced into the human race by the devil. Thus, unregenerate men are his children, not merely because they imitate him, but because they are indwelt by the principle of sin of which he is the source.[33] Bonsirven explains that "We think that to be of the devil implies more than a relation of imitation: the sinner allows himself to be led by the tempter; he is inspired by him; is he not in some measure motivated by him (cf. II Thess. 2:9)? Possessed by him (Jn. 13:2, 27)?"[34]

John supports his statement with the explanation (ὅτι, "because") that the devil is sinning from the beginning. The tense of the verb ἁμαρτάνει is present, depicting continuing action. This usage of the present tense is designated as the present of duration, "denoting that which has begun in the past and continues into the present."[35] Throughout all the years "from the beginning" the devil has been continually engaged in sin. The phrase ἀπ' ἀρχῆς stands first in the clause and is thus emphatic, pointing up

---

33. Dodd, *The Johannine Epistles*, The Moffatt New Testament Commentary, p. 66, n. 1.
34. Bonsirven, p. 163 (my translation).
35. Dana and Mantey, p. 183.

the long period of time during which the devil has been engaging in sin. The time referred to by ἀρχῆς is somewhat debatable. It has been interpreted as pointing to the beginning of the world, the beginning of sin, or the beginning of the devil. It is, however, not reasonable to hold that sin has existed as long as the devil. This would seem to suggest either that God created Satan as an evil being, making God the immediate author of sin, or that Satan eternally co-existed with God in a dualism of good and evil. John no doubt has in mind that period when all things had their beginnings. It was then that sin originated in the first satanic rebellion against the Almighty (John 8:44). Houlden explains the beginning as referring to "the moment of that mysterious primeval disaster."[36] Prior to the creation of the first human beings, the devil was already sinning. It was he who introduced sin to the human race, and thus all who are sinning are his spiritual offspring.

εἰς τοῦτο ἐφανερώθη ὁ υἱὸς τοῦ θεοῦ, ἵνα λύσῃ τὰ ἔργα τοῦ διαβόλου, "The Son of God appeared for this purpose, that He might destroy the works of the devil." The prepositional phrase εἰς τοῦτο, "unto this," expresses the purpose of Christ's coming. Τοῦτο, however, does not look back to an antecedent in the preceding context. Instead it finds its explanation in the ἵνα clause that follows. The sense of the statement is that the Son of God was manifested for this, namely, that He might destroy Satan's works. The same type of construction appears again in verses 10 and 16. The punctiliar action indicated by the aorist ἐφανερώθη, "was manifested," looks back to the incarnation. Here as in verse 5 the selection of the term ἐφανερώθη rather than ἐγεννήθη, "he was born," shows that John was thinking of one who had previously existed in another sphere and then was manifested to men. The aorist λύσῃ, "He might destroy," also depicts point action, referring no doubt to Christ's victory over Satan on the cross (cf. Jn. 12:31; Heb. 2:14). The devil's works are all the sinful attitudes and activities of which he is the source, whether directly or indirectly. Everything that the devil has done was potentially destroyed at the cross and will be destroyed in actuality at the final judgment (Rev. 20:11-15). However, in this context destroying the works of the devil is parallel to taking away sins (see on v. 5). That is to say that Christ is here and now destroying or removing sins. He came to give believers victory over sin, and thus to destroy the sins that otherwise would fill people's lives. The

---

36. Houlden, p. 95.

verb λύσῃ, "destroy," normally means "to loose, to dissolve, to break up, to destroy." Marshall points out that its usage here is "somewhat unusual." What John says is that "the task of Jesus was to undo whatever the devil had achieved, to thwart whatever he tries to do." Specifically Marshall applies this to the devil's work of tempting and enslaving men.[37]

3:9. πᾶς ὁ γεγεννημένος ἐκ τοῦ θεοῦ ἁμαρτίαν οὐ ποιεῖ, "No one who is born of God practices sin." Ὁ γεγεννημένος ἐκ τοῦ θεοῦ reminds us that the keynote of this second main section of the epistle (2:29—4:6) is divine sonship. The perfect tense participle γεγεννημένος refers to a point in the past when the person experienced spiritual birth (was regenerated). Although that occurrence could have been described by using the aorist tense, the perfect tense adds the fact of continuing results. So John refers to one who has been regenerated in the past and who, as a result, is now a child of God.

The words πᾶς, "everyone," and οὐ, "not," combine to produce a universal negative, "no one," having the same meaning as οὐδείς.[38] John makes it clear that there is not a single regenerated person who commits sin. This assertion, however, does not agree with reality or with other statements that the apostle has already made in the first two chapters of the epistle. Experience teaches that the most saintly believers do sin. Furthermore, in 1:8, 10 John insists that to deny the possession of or commission of sin is erroneous. And in 2:1 he explains God's provision for Christians when they do commit acts of sin (aorist tense, ἁμάρτῃ). It cannot be true, therefore, that no regenerated person commits sin.

Various suggested solutions have been proposed, many of which have been listed and analyzed by Marshall.[39]

1. It may be argued that those who do not commit sin are the spiritually elite who have reached the plane of sinlessness. John, however, does not limit this condition to the few; he includes all of the regenerate.
2. Some have limited the sin mentioned here to some particular kind of sin such as willful acts of sin. But such an idea must be read into the passage if it is to be found there, for John in no way indicates that he has anything in mind but sin in general.

---

37. Marshall, p. 185.
38. Ibid., p. 186, n. 35; C. F. D. Moule, *An Idiom Book of New Testament Greek*, p. 182.
39. Marshall, pp. 178-83.

Sonship Tested on Ethical Grounds: Practice of Righteousness 245

3. Some have explained that John is speaking of the Christian ideal. A Christian ought not to sin. This is the aim of the Christian life. The problem with such a view is that the text gives no basis for such an interpretation. John uses simple straightforward indicative mood verbs that declare the fact that regenerated people do not sin. (See οὐχ ἁμαρτάνει, "he does not sin," 3:6; ἁμαρτίαν οὐ ποιεῖ, "he does not commit sin," 3:9). This is not an unrealized ideal; it is an existing reality.
4. Some have seen the statements of 3:6, 9 as implicit imperatives, but faithfulness to John's text demands that full value be given to these indicative statements.
5. Some have made them out to be implicit conditions meaning something like "if one abides in Christ, he will not sin." Again, this is altering John's text. There are no conditional particles or subjunctive moods to be found in these statements.
6. Marshall holds that "John refers to the eschatological reality brought about by Christ's coming, namely the possibility that is open to believers, which is both a fact ('he cannot sin') and conditional ('if he lives in him')."[40] This view likewise fails to preserve the integrity of John's indicative declarations, in that it inserts a conditional element where none is in any way indicated. Furthermore, Marshall fails to explain in what sense the child of God *cannot* sin. In this connection, Bultmann says that the expression "he is not able to sin" speaks of "the possibility of not sinning."[41] But this, too, does damage to John's statement. It does not say "he is *able not* to sin," but "he is *not able* to sin."
7. Some suggest that the contradiction between 1:8, 10 and 3:6, 9 is resolved by recognizing that the two passages refer to two different erors.[42] In 1:8, 10 John combats the Gnostics who believed that through esoteric knowledge they had become perfect, whereas in 3:6, 9 he refutes those who insisted that sin is merely a matter of the material body and thus does not touch the spirit of the enlightened Gnostic. Although some Gnostics did hold to one view and some to the other, this fact does not really solve the problem. The seeming contradiction is still present.

40. Ibid., pp. 182-83; Dodd, pp. 79-80.
41. Bultmann, p. 53.
42. Stott, p. 126; Dodd, p. 80.

8. Still others have explained the passage by saying that John means that the new nature in the believer does not commit sin. John does not say, however, that "that which (neuter) has been born of God does not sin," but "he who has been born (ὁ γεγεννημένος) of God does not sin." No valid distinction can be made between a Christian person and his new nature.
9. The solution to the problem lies in the present tense verbs in 3:6 and 9. It is the normal function of the present tense to express continuing action. There are, of course, exceptions to this pattern such as the aoristic uses of the present. Generally, however, some degree of linear action or continuing state are expressed. This fact is recognized in all grammars.[43]

Numerous examples of intended distinctions between the kinds of action portrayed by differing tenses could be cited. In Matthew 16:24, Jesus said, "If anyone wishes to come after Me, let him deny [aorist tense, point action] himself, and take up his cross [aorist tense, point action] and follow [present tense, continuing action] Me." It is apparent that the self-denial and the taking up of the cross are performed at a point in time before the disciple begins to follow. The following, however, is a linear or continuing action that goes on throughout the disciple's lifetime. Or consider the tense change in John 10:38 where Jesus called on His hearers to believe the works that He was doing. The expressed purpose was ἵνα γνῶτε καὶ γινώσκητε, "that you may know and understand," or more literally (as in the NASB margin) "know and continue knowing." Robertson says concerning this passage, "Jesus is anxious that his hearers may grasp the idea and hold on to it. . . ."[44] Such interpretations of tense are not grammatical subtleties as Dodd and Marshall assert,[45] but are valid distinctions based on recognized differences between the kinds of actions expressed by the aorist and present tenses. The context in 1 John, especially the earlier statements concerning sin and the believer (1:8—2:2), would seem to call for continuing action in contrast with the punctiliar aorists of 2:1. Thus John is declaring, not that the regenerated person does not commit sin, but that he does not continually engage in sinning. The Christian does not follow the example of the devil, who has been continually sinning (ἁμαρτά-

---

43. Blass and DeBrunner, sec. 318 (2); Moule, p. 7; Robertson, pp. 179-80; Dana and Mantey, pp. 181ff; Maximilian Zerwick S.J., *Biblical Greek*, sec. 251.
44. A. T. Robertson, *The Minister and His Greek New Testament*, p. 95.
45. Dodd, p. 80; Marshall, p. 180.

νει, present tense) ever since his fall.

ὅτι σπέρμα αὐτοῦ ἐν αὐτῷ μένει, "because His seed remains in him." This is the reason why the regenerated person does not engage in habitual sin. The term σπέρμα, "seed," reflects the process of human procreation rather than that of plant propagation. This interpretation is borne out by the reference in the last clause of verse 9 to being born of God. The sperm carries the life principle as well as the hereditary characteristics. In the same manner, that which imparts the characteristics of the divine family resides continually (present tense μένει) in the child of God.

Some, basing their interpretation on James 1:18 and 1 Peter 1:23, have viewed the seed as being the Word of God by which men are regenerated. In the latter passage the related word σπόρος, "seed," is used. Strictly speaking, however, as E. G. Selwyn demonstrates, this term refers to the act of sowing seed, rather than to the seed that is sown (σπέρμα).[46] It is also significant that the use of the term seed to refer to the word of God is not found elsewhere in John's writings.

Others view the term σπέρμα as referring to God's offspring. The apostle would then be saying that no one born of God sins because God's children abide in Him. But the use of σπέρμα here to designate God's offspring is quite unexpected. John has referred to Christians as born of God (2:29) and as children of God (3:1-2), but there is nothing in the context to indicate that σπέρμα is being used in this sense. Also the introduction of the idea that God's children do not sin because they abide in Him disrupts the otherwise unified statement of verse 9. John is obviously saying that the reason why believers do not sin is that they have been born of God. Verse 9 begins and closes with this fact.

Still others interpret the word σπέρμα as referring to the Holy Spirit. Although the Spirit is not elsewhere described as the seed, there is good reason for preferring this view. In John 3:5-8 Jesus associates the Holy Spirit with the new birth. And in 1 John 2:27 he speaks of the anointing (Holy Spirit) that "abides in you," (μένει, as in 3:9). In regeneration the active, life-giving agent is the Holy Spirit, whereas the Word of God is the means used by the Spirit. He is also the producer of Christian character in the believer (2 Cor. 3:18; Gal. 5:22-23). It is because of the Spirit's indwelling presence as the σπέρμα of God that the regenerated person does not engage continually in the practice of sin.

---

46. E. G. Selwyn, *The First Epistle of St. Peter,* pp. 150-51.

καὶ οὐ δύναται ἁμαρτάνειν, ὅτι ἐκ τοῦ θεοῦ γεγέννηται, "and he cannot sin, because he is born of God." Here, John goes beyond his previous statement. Not only is it true that the believer does not continually sin, but he cannot do so. Again the present tense verbs are significant. It is not that the Christian cannot commit a single act of sin as the KJV may seem to suggest, but he is continually unable (οὐ δύναται) to engage in habitual sin (ἁμαρτάνειν). He may commit individual acts of sin, but it is not possible for sin to become the pattern of his life. As in the first part of the verse, John sets forth the reason for his assertion. It is ὅτι ἐκ τοῦ θεοῦ γεγέννηται, "because he is born of God." It is the new life principle implanted in the child of God by regeneration that keeps him from continually engaging in sin. Instead the new life principle provides motivation toward righteousness.

3:10. ἐν τούτῳ φανερά ἐστιν τὰ τέκνα τοῦ θεοῦ καὶ τὰ τέκνα τοῦ διαβόλου, "By this the children of God and the children of the devil are obvious." This verse serves both as a summary of the preceding section (2:29—3:9) and as a transition to the following section (3:11-24). The preposition ἐν may be used either with the locative case and be translated "in," or with the instrumental case and mean "by means of." In this instance John no doubt intends the latter, indicating the means by which it is possible to identify the members of the two families mentioned. The demonstrative pronoun τοῦτο may either refer back to the preceding statement or look forward to what follows. John uses the pronoun in both ways in this epistle. Here, however, it makes little difference since both the preceding and the following context speak of the same fact: the family of God is marked by the practice of righteousness. It is probable that τοῦτο refers to the remainder of verse 10, but, since this is a summary of what precedes, the pronoun also refers to the preceding context. The designation τὰ τέκνα τοῦ διαβόλου, "the children of the devil," clearly shows that the phrase ἐκ τοῦ διαβόλου, "of the devil" (v. 8), is to be understood as referring to the source of the persons described. Although John does not go so far as to say that they are born of the devil, he does indicate that, in a spiritual and moral sense, they are derived from the devil. (Cf. John 8:44).

πᾶς ὁ μὴ ποιῶν δικαιοσύνην οὐκ ἔστιν ἐκ τοῦ θεοῦ, "any one who does not practice righteousness is not of God." Here as in verse 9 John combines πᾶς, *everyone,* with οὐκ, "not," to make a universal negative: "No one who is not doing righteousness is of God." It is clear that anyone who is not habitually performing

Sonship Tested on Ethical Grounds: Practice of Righteousness

(present tense ποιῶν) acts of righteousness is not a part of the family of God. The phrase ἐκ τοῦ θεοῦ, "of God," occurs several times in this epistle. In addition to its appearance in 3:10, it occurs six times in 4:1-6. The key to its meaning is found in 3:9-10 where it is clearly parallel with γεγεννημένος ἐκ τοῦ θεοῦ, *"born of God."* Dodd says that the shorter expression appears to be "a briefer synonym" for the longer one.[47] Thus the idea of being born of God is found at the beginning (2:29—3:10) and at the end (4:1-6) of this major section of the epistle.

THEOLOGICAL COMMENTARY (2:29-3:10a)

A. THE APOSTLE'S REASONING IN 2:29-3:10A

This section introduces the second cycle of the epistle, in which the Christian life is viewed as divine sonship. As in the first cycle, John sets up a series of tests by which one can discern who is and who is not a child of God. The first set of tests is ethical in nature having to do with righteousness (2:29—3:10a) and love (3:10b-24).

1. THE STANDARD OF COMPARISON, 2:29

Verse 29 parallels 1:5. In both verses, God's character is pointed up as the standard that is the basis for the ethical test. Anyone who passes the test will be, in some measure, like God. In 1:5-7, likeness is the prerequisite for fellowship; in 2:29 likeness is the sure result of spiritual birth.

John assumes that it is true beyond any shadow of doubt that God is righteous. The righteousness of God is His holiness exercised in relation to His creatures. All His attitudes and actions are thoroughly in keeping with His holy nature. He is morally self-consistent in all that He thinks and does. And it is this holiness in action toward others that John sets up as the standard. Those whose lives are in agreement with this standard give evidence that they are the children of God.

The reason why it can rightly be assumed that this likeness will be present in the life of every believer is to be found in the verb γεγέννηται (2:29). The righteousness of the Father is passed on to His child. This family trait is not merely a matter of the imitation of the Father; it is rather a matter of inherited family characteristics.

47. Dodd, p. 66, n. 1.

2. THE PRIVILEGE OF SONSHIP, 3:1-3

Having stated the basic truth on which 2:29—3:10*a* rests, John pauses to express his own amazement that God would condescend to make us His children. That sinners should be brought into the family of God is beyond comprehension. Behold, what love! Sinners are not only *called* His children—designated as such; by spiritual birth, they actually *become* His children.

These verses speak of both the present and the future state of the children of God. As for the present, Christians are now God's children by regeneration. What they shall become in the future has not yet been spelled out. Only a brief glimpse has been given, but this much is known (v. 2):

- Christ will come again.
- He shall be seen as He really is.
- This is proof that Christians will then be like Him.

As children of God there is currently a family resemblance, but then there shall be full conformity to His likeness and this guarantee concerning the future has a present purifying effect. Even now it is in the process of making His children like Him. Sonship, then, produces sanctification. In the present it results in progressive sanctification—the process by which Christians become more and more like Him. In the future it will result in complete and final sanctification when the sinful nature will be eradicated and His children will be holy as He is holy.

3. THE MARK OF SONSHIP, 3:4-10A

John explains that one of the chief characteristics of the child of God is the practice of righteousness. Like his heavenly Father the believer does what is right toward others as his usual pattern of life. The general tenor of his life is in accord with the divine standard of right and wrong. Any other course is incompatible with his position as a child of God. In verses 4-10 John explains why it is that sin is incompatible for the child of God.

a. It is incompatible because of the nature of sin (v. 4). Sin is not merely a mistake; it is not merely a careless failure to do what is right; it is not simply a matter of finitude or human weakness; nor is it, as the Gnostic would have said, a result of imprisonment in a material body. Sin is a criminal act against God's law. It is rebellion

Sonship Tested on Ethical Grounds: Practice of Righteousness 251

against His rightfully constituted authority. It is, therefore, not consistent for members of God's family to practice sin.

b. Sin is likewise incompatible for the Christian because of the nature of Christ's person and work (vv. 5-7). John describes Christ's person both negatively and positively. Negatively he declares that in Christ there is no sin (v. 5*b*). That is, there is in Him no indwelling depravity, no sinful nature. Sin is totally foreign to His being. Put positively, He (ἐκεῖνος) is righteous (v. 7) just as God is declared to be righteous (2:29). For the follower of Christ to practice sin is, therefore, inconsistent.

Sin likewise is incompatible with the work of Christ. He came to remove sins (v. 5) or, as it is stated in verse 8, to undo all that the devil seeks to accomplish. For the child of God to practice sin, therefore, is to be diametrically opposed to all that Christ came to do. It is to place oneself at sword's points with the Savior. Therefore, for the one who dwells in Him (v. 6) to continually practice sin is totally inconsistent. He who has seen Him and who has come to know Him cannot be in such frontal opposition to Christ's person and to His purpose in coming.

c. Furthermore, sin is incompatible for the Christian because of its source (v. 8). Here John reflects the remarks of Jesus to the unbelieving Jewish leaders (John 8:44). Sin had its origin with the devil, and, since the time of its origin, he has been its most persistent propagator. The practice of sin is, therefore, a characteristic of the devil and his family, and as such, it is incompatible for a member of the family of God.

Not only is sin *incompatible* with the Christian's position as a member of God's family, but, according to verse 9, sin is *impossible* for the child of God. Numerous attempted explanations of this difficult assertion have been advanced, the simplest and most natural of which rests on the significance of the Greek present tense (see pp. 244-46).

When John speaks of the impossibility of sin, it is the impossibility of the habitual practice of sin to which he refers. This does not rule out individual acts of sin, but it does rule out living in sin.

The first cycle of the epistle provides a helpful parallel. John speaks of walking in the light and of walking in the darkness (1:6-7). The metaphorical term "walk" refers to the continuing pattern of life, and this linear idea is strengthened by the Greek present tense. The apostle's point is that anyone who is in fellowship with God will be living continually in the light. But John does not leave room for the idea of sinless perfection. In 1:8-10, he rules out the possibility of sinlessness (both the principle of sin, 1:8, and the acts of sin, 1:10), and he suggests (1:9) that the believer will regularly (Greek present tense) be admitting his sin. Also in 2:1 he allows you the possibility of committing acts of sin (aorist tense, point action). It is clear, therefore, that walking in the light refers to a life whose general tenor is not dominated by sin, but by righteousness.

It is this same pattern that the apostle has in mind in 2:29—3:10*a*. What is impossible (3:9) is not individual acts of sin, but the continuing practice of sin. This is because the divine seed (life principle, nature [2 Pet. 1:4]) that dwells in the believer exerts its influence so that the characteristics of God's family manifest themselves. Consequently, no longer is sin dominant; now it is righteousness that exercises primary control.

The clearest declaration of the two families is found in 3:10—where John speaks of the children of God and the children of the devil—the former marked by the practice of righteousness and the latter by the practice of sin. There is no room here for a universal spiritual fatherhood of God. It may be said that, as Creator, God is the Father of all people; however, God is spiritually Father only of those who have been born into His family. All others are in the family of the devil. There is no third category.

B. THE NATURE AND EFFECT OF SPIRITUAL BIRTH

It should be noted that the believer is not called a son of God (υἱὸς θεοῦ) in 1 John. Instead he is designated as a child of God (τέκνον θεοῦ). Nor is it said that he enters the family of God by adoption, but by birth (2:29; 3:9). Although the term *son* may refer to one who is born into the family (Matt. 1:25), it may also designate one who is adopted. Bonsirven points out that, whereas the word τέκνα designates those who are children by blood, υἱός connotes primarily the legal relationship.[48] Etymologically τέκνον is related to the verb τίκτω, "to bear," and thus could not be rightly used of an adopted child. It assumes a blood relationship, the result of natural procreation. In the spiritual realm it speaks of spiritual procreation, and this is exactly how John explains the action by which a believer enters God's family. He is born of God (γεγεννημένος τοῦ θεοῦ). He shares in the family traits, not merely because he lives in the family environment, but because, by birth,

---

48. Bonsirven, p. 147.

Sonship Tested on Ethical Grounds: Practice of Righteousness 253

he is a recipient of the divine nature.

The concept of spiritual birth goes back to Jesus Himself. In John 3 He insisted that Nicodemus must be born again (vv. 3, 5). The apostle John adopted the doctrine of regeneration as one of the main themes of his writings. It is a concept that assumes a prior condition of death—the New Testament has a previous spiritual death in view. Paul declares that at one time all were dead in trespasses and sins (Eph. 2:1), but God "made us alive together with Christ" (Eph. 2:5). Spiritual death is that state wherein a person is separated from God and so draws no spiritual life or power from him. The person is alive physically and intellectually, but morally and spiritually his soul is dead to all of those life-giving and holy influences of which God is the source. There is no ability to sense or to respond to the sanctifying power that continually flows from a holy God. Man's nature no longer naturally goes out to God; self now has become the all-important center around which his life revolves.

Regeneration restores spiritual life and creates ability to receive and benefit by those sanctifying impulses that come from God. The nature of the regenerated person now responds positively to divine overtures. Depravity, which had full play in the unregenerate state, is now thwarted by a nature renewed in holiness by the Holy Spirit. Although depravity is still present, "the governing disposition of the soul is made holy,"[49] so that the power of sin no longer dominates all of life.

It is to this kind of change that John refers when he speaks of one who is γεγεννημένος ἐκ τοῦ θεοῦ, "born of God" (3:9). Thus, when one comprehends what regeneration actually is, it is not so difficult to understand what John means when he declares that for God's child the practice of sin is impossible.

Having explained the nature of spiritual birth, there is a need to consider its effect. Wesley was correct in referring to regeneration as "the gateway to sanctification."[50] What is begun in new birth is continued in progressive sanctification.

John does not have in mind complete eradication of sin during this life. Complete and final sanctification will not take place until Christ returns (3:2), but a progressive sanctification is taking place in the believer's life now (3:3). The effect of this present sanctifying process is the reversal of the previous general pattern of life.

---

49. A. H. Strong, *Systematic Theology*, p. 809.
50. H. Orton Wiley, *Christian Theology*, 2:423.

Whereas once the tide of activity was largely characterized by sin, since regeneration that tide is largely characterized by righteousness. Whereas before conversion the habitual pattern of life was the practice of sin, since entering God's family the habitual pattern has been the practice of righteousness. Regeneration sets in motion the process of progressive sanctification. And it is because of this sanctifying process that the member of God's family οὐ δύναται ἁμαρτάνειν, "is not able to practice sin" (3:9, Gr.).

C. THE THREAT OF THE FALSE TEACHERS

Only once in this section (2:29—3:10*a*) does John give any hint as to the false teaching that gave rise to the epistle. Nevertheless, it is clear from 3:7 that false teachers were present and that their error had to do with the subject under discussion in these verses. Their attempt to deceive concerned morality for John warns, "Little children, let no one deceive you; the one who practices righteousness is righteous, just as He is righteous." Apparently there were those present in the towns of the province of Asia who insisted that one could be righteous, regardless of his actions, simply because he was one of the πνευματικοί, the spiritual elite.

Irenaeus explains the reasoning of Valentinian Gnostics saying:

> Animal men, again, are instructed in animal things: such men, namely, as are established by their works, and by a mere faith, while they have not perfect knowledge. We of the Church, they say, are these persons. Wherefore also they maintain that good works are necessary to us, for that otherwise it is impossible we should be saved. But as to themselves, they hold that they shall be entirely and undoubtedly saved, not by means of conduct, but because they are spiritual by nature. For, just as it is impossible that material substance should partake of salvation. . . , so again it is impossible that spiritual substance (by which they mean themselves) should ever come under the power of corruption, whatever the sort of actions in which they indulged.[51]

It would appear that it was in response to reasoning such as this that John insisted that the one who is actually *"doing righteousness"* (ποιῶν τὴν δικαιοσύνην) is righteous (3:7).

D. THE PRESENT-DAY APPLICATION

Two quite opposite types of application may be drawn from this passage.

51. Irenaeus *Against Heresies*, 1. 6. 2.

Sonship Tested on Ethical Grounds: Practice of Righteousness

1. A misuse of positional truth

What the Gnostic was claiming for himself was a position or a standing that was not based on his deeds. His standing was secure regardless of what he did. Such an assumption may be paralleled today by those who make a distinction between one's position in Christ and the state of one's day-by-day life. In one's position one is righteous because the righteousness of Christ has been imputed to him. In one's state one is a sinner, because one has a sinful nature and commits sinful acts. Now this is all very true and in accord with the teaching of the New Testament. The danger one must beware of is that of assuming—perhaps quite unconsciously—that since positional righteousness is a guaranteed fact, one can be less concerned about righteousness of life. Seldom does one meet someone who is as crass as to say that salvation by grace allows antinomianism, but the doctrine of standing and state may lead to a growing laxness of life, and to the extent that this is true, one falls into the error against which John was waging war. A most effective expression of positional truth is in terms of "the indicative" and "the imperative."[52] The indicative fact of our righteousness in Christ carries with it the inseparable imperative to be righteous in daily life.

2. Perfectionism

Some who believe in the possibility of living in this life without sinning have used 1 John 2:29—3:10 to argue for what has been called sinless perfection. Clarke, commenting on the words "as He is pure" (3:3), explains that this means "Till he is as completely saved from his sins as Christ was free from sin." To this Clarke adds:

> Now, as he was manifested to take away our sins, ver. 5, to destroy the works of the devil, ver. 8; and as his blood cleanseth from all sin and unrighteousness, chap. i. 7, 9; is it not evident that God means that believers shall be saved from all sin? For if his blood cleanses from all sin, if he destroys the works of the devil, (and sin is the work of the devil,) and if he who is born of God does not commit sin, ver. 9, then he must be cleansed from all sin: and while he continues in that state he lives without sinning against God, *for the*

---

52. George E. Ladd, *A Theology of the New Testament*, p. 493.

seed of God remaineth in him, and he cannot sin because he is born, or begotten, of God, ver. 9.[53]

Although it is true that Clarke is of an earlier day, and such modern commentaries as *The Wesleyan Bible Commentary* do not appear to find perfectionism taught in this passage,[54] some preachers and lay people who are of the perfectionist persuasion still use this passage to support their view.

Such an interpretation, however, overlooks several significant factors:

1. The view disregards the normal significance of the Greek present tense. John does not say that the believer does not commit sin, which would require the aorist tense, but that he does not continue sinning in habitual fashion.
2. Verse 3 states that the believer keeps purifying (present tense) himself as Christ is pure. It does not say that perfection is reached, but that a continuing process is taking place.
3. In verse 5 John says that Christ "appeared in order to take away sins," and in verse 8 it is said that He came to "destroy the works of the devil." These verses, however, do not state that Christ completely takes away sin or destroys Satan's work in any believer's life during this lifetime. Ultimately Christ's goal will be completely reached, but nothing in Scripture indicates that it occurs before His second coming. (See 3:2.)
4. Verse 6*b* says more than the perfectionist really wants it to say. If the present tense is not to be taken in its normal linear sense, this verse declares that "no one who sins [commits sin] has seen Him or knows Him." Clarke attempts to circumvent the difficulty by explaining that the apostle sometimes used the past for the present. Thus this verse would mean that the one who sins "doth not see him nor doth he know him."[55] But this unsatisfactory suggestion fails to relieve the difficulty. The verse, so interpreted, would mean that the person who commits an act of sin does not know the Lord, that is, he is unsaved. According to this interpretation only the person who does not sin at all would be saved. A recognition of the normal linear meaning of

---

53. Adam Clarke, *The New Testament of Our Lord and Savior Jesus Christ . . . A Commentary and Critical Notes,* 2:914.
54. Leo G. Cox, "First, Second and Third John," in *The Wesleyan Bible Commentary,* 4:341-42.
55. Ibid., pp. 914-15.

Sonship Tested on Ethical Grounds: Practice of Righteousness 257

the present tense relieves this difficulty. It is the person who habitually lives in sin who has not seen the Lord nor come to know Him.

5. In verse 9 John declares that "His seed abides in him." It is significant that the verb chosen is μένω, "to abide, remain, dwell," rather than εἰμί, *to be*. The permanence of the indwelling of God's seed is stressed by the use of μένω. Thus the person born of God will not lapse back into a life of habitual sin, because he is permanently indwelt by the Spirit of God.

Paraphrasitic Commentary (2:29—3:10*a*)

(29) If you are sure that all God is and does is in perfect harmony with what is right, then you may correctly conclude that every man who consistently does what is right is God's child, not by adoption but by birth. (3:1) Consider what indescribable love God has lavished on us! He even calls us His children—and that is just what we are! Since people did not know and appreciate Jesus when He was on earth, we can be sure that they will not understand us either. (2) Dear friends, now we are members of God's family, but we do not yet have detailed knowledge concerning our future state. We only know that when Christ comes again we will be like Him both in holiness and in resurrection body. Of this we can be sure, because we know that we will be able to see Him as He really is (and only those who are like Him will be capable of seeing Him in this way). (3) Everyone who has this confident expectation resting upon Christ is even now undergoing a constant sanctifying process so that he is becoming daily more like Christ. (4) The practice of sin is continued rebellion against God and His law; sin, in reality, is refusal to conform to God's will. (5) You well know that the reason That One came was to take away our very acts of sin; furthermore, in Him there dwells none of sin's depravity. (6) No one who has an intimate, saving relationship with Christ engages in sin as a constant habit of life; anyone who does so has not seen Him (with the eye of faith), nor has he come to know Him. (7) Dear children, continue to resist those who would lead you away from the truth: the only one who is righteous like Christ is the one who habitually performs acts of righteousness. (8) The one who is continually committing sin is a child of the devil, because the devil has been committing sin constantly ever since his fall. The reason Christ came was to undo every act for which the devil is responsible. (9) No one born into the family of God constantly performs acts of sin. This is true because God's new life principle forever dwells in the believer. It is impossible for him to live in sin because by new birth he has be-

come God's own child. (10a) This is how you can distinguish beween God's children and those of the devil: The person who does not habitually engage in acts of righteousness has never become a member of the family of God.

STRUCTURAL COMMENTARY (2:29—3:10a)[56]

III. Second cycle: The Christian life viewed as divine sonship, 2:29—4:6.
   A. Sonship tested on ethical grounds, 2:29—3:24
      1. Sonship demands practice of righteousness, 2:29—3:10a
         a. The basic principle, 2:29
            (1) God is righteous.
            (2) Anyone who is like Him is a member of His family.
         b. The privilege of sonship, 3:1-3
            (1) Evidence of unspeakable love, 3:1
            (2) Future effects of sonship, 3:2
            (3) Present effects of sonship, 3:3
         c. The sign of sonship, 3:4-10a
            (1) The incompatibility of sin, 3:4-8
               (a) Because of the nature of sin, 3:4
               (b) Because of the nature of Christ's person and work, 3:5-7
               (c) Because of the source of sin, 3:8
            (2) The impossibility of sin, 3:9
               (a) The regenerate person does not practice sin.
               (b) The regenerate person cannot practice sin.
            (3) The concluding statement, 3:10a

---

56. For previous section of the outline, see p. 223.

11

2. Sonship Tested on Ethical Grounds: Love for Fellow Believers, 3:10b-24

At this point, without introducing a new sentence, John makes a transition from the subject of righteousness to that of love. The two concepts are not unrelated. In fact, they may be viewed as two ways of referring to the same thing. The relationship of righteousness (i.e., keeping the law) and love is explicitly stated by both Jesus (Matt. 22:34-40) and Paul (Rom. 13:8-10). This is the second cycle in John's treatment of love as a test, just as 2:29—3:10a was the second cycle in his treatment of righteousness. In neither instance, however, is the second cycle mere repetition. Each succeeding cycle always advances beyond the content of earlier sections.

In 3:10b-24, the apostle makes his transition from righteousness to love (3:10b) and then reminds his readers of the long-standing love command (3:11). After citing two negative examples (3:12-13), he restates more explicitly the love test (3:14-15) and then proceeds to establish a test to distinguish between genuine and counterfeit love (3:16-18). The chapter closes with a discussion of confidence—the fruit of love (3:19-24).

EXEGETICAL COMMENTARY (3:10b-24)

SONSHIP DEMANDS LOVE FOR FELLOW BELIEVERS, 3:10b-24

3:10b. καὶ ὁ μὴ ἀγαπῶν τὸν ἀδελφὸν αὐτοῦ, "nor the one who does not love his brother." This phrase is parallel to the phrase, ὁ μὴ ποιῶν δικαιοσύνην, "who does not practice righteousness," in the first part of the verse. The two phrases together set forth the two sides of the ethical test of sonship: the practice of righteousness and the love of fellow believers. Bultmann holds that the term "brother," here and in 2:10; 3:15; and 4:20, is not to be limited to fellow Christians, but means "neighbor."[1] John, however, explicitly limits the term to the person who has been born of God (5:1). This is not to say that the love of outsiders is unimportant. But for John's purpose of establishing a series of tests to distinguish the genuine believer from the spurious one, love is limited to the love of believers. Thus limited, the test is easier to handle and, no doubt, more objective.

As in the discussion of righteousness, it is not an isolated instance of love that is in view, in which case the aorist tense would have been used. Instead, John employs the present tense participle ἀγαπῶν to indicate the continuing practice of love.

Although the practice of righteousness is a fairly general test, the love of the brother is more specific. In fact, it is actually a more specific form of righteousness, and thus it provides a more objective test in distinguishing those who are God's children from those who are not. On the other hand, love may be viewed as the sum total of righteousness, for to love one's brother is to fulfill the total obligation the law lays on one (Rom. 13:8-10).

3:11. ὅτι αὕτη ἐστὶν ἡ ἀγγελία ἣν ἠκούσατε ἀπ᾽ ἀρχῆς, ἵνα ἀγαπῶμεν ἀλλήλους, "For this is the message which you have heard from the beginning, that we should love one another." This verse is very similar to the opening statement of the first discussion of love (2:7). The connecting particle (ὅτι) is better translated "for" (NASB) than "because," since it explains the authority on which the statement in verse 10b rests. Christ declared that God's people are a loving people (John 13:34-35). In this epistle the demonstrative pronouns usually point to what follows; in like manner αὕτη here refers to the ἵνα clause with which the verse closes.

The word ἀγγελία, "message," reminds us of the similar statement in 1:5, where we find the only other New Testament occurrence of this noun. The phrase ἀπ᾽ ἀρχῆς, "from the beginning," has several possible interpretations, depending on the context in which it appears (see on 1:1 and 2:7). Here the verb ἀκούσατε, "you have heard," indicates that the beginning re-

---

1. Rudolf Bultmann, *The Johannine Epistles*, Hermeneia, p. 54.

Sonship Tested on Ethical Grounds: Love for Fellow Believers 261

ferred to was the time when the readers first heard the gospel message. In contrast to Gnostic teaching, which was a comparatively late arrival, the command to love was part of the original authoritative message that came from Christ Himself. On ἀγάπη, "love," see on 2:7.

Although some would insist that ἵνα, "that," is here used in a final sense to express purpose,[2] It is clear that the conjunction is used in an objective sense as the equivalent of ὅτι, "that," used in apposition.[3] That this is true is indicated by the presence of αὕτη, "this," which Brooke says excludes any possibility that ἵνα is final.[4] The verb ἀγαπῶμεν occurs in the subjunctive mood, since ἵνα normally takes the subjunctive. The translation "should love," therefore, does not reflect the subjunctive (since the ἵνα is equal to ὅτι and the use of the subjunctive is merely formal), but it gives expression to an implicit command that, no doubt, goes back to John 13:34-35, "A new commandment I give to you, that you love one another." ἀλλήλους, "one another," is to be limited to believers, as the term "brother" in the following context (1 John 3:14-15) indicates. Also see on 3:10b.

3:12. οὐ καθὼς Κάϊν ἐκ τοῦ πονηροῦ ἦν καὶ ἔσφαξεν τὸν ἀδελφὸν αὐτοῦ, "not as Cain, who was of the evil one, and slew his brother." Although this sentence is incomplete, its meaning is obvious. The negative οὐ clearly sets verse 12 in contrast to verse 11. From the context one must attempt to ascertain John's thinking and supply what he omits. He might have meant that believers are not to be of the evil one as Cain was, but this is not likely since John's readers were already members of the family of God. Or it may be taken to mean that they are to love one another in a manner different than Cain who was of the evil one. This is not possible because Cain did not love his brother in any sense of the word. It is best to understand the ellipsis as occurring at the beginning of verse 12 and to read John's intended meaning as follows: "Let us not be like Cain (who) was of the evil one and murdered his brother." In any case it seems necessary to supply the pronoun "who" as the NASB does. This mention of Cain is the only explicit reference to the OT in this epistle (Gen. 4:8), a

---

2. B. F. Westcott, *The Epistles of St. John*, p. 110.
3. H. E. Dana and Julius R. Mantey, *A Manual Grammar of the Greek New Testament*, pp. 248-49.
4. A. E. Brooke, *The Johannine Epistles*, The International Critical Commentary, p. 91.

feature worthy of note when one consider how many references to the OT appear in John's gospel.

On the expression, ἐκ τοῦ πονηροῦ ἦν, "was of the evil one," see the treatment of 3:8. The phrase parallels γεγεννημένον ἐκ τοῦ θεοῦ, "born of God," and refers to the spiritual relationship that existed between Cain and the devil. See τέκνα τοῦ διαβόλου (v. 10). That the adjective πονηροῦ is here used substantivally to refer to the evil one rather than to the abstract quality of evil is indicated by the presence of the article. It is certain that Cain was a member of the devil's family because he manifested the family characteristic. Jesus declared Satan to have been a murderer ἀπ' ἀρχῆς, "from the beginning," that is from the time of his primeval rebellion against God (John 8:44). Cain, in the murder of his brother, fulfilled the proverb, "Like father, like son." His attitude was hatred, and his act was murder.

The verb ἔσφαζεν, "slew," is a strong term that originally meant "to cut the throat." It had come to refer to violent slaughter. Both Otto Michel and Bultmann translate it "butchered." Michel says it is a "vivid and grisly expression for murder."[5]

καὶ χάριν τίνος ἔσφαζεν αὐτόν; ὅτι τὰ ἔργα αὐτοῦ πονηρὰ ἦν, τὰ δὲ τοῦ ἀδελφοῦ αὐτοῦ δίκαια, "And for what reason did he slay him? Because his deeds were evil, and his brother's were righteous." The phrase χάριν τίνος, *on account of what*, is not a very common expression. Χάριν is the accusative case of χάρις and functions as a preposition. As such, it appears only nine times in the New Testament. The expression is a somewhat striking way of pointing up the reason Cain murdered his brother. It was because the wicked person hates righteousness. It is not that he is jealous of the righteous and wishes that he were like him. Instead it is that the righteousness of the righteous puts the wicked person in a bad light. "Godlessness is disturbed by the condemning presence of righteousness in its midst, and it would remove the cause of its discomfort if it could."[6] Whereas Abel brought the offering that God had commanded, Cain disobeyed God,[7] and the obedience of Abel threw the disobedience of Cain

---

5. Gerhard Kittel, ed., *Theological Dictionary of the New Testament*, 1964-76, s.v. "σφάζω, σφαγή," by Otto Michel. 7:932.
6. Donald W. Burdick, *The Epistles of John*, p. 58.
7. The Genesis account assumes that the two brothers both knew what was expected of them. A revelation of the divine will is taken for granted. Abel submitted to God's command, but Cain insisted on bringing the offering that he wanted to bring.

Sonship Tested on Ethical Grounds: Love for Fellow Believers 263

into sharp contrast. Notice that just as Cain was ἐκ τοῦ πονηροῦ, "of the evil one," so his deeds were πονηρά, "evil."

3:13. [καὶ] μὴ θαυμάζετε, ἀδελφοί, εἰ μισεῖ ὑμᾶς ὁ κόσμος, "Do not marvel, brethren, if the world hates you." The United Bible Societies' *Greek New Testament* places καί in brackets to indicate that considerable doubt exists as to whether or not the word belongs in the text. The manuscript evidence is fairly evenly divided with ℵ and C including καί and A and B omitting it. It is possible that scribes inserted it to emphasize the connection between verses 12 and 13, or it may be that it was accidently omitted due to confusion caused by the καί in the immediately preceding δίκαια.[8] It is not translated in the NASB, NIV, RSV, or NEB.

Θαυμάζετε is a present imperative verb preceded by μή, a construction that usually assumes that the action of the verb has already been occurring. The μή then calls for the action to cease. Apparently the readers had been upset by the world's antipathy, and John was urging them to "stop marvelling."[9] "Marvel" is not the best translation of θαυμάζω in the context. The verb was used to express wonder, astonishment, or surprise.[10] The NIV translates it, "Do not be surprised." The world's hatred is not a cause for surprise because it is natural that the wicked hate the righteous. See on verse 12.

This verse is the only instance in which John addresses his readers as ἀδελφοί, "brothers." In all other places he calls them τεκνία, "little children," παιδία, "children," or ἀγαπητοί, "beloved." By using the term, ἀδεγφοί, he puts himself on the same level with his readers. The normal use of εἰ, "if," with the indicative mood in a conditional sentence is to indicate a condition that is viewed as fulfilled. Marshall states that in this verse it means either "that" or "if" and views hatred by the world as a possibility rather than a fact.[11] However, Bauers translate 1 John 3:13, "Do not wonder that the world hates you."[12] Reasons why this antipathy should be taken for granted can be found in Jesus' statement in John 15:18-20.

---

8. Bruce M. Metzger, *A Textual Commentary on the Greek New Testament,* p. 712.
9. See note on 2:15.
10. Kittel, s.v. "θαῦμα, θαυμάζω, κτλ.," by Georg Bertram. 3:28-29, 38.
11. I. Howard Marshall, *The Epistles of John, The New International Commentary on the New Testament,* p. 190, n. 9.
12. William F. Arndt and F. Wilbur Gingrich, trans. and eds., *A Greek-English Lexicon of the New Testament,* by Walter Bauer, p. 219 (II).

On the meaning of κόσμος, see on 3:1. The term is here used in a similar way to designate the people who are enmeshed in this evil world system, who are members of the devil's family. It is the same world that Christ died to save (1 John 4:14). There is a notable parallel between Cain, who hated his brother and murdered him, and the world that hates God's people. The reason for the hatred is the same in each instance—wickedness cannot tolerate the presence of righteousness. Both verses 12 and 13 contain prohibitions, the former implicit and the latter explicit. Both are examples of hatred, the one ancient and the other current.

3:14. ἡμεῖς οἴδαμεν ὅτι μεταβεβήκαμεν ἐκ τοῦ θανάτου εἰς τὴν ζωήν, "We know that we have passed out of death into life." In verses 14-15 John restates the test he had previously advanced in 2:9-11. Love for Christians is evidence that one is saved; hatred for Christians reveals that one is still lost. Since the Greek verb carries its own subject (οἴδαμεν, "we know"), the personal pronoun, ἡμεῖς, "we," is unnecessary, except for emphasis. The world is characterized by hatred (3:13), but believers know they have passed from death to life (v. 14). Οἴδαμεν here, on the one hand, functions like γινώσκω, drawing a conclusion from the experiential fact that one loves the brothers. On the other hand, however, this usage is distinctively characteristic of οἶδα in that it speaks of assured knowledge, a matter commonly known by believers. The verb μεταβεβήκαμεν usually describes geographical movement from one location to another. Here it is used metaphorically to depict movement from one spiritual sphere, ἐκ τοῦ θανάτου, "out of death," to another spiritual sphere, εἰς τὴν ζωήν, "into life." Note the definite articles (τοῦ, τήν) marking out the two distinct spheres into which the entire human race is divided. The perfect tense μεταβεβήκαμεν, "we have passed," indicates that the transfer has already occurred at a point in the past, and, as a result, the sphere of life has already been entered. Eternal life is not a state to be reached only after death; it is an experience that begins at regeneration (John 5:24).

ὅτι ἀγαπῶμεν τοὺς ἀδελφούς, "because we love the brethren." The conjunction ὅτι, "because," serves to explain οἴδαμεν, "we know," rather than μεταβεβήκαμεν, "we have passed." In other words, the assurance of eternal life is based on the fact that one loves fellow believers. Life is not earned by loving the brothers; it is evidenced by such love. As in previous passages (2:10; 3:10) the present tense verb ἀγαπῶμεν, "we love" speaks of the continuing exercise of love, a pattern of life, not merely a

Sonship Tested on Ethical Grounds: Love for Fellow Believers 265

momentary flash of affection. Whereas in 2:9-11, John uses the singular ἀδελφόν, "brother," his use of the plural here makes it more obvious that the term is used in this epistle to refer to spiritual rather than natural kindship.

ὁ μὴ ἀγαπῶν μένει ἐν τῷ θανάτῳ, "He who does not love abides in death." Continuing his pattern of contrast, John follows the positive statement of verse 14a with two negative statements, verses 14b and 15. The use of the present tense ἀγαπῶν indicates that it is the habitual practice of love that is required. Some manuscripts (C K L Ψ 81 88) add the words τὸν ἀδεγφόν, "the brother" (P adds τὸν ἀδελφὸν αὐτοῦ, *his brother*), but the better witnesses (ℵ A B 33 etc.) simply read ὁ μὴ ἀγαπῶν, "he who does not love." Although it may be that John did not repeat the object of the love because he had indicated it in the immediately preceding sentence, it is possible that he was referring to love in the absolute or unlimited sense. A Christian is one who loves; the person who does not love is not a member of the family of God.

John does not say that the one who does not love dies, but that he *remains in death* (μένει ἐν τῷ θανάτῳ). This means that he existed from birth (Eph. 2:1) in the sphere of death, and he continues to stay in that sphere, as opposed to those who love the brothers and have been transferred from death to life.

3:15. πᾶς ὁ μισῶν τὸν ἀδελφὸν αὐτοῦ ἀνθρωποκτόνος ἐστίν, "Every one who hates his brother is a murderer." The adjective πᾶς, "every one," introduces a sweeping declaration. It is limited, however, by the present tense μισῶν, "hates," which speaks of continuing action. John does not refer to one who is caught up in a momentary fit of anger toward someone. The one he designates as a murderer is the one who, as a continuing habit, hates his brother. A comparison of verse 14b with verse 15a seems to equate ὁ μὴ ἀγαπῶν, ("he who does not love") with ὁ μισῶν, ("the one who hates"). John puts matters in stark terms. There is no middle ground; not to love is to hate. One may well ask in what sense the term "brother" is used here. Westcott says, "But hatred may find place among 'the brethren.' . . . There are Cains in the new family."[13] That is, there are counterfeit brothers in the outward fellowship of professed believers. Perhaps the apostle may have the Gnostic errorists in mind, although the application is not limited to them.

---

13. Westcott, p. 113.

The only occurrences in the New Testament of the word ἀνθρωποκτόνος, "murderer," are here and in John 8:44, where Jesus declares the devil to have been a murderer from the beginning. It is apparent that in 1 John 3:8-15 John draws extensively from the teaching of Jesus in John 8. Here, in 3:15, he reflects Christ's equation of anger with overt crime (Matt. 5:21-22, cf. vv. 27-28.) That hatred is the equivalent of murder is apparent when one analyzes this destructive attitude. Bonsirven quotes bishop John of Jerusalem as saying, "The person whom one hates, one desires to see disappear."[14] Hatred is the desire to get rid of someone, whether or not one has the nerve or the occasion to perform the act.

καὶ οἴδατε ὅτι πᾶς ἀνθρωποκτόνος οὐκ ἔχει ζωὴν αἰώνιον ἐν αὐτῷ μένουσαν, "and you know that no murderer has eternal life abiding in him." Οἴδατε, "you know," very aptly expresses knowledge that is generally accepted, axiomatic, or intuitive. Ανθρωποκτόνος is used anarthrously to show the general characteristics of the person. That one who is the possessor of eternal life should characteristically commit murder is unthinkable. John does not mean that a person who has committed murder can never be saved afterward. Instead, he says that a saved person, by nature, does not commit murder. This is true because one of the marks of the Christian is love. It is also true that one who possesses eternal life will value life too highly to destroy it. Αἰώνιον, "eternal," is both a qualitative and a quantitative word, referring to quality of life as well as extent (see on 1:2). This life is described as ἐν αὐτῷ μένουσαν, "abiding in him." The verb μένω speaks of a continuing possession that is experienced now rather than being delayed until the end time.

3:16. ἐν τούτῳ ἐγνώκαμεν τὴν ἀγάπην, ὅτι ἐκεῖνος ὑπὲρ ἡμῶν τὴν ψυχὴν αὐτοῦ ἔθηκεν. "We know love by this, that He laid down His life for us." Having set forth the *love test* (vv. 14-15), John now turns to a discussion of the *test of love*.[15] How can genuine love be recognized? This is crucial since the epistle sets up love as a test of the genuineness of one's salvation.

The pronoun τούτῳ, "this," is to be understood as an instrumental case. As is usually true in this epistle, the pronoun, τούτῳ,

---

14. Joseph Bonsirven, *Épitres de Saint Jean*, vol. 9, *Verbum Salutis*, p. 166 (my translation).
15. Bultmann, p. 55, says that vv. 16 ff. show "what genuine love is, or how it is to be tested."

looks forward, in this case to the ὅτι clause, "that He laid down His Life for us." Ἐγνώκαμεν (γινώσκω) refers to the acquisition of knowledge, therefore meaning *we have come to know.* The perfect tense verb looks back to Calvary where John gained the knowledge of love, but the verb also speaks of the existing results in the form of a continuing understanding of what love is. The presence of the article with ἀγάπην, "love," serves to identify the specific love John has in mind[16]—God's active, sacrificial love manifested at the cross. On ἀγάπη, see on 2:7.

As throughout 1 John (2:6; 3:3, 5, 7) the demonstrative pronoun, ἐκεῖνος, "that one," refers to Christ. The readers were thoroughly familiar with this pointed designation of their Lord. The expression ὑπὲρ ἡμῶν τὴν ψυχὴν αὐτοῦ ἔθηκεν, "He laid down His life for us," is reminiscent of John 15:13, where Jesus explains that the greatest love of all is the kind that leads one to "lay down his life for his friends," τὴν ψυχὴν αὐτοῦ θῇ ὑπὲρ τῶν φίλων αὐτοῦ. In both passages the verb is τίθημι, which speaks of an action that is voluntary and intentional. In John 10:17-18 Christ declared, "For this reason the Father loves Me, because I lay down [τίθημι] My life that I may take it again. No one has taken it away from Me, but I lay it down [τίθημι] on My own initiative" (ἀπ' ἐμαυτοῦ, "from myself"). It is this intentional giving for the sake of others that best explains what ἀγάπη is.

In all of these passages (John 10:11, 15, 17, 18; 15:12, 13; 1 John 3:16) the primary concern is not to treat the subject of Christ's atoning death, but to set forth the characteristics of genuine love.[17] In John 10, Jesus indicates the kind of self-sacrificing love that characterizes the good Shepherd; in John 15, He explains the kind of love that He expects His followers to show; and in 1 John 3:16, the apostle points out the supreme example of what genuine love is. It is doubtful, therefore, that the preposition ὑπέρ, "for," is substitutionary in meaning (although it is used to express substitution in certain contexts; cf. John 11:50; Gal. 3:13).[18] The parallel occurrence of ὑπέρ in the second half of verse 16 is further reason for denying a substitutionary use in this context.[19]

---

16. Dana and Mantey, pp. 141-42.
17. Marshall, p. 193.
18. Dana and Mantey, pp. 111-12.
19. However, see Marshall, p. 193, n. 17, in favor of a substitutionary meaning.

καὶ ἡμεῖς ὀφείλομεν ὑπὲρ τῶν ἀδελφῶν τὰς ψυχὰς θεῖναι, "and we ought to lay down our lives for the brethren." In this clause Christ's example is applied to His followers. Ἡμεῖς, "we," is paralleled to ἐκεῖνος, "He" *(that one)*, as John declares that "we ought" (ὀφείλομεν), like Him, "to lay down our lives for the brethren." Whereas John could have used δεῖ, *one must, it is necessary*, he chose ὀφείλω. The reason for the choice seems to lie in the fact that, while δεῖ leans toward "logical necessity," ὀφείλω speaks of "moral obligation."[20] It is true that δεῖ may also be used to express moral obligation, but this is not its primary connotation, as is true of ὀφείλω. The obligation is based on two facts:

- It is a generally accepted New Testament truth that believers are to become like Christ. Paul declares it to be God's purpose that they become conformed to the image of His Son (Rom. 8:29), and Jesus commanded His disciples to love as He loved (John 13:34-35; 15:12).
- Only as love is put into action does that love become complete and, thus, genuine.

What John meant by laying down lives is not explicitly stated. It is, however, parallel to Jesus' act of self-sacrifice for others. There would, therefore, seem to be no limit to the extent to which one should be ready to go to meet the need of a fellow Christian—any action from sharing a loaf of bread (1 John 3:17) to actually giving up one's life would seem to be included in this statement of obligation. And John uses the same aorist tense verb θεῖναι, "to lay down," in verse 16*b* that he used in verse 16*a* (ἔθηκεν, "He laid down"), depicting voluntary and intentional action.

3:17. ὃς δ᾽ ἂν ἔχῃ τὸν βίον τοῦ κόσμου, "But whoever has the world's goods." The conjunction δέ (δ᾽), "but," introduces an adversative statement, a negative example in contrast to the positive example and command of verse 16. Christ's act proved that He loved with perfect love, whereas the refusal of help in verse 17 indicates that genuine love is totally absent. John's description of the negative example consists of three elements, the first of which is the possession of material things. He introduces the example with an all inclusive expression, ὃς δ᾽ ἂν, ("whoever")—*anyone who fits the description given in verse 17 fails the test.* The word

---

20. G. Abbott-Smith, *A Manual Greek Lexicon of the New Testament*, p. 99; Richard C. Trench, *Synonyms of the New Testament*, pp. 360-61.

Sonship Tested on Ethical Grounds: Love for Fellow Believers 269

βίον, translated "*goods*" in the NASB, actually means "*life*" (see discussion on p. 180). John uses βίον to describe the material things necessary to sustain life in this "world." Κόσμος is not to be understood in a negative sense, but simply as describing the sphere in which this life is lived.

καὶ θεωρῇ τὸν ἀδελφὸν αὐτοῦ χρείαν ἔχοντα, "and beholds his brother in need." The second element in the description of this negative example is the observing of a brother's need. John uses the present tense θεωρῇ, "beholds," to express, not a momentary glimpse, but a continuing observation of the need. As in other passages (1 John 2:9-11; 3:10, 14-16), it is apparent that the brother is a fellow Christian. This heightens both the obligation and the sin of neglect. Paul sets forth the principle that family members are especially obligated to care for needy relatives (1 Tim. 5:8), and this principle surely has some application to the family of God. Of all people, Christians are obligated to take care of those nearest them. Not only is the observation (θεωρῇ) of the need a continuing action, but the state of poverty is likewise a linear situation, as indicated by the present tense participle, ἔχοντα, "having." So the verse describes the continued witnessing of a continuing need.

καὶ κλείσῃ τὰ σπλάγχνα αὐτοῦ ἀπ᾽ αὐτοῦ, "and closes his heart against him." The verb κλείσῃ is in the aorist tense, which speaks of point action.[21] It is significant that John uses three present tense verbs (ἔχῃ, "has"; θεωρῇ, "beholds"; and ἔχοντα, "having") all of which depict continuing action, and then he switches to the punctiliar aorist. Robertson explains the significance of κλείσῃ in a brief comment: "to close, like the door, changed on purpose from present tense to aorist (graphic slamming the door of his compassion . . .)."[22] The word σπλάγχνα is literally translated "bowels" in the KJV, a rendering that has been baffling to many. Years ago, however, Lightfoot explained that the term σπλάγχνα was used to designate the upper internal organs such as the heart, lungs, and liver.[23] (The word ἔντερα referred to lower organs, such as the intestines.) The σπλάγχνα came to be regarded by the Greeks as the seat of the affections, the place where emotions of fear and love are felt. The word came to be used figuratively to refer to the seat of the emotions or to the

---

21. Blass and DeBrunner, sec. 318; Dana and Mantey, p. 194.
22. A. T. Robertson, *Word Pictures in the New Testament*, 6:226.
23. J. B. Lightfoot, *St. Paul's Epistle to the Philippians*, p. 86.

emotions themselves, especially love, mercy, and compassion.[24] When designating the seat of the emotions, as here, "heart" is the best translation. The NASB "against him" represents ἀπ αὐτοῦ, "from him," which speaks of excluding the needy person from access to one's heart.

πῶς ἡ ἀγάπη τοῦ θεοῦ μένει ἐν αὐτῷ; "how does the love of God abide in him?" The genitive case τοῦ θεοῦ has been interpreted in three ways: (1) as a subject genitive, speaking of God as the author of the love (God's love); (2) as an objective genitive, speaking of God as the One being loved (love for God); or (3) as a descriptive genitive (God-like love). Since the immediate context is dealing with love for the brothers (vv. 14-16), it is best not to understand "the love of God" as love for God but as God's kind of love or love of which God is the author. Marshall favors the descriptive genitive because he does not think that John teaches that "our love for others is simply God's love flowing through us."[25] However, there is good reason to hold that 1 John 4:7-16 does teach that God loves through us (see on verses 7-8, 12, 16.) It is best, then, with Bultmann, Stott, and Houlden, to view verse 17 as speaking of the love of which God is the author. If acts of love are not present, it is unreasonable to claim that one is indwelt by God's love. In actual effect, the question John asks is really a denial.

3:18. τεκνία, μὴ ἀγαπῶμεν λόγῳ μηδὲ τῇ γλώσσῃ ἀλλὰ ἐν ἔργῳ καὶ ἀληθείᾳ, "Little children, let us not love with word or with tongue, but in deed and truth." The vocative, τεκνία, "little children," reminds the readers of the spiritual family of which they are a part and of the source of their spiritual life (γεγεννημένος ἐκ τοῦ θεοῦ, "born of God," v. 9). Ἀγαπῶμεν is a hortatory subjunctive verb in the present tense. As such it calls for continuing love (genuine love, of course, rather than mere superficial verbalization). As an exhortation, the verb includes John as well as his readers. In typical Johannine fashion the author makes use of negative-positive contrast (μή, "not" . . . ἀλλά, "but" . . .) to strengthen his exhortation. From the repetition, λόγῳ, "word"—γλώσσῃ, "tongue," it would appear that the most prevalent deviation from genuine love was that of mere talk rather than loving action. The quality of truth (ἀληθείᾳ) is added because even deeds may be hypocritical. John wants them to be genuine expressions of love.

---

24. Kittel, s.v. "σπλάγχνον, σπλαγνίζομαι, κτλ.," by Helmut Köster. 7:551, 557.
25. Marshall, pp. 194-95, n. 24.

Sonship Tested on Ethical Grounds: Love for Fellow Believers 271

3:19. [καὶ] ἐν τούτῳ γνωσόμεθα ὅτι ἐκ τῆς ἀληθείας ἐσμέν, "We shall know by this that we are of the truth." Having established a test by which to ascertain the genuineness of love, whether divine or human (3:16-18), John proceeds to discuss the fruit of genuine love (3:19-24). Verses 19-20 are closely related in content and in grammatical construction. All commentators agree that they are unusually difficult to interpret. The problems essentially are two (1) the meaning of πείσομεν (v. 19) and (2) the interpretation of the two occurrences of ὅτι in verse 20.

Καί appears in brackets in the UBS *Greek New Testament* indicating that the evidence for and against its inclusion is quite equal in weight. The fact that some early manuscripts such as ℵ and C have the word is evidence of an early opinion that verse 19 is related to verse 18. It also favors the view that τούτῳ looks back to verse 18 rather than forward as is usually the case in this epistle (cf. 2:3, 25; 3:8, 11, 16). The apostle here declares that the love that gives evidence that a person is "of the truth" is love in action. It is the kind of love that gives sacrificially to those in need. Mere sentiment or verbalization is not adequate evidence of salvation.

The verb γνωσόμεθα, "we shall know," is used in the classical sense of γινώσκω to indicate the acquisition of knowledge. Here it means something like "we shall ascertain. . . ." The use of the future tense (instead of the present, 2:3, 5) looks forward to the fulfillment of the prerequisite for acquiring the knowledge. When that condition has been met, then "we shall know . . . that we are of the truth." The phrase ἐκ τῆς ἀληθείας, "of the truth," occurs in John's writings only in John 18:37; 1 John 2:21; 3:19. Ἐκ with the ablative case speaks of source, so John here declares that no lie has its source in truth; both of the other passages speak of people whose spiritual experience comes *from* the truth and who therefore are identified *by* the truth. Marshall sees the phrase as being synonymous with "being born of God."[26] The definite article particularizes truth as that truth which is distinctively God's truth, especially the truth of the gospel.

καὶ ἔμπροσθεν αὐτοῦ πείσομεν τὴν καρδίαν ἡμῶν, "and shall assure our heart before Him." The verb πείσομεν, "[we] shall assure," and its clause are parallel to γνωσόμεθα, "we shall know," and its clause. Love in action (ἐν τούτῳ, "by this") produces two results: (1) knowledge that people are of the truth and (2) assurance before God.

One of the major problems of this and the following verse

---
26. Ibid., p. 197, n. 2.

concerns the translation of πείσομεν. The usual meaning of πείθω is "persuade," which demands an object and some explanation, stated or implied, of the content of the persuasion. In this instance, the content may be found in the second ὅτι clause of verse 20, ὅτι μείζων ἐστὶν ὁ θεὸς τῆς καρδίας ἡμῶν. . . , "for God is greater than our heart. . . ." However, it is not clear in what way love in action (v. 18) persuades one that God is greater than our heart. Again, the content may be understood although not stated. In this case, the persuasion would be something like "that we are of the truth," which appears in the first clause of verse 19. This interpretation is very possible. There is, however, another meaning for πείθω that yields an even more natural rendering of the statement. Πείθω can mean "pacify, set at ease, conciliate, assure."[27] For another instance of this usage of πείθω see Matthew 28:14. In this case, it is not necessary to try to ascertain the content of the persuasion. As in the NASB translation, a heart that is lacking in assurance is assumed. John is addressing a heart that is unduly sensitive and troubled by guilt and fear.

The phrase ἔμπροσθεν αὐτοῦ, "before Him," appears in a striking position, standing as it does at the head of the clause. John thereby emphasizes that the assurance is a justified assurance since it is experienced in the very presence of God. Bultmann and Lenski interpret this use as forensic:[28] as though standing before the divine judge, we assure our hearts because of the presence in our lives of active love. Καρδίαν, "heart," is not to be viewed, as current English commonly does, as primarily the seat of the emotions. In Greek parlance, it was the seat of the emotions, instincts, passions, thought, and will.[29] John uses the term to refer to the inner man with special emphasis here on the conscience and the feelings. Bonsirven refers to the heart as the seat of the conscience,[30] and the word is translated as "conscience" in the NEB. The singular καρδίαν, "heart," with the plural possessive pronouns, "their," "your," "our," is found in John's writings ten times (John 12:40, 40; 14:1, 27; 16:6, 22; 1 John 3:19, 20, 20, 21), with John 12:40 being an Old Testament quotation. The construction

27. Arndt and Gingrich, p. 645; Brooke, p. 99; Westcott, p. 117.
28. Bultmann, p. 56, n. 59; R. C. H. Lenski, *The Interpretation of the Epistles of St. Peter, St. John, and St. Jude*, p. 477.
29. Colin Brown, ed., *The New International Dictionary of New Testament Theology*, 1975-78, s.v. "Heart," by T. Sorg.
30. Bonsirven, p. 175.

stresses the oneness of the people in the experience or situation being described.

3:20. ὅτι ἐὰν καταγινώσκῃ ἡμῶν ἡ καρδία, ὅτι μείζων ἐστὶν ὁ θεὸς τῆς καρδίας ἡμῶν καὶ γινώσκει πάντα, "in whatever our heart condemns us; for God is greater than our heart, and knows all things." The major problem in this verse is the interpretation of the two occurrences of ὅτι. There are at least ten different possible ways of understanding verses 19-20. For ease of handling, they are grouped according to major characteristics:

1. Love in action (v. 18) persuades (v. 19) that God is greater than the human heart (v. 20). Under this heading there are two possible translations:
    a. "We shall persuade [assure] our heart, concerning anything about which our heart condemns us, that God is greater than our heart. . . ." Here ὅτι ἐάν is read as ὃ τι ἐάν, with ὅ being understood as a neuter, accusative, relative pronoun used as an accusative of reference. Ἐάν would then be equal to ἄν, as is sometimes the case (Gal. 5:10). The Alexandrinus manuscript and very few others have ἄν rather than ἐάν.
    b. "We shall persuade [assure] our heart that—if our heart condemns us—that God is greater than our heart, and. . . ." In this translation the *if* clause is parenthetical and the conjunction *that* is repeated after the parenthesis.
   In both of the above translations John asserts that love in action serves to persuade the heart that God is greater than the heart and knows all things. It is difficult, however, to see how love could bring one to such a conclusion. The one does not logically follow from the other.
2. Love in action assures one's heart concerning any guilt feeling.
    a. "We shall assure our heart concerning anything about which our heart condemns us because God is greater than our heart, and. . . ."
    b. "We shall persuade [assure] our heart concerning anything about which our heart condemns us, that God is greater than our heart, and. . . ." This translation is the same as (1) (a).

The expression, "concerning anything about which," is a translation of the text altered to read ὃ τι ἐάν. It is not

true, however, that love in action gives assurance concerning *anything* about which we feel guilty. This is far too sweeping an assertion to be true.
3. The *if*-clause is to be viewed as parenthetical.
   a. "We shall persuade [assure] our heart (that we are of the truth) because if our heart condemns us—because God is greater than our heart, and knows. . . ." This translation assumes that John does not explicitly state the content of the persuasion, but expects that the reader will supply it from the immediately preceding context (i.e. "that we are of the truth").
   b. "We shall persuade [assure] our heart that—if our heart condemns us—that God is greater than our heart, and. . . ." This is the same as (1) (b) above.

   Both of these translations treat the *if*-clause as a parenthesis. This is a possibility, but it is very unlikely that, after so short a parenthetical expression, it would have been thought necessary to repeat ὅτι, (*because* or *that*). That this was a problem at least as early as the fifth century is evident from the fact that the Alexandrinus manuscript and the Vulgate and the Coptic versions omit ὅτι.

4. God's greater knowledge is reason to fear rather than to be confident.
   a. "We shall assure our heart for, if our heart condemns us, (it is certain) that God is greater [i.e., His judgment is more severe], and He knows all things." The main features of this interpretation are that it inserts the words, "it is certain," and it explains God's greatness and omniscience as referring to sterner judgment.
   b. "We shall assure our heart because, if our heart condemns us, (it is) because God is greater than our heart, and knows all things." The only way in which this interpretation differs from the preceding one is that it simply inserts "it is" rather than "it is certain."

   The weakness of these two views is that the idea of divine severity does not at all fit the context. The general purpose of verses 19-20 is to instill confidence in the hearts of the readers. To inject the thought of the sternness of God into this context is contradictory to the main thrust of these verses.

5. The statement assumes an ellipsis.
   a. "We shall assure our heart because, if our heart condemns

Sonship Tested on Ethical Grounds: Love for Fellow Believers 275

us, (it is evident) that God is greater than our heart, and knows all things." Here the word δῆλον, *it is evident*, is assumed. In fact, the term δῆλον ὅτι meant "it is plain that, clearly, of course."³¹

b. "We shall assure our heart because, if our heart condemns us, (we know) that. . . ." Bultmann suggests that inserting οἴδαμεν, "we know," is the most reasonable solution to the problem of verse 20. It is his assumption that the text is corrupt and οἴδαμεν has been lost.³² There is no indication in the manuscripts of any such corruption.

It is better, therefore, to assume that John expected his readers to understand that δῆλον, "it is evident" (or possibly οἴδαμεν, "we know"), should be supplied. Such an explanation has the least difficulty of any. Plummer points out that 1 Timothy 6:7 has a similar use of ὅτι, "that," and in this case a number of later manuscripts (ℵ³ D³ K L) read δῆλον ὅτι, "it is evident that."³³

The content of verses 19-20 may be summarized as follows:

- Love in action in one's life is indicative of salvation.
- By this one can pacify an overly sensitive conscience.
- This is true because the omniscient God is superior to the accusing conscience.
- He assures that the presence of self-sacrificing love in one's life is certain evidence that one has eternal life.

3:21. ἀγαπητοί, ἐὰν ἡ καρδία [ἡμῶν] μὴ καταγινώσκῃ, "Beloved, if our heart does not condemn us." Four of the six occurrences of ἀγαπητοί—one of John's favorite terms of address in this epistle—occur in sections where the subject of discussion is love for the brothers. On καρδία, "heart," see 3:19. The accompanying pronoun ἡμῶν, "our," appears in brackets in the United Bible Societies' *Greek New Testament,* indicating that evidence for and against inclusion is fairly evenly balanced.³⁴ Some manuscripts have the pronoun ἡμῶν after καρδία and after καταγινώσκῃ (ℵ K and numerous minuscules). There is, of

---

31. *A Lexicon Abridged from Liddell and Scott's Greek-English Lexicon,* p. 157.
32. Bultmann, p. 57.
33. A. Plummer, *The Epistles of St. John,* Cambridge Greek Testament for Schools and Colleges, p. 88.
34. Metzger, p. 713.

course, the common confusion of ἡμῶν, "our," and ὑμῶν, "your." Some manuscripts have ἡμῶν only after καρδία (C etc.). Some have ἡμῶν (or ὑμῶν) only after καταγινώσκῃ (or καταγινώσκει), "condemn," (A Ψ 33 etc.). It would seem that, where the pronouns (ἡμῶν or ὑμῶν) appear after both καρδία and a form of καταγινώσκῃ, this is evidence of an attempt at conflation (harmonizing two separate texts by including both readings). It is easy to see how the original text could have composed without a pronoun after either word. The article ἡ before καρδία would function as a possessive pronoun, "our heart," and καταγινώσκῃ would not require an object since it appears with an object in the verse immediately preceding. Copyists unintentionally could have inserted one or the other pronoun (or possibly both), thus stating explicitly what John had meant implicitly.

Question may be raised concerning the occasion to which καταγινώσκῃ was intended to apply. Does it refer to a person whose sensitive conscience has been quieted so that it no longer condemns, or is it simply a general statement concerning a person whose conscience does not condemn? At least it is clear that the statement of verse 21 is the opposite of that in verse 20, in keeping with John's practice of placing negative and positive statements back to back. It is best not to press the statement beyond this obvious meaning: verse 20 addresses itself to that condemning heart (ἐὰν καταγινώσκῃ ἡμῶν ἡ καρδία), and verse 21 to the heart that does not condemn (ἐὰν ἡ καρδία [ἡμῶν] μὴ καταγινώσκῃ).

παρρησίαν ἔχομεν πρὸς τὸν θεόν, "we have confidence before God." On παρρησίαν, "confidence," see on 2:28 where confidence is related to Christ's second coming. In 3:21, however, the context is not dealing with the second advent or final judgment, but is more general. The following statement relates the term to prayer, and this is particularly fitting, since παρρησία basically referred to freedom in speaking. If a person's conscience does not condemn him, he can come confidently into God's presence in prayer and freely voice his requests. However, it should be remembered that the confidence and boldness expressed by παρρησία contain nothing of impropriety or brashness. It gives no license to anyone to *command* God to act; it does not erase the distinction between God's infinity and our humanity. Πρὸς τὸν θεόν, "before God," literally means "toward God." See on 1:2. Murray Harris says that πρός when referring to a "relationship between persons" depicts "personal intercourse" rather than mere accompaniment.[35] It has a dynamic rather than a static sense. Confidence that involves an "I-Thou" interpersonal relationship with God is what is available to the believer.

3:22. καὶ ὁ ἐὰν αἰτῶμεν λαμβάνομεν ἀπ' αὐτοῦ, "and whatever we ask we receive from Him." The conjunction καί is probably epexegetical (explanatory of the immediately preceding statement). If so, when John speaks of confidence toward God (v. 21), he refers to the freedom with which one may approach God in prayer (v. 22).

The clause, ὁ ἐὰν αἰτῶμεν, "whatever we ask," is, in itself, all-inclusive and could be taken as a guarantee that one will receive anything one requests. However, both the immediate and the more remote contexts must be taken into consideration. The immediate context indicates that the petitioner is one who is concerned with doing God's will and pleasing Him (v. 22b). Surely, such a person will want to pray in accordance with what God desires. Furthermore 5:14-15 makes it clear that the prayer that may be offered with confidence is prayer "according to His will." Stott lists six conditions that must be fulfilled in order for prayer to be answered: prayer must be offered in Christ's name (John 16:23-24), for God's glory (James 4:2-3), from a heart that does not cherish sin (Psalm 66:18), from a forgiven and forgiving heart (Mark 11:25), with faith (Matt. 21:22) and backed by an obedient life (1 John 3:22).[36]

Both αἰτῶμεν, "we ask," and λαμβάνομεν, "we receive," are present tense verbs. It seems to be straining the sense to insist that they are progressive in force and should be translated "keep on asking" and "keep on receiving." It is better to view both as gnomic presents, describing a fact that is generally or always true.[37] It is a maxim that God answers prayer. Ἀπ' αὐτοῦ, "from Him," clearly refers to God the Father since the confidence of verse 21 is directed to God (πρὸς τὸν θεόν). The preposition ἀπό (ἀπ') speaks of the source from which the answer to prayer comes.

ὅτι τὰς ἐντολὰς αὐτοῦ τηροῦμεν καὶ τὰ ἀρεστὰ ἐνώ-

---

35. Brown, s.v. "Prepositions and Theology in the Greek New Testament," by M. J. Harris.
36. John R. W. Stott, *The Epistles of John*, The Tyndale New Testament Commentaries, p. 149.
37. C. F. D. Moule, *An Idiom Book of New Testament Greek*, p. 8.

πιον αὐτοῦ ποιοῦμεν, "because we keep His commandments and do the things that are pleasing in His sight." This clause begins with the casual conjunction ὅτι, "because," which should not be taken to refer to the ground on which answered prayer rests, but to the condition for answered prayer. It is not a benefit that must be merited; spiritual benefits are gifts of grace. However, there are conditions that God's Spirit enables believers to meet. Stott puts it crisply when he says, "Obedience is the indispensable condition, not the meritorious cause of answered prayer."[38]

The two verbs that stand at the center of this "indispensable condition" are τηροῦμεν, "we keep," and ποιοῦμεν, "[we] do," both of which are in the present tense. Unlike the two verbs in the first part of the verse, these two are progressive presents, speaking of continuing action. It is the habitual keeping of the commands and doing of things that please God that are the conditions of answered prayer. John previously referred to keeping God's commandments in 2:3-5, where he used the same expression, τὰς ἐντολὰς αὐτοῦ τηρῶμεν, "we keep His commandments." (See on 2:3.)

The apostle seems to refer to two categories: τὰς ἐντολάς, "commandments," and τὰ ἀρεστά, "things that are pleasing" to Him. Bultmann thinks that this is a hendiadys, that is, that both terms refer to the same thing.[39] Keeping God's commandments is what pleases Him. While this is true, it is probably better to view the two items as distinct and different. The commands are explicit expressions of God's will that call for obedience, whereas the things that please Him do not refer merely to acts specifically called for by law but to any action that is pleasing to Him. Jesus could say, "I always do the things that are pleasing to Him," (John 8:29). The statement in 1 John 3:22 (ἐνώπιον αὐτοῦ, "in His sight") is more forceful than the simple dative αὐτῷ, "to Him." It describes the pleasing action as taking place before God's very eyes.

3:23. καὶ αὕτη ἐστὶν ἡ ἐντολὴ αὐτοῦ, "And this is His commandment." The change from the plural ἐντολάς, "commandments," to the singular ἐντολή, "commandment," may seem strange, especially when it is followed by two requirements rather than one. The expression is obviously singular with a singular pronoun, a singular verb, and a singular article and noun. It is

---

38. Stott, p. 149.
39. Bultmann, p. 58.

Sonship Tested on Ethical Grounds: Love for Fellow Believers 279

just as clear from the following two subjunctive verbs that the singular command is somehow plural in nature. Marshall explains the seeming paradox by saying that John "sums up the commands as one command, which is then expressed as having two parts; in this way the fundamental unity of the two parts is made quite clear."[40] But in what sense are these two commands a unity? In Galatians 5:6, Paul views the relationship between faith and love as one in which faith works through, or expresses itself through, love. And Lenski says, "You cannot believe without loving nor love without believing."[41] To believe is to be regenerated, and to be regenerated is to love. This dual command to believe and love sums up the two basic tests of 1 John, namely, the Christological test of belief in Jesus Christ as God's incarnate Son and the ethical test of love for fellow believers. The command also deals with our relationship to God (belief) and our relationship to man (love).

John identifies this command as being "His commandment" (ἡ ἐντολὴ αὐτοῦ). In the light of the description of Jesus Christ as "His Son," the pronoun, "His," must refer to God the Father rather than to Christ.

ἵνα πιστεύσωμεν τῷ ὀνόματι τοῦ υἱοῦ αὐτοῦ Ἰησοῦ Χριστοῦ, "that we believe in the name of His Son Jesus Christ." Although ἵνα is normally a telic conjunction *(in order that)*, it is here epexegetical or definitive. It is actually equal to ὅτι, "that," and functions like a noun clause in apposition to ἐντολή, "commandment."

The verb "believe" appears in some texts (B K L etc.) as an aorist (πιστεύσωμεν) and in others (ℵ A C etc.) as a present tense (πιστεύομεν). Although the manuscript evidence slightly favors the present tense, it is easy to see how a scribe knowingly or unintentionally could have changed the aorist to a present in order to harmonize it with ἀγαπῶμεν, "[we] love," which is unquestionably a present form in the manuscripts. The aorist, therefore, seems to have been the original form. The contrast with the present ἀγαπῶμεν is striking. No doubt John used the aorist to point to the initial act of placing faith in Christ as Savior, as over against the continuing practice of loving (ἀγαπῶμεν) one another. Bruce identifies the aorist as ingressive.[42] It is probable that both aspects of the command (belief and love) are set forth with

---

40. Marshall, pp. 200-201.
41. Lenski, p. 479.
42. F. F. Bruce, *The Epistles of John*, p. 100.

the Gnostic false teachers in mind. Reason for such a statement is found in the almost creedal identification, τοῦ υἱοῦ αὐτοῦ Ἰησοῦ Χριστοῦ, "His Son Jesus Christ." The human Jesus is identified both as God's Son and as the Christ. He is, therefore, God's incarnate Son, and it was this enfleshment of Deity that the Gnostic denied. On the use of Χριστός, "Christ," in 1 John see on 2:22. On ὀνόματι, "name," see 2:12. The name in biblical usage is inseparably related to the person who bears it. To believe in the name of Christ is to believe in Him and in all that He is—Divine Son, perfect Man, Savior, Propitiation for sin, and Advocate for the saved.

Belief in 1 John is not to be limited to mere acceptance of a certain doctrine. Indeed it is that, as such passages as 2:22 and 5:5 suggest. But it is also the acceptance of the Person of Jesus Christ (3:23); it is the confession of the incarnate Christ (4:2); it is the kind of genuine inner belief that is associated with new birth (5:1); it is to place one's trust in God's Son, thus receiving eternal life (5:10-12). Believing, then, is a combination both of a creedal confession and of faith in the Person of Jesus Christ.

καὶ ἀγαπῶμεν ἀλλήλους, καθὼς ἔδωκεν ἐντολὴν ἡμῖν, "and love one another, just as He commanded us." The second part of the double command is to love one another. As noted above, the verb ἀγαπῶμεν is in the present tense, thus calling for continuing love in contrast to the point of initial faith indicated by the aorist πιστεύσωμεν. As in 3:11 ἀγγήλους, "one another," refers to fellow believers, just as ἀδελφοί does. See 1 John 5:1.

Bultmann holds that the command that "He gave" (ἔδωκεν) to us is not from Jesus, but from God.[43] Two factors, however, indicate that John has Christ's command in mind: (1) Christ is the nearest possible antecedent, and (2) Jesus used the very words that John employs here—ἀγαπᾶτε ἀλλήλους, "love one another" (John 13:34; 15:12, 17). In referring to this command, John makes it clear (3:23) that what is demanded is an exact correspondence (not ὡς, "as," but καθώς, "just as") with Jesus' requirement.

3:24. καὶ ὁ τηρῶν τὰς ἐντολὰς αὐτοῦ ἐν αὐτῷ μένει καὶ αὐτὸς ἐν αὐτῷ, "And the one who keeps His commandments abides in Him, and He in him." The keeping of God's commandments refers back to verse 22, which makes verse 23 a parenthetical explanation of the content of the commands. As

---

43. Bultmann, p. 58.

demonstrated in the discussion of verses 22-23, the pronoun αὐτοῦ, "His," refers to God the Father, and this continues to be the case throughout verse 24. Just as the practice of keeping God's commandments reminds us of 2:3-5, so also does the subject of remaining in God and He in us (ἐν αὐτῷ μένει καὶ αὐτὸς ἐν αὐτῷ). These two expressions of mutual indwelling describe in mystical terms the close union that exists between a believer and God. It should be noted that the tense of τηρῶν, "keeps," and μένει, "abides," is in both instances present, thus depicting a continued obedience and a continued remaining. It is not that the keeping of the commandments maintains the intimate abiding relationship; rather, obedience is evidence that a person is continuing to abide in God.

καὶ ἐν τούτῳ γινώσκομεν ὅτι μένει ἐν, ἡμῖν, ἐκ τοῦ πνεύματος οὗ ἡμῖν ἔδωκεν, "And we know by this that He abides in us, by the Spirit which He has given us." As previously noted, the pronoun in an expression like ἐν τούτῳ usually refers forward in 1 John. In this instance, most commentators refer the pronoun to the expression ἐκ τοῦ πνεύματος. . . , "by the Spirit. . . ." There is good reason, however, in this case to refer the pronoun back to the keeping of the commandments (τηρῶν τὰς ἐντολάς). Such external activity provides objective evidence of an inner mystical experience. Furthermore, the phrase ἐκ τοῦ πνεύματος, "by the Spirit," is not parallel in form to ἐν τούτῳ, "by this," as one would expect if the latter phrase did indeed refer to the former.[44] If the one were in apposition to the other, the preposition ἐν might be found in both instances, or ἐν in the first phrase and διά in the second. It may, however, be argued that, since in the parallel passage, 1 John 4:13, the pronoun certainly refers forward, it must do so here in 3:24. But closer comparison reveals that the construction in 4:13 is different in that the phrase ἐκ πνεύματος appears in a ὅτι clause, which is more naturally appositional.

The verb γινώσκομεν, "we know," is used here with precision in its classical sense. It speaks of knowledge that is arrived at by drawing a conclusion from the fact of continued keeping of God's commands.

The significance of the divine indwelling (μένει ἐν ἡμῖν, "He is dwelling in us," Gr.) becomes more apparent when parallel

---

44. W. Robertson Nicoll, gen. ed. *The Expositor's Greek Testament*, s.v. "The Epistles of John," by David Smith, 5:188.

passages in 1 John are examined. In 2:3-6 being in Christ and dwelling in Him are parallel to knowing Him, or to being saved. In 2:24 dwelling in the Son and the Father is the result of holding to the gospel message. And in 3:15 divine indwelling is contingent upon confessing that Jesus is God's Son.

The prepositional phrase, ἐκ τοῦ πνεύματος, "by the Spirit," is literally to be translated "from the Spirit." The preposition ἐκ with the ablative case speaks of source. The whole statement may thus be paraphrased as follows: "And by this means (that is, by continued keeping of God's commandments) we know that He is dwelling in us, and this assurance comes from the Holy Spirit whom God has given to us." The Spirit is the source of the knowledge in that He uses the fact of obedience to produce assurance in the believer's heart. Smith says concerning the preposition ἐκ, "The assurance is begotten of the Spirit."[45]

The relative pronoun οὗ could be taken as a partitive genitive case, but such an interpretation is not necessary here, nor does John give any indication in the context that the believer's experience of the Spirit is limited in any way. The case of the relative pronoun is often attracted to the case of the antecedent—in this instance to the ablative case of πνεύματος.

Ἔδωκεν is aorist and speaks of a one-time giving of the Spirit. The NIV properly translates this "he gave."

THEOLOGICAL COMMENTARY (3:10b-24)

A. JOHN'S SECOND DISCUSSION OF LOVE (3:10B-24)

In the first cycle of the epistle, love was set forth as a test of whether or not one is in fellowship with God, i.e., saved (2:7-11). In the second cycle the Christian life is viewed as divine sonship, and love again is employed as a test of whether or not a person is a child of God (especially in 3:14-15).

1. EXAMPLES OF HATRED, 3:10b-13

After making a transition from the discussion of righteousness to the discussion of love (3:10b) John restates Jesus' command to love. Then he cites two negative examples of the kind of attitude and action that a Christian must avoid. Cain's murder of his broth-

---

45. Plummer, p. 91.

er is the first example (v. 12). Although John does not explicitly state that Cain hated Abel, that he did is certainly implied. It was Abel's obedience that rebuked Cain's disregard of God's will. In the presence of his brother's righteousness, Cain stood condemned and he hated his brother because of it. His desire was to get rid of the person who made him miserable. In Cain's life, hatred produced murder. Contrasted to this is the example of Christ (3:16) where love produced self-sacrifice. Hatred seeks to destroy; love seeks to save. The believer, then, does not want to walk in the footsteps of Cain; rather he follows the example of Christ. To be like Cain is to reveal that like him one is a child, not of God, but of the devil.

In the second negative example John moves from the individual to the corporate, from Cain to the world (v. 13). It is true that the apostle does not declare in so many words that he is using the world as an example, nevertheless, it functions as such. Here the attitude of hatred is explicitly mentioned. Christians are not to be surprised that the world manifests hatred toward them. Like Cain the people of the world are members of the devil's family. Consequently, the characteristic trait of unbelieving men is hatred. In the same way that Abel's righteousness rebuked Cain's wickedness, the presence of a godly people in the midst of the world rebukes the world's ungodliness, and the result is hatred.

2. THE LOVE TEST, 3:14-15

John's second treatment of love is not a mere repetition of the first. It is more specific in several ways. First, it more clearly defines what it is that is being tested. The issue is one of life and death. In fact it is eternal life (v. 15) contrasted with death; and it may be assumed that as the life is eternal, the death is likewise eternal. The test then determines whether a person has eternal life or is still living in the sphere of death (v. 14)—1 John 2:9-11 only declared that the one who hates his brother is in darkness.

A second area where this section is more specific is that of the identification of the persons who are loved or hated. In 2:9-11 this person is referred to as "brother." Being singular in number and being accompanied by αὐτοῦ, "his," which in the genitive case serves as a possessive pronoun, it is not altogether clear whether or not the expression refers to one's blood brother.

In 3:14, however, the identification is more specific. Whereas in 3:15 John speaks of hating τὸν ἀδελφὸν αὐτοῦ, "his brother," in 3:14 he speaks of loving τοὺς ἀδελφούς, *the brothers*. The absence of the pronoun indicative of possession and the use of the plural both suggest that John is referring to a fraternal group other than blood brothers. In the context of 1 John, these would be spiritual brothers. It is a question, then, of loving or hating the members of the Christian community. Love for fellow believers is evidence that one has eternal life. Hatred for the members of the community indicates that one is spiritually dead. While John does not mention the Gnostic, it seems clear that he has Gnostic lovelessness in mind.

A third area of greater specificity is that of the explanation of the nature of hatred. In 2:9-11 he does nothing more than to use the word μισέω, *to hate*. However, in 3:15, he associates hatred with murder, saying, "Everyone who hates his brother is a murderer." From this statement, it is clear that John's concept of hatred is not that of mere disagreement with someone. Instead, it is an attitude that would harm or even destroy the person hated. The apostle, of course, is drawing on the teaching of Jesus in the Sermon on the Mount (Matt. 5:21-22). Anyone who has such an attitude toward the people of God reveals that he is not himself a member of that fellowship. If he were, he would love his fellow members.

3. THE TEST OF LOVE, 3:16-18

Whereas 3:14-15 sets forth the love test, 3:16-18 deals with the test of love. In the first instance love is the test; in the second, love is being put to the test. Since love is a subjective attitude, it is not easy to identify its presence. In John's day as in ours, different concepts of love were in circulation. This is apparent from the variety of Greek terms used to express the idea. In addition to ἀγάπη, which John uses in this epistle, love was identified as φιλία, φιλαδελφία, στοργή, and ἔρως. Ἀγάπη, in secular Greek, was the term for high regard and respect; among Christians it was used to describe a selfless, purposeful, outgoing attitude that desires to do good to the one loved (see on 2:7). Φιλία and its verb form φιλέω referred to a warm affectionate regard for another, both friends and members of the family. Θιλαδελφία spoke of brotherly love, στοργή of natural affection between parents and children, and ἔρως of passionate love.

Since love is a test that gives evidence that one has eternal life (3:14-15), it is imperative that the Christian know how to identify genuine ἀγάπη. Is it merely sentiment? Is verbalizing enough to prove its presence? This is the problem with which John deals in 3:16-18.

The passage begins with the supreme example of love, Christ's self-sacrifice on the cross. He did not merely nurture the feeling of love in His heart, nor did He simply declare His love to us. His love was indeed feeling, and He did declare His love for the lost world, but in addition His love expressed itself in self-sacrificing, loving action. "He laid down His life for us" (3:16). Genuine love, then, is active love (3:18) that helps the loved one in his area of need. Such love may express itself in the supreme self-sacrifice of giving one's life for the sake of the one who is loved (3:16), or it may be called on to engage in such an unheroic act as sharing a loaf of bread with a hungry brother (3:17).

The kind of love that gives grounds for the assurance of salvation is that expressed in the biblical use of ἀγάπη. It is love in action, helping, giving, sacrificing for the benefit of the brother in need. It is by this objective evidence that one knows "that we are of the truth" and can "assure our heart before Him" (3:19). In this regard, also, John's treatment of love noticeably advances beyond 2:9-11 in 3:16-18. In the former passage he speaks of love without defining it; in the latter passage he graphically shows what genuine love is.

4. THE FRUIT OF GENUINE LOVE, 3:19-24

In this section the primary theme is assurance. Notice γνωσόμεθα, "we shall know" (v. 19), πείσομεν, "we shall assure" (v. 19), παρρησίαν, "confidence" (v. 21), and ἐν τούτῳ γινώσκομεν, "we know by this" (v. 24). It is obvious that a major fruit of genuine love is assurance of salvation. In addition, a secondary fruit of love is mentioned—answered prayer (v. 22). Although verse 22 is connected to verse 21 by the coorindating conjunction καί, "and," the relationship seems to be that of cause and effect. There is confidence toward God *so that* whatever is asked from God is received. Love in action produces confidence, and confidence in turn results in answered prayer.

Further explanation of the cause of answered prayer is given in verse 22*a*. God responds to prayer because (ὅτι) it is the believer's practice (present tense) to obey God and to please Him. In verse 23 John explains that obedience involves the fulfillment of Christ's command to love one another, and this, of course, is the basis for the confidence spoken of in verses 19-21. God answers prayer, then, because of the confidence in Him; He likewise answers because the petitioners have met the conditions of obeying and pleasing Him. Lenski goes one step further and suggests that answered prayer is itself evidence that we are God's children. "Every answer to our petitions," he writes, "is thus the clearest factual evidence that he treats us as children."[46]

One of John's main purposes in penning this epistle was to give grounds for Christian assurance (5:13). Some have superficially insisted that assurance is to be based solely upon profession of faith. To call upon evidence such as acts of righteousness is thought to be dangerously approaching the fallacy of salvation by works rather than by faith. John would agree that the grounds of assurance must include faith in the incarnate Christ who made atonement for man's sin (2:22-23; 4:9-10; 5:1, 4-5, 10-12; and 5:13). But the apostle places beside faith as a ground for assurance the evidence of a changed life. This ethical test stands alongside the doctrinal test. More specifically the changed life involves the habitual practice of righteousness (2:29—3:10a) and the continuing love of fellow believers (3:14-15). John explicitly declares, "If you know that He is righteous, you know that every one also who practices righteousness is born of Him" (2:29), and he adds, "We know that we have passed out of death into life, because we love the brethren" (3:14a). These two themes of the epistle are succinctly stated as an imperative in 3:23. God's command is (1) belief in God's Son Jesus Christ (the Christological test) and (2) love for one another (the ethical test).

B. SOCIAL CONCERN IN THE EARLY CHURCH

Although 1 John 3:17 is simply an illustration, it nevertheless has a significant bearing on the New Testament teaching concerning giving. It has something to say about the motivation for, and the beneficiaries of, New Testament giving.

A survey of New Testament passages dealing with the subject of giving seems to indicate that the early church was more concerned with giving to the poor than with giving for the support of preachers of the gospel. That contributions were made to Christian workers is clear from a number of passages. The principle is set

---

46. Lenski, p. 478.

forth in Galatians 6:6, where Paul says, "Let the one who is taught the word share all good things with him who teaches." Paul further discusses the fact that the minister of the gospel has the right to expect financial support from those to whom he ministers (1 Cor. 9:6-14). He shows that it is God's will for "those who proclaim the gospel to get their living from the gospel" (v. 14). The same principle is stated in 1 Timothy 5:17-18. And John himself indicates that travelling brothers (missionaries?) should be supported by the believers (3 John 5-8).

Still greater stress is placed on giving to the poor. No doubt this emphasis can be traced, at least in part, to the Old Testament. It is true that there are no New Testament passages that explicitly cite the Old Testament as the source for teaching concerning social concern is clearly evident in the law of Moses (Ex. 22:22-25; Lev. 19:9-10; 23:22; 25:35-37; Deut. 15:11; 24:14-15, 19-22). The psalmists are keenly aware of the plight of the needy (Psalms 12:5; 14:6; 35:10; 37:14; 72:4, 12-14). And the prophets pour out righteous indignation against those who oppress the poor (Isa. 10:1-2; Ezek. 22:29; Amos 2:6-7; 5:11-12; 8:4-6).

It is also certain that Jesus' concern for the poor and His personal display of compassion (Matt. 11:5; 15:32; 19:21; 20:34; Luke 14:13, 21) are reflected in the practice of the early church. Christ is quoted by Paul as saying, "It is more blessed to give than to receive" (Acts 20:35). Again in 2 Corinthians 8:9, Paul points to the supreme example of giving, the grace of our Lord Jesus Christ, who, although He was rich, became poor for our benefit, so that we as a result of His poverty might become rich.

The earliest giving recorded in the history of the church was sacrificial sharing with needy brothers (Acts 2:45; 4:34-35). This concern of the early Jerusalem church is also reflected in the desire of its leaders expressed to Paul in Galatians 2:10. It is likewise apparent in the arrangements for the support of widows practiced by the church (Acts 6:1-6).

The same emphasis is seen in the epistle written—perhaps as early as A.D. 45-50—by James, the leading elder of the Jerusalem church (James 2:14-17). It is his insistence that genuine faith will share with a brother in need, just as it is John's insistence that genuine love will take steps to help the needy.

Paul's ministry demonstrates the same concern. In Acts 11:27-30 it was Barnabas and Saul who took the contributions of the Antiochean church to the famine threatened church in Judea. Later in his ministry Paul instigated an offering from his missionary churches for the poverty stricken believers of Jerusalem (Rom. 15:26). And in connection with that campaign to help the needy, Paul wrote the most extensive stewardship passage in the New Testament (2 Cor. 8-9). Another Pauline program of sharing with the needy is seen in the instructions for the care of widows (1 Tim. 5:3-16).

So, the apostle John writing much later (c. A.D. 90) reveals the same emphasis on sharing with the poor. Genuine Christian love will make it a point to help those in need. In fact, as in the early Jerusalem church (Acts 4:34), there ought to be no needy believer in twentieth-century local churches.

PARAPHRASTIC COMMENTARY (3:10*b*-24)

(10*b*) It is likewise true that the person who does not habitually exercise love for his fellow believer is a member, not of God's family, but of the devil's. (11) My ground for saying this is Christ's command—which you have known ever since you first heard the gospel—that we are to manifest the distinctive mark of His disciples, namely, love for each other. (12) We are not to be like Cain who was a member of the devil's family and who butchered his brother, Abel. And what moved him to commit such a crime? It was hatred, because Abel's obedience was a rebuke to Cain and his rebelliousness. (13) Consider another example of hatred. You are surprised that the people of this evil world are treating you hatefully. Don't wonder at it any longer, for this is to be expected.

(14) As for us, we have assurance that, whereas we were once spiritually dead, now we are spiritually alive. We are sure of this because our lives are characterized by love for God's people. The person who does not have such continuing love remains right where he has always been—in the sphere of spiritual death. (15) To hate a Christian is the same as murdering him, and anyone knows that a person who is eternally saved does not commit murder.

(16) Here is how we know what genuine love is. It was demonstrated by Christ when He voluntarily sacrificed His life for us. In the same way, we should be willing to die for the sake of fellow believers. (17) But suppose that someone who has an adequate income to live on should be aware over some period of time that a fellow Christian is in financial need, and suppose that he responds by slamming shut the door of his heart. How could he possibly be indwelt by God's love? (18) Dear children, let's make sure that our love does not merely consist of words or of empty talk, but of action that is an unhypocritical expression of love.

(19) And it is by this kind of love in action that we will be able to ascertain that we are vitally related to God's truth, and our consciences will be set at ease in the very presence of God Himself, (20) This is true because, if an overly-sensitive conscience makes us feel guilty, we can be sure that God knows better than our conscience that our love in action is proof that we have eternal life. (21) Dear friends, if our conscience does not make us feel guilty, we have perfect freedom to come into the very presence of God, (22) and He will give us anything that we ask for because we are habitually obeying Him and doing those things that make Him happy. (23) And He commands us to do two things: to place our faith in the person of His Son Jesus Christ and to show love continually to one another just as He told us to do. (24) And the one who habitually obeys God's will shows that God is dwelling in him and he in Him. It is by means of this habitual obedience that we can ascertain that God is dwelling in us, and this assurance comes from the Holy Spirit whom God has given to us.

STRUCTURAL COMMENTARY (3:10b-24)[47]

2. Sonship demands love of fellow believers, 3:10b-24
   a. Transition, 3:10b
   b. The command to love, 3:11
      (1) A long standing command, 3:11a
      (2) A command to love fellow Christians, 3:11b
   c. Negative examples, 3:12-13
      (1) Cain, who murdered his brother, 3:12
      (2) The world, that hates the people of God, 3:13
   d. The love test, 3:14-15
      (1) Positive result, 3:14a
         (a) The conclusion: we have passed from death to life
         (b) The criterion: we love the brothers
      (2) Negative result, 3:14b-15
         (a) The criterion: he does not love, 3:14b
         (b) The conclusion: he remains dead, 3:14b
         (c) The explanation, 3:15
            (1a) To hate is the same as murder, 3:15a
            (2a) No Christian commits murder, 3:15b
   e. The test of love, 3:16-18
      (1) The example of genuine love, 3:16
         (a) Christ's act, 3:16a
         (b) Our duty, 3:16b

---

47. For previous section of the outline see p. 258.

(2) The example of spurious love, 3:17
    (a) Ability to help, 3:17a
    (b) Awareness of the need, 3:17b
    (c) Negative reaction, 3:17c
    (d) Conclusion, 3:17d
(3) The consequent exhortation, 3:18
    (a) Negative, 3:18a
    (b) Positive, 3:18b
f. The fruit of love, 3:19-24
  (1) For the condemning heart, 3:19-20
      (a) Assurance based on the presence of loving action, 3:19
      (b) Assurance based on God's Greater knowledge, 3:20
  (2) For the uncondemning heart, 3:21-24
      (a) Confidence, 3:21
      (b) Answered prayer, 3:22-23
          (1a) The promise, 3:22a
          (2a) The prerequisites, 3:22b
          (3a) The commands identified, 3:23
      (c) Assurance of mutual indwelling, 3:24
          (1a) Based on obedience, 3:24a
          (2a) Conveyed by the Spirit, 3:24b

12

B. Sonship Tested on Christological Grounds, 4:1-6

In 1 John 4:1-6 the apostle continues to view the Christian life as divine sonship. In the previous section he insisted that the life of a child of God will be marked by a certain ethical quality. Members of God's family are those who, as a general practice of life, do what is right (2:29—3:10*a*) and who continually manifest love to other members of the family (3:10*b*-24). Now, in 4:1-6, John insists that God's children are those who believe the truth about Jesus. They confess "that Jesus Christ has come in the flesh" (v. 2). After issuing a warning concerning false prophets (v. 1), the author sets up the Christological test (vv. 2-3). This is followed by the test of listening (vv. 4-6).

EXEGETICAL COMMENTARY (4:1-6)

1. A WARNING AGAINST FALSE PROPHETS, 4:1

4:1. ἀγαπητοί, μὴ παντὶ πνεύματι πιστεύετε, "Beloved, do not believe every spirit." Having just completed a major section dealing with love, John uses ἀπαπητοί, "beloved," to express his tender concern for his readers. His first statement is a warning against gullibility, μὴ . . . πιστεύετε, "do not believe." The use of the negative μή with the present tense imperative verb suggests that the readers had shown a tendency to give credence to the false teachers. The Greek construction means, *Stop believing* ... (see on 2:15). Bultmann suggests that the verb πιστεύετε, "believe," carries the same connotation as in 3:23, no doubt because in both places John used πιστεύω with the dative case. He understands that the expression here refers to "faith in the sense of acknowledgement," and he paraphrases it, "Do not come under the power of. ..."[1] Arndt and Gingrich, however, list 1 John 4:1 under the meaning, "give credence to."[2] There is a difference between making a commitment to Christ (3:23) and believing a false teacher. The concept of giving credence to what someone says seems best to describe a person's response to a false teacher.

The use of the term πνεῦμα, "spirit," to describe the heretical teachers is best understood in connection with the term ψευδοπροφῆται, "false prophets." A prophet is a person who speaks under supernatural inspiration. An example is the experience of Saul when the Spirit of the Lord came on him (1 Sam. 10:6, 10). A prophet is a spokesman for some spirit, either a false spirit or the Spirit of God. John so closely identifies the spokesman with the spirit that by synecdoche he uses the term *spirit* to refer to both the prophet and the spirit who inspired him. To believe the prophet was to believe the spirit who spoke through him.

ἀλλὰ δοκιμάζετε τὰ πνεύματα εἰ ἐκ τοῦ θεοῦ ἐστιν, "but test the spirits to see whether they are from God." The contrast between what the readers had been doing (indiscriminately giving credence to various spirits) and what they ought to be doing (testing the spirits) is emphasized by the strong adversative conjunction ἀλλά, "but, on the contrary."

δοκιμάζω, "to test," was commonly used for such tests as the testing of calves for sacrifice, the testing of officials for public office,[3] and the testing of coins to see if they were valid. The word also came to speak of approval as the result of testing, but here in 4:1, it is obviously used to speak of the process of testing with no indication of the outcome.[4] The term suggests that there is an objective standard by which to put the suggested test into effect. This standard is described in verses 2-3. The verb δοκιμάζω is a present tense imperative used in the progressive sense, urging the

1. Rudolph Bultmann, *The Johannine Epistles*, Hermeneia, p. 61.
2. William F. Arndt and F. Wilbur Gingrich, trans. and eds., *A Greek-English Lexicon of the New Testament*, by Walter Bauer, p. 660-61.
3. James Hope Moulton and George Milligan, *The Vocabulary of the Greek New Testament*, p. 167.
4. Arndt and Gingrich, p. 201.

readers to make it a practice to put any and all prophets to the test. The testing of prophets had an Old Testament precedent. Moses gave the people criteria by which to test anyone who professed to be a prophet (Deut. 18:20-22), namely, (1) what he said must agree with what God had previously revealed, (2) he must speak in the name of the Lord, and (3) it must come to pass. See also Deuteronomy 13:1-5; Jeremiah 23:9-22; 28:9.

The expression εἶναι ἐκ with the ablative case is characteristic of John. Various tenses of the expression occur some nineteen times in this epistle (with πατρός, "father," 2:16; with κόσμου, "world," 2:16 and 4:5; with ἡμῶν, "of us," 2:19, 19, 19; with ἀληθείας, "truth," 2:21 and 3:19; with διαβόλου, "devil," 3:8; with πονηροῦ, "evil one," 3:12; and with θεοῦ, "God," 3:10; 4:1, 2, 3, 4, 5, 6, 6, 7; and 5:19). Bultmann says that the expression "designates the origin and thereby the essence."[5] The spirits are to be tested to see if they derive their message and power from God.

ὅτι πολλοὶ ψευδοπροφῆται ἐξεληλύθασιν εἰς τὸν κόσμον, "because many false prophets have gone out into the world." John identifies the persons against whom he warns his readers as ψευδοπροφῆται, "false prophets," a term Jesus had previously used (Matt. 7:15; 24:11, 24; Luke 6:26). In nonbiblical Greek usage, a prophet was one who spoke in the name of a god, declaring the will and counsel of the god.[6] In the Old Testament (Jer. 15:19), a prophet is described as the spokesman of God (Heb., *mouth*). He was one who spoke under the influence of supernatural inspiration. John uses the term prophet similarly in 1 John 4:1. These individuals are not merely teachers as one might conclude from 2 Peter 2:1. They were actually inspired by a spirit—the spirit of the antichrist (1 John 4:3). The NEB designates them as "prophets falsely inspired" (v. 1).

There was, of course, a valid New Testament office of prophet filled by persons who had the gift of prophecy (Rom. 12:6; 1 Cor. 12:10, 28, 29; 14:1, 29-32; Eph. 4:11). It is clear from such passages as Acts 11:27-28; 21:4, 10-11; and 1 Corinthians 12:7-11 that the prophet was one who conveyed information that was supernaturally imparted to him by the Spirit of God. Thus he was not merely a teacher or preacher, relying only on his learning and understanding.

5. Bultmann, p. 61, n. 1.
6. Gerhard Kittel, ed., *Theological Dictionary of the New Testament*, 1964-76, s.v. "προφήτης, κτλ.," by Helmut Kramer. 6:795.

The declaration that "many false prophets have gone out into the world" has been interpreted in several different ways: (1) that they had left the church because of their heretical differences (2:19), (2) that they had gone out as missionaries for their cause,[7] and (3) that they were generally present in the world. It would seem that the last view is the most likely, since the context gives no indication of anything more specific. The perfect tense verb ἐξεληλύθασιν, "have gone out," is intensive in force, laying emphasis on the continuing results of the completed act. That they are now present in the world is what John has indicated by his choice of tense.

2. THE CHRISTOLOGICAL TEST, 4:2-3

4:2. ἐν τούτῳ γινώσκετε τὸ πνεῦμα τοῦ θεοῦ, "By this you know the Spirit of God." In verse 2, John states the Christological test in positive terms, indicating the criterion for identifying the person who speaks under the inspiration of the Spirit of God. The phrase, ἐν τούτῳ, "by this," refers forward, as it usually does in 1 John. (See 2:3; 3:16; 4:9-10, etc.) There is obviously nothing in verse 1 that could conceivably serve as an antecedent for the pronoun. Here again the verb γινώσκω, "know," is used in its classical sense of knowledge arrived at by observation or deduction. In this instance, it is a case of observing the evidence (the confession concerning Jesus) and drawing the conclusion (the "spirit . . . is from God"). The form of γινώσκετε could be either indicative or imperative. Law thinks the imperative is better since it follows the two imperatives μὴ πιστεύετε, "do not believe," and δοκιμάζετε, "test" (v. 1).[8] However, most other commentators prefer the indicative mood. Reasons usually given are: (1) an appeal to the readers' knowledge is more in keeping with the author's method, and (2) ἐν τούτῳ, "by this," is nowhere else joined to an imperative in John's writings. By the criterion advanced in the second half of the verse the readers recognize the presence of "the Spirit of God" in the prophets who come to them.

πᾶν πνεῦμα ὃ ὁμολογεῖ Ἰησοῦν Χριστὸν ἐν σαρκὶ ἐληλυθότα ἐκ τοῦ θεοῦ ἐστιν, "every spirit that confesses

---

7. Joseph Bonsirven, *Épitres de Saint Jean*, vol. 9, *Verbum Salutis*, p. 186, calls it a "diabolic invasion"; B. F. Westcott, *The Epistles of John*, p. 140, says that they "are gone out on a mission of evil from their dark home."
8. Robert Law, *The Tests of Life*, p. 396.

that Jesus Christ has come in the flesh is from God." This is a test that applies to all who measure up to its standard (πᾶν πνεῦμα, "every spirit") just as verse 4 applies to all who fail to measure up. There are no added conditions or mitigating circumstances.

Inasmuch as ὁμολογεῖ, "confesses," is a present tense verb, it is clear that John has in mind a continuing confession rather than a momentary agreement. As in 2:23, the ideas of solemn affirmation and public proclamation are combined. Michel identifies the usage in both passages as that of making a solemn statement of faith.[9]

Many writers point out the three possible ways of understanding the confession: (1) Ἰησοῦν Χριστόν, "Jesus Christ," may be the object, and ἐν σαρκὶ ἐληλυθότα, "come in the flesh," may be a secondary predicate, in which case it would read, ". . . confesses Jesus Christ as come in the flesh." (2) Ἰησοῦν, "Jesus," may be the object, and Χριστὸν ἐν σαρκὶ ἐληλυθότα, "Christ come in the flesh," may be the secondary predicate, which would read ". . . confesses Jesus as Christ come in the flesh." (3) The whole expression may function as direct object, which would be translated, ". . . confesses Jesus-Christ-come-in-flesh." The third view provides the most natural and most direct treatment of the Greek text.

The KJV, NASB, and NIV all translate this confession as follows: "that Jesus Christ has come in the flesh." The weakness of this rendering is that the Greek text does not have the word ὅτι "that," and it is doubtful that it should be supplied in the English translation. Actually, to supply the word ὅτι is not an incidental matter, for it alters the vary nature of the confession. With ὅτι the confession is propositional in nature. It is a declaration *about* what Jesus Christ did; without ὅτι the text contains a confession of Jesus as a person rather than a confession of a proposition about the Person. Brooke puts it aptly when he declares, "It is a confession not of the fact of the incarnation, but of the Incarnate Christ."[10]

The association of the two designations, Ἰησοῦν and Χριστόν, is a significant combination in view of the Gnostic denial that the human Jesus and the Christ were one and the same Person. That John uses the two words together is obvious from their appear-

---
9. Kittel, s.v. "ὁμολογέω κτλ.," by Otto Michel. 5:209-10.
10. A. E. Brooke, *A Critical and Exegetical Commentary on the Johannine Epistles*, The International Critical Commentary, p. 109.

ance in the following passages: John 1:17; 17:3; 1 John 1:3; 2:1; 3:23; 4:2; 5:6, 20; 2 John 3, 7. The fact that σαρκί appears without the article is also significant. The anarthrous construction, rather than speaking of the identity of the flesh referred to, stresses kind or quality. Christ's coming was an enfleshment. It was a coming in flesh. Both Plummer and Marshall point out that John does not say Jesus came εἰς σαρκά, "into flesh," but ἐν σαρκί, "in flesh."[11] Christ did not come upon a man already in existence as Cerinthus claimed. The participle, ἐληλυθότα, "come," is used in the attributive sense modifying "Jesus Christ." It is "Jesus Christ having come" who is confessed.

The perfect tense speaks of an action that occurred in the past with results continuing at least up to the time when John penned those words. Although the perfect tense does not guarantee permanence, as some have assumed here,[12] it does indicate that, at the time of writing, Jesus was still incarnate.[13] He still possessed the resurrection body with which He ascended to heaven (Acts 1:9-11) and with which He will return. On the phrase ἐκ τοῦ θεοῦ, see on 4:1.

This confession, which John sets up as a standard by which to test the identity of those who claimed to be prophets, concerned Jesus Christ incarnate. It is recognized that He is the human Jesus, but at the same time He is the Christ. He is no ethereal aeon or phantasmal being; He is Christ incarnate, living in human flesh. It is impossible to read this confession against the religious background of the first century without recognizing its thrust at the teachings of the Gnostics.

4:3. καὶ πᾶν πνεῦμα ὃ μὴ ὁμολογεῖ τὸν Ἰησοῦν ἐκ τοῦ θεοῦ οὐκ ἔστιν, "and every spirit that does not confess Jesus is not from God." Verse 3 states the Christological test in negative terms, indicating the identifying mark of the person who fails to measure up to the standard. Here again the test and its results are all inclusive. Πᾶν πνεῦμα, "every spirit," leaves room for no exceptions. The use of πᾶν, "all," with the negative οὐκ makes the denial universal and is best translated, "No spirit that does not confess." The repetition of πνεῦμα in verse 3 assumes that the

---

11. A. Plummer, *The Epistles of St. John*, Cambridge Greek Testament for Schools and Colleges, p. 95; I. Howard Marshall, *The Epistles of John*, The New International Commentary on the New Testament, p. 205.
12. John R. W. Stott, *The Epistles of John*, Tyndale New Testament Commentaries, p. 154.
13. Brooke, p. 109; Plummer, p. 96.

Sonship Tested on Christological Grounds 297

speaker is actually inspired by a spirit just as the speaker in verse 2 was. There the spirit is the Spirit of God; here, the spirit of antichrist.

The use of the negative μή with the indicative ὁμολογεῖ, "confess," is an interesting deviation from the normative οὐ with the indicative. F. Blass and A. Debrunner brush it aside as a textual corruption.[14] Robertson finds "a certain aloofness about μή here," and he quotes F. E. Thompson, who refers to Plato's use of μή to express reserve, politeness, or suggestion.[15] C. F. D. Moule's comment on the passage refers the reader to Robert Law,[16] who says, "Here it is used with classical correctness, as expressing the subjective conviction of the writer that there are no exceptions to the statement he is making.[17]

Most manuscripts read μὴ ὁμολογεῖ, *"does not confess,"* but the Vulgate, many Old Latin manuscripts, and a number of Latin Fathers have readings that assume λύει, "looses, destroys, annuls," as original. The Latin texts have *solvit*, ("severs"), and the Fathers have *destruit*, ("destroys"). Some modern scholars have accepted the Latin reading, seeing it as a refutation of the Gnostic assertion that Jesus and the Christ are not the same Person, and thus are "severed," the one from the other. While it is no doubt true that λύει does reflect a polemic against Gnosticism, the evidence that it was the original reading is very slender. Bruce M. Metzger and the Editorial Committee of the United Bible Societies' *Greek New Testament* concluded that λύει arose in the second century controversy with the Gnostics.[18] Westcott saw the variant reading as an added interpretation that crept into the Latin text.[19] The overwhelming weight of the manuscript evidence leaves little doubt that John originally wrote μὴ ὁμολογεῖ. As in the previous verse, the present tense refers to a habitual practice and the word ὁμολογέω speaks of an affirmation made with conviction.

The substance of the confession is expressed in the text as being τὸν Ἰησοῦν, "the Jesus," a reading that caused some difference of opinion among early scribes. Other readings found in various manuscripts are:

---

14. F. Blass and A. Debrunner, *A Greek Grammar of the New Testament*, sec. 428(4).
15. A. T. Robertson, *A Grammar of the Greek New Testament in the Light of Historical Research*, p. 1169.
16. C. F. D. Moule, *An Idiom Book of New Testament Greek*, p. 155.
17. Law, p. 396.
18. Bruce M. Metzger, *A Textual Commentary on the Greek New Testament*, p. 714.
19. Westcott, pp. 165-66. For a thorough discussion stating arguments on both sides of the problem see Marshall, pp. 207-8, n. 11, and Brooke, pp. 110-14.

- Ἰησοῦν Χριστόν, "Jesus Christ"
- τὸν Χριστόν, "the Christ"
- τὸν Χριστὸν ἐν σαρκὶ ἐληλυθότα, "the Christ come in flesh"
- Ἰησοῦν κύριον ἐν σαρκὶ ἐληλυθότα, "Jesus the Lord come in flesh"
- Ἰησοῦν Χριστὸν ἐν σαρκὶ ἐληλυθότα, "Jesus Christ come in flesh"

The preferred reading (τὸν Ἰησοῦν) is given a B rating on a scale of A through D in the United Bible Societies' *Greek New Testament*. This evaluation is based on the assumption that the other readings all appear to be additions taken from verse 2.[20] It seems clear that the variants are attempts to explain the shorter and more difficult τὸν Ἰησοῦν.

Many modern commentators fail to take into consideration the significance of the article τόν before the name Ἰησοῦν. Brooke sees this shorter reading as emphasizing the personal character of the confession, which it no doubt does.[21] However, it goes beyond this. Although it was common in Greek to use the article before proper names,[22] there is good reason for understanding the article in τὸν Ἰησοῦν as indicating previous reference.[23] John insists that it is "this Jesus" who must be confessed—the Jesus of verse 2 who came in flesh (ἐν σαρκὶ ἐληλυθότα). Houlden says that the expression μὴ ὁμολογεῖ τὸν Ἰησοῦν is shorthand for not admitting "that Jesus came in the flesh."[24] Anyone who, because of Gnostic dualism, denied this fact failed the test, that is, he revealed that he "is not from God" (ἐκ τοῦ θεοῦ οὐκ ἔστιν). On the significance of this expression, see on verse 1.

καὶ τοῦτο ἐστιν τὸ τοῦ ἀντιχρίστου, "and this is the spirit of the antichrist." The demonstrative pronoun τοῦτο, "this," is neuter in gender. As such it could refer to the denial (Brooke[25]);

---

20. Metzger, p. 714.
21. Brooke, p. 110.
22. H. E. Dana and Julius R. Mantey, *A Manual Grammar of the Greek New Testament*, pp. 142-44.
23. Ibid., p. 141. It is so interpreted by R. C. H. Lenski, *The Interpretation of the Epistles of St. Peter, St. John and St. Jude*, p. 488, and Law, p. 396.
24. J. L. Houlden, *A Commentary on the Johannine Epistles,* Black's New Testament Commentaries, p. 107.
25. Brooke, p. 110.

or to the whole matter of the antichrist just referred to (Law[26]); or back to the word πνεῦμα, "spirit," which is neuter. It should be noted, however, that τοῦτο and τό must refer to the same thing since they are joined by the copulative verb ἐστιν, "is." These two neuter words most naturally look back to πνεῦμα as their antecedent since it is a neuter noun in close proximity to the pronoun and article in question and the other suggested antecedents are much less obvious possibilities. Also it is most natural to assume that, since the inspiring spirit in verse 2 is identified, the spirit mentioned in verse 3 will also be identified. Thus, John declares, "And this (the spirit who refuses to confess the incarnate Jesus) is the (spirit) of the antichrist."

On the term ἀντίχριστος, "antichrist," see on 2:18.

ὃ ἀκηκόατε ὅτι ἔρχεται, καὶ νῦν ἐν τῷ κόσμῳ ἐστὶν ἤδη, "of which you have heard that it is coming, and now it is already in the world." This statement is similar to 2:18 in that both passages speak of what the readers had heard concerning the antichrist. However, whereas the former passage refers to the antichrist directly, 4:3 refers to the spirit of antichrist. Just as the neuters τοῦτο and τό referred back to the neuter πνεῦμα, "spirit," so consistency suggests that the neuter ὅ, "which," also refers to πυεῦμα. Law overlooks this relationship when he insists, on the basis of this neuter pronoun, that the antichrist is a principle or event, not a person.[27] In 2:18 John says that his readers had heard that the personal antichrist is coming; in 4:3 he states that they had heard that the spirit of antichrist is coming. It would appear that what they had heard might well have come from Paul and/or John, since both speak of such a coming in their writings (2 Thess. 2:3, 7; 1 John 2:18; 4:3).

At first sight, it may be thought, since John is speaking of the antichrist, that the term κόσμῳ, "world," is here used in its ethical sense of that evil order consisting of all the persons, practices, attitudes, and mechanisms that are controlled by sin. However, he no doubt uses the word in a more inclusive sense to refer to the sphere in which people (saved and unsaved) live and where both the Spirit of God and the spirit of antichrist are present and at work. The position of ἤδη, "already," at the end of the clause gives emphasis to the word. It is not true that antichrist will not appear

---

26. Law, p. 396.
27. Ibid., p. 397.

until the end time. He is already on the scene in the form of a spirit working in and through the false prophets (antichrists, 2:18).

3. THE TEST OF LISTENING, 4:4-6

4:4. ὑμεῖς ἐκ τοῦ θεοῦ ἐστε, τεκνία, καὶ νενικήκατε αὐτούς, "You are from God, little children, and have overcome them." In this section, John indicates that a prophet can be identified spiritually by determining who it is who listens to him. That John is speaking of the identification of the speaker rather than the hearers is made clear by verse 6b. Two groups of listeners are referred to in these verses:

- those who are from God (v. 4) and who know God (v. 6)
- the world (v. 5), that is, those who are not from God (v. 6)

Similarly there are two groups of speakers:

- those who are from the world (v. 5)
- those who are from God (v. 6)

John begins this section with a doubly emphatic personal pronoun—ὑμεῖς, "you." It is somewhat emphatic, in the first place, because the verb ἐστε, "*you are*," carries its own built-in subject. Thus ὑμεῖς is unnecessary except to provide emphasis. In addition, the pronoun is emphatic by reason of its position first in the sentence. Its force can best be expressed by translating it "as for you." It serves to place the believers (v. 4) in strong contrast to those who are under the influence of the spirit of antichrist (v. 3).

The prepositional phrase ἐκ τοῦ θεοῦ "from God," is to be understood as a shortened form of γεγεννημένος ἐκ τοῦ θεοῦ, "born of God" (cf. pp. 224, 291). John continues to view the Christian life as divine sonship. It is also significant that in this section (4:1-6) where the phrase ἐκ τοῦ θεοῦ occurs six times John addresses his readers as τεκνία, "little children," a diminutive term of endearment that stresses the fact of birth (see on 2:1). The apostle commends his readers because they "have overcome them." The pronoun αὐτούς, "them," being masculine and plural, does not refer to the spirit (πνεῦμα) of antichrist (v. 4), which is neuter gender, but to the false prophets (v. 1). The perfect tense verb indicates that the believers had previously gained the victory

Sonship Tested on Christological Grounds 301

over these false teachers and were victors when John wrote them. Law insists that the tense means that the results will continue.[28] The perfect tense, however, guarantees nothing concerning the future, only that the results have continued until the time of writing. This victory did not consist of driving the heretics out physically, although the latter had left the congregation of believers (2:19). Instead it was the victory of rejecting their heretical message and continuing to hold fast to the truth as taught by the apostles. It was a doctrinal victory rather than a moral one, although it was bound to have a moral effect.

ὅτι μείζων ἐστὶν ὁ ἐν ὑμῖν ἢ ὁ ἐν τῷ κόσμῳ, "because greater is He who is in you than he who is in the world." Ὅτι, "because," introduces an explanation of what it was that enabled the readers to overcome. An understanding of apostolic truth was involved (2:24), but John here explains the victory as the product of an indwelling enablement. He indicates that the conflict is between Him "who is in you" (ὁ ἐν ὑμῖν) and him "who is in the world" (ὁ ἐν τῷ κόσμῳ). These phrases reveal a change from the neuter terms πνεῦμα, "spirit," τοῦτο, "this," and ὅ, "which" (v. 3), to the masculine article ὁ, "he." Of course the neuter gender in verse 3 is grammatical gender rather than sense gender[29] so that πνεῦμα is neuter even when referring to a personal spirit such as the Holy Spirit. In verse 4, however, John wishes to place emphasis on the personal element; consequently he changes to the masculine gender in order to make it clear that the conflict is between two personal powers.

Ὁ ἐν ὑμῖν seems clearly to refer to one of the persons of the Godhead. Most commentators say it is God (Dodd, Lenski, Brooke, Marshall, Bultmann, Houlden).[30] It could, however, refer to Christ (Plummer:[31] either God or Christ; Westcott:[32] "God in Christ") or the Holy Spirit (Bruce, Stott).[33] The last view, although not the choice of most writers, has the context in its favor. In verses 2 and 3 John has been contrasting the Spirit of God with

---

28. Law, p. 397.
29. Dana and Mantey, p. 35.
30. C. H. Dodd, *The Johannine Epistles*, The Moffatt New Testament Commentary (London: Hodder and Stoughton, 1946), p. 100; Lenski, p. 490; Brook, p. 115; Marshall, p. 208; Bultmann, *The Johannine Epistles*, p. 63; Houlden, p. 110.
31. Plummer, p. 98.
32. Westcott, p. 144.
33. F. F. Bruce, *The Epistles of John*, p. 106; Stott, p. 157.

the spirit of antichrist, and he again refers to these two spirits in verse 6. In 2:27 the anointing (Holy Spirit) is said to dwell in the believers.

On the other side of the contrast is the one "who is in the world," a phrase that most have interpreted as referring to the devil. Bultmann is one possible exception, and he sees here the spirit of error and falsehood, that is, the spirit of antichrist.[34] It would seem best to understand that John is referring to these two spirits—God's Holy Spirit in the believer and the spirit of antichrist (representative of the devil) in the world. It seems apparent that the term κόσμῳ, "world," is used in a somewhat different sense from its use in verse 3, where it was spatial. In verse 4, John is not merely saying that the spirit of antichrist is present in the sphere where people live. By "he who is in the world," the apostle suggests that the world somehow is what it is because "he" dwells there. The term "world," then, is used here in its moral rather than in its spatial sense.

4:5. αὐτοὶ ἐκ τοῦ κόσμου εἰσίν, "They are from the world." Like ὑμεῖς, "you," at the beginning of verse 4, αὐτοί, "they," is doubly emphatic and indicates contrast, not so much with ὑμεῖς, "you," of verse 4 as with ἡμεῖς "we," of verse 6. The false teachers are contrasted, not with the readers, but with the teachers of truth. Like the phrase ἐκ τοῦ θεοῦ, "from God," the parallel expression ἐκ τοῦ κόσμου, "from the world," speaks of source, and in both instances source determines essential character. The word κόσμοs is here intended to be taken in the ethical sense as referring to the entire organism of evil with all of the people, the programs, the activities, the philosophies, the attitudes, the value systems, and the institutions that comprise that organism. It is the pagan world in its totality. The heretical teachers were "from" it in that they spoke its language, reflected its mentality, and followed its promptings.[35]

διὰ τοῦτο ἐκ τοῦ κόσμου λαλοῦσιν καὶ ὁ κόσμος αὐτῶν ἀκούει, "therefore they speak as from the world, and the world listens to them." Διὰ τοῦτο literally means "because of this," and the demonstrative pronoun obviously refers back to the immediately preceding statement, "They are from the world." Just as their thought patterns originated with the world, so do their communications. Their message is determined by their source. The

---

34. Bultmann, p. 106.
35. Bonsirven, p. 195.

verb λαλοῦσιν, "they speak," is a customary present tense verb denoting that which is generally true.[36] The Gnostic teachers customarily reflected the attitudes and philosophies of the pagan world in their teachings.

That the third occurrence of the word κόσμος in this verse refers to the people of the evil world is obvious from the fact that the world listens to them (αὐτῶν ἀκούει). Again the present tense verb seems to be a customary present. Although the basic meaning of ἀκούω is *to hear*, this context requires that it be translated as "listens to," adding the idea of intent to that of mere hearing. See also John 10:8. The test concerns the person who purposefully directs his attention to the message of the false teachers. This is the proof of the affinity of the hearer toward the speaker.

4:6. ἡμεῖς ἐκ τοῦ θεοῦ ἐσμεν ὁ γινώσκων τὸν θεὸν ἀκούει ἡμῶν, ὃς οὐκ ἔστιν ἐκ τοῦ θεοῦ οὐκ ἀκούει ἡμῶν, "We are from God; he who knows God listens to us; he who is not from God does not listen to us." The personal pronoun ἡμεῖς, "we," like the pronouns that began verses 4 and 5, is emphatic both by reason of its *presence*, and by reason of its *position*. It sets the apostolic teachers in pointed contrast to the heretical teachers of verse 5. Its force could be represented by something like, "As for us. . . ." The first person plural is used in some passages to include both author and readers (1:9; 3:14, 16; 4:10-11, 16, 19). Here, however, since ἡμεῖς is contrasted with αὐτοί (v. 5) and since αὐτοί refers to the false teachers, it is most likely that ἡμεῖς refers to John and his associates—teachers of the truth.

On ἐκ τοῦ θεοῦ, "from God," see on 4:1.

Γινώσκω is the correct word to use when speaking of knowing a person, for it characterizes the knowledge gained by experience. This is true of the knowledge of God (Rom. 1:21; Gal. 4:9; 1 John 2:13; 4:8) and of Christ (2 Cor. 5:16; Heb. 8:11; 1 John 2:13, 14; 3:6). The use of γινώσκω here is also significant in that John is combatting the false γνῶσις, *knowledge*, of the Gnostics. The change from ἐκ τοῦ θεοῦ ἐστε, "you are from God," to ὁ γινώσκων, "he who knows God," would seem to indicate that the two expressions are interchangeable. The first is short for γεγεννημένος τοῦ θεοῦ, "born of God" and assumes that the Christian life is a life of divine sonship, as in 2:29—4:6; the second

---

36. Dana and Mantey, p. 183.

views the Christian life as a life of fellowship with God, as in 1:5—2:28.

John next states the test of listening in positive terms. The person who knows God will invariably listen (ἀκούει, customary present) to the apostolic message. He finds an affinity with it and thus is drawn to it. "Like associates with like".[37] The test is then stated negatively. Characteristically, the person who is not born of God does not listen to the truth (ἀκούει, customary present); in fact, he is repelled by it.

ἐκ τούτου γινώσκομεν τὸ πνεῦμα τῆς ἀληθείας καὶ τὸ πνεῦμα τῆς πλάνης, "By this we know the spirit of truth and the spirit of error." This is the concluding summary of the test of listening. Τούτου refers back to the positive and negative statement of the test in the first part of the verse—to the established fact that like listens to like. The preposition ἐκ, *from*, is used here to express means and is correctly translated "by" in the NASB. Γινώσκομεν, rather than οἴδαμεν, was chosen by John to speak of the attainment, not the possession, of knowledge. Discernment of the spirits of truth and of error is arrived at by observing who listens to a person's message. If the people of God are listening sympathetically, the message and speaker are from God; if the world is listening to it, the speaker and message are not from God, but from the world.

The two genitives, ἀληθείας, *"truth,"* and πλάνης, *"error,"* are descriptive genitives, not possessive or subjective genitives as Lenski suggests.[38] The one spirit is characterized by truth; the other, by error.

There is a noticeable parallelism of terminology in the Dead Sea Scroll *Manual of Discipline* (3, 18; 4, 23), which states that God created two spirits, the spirits of truth and of deceit.[39] These spirits are said to struggle for the control of men's hearts. (Both the Vermes[40] and the Gaster[41] translations designate the evil spirit as the "spirit of perversity.") Whether there is any direct connection between John and the Qumran community, it is impossible to say, but the common ideas and common terminology indicate that

---

37. Brooke, p. 114.
38. Lenski, p. 492.
39. P. Wernberg-Møller, trans., *The Manual of Discipline*, pp. 25, 27.
40. A. Dupont-Sommer, *The Essene Writings from Qumran*, pp. 78, 82.
41. Theodor H. Gaster, trans. *The Dead Sea Scriptures* "The Manual of Discipline," pp. 51, 53.

these ideas and terms were in general use in at least some circles of first century Judaism.

The word πλάνη could be used either in the passive sense of *error* or in the active sense of *deceit*. Context, of course, is the determinant in each occurrence of the term. Braun cites numerous uses in apocalyptic and Hellenistic-mystical writings to describe the seduction of men by supernatural powers. In fact the expression, τὸ πνεῦμα τῆς πλάνης, *the spirit of deceit*, occurs in this sense in the *Testaments of the Twelve Patriarchs*. In a context of Gnostic aggressiveness, it is clear that John uses the word πλάνη to mean "deceit" rather than mere "error."

THEOLOGICAL COMMENTARY (4:1-6)

A. JOHN'S SECOND DISCUSSION OF CHRISTOLOGY, 4:1-6

The first discussion of Christology is found in 2:18-28. As in the case of the second passage on love (3:10b-24), the second passage on Christology (4:1-6) noticeably advances its teaching beyond the first cycle (2:18-28).

The second discussion adds more specific doctrinal criteria to the test of belief.[42] The first of these criteria is the fact of the incarnation—"Jesus Christ has come in the flesh" (4:2). While this fact was implicit in the criterion stated in 2:22 ("Jesus is the Christ"), in 4:2 it is explicitly stated as a required confession. The second criterion is the test of listening (4:4-6). According to 4:5-6 a teacher's doctrinal position is revealed by the character of his audience. If his followers are from the world rather than being born of God, he also is from the world. The world is the source of his teaching (4:5), and he is inspired by the spirit of error (4:6). On the other hand, if a teacher's following is made up of those who know God and are born again, this is evidence that he also is born of God and that he is inspired by the spirit of truth (4:6).

The second discussion of the Christological test (4:1-6) also adds at least two new topics not mentioned in the first (2:18-28). One is the explicit mention of the incarnation, discussed above. The second is the part spirits play in the teaching of both truth and error.

Thus, while it is true that John repeats the ethical and the Christological tests, the tests of the second cycle clearly add new details and rise higher than the tests of the first cycle.

---

42. Bonsirven, p. 186.

1. WARNING CONCERNING FALSE PROPHETS, 4:1

For the first time in the epistle there is clear evidence that some of the readers were giving some credence to the Gnostic teaching. John finds it necessary to combat such gullibility with a prohibition. *"Stop believing every teacher who comes along"* is his warning.

However, John does not use the term teacher here. Instead he warns against believing every "spirit." The clue to understanding this unusual designation is found in the term "false prophets" in the latter part of the verse. A prophet was a person who had come under the influence of a supernatural power, whether good or bad. His message came from that power, so that what the prophet spoke was actually the message of the spirit who inspired him.

In 4:1-6 the spirits can be classified under two headings: the evil and the good. The term "false prophets" assumes the presence of false spirits who spoke through these prophets. In verse 3 the spirit responsible for the denial of the incarnation is called "the spirit of antichrist," and in verse 6 what is apparently the same spirit is referred to as "the spirit of error." In contrast, John speaks of the spirit that "confesses Jesus Christ having come in flesh" (v. 2, Gr.), describing this spirit as being from God. It seems that the apostle is saying that this is the Spirit of God, i.e., the Holy Spirit (v. 2*a*). Verse 6 describes this spirit as "the spirit of truth." (The NIV capitalizes Spirit here, thus interpreting the term as a designation for the Holy Spirit.)

If it is correct to see the Holy Spirit in these references, it may also be assumed that the evil spirit, here contrasted with the good, is likewise personal. It is not merely an attitude or an influence; it is the spirit of antichrist, and, ultimately, the devil—"the spirit that is now working in the sons of disobedience" (Eph. 2:2).

2. THE CHRISTOLOGICAL TEST, 4:2-3

The two spirits singled out in these verses are the Spirit of God (v. 2) and the spirit of the antichrist (v. 3). The former inspires the confession of Jesus Christ incarnate; the latter has nothing to do with such a confession. For both the false teacher and the believer this was a crucial confession. The Gnostic could not make such a declaration because of his basic philosophy of dualism where spirit and matter could not exist in the intimate union involved in an incarnate state. The second-century Gnostic avoided this incongruity either by docetism (Christ did not possess an actual body) or by adoptionism (the Divine Christ only came *upon* the human

Jesus). This latter was the teaching of Cerinthus, which 1 John seems to have intended to refute. This confession of the incarnate Christ, then, was a touchstone that served infallibly to identify the false teacher.

For the Christian also, the confession is crucial. It stands at the very heart of his faith. Do away with the confession, and you do away with the Christian faith itself. Christianity is essentially a system of salvation from sin and its condemnation. Without an incarnate Savior it ceases to be, for the Christian faith is essentially soteriological.

The Savior must be both man and God. He must be completely human in order to take man's place and bear the penalty for sin. If He is to represent man, He must be man—an angel could not take upon himself the penalty for sin. Identity of nature is necessary for valid substitution.

On the other hand, it is equally necessary that the Savior be God. Were he merely human, his death would have limited value. It could pay the penalty for one sinner, and no more. If the Savior is to be able to atone for the sins of millions of sinners, His death must have inestimable value. Only deity could fulfill such a requirement. Therefore, the Savior must be both God and man, or there is no salvation from sin. Just as Paul could declare that without the resurrection our "faith is worthless" (1 Cor. 15:17), so it is true that without the incarnation there is no salvation; we "are still in [our] sins" (1 Cor. 15:17).

The denial of the truth of the incarnation is not merely human in origin. The human teacher is the intermediate agent, but the originating agent is the spirit of antichrist operating in the world in advance of the coming of antichrist himself. This spirit of antichrist is, no doubt, the spirit of Satan. Revelation 13:2 reveals that, when the antichrist appears in person, the devil will give him "his power and his throne and his great authority." Just as the antichrist will then be the product of the devil's evil creative influence, so now the spirit of antichrist likewise originates with Satan.

3. THE TEST OF LISTENING, 4:4-6

In verse 4 the rather cryptic singular/plural reference continues. Believers have overcome "them" (the false prophets of v. 1) because they are indwelt by God's Spirit, who is greater than "he" (antichrist's spirit) who is in the world. It would seem that John is referring to one evil spirit who inspires many false prophets, just as there is one Holy Spirit who inspires the many emissaries of the truth. Even though believers had been giving some credence to these false prophets, as μή with the present tense imperative verb in verse 1 seems to indicate ("Stop believing every spirit"), yet John can declare that the believers had not really been taken in by the deception.

The Gnostic teachers are said to come from the world. From that evil sphere, they derive their essential character. Their teachings were drawn from the pagan world and were marked by a pagan orientation. The philosophy of dualism was taken from pagan philosophical systems. Greek philosophy was essentially dualistic as was Zoroastrianism, the religion of Persia. From such sources came Gnostic dualism with its resulting perversions of Christology and morality.

A moral system that viewed immorality as a commendable service to God and that viewed wrong living as right was obviously pagan in its nature and source. It is easy to see why John declared, "They are from the world; therefore they speak as from the world" (v. 5a). And it is no wonder that the pagan world was sympathetic to their message. The very fact that they gained a sympathetic hearing from the world was clear evidence that they belonged to the world rather than to God (v. 5b).

In the same way the messengers of apostolic truth come from God (are born of God). Therefore, their message strikes a responsive chord with those who likewise are God's people, rather than with the people of the world (v. 6a). The nature of the audience a teacher draws is indicative of the nature of the teacher. In fact, it is also indicative of whether he is inspired by "the spirit of truth" (God's Spirit) or "the spirit of error" (antichrist's spirit).

B. PRESENT-DAY RELEVANCE

First John 4:1-6 sets forth two doctrinal tests: The Christological test and the test of listening. The second is a more general test that still applies in many situations. A teacher's doctrine can be identified by analyzing what kind of people listen to him. The first test is more specific and precise. A person's doctrinal identity can be determined by ascertaining what he believes concerning the Person of Christ. Does he believe in the incarnation of Jesus Christ, God's Son?

This was a valid test in John's day for ferreting out Gnostic teachers. It exposed both an adoptionist Gnostic like Cerinthus and the docetic Gnostic, for both denied the actual incarnation of God's Son. We must determine, however, whether the test is still relevant today. Or was it limited to a first-century religious situation that has long passed from the scene? The test is of such a basic nature that it applies to any situation in which the Person of Christ is in question. It excludes anyone, whatever his religious label may be, who rejects the truth of the incarnation.

1. AREAS OF RELEVANCE

Liberal theology. The various forms of liberal theology have historically possessed one feature in common. They have denied the full deity of Christ. It is not that they deny His humanity as the docetic Gnostics did. They do, however, reject the deity of Jesus, and in this sense they are similar to the adoptionist Gnostic, who taught that the Divine Christ merely came upon the human Jesus during his earthly ministry and left him before he died. The Christological test, therefore, would exclude anyone who espouses any form of the theology of liberalism and thus denies the incarnation.

Neo-orthodoxy and its successors. Neo-orthodox theologians disagreed concerning the fact and nature of the incarnation. Sören Kierkegaard, whose theology was the root from which neo-orthodoxy sprang, viewed the incarnation as the most important doctrine of Christianity. And the doctrine was accepted without question by both Karl Barth and Emil Brunner. However, Reinhold Niebuhr and Paul Tillich both rejected the historic understanding of the incarnation. Niebuhr asserts that it is "logical nonsense."[43] To him the concept of incarnation simply means "that Jesus is morally and religiously divine."[44] Tillich sees the incarnation as representing nothing more than essential manhood.[45]

Bultmann described the doctrine of the incarnation as an interpretation of Jesus from the viewpoint of Gnostic redemption myth. The church came to think of Jesus as "a divine figure sent down from the celestial world of light . . . veiled in earthly form. . . ."[46]

It is obvious that John's Christological test is still relevant for the

43. Reinhold Niebuhr, *The Nature and Destiny of Man*, 2:61, 70-71.
44. Bernard Ramm, *A Handbook of Contemporary Theology*, p. 66.
45. Ibid., pp. 67-68.
46. Rudolf Bultmann, *Primitive Christianity in Its Contemporary Setting*, p. 196.

purpose of evaluating systems such as those of Niebuhr, Tillich, and Bultmann. The application of John's standard shows clearly that these systems of theology are not from God. They are deficient at the very core, in that they reject the incarnation, the God-man, the only Person who could possibly save sinful man from his sin.

Modern cults. The test of the incarnation is also relevant for the the purpose of evaluating the many cults that crowd the modern scene. It has very clear application to the teachings of Jehovah's Witnesses concerning the Person of Christ. They declare, "Jesus' birth on earth was not an incarnation. . . . He was not a spirit-human hybrid, a man and at the same time a spirit person. He was not clothed with flesh over an invisible spirit person. . . ."[47] It is clear that John's Christological test rules out such a system as being from God. Like the theology of Niebuhr, Tillich, and Bultmann, it is deficient at the very core.

Similarly John's test is relevant for evaluating Christian Science, New Thought, the Unity School of Christianity, and the Theosophical Society (cf. pp. 136-37). In fact it may be used to assess any religious system in order to determine whether or not it is fundamentally deficient and therefore unable to provide atonement for sin.

2. THE LIMITATION OF THE TEST

As crucial as the incarnation test is, there is reason to question whether or not it is applicable to all heretical teachings. Lenski seems to think that it is adequately comprehensive to include any and all doctrines, saying:

> It would be a serious mistake to think that John speaks of confessing only the one fact or doctrine of the Incarnation . . . so that it is of minor importance when other facts . . . are either not confessed or are denied in some way. "Jesus Christ as having come in flesh" is not merely the center of the gospel but the whole of it. In Christ there inheres all that . . . the whole New Testament and the Scripture contain.[48]

As true as these statements may be in one sense, they do not confront the real problem. The fact is that the incarnation test by

---

47. *What Has Religion Done for Mankind?* p. 231.
48. Lenski, p. 488.

itself does not come to grips with a person who accepts the incarnation but rejects the fact that Christ's death was an atoning sacrifice for sin, or who teaches that salvation is by human effort rather than by God's grace, or who denies the supernatural inspiration of Scripture.

There is a sense in which John's incarnation test is situational. That is, it applies most explicitly to those teachings that, like Gnosticism, have an erroneous view of the Person of Christ. Although the incarnation is central to the Christian faith, when applied as a test it is not capable of ferreting out other doctrinal deviations. To discover that a person believes in the incarnation does not rule out the possibility that he has other heretical views. The incarnation test was intended to be applied to the early Gnostic heresy, and thus it is likewise applicable to any other religious system that, in some way, parallels Gnosticism in its Christology.

3. THE INCARNATION TEST AND EXORCISM

Some have applied the test of 1 John 4:2-3 to the identification of demons or evils spirits. For example, Ernest B. Rockstad, in a mimeographed article entitled "Speaking in Tongues Scripturally Tested," says that 1 John 4:1 commands us to test any supernatural work to discover whether it is from God or from Satan. The test to be used is the incarnation test of 1 John 4:2-3. Rockstad explains how to employ the test. "While the person is speaking in another tongue. . . ," he says, "the spirit inspiring the tongue is to be addressed and asked the question, 'Is Jesus Christ come in the flesh?' " The article continues with several instances in which the test was used, resulting in insolent and violent denials on the part of people who otherwise loved the Lord.[49]

Is such an application of the incarnation test a valid use? The study of the passage and its background gives no indication that the test was originally intended to be a means of determining the presence of demonic powers. It was to be employed in identifying the presence of false teachers, specifically Gnostics, and there is no indication that they were demon possessed. The Spirit of God (and of truth) is contrasted with the spirit of antichrist (and of deceit). The One inspires God's prophets; the other inspires false prophets. That is as far as the explicit statments of the passage take us.

49. Ernest B. Rockstad, "Speaking in Tongues Scripturally Tested," mimeographed, p. 1.

There is, however, a rule of hermeneutics that declares, "Interpretation is one; application is many." According to Bernard Ramm, "This means that there is only one meaning to a passage of Scripture which is determined by careful study. But a given text or a given passage may speak to a number of problems or issues."[50] Thus, although John gave no indication that he was speaking of demon possession, the test he set up may be employed in any situation where its basic principle applies, that is, in any situation where the doctrine of the incarnation may be the issue.

Paraphrastic Commentary (4:1-6)

(1) Dear friends, stop listening gullibly to every prophet who comes along. Instead, make it a practice to put these supernaturally inspired speakers to an objective test to see if what they are and what they say comes from God. You must exercise caution because in the world there are many teachers who are inspired by that great deceiver, the devil. (2) This is how you can recognize when a person is speaking under the inspiration of the Spirit of God. Any prophet who comes from God will solemnly and publicly be affirming his belief in Jesus Christ, God's Son who has taken up His residence in a human body of flesh and bones. (3) But no prophet who refuses to make such a solemn and open confession of the incarnate Christ has his origin in God. He is inspired by the same spirit who will inspire and empower that wicked end-time enemy of God, the antichrist. You have heard that this spirit is going to come. Indeed it is already here.

(4) As for you, you are born of God, dear children, and you have been victorious over the attempts of the false prophets to win you over to Gnosticism. Your victory was possible because the Holy Spirit who indwells you is more powerful than the spirit of antichrist who is now present in this evil world. (5) These false prophets, on the one hand, have their origin in, and derive their characteristics from, the wicked pagan world. As a result, what they have to say comes from that pagan world, and so the people of the world are always ready to listen sympathetically to them. (6) On the other hand, we of the apostolic circle derive our being and message from God. Consequently, anyone who knows God personally listens sympathetically to us. This is how we can recognize the Spirit who is characterized by truth and the spirit who is characterized by deceit.

---

50. Bernard Ramm, *Protestant Biblical Interpretation*, p. 113.

Sonship Tested on Christological Grounds 313

STRUCTURAL COMMENTARY (4:1-6)[51]

B. Sonship tested on Christological grounds, 4:1-6
  1. A warning against false prophets, 4:1
     a. Gullibility discouraged, 4:1a
     b. Discernment encouraged, 4:1b
     c. Reason for compliance stated, 4:1c
  2. The Christological test, 4:2-3
     a. Stated in positive terms, 4:2
        (1) The desired result: to identify the Spirit of God, 4:2a
        (2) The necessary criterion: confession of Jesus Christ incarnate, 4:2b
        (3) The outcome of the test: the confessor is from God, 4:2c
     b. Stated in negative terms, 4:3
        (1) The criterion denied, 4:3a
        (2) The result stated, 4:3b
        (3) The spirit identified, 4:3c
  3. The test of listening, 4:4-6
     a. The victorious people of God, 4:4
        (1) Their source: God, 4:4a
        (2) Their victory: over the false teachers, 4:4b
        (3) Their enablement: the indwelling Spirit, 4:4c
     b. The false teachers, 4:5
        (1) Their source: the world, 4:5a
        (2) The source of their message: the world, 4:5b
        (3) Their audience: the world, 4:5c
     c. The apostolic teachers, 4:6a-c
        (1) Their source: God, 4:6a
        (2) Their audience, 4:6b, c
           (a) Who it is, 4:6b
           (b) Who it is not, 4:6c
     d. The concluding statement, 4:6d
        (1) Identification of the Spirit of truth
        (2) Identification of the Spirit of deceit

---

51. For previous section of the outline see pp. 289-90.

Third Cycle: The Christian Life Viewed As a Closely Woven Integration of the Ethical and the Christological, 4:7—5:12

Various commentators attempt to show that, although it is not at all obvious, there is a relationship between 4:1-6 and 4:7. Plummer says that John's writings are so subtle that it would be rash to deny that there is such a connection. Then he proceeds to find a very tenuous theological relationship.[1] Alford finds a connection, but confesses that the links are "at first sight not very apparent."[2] Westcott tries (unsuccessfully) to find a transitional connection.[3] Instead of stretching the passage in order to find a connection, it would be better to admit, as Marshall does, that John changes his subject "somewhat abruptly."[4] It would be still better, with Bonsirven, to say, "It is impossible to discover any transition or any connection, material or formal, between this paragraph and the preceding."[5]

The abrupt change is evidence that John is beginning a new cycle of thought, a fact that is confirmed by surveying the follow-

1. A. Plummer, *The Epistles of St. John*, The Cambridge Greek Testament for Schools and Colleges, pp. 99-100.
2. Henry Alford, *The Greek Testament*, 4:488.
3. B. F. Westcott, The Epistles of John, p. 147.
4. I. Howard Marshall, *The Epistles of John*, *The New International Commentary on the New Testament*, p. 210.
5. Joseph Bonsirven, *Épitres de Sain Jean*, vol. 9, *Verbum Salutis*, p. 198 (my translation).

ing verses. It will be observed that the same ethical and Christological tests appear here just as in previous cycles (1:5—2:28; 2:29—4:6). The ethical test is discussed in 4:7—5:5 and the Christological in 5:6-12.

13

A. The Ethical Test, 4:7—5:5

In each new cycle John's treatments of the ethical and the Christological tests are no mere repetition of the previous cycle. This is true of 4:7—5:5. In 2:7-11 the love test is set forth in basic terms. The presence or absence of love for fellow believers is the test of whether or not one is saved. In 3:10*b*-24 John adds a test by which one can determine whether one's love is genuine. Since love is a test of the reality of one's salvation experience, one must be able to determine what genuine love is. Now, in 4:7—5:5 the apostle "arrives at the culminating point of his teaching concerning love."[1] He proceeds to explain the logic on which the test of love rests, showing why it is that the presence of love is a sure test of whether or not a person has eternal life. To put it another way, John here explains why it is true that a believer will in fact love his fellow believers.

This section dealing with the ethical test (4:7—5:5) includes discussions of the source of love, namely God (4:7-16); the fruit of love, which is confidence with regard to the day of judgment (4:17-18); and the relationships of love (4:19—5:5).

---

1. Joseph Bonsirven, *Épitres de Saint Jean*, vol. 9, *Verbum Salutis*, p. 198 (my translation).

EXEGETICAL COMMENTARY (4:7—5:5)

1. THE SOURCE OF LOVE, 4:7-16

4:7. ἀγαπητοί, ἀγαπῶμεν ἀγγήλους, "Beloved, let us love one another." It is appropriate that this section on love should begin with the vocative ἀγαπητοί, "beloved." In the Greek text the construction is particularly striking with its repetitive ἀγαπητοί, ἀγαπῶμεν, "Beloved, we love." It should be noted that John does not limit the use of ἀγαπητοί to passages where love is being discussed (see 3:2; 4:1). Even so it is noteworthy that four of the six occurrences of ἀγαπητοί in this epistle appear in love passages. Although the verb ἀγαπῶμεν is usually translated as a subjunctive here, the form could be indicative, in which case it would mean "we love." John would then be saying that it is characteristic of believers to love each other because love comes from God and believers possess this quality since they have been born of God. This would seem to fit the succeeding context better than the exhortation "let us love," which the subjunctive mood would demand. The main point being expressed in verses 7-16 is not an exhortation to love but a declaration that Christians do love because they have been born of God, who is love. To translate the verb, "let us love," would seem to suggest that by loving one is somehow born of God and comes to know God. Actually the sequence is just the reverse. Those who are born of God and know God are therefore able to love. The present tense of the verb indicates that believers habitually love one another. On the words ἀγαπητοί and ἀγαπῶμεν see on 2:7. Bruce describes ἀγάπη as "a consuming passion for the well-being of others."[2] As elsewhere in 1 John the love referred to is a mutual love within the brotherhood of believers.

ὅτι ἡ ἀγάπη ἐκ τοῦ θεοῦ ἐστιν, "for love is from God." The conjunction ὅτι, "for," introduces the explanation of the preceding declaration. The two clauses that follow explain why it is that believers characteristically love one another. The use of the article with ἀγάπη serves to identify and particularize the love John has in mind. It is not love in general, as ἀγάπη without the article might have suggested. Instead it is *the* love which is distinctively divine in source and nature—the self-giving

2. F. F. Bruce, *The Epistles of John*, p. 107.

love John has set forth as uniquely Christian. This love has but one source: God. Love that comes from any other source is not New Testament ἀγάπη.

καὶ πᾶς ὁ ἀγαπῶν ἐκ τοῦ θεοῦ γεγέννηται καὶ γινώσκει τὸν θεόν, "and every one who loves is born of God and knows God." The participle ἀγαπῶν, being in the present tense, indicates continuing action. The ones referred to are those who are characterized by the practice of loving. The kind of love John has in mind is the ἀγάπη that comes only from God. Anyone who (πᾶς ὁ) manifests this kind of love gives evidence that he is born of God. The intensive perfect tense γεγέννηται is another way of saying that he is a child of God. At a point in the past he was born into the family of God. As a result he is now a member of God's family and, as such, reveals the family characteristic of ἀγάπη.

The statement of verse 7 is not couched in the terms of a test as Law suggests.[3] Instead, it is an explanation (ὅτι) of why the believer loves. It is because love originates with God and the believer by virtue of the new birth is related to God.

The explanation introduced by ὅτι seems to be completed with the verb γεγέννηται, "is born," but John goes on to add καὶ γινώσκει τὸν θεόν, "and knows God." The seemingly unnecessary addition was no doubt aimed at the Gnostics, who professed to have special knowledge. They claimed esoteric knowledge, but knew nothing of love for the people of God. John assures his readers that the love manifested in their lives indicates that they are the possessors of genuine knowledge. In reality they are the true Gnostics. On the other hand the boast of the false teachers that they know God is contradicted by their failure to love. Brooke explains that γινώσκω (rather than οἶδα) speaks of "gradually becoming acquainted with God"[4]—knowing by experience through association.

4:8 ὁ μὴ ἀγαπῶν οὐκ ἔγνω τὸν θεόν, "The one who does not love does not know God." John's penchant for stating truth negatively and positively is seen in verses 7-8. The contrasting πᾶς ὁ ἀγαπῶν, "everyone who loves," and ὁ μὴ αγαπῶν, "the one who does not love," serves to emphasize the truth that believers love one another because they are children of God who is love. Just as in verse 7 the member of God's family manifests love as a

---
3. Robert Law, *The Tests of Life*, p. 398.
4. A. E. Brooke, *A Critical and Exegetical Commentary on the Johannine Epistles*, (Reprint edition, 1964), The International Critical Commentary, p. 117.

pattern of life (present tense, ἀγαπῶν), so in verse 8 the one who does not know God is characterized by a pattern of life (present tense, μὴ ἀγαπῶν) from which love is absent. In neither instance is the object of love stated. It is not here a question of the object of love, but of the fact of it. The person is simply identified as one who loves or who does not love.

Instead of the aorist ἔγνω, "know," one might have expected the present tense γινώσκει, which with the negative οὐκ "would mean he does not know." The aorist, however, was chosen for a purpose. It is indicative in mood and thus looks to the past, functioning as an ingressive aorist. John is saying concerning the one who does not love that "he has not come to know God."[5] Not only does he not know God now, but he has never known God. This is a more forceful form of denial than the present tense would provide. John denies that the Gnostic, in spite of all his boasting of a superior knowledge of God, has ever come to know Him, and this is shown by the fact that his life is not characterized by love.

ὅτι ὁ Θεός ἀγάπη ἐστίν, "for God is love." As in the previous verse, the declaration clause is followed by an explanatory clause. It is assumed that since God is love, the one who knows Him will love, and, on the contrary, the one who does not love does not know Him. The article before θεός, "God," and the anarthrous ἀγάπη, "love," make it certain that θεός is the subject and ἀγάπη is the predicate nominative. The clause cannot be translated "love is God." Furthermore, the fact that ἀγάπη has no article emphasizes quality rather than identity. Thus, it is not the identity of God John is declaring, but His essential quality. God in his essence is love. For comparable declarations, see John 4:24; 1 John 1:5.

4:9. ἐν τούτῳ ἐφανερώθη ἡ ἀγάπη τοῦ θεοῦ ἐν ἡμῖν, "By this the love of God was manifested in us." John moves immediately from the abstract statement, "God is love," to the manifestation of that love through Christ. It is in the incarnation that the nature of ἀγάπη can best be seen. In this verse, John seems to be reminding his readers of John 3:16, which they probably already possessed.

The case of τούτῳ, this, is best understood as instrumental rather than locative. "By this means" God's love was manifested. The pronoun τούτῳ as in most Johannine occurrences refers

---

5. Brooke, p. 118; Bruce, p. 107; A. Plummer, *The Epistles of St. John*, The Cambridge Greek Testament for Schools and Colleges, p. 100.

forward, in this instance, to the ὅτι clause. God's love was manifested by this means, namely that God sent His Son. The aorist ἐφανερώθη, "was manifested," depicts punctiliar action and speaks of the incarnation as the point at which love was manifested. The word φανερόω, "manifest," suggests that God's love had previously existed, but at the time of the incarnation it was manifested to men. Westcott says, "That which 'was' eternally was made known in time."[6] The genitive τοῦ θεοῦ, "of God," after ἀγάπη, "love," is clearly a subjective genitive, which means that God is the acting subject, the one who loves. The article before ἀγάπη identifies the love as that particular spontaneous self-giving love characteristic of God. Commentators differ as to the meaning of the preposition ἐν in the phrase ἐν ἡμῖν. Most of them favor the translation, "in us" (Westcott, Smith, Brooke, Lenski, Alford), and understand the phrase to modify ἡ ἀγάπη τοῦ θεοῦ, "the love of God." Brooke says, "The manifestation of His love is made *in* those who have entered upon the life which He sent His Son to give."[7] It could be translated "for us" or "to us," but these are remote meanings that should only be resorted to when the more natural ones do not fit the context. The best translation is that of the NIV and RSV, "among us." When used with a plural noun the preposition ἐν may very naturally mean "among" if the context permits.[8] As noted above, τούτῳ looks forward to the ὅτι clause, meaning that God's love was manifested in the sending of His Son. Thus the manifestation was not an internal experience, "in us," but an objective historical event that happened "among us."

ὅτι τὸν υἱὸν αὐτοῦ τὸν μονογενῆ ἀπέσταλκεν ὁ θεὸς εἰς τὸν κόσμον, "that God has sent His only begotten Son into the world." The KJV translates ὅτι as "because." Although this is a common meaning of this conjunction, since the ὅτι clause is epexegetical of ἐν τούτῳ, "by this," and thus states what it is that τούτῳ refers to, ὅτι should be translated as "that" (NASB).[9] The word order of the ὅτι clause is significant. By putting the direct object, τὸν υἱὸν αὐτοῦ τὸν μονογενῆ, "His only begotten Son," first in the clause, John places noticeable

---

6. B. F. Westcott, *The Epistles of John*, p. 148.
7. Brooke, p. 119.
8. William F. Arndt and F. Wilbur Gingrich, trans. and eds., *A Greek-English Lexicon of the New Testament*, by Walter Bauer, p. 258.
9. Ibid., p. 592.

emphasis on these words.[10] The force of the construction can be felt if it is translated, "His only begotten Son God has sent." Although the above translation of μονογενῆ has followed the NASB (only begotten), it is generally agreed that this is not the meaning of the word. Etymologically the term comes from μόνος, "only," "single" and γένος, "kind." Although it is remotely related to γεννάω, "to bear," the word μονογενῆς is always used to speak of uniqueness rather than of origin. Moulton and Milligan explain that "only begotten" would be μονογέννητος (from μόνος and γεννάω). The same source cites a passage from a third-century imprecatory tablet in which God is called μονογενῆ and another passage from a third- or fourth-century papyrus in which the Holy Spirit is referred to as μονογενές.[11] In 1 Clement 25:2 the term is used to describe a unique bird called the phoenix. "There is a bird called the phoenix. This bird, the only one of its kind (μονογενής), lives five hundred years." In Hebrews 11:17 Isaac is called μονογενῆ, although he was not the only begotten son of Abraham. He was however unique, one of a kind, since he was the child of promise who came by a miraculous birth. In the Old Testament μονογενής often translates יָחִיד, "only, solitary, only one." The Hebrew term is, on other occasions, translated as ἀγαπητός "beloved." Thus Bonsirven says that this untranslatable word carries the ideas of unique Son of God, His beloved, and One who is equal to God.[12] The NASB is one of the very few modern versions that has "only begotten." "Only Son" is found in TEV, RSV, NEB, Phillips, Williams, Beck, and Montgomery. The NIV has "one and only Son," with a footnote, "Or his only begotten Son."

The verb ἀπέσταλκεν, perfect tense form of ἀποστέλλω, "send," has the connotation of being sent on a mission. It is related to the noun ἀπόστολος, "apostle," one sent forth on a mission with an assigned task to fulfill. *The New International Dictionary of New Testament Theology* contrasts ἀποστέλλω and πέμπω, "send,"

---

10. Law, p. 398.
11. James Hope Moulton and George Milligan, *The Vocabulary of the Greek New Testament*, pp. 416-17.
12. Bonsirven, p. 206. For additional discussions of the word, see Dale Moody, "God's Only Son: The Translation of John 3:16 in the Revised Standard Version," *The Bible Translator* 10:4 (October 1959): 145-47; Colin Brown, ed., *New International Dictionary of New Testament Theology*, s.v. "One, Once, Only," by K. H. Bartels; I. Howard Marshall, p. 214, n. 8; Leon Morris, *Commentary on the Gospel of John*, The New International Commentary on the New Testament, pp. 105-6.

pointing out that the former assumes that the envoy is the personal representative of the sender, while the latter "stresses the mere fact of sending."[13] Jesus was sent forth from the Father with a specific mission to perform. Bonsirven points out the significant role that the idea of mission plays in the gospel of John (3:17, 34; 5:36-37; 7:29; 8:42; 10:36; 17:3, 18; 20:21).[14] The perfect tense, ἀπέσταλκεν, emphasizes the continuing results of the mission Christ fulfilled. It does not, however, speak of the permanency of the results as some assert.[15] The perfect tense in itself only indicates that results continue up to the time the statement is being made. Results may continue beyond that time, but the perfect does not guarantee that to be the case.

Τὸν κόσμον, "the world," is not used in the ethical sense, but in its more literal sense of the world as a place where people live. God sent Christ to live among us on this earth and there to accomplish the work assigned to him.

ἵνα ζήσωμεν δι' αὐτοῦ, "so that we might live through Him." The ἵνα clause expresses the purpose for which God sent His Son. It was that He might be the intermediate agent (indicated by δι' [διά], "through," with the genitive case αὐτοῦ, "Him") who would give life to people dead in sin. A number of commentators identify the aorist tense ζήσωμεν as ingressive.[16] God sent His Son so that life might be acquired through Him.

4:10. ἐν τούτῳ ἐστὶν ἡ ἀγάπη, "In this is love." Opinions differ as to the exact meaning of this expression. Alford claimed that it speaks of "love in the abstract";[17] Lenski denies it.[18] Bultmann says it is not a description of "love in and of itself";[19] Marshall insists that it is "love as such."[20] To decide the question one must look more carefully at both the terms and the grammatical construction employed by John. Τούτῳ "this," as in previous instances (see v. 9) looks forward, this time to ἀλλ' and the following ὅτι clause ("but that He loved us"). The latter

13. Brown, s.v. "Apostle," by E. von Eicken and H. Lindner.
14. Bonsirven, pp. 205-6.
15. W. Robertson Nicoll, gen. ed., *The Expositor's Greek Testament*, s.v. "The Epistles of John," by David Smith, 5:191; Plummer, p. 102.
16. Nicoll, 5:191; Bruce, p. 108; Marshall, p. 214, n. 9; A. T. Robertson, *Word Pictures in the New Testament*, 6:232.
17. Henry Alford, *The Greek Testament*, 4:490.
18. R. C. H. Lenski, *The Interpretation of the Epistles of St. Peter, St. John, and St. Jude*, p. 502.
19. Rudolph Bultmann, *The Johannine Epistles*, Hermeneia, p. 68.
20. Marshall, p. 214.

serves epexegetically as an explanation of what is meant by τούτῳ. So John's assertion could be restated as follows: "In the fact that God loved us and sent His Son is love." The preposition ἐν is here used with the locative case and means "in." The whole phrase, "in this is love," means this is that of which love consists, or this is what love is. The article before ἀγάπη and the absence of any qualifiers such as τοῦ θεοῦ, "of God," make it apparent that John is speaking of "love as such." This is what love "in and of itself" is. The article with ἀγάπη is an article of previous reference and indicates that the love referred to is the distinctive love spoken of previously in this epistle.

οὐχ ὅτι ἡμεῖς ἠγαπήκαμεν τὸν θεόν, "not that we loved God." John first states what this distinctive love is not. It is not spontaneous, unsolicited love toward God, or, to put it differently, it does not originate with man. The presence of the personal pronoun ἡμεῖς serves to emphasize the contrast with αὐτός in the following clause—"not that *we* . . . , but that *He*. . . ." The Vaticanus is the only manuscript having the perfect tense ἠγαπήκαμεν. ℵ A K L have a form of the aorist. It is thought, however, that the perfect tense, being the more difficult, is the original. The aorist is probably an attempt to assimilate the reading to the other aorists in this verse.[21] Marshall suggests that the perfect tense was used to stress the idea of continuing love for God.[22] No doubt John did not choose the aorist because he did not have in mind any particular point in the past when man loved God. Instead he seems to be denying that love consists of man having at any time (iterative) loved God.

ἀλλ᾽ ὅτι αὐτὸς ἠγάπησεν ἡμᾶς καὶ ἀπέστειλεν τὸν υἱὸν αὐτοῦ ἱλασμὸν περὶ τῶν ἁμαρτιῶν ἡμῶν, "but that He loved us and sent His Son to be the propitiation for our sins." The conjunction ἀλλ᾽ (ἀλλά), "but," is a strong adversative that expresses sharp contrast between man's love and God's love. It is not in the Christian's love for God that he can see what "love as such" really is; on the contrary this is seen in God's love. The contrast is further heightened by the use of αὐτός in parallel to ἡμεῖς (see above).

In this clause John has chosen to use the aorist ἠγάπησεν, "loved," apparently because he is looking back to the point at which God manifested His love in the incarnation. God's love is

21. Nicoll, 5:191, n. 1.
22. Marshall p. 214, n. 10.

not mere sentiment or verbalization; it is action. The aorist ἀπέστειλεν, "sent," likewise points back to the time of the incarnation. On the idea of mission, which this verb expresses, see remarks on verse 9. Not only did God manifest His love in the sending of His Son, but in the mission the Son came to fulfill, namely the mission of propitiation (ἱλασμόν). His love provided the legal basis on which forgiveness could be offered. On ἱλασμὸν περὶ τῶν ἁμαρτιῶν ἡμῶν, see comments on 2:2.

4:11 Ἀγαπητοί, εἰ οὕτως ὁ θεὸς ἠγάπησεν ἡμᾶς, "Beloved, if God so loved us." For the last time in this epistle, John addresses his readers as ἀγαπητοί, "beloved," and in so doing he, himself, exemplifies what he is urging upon them: "to love one another." The use of εἰ, "if," with the indicative ἠγάπησεν, "loved," assumes what is obvious in this context: "God so loved us." The construction could be paraphrased, "Since God so loved us." This is the fulfilled condition on which John bases his declaration that Christians ought to love one another. The words οὕτως ὁ θεὸς ἠγάπησεν are a reflection of John 3:16, which is another reason for believing that the gospel preceded the epistle. The adverb οὕτως is a pointed reference to verses 9-10, especially to the two facts of incarnation and propitiation. Although the adverb could refer either to extent or manner,[23] it would seem that extent is the most natural way to take the word: God loved us even to the point of providing the means of propitiating His own righteous wrath against our sin. On ἠγάπησεν see on verse 10.

καὶ ἡμεῖς ὀφείλομεν ἀλλήλους ἀγαπᾶν, "we also ought to love one another." The adjunctive καὶ, "also," goes with ἡμεῖς, "we." God loved and "we also" should love. The pronoun ἡμεῖς is somewhat emphatic in comparing what *we* should do with what *God* has done. The present tense verb ὀφείλομεν, "we ought," expresses a continuing obligation to love. This is not necessity due to the nature of the situation, which would more naturally be expressed by δεῖ, "it is necessary." Instead, ὀφείλω, which has a moral connotation, expresses obligation.[24] As is true in most of its uses in this epistle, the verb ἀγαπάω (here the infinitive, ἀγαπᾶν, "to love") appears in the present tense. Our continuing obligation is to love one another continually.

---

23. Nicoll, 5:191.
24. John Albert Bengel, *Gnomon of the New Testament*, 1 Cor. 11:10, as cited by Richard C. Trench, *Synonyms of the New Testament*, p. 360.

4:12. θεὸν οὐδεὶς πώποτε τεθέαται, "No one has beheld God at any time." This statement is arranged in a most striking order. The forcefulness of the declaration is seen in that the direct object, θεόν, "God," is emphasized by being placed first. The word also appears without an article and thus refers to God in His essence or deity. In addition, the negative οὐδείς is a strong denial excluding everyone. The statement, then, might be put as follows: "God in His essential being no one at any time has seen." This striking denial is made all the more striking by its abrupt insertion, seemingly with no connection to what goes before or comes after. The verb τεθέαται, "has beheld," is a perfect tense used iteratively. In comparison to ὁράω, *to see*, θεάομαι often speaks of careful examination, whereas ὁράω merely indicates the fact of seeing. (See on 1:1, pp. 98-99.) Since "God is spirit" (John 4:24), physical eyes cannot see Him (1 Tim. 1:17; 6:16), certainly not His essential nature, God as God. What Moses saw on the mountain (Ex. 33:22-23) was a theophany in which God took a human form for Moses' benefit. Moses did not see God in His essence.

The purpose and function of this statement must be discerned from the context. A connection with the preceding verse may be seen in the expressions ἀλλήλους ἀγαπᾶν, "to love one another" (v. 11) and ἀγαπῶμεν ἀλλήλους, "we love one another" (v. 12). Apparently verse 12*a* has some relationship with our loving one another. Furthermore, God is mentioned both in verses 12*a* and 12*b*. On the one hand, no one has ever seen God; on the other hand, God indwells those who love one another. While the first is denied, the second is affirmed. In some sense, loving one another must replace seeing God in his essential being. Although God cannot be seen in His essence, since He is love (v. 8), He can be seen indirectly in His people when they love one another.

ἐὰν ἀγαπῶμεν ἀλλήλους, ὁ θεὸς ἐν ἡμῖν μένει, "if we love one another, God abides in us." The verb ἀγαπῶμεν, "we love," is present tense depicting continuing action. As in verse 11, ἀλλήλους refers to fellow believers. The conditional clause, ἐὰν ἀγαπῶμεν ἀλλήλους, "if we love one another," is not the condition or the means of God's indwelling; it is the evidence that God lives in us. This is the first fact that the mutual love of believers proves. Both the verb μένει, *abides, dwells,* and its tense (present) speak of continuing action. On μένω, see on 2:6.

καὶ ἡ ἀγάπη αὐτοῦ ἐν ἡμῖν τετελειωμένη ἐστίν, "and His love is perfected in us." This clause indicates the second fact that is proved when believers love one another. Ἡ ἀγάπη αὐτοῦ, "His love," has been understood in at least three possible ways. (1) The genitive case αὐτοῦ, "His," may be a subjective genitive, meaning that God is the acting subject—He is the one who loves. (2) The genitive may be an objective genitive, in which case God is the one who is loved. (3) Αὐτοῦ could be a qualitative genitive, indicating that the love referred to is God's kind of love, in Westcott's words, "the love which answers to his nature."[25] View (2) can be set aside since the immediately preceding context does not speak of loving God.[26] The emphasis here is on loving one another (ἀλλήλους, vv. 7, 11, 12). The reference to loving God is in the form of a denial (v. 10). Law, Westcott, and Marshall are right in combining (1) and (3).[27] Basically this love is God Himself doing the loving. Since love comes from God (v. 7) and God is love (v. 8), when a believer loves, God must be the source of that love. It is God loving through the believer. Of course, when this happens, the love expressed cannot help but be God's kind of love, for God is the source of it.

John adds that this love "is perfected in us." Τετελειωμένη ἐστίν, "is perfected," is interpreted by numerous commentators as a periphrastic. Others say that τετελειωμένη is an adjectival participle modifying ἀγάπη. In this case the entire clause would read "His perfected love is in us."[28] The word order does not favor the second view, as it would if τετελειωμένη, "perfected," occurred after ἡ ἀγάπη αὐτοῦ, "His love," and ἐν ἡμῖν, "in us," came between τετελειωμένη and ἐστίν, "is." But since τετελειωμένη and ἐστίν come together, the periphrastic, "is perfected," is more natural.[29] Of course, God's love is perfect simply because it comes from Him, however, John does not say merely that God's love is perfected, but that God's love is perfected "in us." That is, His love comes to its intended goal in us when it reaches out through us and treats another brother lovingly.

4:13. Ἐν τούτῳ γινώσκομεν ὅτι ἐν αὐτῷ μένομεν καὶ αὐτὸς ἐν ἡμῖν, "By this we know that we abide in Him and He in us." A number of commentators find a new paragraph beginning here (Brooke, Dodd, Law, Marshall, Stott). However most of them recognize that the new section is closely tied to the preceding one. John has not left the subject of love, as 4:16—5:3 clearly shows.

25. Westcott, p. 152.
26. In favor of (2) see Plummer, p. 103; Alford, 4:492.
27. Law, pp. 250, 399; Westcott, p. 152; Marshall, p. 217.
28. See Westcott, p. 152; Plummer, p. 104.
29. See Bultmann, p. 69; Brooke, p. 120.

The demonstrative pronoun, τούτῳ, "this," is rightly regarded by the NASB as instrumental in case, rather than locative. Thus, the phrase ἐν τούτῳ means "by this." It is obvious that it looks forward, as it does in most of its occurrences in this epistle (2:3; 3:10, 16, 24; 4:2, 9, 10, 13; 5:2). Τούτῳ here points to the God-given gift of the Spirit (v. 13b). The verb γινώσκομεν speaks of the process of obtaining knowledge by experience, by observation, or by instruction. In this instance, knowledge is based on the experience of receiving God's gift of the Holy Spirit. By means of this fact one may conclude "that we abide in him and He in us."

The concept of dwelling in Him is first mentioned in this epistle in 2:5-6, where it is synonymous with knowing Christ (2:2-6). The thought of abiding in the Son and in the Father appears in 2:24-25 and is there seen to be synonymous with eternal life (see on 2:25). On the meaning of μένω, "to abide," see on 2:6 (p. 172). The opposite side of man's dwelling in God is the fact that He dwells in man (καὶ αὐτὸς [μένει] ἐν ἡμῖν). In both cases, the verbs μένομεν and μένει (assumed) are, or are assumed to be, in the present tense, thus depicting a continuing dwelling—man in Him and He in man. This concept of God dwelling in believers closely ties verses 13-16 back to verse 12 where divine indwelling is demonstrated by the mutual love of believers. It should also be noticed that verse 13 is a slightly expanded restatement of 3:24.

ὅτι ἐκ τοῦ πνεύματος αὐτοῦ δέδωκεν ἡμῖν, "because He has given us of His Spirit." The connection of this clause with ἐν τούτῳ can be expressed as follows: "We know that we are dwelling in Him . . . by this, namely that He has given us of His Spirit." It can be said that God gave His Spirit to the believer (3:24), but John 4:13 seems to be indicating that there is a sense in which the Spirit is given in limited measure. He has given man *of* His Spirit. Ἐκ τοῦ πνεύματος is a prepositional phrase consisting of ἐκ, "out of," and τοῦ πνεύματος, "the Spirit," in the ablative case. The phrase is thus partitive in sense[30]—God gave *some* of His Spirit. This, of course, does not conceive of the Spirit as being divisible. Instead the statement should be viewed in the light of John 3:34, which indicates that the Spirit was given without limit to Jesus (NIV).[31] By implication, therefore, the Spirit is given to human beings in limited measure because of their finitude.

Some, such as Marshall, suggest that John was referring to charismatic gifts as proofs of mutual indwelling.[32] Although this is

30. Marshall, p. 219, n. 3; Bonsirven, p. 210.
31. Concerning this interpretation of John 3:34, see Morris, pp. 246-47.
32. Marshall, p. 219.

a possibility, since John does not in any way indicate that he has such gifts in mind it is better to understand that the statement refers simply to the presence of the Spirit. (See Rom. 8:15-16.) Dodd says, "Probably, then, we are intended here to think of the 'interior witness of the Holy Spirit,' the immediate, spontaneous, unanalysable awareness of a divine presence in our life."[33]

The perfect tense δέδωκεν, "he has given," is to be contrasted with the aorist tense ἔδωκεν, "he gave" (3:24, NIV). There, John speaks of the simple fact that God gave the Spirit; here it is the continuing possession in addition to the past reception of the Spirit that is in view.

4:14. καὶ ἡμεῖς τεθεάμεθα καὶ μαρτυροῦμεν, "And we have beheld and bear witness." The conjunction of καί, "and," introduces the addition of another basis for knowledge that "we abide in Him and He in us" (v. 13). The subjective experience of the Spirit is supported by the objective, historical fact of the advent of the Savior. There are several possible interpretations of ἡμεῖς, "we." (1) It may refer to the original apostolic eyewitnesses;[34] (2) it may be an editorial "we"; (3) it could speak of John and his readers, all of whom had experienced what Bultmann calls "a seeing of faith";[35] or (4) it may be based on the experience of the church "gathered up in that of its leaders."[36] Some have argued that the first person plural is used in the immediately preceding verses to refer to John and his readers, and therefore it must mean the same in verse 14. However, the emphatic ἡμεῖς, "we," calls for a meaning of adequate significance to justify its appearance. It obviously is not used to show contrast, as in verse 10. Reference to the original apostolic eyewitnesses would surely justify the use of ἡμεῖς. Furthermore, both θεάομαι, "to see," and μαρτυρέω, "to bear witness," remind of 1:1-2, where the reference is to the apostolic witnesses (for discussion of this interpretation, see pp. 28-30). In addition, the word θεάομαι, which speaks of careful, concentrated examination (and was so used in 1:1), more naturally refers to the apostolic eyewitnesses, than to a later generation of believers.

The perfect tense (τεθεάμεθα, "we have beheld"), not only looks back to the time when the apostles carefully and searchingly

---

33. C. H. Dodd, *The Johannine Epistles*, The Moffatt New Testament Commentary, p. 115.
34. Brooke, p. 121; Plummer, p. 104.
35. Bultmann, p. 71.
36. Westcott, p. 153.

looked at the incarnate Savior, but it stresses the fact that what they saw was still remembered. John could still see it with his mind's eye. Μαρτυροῦμεν, a present tense verb, portrays the continuing testimony that was still being borne at the time John penned this epistle. Being the testimony of confessedly careful eyewitnesses, it formed a solid foundation for assurance.

ὅτι ὁ πατὴρ ἀπέσταλκεν τὸν υἱὸν σωτῆρα τοῦ κόσμου, "that the Father has sent the Son to be the Savior of the world." In verses 13-14 the three persons of the Trinity are involved in providing assurance of the fact of the mutual indwelling of God and man. On the perfect tense ἀπέσταλκεν, "he has sent," see on the parallel statement in 4:9. The noun σωτήρ, "Savior," appears in John's writings only here and in John 4:42. In extrabiblical Greek the term was used of pagan gods, of men such as physicians, and of kings or emperors.[37] In Scripture, the term is used of judges who delivered the Israelites from their enemies (Judg. 3:9, 15), of God (Isa. 45:15), and of Christ (16 times in the New Testament).[38] Here in 4:14 the term is parallel with ζήσωμεν δι' αὐτοῦ, "we might live through Him" (4:9), and ἱλασμὸν περὶ τῶν ἁμαρτιῶν ἡμῶν, "propitiation for our sins" (4:10). In other words, Christ delivers from death and from the wrath of God against sin.

John again makes it clear that Christ's salvation is not limited in its sufficiency and its availability (cf. 2:2). He was sent to be "the Savior of the world"—not of the elect alone—the *whole* world. (See 1 Tim. 2:3-4.) However, it is man's unbelief that prevents God's desire from being realized. Τοῦ κόσμου is used here, as in John 3:16, to refer to the world of humanity, lost and in need of the Savior.

4:15. ὃς ἐὰν ὁμολογήσῃ ὅτι Ἰησοῦς ἐστιν ὁ υἱὸς τοῦ θεοῦ, "Whoever confesses that Jesus is the Son of God." ἐάν, which ordinarily means "if," is sometimes used in the place of ἄν to mean "ever." Dana and Mantey explain that ἐάν "is found frequently with relative pronouns and adverbs, and it indicates indefiniteness or generality. . . ."[39] Thus ὃς ἐάν, "whoever," stressing the generality of the statement that follows, is a fitting counterpart to τοῦ κόσμου, "the world" (v. 14). Christ came

---

37. Brown, s.v. "Redemption," by J. Schneider and C. Brown.
38. Ibid., pp. 218-19.
39. H. E. Dana and Julius R. Mantey, *A Manual Grammar of the Greek New Testament*, p. 246.

to be the Savior of the world and anyone in the world ("whoever") can experience this mutual divine indwelling if he meets the condition, i.e., confession. On ὁμολογήσῃ, "confess," see 4:2. In addition, it is clear that the confession is not merely a statement of theological fact; it is a confession of personal trust. The aorist tense indicates that John was thinking, not of a continuing confession, but of that single initial confession that introduces one into a life of faith in the incarnate Son of God. By its very content ("Jesus is the Son of God"), this confession excluded any and all Gnostics since their dualistic philosophy made the incarnation an impossibility. ὁ θεὸς ἐν αὐτῷ μένει καὶ αὐτὸς ἐν τῷ θεῷ, "God abides in him, and he in God." This statement is the reverse of the order in verse 13, but the change should not be viewed as significant in any way. On this statement of mutual indwelling, see remarks on verses 12-13. It is clear that in verses 14-15 John is weaving the idea of belief into the section on love. This fact becomes more apparent in verse 16.

4:16. καὶ ἡμεῖς ἐγνώκαμεν καὶ πεπιστεύκαμεν τὴν ἀγάπην ἣν ἔχει ὁ θεὸς ἐν ἡμῖν, "And we have come to know and have believed the love which God has for us." Although it was argued that ἡμεῖς, "we," in verse 14 referred to John and the other apostolic eyewitnesses, the same pronoun here in verse 16 no doubt refers to John and his readers. The reasons for thinking that there is a difference in reference are two: (1) The change in verbs. In verse 14 τεθεάμεθα, "we have carefully observed," and μαρτυροῦμεν, "we are bearing witness," more naturally apply to the apostles. The verbs in verse 16 (ἐγνώκαμεν, "we have come to know," and πεπιστεύκαμεν, "[we] have believed") are more general, and (2) The obvious meaning of ἡμῖν. Whether ἐν ἡμῖν is translated "in us" or "to us," it naturally refers to believers in general. Therefore, ἡμεῖς must have the same persons in view. It is John and his readers who know and believe, not simply the apostles.

The verb ἐγνώκαμεν characteristically speaks of the acquisition of knowledge and is thus translated "come to know" in the NASB. Being in the perfect tense, it speaks of coming to know in the past with the result that that knowledge is now possessed. Similarly, πεπιστεύκαμεν, also a perfect tense verb, means that one has believed and is now confident. The order in which the two verbs appear is significant. A knowledge of basic facts must precede belief, for it is necessary to know what is to be believed. Faith must be intelligent or it is sheer gullibility. On the other hand, however, these two verbs appear in reverse order in John 6:69, for it is also true that faith precedes knowledge. In spiritual matters, basic facts that are perceived must be received in faith in order for one to go on to fuller knowledge. Advance in knowledge may be blocked by unbelief. Brooke well says, "The growth of knowledge and the growth of faith act and react on each other."[40]

In general there are two interpretations of the prepositional phrase ἐν ἡμῖν. (1) It may be translated "to us" or "for us," in which case the love spoken of is God's love exerted toward man. This is the love that the apostles witnessed during Christ's ministry, and especially at the cross. An instance where the remote meaning "to" or "for" is demanded is John 13:35, ἐὰν ἀγάπην ἔχητε ἐν ἀλλήλοις, "if you have love for one another."[41] It should be noted that most versions of the New Testament translate ἐν ἡμῖν "for us" (NASB, NIV, RSV, NEB, TEV, Moffatt, Phillips, Beck, Williams). The RV, standing almost alone, has "in us," with "in our case" in the margin.

(2) The expression ἐν ἡμῖν may more naturally be translated "in us." Although it is true that this preposition had become "extremely diversified" in use in Hellenistic Greek,[42] the primary usage is best expressed by the English preposition "in." In the context of verse 16, ἐν is used nine times, all of which are translated "in" by almost all modern versions (NASB, NIV, RSV, TEV, NEB, etc.). In a context where one of the main themes is the truth that God, who is love, indwells the believer and the believer dwells in God, it is most reasonable to understand that John in verse 16a is speaking of God's love which is "in us." The remainder of verse 16 confirms this interpretation. The concept of God's love being *in* the believer is not foreign to John as John 17:26 shows. Bruce explains: "In speaking of 'the love which God has in us' John may mean more than his love *for* us; that is included, indeed, but the love which God has for His children is poured into their hearts by His Spirit and flows out to others."[43]

Zerwick refers specifically to this passage:

40. Brooke, p. 122.
41. Law, p. 401.
42. Brown, s.v., "Prepositions and Theology in the Greek New Testament," by M. J. Harris.
43. Bruce, p. 112.

Hence too ἐν is perhaps to be taken its full sense in I Jo 4, 16: we have known and believed τὴν ἀγάπην ἣν ἔχει ὁ θεὸς ἐν ἡμῖν.˙ This does not seem to mean ἣν ἔχει . . . εἰς ἡμᾶς, nor does it seem sufficient to understand it of the love which is manifested ἐν ἡμῖν, i.e., among us, namely the mission and ministry of the Son; but in John's theology the sense seems perhaps to be the communication of divine love whereby we are constituted not only its object but also in a certain wise its subject (cf. Rom 5:5).[44]

In summary, then, John is expressing confidence that God's love is at work in Christians as they love one another. They have come to know (ἐγνώκαμεν) and are now confident (πεπιστεύκαμεν) that God who is love is dwelling in and loving others through them.

ὁ θεὸς ἀγάπη ἐστίν, καὶ ὁ μένων ἐν τῇ ἀγάπῃ ἐν τῷ θεῷ μένει καὶ ὁ θεὸς ἐν αὐτῷ μένει, "God is love, and the one who abides in love abides in God, and God abides in him." It is generally assumed that there is a break in John's thought in the middle of verse 16. For example Brooke sees verses 16b-21 as being a new section dealing with, "Love and faith in relation to judgment,"[45] and Westcott heads the same verses with the title, "The Activity of Love."[46] It is more in keeping with the content of verse 16b, however, to keep it closely tied with the first part of the verse. The statement ὁ θεὸς ἀγάπη ἐστίν, "God is love," looks back to verse 8. Verse 16b also repeats what is implied in verse 12. Christian love is God indwelling the believer and loving through the believer. At the same time verse 16b functions as a summary statement concluding the section dealing with the source of love. This concluding statement draws a deduction from the declaration, "God is love" (see on v. 8). Since God in His essence is ἀγάπη, and since He is the source of ἀγάπη, it follows logically that to dwell in love is to dwell in God. It is also true that if a person is dwelling in love, God, who is love, must be dwelling in him, for love comes from God (v. 7).

The verb μένω, "to dwell, to abide," appears three times in verse 16b, always in the present tense making it doubly durative (by virtue of the durative meaning of the word itself and also of the tense). To dwell in love speaks of living constantly in the

---

44. Maximilian Zerwick S.J., *Biblical Greek*, adapted from the fourth Latin edition by Joseph Smith S.J., sec. 105.
45. Brooke, p. 122.
46. Westcott, p. 155.

sphere of love, so that love is the atmosphere, as it were, in which one lives. Thus one's attitude, one's outlook, and one's actions are permeated with love. To dwell in God is to be in a mystical relation with him so that one is in His presence and in fellowship with him. It is to know Him intimately. It is to be saved.

Although ἀγάπη in the first clause of verse 16b is anarthrous because it is a predicate nominative and stresses quality, ἀγάπη in the second clause is preceded by the article. John's intent is to identify the love of which he speaks as that distinctive love that comes from God and characterizes God's people.

2. THE FRUIT OF LOVE, 4:17-19

4:17. ἐν τούτῳ τετελείωται ἡ ἀγάπη μεθ' ἡμῶν, "By this, love is perfected with us." With verse 17 John moves from his discussion of the source of love to a brief treatment of confidence, the fruit of love, which is put first in positive terms (v. 17) and then in negative terms (v. 18).

There are three possibilities as to what ἐν τούτῳ, "by this," refers: (1) it may look back to the mutual indwelling of verse 16b, (2) it may point forward to the ἵνα clause in verse 17, or (3) it may look forward to the ὅτι clause of verse 17. In at least nine of the twelve 1 John occurrences of ἐν τούτῳ in the instrumental case, it refers to a clause that follows (see on 4:13). While it would be more normal for the phrase to refer to what follows, it may on occasion refer back. To refer it forward to the ἵνα clause makes the *present* perfection of love dependent on *future* confidence in the day of judgment, which is unnatural, if not impossible. It is much more natural to take ἵνα in its full telic sense of "in order that." Love is now perfected in order that believers may have confidence on judgment day. Also ἐν τούτῳ cannot refer forward to the ὅτι clause, because the latter is too far removed for the reader to recognize the connection easily. Apart from the fact that ἐν τούτῳ usually looks forward in 1 John, there is no reason why it cannot refer back to the concept of the intimate mutual indwelling of verse 16b, which serves to develop love in the believer.

The verb τετελείωται is better translated "made complete" (NIV) than "is perfected" (NASB). It is not that love reaches perfection in this life (see on 2:5). Love reaches its intended goal and is fully developed when it produces the fruit of loving action toward others. John does not here specify who is the object of love; therefore it is love per se that he has in mind. The article ἡ before ἀγάπη, "love," may be viewed as an article of previous reference,[47] or simply an article pointing out the particular love that John has in mind—Christian love.

The phrase μεθ' (μετά) ἡμῶν literally means "with us." Since this form of expression seems somewhat unnatural various attempts have been made to alter it. The Sinaiticus manuscript reveals that some copyist tried to alleviate the difficulty by changing the phrase to ἐν ἡμῖν, "in us." Among modern versions, Goodspeed and TEV translate it "in us," the NIV has "among us," the NEB has "for us," Beck omits it, and the whole expression ἡ ἀγάπη μεθ' ἡμῶν is paraphrased as "our love" by the KJV, Williams, and *The Living Bible*. A number of versions translate the phrase literally as "with us" (ASV, RSV, NASB, Moffatt, Montgomery). Law suggests that it could mean "in our case."[48] It would seem better, however, to accept John's expression as he wrote it and to try to understand it. It may indicate that love is "sojourning with us" as Smith expresses it.[49] Or it more probably means that God works with us to bring love to its full development in our lives.[50] The development of love, then, is a cooperative process in which God, who is love, dwells in the believer and works out His love through the believer. It is God's love expressing itself in deeds of love, but at the same time it is the believer himself who loves.

ἵνα παρρησίαν ἔχωμεν ἐν τῇ ἡμέρᾳ τῆς κρίσεως, "that we may have confidence in the day of judgment." This clause expresses a purpose (ἵνα, "in order that") of the full development of love in the believer's life. There are obviously other purposes, but this one is singled out here to indicate one of the values of love. On παρρησίαν, "confidence," see on 2:28. The confidence of which John speaks is an assurance that will enable the believer to stand fearlessly on the judgment day since he has solid evidence that he has been regenerated and possesses eternal life. That evidence is expressed in the ὅτι clause with which the verse closes. With such evidence the Christian can be unafraid since he knows that he will not "come into judgment" (John 5:24). It cannot be argued on the basis of the tense that the confidence is a

---

47. Lenski, p. 511.
48. Law, p. 402.
49. Nicoll, 5:192.
50. Westcott, p. 157.

present possession since both the subjunctive mood and the reference to the day of judgment point to the future.

ὅτι καθὼς ἐκεῖνός ἐστιν καὶ ἡμεῖς ἐσμεν ἐν τῷ κόσμῳ τούτῳ, "because as He is, so also are we in this world." Ὅτι introduces a causal clause that explains why the believer will have confidence on judgment day. It is because of a certain likeness to Christ that is indicated by καθώς, "just as." Notice that here, as elsewhere in 1 John (cf., 3:5, 16), ἐκεῖνος refers to Christ. In what is the believer said to be like Christ? Several suggestions have been offered. (1) Christ has perfect confidence before God, and the believer may also be confident both now and at the judgment.[51] (2) Those who are experiencing the mutual indwelling of verse 16b are involved in a fellowship with God that is, to some extent, similar to Christ's present perfect fellowship with God.[52] (3) Christians are like Christ, not in one attribute, but in His whole character.[53] (4) Believers are like Christ ideally or positionally in what Marshall calls the "eschatological reality."[54] (5) Believers are like Christ in that they love as He loves.[55] The fifth view is preferable in that it is drawn from the context. The fact that Christians characteristically love one another occupies the whole section from 4:7—5:5. Love is singled out in verse 18 as the antidote to fear (apparently fear of judgment, v. 17). Furthermore, John calls for a willingness to lay down our lives in love for each other as Christ did (3:16).

The pronoun ἡμεῖς, "we," emphasizes the comparison with Christ (ἐκεῖνος, "that one"). As *that one* is, *we* also are. The difference between Christ and the believer is that the latter is ἐν τῷ κόσμῳ τούτῳ, "in this world." Κόσμῳ is here used in its locational sense, indicating the sphere in which people live. Believers in this world love one another and thus are like Christ as he is eternally—past, present, and future.

4:18. φόβος οὐκ ἔστιν ἐν τῇ ἀγάπῃ, "There is no fear in love." After pointing out the fruit of love from the positive point of view in verse 17, John next looks at the same subject from the negative side. He turns from παρρησία, "confidence," to its oppo-

---

51. J. L. Houlden, *A Commentary on the Epistles of John*, Black's New Testament Commentaries, p. 119.
52. Brooke, p. 124.
53. Alford, 4:494; Westcott, p. 158.
54. Marshall, pp. 222-23.
55. Plummer, p. 106; Lenski, p. 512; Dodd, pp. 119-20.

site, φόβος, "fear." Φόβος, is the general Greek word for fear. Consequently, the degree and kind of fear it depicts are dependent on the context. In this instance, it does not speak of the proper reverence and respect one should have toward God, but of dread, servile fear, or terror. The absence of the article before the word indicates that John refers to fear in the abstract or in general. Ἀγάπη, however, is preceded by the article and is thus specific. The reference is to the particular love that has been under discussion throughout 1 John—that spontaneous, self-giving love that God himself is (4:8) and of which He is the source (4:7). The two concepts, fear and love, are mutually exclusive and contrary to each other. Fear is self-centered; love is other-centered. Fear, in this context, has to do with condemnation; love, here, has to do with the assurance of salvation.

Although ἀγάπη, "love," is made specific by the article, yet John has left it general in that he did not limit it by indicating that it is God's love for us, our love for God, or our love for one another. It could be simply selfless ἀγάπη wherever it is found. However, this context is primarily concerned with the love of fellow Christians for one another.

ἀλλ' ἡ τελεία ἀγάπη ἔξω βάλλει τὸν φόβον, ὅτι ὁ φόβος κόλασιν ἔχει, "but perfect love casts out fear, because fear involves punishment." That the author intended a strong contrast between the preceding clause and the ἀλλ' (ἀλλά) clause is indicated by the use of the stronger Greek adversative. "There is no fear in love"; on the contrary—instead of fear coexisting with love—"perfect love," casts out fear.

The article with τελεία ἀγάπη, "perfect love," identifies what love John has in mind. It is the love that has been designated by the noun ἀγάπη throughout this epistle. Furthermore, it is τελεία, "perfect." This is the love described by the verb τετελείωται in verse 17. It is not flawless love; only God has that. Instead it is love that has become *complete* (perfect) because it has followed through to the production of loving deeds. Such love has completed its intended course and is fully developed rather than dying in the heart.

Such love joins in mortal combat with fear and "casts" (βάλλει) it out. The present tense verb βάλλει does not indicate a continual expulsion of fear; instead it is a gnomic present referring to a fact that is always true. Under the right circumstances, it will always occur. In this instance, φόβον, "fear," is articular, no doubt be-

The Ethical Test   337

cause it looks back to the specific fear—judgment-day fear—that has already been mentioned. When love has completed its cycle of development and issued in loving deeds, it removes any fear of judgment day, for it assures us that we are God's regenerated people. Ὅτι, "because," explains why "perfect love casts out fear." It is because fear is, in some way, related to "punishment" (κόλασιν). The noun κόλασιν is translated as "torment" in the KJV. However, its use from early Hellenistic to modern Greek consistently demonstrates that the term refers to punishment. In the LXX it was used of divine punishment and of punishment administered before a person was executed. The Testaments of the Twelve Patriarchs speak of κόλασις αἰώνιος, "eternal punishment," an expression used by Jesus (Matt. 25:46). And in modern Greek one of the words for "hell" is κόλασις.[56] The Greek verb ἔχει, "has," has been variously translated or explained. It may mean that fear includes or brings punishment with it, fear involves punishment, fear has to do with punishment, or fear is itself punishment. The last view is favored by Bultmann, who limits the punishment to the present. He says that the concept of eschatological punishment is "historicized," so that present fear here and now becomes itself the only punishment.[57] Dodd, in keeping with his view of realized eschatology, seems to agree,[58] as does J. Schneider.[59] Some, such as Lenski, limit the punishment to the future.[60] It may be, however, that John's somewhat unusual expression, κόλασιν ἔχει, "has punishment," should be taken literally. Fear has punishment in the sense that the punishment comes with fear. Present day psychology recognizes fear as one of the most destructive emotions. To become obsessed with a phobia of some kind is to inflict punishment on one's self. So the judgment day of which John speaks is the occasion of future judgment when Christ returns (verse 17), and the fear referred to is the fear of being called to stand before Christ as judge. The punishment, however, takes place during the present life as one dreads the prospect of judgment.

ὁ δὲ φοβούμενος οὐ τετελείωται ἐν τῇ ἀγάπῃ, "and

---

56. Gerhard Kittel, ed., *Theological Dictionary of the New Testament*, 1964-76, s.v. "κολάζω, κόλασις," by Johannes Schneider. 3:816.
57. Bultmann, p. 74.
58. Dodd, p. 122.
59. Kittel, s.v. "κολάζω, κόλασις," by Johannes Schneider. 3:817.
60. Lenski, pp. 513-514; see also Kittel, s.v., "κολάζω, κόλασις," by Johannes Schneider (especially note 5).

the one who fears is not perfected in love." The conjunction δέ is translated as "and" in the NASB, RSV, and NEB. It can, however, very naturally be a mild adversative and is so taken by numerous commentators. The clause it introduces is set in contrast to ἀλλ' ἡ τελεία ἀγάπη . . . "but perfect love . . ." Perfect love casts out fear, but (δέ) the one who fears is not perfected in love. Φοβούμενος is a present tense participle depicting continuing dread or terror. See on φόβος above. On τετελείωται, see on verse 17. If a person dreads the thought of judgment day, his life is not marked by the perfected love that expresses itself in concrete action. In other words, he has no basis for assurance concerning his welfare when judgment day comes.

4:19. ἡμεῖς ἀγαπῶμεν, ὅτι αὐτὸς πρῶτος ἠγάπησεν ἡμᾶς, "We love, because He first loved us." It is difficult to know for sure whether this verse is more closely related to verse 18 or to verse 20. However it would seem that the relationship to verse 18 is more substantial. There John declares that the one who fears has not been perfected in love. Verse 19 then voices the assurance that, in contrast, believers do love and that the source of their love is His prior love.

This verse echoes what John has already said in verse 10. There he indicated that love in and of itself is a power that God initiated at the cross. Verse 19 is a bit more specific in declaring explicitly that man's act of loving is the result of God's prior act of love (doubtless, at the cross). As in verse 10 the pronouns ἡμεῖς, "we," and αὐτός, "he," are set in contrast to each other.

Ἀγαπῶμεν, "we love," is a present tense verb picturing continuing or habitual action. It is not merely the isolated act of love but the continuing pattern of love that John has in mind. Difference of opinion exists as to whether the mood of ἀγαπῶμεν is indicative or subjunctive. Practically all modern versions translate it as an indicative, and most commentators agree. Law is a lone exception.[61] Three arguments favoring the indicative are: (1) it fits the context better,[62] (2) ἡμεῖς would be more natural with the indicative, and (3) the absence of reference to any object of love surely fits the indicative mood better. Thus, this is a pointed declaration of the cause-and-effect relationship of God's love and man's love.

Some manuscripts show a direct object following the verb. Αὐτόν, "him," is found in K L Ψ, and θεόν, "God," appears in

---

61. Law, p. 402.
62. Westcott, p. 161.

א 33 81 614. However, it seems clear that these two readings are an attempt to supply a word that was mistakenly thought to be missing. Instead, by not indicating the object, John was speaking of love "in its widest possible sense, our very capacity to love, whether the object of our love be God or our neighbor. . . ."[63] The reason why believers love is "because [ὅτι] He first loved us." The conjunction may well indicate that love is (1) because His prior love provides the pre-eminent example of love or (2) because gratitude moves man to love, but primarily it is (3) because He provides the power to love, which is imparted to those who believe on the basis of the cross. Πρῶτος, "first," is intended to be a word of comparison. God's love was prior to the believer's love. As in 4:10, ἠγάπησεν, "loved," being aorist tense, looks back to the point in history when God's love was supremely manifested— the crucifixion.

3. THE NECESSARY ASSOCIATION OF LOVE FOR GOD AND LOVE FOR ONE'S BROTHER, 4:20—5:1

4:20. ἐάν τις εἴπῃ ὅτι Ἀγαπῶ τὸν θεόν, καὶ τὸν ἀδελφὸν αὐτοῦ μισῇ, ψεύστης ἐστίν, "If someone says, 'I love God,' and hates his brother, he is a liar." Ἐάν, "if," begins the description of a hypothetical situation. This does not necessarily mean, however, that it was merely a supposition. The ἐάν clause may reflect the profession of Gnostics, who were known for their vocal claims and their failure to support those claims with ethical action. (On Gnostic lovelessness, see pages 151-52). The heretics may have made loud claims that they loved the Unknown Father while at the same time they despised God's people.

Τὶς, "anyone," is so general that it takes in anyone who fits the description. No allowance is made for exceptions. Ὅτι in this situation is untranslatable, serving only to indicate the beginning of a direct quotation, namely, Ἀγαπῶ τὸν θεόν, "I love God."

It should be noted that the claim is put in highest terms. The word employed is ἀγαπάω, which speaks of the most lofty type of love, patterned after the love of God Himself. It is also put in the present tense, thus depicting continuing action such as a person's life-style or habit. At the same time the speaker is said to hate (μισῇ) his brother. This verb, too, appears in the present tense and describes continuing action. The term ἀδελφόν, "brother," is

63. Dodd, p. 123.

not to be pressed beyond the limits permitted by the context. In this epistle the word refers to one who is regenerated and is therefore a genuine child of God (5:1). However, sometimes when John speaks of the Gnostic heretics he may seem to describe them as being fraternally related to those who are genuinely saved. This is only because the Gnostics apparently had moved in church circles professing to be brothers when in actuality they were not (see 2:18-19). The position of τὸν ἀδελφὸν αὐτοῦ, "his brother," is striking. A literal translation reveals the forcefulness of the word order: " 'I love God,' and *his brother* he hates."

The noun ψεύστης is a strong word used to describe a person who attempts to deceive by conveying misinformation. In 1 John, the person who claims to have fellowship with God but walks in darkness, lies (1:6); the one who professes to know Christ but does not obey Him, is a liar (2:4); and he who says that he loves God but hates his brother is a liar (4:20).

ὁ γὰρ μὴ ἀγαπῶν τὸν ἀδελφὸν αὐτοῦ ὃν ἑώρακεν, τὸν θεὸν ὃν οὐχ ἑώρακεν οὐ δύναται ἀγαπᾶν, "for the one who does not love his brother whom he has seen, cannot love God whom he has not seen." The conjunction γάρ, "for," introduces John's explanation for the strong statement in the first part of the verse. He declares it to be impossible to love God and hate one's brother. On both ἀγαπῶν and τὸν ἀδελφόν see above. The perfect tense verb ἑώρακεν has been misinterpreted by some who treat it as though it were a present tense ("has him continually before his eyes").[64] The perfect does not describe action going on at the time of writing, but rather action completed in the past with *results* continuing to the time of writing.[65] So here the speaker has seen his brother in the past and the vision still lingers in his mind's eye.

Some manuscripts have a question (πῶς δύναται ἀγαπᾶν, *how can he love*) rather than the blunt denial found in our text. Οὐ δύναται, *he is not able,* is supported by ℵ B and others, while πῶς δύναται, *how is he able,* is found in A K L and others. The combination of ℵ B is weighty evidence. Metzger and the United Bible Societies committee give οὐ δύναται a B rating in a scale of A-D.[66] Apparently John's original text contained a categorical deni-

---

64. John R. W. Stott, *The Epistles of John*, The Tyndale New Testament Commentaries, p. 170; Plummer, p. 108.
65. Ernest Dewitt Burton, *Syntax of the Moods and Tenses in New Testament Greek*, p. 37.
66. Bruce M. Metzger, *A Textual Commentary on the Greek New Testament*, p. 715.

al—the person who does not love his brother whom he has seen cannot love God who is invisible.

4:21. καὶ ταύτην τὴν ἐντολὴν ἔχομεν ἀπ' αὐτοῦ, "And this commandment we have from Him." This statement is specifically linked to that of verse 10 by the conjunction καί, "and." Ταύτην τὴν ἐντολήν, "this commandment," is explained by the following ἵνα clause. Opinions differ as to who gave the commandments (ἀπ' αὐτοῦ, "from Him"). Some identify the giver as God (Westcott, Alford, Brooke, Plummer, and Marshall);[67] others, as Christ (NEB, Houlden, Stott);[68] and still another, as both God and Christ (Bonsirven, "from God through Jesus Christ").[69] In favor of the view that the commandment came from God rather than Christ is the fact that Christ is not mentioned in the immediately preceding context, whereas God is. When scholars attempt to identify the specific commandment that John had in mind, many turn to Jesus' quotation of the two greatest commandments (Matt. 22:37-40; Luke 10:27). If this is what 1 John 4:21 refers to, Bonsirven may be right in saying that the command came from God (Deut. 6:4-5; Lev. 19:18) through Jesus Christ (Matt. 22:37-40). John finds it easy to swing back and forth in talking about God the Father and Christ, and in so doing he may use nothing more specific than the third person pronoun.

It may be argued that Leviticus 19:18 speaks of love for one's neighbor, whereas 1 John refers to love for one's brother. (The term brother in 1 John denotes a fellow believer, 5:1). However, since *neighbor* is the broader term, it includes one's brother, and if one is to love one's fellowman (neighbor), one certainly should love one's fellow believer (brother).

ἵνα ὁ ἀγαπῶν τὸν θεὸν ἀγαπᾷ καὶ τὸν ἀδελφὸν αὐτοῦ, "that the one who loves God should love his brother also." Although the conjunction ἵνα ("that") is ordinarily telic, meaning "in order that," it is employed a number of times in a non-final sense simply to mean "that." In this function ἵνα is synonymous with ὅτι and is used to introduce an object clause. In verse 21 the ἵνα clause is in apposition to ταύτην τὴν ἐντολήν, "this commandment."[70]

---

67. Westcott, p. 162; Alford, 4:496; Brooke, p. 127; Plummer, pp. 108-9; Marshall, p. 226.
68. Houlden, p. 120; Stott, p. 171.
69. Bonsirven, p. 222.
70. For an explanation of how ἵνα lost its final sense and came to be used like an imperatival infinitive, see Zerwick, secs. 406-8.

The commandment referred to at least means that it is God's will that anyone who loves him should also love His people. However, Bonsirven shows that there is a logical basis for such an insistence. He says:

> It is easy to pretend to love God whom men do not see, if this love is reduced to a sentiment that no one can verify, but we know that *to love God* is to fulfill his commandments, and, above all the precept of brotherly love: it follows that to violate this precept is not to love God.[71]

5:1 Πᾶς ὁ πιστεύων ὅτι Ἰησοῦς ἐστιν ὁ Χριστὸς ἐκ τοῦ θεοῦ γεγέννηται, "Whoever believes that Jesus is the Christ is born of God." Although this verse begins a new chapter, it does not mark a change in thought. John continues to insist, as he does in 4:20-21, that love for God, if it is genuine, will be accompanied by love for fellow believers. It is clear from this verse that in this epistle John has restricted his discussion to the love of those who have been born again. The interweaving of main themes seen in 4:13-16 becomes apparent here again. Πιστεύων, "believing," being in the present tense speaks of a continuing faith rather than of the initial act of belief. John refers to *everyone who is believing*, that is, to every believer. Although πιστεύων ὅτι is the standard expression for the belief of a statement of truth,[72] it is obvious that John has more in mind than an intellectual acceptance of a statement of fact. In a parallel passage (2:22-23) he speaks of the same truth, Jesus is the Christ, and there uses the term ὁμολογέω, *to confess*, which conveys the idea of solemn affirmation and commitment. (Also see 4:2-3, 15.)

Concerning the declaration Ἰησοῦς ἐστιν ὁ χριστός, "Jesus is the Christ," see on 2:22. The perfect tense γεγέννηται speaks of completed action in the past—"has been born"—with results continuing to the present—"is now born." The emphasis in this instance is on the continuing result. Anyone who believes in the incarnation is a child of God. Stott argues that the combination of the present tense πιστεύων, "believes," and the perfect tense γεγέννηται, "is born," "shows clearly that believing is the consequence, not the cause, of the new birth."[73] This, however, is

---

71. Bonsirven, p. 221 (my translation).
72. Brooke, p. 128.
73. Stott, p. 172.

to miss the significance of these two tenses. Only if it could be shown that the present tense πιστεύων must refer to initial faith and the perfect tense γεγέννηται must be translated "has been born," (as Stott insists) can it be said that this combination of tenses "shows clearly" that believing is the consequence of new birth. It is equally possible—and more in keeping with John's argument in this context—to understand the verse as saying that anyone who believes in the incarnation is a child of God. The point of the passage is that belief is a sign of new birth, not that belief is a consequence of new birth.[74] It can be argued on the basis of John 1:12 that faith is the condition of new birth, but that is not the point of 1 John 5:1 either.[75]

καὶ πᾶς ὁ ἀγαπῶν τὸν γεννήσαντα ἀγαπᾷ [καὶ] τὸν γεγεννημένον ἐξ αὐτοῦ, "and whoever loves the Father loves the child born of Him." Both present tense verbal forms, ἀγαπῶν, "loves," and ἀγαπᾷ, "loves," depict a continuing pattern of love both for God and for fellow believers. On ἀγαπάω, "to love," see on 2:7. The conjunction καὶ is placed in brackets in the United Bible Societies' *Greek New Testament* indicating indecision as to whether or not it belongs in the text. It may have been accidentally omitted from B Ψ 33 vg. etc. or it may have been added after the example of 4:21. On the perfect tense γεγεννημένον, "born," see above on γεγέννηται. Here is an explicit declaration of fact: everyone who loves God also loves His child. Such is the nature of the Father-Son relationship that love for the One will surely be accompanied by love for the other.

4. THE EVIDENCE THAT ONE LOVES GOD'S CHILDREN, 5:2-3A

5:2. ἐν τούτῳ γινώσκομεν ὅτι ἀγαπῶμεν τὰ τέκνα τοῦ θεοῦ, "By this we know that we love the children of God." As the NASB translation indicates, ἐν is used with the instrumental case and is to be translated as "by" rather than "in." It refers to the means of ascertaining whether one loves God's people. In this instance, as in most cases in 1 John, ἐν τούτῳ refers forward, this time to the ὅταν clause. Some have suggested that it would be unnatural for the demonstrative to refer to ὅταν, but it would be no more strange than for it to refer to an ἐάν clause, as it of necessity does in 2:3. Thus, John states that it is by the fact

---

74. Westcott, p. 177.
75. Marshall, pp. 226-27.

of loving God and obeying His commands that one knows that he loves His children. However, there also seems to be a connection with the assertion of verse 1*b* that anyone who loves the father loves His child as well. Westcott actually sees ἐν τούτῳ as referring both forward and backward.[76] γινώσκομεν is inchoative in sense, speaking of coming to know, in this instance of examining the evidence and ascertaining thereby that one loves God's people. As throughout the epistle, John is speaking of the continuing practice of loving God and His children (present tense ἀγαπῶμεν). The τέκνα τοῦ θεοῦ, "children of God," are those who have been born of God (see τὸν γεγεννημένον ἐξ αὐτοῦ, "the one who has been born of him,"5:1). ὅταν τὸν θεὸν ἀγαπῶμεν καὶ τὰς ἐντολὰς αὐτοῦ ποιῶμεν, "when we love God and observe His commandments." Ὅταν is better translated *whenever* to distinguish it from the more specific ὅτε, "when." Whereas ὅτε refers to a particular occasion, ὅταν points to every occasion on which the condition of love for God and obedience to him are fulfilled. Τὰς ἐντολάς, "commandments," appears in the plural in contrast to the singular form found in 2:7-8; 3:23; and 4:21. It is probably true that in 1 John the plural refers to moral commands in general (the Decalog) and the singular refers to the command to love. Compare 2:3-6 and 2:7-8.[77] The plural, however, surely includes the command to love, and there is a sense in which the command to love includes all the commandments (Rom. 13:8-10).[78] The present tense ποιῶμεν depicts the continuing activity of obeying God's commands. It is noteworthy that whereas John uses τηρέω τὰς ἐντολὰς αὐτοῦ, "keep his commandments," five times in 1 John, this is the only occurrence of τὰς ἐντολὰς αὐτοῦ ποιῶμεν, "to do his commandments." In fact, it is the only occurrence in the New Testament. Of course some manuscripts have τηρῶμεν here (ℵ K L P etc.). Ποιῶμεν, on the other hand, is favored because it appears in B and because τηρῶμεν seems to be an adjustment to the form used elsewhere by John, especially in verse 3.[79] The employment of ποιέω, by reason of its literal meaning ("to do") and by reason of its rare use with ἐντολή, speaks pointedly of the actual performance of God's commands. The

---

76. Westcott, p. 178.
77. Law, p. 403
78. Bruce, p. 117.
79. Metzger, p. 715.

NASB rendering, "observe," is inadequate. "Carrying out his commands" (NIV), "do what he orders" (Beck), or "do his commandments" (ASV) are better.

5:3. αὕτη γάρ ἐστιν ἡ ἀγάπη τοῦ θεοῦ, ἵνα τὰς ἐντολὰς αὐτοῦ τηρῶμεν, "For this is the love of God, that we keep His commandments." By introducing this statement with γάρ, "for," John indicates that he is explaining the last clause of verse 2. In effect he makes verse 2b to be a hendiadys—equating τὸν θεὸν 'αγαπῶμεν, "we love God" (v. 2), and τὰς ἐντολὰς αὐτοῦ ποιῶμεν, "we keep his commandments."[80] Αὕτη, "this," obviously refers forward to the ἵνα clause as in 3:11, 23; 2 John 6. The article ἡ with ἀγάπη, "love," indicates that John has in mind the particular selfless love that has been under discussion throughout the epistle. The genitive τοῦ θεοῦ, "of God," is an objective genitive, meaning love "for God," as is obvious from verse 2b. The conjunction ἵνα, which normally means "in order that" is here used in a non-final sense which Brooke calls the "definitive" use. It is simply the equivalent of ὅτι, "that."[81] On τὰς ἐντολὰς αὐτοῦ, "His commandments," see on verse 2. Τηρῶμεν, being present tense, indicates the continued fulfillment of the commands. To love God is to make obedience the pattern of life.

5. THE POSSIBILITY OF OBEYING GOD, 5:3b-5

καὶ αἱ ἐντολαὶ αὐτοῦ βαρεῖαι οὐκ εἰσίν, "and His commandments are not burdensome." For the Christian, God's commands are not βαρεῖαι, "burdensome." This word and its corresponding noun βάρος refer to something that is heavy, whereas the corresponding noun φορτίον, "load," speaks of something carried,[82] (from φέρω, "to bear"). Although the terms sometimes came to be used interchangeably, on other occasions a distinction was made as in Galatians 6:2, 5: βάρη (v. 2) is an oppressive load; φορτίον (v. 5) is a normal load. Thus John in 5:3 is declaring that God's commands are not too heavy to be carried.

5:4. ὅτι πᾶν τὸ γεγεννημένον ἐκ τοῦ θεοῦ νικᾷ τὸν κόσμον, "For whatever is born of God overcomes the world." This clause serves as an explanation of the preceding statement that

---

80. Bultmann, p. 77; Alford, 4:497.
81. Brooke, p. 130.
82. Brown, s.v. "Burden, Heavy, Labor," by W. Mundle.

"His commandments are not burdensome." It is not because the commands are easily obeyed; it is because of the believer's new birth. The neuter gender πᾶν τὸ γεγεννημένον, "whatever is born," is explained by commentators as intended to be more comprehensive or universal[83] or more abstract[84] than the masculine gender would have been. The latter view seems more likely. As Plummer explains, "It is not the man, but his birth from God which conquers."[85] The emphasis is on the new life resulting from the new birth, rather than on the person who is born again. The employment of the perfect participle γεγεννημένον, "is born," reveals John's desire to stress the result of the birth—a continuing, divinely imparted new life.

The present tense verb νικᾷ, "overcomes," may be a progressive present ("continually overcomes"),[86] but it is more likely gnomic in nature since John's statement appears to be in the form of a maxim.[87] It is always true that "whatever is born of God overcomes the world." On the word "world" see on 2:15-17. The fact that the world must be overcome seems to suggest that it is viewed as a hostile power.[88] It includes all that is opposed to God.

καὶ αὕτη ἐστὶν ἡ νίκη ἡ νικήσασα τὸν κόσμον, ἡ πίστις ἡμῶν, "and this is the victory that has overcome the world—our faith." The demonstrative pronoun αὕτη refers forward to its appositive, πίστις, "faith." Put more simply, although less strikingly, the sentence would read, "Our faith is the victory...." Although νίκη, "victory," occurs only here in the New Testament, it was a common word in the Greek world, as both papyri and inscriptions reveal. On the Acropolis the Athenians had erected a small temple in honor of Athena Nike (bringer of victory). It was common to speak of the emperor's νίκη as the ability to gain the victory.[89] In 1 John the believer's faith is the means of gaining the victory over the world.

The aorist participle, νικήσασα, "has overcome," speaks of a conquest at a past point in time. Several suggestions have been advanced: it refers to Christ's victory at the cross; it refers to the church's victory over the false teachers; or it refers to the conver-

---

83. Nicoll, 5:194; Alford, 4:498; Robertson, 6:238.
84. Westcott, p. 179; Plummer, p. 112; Brooke, p. 130.
85. Plummer, p. 112.
86. Dana and Mantey, p. 182.
87. C. F. D. Moule, *An Idiom Book of New Testament Greek*, p. 8.
88. Bultmann, p. 77.
89. Arndt and Gingrich, p. 541.

sion of the believer. That it is not Christ's victory is evident because the means of victory is our faith. While it could be the church's victory, there is nothing in the context that suggests this interpretation. The most natural point of time when faith operated decisively is the point of conversion. When a person turns to Christ in initial faith he gains a victory over the world. Its power over him is broken and he is given the power of continuing victory. Πίστις, "faith," in this instance, is the subjective attitude of confidence in the objective fact of the incarnation, as verse 5 indicates. It is to believe that the human Jesus is also the very Son of God.

5:5. τίς [δέ] ἐστιν ὁ νικῶν τὸν κόσμον εἰ μὴ ὁ πιστεύων ὅτι Ἰησοῦς ἐστιν ὁ υἱὸς τοῦ θεοῦ; "And who is the one who overcomes the world, but he who believes that Jesus is the Son of God?" From the abstract (the neuter πᾶν τὸ γεγεννημένον) and impersonal (ἡ πίστις), John turns now to the personal (τίς, "who") and the specific (Ἰησοῦς ἐστιν ὁ υἱὸς τοῦ θεοῦ, "Jesus is the Son of God"). He asks the question, "Who overcomes the world if it is not the believer?" The obviously implied answer is, "No one!"

The United Bible Societies' *Greek New Testament* has a bracketed δέ after τίς indicating uncertainty as to its inclusion or exclusion. The Sinaiticus manuscript inserts δέ after τίς, while the Vaticanus places if after ἐστιν and A L and the Vulgate omit it. The NASB retains it and translates it "and," thereby tying the personal statement more closely to the impersonal one of verse 4.

The present tense νικῶν, "overcomes," is probably a progressive use portraying continuing victory in the believer's life. On κόσμον, see on 2:15-17. Like νικῶν, the present participle πιστεύων depicts continued believing. Continuing faith results in continuing victory. On πιστεύων ὅτι, see on 5:1. It is not belief itself—an attitude of confidence with no object in view—that results in victory. Rather, it is faith in God's incarnate Son. The term Ἰησοῦς is more than a name; it refers to the human being who bore that name. At one and the same time He is man and He is ὁ υἱὸς τοῦ θεοῦ, "the Son of God." First John employs the two declarations Ἰησοῦς ἐστιν ὁ υἱὸς τοῦ θεοῦ, "Jesus is the Son of God," and Ἰησοῦς ἐστιν ὁ Χριστός, "Jesus is the Christ," synonymously (cp. 5:1 and 5:5). This can also be seen in 2:22-23 where Jesus is identified both as Χριστός and as υἱός. The background for John's emphasis on these synonymous confessions is the Gnostic denial that the man Jesus is the divine Christ. On the usage of the term Christ in 1 John, see on 2:22 and 4:2.

THEOLOGICAL COMMENTARY (4:7—5:5)

A. INTRODUCTORY COMMENTS

This third cycle of the epistle (4:7—5:12) is noticeably different from the other two. Whereas the earlier cycles began with discussions of a holy or a righteous life (walking in the light and obedience, 1:5-7; 2:3-6; practice of righteousness, 2:29—3:10*a*), the third cycle begins with the subject of love (4:7—5:5). This is followed by a shorter Christological section (5:6-12). Some would begin the Christological section with verse 4 since verses 4-5 speak of believing that Jesus is the Son of God. These verses, however, are still tied to the discussion of keeping God's commands as an expression of love for God. (See ὅτι, "because," v. 4.)

The characteristic feature of 4:7—5:5 is that it weaves together the ethical and the Christological themes that have heretofore been dealt with separately. This arrangement is not merely a literary device used for the sake of variety. Instead it grows out of the theology of the Christian life, which is itself an integration of belief, love, and righteousness.

Although the main theme of 4:7—5:5 is love for fellow believers, John weaves in the elements of belief (4:13-16; 5:1, 4-5) and obedience (5:2-3). In 4:13-16 he shows the relationship of love, belief, and mutual indwelling. In 5:1 he demonstrates how belief, regeneration, love for God and love for fellow believers are related. In 5:2-3 he explains how love for Christian brothers, love for God, and obedience to His commands are related. And in 5:4-5 John spells out how belief, regeneration, and obedience to God are related.

B. THE DEVELOPMENT OF JOHN'S ARGUMENT IN 4:7—5:5

1. THE SOURCE OF LOVE, 4:7-16

John begins this third discussion of love for the brothers by laying down the basic theological premises on which the section is built. Those premises are two in number: love comes from God (v. 7) and God is love (v. 8). Although it is not explicitly stated, it is clear that what John means is that God is the only source of the selfless, spontaneous love (ἀγάπη) of which this epistle speaks. Since this is true, anyone who manifests love (ἀγάπη) has received the ability to love from God. He has been born of God (v. 7). Being a child of God he has inherited life from his Father as well as certain family characteristics. He will be like his Father because "His seed abides in him" (3:9). It is not merely that he imitates his Father; he is like his Father because of heredity. It is further assumed that everyone who has been born of God and knows God will manifest the family characteristic of love. Otherwise verse 8a—"the one who does not love does not know God"—would not be true.

John explains that the reason why the one who does not manifest love does not know God is that "God is love." Since God is love, it is necessarily true that everyone who knows God will, without exception, manifest love.

The declaration that God is love has been taken by many to mean only that God possesses the attribute of love and so loves and is loving. However this is to alter and to reduce the meaning of John's statement. As it stands the declaration says that love is not merely one of God's characteristics; love is what He *is* in himself. God in his essence is love. This is not to say that God and love are interchangeable, for the presence of the article with θεός, "God," and the absence of the article before ἀγάπη, "love," will not permit such interchange. Θεός must be the subject of the sentence. Nor is this to say that God in His essence is only love and nothing more. It must be remembered that John also says, πνεῦμα ὁ θεός, "God is spirit" (John 4:24) and ὁ θεὸς φῶς ἐστιν, "God is light" (1 John 1:5). To say that God is light is the same as to say that God is holiness. All three of these statements explain what God is in His essence. Westcott categorizes the three statements as metaphysical ("spirit," John 4:24), moral ("light," 1 John 1:5), and personal ("love," 1 John 4:8).[90] God's essence then is spirit, holiness, and love.

There is no denying that God possesses the attribute of love. The attribute, however, is the expression of the essence. Because God *is* love, He is loving. Concerning the relation of the attributes of God to His essence, Augustus Hopkins Strong lays down four basic propositions: (1) "the attributes have an objective existence," (2) "the attributes inhere in the divine essence," (3) "the attributes belong to the divine essence as such," and (4) "the attributes manifest the divine essence."[91] The attributes find their unity in the one divine essence from which they spring, and it is only as they manifest that essence that what God essentially is can

---
90. Westcott, p. 167.
91. Augustus Hopkins Strong, *Systematic Theology*, pp. 244-46.

be known. In 1 John 4:8 the apostle goes behind the attribute to the very essense of God, expressed by the attribute of love.

That verse 8 is speaking of essence has long been the view of many outstanding commentators on 1 John. Westcott said, "In the O.T. love is an attribute of God, one of many exercised in particular relations. . . . In the N.T. first love can be shewn to be the very Being of God. . . ."[92] Law wrote, "God is love. He is love essentially. Love is not one of God's attributes, but that in which all his moral attributes have their unity."[93] Concerning John's declaration, Plummer stated, "Here as in the other cases, the predicate has no article, and expresses not a quality which He possesses, but one which embraces all that He *is*."[94] Brooke said, "Love is not merely an attribute of God, it is His very Nature and Being. . . ."[95] Alford declared, "Love is the very essence, not merely an attribute of God. It is co-essential with Him: He is all love, love is all of Him: he who has not love, has not God."[96] Walter Conner said, "John's statement that God is love must be accepted. If that be true, then nothing is more fundamental in God than love. Love is the essence of his being. . . ."[97] And Dana was equally specific when he wrote, "Love is not merely an attribute of the Divine Being, nor a demand of divine authority; it is the very essence of God."[98]

Verse 8 assumes that since God is love, one who knows Him will habitually practice love. One cannot know God who in his essence is love and not be oneself manifesting love. This may be because knowing God is being in fellowship with him and fellowship demands likeness (see on 1:5-7). Or it may be because the one who knows God is born of God and thus possesses the nature of God who is love. The latter concept is uppermost in John's mind in verse 8, as the previous verse indicates.

After laying down these basic premises of the theology of love, the author proceeds to discuss the historical manifestation of God's love to a needy world (vv. 9-11). Verse 9 is another expression of the truth previously stated in 3:16. ἀγάπη, "love," is not merely theory, theological proposition, or sentiment; it is action. The kind

92. Westcott, p. 169.
93. Law, p. 78.
94. Plummer, p. 100.
95. Brooke, p. 118.
96. Alford, 4:489.
97. Walter T. Conner, *The Epistles of John*, 2d ed., p. 104.
98. H. E. Dana, *The Epistles and Apocalypse of John*, p. 62.

of love that characterizes the essence of God is love that must and does act, sacrificing and sharing and giving of itself.

This kind of self-sacrificing love does not have its original and chief manifestation in us. The primary exemplar of such love is God, who at one momentous point in history sent His son in order to placate His own wrath by fulfilling the just demands of His own law. This, John declares, is what genuine love is (v. 10), and genuine love has at least three characteristics. *It is spontaneous.* There was nothing of value in the persons loved that called forth such sacrificial love. God of His own free will set His love on us in spite of our enmity and sin. Ἀγάπη is love that is initiated by the lover because he wills to love, not because of the value or lovableness of the person loved. *It is self-giving.* Ἀγάπη is not interested in what it can gain, but in what it can give. It is not bent on satisfying the lover, but on helping the loved one whatever the cost. *It is active.* Ἀγάπη is not mere sentiment cherished in the heart. Nor is it mere words however eloquent. It does involve feeling and it may express itself in words, but it is primarily an attitude toward another that moves the will to act in helping to meet the need of the one loved.

And since God loved man with such unique love, believers ought to love one another with a love patterned after His (v. 11). Although gratitude should move us so to love and new life in Christ ought to empower us so to love, it is sheer moral obligation of which John speaks. It is incumbent upon us to love as He loved. This is the right course for us to follow. God's act of love places on us the obligation to practice such love continually toward one another (v. 11).

From the historic manifestation of God's love on Calvary, the author moves to what may be designated as the ongoing manifestation of God's love (v. 12). No one has seen or can see God in His essence. However, when believers love one another God can be seen in the love of his people for each other, for their love springs from the very nature of God who is love. John states that love for one another proves two facts. First, God's indwelling is proved. The reasoning of verse 12 goes back to the basic premises laid down in verses 8-9. Love comes from God who in His essence is love. When Christians love, it shows that God who is love is dwelling in them. This is a companion truth to the truth of regeneration. To be born of God is to become a partaker "of the divine nature" (2 Pet. 1:4). God in His essence dwells in the believer through His Holy Spirit.

The second fact that is proved by love for one another is that God's "love is perfected in us" (4:12). This does not mean that the point of perfect or flawless love is reached—only God loves in that way. The NIV translates it "his love is made complete in us." It comes to its intended goal when deeds of love for one another are manifested. According to 3:16-17 genuine love, when given full play, will express itself in deeds of love. This is the "perfected" (NASB) or "completed" (NIV) love of 4:12.

Although believers are active in this display of love, it is God's own love that enables, expressing itself and coming to fruition in deeds of love. When a believer actively shows love to another believer, God, who is love, is seen in the life of that believer.

It is now clear why love is a valid ground for the assurance of one's salvation. John has worked out the implications of the basic premises he had laid down in verses 7-8, namely, God is love and He is the only source of love. No one, then, can show true, selfless love unless he draws the ability to love from God. If a person loves, he must be in vital relation to God who is love. When a person is regenerated, he becomes a partaker of the divine nature. God, by His Spirit, takes up His residence in the believer. Thus God, who in His essence is love, indwells everyone who believes. And since God's love is active love, it is bound to manifest itself in the believer's life.

This does not mean that the believer will love everyone all of the time. He will, however, love as a pattern of life. It will be his general practice to show love to the people of God. The presence of such active love in one's life is a valid test of the genuineness of one's salvation.

At this point (vv. 13-16) the first instance of the interweaving of the ethical test (love) with the Christological (belief) occurs. From verse 7 through verse 12 John has been discussing the subject of love; now abruptly in verse 13 he seems to change the direction of his thought. One strand of truth, however, continues on through verses 13-16, namely, the truth of indwelling (vv. 13, 15-16). God dwells in the believer and the believer dwells in God. That God indwells the believer is not difficult to conceive, for the believer is localized in a physical body, but the fact that the believer dwells in God is a different concept, for God is not localized. As has been shown previously, to dwell in God or in Christ is to be in intimate fellowship with these persons of the Godhead. It is to know them personally, and thus be saved (see on 2:5-6; 24-25; 3:24).

John has shown that deeds of love constitute evidence that God lives in a person (v. 12). Now he declares that the reception and presence of the Holy Spirit is also evidence of indwelling—the mutual indwelling of God in the believer and the believer in God (v. 13). In fact, it is through the Holy Spirit that God dwells in the believer, and furthermore it is the Spirit who produces love in the believer's heart (Rom. 5:5) and life (Gal. 5:22).

This mutual indwelling is also dependent on what one believes concerning Jesus. For all generations since the time of the apostles, belief in Christ has, of necessity, rested on apostolic testimony, and it is to that eyewitness testimony that John refers in verse 14. The apostles saw, and indeed were careful eyewitnesses of, the Son of God sent to provide salvation for the world. This eyewitness testimony, when confessed meaningfully, results in the mutual indwelling of which John speaks (v. 15).

John knows nothing of an atonement limited to the elect, for he declares that God sent His Son to be the Savior of the world. A similar statement, more specifically related to the atonement appears in 2:2, where Christ is said to be the propitiation for the sins of "the whole world." Plummer indicates where the limitation lies—and it is not in the purpose of God. He says, "There is no limit to his mission to save, and no limit to its success, excepting man's unwillingness to accept salvation by believing on the Saviour."[99]

In verse 16 John weaves this brief treatment of Christology, of apostolic testimony, and of belief into the larger discussion of Christian love. In so doing he returns to the basic premise of the theology of love—"God is love." In fact he treats God and love as practically identical, so much so that he can say that the one who dwells in love dwells in God, and God dwells in him. Brooke gets at the very heart of John's theology of love when he says, "Thus the test of love can give full assurance. . . . It is a logical deduction from the very nature of God."[100]

John reasons that since God in his essence is love, where God is, love is. If God dwells in a person, love dwells there, for God is love. By the same logic, it is equally true that if love dwells in a person, God dwells there. The doctrine of divine indwelling is really a doctrine of love's indwelling.

But indwelling is tied inseparably to confession of Christ as God's Son. Belief, then, results in indwelling, and indwelling re-

---

99. Plummer, p. 104.
100. Brooke, p. 122.

sults in love. All believers are indwelt by God; thus, all believers are indwelt by love. Furthermore, genuine love is active and will, without fail, produce deeds of love. Therefore, love in action is valid evidence that a person has had a genuine experience of regeneration.

2. THE FRUIT OF LOVE, 4:17-19

There are several passages in the epistle where John discusses the results of perfected love. By perfected love John means that love that has accomplished its goal in producing deeds of love. It is not merely subjective, a matter of thought and emotion; it has objectified itself in action. This objectified love produces at least three fruits according to 1 John. *The fruit of assurance.* Early in the epistle the term τετελείωται, "has been perfected," appears in conjunction with love (2:5). Here, obedience to Christ's word is evidence of the presence of perfected love. Outward action reveals the inner presence of love. And the fruit of this perfected love is assurance of salvation, for John declares, "By this we know that we are in Him" (2:5).

Assurance is again set forth as the fruit of perfected love in 3:19. Here the term perfected is not found, but the fact of it is clearly indicated in verses 16-18, where genuine love is described as love in action. And it is "by this," according to verse 19, that "we shall know . . . that we are of the truth." *The fruit of confidence in prayer (3:21-22).* These verses, like verse 19, are based on verses 16-18. It is love in action, or perfected love, that satisfies the condemning heart and replaces condemnation with assurance. When believers pray they have confidence that God will answer, because perfected love convinces that a right relationship with God exists. His obedient children can be sure that he hears when they pray. *The fruit of confidence on judgment day (4:17-19).* This product of perfected love looks to the future. It is by means of mutual indwelling—the believer in God (who is love) and God in him (v. 16)—that love is brought to the state of completeness (v. 17) in which it expresses itself in action (3:16). This full grown love, in turn, produces confidence that enables one to stand fearlessly before the judgment seat of Christ. Such boldness is based on likeness to Christ—the ability to love as He loves. Thus is fear expelled by perfected love, and the thought of judgment day brings no onslaught of terror. Readiness for that day is clearly proved by the evidence of perfected love showing that God is at work in our lives. Furthermore, this confidence with regard to judgment day is augmented by the consideration of God's prior love (v. 19). Ultimately, assurance rests on "His love for us—in the sending of His Son to be the expiation for our sins."[101]

3. THE RELATIONSHIP OF LOVE FOR ONE'S BROTHER TO LOVE FOR GOD, 4:20—5:5

It may be argued that a person can withdraw in hermit fashion from the world of human beings and love God alone. In fact, it has been suggested that in this section John had in mind Gnostic opponents who thought that love could be aimed directly at God regardless of any hatred they manifested toward God's people.[102] In response John now launches a pointed effort to show that love for God must of necessity be accompanied by love for one's brother in Christ. He offers several reasons this is true. First, it is a logical necessity (4:20). John insists that one cannot love the invisible God if he does not love his visible brother. Three interpretations of this assertion have been advanced: (1) It is impossible to manifest love for God except through love for one's brother. This is said to be true because the brother can be seen but God cannot,[103] (2) Love for God involves obedience to His commands, one of which calls for love for other people. If one does not love his fellow Christian, his disobedience shows that he does not love God either, for love involves obedience,[104] and (3) It is easier to love one whom you can see than one whom you cannot see. Therefore, if a person does not love his brother who is visible, he will find it impossible to love God who is invisible.[105]

View (2), although true, is not set forth in verse 20; instead it is John's point in verse 21. View (1) is really not correct, for God can be loved directly. It is not necessary that He be loved mediately—through loving a brother. He can be loved by any obedience that is rendered to Him. For instance, He can be loved by refraining from worshiping any other person or object and by worshiping Him alone or by refusing to misuse His name. It would seem, therefore, that view (3) is the most reasonable interpretation. In

---

101. Dodd, p. 123.
102. Bultmann, pp. 75-76; Bonsirven, p. 221.
103. Law, p. 252; Nicoll, 5:193; Bultmann, p. 76.
104. Marshall, p. 226; Bonsirven, p. 221.
105. Stott, pp. 170-171; Westcott, pp. 161-162; Alford, 4:496; Plummer, p. 108; Brooke, pp. 126-127.

its favor is the fact that it emphasizes the visibility of the brother and the invisibility of God, which John apparently mentions as the reason why brother love must accompany love for God. John's first reason why love for brother must accompany love for God is that logic demands it. If a person fulfills the more difficult requirements of loving God, he will certainly fulfill the easier requirement of loving his brother.

The second reason that love of God and love of brother are inseparable is found in God's dual command (4:21). The same God who commanded love for Himself also commanded love for one's brother. In Deuteronomy 6:5 He commanded that a person love God with all of his being, and in Leviticus 19:18 He requires that one love one's neighbor as oneself. Jesus placed these two commands side by side as the two greatest commands of the law (Matt. 22:34-39). First John 4:21 also suggests that the nature of genuine love demands that one who loves God must also love his brother. By its nature, love involves not only sentiment but action. Love for another human being involves activity intended for the benefit of that person. Love for God involves obedience to God's commands. Jesus said, "If anyone loves Me, he will keep My word" (John 14:23). Therefore, love for God must by its very nature be accompanied by love for fellow believers. Dodd says, "There is no real love to God which does not show itself in obedience to his commands . . . and God's command is quite explicit: 'that he who loves God is to love his brother also.' "[106]

John's third reason for insisting that love for God and love for one's brother are inseparable companions is the nature of the family relationship (5:1). His reasoning in this verse has been explained in at least two different ways. Plummer, who is followed by Smith, sets up the argument as a double syllogism.[107]

> Everyone who believes the Incarnation
>   is a child of God.
> Every child of God loves its Father.
>   ∴ Every believer in the Incarnation loves God.
> Every believer in the Incarnation loves God.
> Everyone who loves God loves the children of God.
>   ∴ Every believer in the Incarnation loves the
>   children of God.

---

106. Dodd, p. 123.
107. Plummer, p. 110; Smith, p. 193.

It will be noticed that the second premise of the first syllogism is assumed, inasmuch as John does not make such a statement. Furthermore, the conclusion of the second syllogism is not exactly what John was trying to prove in this verse.

There is a simpler and more direct interpretation that does not build on an assumption. It may be represented as follows:

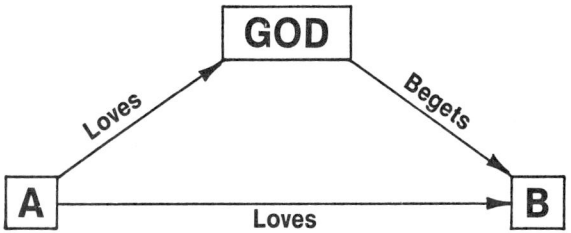

B believes that Jesus is the Christ (v. 1*a*), and
B is born of God (v. 1*b*).
A loves God (v. 1*c*).
A therefore also loves B (v. 1*d*).

The point is that if A loves God who is the Father of B, A will also love B. John does not explicitly say why this is true, but his stress on the idea of spiritual birth suggests what the reason is. The verb γεννάω appears three times in the verse, indicating that A, who loves God, loves B also because B has been born of God. A common nature is possessed by both Father and son. The son has life from the Father and he is the recipient of the family characteristics. Therefore, to love the one is to love the other.[108]

Here in 5:1 the characteristic interweaving of this section is apparent. Belief that Jesus is the divine Christ is shown in its relationship to love for the brothers. The middle term that binds that Christological aspect to the ethical is the fact of regeneration. The believer is born again and therefore the believer loves.

This verse is crucial in determining to whom the term *brother* refers in 1 John. It is clear that the brother is one who has experienced spiritual birth and is a member of the family of God. While a Christian should, like God, love all people everywhere, it is even more incumbent upon him to love fellow believers. John singles out this love of believers for each other because it is easier to demonstrate the necessity of it and therefore easier to use as a test.

---

108. Alford, 4:497.

This verse was not written to prove either the Calvinistic or the Arminian *ordo salutis*. The point the apostle is making is that belief in Jesus as the divine Christ is a sign that one is regenerated. However, it is also true that faith is a prerequisite of regeneration, for John 1:12 declares, "But as many as received Him, to them He gave the right to become children of God, even to those who believe in His name."[109] The sequence John sets forth is as follows:

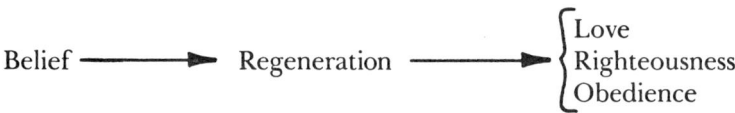

Since it is important to love God's people, it may well be asked, How can one be sure that he loves God's people? John therefore proceeds to discuss the twofold evidence of love for fellow believers (5:2-3a): love for God and obedience to His commands (v. 2). Yet, in another sense this evidence is singular, for to love God is to keep his commandments.

It was not to be expected that John would suggest that love for God is evidence of love for God's people. Instead, the reverse would be assumed, that love for God's people is evidence of love for God. However, what John seems to be saying is that implicit in love for God is love for His people. And this is what verse 1 has already declared—the one who loves the Father also loves His children. So, if there is evidence of genuine love for God, then it is certain there will be love for the people of God. And John indicates in verse 3a how to be sure that one loves God: obey His commands.

There are two possible ways to understand what John means by this assertion. First, obedience to God's commands is evidence that a person loves God, and if a person does love God, he will surely love those begotten by him (v. 1). Second, God's commands include the requirement of love for God's people and thus to obey His commands is to love his people. The immediately preceding context (v. 1) would seem to favor the former view.

So the test of love is in reality the test of obedience.[105] They are

---

109. Marshall, p. 226.
110. Bruce, p. 117.

one and the same. Also the test of love is circular in nature. Love for fellow believers indicates that one loves God, and love for God shows that one loves fellow believers.[106] The two loves are of the same fabric. If a person has one he, logically, must have the other. It should be noticed that John continues the interweaving of main themes. This time it is two aspects of the ethical test—love and obedience (righteousness)—that are woven together.

This section on the ethical test of the genuineness of salvation (4:7—5:5) concludes with an assurance concerning the possibility of keeping God's commands. What is the point of talking about obedience as evidence that one loves God and His children, if obedience is so difficult that it is practically impossible. John's answer is that it is far from impossible. The load is not too heavy to bear (βαρύς), not because it is light, but because of the enabling power the new birth makes available. Being born of God enables a person to make righteousness his life-style (3:9); being born of God results in love for one's fellow believer (5:1); and being born of God provides the ability to obey God's commands (5:3b-4a).

The apostle presses the matter of enablement back to initial faith (v. 4b). Faith in Jesus as God's Christ results in regeneration, and regeneration provides ability to overcome the world and to obey God's commands. And this ability to overcome is a continuing experience for the person who believes that Jesus is God's Son (v. 5).

Here again John's practice of interweaving is obvious. Righteousness (obeying God's commands, overcoming the world) is tied to regeneration, and regeneration is linked to Christology (belief that Jesus is God's Son). And, of course, these items are intimately tied to love for God and His children (vv. 1-3a).

C. PRESENT-DAY APPLICATION

1. APPLICATION TO CURRENT CULTS AND HERESIES

John's teaching is as applicable to the cults and heresies of our day as it was to the Gnosticism of the first century. The reiterated insistence that Jesus is the Son of God (4:9-10, 14-15; 5:5) and the Christ (5:1) clearly excludes Christian Science, Jehovah's Witnesses, Mormonism, Unity, and the Theosophical Society (see pp. 111-12, 164-65, 220-21, 310).

111. Bruce, p. 117; Houlden, p. 123; Westcott, p. 177.

2. APPLICATION TO NOMINAL CHRISTIANITY

The primary thrust of the epistle is like a two-sided coin. One side is the warning against heresy. John's purpose is to identify for the believer those who do not believe the truth, but who subscribe to and propagate error. The other side of the coin has to do with the assurance of the genuine believer. The same tests that exclude the false teachers provide grounds of assurance for the believers.

This third cycle of the epistle characteristically weaves together both the ethical and the Christological grounds for assurance. Faith alone is not an adequate ground. John rules out any form of easy-believism and insists that faith must be accompanied by action. Deeds of love and obedience to God's moral requirements must accompany faith or it is not genuine (5:1-3*a*).

The epistle also rules out any assurance based only on deeds of love and righteousness. John insists that, in order for good deeds to have any assurance value, they must be accompanied by the confession that Jesus is the incarnate Son of God sent to save us by providing propitiation for our sins (4:9-10, 14-15; 5:5).

Marshall indicates two additional points at which application to our day should be made. First, the confession of Jesus as Christ or as Son of God (4:15; 5:1, 5) was surely intended to involve more than mere intellectual acceptance of a theological proposition.[112] At least two reasons for this assertion may be advanced. The term confession speaks of commitment on the part of the one who makes the confession. And the results of the confession (mutual indwelling, 4:15; new birth, 5:1; victory over the world, 5:4-5) also indicate an inner involvement.

In the second place, Marshall warns against a current tendency to speak of "obedient trust in Jesus while denying his metaphysical status as the Son of God. . . ."[113] John's strong emphasis on correct Christology makes it very clear that faith is doctrinally oriented. Apostolic Christianity did not simply believe in Jesus; it believed nothing less than that He is God's incarnate Son. Neither a heartless acceptance of a theological proposition, nor a trust in Jesus that is devoid of theology will do.

Paraphrastic Commentary (4:7—5:5)

(7) Dear friends, we believers are habitually manifesting love to everyone in our fellowship because God enables us to love with

---

112. Marshall, p. 220.
113. Ibid., pp. 220-21.

spontaneous, self-giving love. Anyone who practices such love is a regenerate child of God and knows God by personal experience. (8) The one whose life is not marked by love has never come to know God. This is true because God in his essence is love. (9) We saw God's love in action among men when God sent His unique Son into this world on the mission of securing eternal life for us. (10) Love consists, not in the fact that we on our part have taken the initiative in loving God. Instead, it is that God was the one who manifested His selfess love toward us by commissioning His Son to be the atoning sacrifice for our sins, to satisfy God's just demands so that His wrath might be averted. (11) Dear friends, since God at Calvary manifested such love toward us, we are under a continuing obligation to show the same kind of selfless love to everyone in our fellowship. (12) God in his essence has never been observed by anyone. If we are manifesting love to the other members of our fellowship, it is God living within us and His selfless love which has come to fruitful maturity.

(13) This is how we come to know that we are in close relationship with God and that He is dwelling within us: in limited measure, He has imparted His Holy Spirit to us. (14) In addition, we of the apostolic circle have observed—the memory is still very real—and are continuing to bear eyewitness testimony that God the Father commissioned God the Son to make salvation available for the whole world. (15) If anyone publicly and solemnly confesses his faith in the man Jesus as the incarnate Son of God, God is dwelling within him and he is experiencing a close personal relationship with God. (16) And as for us believers, we have come by experience to know, and we now have confidence in, the love which God has shed abroad in our hearts. God in His essence is selfless love, and the person who dwells in the sphere of love actually dwells in God and God dwells within Him.

(17) It is by this mutual indwelling—God working with us—that love has been brought to fruitful maturity, so that we will be able to stand fearlessly on judgment day. Such confidence is ours because here in this world we are like Christ in manifesting God-like love. (18) Love and fear are mutually exclusive. Love that has come to fruitbearing maturity excludes fear, because terror at the prospect of judgment day is punishment in itself. The person who fears that day does not have the assurance of fruitbearing love in his life. (19) We now are manifesting love, because at Calvary He took the initiative and performed a mighty deed of love in our behalf.

(20) Suppose someone says, "I love God," and yet he hates a fellow church member. He is not telling the truth, because if he does not show God-like love for his brother who is visible to him, he cannot love God who is invisible. (21) Furthermore, God has laid down

this requirement: One who loves God must also love his brother. (5:1) Everyone who is a believer in Jesus as the divine Christ is a child of God, and anyone who loves God, who is the Father, also loves the child who has been born of Him. (2) This is how we can discover if we love God's children: Do we love God and are we obeying His commands? (3) This is what it is to love God. It is to make it a practice to do what He commands. And that is not a burden too heavy to be carried, (4) because, as is well-known, the new life which results from new birth overcomes the wicked pagan world. It was our faith that initially overcame this evil world. (5) Who is the one who is constantly gaining victory over the world? It is the one who continues to believe that Jesus is God's incarnate Son.

STRUCTURAL COMMENTARY (4:7—5:5)[114]

IV. Third cycle: The Christian Life Viewed As a Closely Woven Integration of the Ethical and the Christological, 4:7—5:12
   A. The ethical test, 4:7—5:5
      1. The source of love, 4:7—7-16
         a. Basic premises of John's theology of love, 4:7-8
            (1) Believers love because love comes from God, 4:7
            (2) To know God is to love because God is love, 4:8
         b. The historical manifestation of God's love, 4:9-11
            (1) God sent His Son to bring us life, 4:9
            (2) God took the initiative in manifesting love, 4:10
            (3) We are under obligation to love as He did, 4:11
         c. The ongoing manifestation of God's love, 4:12
            (1) No one has ever seen God, 4:12a
            (2) Mutual Christian love reveals two facts, 4:12b
                (a) God dwells in us
                (b) God's love is perfected in us
         d. The interweaving of the ethical and the Christological as bases for assurance, 4:13-16
            (1) Basis #1—the gift of the Holy Spirit, 4:13
            (2) Basis #2—apostolic testimony, 4:14
            (3) Basis #3—personal confession, 4:15
            (4) Basis #4—the presence of God's love in us, 4:16

---

114. For previous section of the outline see p. 313.

2. The fruit of love, 4:17-19
   a. Positively stated, 4:17
      (1) The means by which love is perfected: mutual indwelling, 4:17a
      (2) The purpose of perfected love: confidence on judgment day, 4:17b
      (3) The basis of confidence: likeness to Christ, 4:17c
   b. Negatively stated, 4:18
      (1) Love excludes fear, 4:18a
      (2) The one who fears does not possess perfected love, 4:18b
   c. His love for us, the ultimate source of our confidence, 4:19
3. The necessary association of love for God and love for one's brother, 4:20—5:1
   a. It is demanded by logic, 4:20
      (1) An impossible situation, 4:20a
      (2) The reason for its impossibility, 4:20b
   b. It is demanded by God's dual command, 4:21
      (1) Love for God
      (2) Love for brother
   c. It is demanded by the nature of the family relationship, 5:1
      (1) Belief in the incarnation is characteristic of a child of God, 5:1a
      (2) Love for the Father will always be accompanied by love for His child, 5:1b
4. The evidence that one loves God's children, 5:2-3a
   a. It is love for God and obedience to Him, 5:2
   b. In reality, to love God is to obey Him, 5:3a
5. The possibility of obeying God, 5:3b-5
   a. His commands are not too heavy to bear, 5:3b
   b. Regeneration enables one to obey, 5:4-5
      (1) New birth brings victory over the evil world, 5:4a
      (2) Faith in God's incarnate Son results in initial and continuing victory, 5:4b-5

14

The Christological Test, 5:6-12

For the third and last time in this epistle John sets forth the Christological test. However, the discussion is not in any sense a repetition of what has been stated in the two previous cycles. Up to this point John has stressed the confession that Jesus is the Christ (2:22; 5:1) or the Son of God (5:5) who has come in the flesh (4:2). In 5:6-12, however, the Christological test is not explicitly stated in those terms. The concept of incarnation is implicit in verses 6-8, and the truth of Christ's Sonship runs through verses 9-12, but these two familiar themes are handled quite differently in this third section.

The organizing factor here is found in the word *witnesses*. John refers to the Holy Spirit, the water, the blood, and the experience of eternal life as witnesses who testify concerning God's Son. The person who receives this combined testimony has eternal life; the one who rejects it does not.

Exegetical Commentary (5:6-12)

1. THE COINCIDENT WITNESS OF HISTORICAL FACTS AND THE HOLY SPIRIT, 5:6-9

5:6. οὗτός ἐστιν ὁ ἐλθὼν δι' ὕδατος καὶ αἵματος, Ἰησοῦς Χριστός, "This is the one who came by water and blood,

The Christological Test   365

Jesus Christ." The demonstrative pronoun οὗτος looks back to the declaration in verse 5, Ἰησοῦς ἐστιν ὁ υἱὸς τοῦ θεοῦ, "Jesus is the Son of God." John proceeds in verse 6 to give a further description of Jesus. He is "the one who came by water and blood." Although it is certain that description means that He became incarnate, this is still a most enigmatic statement. Ὁ ἐλθών, "the one who came," reminds us of the well known messianic designation, the coming one (ὁ ἐρχόμενος). The difference is that the former is aorist tense and the latter is present tense. This, however, does not rule out any relationship between the two expressions. The present tense was commonly used to refer to the Messiah before His advent (John 6:14; 7:27; 11:27; 12:13); the aorist tense looks back on His coming as a historical event.

The most difficult portion of this difficult statement is the phrase δι' ὕδατος καὶ αἵματος, "by water and blood." Of the many suggested interpretations of this expression, three are worth mentioning. (1) Some have understood the terms as referring to the ordinances of baptism and the Lord's supper. However, there is no precedent for using the term blood to refer to the Lord's supper, and the passage speaks of past events in the life of Christ, not of symbolic representations of those events

(2) Others have understood the expression as referring to the piercing of Christ's side on the cross (John 19:34) and the consequent appearance of blood and water. But 1 John 5:6 stresses the fact that Christ came not by water only, which suggests that some were insisting that He did come by water alone. There would be no reason, however, for anyone to assert that water alone came from Christ's pierced side. The denial assumed by John's refutation does not fit the picture as seen in John 19:34. Furthermore, it is difficult to see how the event in John 19:34 could be described by saying, "This is the one who came by water and blood."

(3) The two terms water and blood are seen by many as referring to Christ's baptism and His death.[1] Water easily suggests

---

1. A. E. Brooke, *The Johannine Epistles*, The International Critical Commentary, pp. 131-34; R. C. H. Lenski, *The Interpretation of the Epistles of St. Peter, St. John and St. Jude*, pp. 524-26; I. Howard Marshall *The Epistles of John, The New International Commentary on the New Testament*, pp. 232-33; John R. W. Stott, *The Epistles of John*, Tyndale New Testament Commentaries, pp. 177-79. While Stott accepts the view that John was refuting Cerinthian Gnostics, he also feels that John may have been referring to the two sacraments and to the piercing of Jesus' side.

baptism, as view (1) shows; and blood quite naturally speaks of death, as view (2) reveals. Since the aorist tense ἐλθών depicts a past event and since Jesus is the one involved in the action, it is most reasonable to look to the life of Jesus for the events to which John refers. Also, the presence of Gnosticism in first-century Asia Minor provides a religious background that offers a plausible meaning for John's statement. As we have shown previously, there is good reason to believe that 1 John was intended as a refutation of incipient Gnosticism. Irenaeus places both the apostle John and Gnostic Cerinthus in Ephesus at the same time.[2] Furthermore, Cerinthus taught that at Jesus' baptism the divine Christ came upon the human Jesus but left him at the cross before Jesus died (see on 2:22). It is probable that the terms "water" and "blood" were familiar designations for Christ's baptism and death, understood by John's original readers, but enigmatic to us today. Law thought that these terms were "a kind of verbal shorthand, intended merely to recall to his readers the exposition of those themes which they had heard from his lips."[3]

The difficulty interpreters feel in handling this passage is reflected in the variety of textual variants that appear in the manuscripts. The reading found in the United Bible Societies' text, δι' ὕδατος καὶ αἵματος, is supported by B K Ψ, a number of Old Latin manuscripts, the Vulgate, and the Peshitta Syriac, which combine to provide a fairly broad representation of text types. Several minuscule manuscripts substitute πνεύματος, "spirit," for αἵματος, "blood." Both αἵματος and πνεύματος appear in ℵ A, the Harklean Syriac, and the Coptic. The introduction of the word πνεύματος as a substitute for αἵματος may have been occasioned by the combination of water and Spirit in John 3:5. The addition of πνεύματος may have been a result of John's grouping of πνεῦμα, ὕδωρ, and αἷμα in verse 8 (7). The United Bible Societies Editorial Committee gave the first of the above readings a B rating on a scale of four.

The question as to the exact meaning of ἐλθὼν δι' ὕδατος καὶ αἵματος, "came by water and blood," is not easily answered. Ἐλθών is not to be referred narrowly to the point of time when Christ first became incarnate. It must depict the whole span of His earthly ministry beginning with His baptism and concluding with His death. Baptism is singled out for two reasons. It marked the opening of his ministry, and Cerinthus erroneously taught that it

---

2. Irenaeus *Against Heresies*, 3. 3. 4.
3. Robert Law, *The Tests of Life*, p. 95.

The Christological Test 367

was then that the divine Christ came upon the human Jesus. His death is singled out because it marked the close of His ministry and because it was a point of Gnostic deviation. It was asserted that the divine Christ departed from the human Jesus at the cross before Jeus died.

Blass-Debrunner indicates that διά may be used to denote manner (Acts 15:27) or "the circumstances in which one finds oneself" (2 Cor. 2:4).[4] In the former case, the manner of Jesus' coming was by baptism and death. In the latter, baptism and death were the circumstances in which Jesus came. Bonsirven suggests that δι' ὕδατος καὶ αἵματος, speaks of the region through (διά) which one travels.[5] Viewed in this way, John meant that Jesus Christ came on His redemptive mission by the route of baptism, thus identifying Himself with those He came to save, and by the route of death, he came to be the atoning sacrifice for all who are under the wrath of God.

John insists, in opposition to Cerinthus, that Jesus, the Son of God (v. 5), not only experienced baptism but also death on the cross. To stress this fact, John adds the words Ἰησοῦς Χριστός, "Jesus Christ" (v. 6). The one who was baptized and who died on the cross was not merely the human Jesus. He was Jesus Christ, both human and divine.

οὐκ ἐν τῷ ὕδατι μόνον ἀλλ' ἐν τῷ ὕδατι καὶ ἐν τῷ αἵματι, "not with the water only, but with the water and with the blood." The denial and assertion contained in these words are the key to what John is aiming at in this passage. Some were denying that Jesus' coming was associated with blood. This, of course, could be reflecting a Gnostic denial that Jesus had physical blood and therefore a physical body, but if that were the case, one wonders why blood is mentioned rather than the body. Blood more naturally refers to death, and, in the New Testament, to sacrificial death. It is better, then, to understand John to be saying that Jesus Christ underwent death. The Christ was not merely involved in Jesus' baptism, as Cerinthus asserted, but also in His death.

Attempts have been made to develop a distinction between διά, "by," and ἐν, "with," in this verse. The former is said to speak of the *means* by which Christ's office was revealed and the latter to indicate the *sphere* in which He now fulfills it.[6] But these two prepositions can be, and often are, synonymous. Ἐν may be

---

4. F. Blass and A. Debrunner, *A Greek Grammar of the New Testament*, sec. 233 (3).
5. Joseph Bonsirven, *Épitres de Saint Jean*, vol. 9, *Verbum Salutis*, p. 230.
6. B. F. Westcott, *The Epistles of St. John*, p. 183.

used with the instrumental case to mean *through* or *by*, a usage which appears repeatedly in this epistle (2:3, 5; 3:16, 19, 24; 4:13, 17; 5:2; see also Matt. 5:13; 12:27; 26:52).[7] The NIV translates both prepositions in v. 6 as "by." John changes words for sake of literary variety, but the meaning in both instances is the same. The use of the articles with the repeated occurrences of "water" (ὕδατι) and "blood" (αἵματι) is for the purpose of pointing out previous reference. It is that particular water of which John has been speaking—the water of Jesus' baptism; and that particular blood—the blood of His cross. By using the strong adversative conjunction ἀλλ᾽ (ἀλλά), "but," John forcibly denies the Gnostic position that the Christ came upon Jesus at His baptism but left Him before He died.

5:7. καὶ τὸ πνεῦμα ἐστιν τὸ μαρτυροῦν, ὅτι τὸ πνεῦμα ἐστιν ἡ ἀλήθεια, "And it is the Spirit who bears witness, because the Spirit is the truth." It is here that John introduces the first of the witnesses that will occupy the remainder of this section. (The words μαρτυρέω, "to bear witness," and μαρτυρία, "witness," occur ten times in the Greek in vv. 6-11.) In general, what is meant is that the Holy Spirit bears witness concerning Jesus Christ. The participle μαρτυροῦν, "bears witness," is in the present tense, causing some to find this continuing witness in the "faith, knowledge, and confession of the congregation."[8] Some say it is the inner witness in the heart of the believer; others find the witness in the preaching of the Word.[9]

John, however, is dealing with the two events symbolized by water and blood, namely, with the baptism and the death of Jesus Christ. It would be most logical, therefore, to look for the witness of the Spirit on one or both of these occasions. At the baptism the Spirit descended upon Jesus as a dove (Matt. 3:16), and John the Baptist later explained that this occurrence was the evidence that identified Jesus as the Messiah (John 1:31-33). He concluded, "And I have seen, have borne witness that this is the Son of God" (v. 34). The Holy Spirit, then, at Jesus' baptism was a witness to the deity and the messiahship of Jesus, and through the record of the gospels the Spirit continues to bear witness to Jesus' identity. Jesus, Himself, said that this was the work of the Spirit (John 15:26). In reference to the present tense μαρτυροῦν, "bears wit-

---

7. Law, p. 404; F. F. Bruce, *The Epistles of John*, p. 131, n. 5.
8. Rudolf Bultmann, *The Johannine Epistles*, Hermeneia, p. 80.
9. Marshall, p. 234.

ness," notice the present tense μαρτυροῦντες in verse 8 referring not only to the Spirit but also to the water and blood. What qualifies the Spirit to be a trustworthy witness is that "the Spirit is the truth." It is not enough to explain, as Marshall does, that the Spirit is able to bear witness.[10] The expression τὸ πνεῦμά ἐστιν ἡ ἀλήθεια is a very explicit declaration grammatically identifying the Spirit and the truth as one and the same. When both the subject and the predicate nominative in a copulative sentence have the article the two are usually interchangable.[11] To understand the extent to which this rule applies, it is helpful to look at a parallel in John 14:6 where Jesus declares, "I am the way, and the truth, and the life." "Jesus is the very embodiment of the truth. He is the truth in person."[12] In the same way it may be said that the Holy Spirit is the truth in person or the truth personified, which is much stronger than saying that He is truthful. He is the very source of truth. As such He is supremely qualified to bear witness concerning Jesus.

5:8. ὅτι τρεῖς εἰσιν οἱ μαρτυροῦντες, τὸ πνεῦμα καὶ τὸ ὕδωρ καὶ τὸ αἷμα, "For there are three that bear witness, the Spirit and the water and the blood." The use of the conjunction ὅτι, "because," is not easily discerned. Westcott says that it seems to give the reason for the assertion of verse 5 that Jesus is the Son of God.[13] The problem with this view is that verse 5 is too far back for the connection to be readily apparent to the reader. Westcott, then, concludes that the conjunction may simply explain the addition of the Spirit (v. 7) to the water and the blood (v. 6).[14] Law says that ὅτι is a loosely used connective, and he translates the clause "for in fact, the witnesses are three in number."[15] He thinks that although the water and blood were not at first referred to as witnesses, John has intended to do so, and he now recognizes that there are three witnesses—a significant number for a Jew, as shall be seen. It is certain that the conjunction is loosely used to introduce the noteworthy fact that there are three witnesses, but to attempt to penetrate John's exact train of

---

10. Ibid., p. 234, n. 12.
11. H. E. Dana and Julius R. Mantey, *A Manual Grammar of the Greek New Testament,* p. 149.
12. William Hendriksen, *The Gospel of John,* The New Testament Commentary, p. 268.
13. Westcott, p. 184.
14. Ibid.
15. Law, p. 119, note 1.

thought any further is mere guesswork.

The declaration that there are three witnesses is the main point of verse 8. Its significance must be seen in the light of Jewish jurisprudence, which stems from the Mosaic law. Two or three witnesses were required to convict a person of a crime (Deut. 17:6; 19:15; Matt. 18:16). John is here declaring that there is an adequate number of witnesses to support his assertion that Jesus is the Son of God (v. 5).

The fact that the witnesses are not referred to as οἱ μάρτυρες, "the witnesses," but as οἱ μαρτυροῦντες, "the ones bearing witness," indicates that they are at present actively engaged in witness bearing rather than standing by ready to bear witness. It is also significant that, even though the three nouns, πνεῦμα, "spirit," ὕδωρ, "water," and αἷμα, "blood," are neuter in gender, the participle μαρτυροῦντες, "bearing witness," is masculine. This demonstrates that John viewed all three witnesses as personal, the Holy Spirit as literally personal and the water and blood as personified.

There have been two major interpretations of the meaning of water and blood in verse 8. A number of scholars have argued that, whereas these two elements are to be taken historically in verse 6 to refer to Christ's baptism and death, they are to be understood sacramentally in verse 8 to refer to baptism and the Lord's supper.[16] Most of those who hold this position point out that the present tense participle μαρτυροῦντες demands a currently existing witness, which is impossible if the water and blood are past historical occurrences.

Other scholars argue that water and blood both in verse 6 and verse 8 refer to the historical events of Christ's baptism and His death.[17] It would seem that to find in verse 8 a change of meaning from verse 6 is rather arbitrary since there is nothing in the context that indicates that John has changed the use of the two terms water and blood. (The argument that the present tense participle μαρτυροῦντες demands a change will be discussed below.) Blood is also nowhere used in Scripture as a designation for the Lord's supper. In fact, the failure to mention Christ's body

---

16. Bultmann, p. 80; C. H. Dodd, *The Johannine Epistles*, Moffatt New Testament Commentary, pp. 130-31; J. L. Houlden, *A Commentary on the Johannine Epistles*, Black's New Testament Commentaries, p. 129; Law, p. 121; Gerhard Kittel, ed., *Theological Dictionary of the New Testament*, 1964-76, s.v. "μάρτυς κτλ.," by H. Strathmann, 4:498.
17. Brooke, p. 137; Bruce, p. 121; Marshall, p. 238.

along with the blood is a significant argument against the sacramental view. Finally, it is difficult to see in what sense baptism and the Lord's supper testify to the fact that Jesus is the incarnate Son of God. The explicit explanations of the Lord's supper given by Jesus and Paul do not stress the incarnation of deity (Matt. 26:26-29 and parallels; 1 Cor. 11:25-26).

Since the water and blood in verse 6 symbolize Christ's baptism and death, it is most reasonable that they should have the same significance in verse 8. Thus, John refers to three historical facts, all of which bear witness to the truth that Jesus is the incarnate Son of God. (1) The Holy Spirit descended on Jesus as a dove at the baptism, and John the Baptist later explained that it was this coming of the Spirit that proved to him that Jesus is the Son of God (John 1:32-34). This is the testimony of the Spirit. (2) The testimony of the baptism (water) may well be the voice from heaven that said, "This is My beloved Son, in whom I am well-pleased" (Matt. 3:17). (3) The testimony of the death of Christ (blood) may be the obvious evidence of His humanity. As the baptism spoke of Jesus' deity, the crucifixion revealed Christ's humanity. Only a flesh-and-blood human being could shed his blood and die on a cross. The three witnesses, then, combine their testimonies to declare the truth that Jesus is the incarnate Son of God.

The present tense participle, μαρτυροῦντες, "bearing witness," speaks of a continuing witness still going on when John wrote this epistle, and, it may be assumed, still occurring today. Every time the historical record of Christ's baptism and death is read or proclaimed, these three witnesses testify to the truth of the incarnation of God's Son. Marshall points out that at the time of the writing of Hebrews, Abel, although dead, was still speaking (Heb. 11:4).[18] In this sense many biblical characters, though long dead, continue to speak to us today from the pages of Scripture.

καὶ οἱ τρεῖς εἰς τὸ ἕν εἰσιν, "and the three are in agreement." Translated literally, this clause says, "And the three are unto the one." Numerous versions have translated this phrase as expressing agreement (NASB, RSV, NEB, NIV, TEV). John may be referring to the necessity under the Old Testament legal system for the witnesses to agree (Deut. 17:6) before a conviction could take place. At the trial of Jesus the witnesses did not agree (Mark 14:56, 59), but God's witnesses concerning the fact of the incarnation do agree.

18. Marshall, p. 238.

A comparison of modern versions of the New Testament with the KJV reveals that a substantial portion of verse 7 or verse 8 (depending on the verse division) has not been included in more recent translations. In fact some versions, such as ASV, NASB, RSV, TEV, NEB, and Williams, give no explanation of the omission. The reason, no doubt, is that the material omitted is so obviously not Johannine that its omission was thought to merit no explanation.

The KJV inclusion following the words, "three that bear record," is as follows: "in heaven, the Father, the Word, and the Holy Ghost: and these three are one. And there are three that bear witness in earth. . . ." These words do not appear in a single Greek manuscript of the New Testament prior to about 1520. The earliest Latin Vulgate manuscripts in which they are found come from about A.D. 800. The oldest appearance of the words was in a Latin work from the fourth century, known as *Liber apologeticus*. Because of a rash promise to include the questionable material if it could be found in a Greek manuscript, Erasmas reluctantly placed it in his text of the New Testament. There is no doubt but that the Greek manuscript shown to Erasmus was prepared for the occasion. The Erasmus text, with some alterations, became the basis for the Textus Receptus, from which the KJV was translated.[19]

5:9. εἰ τὴν μαρτυρίαν τῶν ἀνθρώπων λαμβάνομεν, ἡ μαρτυρία τοῦ θεοῦ μείζων ἐστίν, "If we receive the witness of men, the witness of God is greater." The simple conditional clause found in this verse does not express any doubt or uncertainty. Instead, εἰ, "if," with the indicative mood λαμβάνομεν, "we receive," assumes the condition to be a fact. The NIV has rendered the clause, "We accept man's testimony." The verb λαμβάνομεν is a gnomic present tense speaking of a fact that is generally true. It is standard practice to accept human testimony. In this context the reference is probably to the Jewish practice of accepting testimony from two or three witnesses when they agree. See on verse 8. The article before ἀνθρώπων is used to refer to mankind in general.

John argues from the lesser to the greater. If man's testimony (the lesser) is received; how much more should God's testimony (the greater) be received? The conditional sentence that makes up verse 9 is somewhat irregular. Whereas John could have been

---

19. The above material concerning 1 John 5:7-8 is based on Bruce M. Metzger, *The Text of the New Testament,* pp. 101-2.

expected to conclude from the conditional clause that one can surely accept God's testimony, instead he declares that God's testimony is greater. It has been suggested that this means that his testimony is of greater significance and of greater trustworthiness.[20] However, the apostle's point does not concern the significance of the testimony. The fact that one would expect this conditional sentence to say something like, "Since we receive (that is, trust) human testimony, we surely will receive (trust) God's testimony," indicates that trustworthiness is the point John is making. God's testimony, then, is of greater trustworthiness than that of men.

ὅτι αὕτη ἐστὶν ἡ μαρτυρία τοῦ θεοῦ, ὅτι μεμαρτύρηκεν περὶ τοῦ υἱοῦ αὐτοῦ, "for the witness of God is this, that He has borne witness concerning His Son." The first ὅτι is clearly explanatory and should be translated either "because" (NIV) or "for" (NASB). What follows serves to explain why God's testimony is of greater trustworthiness. The first reason is that it is the testimony of God, not of mere men. Αὕτη, "this," has been thought to look forward to the ὅτι clause (as in NASB),[21] to look backward to the three witnesses of verse 8,[22] or to look both backward and forward.[23] In regard to the last view, Westcott says, "This triple witness which has been described, and which is now defined further to be a witness of God concerning His Son: this is the final form of the witness of God."[24] It would seem that Westcott is right in this. Certainly the witness of God is the three-fold witness of Spirit, water, and blood (v. 8), as many commentators will agree.[25]

It may be argued that God's testimony is placed in the past by the perfect tense μεμαρτύρηκεν, "He has borne witness," whereas the three witnesses of verse 8 are testifying in the present. These, however, are not contradictory statements. Both are true: God testified in the past through the descent of the Spirit on Jesus as a dove, through the voice from heaven at Jesus' baptism, and through Christ's death on the cross. This is borne out by the fact that the perfect tense μεμαρτύρηκεν is probably an intensive per-

20. Marshall, p. 239, n. 30.
21. Bultmann, pp. 81-82, n. 10; Marshall, p. 239, n. 31.
22. Law, p. 404.
23. Westcott, p. 185.
24. Ibid.
25. Dodd, p. 132; Houlden, p. 132; Law, p. 404; Lenski, p. 529; Marshall, p. 240; and Stott, p. 181.

fect, stressing the continuing results of God's act of testifying. God had testified in the past, and that witness was still standing when John wrote.[26] The second ὅτι is difficult to interpret. Some have taken it to be causal, setting forth the second reason why God's testimony is greater—because He has testified concerning His Son.[27] Others have construed ὅτι as originally being ὅ, τι. This is God's testimony, that which He has testified concerning His Son.[28] Still others see the ὅτι as declarative—this is the testimony of God that He has testified concerning His Son.[29] The repetition of the causal ὅτι in the first view is unnatural. The reading ὅ, τι seems to solve the problem, but is not Johannine. The last view yields about the same meaning as the ὅ, τι view, and such a usage is not unnatural or unlike John (see John 3:19). There are, therefore, two reasons why God's testimony is of greater trustworthiness: first, the fact that it is God's testimony, not man's; second, the fact that it is God's testimony concerning His Son. Who else could give more reliable testimony concerning a person than his father? And who knows the Son of God better than God the Father?

2. THE EXPERIENTIAL WITNESS OF ETERNAL LIFE, 5:10-12

5:10. ὁ πιστεύων εἰς τὸν υἱὸν τοῦ θεοῦ ἔχει τὴν μαρτυρίαν ἐν ἑαυτῷ, "The one who believes in the Son of God has the witness in himself." John proceeds to speak of the reception of God's testimony. Whereas in 3:23 he uses the aorist tense πιστεύσωμεν, "believe," to refer to the point of initial belief, here he has the present tense πιστεύων, which depicts the continuing life of faith. Although Bultmann claims that any distinction between πιστεύω εἰς and πιστεύω ὅτι or πιστεύω with the dative case is demonstrated by this verse to be nonexistent,[30] careful examination shows the opposite to be true. Πιστεύω εἰς is found thirty-four times in the gospel of John, three times in 1 John

---

26. A. Plummer, *The Epistles of St. John*, The Cambridge Greek Testament for Schools and Colleges, p. 117.
27. Law, p. 404.
28. W. Robertson Nicoll, gen. ed., *The Expositor's Greek Testament*, s.v. "The Epistles of John," by David Smith, 5:196.
29. Brooke, p. 138; Lenski, p. 529.
30. Bultmann, p. 82, n. 12.

(twice here and once in 5:13), and nine times in other New Testament books. Thus, it is a Johannine favorite, used to express the faith of personal commitment and reliance. The first occurrence of πιστεύω in verse 10 speaks of personal trust in and commitment to the Son of God. This is not merely to believe that (ὅτι) Jesus is God's Son (see 5:5). The second πιστεύω refers to the one who does not believe God (dative case), that is, he does not believe what God said about His Son. The third use of πιστεύω speaks of not trusting the testimony of God. As Westcott and Marshall indicate, it looks beyond the testimony to the object of the testimony and speaks of failure to trust Him.[31]

The testimony (τὴν μαρτυρίαν) of verse 10 should be viewed in its contextual relation to verses 8-9. Consequently, it must be the testimony of God (ἡ μαρτυρία τοῦ θεοῦ) spoken of in verse 9, and the testimony of verse 9 must refer back to the three who testify (μαρτυροῦντες) in verse 8. Thus the testimony the believer has "in himself" is the testimony of the three witnesses (v. 8). According to Westcott, "The witness is not of external testimony only, but internal also. . . . The witness of Spirit and water and blood becomes an inner conviction of life and cleansing and redemption."[32]

John says that the believer "has the witness in himself" (ἐν ἑαυτῷ). Manuscripts differ as to the correct form of the pronoun (ℵ ψ: ἑαυτῷ; A B P: αυτω; K: αὐτῷ), but no matter which is correct, the context demands the reflexive translation "himself."

ὁ μὴ πιστεύων τῷ θεῷ ψεύστην πεποίηκεν αὐτόν, "the one who does not believe God has made Him a liar." Failure to believe in (trust) the Son of God is also failure to believe what God has said concerning His Son. Πιστεύω with the dative here refers to the "acceptance of the statement rather than surrender to the person."[33]

By using the perfect tense πεποίηκεν instead of the present or aorist, John has rendered his statement more forceful. Not only did the unbeliever make God a liar in the past, but God continues to be a liar in the unbeliever's mind. (In the perfect tense, the results of a past completed act continue to the time of writing.) See on 1:10, where it is made clear that such an expression must mean "to make God out to be a liar."

31. Westcott, p. 187; Marshall, p. 241, n. 40.
32. Westcott, p. 186.
33. Brooke, p. 139.

ὅτι οὐ πεπίστευκεν εἰς τὴν μαρτυρίαν ἣν μεμαρτύρηκεν ὁ θεὸς περὶ τοῦ υἱοῦ αὐτοῦ, "because he has not believed in the witness that God has borne concerning His Son." The ὅτι clause explains how it is that the unbeliever makes God out to be a liar. By his disbelief, he pointedly says that God's testimony concerning His Son is a lie. Here again the testimony (τὴν μαρτυρίαν) that God has borne must be the testimony referred to in verse 9. The same words are repeated for clarity and emphasis (τὴν μαρτυρίαν, "the witness," and μεμαρτύρηκεν . . . περὶ τοῦ υἱοῦ αὐτοῦ, "[He] has borne concerning His Son"). On the perfect tense μεμαρτύρηκεν, see on verse 9.

5:11. καὶ αὕτη ἐστὶν ἡ μαρτυρία, ὅτι ζωὴν αἰώνιον ἔδωκεν ἡμῖν ὁ θεός, "And the witness is this, that God has given us eternal life." The author ties this statement to the preceding one by the copulative conjunction καὶ, "and." The relationship of the two statements is also confirmed by the continued discussion of "the testimony" (ἡ μαρτυρία), a key term in both verse 9 and verse 10. The demonstrative pronoun αὕτη, "this," as is often the case, clearly points forward to the ὅτι clause. Thus, John declares that the testimony the believer has "in himself" (v. 10) is God's gift of eternal life. (On the word αἰώνιον, "eternal," see on 1:2.) The position of the term ζωὴν αἰώνιον at the beginning of the clause shows the author's intent to emphasize life as being the key concept in the clause. It is also noteworthy that the expression is anarthrous, thus stressing the quality of life, rather than identifying the life as distinct from other forms of life or pointing out that Person who is the source of life (see 1:2), as the article would do.

The aorist tense, indicative mood verb ἔδωκεν, "has given," describes an act at a point in past time. It could be construed as referring to God's act on Calvary by which He made eternal life available or to the historical fact that Christ came to secure eternal life for us.[34] On the other hand, the aorist tense may point to the time of the reception of eternal life.[35] The latter view is preferable, because John is speaking of the possession of life, as verse 12 indicates. He does not have in mind merely the availability of life, but the actual reception of it.

---

34. Brooke, p. 140; A. T. Robertson, *Word Pictures in the New Testament*, 6:242; Stott, p. 183; Westcott, p. 187.
35. Stott, p. 183.

καὶ αὕτη ἡ ζωὴ ἐν τῷ υἱῷ αὐτοῦ ἐστιν, "and this life is in His Son." This clause should not be treated as an addendum. It is, as Brooke points out, part of the witness.[36] What is significant is the fact that God has given eternal life in His Son. That this life is received through Christ testifies to the reality of His deity and His humanity—being man, He could die for man; being God, His sacrifice was of infinite value.

5:12. ὁ ἔχων τὸν υἱὸν ἔχει τὴν ζωήν· ὁ μὴ ἔχων τὸν υἱὸν τοῦ θεοῦ τὴν ζωὴν οὐκ ἔχει, "He who has the Son has the life; he who does not have the Son of God does not have the life." It is a logical conclusion that, since eternal life is in the Son of God, "he who has the Son has the life." The expression ὁ ἔχων τὸν υἱόν, "he who has the Son," has parallels in 2:23 (τὸν πατέρα ἔχει, "has the Father") and 2 John 9 (θεὸν . . . ἔχει, "has God"; τὸν πατέρα καὶ τὸν υἱὸν ἔχει, "has both the Father and the Son"). The verb ἔχω, "to have," suggests possession in the sense of being in a vital spiritual relationship with the Father and the Son, based on the confession of the Son as the Christ (2:23).

The person who is involved in such a relationship "has the life." The verb ἔχει, "has," is in the present tense, indicating a continuing present possession of life. The article with ζωήν, "life," is an article of previous reference looking back to the words αἰώνιον ζωήν, "eternal life," in verse 11. Thus eternal life is not a possession to be experienced only in the future; it is a present possession, as Jesus indicates in John 5:24. John again employs antithetical parallelism (cf. 2:23; 4:7-8), first stating the truth positively, then negatively, to emphasize his point. It will be noticed, however, that the negative restatement contains some variation. Whereas the positive statement simply has τὸν υἱόν, "the son," the negative has τὸν υἱὸν τοῦ θεοῦ, "the Son of God," thus spelling out clearly who is being rejected. In addition, the negative statement places the words τὴν ζωήν, "the life," before the verb, therefore emphasizing that it is *the* life that the person mentioned does not have. The negative form of the statement was no doubt directed against the Gnostics, who denied that Jesus is the Son of God.

The evident purpose of verse 12 is to make it clear that eternal life comes from the Son of God and that the one who has the Son of God has eternal life as the witness within him to the reality of the incarnation.

---

36. Brooke, p. 141.

378   The Letters of John the Apostle

THEOLOGICAL COMMENTARY (5:6-12)

A. INTRODUCTORY COMMENTS

This section contains the third and last presentation of the Christological test. The first Christological passage (2:18-28) centers on the confession that Jesus is the Christ (see on 2:22-23). The second statement of the Christological test appears in 4:1-6. It concerns the confession that Jesus Christ has come in the flesh (see on 4:2-3).

This final Christological section is noticeably different from the two previous ones. It is not that a different Christology is set forth. The Christology is the same, but the manner of presentation is uniquely different. John employs the concept of legal testimony as the structure for this final Christological section. He cites three objective historical witnesses followed by one subjective experiential witness. These four all offer testimony concerning the reality of the incarnation of Jesus Christ, God's Son. By citing three witnesses John fulfills the Old Testament requirement that in a legal case at least two or three witnesses are necessary.

Another unique feature of this Christological section is the rather cryptic use of the water and the blood. Even the reference to the testimony of the Spirit is somewhat obscure.

B. THE HISTORICAL BACKGROUND

As shown in the Introduction (p. 59), there is good reason to believe that the Gnostic Cerinthus lived in Ephesus at the same time as John. Therefore, his heretical teaching would have been a very real threat to the churches of Ephesus and the surrounding area. Cerinthian Gnosticism would seem to have been the chief target of John's letter.

It is significant to notice that the distinctive element of Cerinthus's teaching seems to be the key that unlocks the most cryptic passage of the epistle (5:6). According to Irenaeus,[37] Cerinthus made a distinction between the human Jesus, who was born by ordinary human procreation, and Christ, who is a pure spiritual being, (perhaps viewed by Cerinthus as one of the aeons who eminated directly or indirectly from the Absolute God). Apparently because of the dualistic belief that matter is evil and spirit is

---

37. Irenaeus *Against Heresies* 1. 26. 3.

good, Cerinthus taught that Christ, the pure spirit, descended upon the human Jesus at His baptism. Spirit could have no more intimate relationship with matter than this somewhat superficial accompaniment. Jesus then preached concerning the Unknown Father (the Absolute God) and performed miracles. Before Jesus died, Christ left him. It was impossible that pure spirit should participate in such a physical experience as death. Thus, the baptism of Jesus was a significant part of Cerinthian teaching, but his death was without any significance.

C. THE JOHANNINE REFUTATION

Without naming his opponents or indicating that he is combating heresy, John plunges into this section of his Christological argument. His point will be made by the testimony of significant witnesses.

1. THE COINCIDENT TESTIMONY OF HISTORICAL FACTS AND THE HOLY SPIRIT, 5:6-9

This section is closely tied to the preceding verse where the transition from the discussion of the ethical test to the Christological has already begun. John is preparing to present evidence "that Jesus is the Son of God" (5:5).

In previous statements the two terms, *Christ* and *Son of God*, seem to have been used synonymously. The title *Christ* does not speak of the Jewish Messiah, but of the divine Person who was with God the Father and who became incarnate. This is John's point when he speaks of the denial that Jesus is the Christ (2:22). Jesus the man and the divine Christ are not two persons, but one. (See also 5:1). In 2:22*b*-23 the term Son is apparently synonymous with the term Christ in verse 22*a*. Again in 4:2, the confession that Jesus Christ has come in the flesh assumes that the divine Christ and the human Jesus are one person, deity incarnate. In 5:5-6 the same interchange of terms is seen. The human Jesus is the Son of God (v. 5), and this one is Jesus Christ (v. 6), that is, the human Jesus and the divine Christ in one person. It is this fact of incarnation, which is implicit in these designations, that John proceeds to demonstrate.

Jesus, who is the Son of God, the Christ, is the one who came by water and blood (v. 6). It was the incarnate Son of God who was baptized by John in the Jordan and it was the same God-man who died on the cross. By this insistence John contradicts the Gnostic Cerinthus, who taught that the aeon Christ came upon the human Jesus at his baptism and departed from him before he died. Finally, to the testimony of the water and the blood, John adds the testimony of the Holy Spirit (v. 7).

These three witnesses testify to the fact of the incarnation. The events at Jesus' baptism constitute the first witness. It was a human being who was bodily baptized in the Jordan. Immediately afterward, the voice of God the Father proclaimed that the man Jesus who had just been baptized was His Son. The blood of the cross also bore witness to the humanity of Jesus. It was a physical body that was nailed to the cross, but John also insists that it was the divine Christ who came by blood, that is, who died on the cross. In addition there was the testimony of the Holy Spirit, coming upon Jesus like a dove. That this occurrence was evidence of the incarnation is indicated in John 1:32-34. The coming of the Spirit upon Jesus identified Him to John the Baptist as the one who would baptize with the Holy Spirit (v. 33), and John apparently refers to the same event when he adds, "And I have seen, and have borne witness that this is the Son of God" (v. 34).

These three witnesses testified at Jesus' baptism and at His death to the reality of the incarnation, and they continue to bear witness, as John indicates by the use of the present tense participle, οἱ μαρτυροῦντες, "who are bearing witness" (1 John 5:8). This continued testimony is not the inner testimony of the Holy Spirit. Instead it is the ever-present testimony of the Scripture record of the baptism and the death of Christ.

2. THE INTERNAL TESTIMONY OF ETERNAL LIFE, 5:10-12

In addition to the three witnesses of verse 8, John adds a fourth and different kind of witness whose testimony is experienced only by believers. The person who believes the threefold historical testimony in turn receives the internal testimony of eternal life. Thus, the internal testimony serves to confirm experientially the threefold historical testimony.

That the believer is the recipient of an internal testimony is not merely a matter of subjective opinion. Ramm says concerning the witness of the Spirit, "It is intensely personal without being subjectivistic or individualistic."[38] The New Testament clearly indicates

---

38. Bernard Ramm, *The Witness of the Spirit*, p. 51.

that there is a valid internal witness. Indeed John in this epistle says there is a mutual indwelling with God "because He has given us of His Spirit" (4:13). And Paul declares that "the Spirit Himself bears witness with our spirit that we are children of God" (Rom. 8:16). Again in 2 Corinthians 1:22, Paul refers to the Holy Spirit whom God has placed in our hearts as a pledge. (See also 2 Cor. 5:5; Eph. 1:14.) Concerning Paul's statement in Galatians 4:6, "God has sent forth the Spirit of His Son into our hearts, crying, 'Abba! Father!' " Stevens says, "It is evident that the meaning is: The Spirit inspires in the heart the conviction of sonship which is expressed in the cry, 'Abba, Father'."³⁹

Closely related to the inner witness of the Holy Spirit is the inner witness of eternal life. In fact, the Spirit is the giver of life and in a sense it is true that the witness of eternal life is the witness of the Spirit.⁴⁰

It remains to explain how the subjective experience of eternal life testifies concerning the truth of the incarnation. Obviously it is not by propositional testimony. Rather, the witness is experiential in nature. When a person places his faith in the incarnate Christ, he experiences eternal life with all that such an experience involves (God's Spirit bearing witness with his spirit). This is what John means when he writes, "The one who believes in the Son of God has the witness in himself" (1 John 5:10). Again in 5:11, John says the same thing. The witness is eternal life, and this life is in God's Son; that is, when the Son is received eternal life is experienced. Bultmann says, "The event of faith is the witness. . . . This is confirmed by the remarkable definition of μαρτυρία ('testimony') given in v. 11."⁴¹

D. PRESENT-DAY APPLICATION

It is true that we are not confronted with religious teachers who assert that the divine Christ came upon the human Jesus at the beginning of his ministry and departed from him before his death. However, Cerinthus does have his counterparts today in numerous cults and in various forms of liberal theology. Basic to Cerinthian doctrine was the denial of the union of the human and divine natures in one person, the God-man. Anyone who denies this union today is a counterpart of Cerinthus regardless of how he may differ in incidentals from the first-century heretic.

39. George B. Stevens, *The Theology of the New Testament*, p. 441.
40. Ramm, pp. 59-60.
41. Bultmann, p. 82.

What makes the Cerinthian denial so serious is that it of necessity deprives the sinner of a Savior. The Savior must be both humanity and deity or it is impossible for Him to save anyone from sin's condemnation. He must be a full and complete human being if He is to be qualified to take our place and die in our stead. Only man can die for man's sin. On the other hand, the Savior must be full deity or His death would be sufficient to pay for the sins of but one condemned sinner. Only the death of the Son of God could be of such limitless value that it could be a propitiation for the sins of the whole world (2:2).

There can be no salvation in the message of anyone who denies the incarnation of God's Son. John's witnesses, cited to support the truth of the incarnation, are still weighty today. The voice of God from heaven declaring the human Jesus to be His Son, the coming of the Spirit upon Christ at His baptism, the death of the man Jesus on the cross, the inner experience of life upon acceptance of the incarnate Son of God—these combine to confirm the truth of the incarnation. And all of these facts continue to testify today from the pages of Holy Scripture.

PARAPHRASTIC COMMENTARY (5:6-12)

(6) This Jesus, the Son of God, is the one who was demonstrated at His baptism and at His death to be God incarnate—at one and the same time the human Jesus and the divine Christ. This demonstration occurred not only when He was baptized, but *both* when He was baptized *and* when He shed His blood on the cross. (7) And the Holy Spirit, descending on Jesus as a dove, also is a witness to the incarnation because the Spirit is altogether true. (8) So there are three who, through the years, are witnesses to the incarnation: The Holy Spirit, Christ's baptism in water, and the shedding of His blood on the cross. And these three witnesses agree in the testimony they offer. (9) It is customary in legal cases to accept human testimony. The testimony of God, however, is more trustworthy than human testimony because it comes from God and also because it concerns His own Son. (10) The one who is trusting in God's Son also has an internal witness. The one who is not trusting in God is accusing Him of lying, because he has rejected the testimony that God has borne concerning His Son. (11) Now the internal witness is this: the fact that God has given us eternal life and that this life resides in the Son. (12) The one who has a vital spiritual relationship with the Son has this life now; the one who does not have such a relationship does not have eternal life.

STRUCTURAL COMMENTARY (5:6-12)[42]

B. The Christological test, 5:6-12
  1. The coincident witness of historical facts and the Holy Spirit, 5:6-9
     a. The historical facts, 5:6
        (1) The water of baptism
        (2) The blood of the cross
     b. The Holy Spirit, 5:7
        (1) His activity—bearing witness
        (2) His nature—the truth
     c. The agreement of the three witnesses, 5:8
     d. The superior trustworthiness of the testimony of God, 5:9
  2. The experiential witness of eternal life, 5:10-12
     a. Belief results in a fourth witness—an internal one, 5:10a
     b. Unbelief makes God out to be a liar, 5:10b
     c. The internal witness is eternal life through God's Son, 5:11-12
        (1) The identification of the witness, 5:11a
        (2) The source of life, 5:11b
        (3) The recipient of life, 5:12
           (a) Stated positively, 5:12a
           (b) Stated negatively, 5:12b

---

42. For previous section of the outline see pp. 362-63.

15

Conclusion: Great Certainties of the Christian Life, 5:13-21

This last section of the epistle begins with a summary statement of purpose (v. 13) that is markedly similar to the expressed purpose of the fourth gospel (20:31). The main difference lies in the fact that the gospel's purpose is evangelistic ("that you may believe . . . and . . . have life in His name") whereas the epistle's purpose is edificatory ("that you may know that you have eternal life"). While the gospel's aim is to lead to salvation, the epistle's aim is to give assurance to those who already have been saved.

EXEGETICAL COMMENTARY (5:13-21)

A. THE CERTAINTY OF ETERNAL LIFE, 5:13

5:13. ταῦτα ἔγραψα ὑμῖν ἵνα εἰδῆτε ὅτι ζωὴν ἔχετε αἰώνιον, τοῖς πιστεύουσιν εἰς τὸ ὄνομα τοῦ υἱοῦ τοῦ θεοῦ, "These things I have written to you who believe in the name of the Son of God, in order that you may know that you have eternal life." The antecedent of ταῦτα has been variously identified. Some have viewed the pronoun as referring to the content of the verses immediately preceding (vv. 1-12).[1] Brooke says that the explana-

---

1. A. E. Brooke, *A Critical and Exegetical Commentary on the Johannine Epistles* (Reprinted., 1964) The International Critical Commentary, p. 142; A. T. Robertson, *Word Pictures in the New Testament* 6:242.

Conclusion: Great Certainties of the Christian Life 385

tion that the readers are those who believe in the name of the Son of God "makes the reference to the whole of this section most certain."[2] It is obvious that verse 13 explicitly relates to verses 11-12. Both passages speak of having eternal life, employing the same terms (ἔχω, αἰώνιον, ζωήν), and both refer to the Son of God. There is no doubt but that verse 13 looks back at least to verses 11-12. Others have viewed verse 13 as referring to the whole book.[3] There are several reasons this view is more plausible. Perhaps most important is the obvious parallel that exists between verse 13 and John 20:31. Since it is certain that the latter verse refers to the whole book, it seems most probable that 1 John 5:13 likewise looks back to the whole epistle. Again, the content of the whole of 1 John is clearly designed to provide grounds for the assurance of salvation. The various tests (walking in the light, 1:7; obedience, 2:3-5; love for fellow believers, 2:9-11; 3:14-17; belief in God's incarnate Son, 2:22-23; 4:1-3; 5:1, 5; practicing righteousness, 2:29—3:10a) not only serve to reveal false teachers, but they also identify the children of God. Finally, there is a parallelism between 1:4 and 5:13. In 1:4 John uses the present tense γράφομεν, "we are writing," to describe his task in its beginning, whereas in 5:13 he employs the aorist indicative (ἔγραψα, "I have written") to look back on the task he has completed. Both verses are complementary statements of purpose. If his readers become assured that they have eternal life, John will possess fulness of joy.

It is probably best to view verse 13, on the one hand, as being most closely related to 5:1-12, but, on the other hand, as declaring the purpose of the letter as a whole. Law strikes a commendable balance when he says, "These words accurately define the governing aim of the whole Epistle. Contextually, however, they refer to the contents of 5:6-12, and most directly to 5:11, 12."[4]

---

2. Brooke, p. 142.
3. A. Plummer, *The Epistles of St. John*, The Cambridge Greek Testament for Schools and Colleges, p. 120; B. F. Westcott, *The Epistles of John*, p. 188; C. H. Dodd, *The Johannine Epistles*, The Moffatt New Testament Commentary, p. 133; W. Robertson Nicoll, gen. ed., *The Expositor's Greek Testament*, s.v. "The Epistles of John," by David Smith, 5:197; Henry Alford, *The Greek Testament*, 4:508; Rudolf Bultmann, *The Johannine Epistles*, Hermeneia, p. 83; John R. W. Stott, *The Epistles of John*, Tyndale New Testament Commentaries, p. 184; I. Howard Marshall, *The Epistles of John*, The New International Commentary on the New Testament, p. 243, n. 1.
4. Robert Law, *The Tests of Life*, p. 405.

Some have classified ἔγραψα as an epistolary aorist[5] such as John uses in 2:14, but it is much more likely that in 5:13 the verb is a culminative aorist looking back on the letter now being concluded. The NASB correctly translates it, "I have written." The author exercised a careful choice of words in his selection of εἰδῆτε (perfect subjunctive of οἶδα). It was not his intention to express the desire that his readers might come to know or might grow in knowledge, in which case he would have used γινώσκω. Instead he aimed at assured knowledge. One of the classical uses of οἶδα was "to express knowledge that is characterized by assurance, something known with certainty."[6] This use is clearly seen in Romans 8:28, which could be paraphrased, "And we are sure. . . ."

On ζωὴν αἰώνιον, "eternal life," see on 1:2. As in 5:12, this life is a present possession, not merely a gift to be received in the future.

The construction of the verse is somewhat involved in that the readers, who are referred to in the first part of the verse (ὑμῖν, "you") are again more explicitly identified in the last part of the verse (τοῖς πιστεύουσιν, "who believe"). A very literal translation would read, "These things I have written to you in order that you may know that you have eternal life—you who believe in the name of the Son of God." Because of the seeming awkwardness of the text, several variant readings arose. Some manuscripts (K L P and most minuscules) place the participial phrase (τοῖς πιστεύουσιν . . . "who believe . . .") immediately following ὑμῖν, "you." This seems to have been an attempt to bridge the gap between ὑμῖν, "you," and the explanatory phrase. The same manuscripts add a second purpose clause to the verse, καὶ ἵνα πιστεύητε εἰς τὸ ὄνομα τοῦ υἱοῦ τοῦ θεοῦ, "and in order that you may believe in the name of the Son of God" (as in KJV). This addition seems to have been the result of the influence of John 20:31. In addition, it should be pointed out that the text on which the NASB translation of this verse is based is that found in the original of א, in B, and in the Syriac version.

It is evident that John's reason for placing the τοῖς πιστεύουσιν phrase last was for emphasis (See also John 1:12.) His stress was on

---

5. Ibid.; Plummer, p. 120.
6. Richard N. Longenecker and Merrill C. Tenney, eds., *New Dimensions in New Testament Study*, 'Οἶδα' and 'Γινώσκω' in the Pauline Epistles," by Donald W. Burdick, p. 347.

the fact that it was believers he had in mind, and, more particularly, in view of the Gnostic threat, it was believers in the Son of God. Notice that the identification of Christ as Son occurs seven times in verses 5-12. On the expression πιστεύουσιν εἰς, "believe in," see on 5:10, and on τὸ ὄνομα, "the name," see on 2:12 and 3:23.

B. THE CERTAINTY OF ANSWERED PRAYER, 5:14-17

5:14. καὶ αὕτη ἐστὶν ἡ παρρησία ἣν ἔχομεν πρὸς αὐτόν ὅτι ἐάν τι αἰτώμεθα κατὰ τὸ θέλημα αὐτοῦ ἀκούει ἡμῶν, "And this is the confidence which we have before Him, that, if we ask anything according to His will, He hears us." The conjunction with which this verse begins (καί "and") indicates that there is a connection between verses 13 and 14. Since the believer is certain that he has eternal life, he can also have confidence in prayer. The one naturally flows from the other. In keeping with the predominant pattern in John, the pronoun αὕτη, "this," refers forward to the ὅτι clause. What the author says, to put it in more straightforward language, is "We are confident that, if we ask anything according to His will, He hears us."

On παρρησία, see on 2:28. The original meaning of this word ("freedom of speech") is most fitting in this context.[7] The word is parallel to οἴδαμεν, "we know," in verse 13. Both speak of the believer's assurance. The NASB translates πρός as meaning "before" but adds the marginal explanation that the word literally means *toward*. Basically the preposition means *facing*[8] and speaks of the "active intercourse and fellowship" in which confidence is developed.[9] The pronoun αὐτόν, "Him," may refer to God the Father or to His Son, but because these two are one, John's precise intention may not be too significant. However, most would apply it to God the Father,[10] probably because prayer is more normally addressed to the Father than to the Son.

Most commentators admit that the difference between the active and middle voices of αἰτέω, "ask," is not to be unduly emphasized. Westcott adds that the middle voice suggests a per-

---
7. Brooke, p. 143; F. F. Bruce, *The Epistles of John*, p. 123.
8. H. E. Dana and Julius R. Mantey, *A Manual Grammar of the Greek New Testament*, p. 110.
9. Brooke, p. 143; also see Robertson, 6:242. Stott, p. 185.
10. Alford, p. 508; Bultmann, p. 85; Marshall, p. 244; Westcott, p. 189; and translated thus by the NIV.

sonal reference whereas the active leaves the matter open.[11] Lenski insists that the middle voice speaks of possessing the right to ask, as it does in business dealings.[12] However, Bauer's lexicon declares that there is no real distinction between the active and the middle, and James 4:2-3 is pointed out as an example of interchangeable use.[13] Notice also the use of both middle and active voices in verse 15.

The verb ἀκούει is to be understood in the pregnant sense of hearing favorably, a usage not found outside John (9:31; 11:41-42).[14] Robertson's suggestion that, whereas the accusative case after ἀκούω accents "the intellectual apprehension of the sound," the genitive case "calls attention to the sound of the voice without accenting the sense"[15] does not seem to apply in this instance. God surely understands the meaning of our requests.

5:15. καὶ ἐὰν οἴδαμεν ὅτι ἀκούει ἡμῶν ὃ ἐὰν αἰτώμεθα, "And if we know that He hears us in whatever we ask." The conjunction καὶ, "and," continues the discussion of the certainty of answered prayer. It is followed by a construction somewhat unusual in the New Testament, namely, ἐάν, "if," with the indicative mood (cf. 1 Thess. 3:8). The more usual construction would be ἐάν with the subjunctive mood in a future more probable conditional sentence or εἰ, "if," with the indicative in a simple conditional sentence where the condition is viewed as fulfilled. In the papyri, however, ἐάν occurs in a number of passages with the indicative.[16] Robertson identifies the use in verse 15 as a first class condition (assumed to be true) even though ἐάν is used rather than εἰ.[17] Ernest Burton also says that the construction here was used "apparently to express a simple present supposition."[18] On the use of οἴδαμεν, "we know," see on 5:13. John speaks of full assurance that God hears prayer, an assurance that is based on the

---

11. Westcott, pp. 189-90.
12. R. C. H. Lenski, *The Interpretation of the Epistles of St. Peter, St. John, and St. Jude*, p. 533.
13. William F. Arndt and F. Wilbur Gingrich, trans. and eds., *A Greek-English Lexicon of the New Testament*, by Walter Bauer, p. 25.
14. Westcott, p. 190; Stott, p. 186.
15. A. T. Robertson, *A Grammar of the Greek New Testament in the Light of Historical Research*, p. 506.
16. Ibid., p. 1009-1010; F. Blass and A. Debrunner, *A Greek Grammar of the New Testament*, (3d English ed. rev.), sec. 372 (1) (a).
17. Robertson, *Word Pictures*, 6:243.
18. Ernest Dewitt Burton, *Syntax of Moods and Tenses in New Testament Greek*, sec. 247.

fact that what believers request is in accordance with His will. The conjunction ἐάν, which normally means "if," is used in the second instance instead of the particle ἄν. It adds indefiniteness to the relative pronoun, ὅ, "that which," with the result that the combination of the two terms means "whatever." On the interchangeable use of the active and middle voices of αἰτέω, "ask," see on verse 14.

οἴδαμεν ὅτι ἔχομεν τὰ αἰτήματα ἃ ᾐτήκαμεν ἀπ' αὐτοῦ, "we know that we have the requests which we have asked from Him." It might have been expected that γινώσκω, "know," would have been used here, since the knowledge that one receives what is asked for is drawn from the fact that God hears favorably when requests are made according to His will. Knowledge arrived at by an intermediate means such as observation was normally expressed in Classical Greek by γινώσκω. However, it would seem that John used οἶδα here to express assurance, a common function of this verb.

The present tense ἔχομεν, "we have," is not to be construed as a futuristic use of the present tense. Rather, it is a regular use of the present to indicate that there is a sense in which, at the moment of prayer, that which is asked for is received. Brooke explains, "In the certainty of anticipation there is a kind of possession of that which has been granted.... The things asked for ... are in a sense already ours."[19] The use of the active voice ᾐτήκαμεν, "we have asked," is proof that John is here using the active and middle voices of αἰτέω interchangeably.

5:16. Ἐάν τις ἴδῃ τὸν ἀδελφὸν αὐτοῦ ἁμαρτάνοντα ἁμαρτίαν μὴ πρὸς θάνατον, "If any one sees his brother committing a sin not leading to death." This is the protasis of a more probable future condition, which expresses a possibility that could involve any believer, as τὶς, "any one," indicates. Τὸν ἀδελφόν αὐτοῦ ("his brother") makes it clear that both the one who sees and the one who is seen are Christians. It is to be noted that, although the person sinning is a believer, his act is described with a present tense participle, referring to its continuing nature. In other passages it is denied that believers engage in a continuing practice of sin. (See Theological Commentary on 5:13-21 for the explanation of this usage.)

The anarthrous noun ἁμαρτίαν has been interpreted either as a specific sin the believer is committing or as the kind of sin that

---

19. Brooke, p. 144.

does not lead to death. Both views are true. The sin being committed is specific enough for others to see (ἴδῃ) and identify, and thus it can rightly be referred to as "a sin." On the other hand, inasmuch as the absence of the article stresses quality, the sin is viewed by John as a particular kind of sin—one of such a nature that it will not result in death. The preposition πρός means "leading to" or "moving in the direction of." It does not speak of a finally determined outcome. A parallel usage appears in John 11:4, which Bauer translates, "this disease is not of the kind that will lead to death."[20] It may be assumed that the use of the negative μή rather than οὐ makes the negation tentative rather than sure. However, the μή is no doubt used because it is related to the participle ἁμαρτάνοντα, "sinning," which grammatically requires μή. This is confirmed by the appearance of οὐ in verse 17.

αἰτήσει, καὶ δώσει αὐτῷ ζωήν, τοῖς ἁμαρτάνουσιν μὴ πρὸς θάνατον, "he shall ask and God will for him give life to those who commit sin not leading to death." Αἰτήσει may be viewed as a cohortative future indicative, functioning as a mild command to ask;[21] or it could be a statement of fact assuming that the one who sees his brother sinning will ask.[22]

The NASB translates δώσει as "*God* will . . . give," printing the word *God* in italics. It is debatable whether the subject of δώσει is the praying brother or God. Some point out that in the context of prayer God is always the Giver and Christians are the suppliants, and therefore the word "God" must be supplied as subject. Others, however, point to the two parallel verbs αἰτήσει and δώσει, "he shall ask" and "he shall give," neither of which has an explictly stated subject. It would seem that, if the author had intended that the second verb have a different subject than the first, it would have been necessary to state that subject explicitly. Therefore, since he did not do this, the subject of both verbs should be understood to be the praying brother:[23] "He shall ask and give life to him."

However, in spite of the seeming logic of this interpretation, it nevertheless appears to be better to understand God as the subject of δώσει, "will give." First, it is unnatural to speak of the one who

---

20. Arndt and Gingrich, p. 710 (III. 3. b).
21. Plummer, p. 122.
22. Brooke, p. 146, suggests that it could be either.
23. Bultmann, p. 87, also n. 16. Westcott, p. 191; Brooke, p. 146; Plummer, p. 122.

prays as the giver; God is Giver. Second, the two dative expressions, αὐτῷ, "him," and τοῖς ἁμαρτάνουσιν, "those who commit sin," are more naturally translated "God will give *him* life *for those who commit sin* not to death" (see KJV, RSV, Beck, Centenary). In changing to the plural τοῖς ἁμαρτάνουσιν, "those who commit sin," John broadens the reference to include all brothers who commit sin not leading to death. The participle ἁμαρτάνουσιν, "commit sin," is a present tense, depicting continuing action as does the singular form above. (See Theological Commentary on 5:13-21.)

ἔστιν ἁμαρτία πρὸς θάνατον· οὐ περὶ ἐκείνης λέγω ἵνα ἐρωτήσῃ, "There is a sin leading to death; I do not say that he should make request for this." On the anarthrous ἁμαρτία, "a sin," see above. On πρὸς θάνατον, also see above. The placement of οὐ περὶ ἐκείνης first in the sentence is an emphatic construction—"Concerning *that* I do not say that he should pray." Ἵνα may have been intended as a telic conjunction, in which case the sentence would be translated, "I am not speaking about that (sins, leading to death and not leading to death) *in order that* one should question or debate it."[24] But it is more reasonable to take ἵνα as nontelic, simply meaning "that" like ὅτι.

The change of verbs meaning *ask* (αἰτέω to ἐρωτάω) has occasioned some discussion. On the one hand many have seen an intended distinction. It is said that ἐρωτάω indicates a request that assumes greater intimacy than that expressed by αἰτέω.[25] Although such a distinction may seem to be present in some passages, it does not fit the sense of verse 16. There is no reason John should change to a more intimate word. Marshall is right when he says that attempts to find such a difference between the two verbs "are fanciful."[26] It is better to understand that John here has used the two verbs interchangeably.

5:17. πᾶσα ἀδικία ἁμαρτία ἐστίν, καὶ ἔστιν ἁμαρτία οὐ πρὸς θάνατον, "All unrighteousness is sin, and there is a sin not leading to death." The first clause in this verse is similar to

---

24. P. Trudinger, "Concerning Sins, Mortal and Otherwise: A Note on 1 John 5:16-17," *Biblica*, 52 (December, 1971):541-42.
25. Colin Brown, ed., *New International Dictionary of New Testament Theology*, s.v. "Prayer, Ask, Kneel, Beg, Knock," by H. Schönweiss, 2:855-56; Gerhard Kittel, ed., *Theological Dictionary of the New Testament*, 1964-76, s.v. "αἰτέω κτλ.," by Gustav Stählin, 1:192-93; Richard C. Trench, *Synonyms of the New Testament*, pp. 138-140; Westcott, p. 192.
26. Marshall, p. 246, n. 19.

3:4. By declaring that all unrighteousness is sin, John is insisting that he is in no way minimizing the serious nature of sin when he speaks of a sin that does not lead to death. His use of the word ἀδικία, "unrighteousness," shows that he is thinking of that which fails to measure up to God's objective standard. Ἁμαρτία is the most common word for sin in the New Testament. Thus, all acts that deviate from God's standard are sins. But of all the acts that are rightly classified as sins, there are some that do not lead to death, and it is for these that prayer may be made with full confidence.

It may be that John has the Gnostics of his day in view here as he insists that every departure from the right is sin. They denied that acts commonly designated as unrighteous are sins. (On the change from μὴ πρὸς θάνατον to οὐ πρὸς θάνατον, see on v. 16.)

C. THE CERTAINTY OF VICTORY OVER SIN AND THE DEVIL, 5:18

5:18. Οἴδαμεν ὅτι πᾶς ὁ γεγεννημένος ἐκ τοῦ θεοῦ οὐχ ἁμαρτάνει, "We know that no one who is born of God sins." On οἴδαμεν, "we know," see on εἰδῆτε, "you may know," verse 13. On πᾶς ὁ γεγεννημένος . . . ἁμαρτάνει see on 3:9. The only difference is the substitution of ἁμαρτάνει, "sins," for ἁμαρτίαν . . . ποιεῖ, "practices sin"—both expressions describe continued sinning.

ἀλλ' ὁ γεννηθεὶς ἐκ τοῦ θεοῦ τηρεῖ αὐτόν, καὶ ὁ πονηρὸς οὐχ ἅπτεται αὐτοῦ, "but He who was born of God keeps him and the evil one does not touch him." Emphatic contrast with the first part of this verse is indicated by the strong conjunction ἀλλ' (ἀλλά), "but." Rather than continuing the practice of sin, the child of God is securely preserved from Satan's attacks. The change from ὁ γεγεννηένος, "who is born," to ὁ γεννηθείς, "who was born," is taken by the NASB and a number of commentators[27] to indicate a change of person. The first participle, being a repetition of the expression in 3:9, is seen as designating born again believers; the second participle is viewed as referring to Christ. This is a reasonable differentiation. First, the change in tense must indicate that a difference of some kind was intended. Second, throughout 1 John when believers are designated as regenerated, John always employs the perfect participle.

---

27. Westcott, p. 194; Plummer, p. 125; Brooke, pp. 148-49; Marshall, p. 252; Stott, p. 192; Bultmann, p. 88.

Conclusion: Great Certainties of the Christian Life 393

Third, the aorist tense, used in the gnomic (timeless) sense very accurately describes Christ's eternal relationship to the Father as Son. Fourth, the concept of the believer keeping himself is not taught elsewhere in Scripture; in fact, it is quite contrary to what the Bible teaches on the subject. However, if ὁ γεννηθείς does refer to the regenerated believer, τηρεῖ αὐτόν must be translated "keeps him," or the alternate reading, τηρεῖ ἑαυτόν, "keeps himself," must be adopted. But it was precisely because of the assumption that ὁ γεννηθεὶς refers to Christ that the Editorial Committee of the United Bible Societies' *Greek New Testament* opted for the reading τηρεῖ αὐτόν, "keeps him," rather than τηρεῖ ἑαυτόν, "keeps himself."[28] The verb τηρεῖ is a progressive present describing the continued act of preserving the believer.

The presence of the article before the masculine adjective πονηρός, "evil," makes the adjective definite and suggests that the term refers to "the evil one," that is, the devil. To translate ἅπτεται as "touch," as the NASB does, is to miss the force of the word. The basic meaning of the active form ἅπτω is "fasten to" and in the middle voice, "fasten oneself to." Hence, the middle ἅπτεται means "take hold of, cling to."[29] So John declares that the evil one does not lay hold of the child of God to harm him.

D. THE CERTAINTY OF THE BELIEVER'S RELATION TO GOD, 5:19

5:19. οἴδαμεν ὅτι ἐκ τοῦ θεοῦ ἐσμεν, καὶ ὁ κόσμος ὅλος ἐν τῷ πονηρῷ κεῖται, "We know that we are of God, and the whole world lies in the power of the evil one." (On οἴδαμεν, "we know," see on v. 13; on ἐκ τοῦ θεοῦ, "of God," see on 4:1, 4.) The first relationship mentioned here is the relation of the believer to God. He has been born of God and is now His child.

The second relationship is that of the world and the devil. The word κόσμος, "world," in this passage is used in a somewhat similar sense to that found in 2:15-16 and 4:4-5. Here, however, being set in contrast to the children of God, the term must refer to people who are estranged from God. As in verse 18, τῷ πονηρῷ is a designation for the devil. The text literally declares that "the whole world lies *in* the evil one." The NASB has added the words "the power of" to help explain the enigmatic expression, "lies in

---

28. Bruce M. Metzger, *A Textual Commentary on the Greek New Testament*, p. 719.
29. H. G. Liddell and Robert Scott, *A Greek-English Lexicon*, p. 231; G. Abbott-Smith, *A Manual Greek Lexicon of the New Testament*, p. 56.

the evil one." It is obvious, because of the contrast with God's children in the first part of the verse, that, whatever else the expression means, it at least describes the relationship the world's people sustain with the evil one. Everyone is related either to God or to the devil. The word κεῖται, "lies," suggests that the world is passive and under the control of the devil. Thus, the unsaved people of the world are helpless under Satan's power.

E. THE CERTAINTY OF THE INCARNATION, 5:20

5:20. οἴδαμεν δὲ ὅτι ὁ υἱὸς τοῦ θεοῦ ἥκει, καὶ δέδωκεν ἡμῖν διάνοιαν ἵνα γινώσκωμεν τὸν ἀληθινόν, "And we know that the Son of God has come, and has given us understanding, in order that we might know Him who is true." (On οἴδαμεν see on v. 13.) In this verse John is not adding anything new to the teaching of the epistle. He has previously referred to Jesus as the Son of God (1:3; 2:22, 23; 3:23; 4:9, 10, 15; 5:5, 9-12), and he has before spoken of the incarnation of Christ (1:2; 3:5, 8; 4:2, 9, 10, 14). Here, however, he is placing emphasis for the last time in this epistle on these great truths.

The verb ἥκει is a present tense form built on a perfect stem, and thus its basic meaning is "has come." Numerous commentators treat the verb as an intensive perfect,[30] placing emphasis on existing results.[31] It is, nevertheless, doubtful that this is what John intended. Correctly understood, the intensive perfect of ἥκει would mean "he has come and as a result is now here." But instead of placing emphasis on Christ's continuing presence, John is stressing the fact that in the past He has come. The same commentators also treat δέδωκεν, "has given," as intensive, which is more possible, although even this is doubtful. The word translated "understanding" (διάνοιαν) should not be interpreted as designating knowledge or thought content. In the light of its general New Testament usage, it can only refer to the capacity to understand. Behm explains that it means that Christ has "awakened in us the mind and given our thinking the orientation to know God, to receive His revelation. . . ."[32] So it is the capacity to receive spiritual knowledge that Christ in regeneration imparts to the believer, and the purpose (ἵνα) for this enablement is "that we might know [γινώσκωμεν] Him who is true." The use of οἴδαμεν and γινώσκωμεν in the same sentence points out the difference

---

30. Dana and Mantey, p. 202.
31. Westcott, p. 195; Plummer, p. 127; Stott, p. 194.

Conclusion: Great Certainties of the Christian Life 395

between the two words. οἴδαμεν describes knowledge that is held with assurance; γινώσκω speaks of the acquisition of knowledge. So John is saying that Christ has given the ability to come to know the One who is true, and it is to be assumed that John understands that this growth in knowledge is gained by experience. Although the United Bible Societies' Third Edition text has the subjunctive γινώσκομεν (B³ K), "we might know," the manuscript evidence strongly favors the indicative γινώσκομεν (ℵ A B L P 98 99 101 180). Various explanations have been offered for the differences: (1) the original text had the subjunctive and the indicative is an error of hearing on the part of an early scribe (ω was pronounced like ο); (2) the original text contained the indicative and a scribe changed it to the subjunctive intentionally or unintentionally to bring it into line with the usual form after ἵνα; (3) Robertson suggests that ἵνα with the indicative was original and is a result clause.[33] In this case it should be translated "so that we know him." The weight of the external evidence is not easy to overlook. In addition, the indicative is the most difficult reading and as such more likely to be the original. There is evidence that the indicative was occasionally used with ἵνα. Brooke lists a number of occurrences with the future indicative and some possible examples with the present indicative.[34] In this context it seems best to view the expression as a purpose clause, even though the original text read γινώσκομεν. It was probably an irregularity in spelling.

God the Father is here described as "Him who is true." However, in numerous contexts, the term ἀληθινός may mean "real" or "genuine."[35] The reference to idols in verse 21 indicates that in verse 20 John has in mind the real God as over against counterfeit gods.[36] See John 17:3 for a parallel passage describing God as the genuine God rather than a spurious one. (Also see John 6:32; 15:1.)

καὶ ἐσμὲν ἐν τῷ ἀληθινῷ ἐν τῷ υἱῷ αὐτοῦ Ἰησοῦ Χριστῷ, "and we are in Him who is true, in His Son Jesus Christ." Not only does the believer come to know God more

---

32. Kittel, s.v. "διάνοια," by J. Behm. 4:967.
33. Robertson, *Word Pictures* 6:245; Marshall, p. 253, n. 44; Dana and Mantey, p. 286.
34. Brooke, pp. 150-51.
35. Kittel, s.v. "ἀληθινός," by Rudolph Bultmann. 1:249.
36. J. L. Houlden, *A Commentary on the Johannine Epistles* Black's New Testament Commentaries, p. 138; Dodd, p. 139.

and more, but he is *in* God, a phrase that describes the mystical saving relationship with God that the believer enjoys. The designation of Jesus as "His Son" makes it plain that the Person described as ἀληθινός is God the Father—the second ἐν phrase is not to be taken as appositional to the first, but as an explanation of the first. The relationship of being in God is enjoyed because believers are first in His Son.

οὗτός ἐστιν ὁ ἀληθινὸς θεὸς καὶ ζωὴ αἰώνιος, "This is the true God and eternal life." Commentators have engaged in vigorous debate concerning the antecedent of οὗτος, "this," and arguments have been marshaled on both sides of the question. Some insist that it refers to Jesus Christ, the nearest antecedent; others say it refers back to the subject being discussed in most of the verse, namely, God the Father. In favor of the former view are Bruce, Bultmann, and Marshall.[37] In favor of the latter view are Brooke, Dodd, Law, Robertson ("probably"), Stott, and Westcott.[38] Those who see the pronoun as referring to Christ advance such arguments as the following:

- To understand οὗτος as referring to God makes the clause superfluous
- Grammatically it is argued that οὗτος should refer to the nearest preceding antecedent
- It seems to be John's intention to begin and end both the gospel (1:1; 20:28) and the epistle (1:1 and 5:20) with an assertion of the deity of Christ (Marshall)
- Christ is called the life, both in the gospel (11:25; 14:6) and in the first epistle (1:2; 5:12).

On the other hand, those who view οὗτος as referring to God offer such arguments as:

- The pronoun does not necessarily refer to the subject that is spatially nearest in the sentence; it may refer to the idea that is uppermost in previous discussion—in this case God the Father whom the Son reveals (Westcott, Law)
- John's style is to repeat what has been said and to add to it (Plummer)
- John 17:3, on which John here seems to be drawing, argues for God as the antecedent (Stott)

37. Bruce, p. 128; Bultmann, p. 90; Marshall, p. 254, n. 47.
38. Brooke, pp. 152-53; Dodd, p. 140; Law, p. 413; Robertson, *Word Pictures*, 6:245; Stott, p. 196; Westcott, p. 196; Plummer, p. 121.

- The next verse, which warns against idols, seems to be more in line with the view that οὗτος refers to God (Plummer)
- Rather than being *tautological*, the repetition is *impressive* (Law).

When the arguments pro and con are compared, there is little doubt but that the case for God as the antecedent is the stronger. It successfully explains the assertion of tautology, and it rightly points out that the antecedent may be mentally rather than spatially nearest.

On ζωὴ αἰώνιos see on 1:2; 5:11.

F. A CONCLUDING EXHORTATION, 5:21

5:21. τεκνία, φυλάξατε ἑαυτὰ ἀπὸ τῶν εἰδώλων, "Little children, guard yourselves from idols." On τεκνία see on 2:1. The aorist imperative φυλάξατε, "guard," is a call for immediate action.[39] By its very nature the aorist imperative is a sharper, more authoritative command than the present imperative.[40] Brooke describes it as a "peremptory aorist imperative,"[41] that is, it is urgent, absolute, and final.

The idols against which John warns have, in general, been interpreted in two ways. Most scholars take them to be the false conceptions of God taught by the false teachers against whom John wrote. It is said to be surprising that John introduced the subject so abruptly at the end of the letter. If it is a figurative reference to the false doctrine referred to repeatedly on earlier pages of the letter, the appearance of the subject would not be so abrupt.

But, even though such an interpretation is reasonable, it is unnecessary. Simply to walk among the ruins of Ephesus, Sardis, Hierapolis, or Miletus is enough to impress one with the overwhelming reality of pagan worship. As 1 Corinthians 8-10 reveals, it was a very pressing problem for Christians. As a parting word—almost a postscript—it would have been most fitting for John to add this brief warning.

Furthermore, it has been pointed out that Paul used the term idols to represent such things as greed (Eph. 5:5; Col. 3:5). This is true, but he explicitly explains just what he intended the figure of idolatry to represent. John, however, gives not the slightest hint

---

39. Dana and Mantey, p. 300.
40. Robertson, p. 856.
41. Brooke, p. 154.

that he is using the term idols in a figurative sense. It is only reasonable, therefore, to take the term literally.

THEOLOGICAL COMMENTARY (5:13-21)

A. INTRODUCTORY CONSIDERATIONS

This concluding section contains little that is new to the epistle. It is basically a recapitulation of truth that has already been developed in the earlier portion of the letter as the following comparison shows:

Subjects	Conclusion	Previous Sections
Eternal life	5:13, 20	1:1-2; 2:25; 5:11-12
Belief	5:13	2:23; 5:1, 10
Confident prayer	5:14-17	3:21-23
Practice of sin	5:18	1:6; 2:4; 3:9
New birth, children of God, (born) of God	5:18, 19	2:29; 3:1, 9, 10; 4:4, 6, 7; 5:1
Evil one (the devil)	5:18, 19	2:13-14; 3:8, 10-11
World	5:19	2:15; 3:1, 13; 4:4-5; 5:4
Incarnation	5:20	1:1-2; 3:5, 8; 4:9
Christ's Sonship	5:18, 20	2:22-24; 3:8; 4:9, 10, 14; 5:5, 9-12

The conclusion of this epistle, therefore, is markedly different from those of most other New Testament epistles. Paul's letters, for example, close with personal greetings and miscellaneous instructions that are added almost as a postscript to the body of the document (cf. Col. 4:7-18). The closing instructions have little to do with the main thrust of the letters.

In 1 John, however, the concluding section (5:13-21) is an integral part of the epistle, a genuine conclusion of the author's line of thought. The apostle has been developing a dual argument. On the one hand, he has established tests that identify the false teachers (ethical tests, 1:6-7; 2:3-4; 2:7-11; 3:8-9, etc., and Christological tests, 2:22-23; 4:2-3, etc.), but, on the other hand, he has been providing bases for the believer's assurance of salvation (5:13). In fact, the tests that serve to unmask false teachers also serve to identify genuine believers and thus give grounds for assurance. And it is the keynote of assurance that the author sounds repeatedly in this concluding section.

It will be noted that the word οἶδα, "know," occurs six times in these verses (vv. 13, 15, 15, 18, 19, 20) as John lays stress on some of the areas of assurance that are open to the believer. Somewhat like a symphonic composition, the concluding section takes up the theme of assurance that has been heard throughout the letter and sounds it again and again in a glorious climax: "We know! We know! We know!"

B. IN CONCLUSION: TRACING JOHN'S THOUGHT THROUGH 5:13-21

1. A STATEMENT OF OVERALL PURPOSE, 5:13

This statement of purpose is one of several that appear in the epistle. (See also 1:4; 2:1.) When viewed as a whole the purpose of the letter is twofold: to expose false teachers and to give believers assurance of salvation. John's aim of exposing the Gnostic false teachers is implicit in his statement of 2:26, "These things I have written to you concerning those who are trying to deceive you." Other statements throughout the book make it clear that one major aim of the letter was to combat false teaching. (See 2:18-19, 22; 4:1-6; see also 1:1; 5:6-12.) The declaration of purpose appearing in 2:1 is likewise related to the aim of exposing heretics. It warns against becoming involved in the sinful practices of the Gnostics.

John's aim of helping believers to come to assurance of salvation is most clearly stated in 5:13, but it is also to be seen in numerous other statements in earlier sections of the letter. Many of these passages have to do with the believer's behavior. In 1:5-7, walking in the light is proof that one is in saving relationship (fellowship) with God; in 2:3-5, obedience confirms one's profession to know Him; and in 2:29 and 3:9-10*a*, practicing righteousness shows that a person is a child of God. Again in 3:16-19, especially verse 19, love for fellow believers demonstrates that one is of the truth; in 4:7, love for one another shows that one has been born of God and knows Him; in 4:12, mutual love reveals God's indwelling; and in 4:17-18, love expressed in deeds will give the believer confidence on the day of judgment.

Other statements that bear on the believer's assurance have to do with Christology, particularly with the doctrine of the incarnation. In 2:23, belief in the incarnation is evidence that a person "has the Father"; in 4:2, acknowledgment "that Jesus Christ has come in the flesh" proves that one "is from God"; in 4:6, listening sympathetically to the message of the incarnation shows that the listener "knows God"; and in 5:1 believing that Jesus is the divine Christ is evidence that a person "is born of God."

These are the "things" to which John refers in 5:13. Thus, when believers find such evidences present in their lives, they have solid grounds for assurance of eternal life.

Another statement of purpose is found in 1:4—"so that our joy may be made complete." Here John explains that he wrote this epistle so that when his readers responded favorably to what he had written—that is, when they rejected the heretical teaching and when they came to have assurance concerning their salvation—then John would be full of joy.

2. CONFIDENCE CONCERNING ANSWERED PRAYER, 5:14-17

Closely related to assurance of eternal life is certainty of answered prayer, for prayer is the most natural activity of the child of God.

a. The certainty stated (5:14-15). These verses contain two statements of certainty: (1) "He hears us" (v. 14) and (2) "we have the requests which we have asked from Him" (v. 15). It is assumed that He listens favorably, and therefore what is requested is received. There is, however, a condition that must be met: "if we ask . . . according to His will" (v. 14). At least two interpretations of this conditional clause have been suggested. It has been said that it does not mean that God's will must be ascertained first, but that requests should be qualified by the condition, "If it is your will." While it is true that prayer should be so conditioned, this cannot be what John means here. This passage is explaining how one can know that our prayer will be answered—"we know that we have the requests. . . ." However, to condition the request by "If it is your will" does not give assurance that what has been requested will be received. In fact, it leaves the matter wide open. If it is God's will it will be received; if it is not His will, it will not.

A second interpretation takes the condition more literally. It views the clause as meaning that what is requested is in harmony with the will of God. This view is much more in keeping with the overall thrust of the passage. If believers ask for something that is in keeping with God's will, they can be sure they will receive it. As Marshall puts it, when Christians come to the place where they "want what God wants," they will receive what they request.[42]

The question that naturally comes to mind is, "How can we know what is in harmony with God's will?" Jesus' words in John 15:7 suggest a twofold answer: (1) abiding in Christ and (2) being indwelt by His words. To be in close spiritual union with Christ is to know Him personally and thus to be in a position to know His mind and to be in sympathy with His desires. To be indwelt by His words is to possess His truth in mind and heart. Put differently, it is to understand and to agree with God's revealed truth. By bringing interests and desires into harmony with the Scripture, believers learn to pray for what God Himself wants, and when they do so they receive what is requested.

b. The certainty illustrated (5:16-17). It is most natural to take this short section as illustrating the kind of request that can be made with assurance that it will be granted. Taken in any other way, these verses introduce an irregularity into an otherwise harmonious context. John refers to two different kinds of sin, one that does not lead to death and one that does. It is with the former sin that the passage is mainly concerned. Sin that leads to death is only mentioned in passing and in contrast to sin that does not lead to death.

Sin that does not lead to death—this kind of sin is said to be committed by a "brother" (v. 16). Since the term brother has been used throughout 1 John to refer to a believer (see 2:9-11; 3:14-15; and especially compare the family relationship described in 5:1), it is to be expected that in 5:16 a fellow believer is meant. It is not said that sin that leads to death is committed by a brother.

Although the specific sin is not identified, that it is sin that is visible and identifiable is obvious from the aorist ἴδῃ, "sees." It is also a continuing practice, as is evident from the present tense participle ἁμαρτάνοντα, "committing a sin." Heretofore in this letter, the present tense has been used to describe the continuing sin of the libertine opponents against whom John writes. The sin referred to in verse 16 is committed by a brother, not a heretic. It is therefore necessary to ascertain in what way the continuing practice of this brother differs from the continuing practice of the opponents. First John 2:1 indicates that John expected that a believer may commit acts of sin (aorist tense ἁμάρτῃ, "sins").

---

42. Marshall, p. 245.

However, 1:6-7 makes it clear that a believer will not continue, as a life-style, in moral darkness. Sin will not be the sphere in which his total life is lived. The way in which the *doing* of sin and of righteousness is referred to in 2:29 and 3:6-10 suggests that John refers to two different patterns of life.

The sinful practice referred to in 5:16 is different. Since it is committed by a believer, and since it is a specific identifiable sin it would seem to be a sinful habit in which a brother has become involved—a single sin committed repeatedly, but not a total lifestyle such as was characteristic of the Gnostics.

The whole point of verse 16a is that this sinful habit of a believer is an object of confident prayer. Prayer concerning it is in accord with the will of God, and therefore the one making the request can be sure that it will be granted. (The question concerning what is meant by death and life will be treated below.)

Sin that leads to death—this type of sin is also apparently identifiable. Nothing is said as to whether it is committed by a believer or an unbeliever or as to whether or not it is a continuing practice or a single act. What John says is that it leads to death. He does not say that prayer should be made concerning it. On the other hand, he does not say that one should not make request concerning it. In the context he is only saying that such a sin is not an object of confident prayer. Whether or not God will answer is an open question, no doubt dependent on the particular person and circumstances involved.

Numerous explanations of this sin have been given. Arminian theologians would identify the death referred to as spiritual death, and the person who commits the sin leading to death is said to be a believer. Accordingly a person who has eternal life commits sin that results in spiritual death. This, however, is impossible in the light of Jesus' clear declaration that He gives His sheep eternal life and "they shall never perish" (John 10:28). Here is a categorical statement of the strongest possible denial, made up of the double Greek negative, οὐ μή, and the temporal phrase εἰς τὸν αἰῶνα, which means "to eternity, eternally, in perpetuity," or with the negative, "never, not at all, never again."[43] A person who has eternal life will most certainly never perish. He will never so sin that spiritual death is the result.

Others insist that the sin that leads to death is that of a believer who continues to sin until God removes him from this life. In this

---

43. Arndt and Gingrich, p. 27.

Conclusion: Great Certainties of the Christian Life

case the death is physical and thus no loss of the sinner's eternal life is involved. That God may visit a sinning Christian with sickness or death is stated by Paul in 1 Corinthians 11:30 and perhaps is the meaning of 1 Corinthians 5:5. If this interpretation is correct, John has introduced a subject that finds little relationship to the rest of the epistle. Elsewhere in 1 John death is spiritual death and life is eternal life (see 1:2; 3:14, 15; 5:11, 12, 13, 20).[44] It would seem that this view would be acceptable only if no more fitting view presents itself. Or, to put it differently, the physical death view is possible, but not probable.

A third interpretation of the sin that leads to death is one that rests mainly on the context of the whole epistle. Sin is spoken of in two ways in 1 John. In one passage the Greek aorist tense is used (2:1), thus viewing it as a single act. This type of sin may be committed by believers, as is clear from the personal pronouns employed. In numerous passages sin is spoken of in the present tense and thus viewed as a continuing practice. As such it is described by such expressions as walking in the darkness (1:6), failure to keep God's commands (2:4), and "doing sin" (Gr. 3:8). As has been demonstrated in previous comments on the above passages, the persons to whom John referred were the early Gnostic false teachers and their followers.

In 5:16-17, John takes it for granted that his readers will understand what he means by the two categories of sin. This may have been because of previous oral teaching, but the reason why he does not stop to explain may lie nearer at hand. Since verses 16-17 occur in the concluding section of the epistle, his readers have already become familiar with the concepts of sin dealt with in the letter. It would be natural for them to understand verses 16-17 in the light of what has gone before. Therefore sin that leads to death would be seen as the continuing sin of the false teachers. In addition to disobedience and walking in the darkness, this was a sin that involved hatred for the people of God (2:9, 11; 3:10, 14, 15; 4:20) and rejection of the truth of the incarnation (2:22; 4:3).[45]

If this last interpretation is correct, the death referred to is spiritual death. The sin that does not lead to eternal death is any

---

44. Law, p. 139.
45. Law, pp. 135-42; Walter T. Conner, *The Epistles of John*, 2d ed., pp. 129-31. For a fuller explanation of various interpretations of 5:16-17, see David M. Scholer, "Sins Within and Sins Without: An Interpretation of 1 John 5:16-17," in *Current Issues in Biblical and Patristic Interpretation*, pp. 230-46.

sin that does not, by its very nature, rule out salvation through the death of God's incarnate Son.

One question remains. It concerns the sense in which God gives life to the sinning brother in answer to a fellow Christian's prayer. Since the brother already has life (John 5:24), one may wonder what kind of life is imparted to him. Stott argues that the term "brother" is used in the broader sense of neighbor. Since the person is unsaved, he then is given eternal life in answer to a Christian's prayer.[46] The difficulty with this view is that the term "brother" is used elsewhere in 1 John to refer to a believer (see 2:9-11; 3:10, 14, 15; 4:20; and especially notice the family relationship described in 5:1). Marshall points out that there is nothing in the context that would suggest a broader use of "brother" here.[47] Most interpreters hold that the life given in answer to a brother's prayer is the restoration of fulness of life.[48] Such a view is in agreement with passages that promise a crown of life to those who are believers, even though they already possess eternal life (James 1:12; Rev. 2:10).

3. ASSURANCE CONCERNING VICTORY OVER SIN AND THE DEVIL, 5:18

The statement, "no one who has been born of God sins," is a virtual restatement of 3:9a. The only difference is that, whereas 5:18 has οὐχ ἁμαρτάνει, "does not sin," 3:9a has ἁμαρτίαν οὐ ποιεῖ, "does not do sin." Since 3:9b has the verb ἁμαρτάνειν, it seems clear that the two expressions are interchangeable. They are both in the present tense and therefore both refer to a continual practice, a life-style. The NASB fails to recognize this interchangeable use.

In both passages John declares that a child of God does not live a life of sin. While he may, and does sin (2:1), sin is not the overriding characteristic of his life. In 3:9 the reason given for this statement is that God's seed (divine life principle) dwells in him and as a result a sinful life-style is impossible. Here in 5:18 the reason given is that God's Son (ὁ γεννηθεὶς ἐκ τοῦ θεοῦ, "He who was born of God") continually keeps him so that the devil does not lay hold on him to do him spiritual harm.

Thus, there are two sides to the victory over sin that is charac-

---

46. Stott, p. 190.
47. Marshall, p. 246, n. 15.
48. Ibid., pp. 249-50, n. 27; Scholer, p. 240.

teristic of the believer. On the one hand, he is regenerated by the divine life principle so that he is now a child of God. As God's offspring he has the ability to gain victory over sin (see 5:3-5) and in fact does, to a considerable degree, overcome it (3:9). On the other hand, he is kept by God's Son, and thus Satan cannot drag him off into a life of sin. By reason of his own regenerated nature and of Christ's keeping power, the believer is victorious. And this is a fact of Christian knowledge concerning which there is no doubt (οἴδαμεν, "we know"), 5:18. John's statement is not a hortatory subjunctive ("let us not"), nor is it a prohibition ("stop"), nor is it a conditional statement ("the child of God does not sin *if*..."). Instead it is an indicative declaration of fact. The child of God *does not* continue to practice sin. Righteousness, not sin, is the family characteristic (see 3:9-10).

The experience of being kept by the Son of God is not a passive one in which the believer is at rest while Christ alone exerts effort. It is synergism in the best sense of the term. Both the believer's new nature (3:9) and Christ (5:18) are active. See 1 Peter 1:5 for a similar statement of cooperative activity.

4. ASSURANCE CONCERNING THE BELIEVER'S RELATIONSHIP TO GOD, 5:19

This verse contains another declaration of certainty—οἴδαμεν, "we know." What is known is the fact of two significant spiritual relationships. To say that "we are of God" is the same as asserting that one is *born* of God. The Greek preposition ἐκ speaks of source: God is the source of spiritual life and characteristics. Since believers are born of God, they are the ones who do not practice sin, who are kept continually by Christ, and on whom Satan cannot gain a grip (v. 18).

In contrast, the world sustains a parallel relationship to the devil. It lies "in" him, that is, under his power and control. Whereas the child of God is not in Satan's grip (v. 18), the world lies passively under his control (v. 19).

Verse 19 is a restatement of truths set forth in 3:7-10, where Satan's offspring are contrasted with the children of God.

5. ASSURANCE CONCERNING THE INCARNATION, 5:20

This declaration of certainty is basically a statement concerning the incarnation. However, it breaks down into four distinct assertions:

- The Son of God has come
- He has given us understanding
- We are in the One who is true and in His Son
- This One (of whom we speak) is the true God and eternal life

"The Son of God has come. . . ." Basic to the whole epistle is the fact of the incarnation, a truth that was at the very heart of apostolic Christianity. To affirm this tenet was implicitly to reject the Gnostic error. The statement with which the epistle opens assumes the reality of the incarnation, and the doctrinal test stated in the epistle (2:22; 4:2-3) centers in this very point—"Jesus Christ has come in the flesh" (4:2). Now at the conclusion of the letter the truth of the incarnation is affirmed one last time.

"[He] has given us understanding. . . ." Christ has provided illumination for us through the Holy Spirit so that man may come to know God ("Him who is true"). The subject of the verb "has given" is the Son of God. As was explained in the Exegetical Commentary, the word διάνοια, "understanding," refers not to knowledge but to the ability to understand, the capacity to receive spiritual knowledge. Thus Christ provides illumination. The purpose of this gift is "in order that we might know" God. The word γινώσκω speaks of the process of coming to know, a process that actually starts prior to conversion as the Holy Spirit begins to enable us to comprehend and appreciate spiritual truth. Without such enablement no one would ever come to know God. This process, begun before conversion, continues throughout the life of a believer. It is akin to the teaching ministry of the Holy Spirit (see on 2:27).

"We are in Him who is true, in His Son. . . ." Here another truth developed earlier in the book is reiterated (see 2:5-6, 24, 27-28; 3:13, 15-16). The expression "to be in Him" describes the spiritual union with God and His Son that is true of all believers. To be saved is to know God and His Son personally, to have the closest fellowship with them. And this is made possible by the fact that "the Son of God has come."

"This is the true God and eternal life." The verse division that follows this statement is unfortunate in that it suggests that there should be a break in thought between verses 20 and 21. Instead John seems to have been making a contrast between the "true God" of verse 20 and the idols of verse 21. Ἀληθινός, "true," means " 'real' or 'true' in contrast to the vanity of idols."[49] Living

---

49. Kittel, s.v. "ἀληθινός," by Rudolph Bultmann. 1:249.

in the midst of idolatry in the pagan cities of the province of Asia as John and his readers were, the apostle could not close his letter without appending a warning. False gods were everywhere in evidence in temples and homes and along public thoroughfares. Ephesus provides a prime example of the manner in which idolatry pressed itself on the attention of people. The temple of Artemis was a matter of civic pride around which many aspects of Ephesian life revolved. People flocked from all parts of the Roman world to see the famed temple and its goddess. At the northeast corner of the commercial agora (marketplace) stood a temple of the Egyptian god Serapis, which was probably built by Antony and Cleopatra. A temple dedicated to Domitian, who proclaimed himself to be lord and god, stood just below the state agora. The statues of Artemis, Zeus, Dionysus, Nike (winged goddess of victory), and the god Bes are testimony to the many signs of idolatry with which the city was filled. Obviously many more remains of statutes of gods would have been found had not Nero ransacked the city to augment his own personal collection.[50]

With such ubiquitous idolatrous influence, it is no wonder that reference to the *real* God led John to warn his readers, many of them converts from paganism, that they should guard themselves from idols. Earlier Paul likewise found it necessary to warn the Corinthians concerning the insidious influence of idolatry (1 Cor. 8:1-13; 10:14-33; 2 Cor. 6:14-18).

C. PRESENT-DAY APPLICATION

1. ASSURANCE NO LICENSE TO SIN, 5:13, 18

It has been charged that the doctrine of the eternal security of the believer, and the assurance the Christian therefore enjoys, are not biblical because they result in license for unbridled sin. However the concluding verses of 1 John make it clear that such is not the case.

In the first place, John plainly declares that he writes this epistle so that his readers may come to know that they have eternal life. This is a statement of assurance ("know") based on a security that is eternal. Life that is eternal is life that is qualitatively above and beyond any other level of life, but it is also unending.

50. Edwin M. Yamauchi, "Recent Archaeological Work in the New Testament Cities of Western Anatolia," *Near East Archaeological Society Bulletin*, New Series, no. 13 (1979): 72-73.

It is natural that the question should be asked: Does the assured possession of eternal life give one permission to engage in unbridled sin? The answer is to be found in verse 18, where John declares that the one who is born of God does not make sin the habit of his life. The reasons why he does not are two: (1) He is born of God and His regenerate nature, of necessity, results in a life-style marked by righteousness, and (2) Christ Himself protects him from the devil's power. Therefore, rather than giving license to sin, the truth of eternal security contains a built-in guarantee that regenerated persons will not live in unbridled sin.

2. PRAYER FOR THOSE WHO SIN, 5:14-17

While John's purpose in verses 16-17 is primarily to illustrate what may be prayed for with assurance that God will answer, these verses also give instruction concerning prayer for those who sin. It is surprising that Dodd should conclude that John "emphatically discourages" prayer for a person "who is in deadly sin." Dodd apparently assumes that John suggests that it is contrary to God's will to pray for such persons.[51]

However, this is not what John says explicitly or implicitly. After declaring that there is a sin that leads to death, he simply refrains from encouraging prayer for a person involved in such sin (5:16*b*). This fact must be understood in light of the preceding context. John is not primarily discussing sin; instead his main subject is the type of request that can be made with the assurance that God will answer. Therefore, the reason why, in this context, he does not encourage prayer for sin that leads to death is that it is not the type of request that can be made with assurance. This does not mean that prayer for such sin is discouraged. It only means that such prayer is not an example of the kind that we can be sure will be granted. The reason why it may not be granted is probably that the stubborn will of the sinner may not bend. God, though sovereign, chooses not to coerce the will and thus violate the integrity of the personality He created in His own image.

We may conclude from this passage that prayer for the sinner is always in order, regardless of what his sin may be. If it is adamant rejection of revealed truth that has been intellectually comprehended, the answer may not be forthcoming. Compassion, however, should move us to pray, since the stubborn will after all may

51. Dodd, pp. 136-37.

Conclusion: Great Certainties of the Christian Life

yield to divine overtures. If it is a sin that is less adamant and less final, we may pray with assurance that God will grant our request.

PARAPHRASTIC COMMENTARY (5:13-21)

(13) I am sending this letter to you—you who are trusting in the person of God's Son—so that you may have assurance that you possess life that is both abundant and unending. (14) And this is the kind of bold confidence we have when we come to Him in prayer: we are sure that, if we are careful to ask for what is in keeping with His plan for us, He will listen favorably to our request. (15) And if we are sure of that, we are likewise sure that what we have requested is already ours. (16) To illustrate—suppose a Christian brother is involved in a sinful practice that does not destine him for eternal destruction. If you pray for such a person, you can be sure that God will restore him to abundant life. There is sin that (because of its persistent and adamant rejection of God's incarnate Son—the kind of attitude that characterizes the Gnostics) will lead to eternal death. Concerning prayer for that kind of sin I cannot give any assurance that God will answer. (17) All wrong doing is serious—it is nothing less than sin. Nevertheless, some kinds of sin do not destine a person for eternal hell.

(18) We are sure that no child of God lives a life of habitual sin; on the contrary, God's Son keeps protecting him so that the devil does not lay hold on him. (19) We are sure that we are members of God's family; on the other hand, we know that the people of this sinful world are under the domination of Satan. (20) Again we are sure that God's Son has become the God-man and has given us the spiritual capacity necessary to come to know God. And we are involved in a close spiritual union with the true God and with His Son Jesus Christ. Our God is the real God and in and of Himself He is the essence and the source of eternal life. (21) Dear children, make sure that you guard yourselves from all representations of false gods.

STRUCTURAL COMMENTARY (5:13-21)[52]

V. Conclusion: Great certainties of the Christian life, 5:13-21
   A. The certainty of eternal life, 5:13
      1. The epistle was written to give assurance, 5:13a
      2. Assurance is based on belief in Christ's name, 5:13b

---

52. For previous section of outline see p. 383.

B. The certainty of answered prayer, 5:14-17
  1. Assured prayer described, 5:14-15
     a. God listens favorably to prayers that are in accord with His will, 5:14
     b. Thus, we may know that when we pray, we already have what we request, 5:15
  2. Assured prayer illustrated, 5:16-17
     a. Prayer for sin not leading to death will be answered, 5:16a
     b. John does not command prayer for sin that leads to death, 5:16b
     c. By speaking of sin that does not lead to death, John does not minimize sin, 5:17
C. The certainty of victory over sin and the devil, 5:18
  1. God's regenerated child does not practice sin, 5:18a
  2. Christ keeps the believer, 5:18b
  3. Satan cannot lay hold of the believer, 5:18c
D. The certainty of the believer's relationship to God, 5:19
  1. We are sure that we are members of God's family, 5:19a
  2. In contrast, the evil world is under Satan's control, 5:19b
E. The certainty of the incarnation, 5:20
  1. We are sure that God's Son has come, 5:20a
  2. He has given us the capacity to know God, 5:20b
  3. We are involved in a mystical union with God and His Son, 5:20c
  4. This God is the true God, 5:20d
  5. He is also the source and the reality of eternal life, 5:20d
F. A concluding exhortation, 5:21
  1. A closing word to Christians, 5:21a
  2. A call for separation from idolatry, 5:21b

PART 3
The Second Epistle of John

16

Introduction to 2 John

Because of the shortness of this letter, question has been raised concerning its inclusion in the New Testament canon. However, in addition to the glimpse of early church practices it provides, the epistle embodies a significant principle that should govern one's contribution toward the financial support of pastors, missionaries, and other Christian workers.

Since 2 John is closely related to 1 John in matters of introduction, the discussion of such topics will be much abbreviated.

THE AUTHORSHIP OF THE EPISTLE

The Johannine authorship of 2 John is not as well documented by early church writers as is the authorship of the gospel and the first epistle. The brevity of the letter no doubt explains why it was not more widely used.

Irenaeus (c. A.D. 130-200) quoted 2 John 7-8 and 2 John 11 as from John the disciple of the Lord.[1] The Muratorian Fragment (c. A.D. 170-215) refers to two Johannine letters, one of which was 1 John and the other of which seems most likely to have been 2 John.[2] Clement of Alexandria (c. A.D. 155-215) refers to more

---

1. Irenaues *Against Heresies* 3. 16. 8 and 1. 16: 3 repectively.
2. Donald Guthrie, *New Testament Introduction,* p. 885.

than one Johannine epistle[3] and speaks of 2 John in a Latin fragment called *adumbrationes*.[4] Origen (c. A.D. 185-253) speaks of three Johannine epistles and says that not everyone agrees that they are genuine.[5] Dionysius of Alexandria (c. A.D. 200-265) states that John does not name himself in 2 and 3 John but simply calls himself the elder.[6] And Eusebius (c. A.D. 260-340) placed 2 John among the *antilegomena*.[7]

When one looks at the epistle itself for evidence of authorship, one is impressed with the very noticeable similarity of the epistle to 1 John. Both letters are shot through with similar terms and expressions.[8] The following chart shows the extent of similarity existing between 1 and 2 John.

Term or Expression	No. of Occurrences in 2 John	No. of Occurrences in 1 John
truth	5	9
love (noun & verb)	4	39
love one another	1	5
walk	3	4
command	4	14
new command	1	2
His commands	1	8
from the beginning	1	8
heard from the beginning	1	3
had from the beginning	1	1
confessing Jesus Christ coming in flesh	1	1
antichrist	1	4
this is love that we walk according to his commands	1	1 ("keep" instead of "walk")
dwell, remain, abide	3	23
gone out into the world	1	1

3. Clement of Alexandria *Stromata* 2. 15. 66.
4. Guthrie, p. 885, n. 6.
5. Eusebius *H. E.* 6. 25. 10.
6. Ibid., 7. 25.
7. Ibid., 3. 25. 3.
8. A. E. Brooke, *A Critical and Exegetical Commentary on the Johannine Epistles*, The International Critical Commentary, p. lxxiv.

have God, have Father and Son	2	4
joy may be full	1	1

In the above chart there are six words and eleven expressions that are found one or more times in each epistle. Considering that 2 John contains only thirteen verses, this is a remarkably heavy similarity. It must mean either that the author of 2 John purposefully took these terms and expressions from 1 John or, as is more reasonable, that the same person wrote both letters. The latter view is more plausible because these terms and expressions are used in the same sense in both epistles. Furthermore, there is no telltale unnatural or strained employment of the terms or expressions as often results when one tries to use the style and vocabulary of another.

It is, therefore, most reasonable to conclude that the author of 1 John also wrote 2 John, or, to be more specific, that both epistles came from the pen of the apostle.

Recent scholarship has spoken extensively of a Johannine school from which the various writings traditionally ascribed to John are said to have come (for further discussion, see pp. 11-13). Some are no more explicit than to say that it was the Johannine community that produced the three epistles.[9] Barrett says that 2 and 3 John may have been written by someone other than the person who wrote 1 John.[10]

THE RECIPIENTS OF THE EPISTLE

There have been two major views as to the identity of "the chosen lady and her children" (v. 1). Either the reference is to an individual woman and her children, or it is to a local church and its members. Several variations of these views have been set forth. Some have said that the church universal was meant. Others have suggested that either one or both of the words ἐκλεκτῇ κυρίᾳ, "chosen lady," were proper names. John would then be addressing the lady Electa, or the elect Kyria or Electa Kyria. However, the fact that the sister mentioned in verse 13 is also called ἐκλεκτῆς, "chosen," seems to show rather clearly that the term is not a name. And studies have not shown it to appear elsewhere as a proper name. Furthermore, the word κυρία is seldom found as a proper name. The two most probable views are that the designa-

---

9. Oscar Cullmann, *The Johannine Circle,* pp. 53-54.
10. C. K. Barrett. *The Gospel According to St. John,* p. 113.

tion, "chosen lady," refers to an unknown woman or to a local church somewhere in the province of Asia. Several reasons have been advanced in favor of both views. (1) That the "chosen lady" was loved by "all who know the truth" is said to be more reasonable if a local church was intended, since a church would be more apt to be known by Christians everywhere. However, an outstanding woman of means could well be widely known, and John's language probably should be understood as hyperbole used to indicate widespread acquaintanceship. (2) The use of the second person plural is said to favor a church. However, that the letter is addressed to a group—"the chosen lady and her children"—should not be overlooked. This fact easily explains the second person plural, especially if it is understood that the children are not infants but grown. (3) The main thrust of the letter as a warning against false teachers is assumed to be more applicable to a church than to a family, but if the family had been accustomed to showing hospitality to travelling teachers, the letter would apply as well to such a family as to a church. (4) It is said that the command to love one another (v. 5) fits a local church situation better than an individual family. This is not necessarily true since the circle of love referred to may be the larger circle of all Christians. This may be a general statement in which John was emphasizing the need to show love before he addressed the chosen lady's misuse of Christian love receiving false teachers into her home. He did not want to minimize the importance of love, so he emphasized the need for it first of all.

None of the above arguments is compelling. In fact, they are of such a nature that they allow for understanding either a local church or an individual lady known to John. Since such is the case, the principles of biblical interpretation would seem to direct one to adopt the most natural meaning of the passage, namely that an individual lady and her children were the intended receivers of the letter. It is unnatural that such a simple letter should contain such a lengthy and involved figure of speech. Smith says the simplicity and tenderness of the letter stamp it "as a personal communication."[11] And Plummer points out that the change from σε, "you," singular (v. 5), to ὑμῖν, "you," plural (v. 12), seems to fit a woman and her children better than a church and its members.[12] Furthermore, since 3 John was clearly written to an indi-

11. W. Robertson Nicoll, gen. ed., *The Expositor's Greek Testament*, s.v. "The Epistles of John," by David Smith, 5:162.
12. A. Plummer, *The Epistles of St. John* in the Cambridge Greek Testament for Schools and Colleges, p. 141.

vidual, the close similarity of the conclusions of the two letters suggests that 2 John also was sent to an individual.

THE DATE OF THE EPISTLE

Because of the close similarity to 1 John, not only in vocabulary, but in subject matter, 2 John should be dated about the same time as the first epistle, sometime between A.D. 90 and 95. There is little evidence to indicate which book was prior to the other, although Harrison claims that the reference to antichrist in 2 John 7 seems to assume the background of the teaching of 1 John on the subject.[13]

THE OCCASION AND PURPOSE OF THE EPISTLE

One of the contributions of the Roman Empire to the spread of the gospel was the excellent road system that spanned the Empire from one end to the other. Portions of two of those roads on which Paul travelled are visible yet today. The Appian Way is still in use as it approaches Rome, and in the vicinity of Kavalla (New Testament: Neapolis), Philippi, and Thessalonica, the Egnatian Way may still be seen. The location of Roman colonies and the presence of Roman troops made travel relatively safe. Consequently Christian preachers and teachers journeyed extensively in the interests of the gospel. This fact is to be seen in such NT passages as Acts 13-21; Romans 15:23-29; 16:1-2; 1 Thessalonians 3:1-2, 5; Titus 3:12-13, as well as in the *Didache* (c. A.D. 140-50).

Christian people were urged to show hospitality to travelling brothers (Rom. 12:13; Heb. 13:2). Thus, it became customary to lodge such people and to provide them with food for the next leg of their journey. See 3 John 5-8.

Not all who frequented the roads as travelling teachers were apostolic in their sympathies and doctrine. The propagators of incipient Gnosticism also travelled widely, posing as genuine Christian teachers. By this means unsuspecting and untrained Christian people were led astray. It was in the name of sincere Christian love that some believers made the mistake of taking in false teachers and helping them spread their destructive message.

Second John was written to urge a certain Christian lady of Asia Minor to exercise discernment in the manifestation of Christian love. The practice of doctrinal discrimination was a way to determine whether or not one should assist religious teachers financial-

---

13. Everett F. Harrison, *Introduction to the New Testament*, p. 426.

ly by providing food and lodging for them, for to do so was to participate in the spread of their message (see vv. 7-11).

An Outline of the Epistle

I. Introduction, vv. 1-3
   A. Author and recipients, vv. 1-2
   B. Greeting, v. 3
II. Commendation, v. 4.
III. Exhortation and warning, vv. 5-11
   A. The believer exhorted to love, v. 5
   B. Love explained, v. 6
   C. The exhortation justified, v. 7
   D. The believer warned of loss of reward, v. 8
   E. The enemy and the believer contrasted, v. 9
   F. The believer instructed, vv. 10-11
IV. Conclusion, vv. 12-13

17

Commentary on 2 John

Unlike the first epistle, this letter begins with the customary format for a first century letter by identifying the writer and the recipient. What is different from most ancient letters is that the specific names of the persons are not mentioned. However, the designation "elder" probably was such a well known title of the author that it served as well as a proper name to identify him. The recipient is not as clearly identified to modern readers, but, since the letter was probably delivered directly to the recipient, there would be no need for a more explicit identification.

The remainder of the letter also follows the general pattern for a first century letter, with a commendation of some kind, the main body of the letter, and concluding remarks.[1]

EXEGETICAL COMMENTARY (vv. 1-13)

I. INTRODUCTION, VV. 1-3

A. AUTHOR AND RECIPIENTS, VV. 1-2

v.1. Ὁ πρεσβύτερος ἐκλεκτῇ κυρίᾳ καὶ τοῖς τέκνοις αὐτῆς, "The elder to the chosen lady and her children." On ὁ πρεσβύ-

---

1. Francis Xavier J. Exler, *The Form of the Ancient Greek Letter of the Epistolary Papyri*.

τερος, "the elder," see Introduction to 1 John (pp. 13-16). On ἐκλεκτῇ κυρίᾳ..., "elect lady...," see Introduction to 2 John. οὒς ἐγὼ ἀγαπῶ ἐν ἀληθείᾳ, "whom I love in truth." Any suggestion that John is here voicing romantic love is refuted on four counts: (1) The οὒς, "whom," which is plural, must include both the lady and her children; (2) the phrase ἐν ἀληθείᾳ, "in truth," in this context (see vv. 1*b*-3) most probably refers to the truth embodied in the gospel and should thus be translated "in the truth"; (3) the last clause of verse 1 suggests that others who know the truth love this family in the same way that John does; and (4) the same expression is used in 3 John 1 concerning Gaius. On the meaning of ἀγαπάω, "I love," and ἀγάπη, "love," see on 1 John 2:7.

καὶ οὐκ ἐγὼ μόνος ἀλλὰ καὶ πάντες οἱ ἐγνωκότες τὴν ἀλήθειαν, "and not only I, but also all who know the truth." Here the article before ἀλήθειαν, "truth," makes it clear that the Christian gospel is meant. Since ἐγνωκότες, "know," is in the perfect tense and since γινώσκω is ingressive in nature, the participle indicates that they have come to know and as a result now know. Thus the NASB translates it as an intensive perfect, "know." On γινώσκω, "know," see note on 1 John 2:3.

v.2. διὰ τὴν ἀγήθειαν τὴν μένουσαν ἐν ἡμῖν, καὶ μεθ' ἡμῶν ἔσται εἰς τὸν αἰῶνα, "for the sake of the truth which abides in us and will be with us forever." Here again that the truth is Christian truth as in verse 1 is indicated by the presence of the article τήν before the noun. The prepositional phrase διὰ τὴν ἀγήθειαν, *because of the truth,* no doubt modifies the verb ἀγαπῶ, "I love," in verse 1. Christian love is the product of Christian truth indwelling the believer (see 1 John 5:1; also see 1 John 2:24, where the truth is referred to but not explicitly designated). On εἰς τὸν αἰῶνα, "forever," see on 1 John 1:2 and 2:17.

B. GREETING, V. 3

v.3. ἔσται μεθ' ἡμῶν χάρις ἔλεος εἰρήνη παρὰ θεοῦ πατρός, "Grace, mercy and peace will be with us, from God the Father." The form of the typical salutation in a Greek letter may be seen in Acts 15:23 and James 1:1, in which the writer is named, the recipient is designated, and the greeting is expressed. The salutation in James 1:1, stripped of modifying terms, would read, "James to the twelve tribes, greetings." The usual Greek word for greeting was χαίρειν, literally, "to rejoice," in contrast to the Hebrew greeting of שָׁלוֹם, "peace" (see Luke 10:5). New Testament letters reveal a distinctive form of greeting with the author and recipients identified according to the standard format, but instead of χαίρειν, a separate statement of benediction follows. It has been suggested that it may have been Paul who developed this distinctive form of greeting.[2] A simple example is found in Romans 1:7, "Grace to you and peace from God. . . ." See also 1 Corinthians 1:3; 2 Corinthians 1:2; Galatians 1:3; 1 Peter 1:2. In his letters to Timothy, Paul expands the greeting to read "grace, mercy, and peace" (1 Tim. 1:2; 2 Tim. 1:2). John, in his one use of the greeting (2 John 3) adds another distinctive touch in that he does not express it as a prayer or a desire, but as a statement of fact, using the future indicative ἔσται.

Χάρις, "grace," in Paul's writings is, in most instances, the unmerited favor of God to sinful man. This is the meaning of the word both in the greetings and the closing benedictions of Paul's letters.[3] John here uses the Pauline greeting, no doubt with Paul's meaning.

Ἔλεος, "mercy," was used in secular Greek to refer to "the emotion roused by contact with an affliction which comes undeservedly on someone else."[4] In NT Greek, the word has a similar meaning.

Εἰρήνη, "peace," in the New Testament, reflects the Hebrew parallel *shālôm* and refers to the well-being of an individual or community.[5] In the greetings of New Testament letters the writers have spiritual welfare in mind.

καὶ παρὰ Ἰησοῦ Χριστοῦ τοῦ υἱοῦ τοῦ πατρός, ἐν ἀληθείᾳ καὶ ἀγάπῃ, "and from Jesus Christ, the Son of the Father, in truth and love." This expansion of the greeting no doubt was occasioned by the incipient Gnostic teaching against which John warns in verses 7-10. The emphasis on Jesus' identity as God's Son (see 1 John 5:5) and the stress on truth and love both are attempts to counter the heresy. It is significant that, as Westcott points out,

---

2. I. Howard Marshall, *The Epistles of John*, The New International Commentary on the New Testament, p. 63.
3. Colin Brown, ed., *The New International Dictionary of New Testament Theology*, 1976, s.v. "Grace, Spiritual Gifts," by Hans-Helmut Esser; Gerhard Kittel, ed., *Theological Dictionary of the New Testament*, 1964-76, s.v. "Χάρις," by Hans Conzelmann. 9:394.
4. Kittel, s.v. "ἔλεος, ἐλεέω," by Rudolph Bultmann. 2:477.
5. Brown, s.v. "Peace," by H. Beck and C. Brown.

the combination of truth and love is found only here.⁶ The chief point John makes in this epistle is that love must always be conditioned by truth. That is, one must not exercise love (give material aid) in such a way that it hinders truth and propagates error. As in verse 1, even though ἀλήθεια, "truth," is without the article, it is to be understood as definite, referring to the truth that constitutes the substance of the gospel. The prepositional phrase cannot mean "truly," for that would necessitate that ἀγάπῃ, "love" mean "lovingly," which is most unlikely.

II. COMMENDATION, V. 4

v.4. Ἐχάρην λίαν ὅτι εὕρηκα ἐκ τῶν τέκνων σου περιπατοῦντες ἐν ἀληθείᾳ, "I was very glad to find some of your children walking in truth." This statement of commendation takes the place of the thanksgiving that occurs in most of Paul's letters (see Rom. 1:8; 1 Cor. 1:4-8; Phil. 1:3-8; Col. 1:3-8; 1 Thess. 1:2-4; and 2 Thess. 1:3.). The aorist passive ἐχάρην, "I was . . . glad," has the same meaning as the active voice. The aorist looks back to some point in the past when John had this pleasant experience, but he does not indicate when it took place.⁷ The prepositional phrase, ἐκ τῶν τέκνων, "some of your children," is an elliptical expression.⁸ That John speaks of some of the lady's children does not necessarily mean that her children were not all faithful. It may mean that John had come in contact with some, but not all, who were "walking in truth." The present participle, περιπατοῦντας, "walking," here, as in 1 John 1:6-7, speaks of a continuing activity, a pattern of life. Once more, even though ἀληθείᾳ, "truth," is anarthrous, it clearly means "the truth," as in verses 1 and 3. The lady's children conducted their lives in the sphere (locative case of sphere) of Christian truth.

καθὼς ἐντολὴν ἐλάβομεν παρὰ τοῦ πατρός, "just as we have received commandment to do from the Father." Καθώς, "just as," suggests that there was a close correspondence between the children's lives and the divine command. It has been suggested that, since verse 5 speaks of the new command to love (John 13:34), this must be the command referred to in verse 4; others have

---

6. B. F. Westcott, *The Epistles of St. John*, p. 226.
7. *A Lexicon Abridged from Liddell and Scott's Greek-English Lexicon*, p. 774.
8. A. T. Robertson, *A Grammar of the Greek New Testament in the Light of Historical Research*, p. 515.

assumed that the command in 1 John 3:23 is what John has in mind. However, the commands referred to in those passages are commands to believe and to love, whereas the command in verse 4 is a specific command to walk in the truth. Furthermore, it is a command from the Father. But there is no recorded command in Scripture that, in so many words, calls for walking in the truth. Both John 3:21 and 1 John 1:6 speak of doing the truth, and in the former passage the context is clearly referring to doing deeds that are the opposite of evil deeds—deeds of holiness or righteousness. Scripture, in numerous places, records God's call to holy and upright living, e.g., Exodus 20:1-17; Micah 6:8; 1 Peter 1:15-16. Thus 2 John 4 may refer to the general teaching of Scripture rather than any specific command.

III. EXHORTATION AND WARNING, VV. 5-11

A. THE BELIEVER EXHORTED TO LOVE, V. 5

v.5. καὶ νῦν ἐρωτῶ σε, κυρία, "And now I ask you, lady." The νῦν, "now," is not so much temporal as it is transitional. John has completed the introductory matters (salutation, greetings, and commendation); he is now turning to the major topic of the letter, the relationship of truth and love. He does not say παρακαλῶ σε, "I urge you," or αἰτῶ σε, "I beg you," but ἐρωτῶ σε, "I ask you." The latter term is more authoritative and carries more dignity with it.[9] With fitting dignity and with carefully employed authority, John requests this influential lady to manifest love.

οὐχ ὡς ἐντολὴν καινὴν γράφων σοι ἀλλὰ ἣν εἴχομεν ἀπ᾽ ἀρχῆς, ἵνα ἀγαπῶμεν ἀλλήλους, "not as writing to you a new commandment, but the one which we have had from the beginning, that we love one another." The similarity that exists between this verse and 1 John 2:7 is inescapable, and, of course, both verses clearly reflect John 13:34. It is assumed that the statement in the gospel preceded those in the epistles. It may likewise be assumed that 1 John preceded, and is thus reflected in, 2 John, but this cannot be demonstrated with any certainty. What does seem clear is that both letters came from the same author.

There are two differences between the two statements. (1) The personal pronoun designating the recipients is plural in 1 John 2:7 and singular in 2 John 5. This is not surprising since 1 John was a

---

9. Richard C. Trench, *Synonyms of the New Testament*, p. 140.

circular letter and 2 John was addressed primarily to "the chosen lady" and only secondarily to "her children." (2) The statement in 1 John is more explicit in that it includes the words ἐντολὴν παλαιάν, "an old commandment," whereas they are omitted from 2 John 5. On all other words or phrases, see on 1 John 2:7.

B. LOVE EXPLAINED, V. 6

v.6. καὶ αὕτη ἐστὶν ἡ ἀγάπη, ἵνα περιπατῶμεν κατὰ τὰς ἐντολὰς αὐτοῦ, "And this is love, that we walk according to His commandments." Here again 2 John reveals a noticeable similarity to 1 John (see 5:3). The difference is that the statement in 1 John is fuller and more explicit. It is love for God to which 1 John refers, whereas 2 John merely says, "this is love." Even so, it is quite certain, since 2 John speaks of keeping "*His* commandments," that love for God is what the author has in mind. The two different expressions used to speak of obeying the commands are synonyms with no intended distinction in meaning. For further discussion of terms in 2 John 6*a*, see on 1 John 5:3. On περιπατῶμεν see 1 John 1:6.

αὕτη ἡ ἐντολή ἐστιν, καθὼς ἠκούσατε ἀπ᾽ ἀρχῆς, ἵνα ἐν αὐτῇ περιπατῆτε, "This is the commandment, just as you have heard from the beginning, that you should walk in it." With the second person, plural, ἠκούσατε, "you have heard," John makes his statement to be more pointedly personal than in verse 5 where the first person plural appears. He applies his words directly to the chosen lady and her children. The alternate use of "commandment" (sing., v. 5), "commandments" (pl., v. 6*a*), and "commandment" (sing., v. 6*b*) is worthy of note. The singular and plural are not used as loosely identical; instead John, by a kind of circular reasoning, is showing the relationship between love and obedience to God's commands. The steps in his reasoning are as follows:

- Obedience to God's command produces love (v. 5)
- Love in turn produces obedience to God's commands (v. 6*a*)
- Obedience to Christ's command produces love (v. 6*b*)

Thus love and obedience are integrally tied together. To love is to obey, and to obey is to love. (See Matt. 22:35-40; Rom. 13:8-10.) On ἀπ᾽ ἀρχῆς see comments on 1 John 2:7 (pp. 140-42).

C. THE EXHORTATION JUSTIFIED, V. 7

v. 7. ὅτι πολλοὶ πλάνοι ἐξῆλθον εἰς τὸν κόσμον, "For many deceivers have gone out into the world." The subordinating conjunction, ὅτι, "for," is explanatory supplying the reason for the exhortation given in verses 5-6. Bultmann says that verses 5-6 are intended to prepare the reader for the corrective set forth in verses 7-11.[10] Christian love must be exercised toward fellow believers, John declares in verses 5-6, but he adds in verses 7-11 that it must not be practiced indiscriminately. To be more specific the apostle says that Christians must love one another *because* many false teachers are present in the world. The unity produced by such mutual love enables believers to recognize and resist deceptive error.

This verse is parallel to 1 John 4:1*b* where similar heretics are designated as false prophets. On ἐξῆλθον see on ἐξεληλύθασιν in 1 John 4:1. The persons designated as πλάνοι, "deceivers," were the same early Gnostic teachers against whom John warns in 1 John (see 2:26; 4:1-3). They constituted an insidious danger to the Christian lady and her family to whom this letter is addressed.

οἱ μὴ ὁμολογοῦντες Ἰησοῦν Χριστὸν ἐρχόμενον ἐν σαρκί, "those who do not acknowledge Jesus Christ as coming in the flesh." That these deceivers were the heretics combatted in 1 John is evident from the obvious parallel between this verse and 1 John 4:2-3. For discussion of ὁμολογοῦντες . . . σαρκί, "acknowledge . . . flesh," see on 1 John 4:2. The one significant difference is that 1 John has ἐληλυθότα, "having come," whereas 2 John has ἐρχόμενον, "coming." Grammatically it is possible that the former refers to Christ's first coming while the latter speaks of His second coming. In this case the present tense participle would be a futuristic present. Lenski, however, argues that it is a timeless present,[11] and there are several reasons for agreeing with his view. (1) No known first century heresy denied Christ's second coming in the flesh. (2) The Gnostics denied Christ's first coming in the flesh. (3) The same phrase occurs in 1 John 4:2, where the perfect tense ἐγηθυθότα, "having come," clearly refers to Christ's first coming. (4) Flesh is more naturally used to

---
10. Rudolph Bultmann, *The Johannine Epistles*, Hermeneia, p. 112.
11. R. C. H. Lenski, *The Interpretation of the Epistles of St. Peter, St. John and St. Jude*, p. 566.

refer to the present mortal body than to the immortal resurrection body. οὗτός ἐστιν ὁ πλάνος καὶ ὁ ἀντίχριστος, "This is the deceiver and the antichrist." The demonstrative pronoun, οὗτος, "this," refers to the one who does not accept the incarnation. The articles before πλάνος, "deceiver," and ἀντίχριστος, "antichrist," serve to single out the individual referred to as being in a particular way *the* deceiver and *the* antichrist par excellence. On ἀντίχριστος, see on 1 John 2:18.

D. THE BELIEVER WARNED OF LOSS OF REWARD, V. 8

v.8. βλέπετε ἑαυτούς, ἵνα μὴ ἀπολέσητε ἃ εἰργασάμεθα ἀλλὰ μισθὸν πλήρη ἀπολάβητε, "Watch yourselves, that you might not lose what we have accomplished, but that you may receive a full reward." By use of the present, imperative, βλέπετε, "watch," John urges that his readers place themselves under continuous guard. The purpose of such guard is so that spiritual gains already made may not be lost. Because of the context immediately preceding and following, it is clear that the author has the influence of the Gnostics in mind. A textual problem appears here with regard to the words, ἀπολέσητε, εἰργασάμεθα, and ἀπολάβητε. The following chart shows the distribution of the uncial manuscript evidence:

ἀπολέσητε	εἰργάσασθε	ἀπολάβητε
"you may lose"	"you accomplished"	"you may receive"
ℵ (-λησθε) A B Ψ	ℵ A Ψ	ℵ A B
ἀπολέσωμεν	εἰργασάμεθα	ἀπολάβωμεν
"we may lose"	"we accomplished"	"we may receive"
K L P	B (ἠργ-) K L P	K L P

It seems apparent that the evidence favors ἀπολέσητε and ἀπολάβητε, but, because B switches from the second person plural to the first plural, the decision between εἰργάσασθε and εἰργασάμεθα is more difficult to make. The Editorial Committee of the United Bible Societies' *Greek New Testament* opted for the first person plural εἰργασάμεθα, not because it is supported by B, but because of the weight of transcriptional and internal evidence. Transcriptional: it is thought that εἰργάσασθε was the result of a levelling process that sought to make all three verbs second person plural. Hence the best reading would be εἰργασάμεθα. Internal: the "delicate nuance"—*that you do not lose the things we apostles have accomplished, but that you may receive* . . .—is more apt to have come from the author than from a copyist.[12] The apostle does not want the results of his labor as missionary and teacher to be lost. Instead he desires to see lasting fruit in the lives of the chosen lady and her children.

E. THE ENEMY AND THE BELIEVER CONTRASTED, V. 9

v.9. πᾶς ὁ προάγων καὶ μὴ μένων ἐν τῇ διδαχῇ τοῦ Χριστοῦ θεὸν οὐκ ἔχει, "Any one who goes too far and does not abide in the teaching of Christ, does not have God." The KJV reading, "Whosoever transgresseth, and abideth not in the doctrine of Christ . . ." is based on inferior manuscripts (K L P), which have the word παραβαίνων, "transgress," rather than προάγων, "go on, advance, go too far," which is found in ℵ A B. The verb προάγων, as used here, speaks of professed progress, reflecting the Gnostic claim to have progressed to a higher understanding of God, of the human predicament, and of the secret way of salvation from the predicament.

Brooke points out the non-repetition of the article before μὴ μένων, which serves to limit the kind of progress that is being condemned.[13] John warns against the so-called progress that does not remain within the framework of apostolic teaching. Plummer aptly declares, "There is an advance which involves desertion of first principles; and such advance is not progress but apostasy."[14] The concept of having God (θεὸν οὐκ ἔχει) is also found in 1 John 2:23, which may well have been the original statement (see on 1 John 2:23).

The genitive τοῦ Χριστοῦ may be either a subjective or an objective genitive. If it is the former, it refers to what Christ Himself taught; if the latter, it speaks of teaching about Christ. Numerous commentators favor the subjective genitive here (Brooke, Bruce, Lenski, Plummer, Schnackenburg, Stott, Westcott). However, the context of 2 John 9 calls for an objective genitive. Verse 7 warns against those who deny the incarnation, and the similarity of verses 7 and 9 to passages in 1 John (2:22-23;

---

12. Bruce M. Metzger, *A Textual Commentary on the Greek New Testament*, p. 721.
13. Brooke, p. 177.
14. Plummer, p. 138.

4:2-3) suggests that in 2 John 9 the author refers to heretical Christology, that is, to erroneous teaching about Christ.[15] ὁ μένων ἐν τῇ διδαχῇ, οὗτος καὶ τὸν πατέρα καὶ τὸν υἱὸν ἔχει, "the one who abides in the teaching, he has both the Father and the Son." See on 1 John 2:22-23. Here in 2 John the description of persistent belief is stated in exactly opposite terms from those found in 1 John 2:24. There, John refers to truth remaining in the believer; here (2 John 9) John speaks of the believer remaining in the truth. There is no essential difference between the two ways of decribing the situation.

F. THE BELIEVER INSTRUCTED, VV. 10-11

v.10. εἴ τις ἔρχεται πρὸς ὑμᾶς καὶ ταύτην τὴν διδαχὴν οὐ φέρει, "If any one comes to you and does not bring this teaching." It is significant that John uses εἰ, "if," with the indicative mood rather than ἐάν, "if," with the subjunctive. By the use of εἰ he assumes the reality of the condition rather than merely stating the possibility of it.[16]

The elect lady and her family had been visited by teachers who denied the incarnation of Christ. The "coming" described by ἔρχεται was not merely a chance, personal contact; it was a visit with a specific purpose—in this case, to spread the Gnostic teaching. For instances of other intentional, personal "comings," see Mark 10:45; John 10:10; 3 John 3, 10; *Didache* 11. 1, 4.

The doctrine described as ταύτην τὴν διδαχήν, "this doctrine," refers back to the doctrine about Christ spoken of in verse 9. More specifically, it is the teaching that Jesus Christ is God incarnate. To "bring" (φέρει) this doctrine is, at least, to bring it as one's personal possession, which has been received by faith, but it is probable that John had more in mind than possession or the lack of it. The reference to evil deeds in verse 11 may well speak of the activity of denying the doctrine of incarnation.

μὴ λαμβάνετε αὐτὸν εἰς οἰκίαν καὶ χαίρειν αὐτῷ μὴ λέγετε, "do not receive him into your house, and do not give him a greeting." At first glance, one may think that John has reversed the usual order of first greeting a visitor and then inviting him to come into the house. But χαίρειν, "greeting," was used both at the arrival of a visitor and at his departure. It is, therefore, probable that the reception into the house looks at the arrival, and the

---

15. See Bultmann, p. 113; Marshall, pp. 72-73, n. 13; also see NEB.
16. Westcott, p. 230.

greeting refers to the departure (see 2 Cor. 13:11). The word χαίρειν is the present tense infinitive of χαίρω, "rejoice." The term was the common greeting used in the Greek world just as "Peace be to you" (שָׁלוֹם, Gen. 43:23; εἰρήνη ὑμῖν; John 20:19) was the common Hebrew greeting. Both in the letter dispatched by the Jerusalem council (Acts 15:23) and in the epistle of James (1:1), the Greek greeting occurs. It was an uplifting expression that showed desire that the traveller may experience joy either at his destination or on his prospective journey.

The prohibitions μὴ λαμβάνετε, "do not receive," and χαίρειν . . . μὴ λέγετε, "do not give . . . a greeting," both consist of the negative particle μή and a present tense imperative verb, a construction that in numerous instances is a command to put a stop to an action already in progress.[17] The Christian family to whom this letter is addressed may well have been showing hospitality to travelling Gnostic teachers, thus giving reason for John to pen the epistle.

v.11. ὁ λέγων γὰρ αὐτῷ χαίρειν κοινωνεῖ τοῖς ἔργοις αὐτοῦ τοῖς πονηροῖς, "for the one who gives him a greeting participates in his evil deeds." The conjunction γάρ, "for," introduces John's reason for issuing such sharp prohibitions. To show hospitality to the false teachers is to take an active part in their heretical activities. Κοινωνεῖ speaks of a close union, an active participation, never a casual, superficial involvement.[18] Thus, the seemingly justifiable act of hospitality involves one deeply in helping to propagete error, which John here describes as a wicked act. The emphatic construction, τοῖς ἔργοις αὐτοῦ τοῖς πονηροῖς, "his evil deeds," lays stress on the adjective πονηροῖς, "evil." The emphasis is distributed equally between the noun, ἔργοις, "deeds," and the adjective πονηροῖς, "evil," thus placing more emphasis on the adjective.[19] The teaching of error is characterized as a wicked activity.

IV. CONCLUSION, VV. 12-13

v.12. Πολλὰ ἔχων ὑμῖν γράφειν οὐκ ἐβουλήθην διὰ χάρτου καὶ μέλανος, "Having many things to write to you, I do not want to do so with paper and ink." The participle ἔχων, "having,"

---

17. H. E. Dana and Julius R. Mantey, *A Manual Grammar of the Greek New Testament*, pp. 301-2; F. Blass and A. Debrunner, *A Greek Grammar of the New Testament*, sec. 336 (3).
18. Brooke, p. 179.
19. Dana and Mantey, p. 152.

is causal in sense, meaning "since I have many things to write (impart) to you, I did not want to write with paper and ink." What the "many things" were that John wanted to say to this Christian family he does not tell us. It has been suggested that he was referring to the kind of things that are found in 1 John,[20] but, while this may be true, it is only a guess. Ἐβουλήθην is an aorist indicative literally meaning "I *did* not want." The past tense was here used in keeping with the Greek idiom known as the epistolary aorist, "whereby the writer courteously projects himself in imagination into the position of the reader, for whom actions contemporaneous with the time of writing will be past."[21]

The paper (χάρτου) to which John refers would have been papyrus rather than parchment (μεμβράνα, 2 Tim. 4:13), which was much more costly. Probably this letter was written on a single sheet of papyrus. The word μέλανος, "ink," literally means "black," coming from the fact that the ink then used was made of lampblack, carbon, or soot mixed with a gum and some water. This mixture was shaped into sticks and hardened. It could then be cut and moistened when needed.[22]

ἀλλὰ ἐλπίζω γενέσθαι πρὸς ὑμᾶς καὶ στόμα πρὸς στόμα λαλῆσαι, ἵνα ἡ χαρὰ ὑμῶν πεπληρωμένη ᾖ, "but I hope to come to you and speak face to face, that your joy may be made full." Some have struggled to find some distinctive meaning in γενέσθαι,[23] but Bultmann is right when he points out that the verb γίνομαι is often used as synonymous with ἔρχομαι, "come."[24] The expression "face to face," is even more personal in the Greek text where στόμα πρὸς στόμα appears, meaning "mouth to mouth." This phrase, which may have come from Numbers 12:8, speaks of the most personal kind of fellowship.

The purpose clause, ἵνα ἡ χαρὰ ὑμῶν. . . , "that your joy. . . ," reflects 1 John 1:4. Whereas the NASB has "your joy," the Bible Societies' *Greek New Testament* has ἡμῶν, "our." The confusion between ὑμῶν (your), and ἡμῶν (our), was commonplace. It is probable that the early alteration of ἡμῶν to read ὑμῶν was due to the presence of ὑμῖν and ὑμᾶς in the immediately preceding context.[25] On πεπληρωμένη ᾖ, see on 1:4.

20. Plummer, p. 141.
21. C. F. D. Moule, *An Idiom Book of New Testament Greek*, p. 12.
22. *Wycliffe Bible Encyclopedia*, 1975 ed., s.v. "Ink."
23. Plummer, p. 141; Brooke, p. 179.
24. Bultmann, p. 115, n. 2.
25. Metzger, p. 722.

v. 13. Ἀσπάζεταί σε τὰ τέκνα τῆς ἀδελφῆς σου τῆς ἐκλεκτῆς, "The children of your chosen sister greet you." Many interpret this statement as a greeting from the church in Ephesus sent to the church designated as the "chosen lady" in verse 1. Others, however, view the verse as referring to two Christian women and their children. If this is the correct view, it would seem that the children were in Ephesus where John supposedly wrote this letter. Their mother was not included, either because she was dead or because she was not at the place where John was writing. It may be that these children were the ones who had informed John concerning their aunt's mistaken application of the principle of Christian love. It is difficult to see how, in each instance, both the lady and her children could represent the church. The two designations more naturally suggest separate and different individuals.

THEOLOGICAL COMMENTARY (VV. 1-13)

A. INTRODUCTORY EMPHASIS ON TRUTH AND LOVE, VV 1-4

The words ἀλήθεια, "truth," and ἀγαπάω (ἀγάπη), "love," play significant parts in the first four verses of this letter. Ἀλήθεια occurs five times (vv. 1, 1, 2, 3, 4), and ἀγαπάω (ἀγάπη) occurs twice (vv. 1, 3). This double emphasis sets the tone for the entire letter as John proceeds to show the careful balance in which these two elements of the Christian life must be held.

1. LOVE, THE PRODUCT OF TRUTH, V. 2

The expression διὰ τὴν ἀλήθειαν. . . . indicates that John loved the elect lady and her family because of the truth that dwelt in him. Several facts should be noticed concerning this statement. (1) To be indwelt by truth refers to holding the truth or believing the truth. (2) The NASB translation of διά as "for the sake of" is not an adequate rendering in the context. The translation "because of" is much better. (3) The passage does not say that the apostle loved this Christian family because they were believers, instead, (4) it was because of the truth dwelling in John and other Christians that they loved her and her family.

While this explanation of Christian love could refer to the persuasive power of truth, it no doubt goes beyond this. Believers do love each other because they are taught by God to do so (1 Thess.

4:9). They also love one another because they possess a common bond in the truth they share. It is natural to love someone who holds the same convictions one holds dear. However, there is a more basic way in which truth produces love. First John 5:1 indicates that the truth, "Jesus is the Christ," when believed, results in being born of God, and being born of God in turn results in love for other members of God's family. Truth, then, results in regeneration, and regeneration results in love for other believers.

2. THE OCCASION FOR THIS DOUBLE EMPHASIS

Truth and love are closely related; in fact they are necessary companions. Genuine love does not exist apart from truth. This foundational fact is at the heart of John's message to the elect lady and her family. Love must not be divorced from truth. Instead it should always be exercised within the guidelines of truth.

Apparently the lady to whom John writes had been exercising love at the expense of truth. The remainder of the letter suggests that she had been showing hospitality to traveling teachers who were denying basic Christian doctrines. Truth should have been her guide in the exercise of love. If showing loving hospitality will result in the advance of error and the decline of truth, such hospitality ought to be withheld. Love should not violate truth; instead it should uphold truth and make it known to the greatest possible number of people.

Because of the elect lady's failure to use discernment in the exercise of love, John devotes this short letter to the task of showing the relationship between truth and love. He indicates that his love for this Christian family is in the sphere of truth (v. 1*a*). Others who also love them are people who hold to the truth (v. 1*b*). Such love is the product of Christian truth (v. 2). In fact, the spiritual benefits God bestows likewise exist in the sphere of truth and love (v. 3). And in addition John rejoices because he has encountered members of the elect lady's family who are living in accord with the truth (v. 4).

3. WALKING IN TRUTH, V. 4

The term *walking* is a very common metaphor for living, occurring frequently in both the Old and New Testaments. To walk in truth is to live in truth. The use of the present tense verb suggests that John had in mind a continuing life-style of living in truth.

For the apostle, truth was not merely a corpus of doctrine to be understood intellectually and confessed orally. It was that, to be sure, but truth for John was also meant to impinge upon life so that it molded and shaped the way a person conducted himself. John saw truth, not as mere abstraction, but as intensely practical (see 1 John 1:6). He rejoiced that the children of the elect lady were living in the sphere of truth. It was the area in which their lives were conducted and thus it shaped their total conduct.

B. AN EXHORTATION TO LOVE, VV. 5-6

John's primary purpose in writing this letter was to warn against showing Christian love in the form of hospitality toward those who hold to and who teach false doctrine. However, before he actually begins to sound that warning, he calls for the practice of mutual Christian love. Perhaps this was to avoid any false conclusion that might otherwise have been drawn from his seemingly negative attitude toward the practice of love.

The reasoning of verses 5-6 proceeds, not unjustifiably, in a circle. Verse 5 sounds the command Jesus had given in the upper room (John 13:34-35) to continually exercise love toward each other. Here, obedience to the Lord's command results in love. Verse 6*a* then declares that to love is to live in accordance with God's commands (plural). In other words, love results in obedience to God's commands. This, too, Jesus had taught when, after quoting the two great commandments to love God with one's whole being and one's neighbor as one's self, He declared, "All the Law and the Prophets hang on these two commandments" (Matt 22:40, NIV). Paul put it even more explicitly when he wrote, "Love is the fulfillment of the law" (Rom. 13:10, NIV). John then returns again in verse 6*b* to the command (singular) to love. As in verse 5, obedience to the Lord's command results in love. John's rather involved reasoning in these two verses reveals how closely the two concepts of love and obedience are interwoven.

C. WARNING AGAINST CONTRIBUTING TO THE PROPAGATION OF ERROR, VV. 7-11

In these verses the reader finds himself at the heart of the letter. Here the apostle divulges his purpose in writing.

1. THE OCCASION FOR WRITING, V. 7

At the end of the first century Christians in Asia Minor were being confronted by an early form of a heresy that came to be known as Gnosticism. A number of the early Gnostic teachers denied that the divine Son of God actually became incarnate. The basis for such a denial was the dualistic philosophy that regarded matter as evil and spirit as good. Thus deity, which is spirit, could not become incarnate in a human body, which is matter. (On Gnosticism, see chapter 4, The Occasion and Purpose of the Epistle.) It was to warn against this threat that John wrote both 1 and 2 John.

2. A WARNING TO THE ELECT LADY AND HER FAMILY, V. 8

Because of the presence of numerous early Gnostic deceivers, John urges this Christian family to be on constant spiritual alert. It would appear that these Asian believers in some way owed their spiritual status to John. Either he was instrumental in their conversion or he had played a part in their spiritual development. Consequently he is concerned that these friends should not be swayed by the Gnostic deceivers. If this were to occur, it would result in loss of reward when believers stand at the judgment seat of Christ (see 2 Cor. 5:10).

3. THE ENEMY AND THE BELIEVER CONTRASTED, V. 9

A distinctive characteristic of the early Gnostic was that of "advance." He viewed the traditional believer in apostolic Christianity as hopelessly mired down in a totally inadequate system of salvation by faith. At the same time the Gnostic viewed himself as progressive. He was confident that he had gone beyond (προάγων, "go on, advance, go before") traditional Christianity with its incarnational Christology (τῇ διδαχῇ τοῦ Χριστοῦ). But John's verdict was that this "progressive" teacher, by his "advance," revealed that he was without God.

In contrast the apostle describes the believer as one who, rather than departing from apostolic Christology (τῇ διδαχῇ τοῦ Χριστοῦ, "the doctrine of Christ"), continues in that teaching. His characteristic is doctrinal steadfastness. He is not carried away with a desire for new teaching or for doctrinal progress. He knows that in the area of truth progress may well lead to error because it may mean departure from the truth. To be specific, to advance in the area of Christology as the Gnostic claimed to have done was to give up the doctrine of the incarnation of the Son of God. In reality, what might be called progress was actually retrogression to paganism and unbelief.

4. THE DANGEROUS INVOLVEMENT PROHIBITED, VV. 10-11

In verse 10 what specifically led to the writing of this letter is revealed. The Christian lady to whom John addressed his remarks had been showing hospitality to various travelling teachers, a commendable action if those teachers were proclaiming the truth. The practice to which John refers is also seen in 3 John 5-8 where Gaius is commended for taking in Christian brothers who were travelling for the sake of Christ's name. John is reflecting the first century practice of providing food and lodging for travelling teachers and missionaries and of sending them on their way with provisions for their journey ("to send them on their way in a manner worthy of God," 3 John 6). Paul likewise instructed Titus to provide for the journey of Zenas and Apollos (Titus 3:13). This practice is also reflected in the *Didache* (11, 1-6).

It appears, however, that the elect lady had been extending such hospitality indiscriminately, all in the name of Christian love. She had not been careful to make sure that everyone to whom she showed hospitality held to the teaching that Jesus Christ is God's incarnate Son. The result was that she had been providing food and lodging for persons who were denying the truth and proclaiming a Christ who could not save.

John therefore urged her to stop this practice. On the surface, it appears that he is warning her not to let them into the door, not even to speak to them. Such an interpretation, however, overlooks the practice explained above and documented in 3 John 5-8 and Titus 3:13. What she had been doing and what John forbids was a practice that actually contributed to the work of the false teachers. Verse 11 indicates that the greeting was of such a nature that it actually involved the greeter in the work of those who were greeted. By lodging these teachers, the elect lady had been investing money in their destructive ministry.

D. PRESENT-DAY APPLICATION

In the first century, missionary support was a very simple matter. There were no formal mission societies to send out missionaries, nor were there denominational organizations to sponsor itinerant teachers. This was done on an individual and a local basis. Even if a church leader such as the apostle John sent out such teachers or preachers, they were supported while travelling by believers in towns where they ministered or through which they passed. This practice is substantially different from current methods of missionary support. There is a basic principle, however, that transcends the centuries and applies equally today. John declares that the one who contributes to the teacher actually participates in his ministry, whether it is good or evil. In 3 John 8 we are told that we ought to become involved in the ministry of the truth, but in 2 John 10-11 we are warned against participating by our contributions in the propagation of error.

Paraphrastic Commentary (vv. 1-13)

(1) From the Elder to a dear lady who is one of God's own and to her family, I love them as believers in the truth of the gospel. And I am not the only one who holds this family in high regard. All those who have likewise come to know the truth love them, (2) and we do so because that life-changing truth dwells permanently in our hearts. (3) The blessings of undeserved favor, of tender compassion, and of spiritual well-being, all of which come from God and His Son Jesus Christ, will ever be our companions in the spheres of truth and love.

(4) I was especially pleased when I came across some members of your family who are daily putting their faith into practice just as God has commanded us to do.

(5) Now, I ask you, dear lady, to submit, not to a new command, but to an old one that we have known since the beginning of our Christian experience, namely that we should make it a habit to demonstrate love to each other. (6) And this is what Christian love is: It is to live continually in obedience to God's standards of right and wrong. All of this is included in one command which we are to obey continually—namely that we should love one another. We have heard this ever since we came to know the Lord.

(7) We should love in this way because there are so many false teachers travelling from place to place, bent on leading people astray. They refuse to affirm sincere belief in Jesus Christ, God's Son who came to live in a human body of flesh and bones. A false teacher like this one is the deceiver par excellence; he is the present-day manifestation of the coming antichrist. (8) Keep continual guard over yourselves so that you will not lose the spiritual ground

we have helped you to gain, but will receive the greatest possible reward when you stand before Christ's judgment seat. (9) No person who "advances" beyond what the apostles have taught concerning the incarnate Christ has any meaningful relationship with God. The one who does not renounce his belief in apostolic Christology but remains fully committed within the boundaries of the truth—he has a personal relationship with both God the Father and God the Son. (10) When travelling teachers come desiring lodging at your house, stop granting such requests if those who make them do not come proclaiming that Jesus Christ is God's incarnate Son. Also stop the practice of putting such persons up for the night and sending them on their way with provisions for their journey. (11) If you show such hospitality to them, you are participating in their evil work.

(12) I have much that I would like to say to you, but I do not want to say it by letter. Instead, I expect to visit you. Then we can talk face to face so that our joy will overflow. (13) The family of your godly sister sends its greetings.

STRUCTURAL COMMENTARY (vv. 1-13)

I. Introduction, vv. 1-3
   A. Author and recipients, vv. 1-2
      1. The author: the elder, v. 1*a*
      2. The recipients: a beloved Christian family, vv. 1*b*-2
         a. A Christian woman, v. 1*b*
         b. Her children, v. 1*b*
         c. People widely loved, v. 1*c-d*
         d. A love that results from a knowledge of the truth, v. 2
   B. Greeting, v. 3
      1. A promise of spiritual blessings
      2. The givers of blessing: the Father and the Son
      3. The spheres of blessing: truth and love
II. Commendation, v. 4
   A. Expressing John's joy
   B. Based on the consistent living of some of the elect lady's children
III. Exhortation and warning, vv. 5-11
   A. The believer exhorted to love, v. 5
      1. A command known since conversion, v. 5*a*
      2. A call for mutual love, v. 5*b*
   B. Love explained, v. 6
      1. Love is obedience to God's commands, v. 6*a*

2. The readers have known the command since conversion, v. 6b
3. It is a command intended to affect life, v. 6c
C. The exhortation justified, v. 7
1. By the fact that there are many deceivers in the world, v. 7a
2. By the fact that they deny the incarnation of Christ, v. 7b
3. By the fact that they are forerunners of the antichrist, v. 7c
D. The believer warned of loss of reward, v. 8
1. Constant guard commanded, v. 8a
2. A full reward desired, v. 8b
E. The enemy and the believer contrasted, v. 9
1. The enemy, v. 9a
 a. He "advances" (beyond the truth)
 b. He does not persist in belief in the incarnation
 c. He is without God
2. The believer, v. 9b
 a. He continues to hold to the incarnation
 b. He has a personal relationship with both Father and Son
F. The believer instructed, vv. 10-11
1. The practices to be discontinued, v. 10
2. The reason for discontinuing them, v. 11
IV. Conclusion, vv. 12-13
A. Plans for a visit in the near future, v. 12
B. Greetings from the children of the elect lady's sister, v. 13

PART 4
The Third Epistle of John

18

Introduction to 3 John

The fact that 3 John found its way into the New Testament canon is of itself weighty evidence in favor of the genuineness of the letter. It is not surprising that Romans or 1 Corinthians should be thought worthy of a place in the canon, but the inclusion of such a personal letter as 3 John rules out any possibility that it was a fraud. Dodd says "we could not understand why anyone should have taken the trouble to fabricate it."[1]

THE AUTHORSHIP OF THE EPISTLE

The writings of the early church provide less support for 3 John than for the gospel or the first or even the second epistle. The first church father to refer to the third letter explicitly was Origen (c. A.D. 185-253). He is reported to have said that John wrote the first epistle "and maybe a second and a third; for not all say they are genuine."[2] Dionysius of Alexandria (c. A.D. 200-265) said that John does not indicate his name in 2 and 3 John, but merely calls himself the elder.[3] Eusebius (c. A.D. 260-340) assigned

---

1. C. H. Dodd, *The Johannine Epistles,* The Moffatt New Testament Commentary, pp. lxiii-lxiv.
2. Eusebius *H. E.* 6. 25. 10.
3. Ibid., 3. 7. 25.

both letters to the *antilegomena*.[4] And Jerome (c. A.D. 340-420) held that the two letters were written by John the elder rather than by John the apostle.[5] Such evidence is not impressive.

However, it is the internal evidence that justifies the traditional view of apostolic authorship. The letter's similarity to 2 John is obvious to the most casual reader:

(1) Both letters open in the same way. The author calls himself the elder and he addresses his letters to people whom he loves in truth (2 John 1; 3 John 1).
(2) Both express joy because the recipients are walking in truth (2 John 4; 3 John 4).
(3) Both letters are concerned with itinerant teachers, either false or genuine (2 John 7-10; 3 John 5-8, 10).
(4) The structure of the two letters is similar.
(5) The concluding remarks in both are very much alike.
  (a) In both the author has much more to say but does not want to put it in writing (2 John 12; 3 John 13).
  (b) Instead the author plans to come soon to speak with the recipients personally (2 John 12; 3 John 14).
  (c) The two letters conclude with greetings from persons known to both the author and the recipients (2 John 13; 3 John 14).

The following chart gives further evidence of the similarity between the two letters.

Term or Expression	No. of Occurrences in 3 John	No. of Occurrences in 2 John
The elder	1	1
love (verb ἀγαπάω)	1	2
love (noun ἀγάπη)	1	2
truth	6	5
I was very glad	1	1
walking in (the) truth	2	1

---

4. Ibid., 3. 25. 3.
5. Jerome, *Lives of Illustrious Men* XI. 18.

walk, walking	2	3
many things to write	1	1
I hope to see (come)	1	1
face to face	1	1
greet	2	1

Here are five words and six expressions that serve to tie 2 and 3 John together. In fact, the three Johannine epistles fit together like pieces of an interlocking puzzle. Raymond Brown says, "The fact that the same doctrinal and moral issues are being combatted in 1 and 2 John and that both 2 and 3 John are concerned with traveling teachers interlocks the epistles."[6] The Introduction to the first epistle has already argued that the relationship between the gospel of John and 1 John indicates that both writings came from the same author (see pp. 16-24). Further evidence has been provided to show that the gospel and the first epistle were written by John the apostle (see pp. 33-37).

The Recipient of the Epistle

There is no doubt but that this letter was written to an individual, since the recipient's name is given. However, the fact that the name is known does not enable us to identify the person intended. There are three persons called Gaius in other NT passages, namely Gaius of Macedonia (Acts 19:29), Gaius of Derbe (Acts 20:4), and Gaius of Corinth (Rom. 16:23; 1 Cor. 1:14). There is, however, no reason for identifying the Gaius of 3 John with any one of these three.

Since evidence links John with the churches of the province of Asia, it seems most reasonable to assume that the Gaius of 3 John was a fourth individual by that name who was a member of one of those churches. This identification is rendered all the more plausible since the name Gaius was as common as the name John is today.[7]

Nothing is definitely known of Gaius except what is to be found in this letter. He was spiritually prosperous (v. 2); he lived a life

---

6. Raymond E. Brown, *The Community of the Beloved Disciple*, p. 94.
7. James Hope Moulton and George Milligan, *The Vocabulary of the Greek New Testament*, p. 120.

consistent with the truth (v. 3); and he was outstanding for his hospitality shown to travelling brothers (vv. 6-8). Nothing of his official position in the church, if indeed he filled any such post, is known.

THE DATE OF THE EPISTLE

Little more can be said concerning the date of 3 John than that its similarity to 2 John would seem to place it between A.D. 90 and 95, in the same general time period as the second letter. There is no way of knowing whether 3 John originated before, at the same time as, or after 2 John unless it is theorized, as some do, that 2 John was sent to the church in which Diotrephes was exercising his dictatorship.[8] In that case, the letter mentioned in 3 John 9 may have been 2 John, but that is unlikely.[9]

THE OCCASION AND PURPOSE OF THE EPISTLE

The occasion for the letter grew out of the early church practice of supporting travelling Christian teachers and missionaries by providing food and lodging for them. John commends Gaius for outstanding service in this regard (vv. 5-8), but Diotrephes had refused to show such hospitality to emissaries sent out from John. In fact he absolutely refused to receive them and even went so far as to try to excommunicate anyone who did.

John wrote the letter for several reasons. (1) Its primary purpose was to commend Gaius for faithfulness in spite of Diotrephes' threats (vv. 5-8). (2) It was intended to carry an indirect warning to Diotrephes (v. 10). (3) John wanted to commend Demetrius, who was perhaps one of the travelling teachers and/or the bearer of the letter (v. 12). (4) He also wanted to inform his readers of his plans to visit them soon (v. 14).

AN OUTLINE OF THE EPISTLE

I. Introduction, vv. 1-2
   A. Author and recipient, v. 1
   B. Prayer, v. 2
II. Commendation of Gaius, vv. 3-8

---

8. R. C. H. Lenski, *The Interpretation of the Epistles of St. Peter, St. John and St. Jude*, pp. 549-50.
9. Donald Guthrie, *New Testament Introduction*, p. 899, note 6.

Introduction to 3 John

    A. Commendation for Christian conduct in general, vv. 3-4
    B. Commendation for Christian hospitality in particular, vv. 5-8
III. Condemnation of Diotrephes, vv. 9-10
    A. His rejection of John's letter, v. 9
    B. John's warning that he will deal with Diotrephes' deeds, v. 10
IV. Exhortation to Gaius, v. 11
V. Recommendation of Demetrius, v. 12
VI. Conclusion, vv. 13-14

19

Commentary on 3 John

The introduction to this third epistle of John is both similar to and different from the introduction to 2 John. Both are from "the elder," but whereas the recipient of 3 John is named, 2 John is simply addressed to "the chosen lady."

Like 2 John, the third letter follows the usual overall pattern for a first century letter. A standard first century feature found in 3 John but not in 2 John is the prayer for health and prosperity to be seen in verse 2.

Exegetical Commentary (vv. 1-14)

I. INTRODUCTION, VV. 1-2

A. AUTHOR AND RECIPIENT, V. 1

v.1. Ὁ πρεσβύτερος Γαΐῳ τῷ ἀγαπητῷ, ὃν ἐγὼ ἀγαπῶ ἐν ἀληθείᾳ, "The elder to the beloved Gaius, whom I love in truth." On ὁ πρεσβύτερος, "the elder," see Introduction to 1 John. On Γαΐῳ see Introduction to 3 John: "The Recipient of the Epistle." The adjective ἀγαπητῷ, "beloved," reflects the heartfelt regard in which Asian Christians held Gaius. To this indication of the attitude of believers in general John adds a statement of his own high regard, describing Gaius as one "whom I love in truth." On ἀγαπάω (I love), and ἀγάπη (love), see on 1 John 2:7. On ὅν ἐγὼ ἀγαπῶ ἐν ἀληθείᾳ, "whom I love in truth," see on 2 John 1. That ἀληθείᾳ is to be taken as definite even though it is anarthrous is evident from the further use of the word in verses 3-4. There ἀληθείᾳ is used interchangeably with τῇ ἀληθείᾳ, in both instances having to do with walking in the truth. Clearly John is speaking of living in accordance with *the* truth, that body of truth that lies at the heart of the Christian faith. (Cf. 2 John 4). The two constructions also are used interchangeably in John 8:45-46.

B. PRAYER, V. 2

v.2. Ἀγαπητέ, περὶ πάντων εὔχομαί σε εὐοδοῦσθαι καὶ ὑγιαίνειν, "Beloved, I pray that in all respects you may prosper and be in good health." Instead of the typical Christian greeting (cf. 2 John 3) John includes this standard epistolary formula of concern for the reader's welfare. By using the vocative ἀγαπητέ, "beloved," John continues to stress the high regard in which Gaius was held. It is one of the apostle's favorite words of address, occurring six times in 1 John (2:7; 3:2, 21; 4:1, 7, 11) and in two other places in 3 John (vv. 5, 11). However, even though he declares his love for the chosen lady and her children in 2 John 1, he neither uses the term "beloved" of the lady nor of her children.

The verb εὔχομαι, "I pray," has been interpreted both as referring to a prayer and as referring to a wish.[1] Numerous modern versions translate it "I pray" (RSV, NEB, NASB, TEV, NIV, Williams, Beck, Montgomery), and there is good evidence that the formula in Koine letters often referred to prayer. *The Loeb Classical Library* volume, *Select Papyri*, contains letters reading as follows: "I pray to God that you are prosperous"; "I pray for your prosperity daily before all the gods"; "I pray to God that my letter finds you well."[2] This kind of prayer occurs in papyrus letters of the second century with noticeable frequency, although the form varies from letter to letter. However, the combination of εὐοδοῦσθαι and ὑγιαίνειν in one statement similar to John's use was limited in frequency.[3] Paul uses the verb εὐοδόω, "lead on a good path," in its literal sense in Romans 1:10 and again in 1 Corinthians 16:2 in its figurative sense of prospering financially.

1. Rudolf Bultmann, *The Johannine Epistles*, Hermeneia, p. 97.
2. A. S. Hunt and C. C. Edgar, trans. *Select Papyri*, The Loeb Classical Library, 1:367, 369, 389.
3. Robert W. Funk, "The Form and Structure of II and III John," *Journal of Biblical Literature* 86 (December, 1967): 425.

That it is this latter idea of success in a financial way that John has in mind is clear from the fact that he compares it with prosperity of soul. The more common term, used both in the introductions to and the conclusions of letters, was ὑγιαίνω, "be in good health." Although it was frequently used in secular letters to refer to mental health and general well being, its comparison here with the concept of prosperity of soul indicates that physical health is in view.

καθὼς εὐοδεῦταί σου ἡ ψυχή, "just as your soul prospers." John prays that Gaius may prosper materially and be in health physically in the same way as he prospers spiritually. Καθώς, "just as," calls for a close parallel between the two spheres of prosperity. That the author repeats εὐοδόω, "prosper," rather than ὑγιαίνω, "be in good health," in the second member of the comparison is noteworthy. The choice of εὐοδόω is probably due to the extended use of this word in the LXX, where it reflects the idea that it is God who causes his people to prosper.[4] Gaius is outstanding because his spiritual prosperity has outdistanced his material prosperity rather than the opposite, as is often the case.

II. COMMENDATION OF GAIUS, VV. 3-8

A. COMMENDATION FOR CHRISTIAN CONDUCT IN GENERAL, VV. 3-4

v.3. ἐχάρην γὰρ λίαν ἐρχομένων ἀδελφῶν καὶ μαρτυρούντων σου τῇ ἀληθείᾳ, καθὼς σὺ ἐν ἀληθείᾳ περιπατεῖς, "For I was very glad when brethren came and bore witness to your truth, that is, how you are walking in truth." Studies of numerous Greek personal letters show that ἐχάρην λίαν, "I was very glad," or variants of it was a "common epistolary formula" in introductions to letters about A.D. 100 and later.[5] Sometimes joy was expressed because of the receipt of a letter; often it was because of good news received as in 3 John 3, 4. John's joy was occasioned by reports of Gaius's truth. The present tense participles ἐρχομένων and μαρτυρούντων, "coming" and "bearing witness," are iterative in nature and thus refer to an occurrence that took place repeatedly. It seems that at various times traveling teachers coming from Gaius's locality had reported concerning his devotion to

---

4. Gerhard Kittel, ed., *Theological Dictionary of the New Testament*, s.v. "εὐοδόω, " by Wilhelm Michaelis. 5:114.
5. Funk, pp. 425-27.

the truth. The articular τῇ ἀληθείᾳ does not refer to Gaius's truthfulness, but rather to his devotion to the truth of the gospel as set forth in the Scripture. This devotion to truth, however, was not limited merely to acceptance and belief; it was faithfulness that expressed itself in practice. The adverb καθώς, "just as," here is synonymous with πῶς, "how," and was used to introduce indirect discourse, namely the content of the report given by the traveling brothers. On ἐν ἀληθείᾳ περιπατεῖς, "you are walking in truth," see remarks on 2 John 4. The fact that ἀληθείᾳ, "truth," is not accompanied by an article in its second occurrence in the verse does not make the word indefinite. Since it was used with an article but a half dozen words before, it was not necessary to repeat the article. It means *the* truth in both instances.

v.4. μειζοτέραν τούτων οὐκ ἔχω χαράν, ἵνα ἀκούω τὰ ἐμὰ τέκνα ἐν τῇ ἀληθείᾳ περιπατοῦντα, "I have no greater joy than this, to hear of my children walking in the truth." The demonstrative pronoun τούτων, "this," is plural in number and could literally be translated "these things." However, the added explanation in the remainder of the verse speaks of one single piece of good news—his children are walking in the truth. Three interpretations of the plural have been suggested. (1) The use of the plural for the singular is said to be a common usage.[6] (2) By using the plural John recalls a number of occasions when brothers came with news of the faithfulness of Gaius.[7] (3) The most reasonable suggestion sees the plural as referring to the things included in such reports—the activities of Gaius the brothers reported.[8] These activities could all be described as aspects of "walking in the truth." The variant reading χάριν, "grace, favor," which appears in B and the Vulgate, is no doubt the error of a scribe who carelessly wrote the more common χάριν instead of χαράν. Both manuscript evidence (א A C K L P) and Johannine usage (seven occurrences in the gospel as well as occurrences in 1 John 1:4 and 2 John 12) favor χαράν.

Although the conjunction ἵνα usually expresses purpose ("in order that"), it is used in numerous places in a nonfinal sense as

---

6. W. Robertson Nicoll, gen. ed., *The Expositor's Greek Testament*, s.v. "The Epistles of John," by David Smith, 5:206.
7. A. E. Brooke, *The Johannine Epistles*, The International Critical Commentary, p. 183.
8. R. C. H. Lenski, *The Interpretation of the Epistles of St. Peter, St. John and St. Jude*, p. 581.

the equivalent of ὅτι, "that."[9] It serves in this passage to introduce an epexegetic clause explaining the sum and substance of τούτων, "these things," more fully. Τὰ ἐμὰ τέκνα, "my children," may designate John's converts or it may be his word for all who were under his spiritual care. It would seem better to interpret the term as including all under John's care, since many of the churches in the province of Asia could trace their history back to the days of Paul's ministry in Ephesus (c. A.D. 53-55), and many had been won to Christ before John arrived in Ephesus (c. A.D. 70).

B. COMMENDATION FOR CHRISTIAN HOSPITALITY IN PARTICULAR, VV. 5-8

v.5. ἀγαπατέ, πιστὸν ποιεῖς ὃ ἐὰν ἐργάσῃ εἰς τοὺς ἀδελφοὺς καὶ τοῦτο ξένους, "Beloved you are acting faithfully in whatever you accomplish for the brethren, and especially when they are strangers." On ἀγαπατέ, "beloved," see on verse 2. The reports from traveling brothers apparently had specifically mentioned the hospitality of Gaius. John describes this activity as πιστόν, "a faithful thing." Although such activity sprang from faith, as do all good works (Eph. 2:8-10; James 2:14-26), the word πιστόν is no doubt used in the passive sense meaning trustworthy, dependable, loyal.[10] The NASB translation of ἐργάσῃ as "accomplish" is a bit heavy; a simple "do" would be an adequate rendering in the context. In the Johannine epistles the word ἀδελφός, "brother," is regularly used of fellow Christians (thirteen times in 1 John and three times in 3 John; see on 1 John 2:9). Although ξένος "stranger," sometimes refers to foreigners, this is not the meaning intended here. These individuals are simply not known personally to Gaius.

v.6. οἳ ἐμαρτύρησάν σου τῇ ἀγάπῃ ἐνώπιον ἐκκλησίας, "and they bear witness to your love before the church." The traveling brothers had returned to the congregation in John's locality and had reported concerning Gaius's loving reception of itinerant Christian teachers. In verse 3 the present tense participle is used (μαρτυρούντων, "bearing witness"), signifying the numerous occasions when the brothers came with reports of Gaius's faithfulness. Here in verse 6, however, John employs the aorist tense ἐμαρτύρησαν, "bore witness," which views the repeated reports as a single fact. The NASB causes some confusion by translating

---

9. H. E. Dana and Julius R. Mantey, *A Manual Grammar of the Greek New Testament*, p. 248.
10. William F. Arndt and F. Wilbur Gingrich, trans. and eds., *A Greek-English Lexicon of the New Testament*, by Walter Bauer, pp. 664-65.

Commentary on 3 John

both occurrences of the word in the wrong tense ("bore" instead of "bearing," v. 3, and "bare" instead of "bore," v. 6). The substance of the reports is summed up in the single word ἀγάπη, "love." In the epistles of John, love is never mere sentiment or verbalization. Instead it is action, as the following context (vv. 6b-8) bears out. On love as action, see on 3:16-18. The church before which the travelling brothers bore witness may well have been the local church in Ephesus since early church tradition indicated that John spent his latter years in that city.

οὓς καλῶς ποιήσεις προπέμψας ἀξίως τοῦ θεοῦ, "and you will do well to send them on their way in a manner worthy of God." The expression οὓς καλῶς ποιήσεις, "you will do well," followed by a participle, was a very common introduction to a request. It was comparable to *please*. Moulton and Milligan give a number of examples from papyri of the first three centuries A.D. where this idiom appears.[11] The word προπέμψας, "send on their way," was something of a technical term among early Christians for the act of providing the traveller with goods for his journey.[12]

The way in which such hospitality was to be shown is described as ἀξίως τοῦ θεοῦ, "in a manner worthy of God." The Greek text literally reads *worthily of God*. This may refer to: the way God should be treated (see Matt. 10:40);[13] the way God has treated us;[14] or (3) the kind of treatment that will bring praise to God (Col. 1:10; 1 Thess. 2:12). While all three possibilities should be true of any Christian conduct, the third suggestion seems to best represent John's intended meaning.

v.7. ὑπὲρ γὰρ τοῦ ὀνόματος ἐξῆλθον μηδὲν λαμβάνοντες ἀπὸ τῶν ἐθνικῶν, "For they went out for the sake of the Name, accepting nothing from the Gentiles." The conjunction γάρ, "for," indicates that what follows is intended to provide reasons for the action prescribed in the preceding statement.[15] The first reason why the itinerant teachers ought to be assisted on their way was because they set forth, not for themselves, but for the Name. The article τοῦ before ὀνόματος, "Name," particularizes

---

11. James Hope Moulton and George Milligan, *The Vocabulary of the Greek New Testament*, pp. 522-23; also see NEB, Williams.
12. C. H. Dodd, *The Johannine Epistles*, The Moffatt New Testament Commentary, p. 160.
13. John R. W. Stott, *The Epistles of John*, Tyndale New Testament Commentaries, p. 221.
14. Donald W. Burdick, *The Epistles of John*, p. 119.
15. Dana and Mantey, p. 243.

the name and sets it off as the name distinct from all other names. For Christians *the* Name could be none other than the name Jesus Christ. On the biblical usage of the term *name*, see on 1 John 2:12. Ἐξῆλθον, "they went out," was used to describe the initiation of a mission such as a missionary journey (Acts 15:40) or a campaign to spread false doctrine (2 John 7). The itinerant missionaries to whom John refers in 3 John 7 probably set out from the church in Ephesus, perhaps being dispatched by John himself.

The second reason why these itinerant brothers should be provided for was because of the sacrificial manner in which they set out. They went taking nothing (λαμβάνοντες, a participle expressing manner). Τῶν ἐθνικῶν, "the Gentiles," is not to be understood primarily as an ethnic term, but as a moral and religious description, referring to unbelievers living in moral and spiritual darkness. Since such people were mostly Gentiles, the term ἐθνικός came to be used as the terms "heathen" (RSV) and "pagans" (NIV) are used today. The missionaries made it a policy not to receive any support from the unbelievers to whom they were taking the gospel message.

v. 8. ἡμεῖς οὖν ὀφείλομεν ὑπολαμβάνειν τοὺς τοιούτους, "Therefore, we ought to support such men." The pronoun ἡμεῖς, "we," is emphatic. Since the missionaries do not rely on unbelievers for support, "we" Christians must provide what is needed. The word "ὑπολαμβάνειν is translated by the NASB as "to support." However, the marginal reading, "receive such men as guests," is more specific. The kind of support referred to is that of providing food and lodging. In addition, the verb carries the idea of providing protection (for the persecuted).[16] The persons who should be received hospitably are designated as τοὺς τοιούτους, "such men." The article τούς serves to point out the particular persons John has in mind[17] and the qualitative correlative demonstrative pronoun speaks of their characteristics,[18] namely, they were the kind of persons who made it a point on their missionary journeys to take no support from unbelievers (v. 7).

ἵνα συνεργοὶ γινώμεθα τῇ ἀληθείᾳ, "that we may be fellow-workers with the truth." Although the verb γίνομαι usually

---

16. Kittel, s.v. "ὑπολαμβάνω," by G. Delling. 4:15.
17. F. Blass and A. Debrunner, *A Greek Grammar of the New Testament*, sec. 274.
18. A. T. Robertson, *A Grammar of the Greek New Testament in the Light of Historical Research*, pp. 709-10.

means *become*, it seems to be used here as the equivalent of εἶναι, "to be," and is thus translated "we may be." Gaius, by virtue of the fact that he was engaged in such a helping ministry, had already become a fellow worker with the truth. Συνεργοί . . . τῇ ἀληθείᾳ may be translated in two different ways. The truth personified may be understood as that with which Christians may work: "fellow-workers with the truth" (NASB), or John may be speaking of the cooperation of Christians in the interest of the truth: "we may work together for the truth" (NIV). Although the noun συνεργός is not used with the instrumental case elsewhere in the New Testament, the verb συνεργέω, "work together," is used with the instrumental in James 2:22, where faith is said to work together with deeds (συνήργει τοῖς ἔργοις). The noun is more commonly followed by the genitive case as in 1 Corinthians 3:9: θεοῦ γάρ ἐσμεν συνεργοί, "for we are God's fellow-workers." The noun is also used with εἰς as in Colossians 4:11: συνεργοὶ εἰς τὴν βασιλείαν, "fellow-workers for the kingdom." Since the preposition σύν is generally used with the instrumental case to mean "with" or "together with,"[19] it is to be assumed that the meaning is the same in this instance. Thus John is speaking of working together with the truth. The only justification for the translation, "workers together for the truth," would be if the text contained an explicit identification of the person(s) with whom work is done for the truth, i.e., workers for the truth together with (σύν) the itinerant missionaries.

III. CONDEMNATION OF DIOTREPHES, VV. 9-10

A. HIS REJECTION OF JOHN'S LETTER, V. 9

v.9. Ἔγραψά τι τῇ ἐκκλησίᾳ, "I wrote something to the church." The aorist tense ἔγραψα, "I wrote," ought to be taken as a simple constative aorist expressing a past action. There is no justification for interpreting it as an epistolary aorist. The indefinite pronoun, τι, "something," may have one of three possible meanings. (1) It may mean something special, similar to what is meant today when someone says, "Now, *that* is *something!*" (2) It may be a term of belittlement. John doesn't bother to dignify what he wrote as a letter—it is just something. (3) Or, as Brooke says, it may suggest neither something great nor something insig-

---

19. Dana and Mantey, p. 111.

nificant.[20] The last view seems to be the best of the three. It is difficult to understand why John would play down the significance of his letter to the church, and it is certain that he was not insinuating that his letter was something great. No doubt what he wrote was a letter commending itinerant missionary teachers and urging the church to receive them and provide for their needs.

Since ἐκκλησία, "church," is preceded by an article, it is reasonable to assume that the church to which the letter was sent was the church with which Gaius was associated. Τῇ ἐκκλησίᾳ could in itself refer to the universal church, but it would have been rather difficult for John to distribute his letter to the whole church and the apparent subject of the letter seems to assume a local church.

ἀλλ᾽ ὁ φιλοπρωτεύων αὐτῶν Διοτρέφης οὐκ ἐπιδέχεται ἡμᾶς, "but Diotrephes, who loves to be first among them, does not accept what we say." John chose to use the stronger adversative conjunction ἀλλά, "but," rather than the less forceful δέ in order to heighten Diotrephes' rejection of his communication. The present tense participle, φιλοπρωτεύων, "loves to be first," indicates that loving to be first was the persistent pattern that characterized Diotrephes. The verb φιλοπρωτεύω, like the simple πρωτεύω, "be first," takes the genitive case to designate the person(s) who are being exceeded. Diotrephes loved to be first among them, that is, to be the first one *of* the group. The context (v. 10) indicates that αὐτῶν, "them," refers to the members of the local church in which both Gaius and Diotrephes were involved. The name Diotrephes, which means "nourished by Zeus," may indicate that its bearer had himself come out of a pagan background rather than being a second or third generation Christian. The present tense οὐκ ἐπιδέχεται, "does not accept," indicates Diotrephes' customary reaction toward John and his associates (ἡμᾶς, "us"). He refused to recognize John's authority.[21] The NASB "what we say" is an explanatory paraphrase for the Greek ἡμᾶς, "us."

B. JOHN'S WARNING THAT HE WILL DEAL WITH DIOTREPHES' DEEDS, V. 10

v.10. διὰ τοῦτο, ἐὰν ἔλθω, ὑπομνήσω αὐτοῦ τὰ ἔργα ἃ ποιεῖ, λόγοις πονηροῖς φλυαρῶν ἡμᾶς, "For this reason, if I come, I will call attention to his deeds which he does, unjustly

20. Brooke, p. 187.
21. Arndt and Gingrich, p. 292; Moulton and Milligan, p. 237; Bultmann, p. 100.

Commentary on 3 John 455

accusing us with wicked words." It is clear that in this instance τοῦτο, "this," refers back to the preceding statement. What John proposes to do in verse 10 is based on Diotrephes' refusal to recognize the apostle's authority. The conditional conjunction ἐάν, "if," was probably not intended to cast doubt on the certainty of John's proposed visit. This conjunction is sometimes practically synonymous with ὅταν, "whenever." John himself used it in this manner in 1 John 2:28; 3:2, where he speaks of Christ's return. It is certain that he was not voicing doubt concerning the fact of the second advent; only about the time. (See also John 12:32.) So here in 3 John 10, there is no doubt that John intends to come; in verse 14 he declares his plan to see Gaius shortly. He is not sure when that will be, but whenever he comes, he "will call attention to his [Diotrephes'] deeds." The verb ὑπομιμνήσκω, "remember," in 25 percent of its usages in secular Greek, meant "to mention," "to bring up,"[22] and it is this meaning that many modern translations (NASB, NIV, RSV, NEB, TEV, Beck, Moffatt, and Goodspeed) and commentators find in this passage.[23] The apostle warns that he will bring up for official, public discussion what Diotrephes has been doing and saying.

Diotrephes' verbal attack against the Elder is described by the participle φλυαρῶν. The present tense describes the action as continually going on. The verb itself was used of unjust accusation, but its more common meaning was "to talk nonsense."[24] (See 1 Tim. 5:13 for the occurrence of the adjective φλύαρος, "gossipy.") In 3 John 10 the malicious statements (λόγοις πονηροῖς) were also nonsense, so far were they from the truth. The adjective πονηρός, "wicked, evil, malicious," refers to one who is engaged in aggressive evil, in active malignity.[25] Thus, Diotrephes' words were vicious attacks designed to destroy the standing of the accused.

καὶ μὴ ἀρκούμενος ἐπὶ τούτοις οὔτε αὐτὸς ἐπιδέχεται τοὺς ἀδελφούς, "and not satisfied with this, neither does he himself receive the brethren." The plural demonstrative pronoun τούτοις, translated as "this" in the NASB, is by its plural nature

---

22. Colin Brown, ed., *The New International Dictionary of New Testament Theology*, 1975-78, s.v. "Remember, Remembrance," by K. H. Bartels.
23. Brooke, p. 189; Bultmann, p. 101; Dodd, p. 165; A. Plummer, *The Epistles of St. John*, Cambridge Greek Testament for Schools and Colleges, p. 149; Stott, p. 227; B. F. Westcott, *The Epistles of St. John*, p. 240.
24. Moulton and Milligan, p. 673.
25. Richard C. Trench, *Synonyms of the New Testament*, p. 304.

referring back to the malicious words (λόγοις πονηροῖς). Diotrephes was not satisfied with mere talk, as forceful as his vicious utterances had been. He backed up his verbal attacks with malignant actions. The verb ἐπιδέχεται, "receive," here refers to hospitality rather than recognition of authority as in v. 9. The use of the present tense makes it clear that Diotrephes' continuing policy was to refuse lodging to the itinerants.[26] The brothers (τοὺς ἀδελφούς) are no doubt the ones referred to in verses 3, 5-8 who had been engaged in itinerant missionary work and had reported back to John concerning their reception.

καὶ τοὺς βουλομένους κωλύει καὶ ἐκ τῆς ἐκκλησίας ἐκβάλλει, "and he forbids those who desire to do so, and puts them out of the church." The combining of a negative and a positive (οὔτε, "neither," and καί, "and") is not common in classical Greek or in the NT (see John 4:11), but it does appear more often in later Greek.[27] However, although the construction was acceptable Greek idiom, it is strange to the English ear, and ought to be restated in corresponding English idiom. See RSV, NEB, NIV, and TEV, all of which simply replace the word "neither" with a negative term such as "refuses" (to welcome) or "will not" (welcome).

κωλύει, translated "forbids" in the NASB, is really a broader term that may mean "prevent, restrain, hinder, forbid" (Acts 8:36; 27:43; 2 Pet. 2:16). Diotrephes may have been forbidding people orally, whether or not he was successful in his intention; he may have been hindering people by placing obstacles in their way, thus making it difficult for them to show hospitality to the itinerant missionaries; or he may have been trying to prevent people from showing such hospitality. The third possibility understands the present tense κωλύει as a conative present describing an attempt, which may or may not have succeeded. The parallel verb ἐκβάλλει, "puts out," could refer to actual physical expulsion from the church meetings, although this is not likely. The verb could be describing an actual fact—Diotrephes was succeeding in excommunicating people. Or this verb also could be a conative present in which case Diotrephes would have been attempting to excommunicate members of the church. Whether or not he was succeeding is not indicated. Inasmuch as Gaius does not seem to have been excommunicated even though he had been showing hospitality to the travelling evangelists (vv. 5-7), it would seem that Diotrephes' efforts, both to prevent such hospitality and to excom-

---

26. Brooke, p. 190.
27. Blass and Debrunner, sec. 445.

municate those who exercised it, had failed. Thus, the two verbs, κωλύει and ἐκβάλλει, should probably both be interpreted as conative. That John is not referring to a single occurrence is apparent from his use of the present tense, which depicts continuing action. As both Brooke and Bultmann indicate, the present tense verbs speak of Diotrephes' policy or practice.[28] Because of the article with ἐκκλησίας, "church," the term should be understood as referring to the local church, as in verse 9.

IV. EXHORTATION TO GAIUS, V.11

v.11. Ἀγαπητέ, μὴ μιμοῦ τὸ κακὸν ἀλλὰ τὸ ἀγαθόν, "Beloved, do not imitate what is evil, but what is good." On ἀγαπητέ, see on verse 2. The change from the discussion of Diotrephes to the exhortation to Gaius is somewhat abrupt, marked as it is by asyndeton. This absence of any connecting particle makes the subsequent prohibition with its vocative ἀγαπητέ, "beloved," the more striking. As a general rule, the construction consisting of μή and the present tense imperative (μὴ μιμοῦ, "do not imitate") prohibits the continuation of an action already in progress.[29] Such an interpretation would assume that Gaius was actually imitating Diotrephes, and John would be saying, "Stop imitating what is evil." This, however, does not agree with the practice for which John commends Gaius in verses 5-7. Consequently, it may be that John was merely reflecting Gaius's tendency to be too easily influenced by Diotrephes' evil ways. The apostle would, therefore, be attempting to put a stop to this tendency. Instead Gaius is urged to imitate "what is good." It is to be assumed that the present tense, imperative verb μιμοῦ carries through to the end of the clause, thus calling on Gaius to make it his practice to imitate the good.

ὁ ἀγαθοποιῶν ἐκ τοῦ θεοῦ ἐστιν· ὁ κακοποιῶν οὐχ ἑώρακεν τὸν θεόν, "The one who does good is of God; the one who does evil has not seen God." The prohibition stated in the first part of the verse is here undergirded by means of a general principle. The two participles, ἀγαθοποιῶν, "does good," and κακοποιῶν, "does evil," because they are in the present tense, speak of the continuing practice of doing good and evil. As in 1 John 2:29;

---

28. Brooke, p. 190; Bultmann, p. 101.
29. Blass and Debrunner, sec. 336; Robertson, p. 950; Dana and Mantey, secs. 289-90; Ernest Dewitt Burton, *Syntax of the Moods and Tenses in New Testament Greek*, sec. 165; William Douglas Chamberlain, *An Exegetical Grammar of the Greek New Testament*, p. 86.

3:7-10, it is the general pattern of life, not the isolated act, that reveals a person's spiritual relationship. The expressions ἐκ τοῦ θεοῦ ἐστιν, "is of God," and οὐχ ἑώρακεν τὸν θεόν, "has not seen God," remind us of 1 John 3:10; 4:4, 6; and 3:6 respectively. There, as here, the practice of righteousness is the evidence that one has been born of God and has seen God in intimate personal experience. It is such similarities that tie these three epistles together as coming from the same author. On the phrase ἐκ τοῦ θεοῦ as short for γεγεννημένος ἐκ τοῦ θεοῦ, see on 1 John 3:10a.

V. RECOMMENDATION OF DEMETRIUS, V. 12

v.12. Δημητρίῳ μεμαρτύρηται ὑπὸ πάντων καὶ ὑπὸ αὐτῆς τῆς ἀληθείας, "Demetrius has received a good testimony from everyone, and from the truth itself." The name Demetrius occurs but twice in the New Testament, here and in Acts 19:24 where it refers to the Ephesian silversmith who stirred up a riot because of Paul's successful ministry there. However, outside of the fact that both lived in the province of Asia, there is no reason to assume that the two individuals were the same. It was a common name, as Greek inscriptions reveal.[30] Some have thought that the name Demas (Col. 4:14; 2 Tim. 4:10; Philem. 24) is a shortened form of Demetrius, but this is only conjecture. Most commentators take him to be the bearer of this letter and/or one of the itinerant teachers mentioned in verses 5-8. It is virtually certain that he carried the letter, a thought also held by Marshall.[31] The most plausible reason for commending him would have been that he was coming to Gaius from John. In view of Diotrephes' rejection of John's messengers, the apostle wanted to make sure that Demetrius was well received.

Μεμαρτύρηται, "has received a good testimony," is a perfect tense verb, and therefore depicts an action that was completed in the past. People have previously given testimony concerning Demetrius' character, and that testimony now stands as an assured fact. That this testimony was given by everyone (ὑπὸ πάντων, "by all") is hyperbole, not exaggeration. John desires to emphasize the widespread character of the testimony. At least it was true of all who knew him.

The word ἀληθείας, "truth," does not refer to truth as an abstract quality, which could be the case if the noun were anarth-

---
30. Moulton and Milligan, p. 144.
31. I. Howard Marshall, *The Epistles of John, The New International Commentary on the New Testament*, p. 93.

rous. The fact that the word is preceded by an article (τῆς ἀληθείας, "the truth") points to a specific *body* of truth, the revealed corpus of truth at the heart of the Christian faith (see on v. 3.) This corpus John personifies as a witness to Demetrius' character.[32] The apostle no doubt means that Demetrius lives in harmony with revealed truth, and in this way the truth testifies to the kind of man he is.

καὶ ἡμεῖς δὲ μαρτυροῦμεν, καὶ οἶδας ὅτι ἡ μαρτυρία ἡμῶν ἀληθής ἐστιν, "and we also bear witness, and you know that our witness is true." To the testimony of others (καί, "also"), John adds his own word, which, as the present tense μαρτυροῦμεν, "bear witness," indicates, is a continuing affirmation. Whereas the preceding testimony came from the past, John's was a current witness concerning things as they were at the moment he wrote. The pronoun ἡμεῖς, "we," is somewhat emphatic. In addition to others, *we* bear witness. The "we" is probably an editorial "we," although it could be a reference to those personally associated with John in Ephesus.[33] John adds his personal testimony, not because the preceding witnesses are inadequate, but because he knows that Gaius is sure (οἶδα represents knowledge held with assurance; see on 1 John 2:29) that John is utterly truthful.

VI. CONCLUSION, VV. 13-14

v.13. Πολλὰ εἶχον γράψαι σοι, ἀλλ' οὐ θέλω διὰ μέλανος καὶ καλάμου σοι γράφειν, "I had many things to write to you, but I am not willing to write them to you with pen and ink." For basic commentary on this statement, see on 2 John 12*a*, which is essentially the same as this verse. Although there is some change in vocabulary and grammatical structure, the meaning is not different. The imperfect verb εἶχον, "I had," looks at John's previous intention. Perhaps when he contemplated writing, his original plan was to write more. The aorist infinitive γράψαι, "to write," looks at the letter as a whole, whereas the present infinitive γράφειν, "to write" (2 John 12; 3 John 13) speaks of the process. In 2 John 12, the epistolary aorist ἐβουλήθην, "I do not want," was used—this is not essentially different from the present tense θέλω, "I am not willing." Although some have tried to develop a difference in meaning between these two verbs, the resultant disagreement seems to indicate that there is no real distinction. In

---

32. Bultmann, p. 102; Marshall, p. 93, note 6.
33. Marshall, p. 93, note 8; Westcott, p. 242.

place of the writing paper referred to in 2 John 12 (χάρτου, "paper"), 3 John 13 speaks of the writing instrument (καλάμου, "a reed pen"). John's reason for not writing a more lengthy letter may have been the cost of writing materials, the labor of writing with materials then available, or the personal nature of what he had to say. The last explanation seems most plausible.

v.14. ἐλπίζω δὲ εὐθέως σε ἰδεῖν, καὶ στόμα πρὸς στόμα λαλήσομεν, "but I hope to see you shortly, and we shall speak face to face." Again, because of the similarity of this verse to the conclusion of 2 John, see verse 12b of that epistle. There is no essential difference between γενέσθαι, "to come" (2 John), and ἰδεῖν, "to see" (3 John). In 3 John the Elder adds εὐθέως, "shortly," probably because of the urgent need to confront Diotrephes. And there is no real difference between λαλῆσαι, "to speak" (2 John), and λαλήσομεν, "we shall speak" (3 John). A better alternative than extended communication by letter is that of speaking "face to face" (στόμα πρὸς στόμα, *mouth to mouth*).

εἰρήνη σοι. ἀσπάζονταί σε οἱ φίλοι. ἀσπάζου τοὺς φίλους κατ' ὄνομα, "Peace be to you. The friends greet you. Greet the friends by name." Whereas the English text includes what follows in verse 14, the Greek text has for years begun verse 15 at this point. Εἰρήνη σοι, "Peace be to you," is the traditional Hebrew expression for both greeting and farewell, used to this day and adopted by Christians as well. See Christ's use of it as a greeting (John 20:19, 21, 26). It was particularly appropriate considering the upsetting nature of Diotrephes' actions. Whereas 2 John identifies specifically those sending greetings (v. 13), 3 John simply calls them οἱ φίλοι, "the friends." This is the only place in the NT that fellow Christians are called "friends," although Jesus employed the term to refer to those for whom He was about to give His life (John 15:13). The reason why John wanted the friends greeted "by name" may have been twofold. First, it was more personal and more readily conveyed John's warm affection to them, and second, because of Diotrephes' stranglehold on the church, the greetings could not be conveyed in a corporate fashion.

THEOLOGICAL COMMENTARY (vv. 1-14)

A. THE SPIRITUAL PROSPERITY OF GAIUS, VV. 2-8

The contrast between Gaius's physical and material condition, on the one hand, and his spiritual condition, on the other, was rather striking. His spiritual prosperity seems to have exceeded his material prosperity. Too often in that day, as well as this, just the reverse was true. Evidence of Gaius's spiritual prosperity is to be seen in verses 3-8.

1. GAIUS WALKED IN THE TRUTH, VV. 3-4.

In verse 3 John refers to Gaius's truth, which might at first glance be taken to mean his truthfulness. However, the concluding clause of the verse, καθὼς σὺ ἐν ἀληθείᾳ περιπατεῖς, "how you are walking in truth," explains that John has in mind the practice of the truth in daily living. The term *walk* is a metaphor for "live." To live in the truth is to make the truth the sphere in which life is conducted; it is to live in accordance with the truth. On the interpretation of truth as that body of truth on which Christianity rests, see the exegetical commentary on verse 1.

To John the normal Christian life is not one of intellectual belief alone. Truth is not to be merely theoretical, something to be held in the mind but not expressed in life; it is not to be speculative, something to be argued in debate but not applied in the struggle of life; it is not merely to be believed, it is also to be lived. In four places in his gospel and in his three letters John speaks of walking in or doing the truth. In John 3:21 the one who is doing the truth is contrasted with the one whose actions are evil (vv. 19-20). In 1 John 1:6 the person who is walking in the darkness is not doing the truth. In 2 John 4 some of the children of the chosen lady are walking in the truth. In 3 John 3, 4 Gaius is walking in the truth, and John rejoices to hear that his children are walking in the truth. Belief, then, is to be the kind of commitment that involves life as well as thought. In this regard, Gaius prospered spiritually.

2. GAIUS ACTED FAITHFULLY, V. 5.

What he did for the itinerant brothers was πιστόν, "a faithful thing." As stated in the exegetical commentary, this term does not speak merely of action that flows from faith, but of deeds that were faithful and loyal in and of themselves. Gaius was dependable; he could be counted on to help when help was needed. When travelling missionaries came to his town, he was sure to take them in and provide for them, even at the risk of incurring the wrath of Diotrephes. In this regard, too, Gaius enjoyed prosperity of soul.

3. GAIUS MANIFESTED GENUINE LOVE, V. 6.

The motivation that moved Gaius to do what he did for the brothers, even when they were strangers, was love. Here, as elsewhere in the Johannine letters, the word translated "love" is ἀγάπη, which speaks of the self-giving, spontaneous but deliberate, outgoing love seen first in God and reproduced in His children. In this passage it expresses itself even to people who are not personally known (v. 5). Furthermore, it clearly is not mere sentiment, but love in action (cf. 1 John 3:16-18), expressing itself in Christian hospitality for itinerant missionaries. In this also Gaius revealed his genuine spiritual prosperity.

B. AN EARLY FORM OF MISSIONARY SUPPORT, VV. 5-8

In the early days of Christianity there was as yet little or no formal provision for the support of missionaries and other travelling Christian teachers. Mission boards were things of the distant future. Whatever arrangements were made were not organized but were dependent on the spontaneous giving of believers. Actually, such support came in the form of hospitality shown to the traveller. He was received and put up as a guest while in the vicinity, then he was sent on his way to his next place of ministry with adequate provision for his journey. This practice is seen in Titus 3:13, where Paul instructs Titus to help Zenas and Apollos on their way so that they lack nothing for their journey. This, no doubt, was also the intended meaning in Acts 15:3; Romans 15:24; 1 Corinthians 16:6, 11; and 2 Corinthians 1:16.

Such support would involve food and perhaps money. It should be remembered that the roads were not lined with restaurants and fast food outlets. Inns, while they were present along most Roman roads, were most unpleasant facilities infested with vermin and robbers. Such conditions amplified the need for Christians to show hospitality to fellow Christians, especially those travelling for the purpose of spreading the Christian message. It was such Christian workers that John had in mind, as verse 7 makes clear.

Two enduring principles governing mission giving emerge from this passage. First, support for Christian work is not to be expected from unbelievers (v. 7). On the contrary, such support is to be provided by God's people. The propagation of the gospel is to be underwritten by the voluntary giving of believers, who give because God first gave to them. (See 2 Cor. 8, 9.) The second principle is found in verse 8. To support those who are proclaiming the gospel is to become a participant with the good news as it effects a work of saving grace in the lives of people. (See Exegetical Commentary on v. 8.) John is not merely saying that believers become fellow preachers of the gospel with those supported; instead, he declares that those who give work together with the message itself. They have a part in impressing the truth of the gospel on the minds and hearts of people who hear it.

C. DIOTREPHES' POSITION IN THE CHURCH, VV. 9-10

In these two verses something of the characteristics of Diotrephes and the nature of the authority he exercised is observed. He habitually pushed himself into the place of preeminence (v. 9). He attempted to foist upon the church his own personal policy of rejecting the travelling teachers (v. 10). He went so far as to try to excommunicate church members who refused to comply (v. 10).

What was the position of Diotrephes in the church? There are at least three possibilities. (1) He was a lay member who had gained a stranglehold on the church and was grasping for the power of excommunication. (2) He was one of the church elders (overseers) who had gained dictatorial power. (3) He was a bishop (overseer) of the kind found in the second century church, who possessed the power of determining church policy and of excommunication.

Although Diotrephes' exercise of authority may suggest that he was indeed a second century bishop of the monarchical type, the description of him given in these verses favors a person who had arrogated to himself power that did not rightfully belong to him. The description of him as one who loved to be preeminent seems to describe a person who does not possess the position of preeminence, but who has usurped it. As Bruce says, "The language suggests a self-promoted demagogue rather than a constitutional *presbyteros* or *episkopos.*"[34] Lenski believes that the absence of any reference to Diotrephes' official position agrees best with the view that he was simply a member of the congregation who had been able to dominate both elders and congregation.[35]

If Diotrephes was but a lay member of the church, he serves as a warning to any and all church people of the danger of such self-exalting attempts at church control. It should be noted that the root of Diotrephes' problem was his own attitude toward himself.

---

34. F. F. Bruce, *The Epistles of John*, p. 152.
35. Lenski, p. 588.

He loved to be first, and this produced the vicious and dictatorial actions described in verse 10.

Something of John the elder's authority is also seen in verse 10. He does not speak merely as a lay person, but as one who possesses authority to deal effectively with the troublesome person. However, it is not ecclesiastical authority that enables John to command that Diotrephes be summarily dealt with and removed. He simply says, "I will 'bring up' what he is doing," no doubt for congregational discussion and action.

D. CONCLUDING COMMAND AND WARNING, V. 11

John's typical negative-positive construction reminds us of passages such as 1 John 1:6-7; 2:4-5, 9-11; 3:7-8. The command was doubtless occasioned by the acts of Diotrephes who showed himself to be evil. The warning is stated as a general principle, but in light of the preceding context it would seem to have a specific reference to Diotrephes. Such evil practices (note the present tense verbs in v. 10 describing his acts) show that he was not born of God. The mark of God's people is the continuing practice of good or, more specifically, the continuing manifestation of love for the people of God, rather than the antipathy shown by Diotrephes.

PARAPHRASTIC COMMENTARY (vv. 1-14)

(1) From the Elder to Gaius, who is dearly loved, whom I hold in high regard as a believer in the truth of the gospel. (2) Dear friend, I am asking God that you will be as prosperous financially and physically as you are spiritually. (3) I was most happy when, time and again, our travelling missionaries came and gave us firsthand reports of your devotion to God's truth, and how you are living in accordance with it. (4) Nothing causes me to rejoice more than the things I am hearing—how those under my spiritual care are patterning their lives after the truth of God.

(5) Dear friend, what you have done for these travelling missionaries—even for those you have never met before—shows how trustworthy you are. (6) They have told the congregation here about your acts of love. When they set forth on their way, please provide what they need for their journey. And do so with the kind of generosity that will bring praise to God. (7) This is only right because they have set out on their mission for the sake of Christ, and they are not depending on unbelievers for support. (8) So we

are under obligation to take these itinerant brothers into our homes as guests. One purpose for doing so is in order that we may work side-by-side with the truth which these brothers are proclaiming.

(9) I sent a letter to the church where you are a member, but Diotrephes, who is obsessed with the desire to be in a place of preeminence does not recognize our authority. (10) So whenever I come, I will bring up (for official discussion) what he is doing, ranting maliciously against us. And, as if this were not enough, he himself does not show hospitality to the travelling missionaries, and in addition he tries to stop anyone who wants to do so. He even goes so far as to try to excommunicate them.

(11) Dear friend, root out any tendency to be influenced by the evil practices of Diotrephes; instead make it your practice to follow good examples. The person whose life-style can be characterized as good shows that he is God's child; the one who habitually does evil has never come to know God.

(12) Everyone has a good word for Demetrius (who brings you this letter); even the truth of God bears witness that he lives in harmony with God's word. We also add our word, and you can be sure that it is altogether true.

(13) There are many things I had wanted to write to you, but I would rather not put them in writing now. (14) Instead I want to come and see you soon. Then we can talk face to face. May you have peace. Your friends here send you greetings. You also give greetings by name to the friends there.

STRUCTURAL COMMENTARY (vv. 1-14)

I. Introduction, vv. 1-2
   A. Author and recipient, v. 1
      1. The author: the elder, v. 1a
      2. The recipient: Gaius, a beloved fellow Christian, v. 1b
   B. Prayer, v. 2
      1. For financial prosperity
      2. For good health
II. Commendation of Gaius, vv. 3-8
   A. Commendation for Christian conduct in general, vv. 3-4
      1. It was reported by travelling brothers, v. 3a
      2. It constituted living in accordance with the truth, v. 3b
      3. To hear such reports was John's greatest joy, v. 4

B. Commendation for Christian hospitality in particular, vv. 5-8
   1. Gaius's faithful act, v. 5
   2. The subject of a report before the church, v. 6a
   3. A request that provisions for the road be given travelling missionaires, v. 6b
   4. Reasons why these brothers should be helped, vv. 7-8
      a. They went out to represent Jesus, v. 7a
      b. They accepted nothing from unbelievers, v. 7b
      c. To help them is to work together with the truth, v. 8

III. Condemnation of Diotrephes, vv. 9-10
   A. His rejection of John's letter, v. 9
   B. John's warning that he will deal with Diotrephes' deeds, v. 10
      1. His unjust and nonsensical accusations
      2. His refusal to receive the brothers
      3. His insistence that no one receive them

IV. Exhortation to Gaius, v. 11
   A. The prescribed course of action
      1. Not to imitate what is evil
      2. To imitate what is good
   B. The principle involved
      1. The one practicing good is God's child
      2. The one practicing evil has never had any personal relationship to God

V. Recommendation of Demetrius, v. 12
   A. By everyone
   B. By the truth
   C. By John

VI. Conclusion, vv. 13-14
   A. Plans to come soon and communicate face to face rather than by letter, vv. 13-14a
   B. A brief benediction: Peace to you, v. 14b
   C. An exchange of greetings, v. 14c

Bibliography

REFERENCE WORKS

Abbott-Smith, G. *A Manual Greek Lexicon of the New Testament.* Edinburgh: T. & T. Clark, 1948.
Barclay, William. *New Testament Words.* London: SCM, 1964.
Bauer, Walter. *A Greek-English Lexicon of the New Testament.* Translated and edited by W. F. Arndt, F. W. Gingrich, and F. W. Danker. Chicago: U. of Chicago, 1979.
Blass, F., and Debrunner, A. *A Greek Grammar of the New Testament.* Translated and edited by Robert W. Funk. 3d English ed. rev. Chicago: U. of Chicago, 1970.
Brown, Colin, ed. *The New International Dictionary of New Testament Theology,* 3 vols. Grand Rapids: Zondervan, 1975-78.
Burton, Ernest Dewitt. *Syntax of the Moods and Tenses in New Testament Greek.* Chicago: U. of Chicago, 1923.
Chamberlain, W. D. *An Exegetical Grammar of the Greek New Testament.* New York: Macmillan, 1954.
Dana, H. E., and Mantey, J. R. *A Manual Grammar of the Greek New Testament.* Toronto: Macmillan, 1957.
Dupont-Sommer, A. *The Essene Writings from Qumran.* Cleveland: World Publishing, 1962.
Gaster, Theodor H., trans. *The Dead Sea Scriptures.* Garden City, N.Y.: Anchor Books, 1964.
A Lexicon Abridged from Liddell and Scott's Greek-English Lexicon. Oxford: Clarendon, 1935.

Liddell, H. G., and Scott, Robert. *A Greek-English Lexicon.* Edited by H. Stuart Jones and R. McKenzie. 9th ed. Oxford: Clarendon, 1940.
Kittel, G., and Friedrich, G. *Theological Dictionary of the New Testament.* Translated by G. W. Bromiley. 10 vols. Grand Rapids: Eerdmans, 1964-76.
Metzger, B. M. *A Textual Commentary on the Greek New Testament.* New York: United Bible Societies, 1971.
Moule, C. F. D. *An Idiom Book of New Testament Greek.* Cambridge: University Press, 1968.
Moulton, James Hope, et al. *A Grammar of New Testament Greek.* 4 vols. Edinburgh: T. & T. Clark, 1908-1976.
Moulton, James H., and Milligan, George. *The Vocabulary of the Greek New Testament.* Grand Rapids: Eerdmans, 1930.
Robertson, A. T. *A Grammar of the Greek New Testament in the Light of Historical Research.* New York: Harper and Brothers, 1923.
Trench, Richard C. *Synonyms of the New Testament.* London: Macmillan, 1876.
Turner, Nigel. *Style.* Vol. 4 of *A Grammar of New Testament Greek.* Edinburgh: T. & T. Clark, 1908-1976.
———*Syntax.* Vol. 3 of *A Grammar of New Testament Greek.* Edinburgh: T. & T. Clark, 1908-1976.
Wernberg-Møller, P. *The Manual of Discipline.* Grand Rapids: Eerdmans, 1957.
Zerwick S. J., Maximilian. *Biblical Greek.* Adapted from the fourth Latin edition by Joseph Smith, S. J. Rome: Scripta Pontificii Instituti Biblici, 1963.

COMMENTARIES ON THE JOHANNINE EPISTLES

Alexander, William. *The Epistles of St. John.* The Expositor's Bible. London: Hodder and Stoughton, 1889.
Alford, Henry. *The Greek Testament.* 4 vols. London: Rivingtons, 1875.
Bengel, J. A. *Gnomon of the New Testament.* Edinburgh: T. & T. Clark, 1863.
Bonsirven, Joseph. *Épitres de Saint Jean.* Vol. 9 of *Verbum Salutis, Commentaire du Nouveau Testament.* Paris: Beauchesne et ses fils, 1954.
Braune, Karl. "The Epistles General of John." In *A Commentary on the Holy Scriptures,* edited by J. P. Lange. New York: Scribner's, 1868.

Brooke, A. E. *The Johannine Epistles*. The International Critical Commentary. 1912. Reprint. Edinburgh: T. & T. Clark, 1964.
Brown, Raymond E. *The Epistles of John*. The Anchor Bible. Garden City, N.Y.: Doubleday, 1982.
Bruce, F. F. *The Epistles of John*. Old Tappan, N.J.: Revell, 1970.
Bultmann, Rudolf. *The Johannine Epistles*. Hermeneia. Philadelphia: Fortress, 1973.
Burdick, Donald. *The Epistles of John*. Chicago: Moody, 1970.
Conner, Walter T. *The Epistles of John*. 2d ed. Nashville: Broadman, 1957.
Cox, Leo G. "First, Second, and Third John." In *The Wesleyan Bible Commentary*, vol. 6, edited by Charles W. Carter, Ralph Earle, W. Ralph Thompson, and Lee Haines. Grand Rapids: Eerdmans, 1966.
Dana, H. E. *The Epistles and Apocalypse of John*. Kansas City, Kan.: Central Seminary Press, 1947.
Dodd, C. H. *The Johannine Epistles*. The Moffatt New Testament Commentary. London: Hodder and Stoughton, 1946.
Findlay, George C. *Fellowship in the Life Eternal*. London: Hodder and Stoughton, n.d.
Houlden, J. L. *A Commentary on the Johannine Epistles*. Black's New Testament Commentaries. London: Adam & Charles Black, 1973.
Law, Robert. *The Tests of Life*. Edinburgh: T. & T. Clark, 1909.
Lenski, R. C. H. *The Interpretation of the Epistles of St. Peter, St. John and St. Jude*. Columbus, Ohio: Wartburg, 1945.
Marshall, I. Howard. *The Epistles of John*. The New International Commentary on the New Testament. Grand Rapids: Eerdmans, 1978.
Perkins, Pheme. *The Johannine Epistles*. Vol. 21. The New Testament Message. Wilmington: Michael Glazier, 1979.
Plummer, A. *The Epistles of St. John*. The Cambridge Greek Testament for Schools and Colleges. Cambridge: University Press, 1894.
Robertson, A. T. *Word Pictures in the New Testament*. Vol. 6. New York: Harper and Brothers, 1933.
Ross, Alexander. *The Epistles of James and John*. The New International Commentary on the New Testament. Grand Rapids: Eerdmans, 1954.
Smith, David. "The Epistles of John." In *The Expositor's Greek Testament*, vol. 5. Grand Rapids: Eerdmans, n.d.
Stott, J. R. W. *The Epistles of John*. Tyndale New Testament Com-

mentaries. Grand Rapids: Eerdmans, 1964.
Vincent, Marvin R. *Word Studies in the New Testament.* Vol. 2. New York: Scribner's, 1908.
Westcott, B. F. *The Epistles of John.* Grand Rapids: Eerdmans, 1950.
White, R. E. O. *Open Letter to Evangelicals.* Grand Rapids: Eerdmans, 1964.

OTHER WORKS DEALING WITH JOHANNINE LITERATURE

Albright, W. F. "Recent Discoveries in Palestine and the Gospel of John," In *The Background of the New Testament and Its Eschatology,* edited by W. D. Davies and D. Daube. Cambridge: University Press, 1956.
Bacon, B. W. *The Fourth Gospel in Recent Research and Debate.* New York: Moffat, Yard and Co., 1910.
Barrett, C. K. *The Gospel According to St. John.* New York: Macmillan, 1955. 2d ed. Philadelphia: Westminster, 1978.
Braun, F.-M. *Jean Le Théologien.* Paris: Gabalda, 1959.
Brown, Raymond E. *The Community of the Beloved Disciple.* New York: Paulist, 1979.
―――. *The Gospel According to John.* The Anchor Bible. Garden City, N.Y.: Doubleday, 1966, 1970.
Bultmann, Rudolf. *The Gospel of John: A Commentary.* Philadelphia: Westminster, 1971.
Carson, D. A. "Historical Tradition in the Fourth Gospel: After Dodd, What?" In *Gospel Perspectives,* 2:83-145, edited by R. T. France and David Wenham. Sheffield, England: JSOT Press, 1981.
Cullmann, Oscar. *The Johannine Circle.* Philadelphia: Westminster, 1976.
Culpepper, R. Alan. *The Johannine School: An Evaluation of the Johannine School Hypothesis Based on an Investigation of the Nature of Ancient Schools.* Missoula, Mont.: Scholar's Press, 1975.
Dodd, C. H. "The First Epistle of John and the Fourth Gospel." *Bulletin of the John Rylands Library* 21 (April 1937): 129-56.
Encyclopaedia Biblica, 1901 edition. S.v. "John, the Son of Zebedee."
Hendriksen, William. *The Gospel of John,* The New Testament Commentary. Grand Rapids: Baker, 1970.
Hoskyns, E. C. *The Fourth Gospel.* 2d ed. Edited by F. N. Davey. London: Faber and Faber, 1947.

Howard, W. F. "The Common Authorship of the Johannine Gospel and Epistles." *Journal of Theological Studies* 48 (January 1947): 12-25.

International Standard Bible Encyclopedia, 1939 edition. S.v. "The Epistles of John."

Moody, Dale. "God's Only Son: The Translation of John 3:16 in the Revised Standard Version." *The Bible Translator* 10 (October 1959): 145-47.

Morris, Leon. *Commentary on the Gospel of John*. The New International Commentary on the New Testament. Grand Rapids: Eerdmans, 1971.

———. *Studies in the Fourth Gospel*. Grand Rapids: Eerdmans, 1969.

Piper, Otto. "I John and the Didache of the Primitive Church." *Journal of Biblical Literature* 66 (December 1947): 437-51.

Robinson, J. A. T. "The New Look on the Fourth Gospel." In *Twelve New Testament Studies*. Studies in Biblical Theology, no. 34. Naperville, Ill.: Allenson, 1962.

Salom, A. P. "Some Aspects of the Grammatical Style of 1 John." *Journal of Biblical Literature* 74 (June 1955): 96-102.

Schnackenburg, Rudolf. *The Gospel According to St. John*. Herder's Theological Commentary on the New Testament. New York: Herder and Herder, 1968.

———. "On the Origin of the Fourth Gospel." In *Jesus and Man's Hope*. Vol. 1. Pittsburgh: Pittsburgh Theological Seminary, 1970.

Scholer, David M. "Sins Within and Sins Without: An Interpretation of 1 John 5:16-17." In *Current Issues in Biblical and Patristic Interpretation*. Edited by Gerald F. Hawthorne. Grand Rapids: Eerdmans, 1975.

Songer, Harold S. "The Gospel of John in Recent Research." *Review and Expositor* 62 (Fall 1965): 418-28.

Stevens, George B. *The Johannine Theology*. New York: Scribner's, 1894.

Trudinger, P. "Concerning Sins Mortal and Otherwise: A Note on 1 John 5:16-17." *Biblica* 52 (December 1971): 541-42.

Westcott, B. F. *The Gospel According to St. John, The Greek Text with Introduction and Notes*. Grand Rapids: Eerdmans, 1954.

Wilson, W. G. "An Examination of the Linguistic Evidence Adduced Against the Unity of Authorship of the First Epistle of John and the Fourth Gospel." *Journal of Theological Studies* 49 (July 1948): 147-56.

Winn, Albert Curry. *Tests of Real Christianity.* Richmond, Va.: John Knox, 1948.

GENERAL WORKS

Bultmann, Rudolf. *Primitive Christianity in Its Contemporary Setting.* New York: Meridan Books, 1956.

Burdick, Donald W. "Οἶδα and Γινώσκω in the Pauline Epistles" In *New Dimensions in New Testament Study.* Edited by Richard N. Longenecker and Merrill C. Tenney. Grand Rapids: Zondervan, 1974.

Clark, Adam. *The New Testament of Our Lord and Saviour Jesus Christ.* Vol. 2. New York: Phillips and Hunt, n.d.

Corwin, Virginia. *St. Ignatius and Christianity at Antioch.* New Haven, Conn.: Yale U., 1950.

Drane, John W. "Gnosticism and the New Testament" 1 & 2. *TSF Bulletin* 68 & 69 (Spring and Summer 1974).

Eddy, Mary Baker. *Science and Health with Key to the Scriptures.* Boston: First Church of Christ Scientist, 1932.

Fletcher, Joseph. *Situation Ethics, the New Morality.* Philadelphia: Westminster, 1966.

Goodspeed, Edgar J. *An Introduction to the New Testament.* Chicago: U. of Chicago, 1937.

Grant, Robert M. *Gnosticism.* New York: Harper and Brothers, 1961.

———. *Gnosticism and Early Christianity.* New York: Columbia U., 1959.

Greenlee, J. Harold. *Introduction to New Testament Textual Criticism.* Grand Rapids: Eerdmans, 1964.

Guthrie, Donald. *New Testament Introduction.* Downers Grove, Ill.: InterVarsity, 1974.

Harrison, Everett F. *Introduction to the New Testament.* Grand Rapids: Eerdmans, 1964.

Hill, David. *Greek Words and Hebrew Meaings.* Cambridge: University Press, 1976.

Hunt, A. S., and Edgar, C. C., trans. *Select Papyri.* The Loeb Classical Library, Cambridge, Mass.; Harvard U., 1952.

Hunter, A. M. *Interpreting the New Testament 1900-1950.* Philadelphia: Westminster, 1951.

Jonas, Hans. *The Gnostic Religion.* Boston: Beacon, 1958.

Ladd, George E. *A Theology of the New Testament.* Grand Rapids: Eerdmans, 1974.

Lightfoot, J. B. *St. Paul's Epistle to the Philippians.* London: Macmillan, 1913. Reprint. Grand Rapids: Zondervan, 1953.

Longenecker, Richard N.; and Tenney, Merrill C., eds. *New Dimensions in New Testament Study.* Grand Rapids: Zondervan, 1974.

McNeile, A. H. *An Introduction to the Study of the New Testament.* Oxford: Oxford University, 1953.

Martin, Walter R. *The Kingdom of the Cults.* Grand Rapids: Zondervan, 1965.

Metzger, Bruce M. *The Text of the New Testament.* New York: Oxford U., 1964.

Moffatt, James. *An Introduction to the Literature of the New Testament.* Edinburgh: T. & T. Clark, 1933.

Morris, Leon. *The Apostolic Preaching of the Cross.* Grand Rapids: Eerdmans, 1965.

Munck, Johannes. "The New Testament and Gnosticism." In *Current Issues in New Testament Interpretation.* Edited by William Klassen and Graydon F. Snyder. New York: Harper and Brothers, 1962.

Nicole, Roger. "C. H. Dodd and the Doctrine of Propitiation," *Westminster Theological Journal* 17 (1954-55): 117-57.

Niebuhr, Reinhold. *The Nature and Destiny of Man.* New York: Scribner's, 1951.

Perkins, Pheme. *The Gnostic Dialogue.* New York: Paulist, 1980.

Ramm, Bernard. *A Handbook of Contemporary Theology.* Grand Rapids: Eerdmans, 1966.

———. *Protestant Biblical Interpretation.* 3d revised ed. Grand Rapids: Baker, 1970.

———. *The Witness of the Spirit.* Grand Rapids: Eerdmans, 1959.

Ramsay, William M. *Luke the Physician.* London: Hodder and Stoughton, 1908.

Robertson, A. T. *The Minister and His Greek Testament.* Grand Rapids: Baker, 1977.

Robinson, J. A. T. *Redating the New Testament.* Philadelphia: Westminster, 1976.

Rockstad, Ernest B. N.d. "Speaking in Tongues Scripturally Tested." Wichita, Kan. Mimeo.

Rogers, L. W. *Elementary Theosophy.* Wheaton, Ill.: Theosophical Press, 1956.

Ryrie, Charles. *Biblical Theology of the New Testament.* Chicago: Moody, 1959.

Salmon, George. *An Historical Introduction to the Study of the New*

Testament. London: John Murray, 1904.
Selwyn, E. G. *The First Epistle of St. Peter.* New York: St. Martin's, 1955.
Stevens, George B. *The Theology of the New Testament.* New York: Scribner's, 1914.
Strong, A. H. *Systematic Theology.* Philadelphia: Judson, 1942.
Tenney, Merrill C. *The New Testament, An Historical and Analytical Survey.* Grand Rapids: Eerdmans, 1953.
Theron, Daniel J. *Evidence of Tradition.* Grand Rapids: Baker, 1958.
Unger, Merrill F. *Archaeology and the New Testament.* Grand Rapids: Zondervan, 1962.
Van Unnik, W. C. *Newly Discovered Gnostic Writings.* Studies in Biblical Theology, no. 30. Naperville, Ill.: Allenson, 1960.
What Has Religion Done for Mankind? Brooklyn: Watchtower Bible Society, Inc., 1951.
Wiley, H. Orton. *Christian Theology.* 3 vols. Kansas City, Mo.: Beacon Hill, 1940-58.
Wood, Henry. *New Thought Simplified.* Boston: Lee and Shepard, 1903.
Yamauchi, Edwin M. *Pre-Christian Gnosticism: A Survey of the Proposed Evidence.* Grand Rapids: Eerdmans, 1973.
———. "Recent Archaeological Work in the New Testament Cities of Western Anatolia." *Near East Archaeological Society Bulletin,* New Series, no. 13 (1979): 37-116; no. 14 (1979): 5-48.
———. "Some Alleged Evidences for Pre-Christian Gnosticism." In *New Dimensions in New Testament Study.* Grand Rapids: Zondervan, 1974.
Zahn, Theodor. *Introduction to the New Testament.* 3 vols. Grand Rapids: Kregel, 1953.

EARLY CHRISTIAN WRITINGS

Clement of Alexandria. *Stromata.* The Ante-Nicene Fathers. Edited by Alexander Roberts and James Donaldson. Grand Rapids: Eerdmans, 1951.
Clement of Rome. *Epistle to the Corinthians.* The Ante-Nicene Fathers, Edited by Alexander Roberts and James Donaldson. Grand Rapids: Eerdmans, 1950.
Clementine Homilies. The Ante-Nicene Fathers. Edited by Alexander Roberts and James Donaldson. Grand Rapids: Eerdmans, 1951.

Cyprian of Carthage. *Epistles*. The Ante-Nicene Fathers. Edited by Alexander Roberts and James Donaldson. Grand Rapids: Eerdmans, 1951.

Eusebius. *Ecclesiastical History.* A Select Library of Nicene and Post-Nicene Fathers of the Christian Church. Edited by Philip Schaff and Henry Wace. Grand Rapids: Eerdmans, 1952.

Ignatius. *Epistles.* The Ante-Nicene Fathers. Edited by Alexander Roberts and James Donaldson. Grand Rapids: Eerdmans, 1950.

Irenaeus. *Against Heresies.* The Ante-Nicene Fathers. Edited by Alexander Roberts and James Donaldson. Grand Rapids: Eerdmans, 1950.

Jerome. *Lives of Illustrious Men.* A Select Library of Nicene and Post-Nicene Fathers. Edited by Philip Schaff and Henry Wace. Grand Rapids: Eerdmans, 1953.

Tertullian. *Against Marcion.* The Ante-Nicene Fathers. Edited by Alexander Roberts and James Donaldson. Grand Rapids: Eerdmans, 1951.

Index of Subjects and Persons

Abide. *See* Remain
Abiding in Him, 138-40, 159, 208, 238-39, 326, 327
Advocate (παράκλητος), 76, 130, 157-58
Anointing, 196-97
Antichrist(s), 50, 51, 83-84, 193-94, 199-201, 213-14, 220, 299, 426
Anti-Marcionite Prologue, 33
Antinomian (libertine), 53, 59, 60, 64, 148-49, 155, 166
Apostasy, 219
Apostles' teaching, 214-15
Asia, province of, 3, 4, 5, 6, 7, 43, 48, 443
Assurance, 65, 81-82, 160-61, 171, 182, 264, 271-72, 275-76, 282, 285-86, 326-27, 328-29, 334, 337, 338, 354, 360, 385, 386, 389, 392, 393, 394, 399, 400
Atonement, 132
Authorship of fourth gospel, 33-37

Baptism of Christ, 61, 365-68
Basilides, 149

Beginning, 75, 97, 142-43, 173-74, 202-3, 262, 424
Belief, 342, 356-57, 358, 359, 374-76
 continuing, 217-19, 374
 in the incarnation, 110, 115, 342, 360
Beloved, 43, 47, 140
Beloved disciple, 7, 9, 10, 11
Bishop, office of, 43
Blood, 364-69
Brother(s), 145-46, 260, 261, 265, 339-40, 404, 450

Cain, 261, 282-83
Carpocrates, 149, 150
Charismatic gifts, 327-28
Children, of the devil, 248
 of God, 230-31, 248, 344, 393
 little, 42, 43, 47, 129, 172, 174-75, 300
Christ, sinlessness of, 238
 usage of term in 1 John, 51, 54, 72-73, 131, 200, 201, 342, 347, 379
Christian Science, 111, 164, 220, 310

Index of Subjects and Persons 477

Christological test, 51-52, 64, 90, 152, 192-223, 291-312, 378, 427-28, 434
Church, 453, 454, 456, 457
Clementine Homilies, 58-59
Coming (παρουσία), 209
Commandment(s), 134-35, 141, 278-81, 344, 358, 422-23, 424
  old/new, 141-43, 161-63
Confess, confession, 126, 155-56, 158, 202, 252, 295, 296-98, 330, 360
Confidence (παρρησία), 208-9, 333, 354, 387, 392
Conscience, 275-76
Corinthus (Corinthianism), 58, 59, 60, 61, 62, 107, 109, 110, 149, 150, 200, 210, 216, 296, 306-7, 366-67, 378-80
Cults, modern, 111, 220-21, 310

Darkness, 75, 120-22, 143-44, 146, 147-48, 153-54
Dead Sea Scrolls. *See* Qumran
Death, 264, 265
Deceivers, 425-26
Demetrius, 458
Demiurge, 150
Demons, exorcism of, 311-12
Deny, 200-201, 202
Devil, 75, 174, 187, 242-44, 262, 307, 392-93, 404-5
Didache, 417
Diotrephes, 454-57, 463-64
Docetism, 44, 54, 56, 58, 60-61, 62-63, 107, 108, 306
Domitian, 41, 44
Dualism, 5, 55, 306, 308, 378-79

Elder, office of, 43
Ephesus, 40, 47-48
Epistolary format, 68-70
Eschatology, 193-94
Eternal life, 80-82, 102, 204, 217, 264, 266, 376-77, 386
Eternal security. *See* Perseverance
Ethical tests, 90
Excommunication, 456-57
Expiation. *See* Propitiation
Eyewitnesses, 28-30, 102, 106

Faithfulness of God, 126
False prophets, 51, 293-94, 306
False teachers, 83, 302, 303
Fathers, 172, 173, 175
Fear, 335, 338
Fellowship (κοινωνία), 104-5, 109, 111, 115-16, 117, 121, 123, 129, 152-53, 156-57, 159, 192-93, 216-20
Flesh (σάρξ), 178-79
Forgive, forgiveness, 127, 156-57, 172-73, 182-83

Gaius, 443, 444, 446, 447
Gentile recipients, 45-46
Giving, 286-87
Gnosticism, Gnostic(s), 4, 6, 7, 51-61, 121, 148-52, 160, 163, 189-90, 194, 196, 198, 200, 201, 205, 216, 229, 237, 241, 245, 255, 279-80, 303, 306, 308, 318, 319, 378-79, 427, 428, 429, 434
  incipient, 44, 49, 57, 75, 132, 136, 155, 158, 183-84, 210, 366-67, 417, 425
God the Father, 197-98, 200-202, 205, 406-7
Goods (Bίον), of this world, 180, 268-69
Gospel of John, 7, 8, 9
Greek verb tenses, 246-47, 269, 279, 322, 373, 397
Greeting, 420-22, 428-29

Hate, hatred, 145, 147-48, 262, 263, 265, 266, 282-83, 284
  continuing action, 265
Heart (καρδία), 271, 272
Heart (σπλάγχνα), 269-71
Hellenization, 3, 4
High Priest, 130
Holy One, 197-98
Holy Spirit, 197, 205, 281-82, 301-2, 306, 327, 368-71
  teaching ministry of, 74, 205-7, 214-15, 406
Homosexuality, 166
Hope (ἐλπίς), 235
Hospitality, 417, 429, 432, 435, 451, 456, 462

Idols, 397-98
Illumination by the Spirit, 74, 406
Incarnation, 52, 53, 95, 101, 102, 104, 237, 243, 291, 294-96, 305, 306-7, 308-9, 347, 371, 377, 379, 381-82, 406, 428, 434
Indicative/Imperative, 255
Indwelling, 205-6, 281, 325, 327, 330, 331, 332, 352-53

Jehovah's Witnesses, 310
Johannine School (Circle), 10, 11, 17, 415
Johannine writings, relationships between, 17-22, 38-40
John, epistles of. *See also* Theology (Johannine epistles)
 authorship, 7-37, 413-15, 441-43
 background, 3-5
 character and content, 68-92
 date, 38-44, 417, 444
 occasion and purpose, 49-67, 417-18, 444
 place, 42, 44
 recipients, 44-48, 415-17, 443-44
 structure, 85-92, 95
 style, 17, 18, 20, 27-28
John the Baptist, 11, 368
John the Elder, 14-16
Joy, 106
Judaizers, 54
Judgment day, 85, 189, 333, 334, 337-38, 354

Know, knowledge (γινώσκω, γνῶσις), 55, 133, 159-60, 173, 183-84, 198, 214-15, 232-33, 264, 281, 303, 304, 318, 319, 327, 330-31, 344, 394-95, 406-7, 420

Lady, chosen, 415-17
Last hour, 82-83, 193-94, 208, 211-12
Lawlessness, 75, 236-37
Liar, 128, 136, 340, 375, 376

Liberalism, 309
Life, 180, 264, 404
Light, 118-120, 122-23, 144, 153-54
Listening, the test of, 300-305, 307-8
Lord's supper, 370
Love (ἀγάπη), 140-41, 159-60, 230, 284-85, 317-18, 320, 322, 336, 351, 451, 462
 characteristic of God's family, 260, 318, 348-49
 discernment in the exercise of, 431, 432, 435
 essence of God, 319, 332, 349-50
 for brothers, 53, 146-47, 161-63, 280, 283-84, 324-26, 339-41, 358, 420, 423
 for God, 137-38, 178, 339-41, 345, 355-58, 424
 for the world, 176-78
 fruit of, 271, 333-39, 354-55
 God's, 229-30, 270, 332, 333
 manifestation of, 350-52
 perfected, 138, 159-60, 326, 333, 334, 336, 352, 354
 practice of, 260-64, 271, 280, 286, 317, 318-19, 338, 344
 product of truth, 431
 source of, 317-33, 338, 348-355
 tested, 266-70, 284-85
 test of salvation, 140-48, 259-82, 283, 316, 352
 theology of, 348-50
Lovelessness, 53, 151-52, 318, 339
Lust, 178-181

Main themes, interweaving of, 348, 352, 357, 359, 360
Message, 97
Messiah. *See* Christ
Missionary support, 435-36, 444, 452, 461, 462-63
Muratorian Canon, 24-25, 33
Murder, murderer, 53, 266, 282-83, 284
Mystery religions, 4, 5

Nag Hammadi, 4, 63
Name, 173, 183, 280, 451-52
New Morality, 166
New Thought, 111, 310
Nicolaitans, 59, 62, 149

Obedience, 158-60, 281, 344-46, 358
Only begotten, 321
Overcome. *See* Victory

Patmos, John's exile on, 42
Perseverance, 194-96, 218, 407-8
Prayer, 277-78, 285-86, 354, 387-89, 390-91, 392, 400-404, 408-9
  in God's will, 400-401
Pride, 179
Propitiation (ἱλασμός), 19, 76, 78-79, 131-32, 157, 324
Prosperity, spiritual and material, 447-48, 460-61
Punishment, 337

Qumran, 21, 119, 120, 122, 153, 304

Realized eschatology, 18, 21, 211. *See also* Eschatology
Regeneration, 80-82, 227, 244, 246-48, 249, 253, 300, 318, 342-43, 345-46, 357-58, 359, 393, 404-5
Remain (abide, dwell), 203, 216-20, 257, 281-82, 327, 428
Revelation, book of, 8, 9, 11
Righteous (δίκαιος), 228, 262
Righteousness of God, 126-27, 227, 249
Righteousness
  practice of, 53, 228, 241, 242, 252, 254, 286
  as test of salvation, 117-40, 224-49

Sanctification, 84, 123-24, 128, 233-34, 250, 253, 254
Second advent, 84-85, 188-89, 208-9, 232-33
Seed, 247, 404

Simon Magus (Simonianism), 57, 58, 62
Sin (depravity), 124-25, 253
  impossibility of, 251-52
  incompatibility of, 250-51
  individual acts of, 53, 76, 77, 123, 124, 128, 129-30, 157, 244, 248
  leading to death, 76, 391, 402-3
  not leading to death, 389-90, 391-92, 401-2, 403-4
  source of, 251
Sin (as life-style), 53, 64, 75, 77, 129-30, 236, 238, 240, 242, 246-47, 248, 252, 392, 404-5
Sinful habit, 391, 402
Sinless perfection, 164-66, 239, 255-57
Social concern (in the church), 286-88
Son of God, 51, 54, 72, 347, 373-77, 379, 392, 393, 394, 421
Spirit(s), 50, 51, 292-300, 306
Spirit of error (antichrist), 51, 299, 302, 304-5, 306
Spirit of truth (God), 304, 306
Stumbling block (σκάνδαλον), 146-47
Syncretism, 4, 5

Test, 292
  ethical, 152, 316
  of likeness, 117-24, 153
  of obedience, 159-60
Teach, 206
Theology (Johannine epistles) *See also* John, epistles of
  Christ, 71-73
  God, 70-71
  Holy Spirit, 73-75
  last things, 82-85
  salvation, 78-82
  sin, 75-77
Theosophical Society, 112, 220, 310
Travel (first-century Roman roads), 462

Truth, 122, 136, 155, 198, 199, 217, 271, 369, 420, 421-22, 458-59

Unity School of Christianity, 111, 220, 310

Valentinus, 57, 151, 254
Victory, 174, 176, 184-86, 300-301, 345-47, 404-5

Walking
in darkness, 121-22, 154-55
in the light, 154-55, 251-52
in the truth, 422-23, 432-33, 447, 449, 461
Water, 364-68
Witness(es), 102, 364, 368-74, 377
Word, 72, 96, 98, 129, 177, 197
World (κόσμος), 176-77, 186-88, 189-90, 231, 263, 264, 283, 302, 303, 308, 329, 335, 345-46, 393-94

Young men, 75, 172, 174-76

Index of Scripture

Leviticus	
19:18	341

Deuteronomy	
17:6	370, 371

Daniel	
7	213

Matthew	
5:21-22	284
6:24	188
10:32	202
17:1	32
22:37-40	341
24:4-14	83
24:5	194
24:5-12	212
26:36	32

Mark	
3:17	31
5:37	32
9:38	31
12:44	180

Luke	
9:54	31
24:58	98

John	
1:1	72, 73, 97, 101, 103
1:1-2	40, 72
1:4	72
1:4-9	119
1:14	99, 101
1:29	22, 34
1:31-33	368
1:35	34
1:35-51	35
1:38	33
1:41	33
1:43	34
2:1	34
2:6	34
2:12	34
2:20	34
2:24-25	35
3:3,5	253
3:5-8	18
3:14-19	22
3:15-16	40
3:16	324
3:19-21	119
3:20-21	122
3:23	34
3:34	327
3:36	40

4:1	35	15:12	40
4:1-45	35	15:13	267
4:9	33	15:17	40
4:18	34	15:23	39
4:24	21, 319, 349	15:26	18, 40
4:27	34	16:8-11	18
4:40	34	16:13-14	40
4:52	34	17:2-3	40
5:2	34	17:3	184
5:5	34	17:13	106
5:24	334	19:25-27	32
5:28-29	21	19:34	365
6:1	34	20:31	39, 385
6:5-7	34	21:20	32, 35
6:6	35	21:24	35
6:19	34		
6:51	22	Acts	
6:61	35	2:17	193
6:64	35	2:32	98
6:69	331	2:45	287
7:37	34	4:13	27
8:12	21, 118	5:32	18
8:20	34	8:9-24	58
8:44	39, 75, 243, 248, 262	10:39	98
10:11	22, 267	17:13	72
10:15	22, 267		
10:28	40, 218, 402	Romans	
11:18	34	1:18	76
11:33	35	1:32	76
11:49-52	22	2:1-9	76
12:21-22	34	3:10-18	128
12:23	21, 32	5:8	230
12:31	21	8:34	131
13:1	35	13:8-10	260
13:3	35	15:26	288
13:11	35		
13:21	35	1 Corinthians	
13:23-26	34	2:10-16	22
13:31	21	9:6-14	287
13:34-35	40, 141, 261, 331, 423	Galatians	
14:5	34	2:9	41
14:6	74	3:10	76
14:8-9	34	5:6	279
14:16-17	101, 201	6:2,5	345
14:17	207	6:6	287
14:21,23,24	138		
14:26	39, 197	Ephesians	
15:4-7	217	2:2	306
15:11	106	3:16	22

Index of Scripture   483

Colossians		1:5-10	64
1:1	68	1:6	31, 53, 121-22
		1:6-7	28, 70
2 Thessalonians		1:6-8	30
2:3-4	213	1:6-10	70
2:4	194	1:7	65, 78, 79, 122-24
		1:8	53, 76, 77, 124-26
1 Timothy		1:8-9	28
1:3	42	1:8-10	70, 150, 164-66,
1:3-4	6		244, 245
4:1-3	6	1:9	76, 77, 126-28, 156-57,
5:8	269		183, 228
6:20-21	6	1:10	30, 53, 76, 77, 128-29
		2:1	30, 42, 47, 72, 76, 77,
2 Timothy			80, 129-31
3:1	193	2:1-2	76, 157-58
3:1-9	212	2:2	18, 76, 77, 78, 131-32
		2:3	53, 65, 132-35
Titus		2:3-4	31, 81, 219
3:13	435	2:3-6	159, 164, 166, 278
		2:4	31, 51, 135-36, 148
Hebrews		2:4-5	28, 30
1:2	193	2:5	53, 65, 136-38, 160
4:15-16	131	2:5-6	33, 81, 219
7:25	157-158	2:6	139-40, 160
		2:7	97, 140-43, 260, 423
James		2:7-8	40, 45
2:14-17	288	2:7-11	151
4:4	188	2:8	143-44
		2:9	65, 145-46
1 Peter		2:9-10	28
1:1	15	2:9-11	31, 33, 53, 109, 285
1:20	193	2:10	65, 146-47
5:1	15, 16	2:11	65, 147-48
		2:12	30, 42, 76, 172-73
2 Peter		2:12-14	45, 171, 172-76
3:3	193	2:13	75, 173-75
		2:13-14	40, 45, 72,
1 John			183-84, 185
1:1	32, 52, 72, 96-101, 260	2:14	175-76
1:1-2	30, 72, 108-9	2:15	30, 31, 176-78
1:1-3	32, 73	2:15-17	171, 176-81,
1:1-4	28-29, 96-113, 115		186-88, 189, 190
1:2	32, 72, 81, 101-4	2:16	178-80
1:3	30, 32, 50, 80, 104-6	2:17	181
1:3-4	109	2:18	31, 45, 46, 50, 51,
1:4	70, 106-7, 385		83, 193-94
1:5	18, 21, 53, 70, 117-21,	2:18-19	25, 44, 54, 66, 340
	159, 249, 319, 349	2:18-22	24
1:5-7	71, 74, 81, 154	2:18-23	64

2:19	50, 194-96	3:22	277-78
2:20	22, 45, 74, 196-98	3:23	278-80
2:20-21	40, 45, 214	3:24	22, 33, 74, 280-82
2:21	198-99	4:1	30, 43, 46, 47, 50, 51, 66, 291-94
2:22	31, 39, 44, 46, 51, 61, 64, 72, 83, 199-201, 220	4:1-3	25, 73
2:22-23	30, 51, 81, 215-16, 221, 347	4:1-6	51, 74
2:23	65, 201-2	4:2	64, 65, 72, 73, 74, 294-96
2:24	30, 33, 45, 67, 81, 202-4	4:2-3	44, 51, 81, 83, 425
2:24-28	216-20	4:3	45, 46, 64, 66, 296-300
2:25	40, 81, 204	4:4	30, 47, 74, 185, 300-302
2:26	43, 50, 64, 66, 204-5	4:5	302-3
2:27	22, 39, 40, 45, 67, 74, 205-8	4:5-6	65, 66
		4:6	303-5
2:27-28	33, 81, 203	4:7	43, 47, 65, 317-18
2:28	30, 42, 47, 84, 208-9	4:7-8	80
2:29	53, 65, 82, 133, 226-29	4:7-5:12	314-15
		4:8	18, 21, 71, 120, 318-19, 332
2:29—4:6	224-25		
3:1	229-32	4:9	319-22
3:2	232-34	4:9-10	72
3:2-3	21, 43, 47, 72, 84	4:10	76, 78, 322-24, 329
3:3	234-35	4:11	43, 47, 324
3:4	46, 75, 76, 79, 235-37	4:12	325-26, 332
3:4-10	64	4:13	22, 33, 74, 326-28
3:5	45, 72, 76, 78, 79, 237-38	4:14	28, 72, 328-29
		4:15	51, 73, 329-30
3:6	77, 238-40	4:16	330-33
3:7	30, 47, 53, 240-41	4:17	85, 333-35
3:8	39, 53, 75, 78, 241-44	4:18	335-38
3:8-9	77	4:19	338-39
3:9	53, 80, 82, 244-48	4:20	339-41
3:9-10	65, 80	4:21	40, 341-42
3:10	64, 65, 109	5:1	51, 65, 72, 80, 109, 260, 342-43, 432
3:10a	248-49		
3:10b	259-60		
3:10-15	109	5:2	343-45
3:11	40, 45, 260-61	5:3a	345
3:12	75, 261-63	5:3b	345
3:13	263-64	5:4	345-47
3:14	65, 133, 264-65	5:4-5	80, 185
3:14-15	53	5:5	72, 347
3:15	45, 265-66	5:6	18, 61, 364-68
3:16	78, 266-68	5:7	74, 368-69
3:17	268-70, 286	5:7b-8a	372
3:18	30, 47, 270	5:8	22, 74, 369-72
3:19	133, 271-73	5:9	372-74
3:20	273-75	5:10	374-76
3:21	43, 275-77	5:11	81, 276-77

5:12	81, 377	3 John	
5:13	39, 40, 65, 81, 384-87, 399-400	1	14, 24, 446-47
5:14	387-88	2	447-48
5:14-17	400-404	3	448-49
5:15	133, 388-89	4	449-50
5:16	46, 389-91	5	450
5:16-17	76, 77	5-8	435
5:17	76, 391-92	6	450-51
5:18	75, 392-93, 404-5	7	451-52
5:19	75, 393-94, 405	8	452-53
5:20	40, 72, 394-97, 405-7	9	453-54
5:21	30, 42, 45, 46, 47, 397-98, 406-7	10	454-57
		11	457-58
		12	458-59
		13	459-60
2 John		14	460
1	14, 24, 419-20	15 (Greek text)	460
2	420		
3	420-22	Revelation	
4	422-23	1:9	41
5	423-24	1:11	48
6	424	2:1-7	66
7	83, 213, 425-26	2:6	62
7-10	23	2:9	5
7-11	50	2:15	62
8	426-27	11:7	213
9	427-28	13:1	213, 307
10	428-29	13:15	194
11	429		
12	429-30		
12-13	24		
13	431		

Index of Authors

Albright, W. F., 57
Alexander, W., 32
Alford, H., 124, 199, 231, 233, 233 n. 17, 314, 320, 322, 335 n. 53, 341, 350
Arndt, W. F., and F. W. Gingrich, 292

Bacon, B. W., 8
Barrett, C. K., 9-10, 28, 34, 35, 36, 133
Barth, Karl, 309
Bauer, W., 263, 388, 390
Behm, J., 394
Bengel, J. A., 86
Blass, F., 297, 367
Bonsirven, J., 71, 72, 98, 118, 119, 123, 125, 158, 159, 212-13, 237, 242, 252, 266, 272, 294 n. 7, 314, 316, 321, 322, 327 n. 30, 341, 342, 367
Braun, F. M., 36
Brawne, K., 44
Brooke, A. E., 23 n., 39, 40, 66, 86-87, 102-3, 127, 131, 137, 196, 227 n. 1, 231, 261, 295, 298, 301, 318, 320, 326, 331, 332, 335 n. 52, 341, 345, 350, 353, 377, 384, 385, 389, 397, 427, 453-54, 457
Brown, R., 10, 13, 34, 57-58, 63, 88, 443
Bruce, F. F., 134, 163, 195, 279, 301, 317, 319 n. 5, 331, 463
Brunner, E., 309
Bultmann, R., 8, 9, 102, 125, 134, 139, 159, 177, 195, 216, 227 nn. 1,3, 229, 237, 238, 245, 260, 262, 266 n. 15, 270, 272, 275, 278, 280, 292, 301, 302, 309, 322, 328, 337, 374, 381, 425, 428, 430, 457
Burton, E. D., 388

Calvin, John, 11, 157
Clarke, A., 165, 255-56
Clement of Alexandria, 25, 33, 41, 42, 47-48, 149, 150, 413-14
Clement of Rome, 43
Conner, W. T., 185, 350
Cox, L., 256
Cullmann, O., 11, 13
Culpepper, R. A., 11 n. 15
Cyprian, 25

Dana, H. E., 69, 230, 350
Debrunner, A., 297, 367
De la Potterie, I., 197
Dionysius of Alexandria, 26, 33, 60, 149, 414, 441
Dodd, C. H., 14, 15, 17-20, 28-29, 43, 68, 85, 91 n., 120, 133, 134, 177, 182, 189, 197, 211, 242, 246, 249, 301, 326, 328, 335 n. 55, 337, 339, 356, 408, 441, 451 n. 12

Eddy, M. B., 111, 112, 164, 220
Edwards, R. A., 35
Eusebius, 13, 14, 15, 26, 33, 40, 41, 42, 44, 47, 414, 441-42

Findlay, G., 69, 177
Fletcher, J., 166 n. 85

Godet, F. L., 11, 133
Goodspeed, E. J., 24
Grant, R. M., 57, 150 n. 64, 183-84
Greenlee, J. H., 231
Gutbrod, W., 237
Guthrie, D., 12, 27, 39, 44

Harris, M. J., 276-77
Harrison, E. F., 31
Hendriksen, W., 12, 133
Higgins, A. J. B., 35
Hoskyns, E. C., 110
Houlden, J. L., 132, 172, 207, 229, 243, 270, 298, 301, 335 n. 51, 341
Howard, W. F., 19, 22
Hunter, A. M., 8

Ignatius, 42, 43, 60-61, 62, 63, 107, 152, 163
Irenaeus, 24, 33, 40, 41, 42, 58, 59, 62, 149, 150, 151, 163, 254, 366, 378, 413

Jerome, 149, 442
Jonas, H., 3, 4, 153

Kramer, H., 379

Index of Authors 487

Ladd, G. E., 74, 77, 79
Law, R., 11, 28, 69, 71, 72, 76, 79, 80, 86, 87, 105, 116, 125, 133, 134, 137, 138, 175, 177, 200, 215, 227 n. 4, 228, 231, 237, 294, 297, 299, 301, 318, 326, 334, 338, 350, 366, 369, 385, 396, 397
Lenski, R. C. H., 91, 110, 133, 233, 233 n. 17, 272, 279, 286, 301, 304, 310, 320, 322, 334, 335 n. 55, 337, 388, 425, 463
Lightfoot, J. B., ix, 39, 133, 269
Luther, Martin, 11

Manson, T. W., 36
Marshall, I. H., 16, 88, 97, 120, 127, 174, 195, 197, 199, 227 n. 3, 237, 244-46, 263, 267, 267 n. 19, 270, 271, 279, 296, 301, 314, 322, 323, 326, 327 n. 30, 327, 335 n. 54, 341, 360, 369, 371, 375, 391, 396, 401, 404, 428, 458
Metzger, B. M., 297, 340, 372
Michaelis, W., 68
Michel, O., 262, 295
Moffatt, J., 8, 25, 68
Moody, D., 321 n. 12
Morris, L., 12, 33-36, 78, 132 n. 29, 133, 327 n. 31
Moule, C. F. D., 297

Niebuhr, R., 309

Origen, 25, 414, 441

Papias, 13, 14, 15, 16, 47
Perkins, P., 56, 63
Plummer, A., 11, 85, 133, 143, 199, 209, 275, 296, 301, 314, 319 n. 5, 335 n. 55, 341, 346, 350, 353, 356, 396, 397, 427
Polycarp, 42, 47, 59, 149

Ramm, B., 312, 380
Ramsay, W. M., 3
Robertson, A. T., x, 133, 233, 233 n. 17, 246, 269, 297, 388, 395

Robinson, J. A. T., 12, 13, 36, 46
Ross A., 43
Ryrie, C., 110

Salom, A. P., 19
Schlier, H., 200
Schmiedel, P. W., 8
Schnackenburg, R., 10-11
Schneider, J., 337
Seesemann, H., 133, 277 n. 1
Selwyn, E. G., 247
Smith, D., 233, 233 n. 17, 239, 320, 334, 356
Songer, H. S., 8
Stevens, G. B., 70, 79, 381
Stott, J. R. W., 12, 87, 110, 166, 217, 227 n. 1,4, 231, 233, 270, 277, 278, 301, 326, 341, 342, 343, 396, 404
Strong, A. H., 349

Tertullian, 25, 33
Theophilus of Antioch, 33
Tillich, P., 309
Trench, R. C., 141

Trudinger, P., 391
Turner, N., 20, 27, 133

Van Unnik, W. C., 4
Vincent, M. R., 28, 133
Von Eicken, E., 322

Wesley, John, 253
Westcott, B. F., 11, 12, 33-36, 39, 66, 68, 128, 133, 137, 163, 177, 193, 196, 227 n. 1,2, 231, 239, 265, 294 n. 7, 297, 301, 314, 320, 326, 332, 334, 335 n. 53, 341, 344, 349, 350, 369, 373, 375, 387-388, 396, 421-422
White, R. E. O., 69
Wiley, H. O., 165
Wilson, W. G., 19
Wood, H., 111, 220

Yamauchi, E. M., 407

Zahn, T., 30
Zerwick, M., 331-32

Moody Press, a ministry of the Moody Bible Institute, is designed for education, evangelization, and edification. If we may assist you in knowing more about Christ and the Christian life, please write us without obligation: Moody Press, c/o MLM, Chicago, Illinois 60610